Psychology

for

the Classroom

Psychology
for
the Classroom

ROBERT D. STROM

Professor of Education and Psychology
The Ohio State University

PRENTICE-HALL, INC., Englewood Cliffs, New Jersey

Current printing (last digit):

10 9 8 7 6 5 4 3 2 1

Prentice-Hall International, Inc., London
Prentice-Hall of Australia, Ptd. Ltd., Sydney
Prentice-Hall of Canada, Ltd., Toronto
Prentice-Hall of India Private, Ltd., New Delhi
Prentice-Hall of Japan, Inc., Tokyo

To GORDON W. ALLPORT, late professor of psychology, Harvard University, and E. PAUL TORRANCE, professor of educational psychology, University of Georgia, whose wisdom as scholars and behavior as men has enabled a better life for the many they have served.

Preface

Perhaps there was a time when it was reasonable to expect the author of a basic text in educational psychology to include some discussion of *every* aspect of the field. Today, however, a sampling of the entire range of concerns in the field is hardly a reasonable expectation for an introductory text. Only the pretender would suggest that limited space and lack of time are the reasons his text omits certain issues and thus does not match in content the totality of educational psychology. The truth is that the number of issues being urged for consideration as properly within the scope of educational psychology is increasing at a more rapid pace than the ability each of us has for accommodation. While there is general agreement among writers concerning the goal to make explicit a psychology for the classroom so that teachers can improve their influence, we quite naturally differ in perceiving the requisite elements and design.

Therefore, it is essential that the unique purposes for which a text is intended represent the primary criteria for judging the book. It follows that only the reader who is aware of what an author intends to accomplish can properly evaluate whether or to what degree the writing purposes have been met. My objectives have been: (1) to present ways by which teachers can maintain pupil respect without recourse to coercion and punitive techniques; (2) to enable a better understanding of the student view regarding school life, its problems and their resolution; (3) to define the ethic and its proper teacher response in relating to pupils, parents, and colleagues; (4) to describe certain prominent theories of learning as well as the consequent methods of teaching; (5) to urge the recognition, acceptance, and encouragement of creative behavior in the classroom; (6) to indicate the importance and process of evaluation as a part of teaching; and (7) to suggest an orientation for ensuring student mental health and personality development.

I wish to acknowledge the help afforded me by the several scholars who have reviewed this book: The late Dr. Gordon W. Allport, Emeritus Professor of Psychology, Harvard University; Dr. Edgar Dale, Professor of Education, The Ohio State University; Dr. Don E. Hamachek, Professor of Education, Michigan State University; Dr. Sidney Pressey, Emeritus Professor of Psychology, The Ohio State University; and Dr. E. Paul Torrance, Professor of Educational Psychology, University of Georgia. Appreciation is also extended to Mrs. Viriginia Hake for her bibliographic assistance and to my wife, Shirley, for her questions and concern for clarity.

Robert D. Strom

Table of Contents

Psychology

for

the Classroom

CHAPTER I

Respecting Differences

Among Pupils

"Respect your elders" is an admonition that has persisted for centuries. It has implied everything from blind acceptance of adult advice to simple good manners and tact in refraining from contradicting parents and teachers. But regardless of intent, it assumes that adult-youth relationships might be mutually more rewarding if children were more reverent. Challenging authority, asserting independence, confiding in peers, and generally ignoring the advice of more experienced adults are but a few of the child behaviors that supporters of the precept find disconcerting. If the much abused word "respect" had not been used as a synonym for "obey," and age had not pretended to go hand in hand with wisdom, the precept might have been correctly interpreted as counsel to profit by the learning and experience of others. Currently, in our society of accelerated pace, the respect directive for childrearing is less widespread but even more unreasonable; indeed, its feasibility declines with every passing day. Although history may pardon our time for many misdeeds, there can be no sanctuary for those who run from reason, from understanding their young.

The rapidity of change in America has reshaped child life so that today it only vaguely resembles what it was a few years ago. This tends to decrease the experiences the young and not so young share in common, separating persons of different generations. Yet many a well-intentioned adult fails to recognize that a child's world can be populated only by children, that its reality grows less with age, and that the life space of a youngster today cannot be duplicated by the retrospect of adults who

1

were children in another time. Evidence for this thesis abounds and is especially replete in the evolving nature of verbal exchange between youth and elders.

Consider a typical comment by boys and girls in a recent opinion survey. When approached with the complaint of parents that communication with teen-agers seems to be diminishing, the respondents said, "They're removed from our world pretty much. Oh, we know they say they were young once, but we don't believe it" (Hogan, 1964).* The wise response of grown-ups to this statement should be a new awareness that one cannot remember something that never happened to him—and what is happening to youth today is unique in history to their age group. Undoubtedly, it is the discrepancy between what each of us remembers our early years to have been and what life's first two decades are now that renders some of our advice irrelevant, certain of our experiences obsolete, and many of the analogies anachronistic. For many future citizens, the response is a persistent lament, "Why don't the grown-ups try to understand us!"

The double search in which adults seek respect from children and children look to their elders for understanding often leads to an impasse. This result is not born of necessity, the consequence is not inevitable; it can and should be rectified. Since both age groups share the common goal of recognition and esteem, and as we cannot demand of others what we would deny to them, there is a need for one element to demonstrate the initiative of accommodation. For most men and women, particularly those who would instruct the young, this means we must direct more of our energies toward understanding children; we must activate the reciprocal of our dictum for boys and girls—we must *respect* the child. To do less is to fail as a parent or teacher. Although this idea is not a new alternative, in the speed of current social change it becomes a new imperative.

Almost all prospective educators are required to elect college courses designed to sensitize them to the variety of emotional, intellectual, physical, and social differences one may expect to encounter in a classroom. This is as it should be. But we cannot respect the differences among children unless we first accept the differences between children and adults. Until we are convinced that solutions to many of the problems facing today's youth are beyond memory, the dangerous tendency to resolve issues by retrospect will continue to obstruct our understanding of the young. This is one of the greatest deterrents to becoming a good teacher, since it ignores the characteristics indigenous to certain age groups and denies the unique identity of individuals. Adults too often suggest, "When you've lived as long as I have, you will understand"; a more proper assertion is, "When you have lived my years in my time, you may better know something of what I feel."

* References in parentheses refer to the Bibliography at the back of this book.

Perhaps the problem is less acute in nations other than ours where more cultural uniformity and a slower rate of progress have allowed adults and children to retain more common experiences, better communication, and closer relationships. For example, consider Figure I-1, which depicts the activity space of a child in a society where life is simple, the collective experiences of his adult fellows, and the context in which these age groups share experiences. Note that only a minor portion of contemporary child life lies outside the background of the culture's adult membership. In this setting, a father might reasonably say to his son, "Let me tell you about life and what to expect. I'll give you the benefit of my experience. Now, when I was your age. . . ." The fact that the youngster could expect to confront circumstances essentially similar to those which his father had earlier encountered would seem to lend credence to parental counsel.

In contrast, juxtapose life in modern America as illustrated by Figure I-2. Here, of course, the pace of change is more rapid than in the simple society and, as a result, a larger portion of contemporary child experience becomes foreign to the culture's adult membership. There may be some things we adults are too old to know simply because we are not young now. In fact, some anthropologists are predicting that the rate of change in our society will so increase during the next few years that children now being born will find few contemporary adult behavior patterns that will stand them in good stead when they reach maturity. Therefore, youngsters may be forced to turn more and more to one another to work out effective and satisfying modes of behavior. Figure I-2 suggests that while children are having experiences that are unique in history to their age group, there seems to be a coincident decline in the range of day-to-day activities they share with adults; the context of mutual endeavor appears to shrink. Most men and women are vitally concerned about reversing this tendency because they love their children, dislike misunderstandings, and wish to have more in common with sons and daughters. Teachers join parents in this concern, since to know students better is to be a better teacher. Unfortunately, many grown-ups who desire to share more of life with children fail to demonstrate the logical concomitant of this attitude in that they choose relationships that are incompatible with a child's best interests.

A dangerous but frequently selected path is that of constricting the tenure of childhood. By insisting that a boy behave as an adult, that he simulate maturity, the child is obliged to substitute patterns of behavior we understand for those behaviors characteristic of his age. Thus, unwilling to understand the actions of youth which puzzle us, we attempt to shorten the duration of their occurrence. In other words, the burden of accommodation is incumbent upon the child, for not only is he expected to be more like an adult than a child, but he must make the transformation in less time than ever before, quicker than nature would dictate. The emotional cost of this practice is beyond assessment, because in requesting a child to forfeit part of himself, we render incalculable expense to every aspect of his personality development. And this is so unnecessary, for we now know that children who are permitted a chance for normal growth and development are more likely to be emotionally stable than children who are denied the opportunity. In the twentieth century, for the first time in history, Americans have a life cycle that permits full development. Today, with the life expectancy of three score and ten, there can be lengthy periods of childhood, adolescence, young adulthood, middle years, and even aging. Despite this fact, there are mounting pressures for children to grow up faster than ever before, to imitate adulthood, to be men before they are boys, to omit childhood (Strom, 1965a, 1965b).

Another adult contingent, equally supportive of closer association with the young, has formulated a somewhat opposite strategy. Instead of requiring children to be adultlike, this group advocates emulation of youth. Their rationale stems from a sincere belief that students, especially teen-agers, will accept, favor, and respect only those grown-ups who demonstrate an understanding of young life. Further, adolescents will distinguish between the understanding and the uninformed adults by observing our behavior patterns. Therefore, the reasoning continues, the initiative lies with us: show that we do understand them by acting more like them, particularly by adopting certain of their actions (which adults in the main severely criticize) such as dance types, clothing styles, and illogical expenditures of time and energy. So goes the reasoning. However, it is disheartening to watch supposedly mature persons who, apparently distressed by their inability to communicate with youth, have capitulated to imitating youth, striving for a second adolescence in order to be closer to their teen-agers. By adopting juvenile behaviors and interests, the adult is unwittingly forced to trade that vital part of himself which could be the only reasonable base for the type of companionship he seeks with his son or daughter. Children do not request that adults become children again, but that adults understand children—by learning rather than memory. Otherwise, the position of leadership is vacated; and in our time, as in every other, boys and girls seek counsel from the mature. Without some responsible adult direction, children are destined to follow a restless movement, a planless self-development, an aim of living that has no criteria for value, in which happiness always lies in the future, never in any present achievement.

Both propositions suggested thus far are unacceptable, since they call for the ultimate desertion of an individual from himself. On the one hand, children are directed to enter an adult society before they are ready; the other alternative implies the need for adults to revert to childhood. Neither path allows the person to remain essentially what he is, a member of an age group at a given point in the life cycle, whose behavior should reflect his present situation. Yet it should be obvious that when any activity

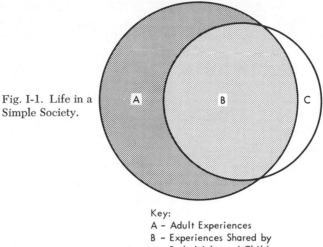

Fig. I-1. Life in a Simple Society.

Key:
A – Adult Experiences
B – Experiences Shared by
    Both Adults and Child
C – Child Experiences

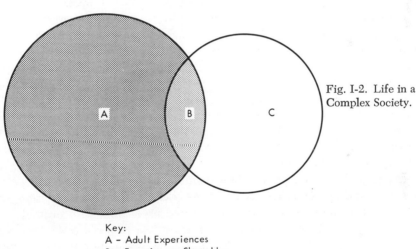

Fig. I-2. Life in a Complex Society.

Key:
A – Adult Experiences
B – Experiences Shared by
    Both Adults and Child
C – Child Experiences

is jointly carried forth under either of these imposed conditions, there can be no mutual satisfaction or feeling of sharing. Sharing involves more than doing things together or spending time with one another—its most meaningful dimension is *communication*. When there is communication between the young and the mature, there is sharing, even though separate schedules may prevent or limit extended periods of time together.

But how do we communicate with children if our backgrounds make us illiterate in the language of their experience? Some wish to be told this task is easy or impossible; in truth it is both difficult and possible. To begin with, tolerance and humility are essential, a realization that children may know things that are unknown to us (a notion that should change our view of teaching). This means that the Victorian admonition, "Children are to be seen and not heard," is inappropriate as a modern guide for nurture and classroom management. Rather, we must learn to listen to the young, to what they say and what they are trying to say— ever as mindful as they that masks have no ears.

We need to discontinue parataxic relations. These relations occur when a youngster's comment is halted by an adult on the insulting assumption that we know what he is going to say before he says it, or when a teacher prematurely interrupts a student on the premise that his response is irrelevant. Such a mindreading view fails to recognize that for most children answers may begin with what we, as adults, consider extraneous information before the pertinent data is given. Bear in mind that a child's supposedly irrelevant preamble to those answers adults seek may be germane as seen from the youthview (Strom, 1966a). In the way a teacher listens and communicates concern and regard, children perceive whether they are viewed as valued and respected persons. To these young people, as to their parents and teachers, respect is important because it distinguishes one as an individual, a unique being. It follows that each of us tends to learn more rapidly from one who gives consideration to our desires, feelings, and wisdom, a person whom we hold in high esteem.

There is a distinction between recognizing differences among pupils and respecting these differences. When respect is lacking, the teacher makes no attempt to retain the identity of every student. Instead, he establishes uniform expectations, fosters conformity, and tries to make all students alike. Under these conditions, many children are destined to stand in the shadow of their potential. On the other hand, a more effective instructor is careful not to constrict the range of diversity among students. He feels the best way to respect individual differences is to make provision for them by modifying lessons and assignments both in nature and length corresponding with the capacity of each pupil. Accordingly, he seeks insights, new ways of assisting each student to profit from classroom instruction, recognizing that to deny a child understanding is to deny him an education. In part, this vital understanding implies knowing how children differ in their *facility to learn, environmental support,* and *readiness for instruction.*

FACILITY TO LEARN

Intelligence

For years the concept of facility to learn was restricted to considerations of hereditary influence. As the nature of intelligence and its measure had yet to be described, there were few scientists who would concede that environment might appreciably alter human development. Biological inheritance alone was regarded as the key to academic and life success. Then, with the advent of testing, an optimistic conviction arose that the term *mind* was understood, its dimensions had been determined, its assessment was possible. Unfortunately, the number of man's mental functions was grossly underestimated in the first tests of intelligence and as a result schools have endeavored to improve certain aspects of the learning process to the exclusion of other equally important components of potential. Only during the past decade have we come to envisage a more complex structure of intellect, a wider view of the human mind and, from this vantage, introduce an educational setting that is without precedent in its curricular scope and humane regard. The story of how it all came about is both interesting and gratifying.

Before 1860, little attention was offered the notion that children markedly differ in mental functioning from their parents as well as from one another. Instead, the observational propensity of adults was to seek out and explain familial similarities as evidenced in such statements as, "She has her mother's intuition," "He has his grandfather's wit and temper," "He's a chip off the old block—like father, like son." In order to ensure the best destiny possible for their offspring, many parents of the nineteenth century felt inclined to adopt a popular doctrine known as the *inheritance of acquired characteristics*. This miscarriage of science, first put forth by the French zoologist Jean Lamarck in his *Philosophie Zoologique* (1830), maintained that acquired changes in thinking and behavior could be passed on from parent to offspring and that this was the chief cause of evolution. Lamarck stated in effect that parents could improve the biological endowment of their children by participating in mental and physical ventures of self-improvement. For example, if in his youth a father had been interested in painting, the affinity toward artistic expression would likely be transferred to his son. The same transmission would obtain for athletic or mechanical ability. A mother who previous to the birth of her daughter had been trained to regard classical music might expect the girl to manifest a similar interest. The fact that most parental characteristics believed to be conveyed at the moment of conception were culture-obtained attributes did not seem to threaten Lamarck's theory or in any way render it dubious.

To persuade the reluctant element whose distrust of scientific method and direction was based on a religious orientation, proponents of the acquired characteristics theory claimed theological support by citing biblical accounts in which even intrauterine life had been advantageously affected under certain conditions. For large numbers of people, Lamarck's basic rationale seemed to provide inferences upon which one could postulate a convenient explanation for many of nature's unknowns. Perhaps the snake lost his legs because of his ancestor's predilection for crawling through tight spaces, narrow holes and clefts; maybe the long neck of the giraffe was acquired because his progenitors spent much of their time reaching into the trees for food (Weismann, 1891, p. 86). However foolish the theory of acquired characteristics and its unscientific variants now appear to us, these viewpoints enjoyed an acceptance which is difficult to overestimate.

When the general principles of genetic transmission were finally discovered in 1857 by the brilliant Austrian monk Gregor Mendel, they were ignored. In fact Mendel lived to see his published findings (1865) denied even the courtesy of attentive study; not until several decades after his death (1900) were the Mendelian laws given serious consideration and thereafter became the basis for future studies in genetic transmission. During the interval between Mendel's discovery and the acceptance of his hypotheses, there were other men who tried to dissuade popular opinion from the prevailing fiction about heredity. Among the more eloquent spokesmen was August Weismann who, in 1889, released a series of essays in which he suggested that heredity is brought about by the transference from one generation to another of a substance having a definite chemical molecular constitution. This substance called germ plasm is uninfluenced by that which happens in the life of an individual who bears it. Therefore, while the rest of the body may be altered through illness, injury or exercise, the germ plasm that an individual passes on to his children at their conception does not ordinarily change. And as genes are not subject to the usual influences that either improve or deteriorate our bodies and minds, it follows that the genes of a sick but well-educated man of middle age are no different from those he possessed as a robust but unschooled youngster of seventeen. In short, changes in the rest of the body do not effect the genetic characteristics of the germ plasm that is passed on to our progeny (Weismann, 1891, pp. 71–106). This is not to say that parental self-improvement is unimportant for proper child growth and development but rather that it is ineffectual as a determinant in genetic transmission. Certainly a child inherits not only his father's genes but his father as well.

A contrasting method for improving intellectual facility of children arose from studies conducted by Sir Francis Galton. His curiosity about the differences among people, and particularly the differences between families, may have been stimulated by the earlier ideas of a cousin, Charles Darwin, whose monumental work *The Origin of Species* (1860), had reflected a concern for biological variations. In pursuit of the quest to determine what relationships obtain between family background and recognized achievement, Galton learned that a comparatively small number of English families were responsible for the rearing of most of the Crown's scientists. Reporting these findings in *English Men and Science* (1874), Galton concluded that genius is inherited. Other genealogical studies of the time seemed to lend credence to his hypothesis that mental inheritance is relatively consistent in families over time. For example,

Dugdale (1877), a New York prison association inspector, published a study of the infamous Jukes family, who by their vice, crime, and pauperism during a period of seven generations cost the State of New York over one million dollars. Apparently adverse characteristics are genetically transferred as readily as culture-termed genius.

Precisely because this appeared true, Galton felt disposed to suggest that for the human race to improve itself, there was need for a selective breeding process by which intellectually able persons would choose as mates only those of similar inheritance. Known as *eugenics* (based on the Greek word *eugenes*, meaning "well-born") this concept suggested that citizens might be bred as we now breed race horses and pedigree pups. Eugenics should not be confused with the term genetics, which did not come into being until 1900. Needless to say, acceptance of the selective breeding principle was initially confined to persons within the favored societal element, to those individuals convinced that their offspring would profit the culture. Yet by the beginning of the twentieth century, a host of British psychologists had joined Galton, Darwin, Spencer, and Huxley in the belief that the laws of individual variation and heredity apply to men as well as animals, mind as well as body. Many who remained unsure, still wavering over the social implications, were to be won over by Huxley's celebrated essay, "On the Natural Inequality of Men" (1890). In the main, teachers were already converted by firsthand experience under the relatively new scheme of universal education (Burt, 1958).

The theories of both Lamarck and Galton were similar in their objective as each sought to enhance the mental facility of the unborn by first modifying some dimension of parental behavior. On the one hand, Lamarck believed that the benefit of any parental effort toward self-improvement would necessarily be effectual for one's offspring as well. To Galton, however, only careful mate selection would obviate those difficulties that led to producing less able, low-achieving children. Neither man proposed to understand inheritance so much as to improve it. Nonetheless, the aims of Galton—to determine differences among individuals—was a noble beginning, for not until the individual became the focus of concern did the research orientation shift from an emphasis on who inherits most to the question of what is genetically transferred. The need for more accurate instruments to measure and describe the physical and psychological differences in which Galton was interested required a new field of concentration for psychology—a concern for statistics.

It is interesting to note that recent research involving the preservation of human sperm by freezing and freeze-drying may serve to encourage those who embrace some modified version of the Lamarck or Galton theories. In brief, the frozen sperm experiments, originated by Dr. Jerome K. Sherman, University of Arkansas Medical School, proceed by mixing an ejaculation of sperm cells with a 10 percent solution of glycerol, which protects these cells from adverse effects of freezing and thawing. The mixture is then bottled in ampules and suspended over nitrogen vapor in a container at –168°C. When samples are thawed, about 30 percent of the sperm cells are lost; the surviving 70 percent, which can be preserved perhaps indefinitely, retain their power of motility and fertility. As the process does not damage or alter chromosomal structure, there is no increased probability of abnormal offspring.

Consider the prospect stored semen offers in relation to the theories of Lamarck and Galton respectively. Most geneticists agree that the reproductive cells of a young man are more fertile, more motile, more capable of doing the job they were destined to do than is his semen at an older age. However, many young couples today wish to defer the task of rearing a family until their economic circumstance is such that they can more easily provide the material things children may require. In short, they perceive their self-improvement a requisite for parenthood. Suppose a bridegroom of 21 years of age deposits spermatozoa in a frozen sperm bank and then later, at age 30, having achieved some degree of affluence, he and his wife decide they wish to become parents. However, during the interval between ages 21 and 30, the husband has suffered an illness which resulted in sterility. Under these conditions, there usually would be no chance to produce children but this man is still capable of fathering youngsters via his stored semen. Or take a different circumstance: At age 35 a similar couple, except that the man is not sterile, attempts to have children but without success. This is not uncommon, as medical estimates indicate some 10 to 25 percent of all married couples suffer problems of infertility at one time or another. Using the stored semen, injected by a physician on days to coincide with the woman's ovulation, some of these couples can be helped. According to Dr. Sherman, a half dozen or so consecutive inseminations with concentrated spermatozoa—sperm cells collected and frozen over a time span of several months, then thawed, pooled, and centrifuged so that the resultant sperm cell count is eight to ten times higher than the original count in any possible ejaculation—has resulted in pregnancies where couples have previously tried in vain to beget a child.

The idea of establishing regional banks for frozen sperm has implications also for those who support a variant of Galton's eugenic mate selection concept. An example: After learning of his sterility, caused either by a chromosomal abberation or illness, a husband and his wife decide artificial insemination is the way by which their child should arrive. At the sperm bank, the couple looks at the master catalogue which contains vital statistics and unnamed colored photographs of men who have contributed semen. They may decide to select the semen of one whose build, background, and eye or hair color approximates that of the father. Perhaps they choose to endow the infant with characteristics of mind or body better than their own and so pick the most intelligent or good-looking candidate. To those couples who will have no difficulty in producing children, this discourse may seem repulsive; to those couples who wish to have children and cannot for one of the reasons mentioned here, this becomes a tenable alternative.

Leo Szilard, one of our most versatile scientists, without whom atomic energy might not have been developed, said before his death, "This system gives a couple a germinal choice of parental selection. Just imagine if we had a bank containing the sperm of such notables as Albert Einstein, George Gershwin, John F. Kennedy, Albert Schweitzer . . . we could improve the human breed . . . look at the tremendous strides made by farmers and cattlemen in improving their cattle. I know it sounds harsh and clinical but with human beings it can be very much the same." Dr. Herman J. Muller, Nobel Prize–winning geneticist of Indiana University, entertains a similar belief in hoping that the concept of parental selection may one day extend beyond couples with one sterile or infertile member, that it may be practiced by those fertile couples who wish to improve upon the genetic constitution of their young (Shearer, 1964, pp. 4–5).

After this digression regarding frozen sperm, let us return to the influence of Galton. Although it is little known, he anticipated Charles Spearman, a pioneer in factor analytic technique, by postulating a two-factor theory of intelligence. In Spearman's initial papers, he expressly states that he borrowed the distinction between general and specific abilities from Galton (Spearman, 1904). Advocates of the two-factor theory have believed that intelligence is made up of a g or general factor and a number of s or specific factors. Whereas the g factor is operative in all types of intellective activity, various endeavors require special abilities (s) in addition to the general (g) ability factor. What is ordinarily termed general achievement then is attributed to the g factor while excellence in one subject or another is due to the presence of greater specific factors for that area of endeavor. Until this reorientation—an emphasis on trying to understand the nature of intelligence—school experience for many children was a daily exercise of inequity.

When techniques in mental testing were first devised, their initial application involved persons at the lower end of the intelligence scale. Puzzled by the difficulties of identifying pupils whose mental abilities were insufficiently developed to profit from instruction in the public schools of Paris, educational authorities of that city enlisted the support of Alfred Binet and his colleague Theophile Simon, who together constructed the first test of intelligence (1905). However, administration of the test was not confined to unfortunate deviates; its measure did more than express in a uniform way the degree of mental defect among maladjusted students. That first series of mental tasks ultimately grew into the whole complex of today's familiar intelligence tests. In our country, Lewis Terman (1916) translated Binet's work into several versions, the most influential of which is the Stanford Binet.

According to Binet, intelligence is not a single mental function but rather an aggregate of abilities involving censorship, comprehension, direction, and invention. Critics of the French psychologist point out his tests do not meet the criteria of his own definition. That is, invention, originality, and fertility of ideas are not considered on Binet's selected items; neither is motivation, which ostensibly is an integral part of direction. But Binet never stated that his tasks measure the composite of man's mental abilities; instead he clearly recognized there are many functions not assessed by the tests (1909). He perceived his work to be a beginning, and a good beginning it was. However, Binet's reluctance to claim more for the scope of intelligence tests than their measure did not prevent others from misusing the instrument by adopting the tool as a comprehensive index of mental functioning. In school, especially, many decisions regarding the future of children were based exclusively upon the IQ score—important decisions involving academic expectations, instructional grouping, and evaluation of progress.

The tragedy of this persuasion appears clear in retrospect. Guilford, an eminent psychologist who has devoted a long and productive career studying the mental abilities, estimates the number of mental functions to be 120, perhaps only 6 of which are considered on traditional intelligence tests: vocabulary ability, general reasoning, memory for ideas, number ability, ability to visualize spatially, and perceptual speed. Even more significant than the relatively small portion of abilities that IQ tests measure is the importance of these abilities in today's world. For example, in one study scientists were presented a list of 28 functions of the mind and requested to rank-order these in terms of their relevance for successful work in the physical sciences. All but one of the traditional intelligence test factors ranked below 20th on the list; that is, 19 out of the 20 characteristics considered by scientists most important on the job were not included on the traditional IQ test (Taylor, 1961, p. 65). The prospect of this discrepancy applying to other vocations as well as life in general becomes apparent upon the realization that for years educational curricula and materials have been shaped to bring out only the kinds of growth and achievement related to the abilities measured by IQ tests; measures of scholastic achievement have also been patterned along these lines. Furthermore, IQ has always been the major instrument used in assessing intellectual potential and mental growth, for determining giftedness and mental retardation. (Strom, 1964b, pp. 27–29).

Alfred Binet never abandoned his hope that one day psychologists would envision a broader view of the mind, a more adequate, complex image of mental functioning. This aspiration, though as yet not fully realized, continues as the focus of regard for many dedicated investigators. Chief among the obstacles to their success has been the circular logic employed in granting acceptability to new measures of intelligence and the absence of a comprehensive theoretical structure of intellect. Consider each of these difficulties.

For a test to be acceptable, it must be judged valid; in other words, evidence must exist that the test measures what its authors intend. To establish validity, it has been customary for new tests to show a satisfactory correlation (relationship) with an existing measure (test) of the same function. The irony here is that no single intelligence test measures the composite of abilities implied in the term *intelligence*. Thus, when a new test is to be validated, it must measure the identical components of intelligence that the accepted test measures or validity is lost. Naturally, new tests alleging to measure abilities other than those few called for in traditional intelligence tests may expect low validity. As a consequence, it has been difficult to initiate a departure from the narrow definition that "intelligence is what intelligence tests measure." It is to be hoped that IQ tests, tests of creative thinking, and other instruments will be used in combination as indices of potential. Certainly all of our present tests combined do not consider the whole measure of man's mind, but in measurement as in all of education we must preserve what is good and work for what is better (Strom, 1965c, p. 91).

Knowledge about the matrices of intellectual functions is recent and incomplete. Among those who have most influenced advance in perspective are Thorndike, Thurstone, and Guilford. It was Thorndike who proposed the idea that there are three types of intelligence, with the distinctions made on the basis of content: the ability to work with symbols he called abstract intelligence; the ability to manipulate objects is mechanical intelligence; and the ability to relate well with one's fellows is social intelligence (1927, p. 5). Thurstone (1938) was the first to approach a study of intelligence by using factor analysis. Basing his research on Spearman's two-factor theory, Thurstone came to believe the mind of man harbors seven primary mental abilities in addition to a g or general factor. Separately, the contributions of both Thorndike and Thurstone in this context appear less important than when viewed as influences in the work of a more recent scientist, J. P. Guilford, to whom credit is due for conceptualizing a structure of intellect (1959, pp. 342–406).

A theoretical model for the complete structure of intellect (Figure I-3) is shown by a solid figure of three dimensions in which each of the individual cells or factors is also three dimensional. At each intersection of the dimensions there is a certain mental *operation* performed upon a certain kind of *content* resulting in a certain type of *product*. In combination, given Guilford's hypothesis that there are five mental operations, four kinds of content and six types of products, a total of 120 cells or factors are estimated, nearly 50 of which are now known.

Four categories appear under the dimension of content, the materials upon which mental operations are performed: figural, symbolic, semantic, and behavioral. *Figural* content involves the senses of audition, vision, and kinesthetics. In his classification of intelligence types, Thorndike would have considered this as mechanical intelligence but, as the scope of figural content is more extensive than Thorndike's earlier typology, it is now generally regarded as concrete intelligence. *Symbolic* content refers to letters, words, sentences, or numbers (their structures as opposed to meanings), while *semantic* content is of a conceptual nature, dealing with meanings expressed in verbal form. Considered by some as verbal intelligence, the semantic category is frequently used in current tests of intelligence. It is clear that what Thorndike termed abstract intelligence subsumes both the symbolic and semantic categories of Guilford. What Thorndike thought of as social intelligence or empathy (the ability to be effective with people) is close to *behavioral* content, which is the ability to infer the perceptions, attitudes, thoughts, and feelings of others from their behavior.

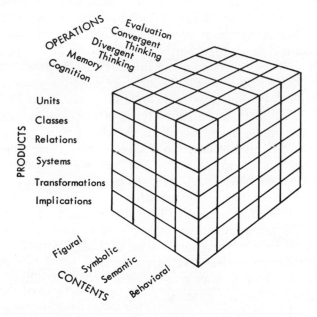

Fig. I-3. Theoretical model for the complete structure of human intellect. From *Personality* by J. P. Guilford (New York: McGraw-Hill Book Company, 1959), p. 397. Used by permission.

The second dimension of intellect is made up of the five kinds of mental operations performed on the content categories: cognition, memory, convergent production, divergent production, and evaluation. *Cognition* involves the discovery of information while *memory* is the recall or reproduction of what has been cognized. What is done with information that has been remembered or cognized depends on which of two productive thinking types are employed (convergent-divergent). *Convergent production* is directed toward a single solution or right answer whereas *divergent production* entertains the prospect that there may be several alternatives or possible solutions. Clearly most tests given in classrooms favor convergent production. *Evaluative* abilities are activated when it becomes necessary to determine whether information cognized, remembered, or produced is adequate, correct, or suitable.

Applying certain mental operations to categories of content results in various kinds of products. These products, which constitute the third dimension in the structure of intellect, consist of units, classes, relations, systems, transformations, and implications. *Units* are made up of discrete concepts or symbolic structures, while *classes* include informational elements grouped with one another because of some commonality. When units of information are recognized as bearing reference to others, the connection is termed a *relation*. A structured complex of informational relationships constitutes a *system*. *Transformations* occur when items are improvised or placed in new combinations such as in divergent production. Finally, products known as *implications* occur when inferences drawn from information govern future expectations or predictions. Admittedly, these dimensions form a purely theoretical structure of intellect and, like Binet, Guilford has emphasized the tentativeness of his model, and the necessity for its improvement as additional information is acquired.

To summarize, for years the study of man's intellectual facility to learn was more concerned about the source of mental inheritance than with its dimensions, placing greater stress upon the causal factors that account for differences among individuals than upon the ways in which individuals differ. This problem was exacerbated when instruments were first devised to assess limited aspects of intellect, for many eager but unwise persons embraced intelligence tests as adequate indices of all mental functioning. Believing the dimensions of intellect already determined, many educators felt little inclination to understand the mind—their task was to improve it, and as the mind's improvement involved development of only those functions considered on the tests, curriculums were structured so as to correspond with the measures of intellect. Naturally, this arrangement worked to the disadvantage of all children, for many inhumane decisions were made regarding educational prospect and achievement. To some teachers, intelligence was considered a central factor of personality; by knowing the intellectual quotient of an individual, it was believed one could know many other things about him, including his honesty, leadership, and value structure. Today we are less certain that high IQ scores ensure loyalty, trust, or other positive attributes. Even when confronted by anomalies in the achievement levels of certain children, educators did not permit their perplexity to interfere with fidelity to the system. Creative children, for example, unable to obtain elevated scores on the IQ tests, have always been labeled "overachievers" instead of "gifted," since their success has been considered the result of motivation rather than of mental ability. In truth, of course, such children have not exceeded their intellectual potential; instead their potential has been miscomputed.

This is not an indictment of intelligence tests, as for years such measures have been useful and will continue to be if we expect of them what their results can offer us. The greatest limitations of the IQ tests have been the unrealistic expectations of those who use them. Whenever more is expected from a test than its findings can provide, those using the results misperceive the instrument to be a horoscope. Each of us who teach must daily make judgments about the intelligence of students, their ability, and their levels of achievement. These decisions are important, for they govern our aspirations regarding a pupil, our expectations of his performance, the type of instruction, and the level of content. Such decisions are destined to be erroneous if we oversimplify their predicate—that is, no judgment should be made on the basis of a single index, a measure of only limited aspects of intelligence. There is less danger now that we shall disregard talent than that we shall fail to recognize it and so promote conditions under which certain abilities can neither be demonstrated nor developed. This much is certain: We can no longer afford to sustain a history of disrespect for the entire spectrum of intelligence. To remain indifferent or myopic about developing any of the mental functions (Figure I-3) of children is to forfeit much of their potential as individual citizens and in turn much of our greatness as a nation.

Motivation

An examination of school report cards for any grade or class would show that great differences often obtain in achievement levels between pupils having the same measured intelligence. Although Roger and Larry both score an IQ of 100 on their intelligence test, Roger receives all A's on his report card while Larry is judged to be a C student. This discrepancy in accomplishment between the two boys occurs because the facility to learn involves more than just mental ability; it incorporates a number of nonintellectual factors as well. Among the nonintellectual elements which most appear to influence success in school are motivation, aspiration, self-concept, and social adjustment. To illustrate the impact such factors can have on educational process, let us consider the field of motivation. As motives direct behavior, they are of considerable interest to both psychologists and educators.

In every age, mankind has engaged in speculation about the source of behavior, the reasons for actions, the acquisition of motives. For millenniums, a common practice was to interpret human behavior by one set of concepts and explain animal behavior in terms of another. Thus, while the soul was considered responsible for impelling man to act or respond,

Descartes postulated that animals, being machinelike, were driven by certain fluid spirits rushing through their nerves. This type of explanation was not discarded until the influence of Darwin became widespread. In his *The Origin of Species* (1860) discussion about the anatomical and physiological continuity between animals and human beings, Darwin suggested there might also be a corresponding continuity in their behavior. He later gave elaboration to this thesis in *The Expression of the Emotions in Man and Animals* (1872). Thereafter, studies of animal behavior rapidly increased in number for many investigators came to regard the observation of lower forms of life as clues to the more complex but essentially similar patterns of human beings. It was during this transition as numerous biological concepts were being received into psychology that the term *instincts* replaced *soul* and other animistic references as the dynamic agents that are responsible for moving organisms to perform different kinds of activity (Bindra, 1959, pp. 5–10).

Among the first psychologists to accept the instinct theory was William James, who in 1890 contended that man possesses more instincts than any other animal. Unlike most of his colleagues, however, James was dissatisfied with the limited task of merely enumerating innate propensities: jealousy, curiosity, rivalry, pugnacity, and crying. Instead he sought to encourage additional investigation into causation, the why of human behavior and to overcome the ambiguity which characterized discussions on the topic of instincts. To James, an instinct was "the faculty of acting in such a way as to produce a certain end without foresight of that end and without the individual's having previous education in the performance." But instincts are neither blind nor invariable because experience (memory) combines with the innate factors to evoke later behaviors that often differ from the original act. Thus, ". . . every instinctive act in an animal with memory, must cease to be blind after being once repeated and must be accompanied with foresight of its end just so far as that end may have fallen under the animal's cognizance" (James, 1890, pp. 383–441). This broad conception of instincts containing experiential, cognitive, and perceptual elements was largely ignored by theorists of the twentieth century, who chose instead to embrace mechanistic definitions of less complexity, definitions that allowed them to believe they were solving the problems of instincts by merely naming them (instincts).

Most popular among the instinct doctrines was that first advanced by McDougall (1908). Characterizing the instincts as a complex of innate emotional strivings that predispose an individual to either approach or avoid stimuli, McDougall emphasized the purposive nature or goal-directedness of all animal and human behavior. The most important aspect of instinct to him was its supposed control over perception in that instincts would predetermine the avoidance or acceptance of stimuli. Initially, McDougall believed he might subsume all behaviors under perhaps a dozen instincts. As time passed, however, the number of native propensities grew so that by 1933 his list had reached seventeen: fear, sex, disgust, curiosity, food-seeking, parental propensity, gregariousness, self-assertion, submission, constructive propensity, anger, appeal, acquisitive propensity, comfort, laughter, migratory propensity, and rest (McDougall, 1933, pp. 97–106).

Before long, the term instinct was a favored one in psychological parlance used by such notables as Thorndike (1913), Dewey (1917), Watson (1914), and Woodworth (1918). Whenever behavioral antecedents were discussed, the instinct reference seemed an appropriate interpretation. Few people seemed bothered by the difference between describing something and explaining it. Under these conditions, it was natural for the number of suggested instincts to increase so that after his survey of approximately five hundred books in which authors employed the instinct concept, Bernard (1924) reported that no fewer than 849 separate types of instincts had been hypothesized.

But instinct theory was not without opposition. A number of psychologists felt the concept had to be discredited as an explanation for all behavior if genuine inquiry was to persist regarding motivation. In his attack entitled *Are There Any Instincts?* (1919), Dunlap asserted that much activity considered as instinctive is really a combination of learned and unlearned responses. From sociology came the complaint that certain of the instincts such as maternal love were too complex and variable between cultures to be considered as innate; instead these were behaviors that had been acquired from environmental influence. Scholars from other disciplines mused over the apparent inability of psychologists to agree on the exact number or even the nature of instincts. Perhaps the greatest challenge came from John B. Watson, who appealed for proof that certain responses were innate rather than learned. He argued that the instinct concept was being used as an ever-ready substitute for true explanations of observed activities. When silence was his answer, Watson set out to design research studies that would answer his own inquiry, hasten the demise of instinctive psychology, and earn for him the title "Father of Behavioristic Psychology."

As there was no reliable data on the human infant, Watson launched his series of pioneer studies into the behavioral and emotional responses of the human young. For a generation, scientists had been gathering a substantial collection of facts about the young of practically every species except man. To test for native emotions (instincts), Watson introduced various furry objects and animals to his sample babies, things that children are supposed instinctively to fear. It was found that infants exhibit no fear in their behavior of the proverbial black cat, reptiles, white rats, pigeons, or dogs. Watson's results seemed incredible, for if the average infant has practically no fears, no instincts of avoidance, how does it happen that a few years later in their lives practically all children are so fearful of many things? To this question, Watson replied that hampering fears are learned or built into human behavior by social environment. To prove this he decided upon a daring experiment in which he would build up fears in an infant and then study practical ways by which these fears might be removed. For his subject, Watson chose a happy, chubby infant of eleven months named Albert B. The first task, using a conditioning process, was to produce a fear response in Albert to a white rat. As the white rat with which Albert had played for some weeks was taken from the basket and presented to him in the usual manner, a metal bar was struck immediately behind the infant's head. Albert jumped! In turn, rabbits, reptiles, and other objects were presented. The results showed how infants can build up fear by transferring a conditioned, emotional reaction acquired in connection with another stimulus—in this case, the rat. If emotional responses, fears, habits, the so-called instincts, could be so easily built in, why couldn't educators and psychologists assist parents in removing these fears and other handicaps which hampered the development of so many children (Watson, 1930, pp. 158–166).

Under a grant from the Rockefeller Memorial Fund, Watson worked with Mary Cover Jones on a project involving the elimination of children's fears. Together they studied some seventy children who had shown pronounced fears of snakes, rabbits, frogs, and other animals. Seven techniques were employed in the attempt to remove fears. This was a practical problem as parents were always fussing about the anxiety of their youngsters. There was a good deal of dispute about the proper course to follow when a youngster was afraid of such things as a neighbor's dog—should one ridicule him, distract him, or reason with him? These questions were answered by the Watson-Jones project and from their findings it was apparent that environmental influences have a good deal to do with shaping behavior (Watson, 1930, pp. 167–195).

At the conclusion of his studies, Watson believed there no longer was a need for the term *instinct,* that everything psychologists had been in the habit of calling instinctive really belonged to man's learned behavior. He indicated there are no human instincts in the old meaning of the term but only learned and unlearned (rage, fear, love) emotional responses—no inherited capacities of any sort. In fact, Watson went on record as saying, "There are inheritable differences in structure but we no longer believe in inherited capacities. Give me a dozen healthy infants and my own world to bring them up in and I will guarantee to train any one of them to become any type of specialists I might select—doctor, artist, merchant or chief, beggarman, or thief" (Watson, 1930, p. 104).

In general, behaviorists accepted the idea that human activity is almost entirely a matter of conditioning and that any child can be caused to develop in whatever direction those who train him so desire. In support of this thesis, much credence has been given at various times to stories of babies or young children whose deviant behavior can ostensibly be attributed to their rearing by animals. Almost all of these stories emanating from a number of countries have been rendered untenable by subsequent investigation. There was the baboon boy, allegedly found in South Africa (1903) living with a troup of baboons and exhibiting the mannerisms of these animals. Later inquiry revealed that the youngster was suffering from a severe mental disorder. Great attention was extended to the gazelle boy episode (1946), a wild Arab lad who was believed to be grazing and living with a herd of gazelles in the Syrian Desert. Reportedly he fled from hunters at the phenomenal speed of 50 miles per hour. When truth caught up with the human gazelle, he was identified as a very ill child who had strayed from his parents and who may or may not have been racing with animals. As for the phenomenal speed, magazine writer Michael Stern, who subsequently visited the boy's village, said he ran a foot race with the human gazelle and left him far behind (Scheinfeld, 1950, pp. 394–410).

Many stories of environmental determinism have come from India, where the myth of lower-class children reared by animals is widespread. There was the instance of the two wolf girls, Kamala and Imala, reported as having been reared by a she-wolf after their mother had abandoned them. When the girls were found, they allegedly were running on all fours, unable to stand upright, drank by lapping their long tongues, howled at night, ate live chickens, and were able to see in the dark. The male sequel to this story, reported in 1960, involved an adolescent mowgli (a human being raised by wolves) named Ramu (*Newsweek*, 1960, p. 82). As the tale goes, Ramu had been found several years earlier inside a dirty clothes bundle in a railroad depot at a time when four million Indians had crowded into the city of Lucknow for a fair. As the moving bundle attracted the attention of passersby, police were summoned and upon opening the bundle found therein a nine-year-old boy who was unable to speak and crawled on all fours. Speculation had it that the boy was abandoned by a Hindu beggar who intended to use him to attract the pity of fairgoers.

Dr. Dev Narayan Sharma, medical superintendent at Balrampur Hospital in Lucknow, stated, "Ramu's behavior at the hospital gave us the impression that wolves had reared him." Hospital authorities indicated that upon his arrival Ramu was unable to walk, lapped milk like an animal, howled like a wolf, preferred raw meat to other fare, bit people, but when approached by a dog, he jumped about happily on all fours. For many Indians, the mowgli story is feasible as he obviously had been kidnapped during infancy by wolves who raised him like a cub. Already there is much to suggest that this story is in the same dubious category as the others that precede it.

Perhaps the most obvious questions involve whether any child could survive for an extended period of time under the life conditions and care of a wild animal, and whether any animal would extend the affection and kind of assistance needed for the years required before a child can shift for himself. The serious point speculative observers sometimes overlook is that human beings require a more lengthy period of dependency from birth to independence than do the young of other species. Closest to us in this context are the higher apes, whose maturity does not occur until they are nine years old. Such prolonged dependency among the human young provides the elders who comprise their social environment a greater opportunity for shaping child life. Therefore, whatever the inherited behavioral tendencies may be with which a child begins, the difficulty of disentangling the natural or what has been termed instinctive elements of behavior from those that have been acquired from his environment becomes increasingly difficult for each later stage of development.

Largely because of Watson's findings and the research of other behavioristic psychologists, the instinct concept was judged anathema. Drives and conditioned reflexes—these became the sanctioned adjectives, the new constructs under which all human motives could be subsumed. In order to accommodate the influence of biology and social environment upon man's direction for striving, two drive types were hypothesized. Primary drives, shared by all mankind, consist of the biologic (innate) urges of sex, hunger, pain, and thirst. There are also a host of secondary drives or motives learned from the environment (not innate) that are presumably built up in the course of attempting to satisfy primary needs. Just as certain objects (food, water) and circumstances (sex expression or activity) in providing for the reduction of primary drives tend to reinforce these drives, so too our secondary (environmentally derived) motives need reinforcement if they are to persist.

Questions of application arose almost immediately: What are the implications of drive theory for the school setting? More particularly, what does it mean in terms of academic competition, teacher-pupil roles, or relationships and home-school conjunctive efforts? Most investigators believed the scope of motivational concern had been enlarged from the restricted topic of motive acquisition to include the nurture of certain motives. That is, the principle question no longer was, how are motives acquired but rather how can we be sure that certain motives will be sustained? Educators could afford to be unconcerned about the acquisition of motives because most of the students who would remain to graduate (upper-middle and upper class) arrived in the educational setting with school-oriented motives. The fact that children had already acquired the secondary drives of interest in learning and the desire to read and inquire made the new task of motivation one of reinforcement, of sustaining educational motives. This took the form of incentives.

As a consequence, most of the research in learning situations has dealt with the extent to which certain rewards and punishments, extrinsic to the individual, effect his achievement. A myriad of incentives were introduced such as prizes, honor rolls, gold stars for good work, rewards for completing assignments on time—all designed to reinforce the motivation toward accomplishment. Negative techniques were included as well to punish certain of the undesirable behaviors. Taking away privileges such as recess or gym was believed an effective motivational goal, as was homework, failing a child, or inducing shame by banishing one from the classroom. It is difficult to understand how a pupil sent out to the cloakroom was to learn much unless it was assumed he was going to become a clothing salesman. Another technique was the familiar satellite system in which children who for one reason or another did not perform well were relegated to sit in other parts of the room, away from their fellows. Numerous studies have been done regarding the effect of praise and reproof by the teacher (Hurlock, 1925; Thompson and Hunnicutt, 1944; Page, 1958). In most research, the effect of motivational techniques has been limited to assessing improvement or retardation in performance rather than determining the real effect that such practices have in terms of pupil self-concept and personality adjustment. The important thing was to change and sustain certain behaviors rather than understand motivation. All these efforts were tantamount to an admission that education cannot be interesting, enjoyable, or fun—that we need to make payments to children to endure the process—that satisfaction must come from incentives outside the learning process.

The problems of a constricted focus in motivational research have long been compounded by widespread teacher misunderstanding regarding the drive concept. Finding the language of Hull, Miller, Dollard, Mowrer, and other theorists foreign to familiar reference points, a number of educators have been inclined to conjure their own interpretation. The most common of these interpretations construes drive for academic success to be synonymous with the idea of will; that is, drive relates to volition and therefore is a matter of choice. So, in a sense, achievement can either be chosen or rejected by a learner—if he wants success he can have it—perseverance will make it so. Little credence was given the notion that effort becomes important only when a goal is within reach of one's ability and that otherwise desire of itself cannot produce competence. For certain instructors, the virtue of perseverance was an achievement in itself, so that one might speak in terms of giving a child an A for effort. This emphasis on industry, reflecting the goal that a busy child is a well-behaved child, was indicative of the greater importance attached to a child's motives for pleasing his supervising adults than for his drive to learn. That motivation might be more a question of interest than of effort was considered unlikely; instead, belief had it that motives or drives could be inferred from performance. Low achievement then obviously is caused by low motivation and therefore those earning poor grades need but to do more work, increase their striving, put forth greater effort. Invariably such children receive report cards indicating that "Johnny could do better if he would only try harder."

Naturally parents adopted the teacher viewpoint that their child could be more successful if he would exert greater effort, he could attain higher marks if he would just work harder, exhibit more industry, demonstrate greater drive. This persuasion continues in spite of evidence that trying and producing are not necessarily synonymous. Otherwise, many of those who have failed, others who are retarded, and those who have dropped out are persons who by definition have not tried. To so imply is to assume that responsibility for motivation is exclusive to the child alone and does not charge the institution he attends. It means that failure is chosen by the pupil rather than sometimes induced by the school. It means that success is possible for all students in spite of the fact that an archaic educational structure remains that necessarily acts as an impediment to preclude the success of some.

The problem of whom should we motivate is a very important question for the public schools to answer today. Our student population has been extended in recent years so that we now attempt to educate more than just the chosen few; we intend to educate the children of all. Whether this goal is realized, whether all children are able to achieve and complete their studies with success is contingent upon whether we expand our concept of motivation to include all children. Until now many students have been exploited, used as the pawns of success for others. In the main we have failed to recognize that there is something wrong with a system in which certain pupils need to be punished in order that others might be rewarded, that able students might succeed at the expense of less able, that grading should reward only biological inheritance. Adherence to the curve evaluation system has resulted in a philosophy of scarcity, which insists that since only a few can do well in school, a number must necessarily do poor—in spite of the fact that in an adequate educational system all might do well.

Previously our society has believed we could afford to lose those children who, after a period of repeated failure, would say they no longer care to attend school and would leave to enter the labor market. Indeed their exodus was considered a confirmation of teacher judgment that such pupils are uncooperative, lazy, indolent, unmotivated. However, in our time, we can no longer afford to assume that the labor market will absorb the mistakes made in the educational system. The number of unskilled jobs is steadily declining so that now when a youngster quits school, he is no longer socially invisible. Nearly one million adolescents who drop out each year form a dismal picture of limited opportunity, restricted choice, and futility. Because this is so they represent an indictment against all the school systems that have disallowed their success.

In a report to the U.S. Commissioner of Education, the Panel on Educational Research and Development (1964, pp. 11–13), predicts that in the future all people will need to learn throughout much of their life as continued education will be necessary for vocational adaptation and survival. Given this prospect, the panel indicates one of the great needs in our time is to find ways by which we can stimulate in all children the desire to learn. In short, this implies the need to find ways to make motivation intrinsic rather than extrinsic, making school pleasant and helping children to become absorbed in their studies. We want our educational structure to offer satisfactions for all who attend, not just those whose accomplishments exceed that of their fellows. We must desist in the persuasion that learning is by nature uninteresting and that children need to endure it, to put up with it so that they might obtain future rewards outside of school. Somehow we must be able to exchange the positions of reward and learning so that satisfaction derives from the gain of knowledge rather than from what one receives as a gift after he has learned something he finds uninteresting.

All of these considerations suggest a reorientation, a need to shift some of the responsibility for motivation from the individual to the school. Chances for such a move are resented by those who point out that we need but to consider new types of extrinsic motivation and then we shall be successful. For example, the dropout rate has been diminished in certain European countries where continued attendance is maintained by offering monetary incentives to the parent or child. As a child advances through the grades in Belgium, his parents are paid an ever-increasing stipend. However enthusiastic its advocates, this approach is really not a positive one, for it results in a strain if not a dislocation of a student's motivation in that his parents are the ones who are motivated to keep him in school in order that payments are continued. In East Germany, money grants are given directly to the pupil, supposedly to reduce the lure of material things that one might gain by quitting school and taking a job. The real purpose, however, is to reestablish the dependence of a child from his parents to the state and thus encourage greater allegiance to the revered political entity than to the family (Strom, 1964c). These methods of either East Germany or Belgium are inappropriate for our culture, as we cannot be content by insisting children find school interesting; rather part of our task is to make learning interesting for them.

Whether we see motivation as intrinsic or extrinsic has a great deal to do with how each of us teaches or whether in fact we teach at all, as one point of view recognizes the individual while the other ignores him as a person; one allows for individual expectations whereas the other insists upon a uniform standard. To achieve any form of intrinsic reward for each pupil, a staff must be ever sensitive to the fact that each youngster has purposeful motives even when these aims are inconsonant with classroom objectives. Where dissonance occurs between the school and student purposes, we need not suppose the child lacks motives and attempt to manufacture them by punishment or reward but rather recognize the course of his drives.

The problem then becomes one of redirection rather than of manufacture. This redirection process begins with respect, a respect that is initial—not one that is reserved for what a child may be or will become. Redirection begins when all children are honored, not just those who are on the honor roll. So redirection implies getting to know each child; for unless each is known as an individual, the teacher cannot use a pupil's unique strength or interests. For too long, motivation has been viewed as a function of effort rather than as a function of interest. By now we should have come some educational distance from the time when the motives of an institution would preempt the motives of an individual on every occasion; when the school was too rigid to consider the unique abilities of its patrons. Unless we repudiate this tradition, it is tantamount to saying we still suppose that it is easier for a youngster to modify his needs than for the school to alter its requirements or change its expectations. It is doubtful whether an inflexible institution can train its students to adapt to change.

As new approaches are developed, it will be possible to face certain kinds of motivational problems that heretofore have been ignored. For example, little attention has been given to the conflict of motives children face, to the fact that wishing to do well and desiring to be well thought of may not both be possible under present conditions. A child ought not to have to choose between his need for affiliation with peers and his need for academic achievement. But if a school is so structured that to achieve academically one must succeed at the expense of his peers, he runs the risk of exclusion and the label of "curve raiser." The problem is not merely that the need for affiliation will more often dominate one's need for achievement; rather the difficulty is that one must gain fulfillment of one noble purpose at the expense of another. The so-called other-directed person, which most of us are, is very responsive to social pressure, but in emphasizing the need for mastery we in the schools often have overlooked student need for affiliation. As a result, we have failed to see that for a pupil, being adequate does not necessarily mean to be alone. Need-affiliation, like many other problems indigenous to humanity, has been overlooked largely because our research has historically emphasized more studies of sick and anxious rats than inquiry regarding the attributes and mechanisms by which happiness and adjustment are attained for human beings.

Schoolmen today should accept the broad definition of motivation, understand that it involves all of those variables that arouse, sustain, and give direction to behavior. As these variables differ between individuals, it is obvious that motivation must involve more than extrinsic rewards, which by their very nature are impersonal and under the present circumstance reserved for only a small element who can attain them. We have the task of arousing school-oriented motives in those persons who have been unable to see their need for education; we have the job of sustaining culture-favored motives for those who need our support and encouragement as expressed by a consideration for their interests and abilities. Finally, our job involves helping all students direct their behavior toward goals compatible with personal advance and the gain of our culture. These are noble purposes, lofty goals, motives our profession would do well to embrace (cf. Frymier 1965; Hilgard 1958; McClelland 1955).

ENVIRONMENTAL SUPPORT

At one time or another, most of us have wondered about the relative influence of nature and nurture, the extent to which each of these factors effects life style and accomplishment. Rarely can one note an instance of egregious behavior or youth crime without pondering whether the misdeed would have occurred had the individuals involved been reared under different environmental conditions. Similarly, whenever low achievement or pupil failure occurs in the classroom, teachers want to know if the obstacles to success might be overcome by modifying some dimension of the student's home or school environment. Because most of our society now believes environmental support to be essential for achievement in school and life, there is increasing encouragement for educational researchers to pursue long-neglected areas of inquiry: How do adult-imposed aspirations influence pupil performance? In what ways does the home inadvertently obstruct mental health and learning? What are the mechanisms through which parental influence is mediated? How can the school and home sustain more beneficial conjunctive efforts? Before any of these topics could be investigated, it first was necessary to secure popular conviction for the belief that social environment is a crucial determinant in the process of child growth and development.

A favored procedure for assessing the impact of environment on intelligence has been to use subjects whose heredity is the same or similar but whose places of rearing have differed. This type of sample is not easily obtained, for on the average there is about one pair of twins in every ninety births; even more infrequent are the cases of twins who have been separated during infancy and reared in disparate environments. Nevertheless, in spite of these limitations, there have been a few major studies of the two classes of twins, identical and fraternal.

Since identical twins, sometimes called uniovular or monozygotic, are exactly alike genetically, they are from the standpoint of heredity the same individual in duplicate (see Figure I-4). Products of a single fertilized egg which splits in half to form two individuals, identical twins must always be of the same sex and often are so much alike that even members of their own family have difficulty in recognizing who's who. On the other hand, fraternal twins, referred to as nonidentical binovular or dizygotic, have a dissimilar mode of genesis. As products of two

HOW TWINS ARE PRODUCED

IDENTICAL TWINS	FRATERNAL TWINS
Are products of	Are products of TWO different eggs fertilized by TWO different sperms

IDENTICAL TWINS

A single sperm and A single egg

In an early stage the embryo divides

The halves go on to become separate individuals

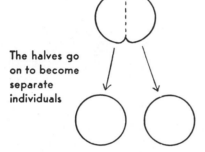

Usually — but not always — identical twins share the same placenta and fetal sac

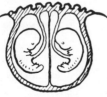

But regardless of how they develop, they carry the same genes and are therefore

Always of the same sex — two boys or two girls

FRATERNAL TWINS

Are products of TWO different eggs fertilized by TWO different sperms

They have different genes and may develop in different ways, usually— but not always — having separate placentas and separate fetal sacs

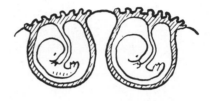

Also, as they are totally different in-dividuals, they may be

Both of the same sex

Two boys

—or two girls

—Or a mixed pair

One boy   One girl

Fig. I-4. How twins are produced. From *The New You and Heredity* by Amram Scheinfeld (Philadelphia: J. B. Lippincott Co., 1950), p. 132. Used by permission.

entirely different eggs that are fertilized at approximately the same time by two entirely different sperms, nonidentical twins need be no more or less alike than ordinary brothers and sisters.

In 1937, Newman, Freeman, and Holzinger reported the results of their investigation involving 50 pairs of identical twins who had been reared together and 19 pairs of identical twins who had been reared apart. Our concern is with the 19 identical twins, separated at ages ranging from two weeks to six years; when studied as a group their ages ranged from twelve to sixty years. The span of differences in IQ between these twins ran from 1 to 24 points with an average difference of 8.21. This was statistically significant when compared with the average IQ difference of 5.35 between identical twins reared together. Newman's findings (1937) seem to indicate that when heredity is constant, as in identical twins, diverse environs produce differences in intelligence. Subsequent studies of separated monozygotic twins (Burt and Howard, 1956; Shields, 1962), lend credence to the view that at least some variability can be attributed to environmental setting. (The study of twins as a measure of environmental influence is being replaced by a superior method known as multiple abstract variance analysis [Cattell, 1965, pp. 32–38].)

The wide range of differences in IQ that obtains when identical twins are separated (24 points in the Newman study) has prompted other types of inquiry. From her analysis of data, using numerous studies of twins, Anastasi (1958, pp. 295–300) concluded that differences in educational opportunity seem to account for some of the variance in IQ. Indeed, the correlation between educational advantages, as estimated from schooling and other information, and the magnitude of the differences in IQ between the pairs of twins was .79. (See pages 324–25 for an explanation of how to interpret coefficients of correlation.) Anastasi's (1965, pp. 4–42) findings suggest that individuals with the same heredity will tend to differ in intelligence to the degree that their educational opportunities differ. The obvious implication here is that home support for the schooling process is an important variable influencing child achievement.

Precisely how much difference can environment mean in the development of intelligence? There is considerable disagreement regarding this matter among scholars who have estimated proportions of the variance in intelligence that might be attributed to heredity and environment. Burt (1958) suggests 12 to 23 percent derives from environment; Cattell (1965) indicates 20 percent; Leahy's (1935) appraisal is 22 percent; Burks (1928) believed 34 percent; Newman, Freeman, and Holzinger (1937) judged 20 to 35 percent; while Woodworth (1941) calculated 40 percent attributable to environment. Their differences of estimate notwithstanding, all of the scholars agree that at least some proportion of the variance must relate to the environmental influence in which children are reared, the homes from which they come. This conclusion raises an issue that perhaps is more germane than determination of how much environment makes a difference, the question of how can we render more likely the prospect that the environment will do its best job?

Familial influence has many dimensions. Currently nationwide attention is focused upon those homes in which support for the schooling process is lacking. Since to be a functional citizen in our time requires more education than ever before, it is undesirable that parents discourage children from academic pursuits. Unfortunately, in some families in which the educational experience of the adults has been less than satisfying, there is a tendency to delimit advantages of learning, to view the skills of reading and writing simply as demands made upon the individual by his society. The extent to which a student is willing to meet these "demands" often depends on the attitude he has adopted at home. A feeling on the part of some students in San Francisco's Special Reading Laboratory that learning to read well or to read at all is worthless in value has been traced to family settings in which there is constant repetition of the theme that no matter how well one does, he will never be allowed by society to practice his skills (Abbott, 1964). Obviously this type of environment tends to restrict the aspiration level of children.

Research findings confirm the belief that negative parental attitudes adversely affect pupil achievement, whereas encouragement and support usually result in school progress. In their study of school dropouts, Bowman and Matthews (1958) found that when intelligence and social class are controlled, the major factor distinguishing pupils who remain in school from those who leave before graduating is the attitude of the parents. Most of the parents of dropouts register no objection to the decision of their youngster to leave school, while most of the parents of children who stay in school place great value on education themselves and vigorously insist that their child remain to complete his studies. This same theme of difference in levels of aspiration holds when comparing high achievers with low achievers in a group of very bright high school students (Pierce and Bowman, 1960). Among the family factors characteristic of the high-achieving students were: parents are better educated, hold higher aspirations for their children, consider their children more independent and responsible, encourage more verbalization, and are more often named by the children as having been significant influences in their lives.

Equally disappointing as the homes in which low aspirations prevail are those families that set unrealistically high goals for the young. Viewing sons and daughters as extensions of themselves, some parents seek to accomplish in the lives of their children goals that eluded them during their own youth. As a result, the concept of preparation for college becomes a paramount concern from the day a child enters kindergarten. Realizing that promotions, honors, awards, and scholarships are contingent upon marks, many parents early choose grades rather than growth

as a goal for their child in school. The student, if successfully indoctrinated, relocates his interest from subject to grade. It is disappointing
to encounter parents who view the report card of their child as a status
symbol, parents for whom youngsters have replaced French poodles as
an indication of snobbery, mothers and fathers whose first topic of conversation with friends and associates takes the form of comparing how
well offspring are doing in school. Given the premium placed on marks
we can expect that some parents will bribe, cajole, or threaten their children to obtain enviable records.

Underlying the pressures for academic excellence imposed on many
children is an assumption that most if not all can have high grades if
they but work hard enough. A report on high school students in New
Jersey indicates, "There is an almost unanimous evaluation of each child
by his parents and teachers as one who is capable of doing better"
(Jackson, 1965). This kind of pressure, in many cases, results in a student
making lower marks than his industry would normally permit him to
make simply because his concern impedes effective concentration. Some
pupils whose schoolwork has become grade-oriented are unduly disappointed as they perceive failure to get a certain grade as complete failure
and hence lose even that which is within their reach. Although one cannot
accurately assess the degree to which preoccupation with grades retards
learning, few psychologists would deny the amount as influential. Indeed,
all of us should be acquainted with the unnecessary anxiety, disappointment, and parental disfavor accompanying report card time for some
youngsters. By the nature of most grading systems, of course, the weaker
student is forced to endure failure over and over again. Aside from the
questionable desirability of such negative motivation, the blighting
effects of constant frustration on personality development should be a
matter of grave concern (Strom, 1965d, 1966b).

Even if youngsters are capable of attaining high marks, the consequences of attaching excessive worth to academic achievement can be
damaging to personal and social development. For one thing it can lead
to a child having his fundamental values dependent not upon his character, personality, or relations with others but solely on his academic
prowess. When a youngster perceives his school success to be the most
operational base for evoking parental response and affection, he may be
expected to adopt this method. In certain cases there is danger that
reliance on educational attainment to elicit adult approval might replace
emotional bases as criteria for personal relations. Moreover, a time comes
for each person when behavior is no longer precocious, when accomplishments cannot be traded for affection. At that point, persons who have
used gains in school as their base of affinity for personal association find
they lack the capacity for intimate relations in adulthood (Strom,
1965 a, b).

For many pupils who are led to adopt goals beyond their reach there is a withdrawal from important areas of child life. Large numbers of students today experience recurring guilt as they struggle along, living up to desired standards only on rare occasion. One high-school girl put it this way, "I think that having your parents' confidence is what builds up the pressure. You have these people looking toward you with all their hopes instilled in you and it's up to you to fulfill them by getting good grades—you feel you have to do it." Evidence is replete for the contention that many students are unable to cope with the stress brought to bear upon them for academic attainment. Dr. Paul Patterson, Chairman of the Department of Pediatrics at the Albany Medical College, cites the example of youth in Scarsdale, New York, a community that spends four times as much per pupil as the national average, sustains a dropout rate of only 1 percent, sends 80 percent of its graduates to college—and yet reports a 5 percent incidence of suicide among adolescents, far above the national average (Patterson, 1965a, 1965b). Alarm is also being expressed over the rising rate of suicide at a number of our nation's universities and colleges. One estimate has it that two out of ten American students need psychiatric help during their undergraduate career, half of whom will receive it. The mental health facilities of colleges and universities report they are more busy than ever before. One example: At Massachusetts Institute of Technology the number of students seen by psychiatrists has increased 49 percent over a three-year period (Jackson, 1965).

These same problems of strain, distress, and urgency to excel are present although less visible in most secondary and elementary schools. In fact, at any grade level one can find students with learning disabilities who after incorporating parental expectations receive little or no assistance from their mother and father in learning how to reach the desired goals. While concern about the future of their offspring is commendable, there are far too many parents who have a total lack of regard for such factors as, "Does my child's potential indicate he can be successful in college? What are his curricular and vocational interests? Are our present achievement expectations in line with his capacity to perform?" These are important questions. How they are answered could be an index of environmental support.

Although we could argue that inordinate parental expectations represent only one of many environmental factors impinging upon student performance, it is also true that, in the absence of unreasonable adult-imposed goals, a host of other pupil difficulties might not arise. Surely the number of students experiencing feelings of frustration and despair, failure and guilt, could be appreciably diminished were the reference point for acceptable learning rates, as established by familial aspiration, more compatible with pupil ability and environmental support. To the extent that a child's needs, interests and abilities differ from those objectives imposed on him by the "significant others" in his life, obstacles are set up that no amount of time and effort alone can overcome. Rather than expect a child to alter his ability to coincide with our desire for his future, the real change must emanate from parents—in terms of revised expectancies and ample support to meet realistic goals.

Many parents could maintain more reasonable scholastic expectations were they to possess greater knowledge regarding sons and daughters— knowledge about their abilities, aptitudes, interests, strengths, weaknesses —items of information currently known best by school staff. Conversely, if the school systematically sought from every parent their store of information about aspects of the child's out-of-school life including his goals, fears, friends, and areas of excellence, classroom learning might proceed more effectively toward appropriate ends. In combination, the mutual needs of the two institutions represent a sufficient cause for home-school conjunctive effort. By working together there would be less chance of defeating the other's purpose, of undermining the other's influence. Instead, expectancies of the child might be more coincident, realistic, and supporting. Then too, under these conditions it is possible to focus on the child as an individual using him as the reference point for his own aspirations rather than referring to some extrinsic standard or adult wish that could interfere with educational progress.

However desirable close parent-teacher relationships might appear to be, they often fail to materialize. Unlike others who hold joint responsibility for human welfare, parents and teachers spend little time together in mapping strategies, sharing information and planning for a student's well-being despite the fact that both have a genuine interest in the child, are committed to his development, and claim to seek the best help available where his advancement is concerned. Often the interchange of ideas between classroom and home is limited to several written or verbal communiques per year. How two or three adults, parents and teacher, who share such a regard for and investment in the same child have so little to do with one another is difficult to accept if not to understand.

Some educators are convinced the problem is a simple one and that relations would undoubtedly improve if the frequency of contact between teacher and parent were increased. To test this hypothesis, Bowman (1965) conducted a two-week summer session designed for teachers and parents. By the beginning of the second week, a number of parents were complaining that the teachers spoke a language all their own, engaged in clique behavior, were uninterested in the parents and appeared more concerned about the development of curricula than children. Teachers dismissed these claims as overcritical although they admitted to sharing few interests with the group of parents. An open conflict ensued that was never bridged—this within a group of persons selected because of their interest in improving the understanding between home and school.

To depreciate the value of greater contact between home and school is not the purpose of this discussion; nor is the author's intent to under-rate the importance of improved communication. Few would deny that the school must continue to foster a two-way exchange with the home by organizing better routes of communication. This in itself is a major attitudinal and mechanical problem because parents must first be convinced that their views are sincerely sought. A time, place, and means must be understood for the communication. Since many parents are employed, they should know what kinds of difficulties can be handled over the telephone, how and when to reach the instructor of their child, and when problems arise with the teacher that they feel cannot be discussed directly with him, parents ought also to know the name and telephone number of another staff member with whom they might speak. These may seem like simple things but often prove to be significant.

However, the underlying cause for lack of joint effort between home and school seems to center more about goal interpretation than any other factor. In the absence of commonly understood specific societal expectations, both parents and teachers tend to guard certain functions jealously while assuming different tasks to be within the other's province. Seldom are the assumed responsibilities conjunctive. Thus failure is always considered the fault of the other party; advice is considered an imposition, always objectionable because it is given for matters outside one's responsibility. A common attitude seems to be, "You mind your business and we will mind ours." While this devotion to duty is commendable, the delineation of responsibility remains unclear, always producing doubt in the minds of teacher and parents regarding their real role (Strom, 1965c, pp. 20–26).

Somehow in the training of teachers more attention must be given to role specificity for both educator and parent. In general there has been a tendency among professors to overestimate teacher influence and under-estimate the influence of the home. Perhaps this appraisal will be reversed by current research indicating the strong relationship between academic achievement and the self-concept children have of their own ability. It seems that, as self-concept of ability is altered, corresponding changes occur in the grade-point average of students. In attempts to elevate pupil self concept by (1) formal learning groups and information sessions, (2) group and individual counseling, and (3) training parents to promote the improvement of child self-view, only the last method resulted in a significant change as shown by improved grades (Brookover, 1964). These results seem to indicate that parents are the primary influence on self-concepts of children, more important than teachers or counselors, and that their influence can be positively modified by training. When it is appropriate, perhaps school and home together can consider ways by which the family might assist in developing a more positive self-image for students. Meetings with this objective would be far more meaningful than periodic social encounters at the school.

Pupil self-concept and confidence can be enhanced by parents who, in using guidance and encouragement, foster their child's successful completion of tasks without driving him or removing his freedom to fail. The freedom to fail, essential as it is to developing confidence, growth, and success, is lost when parents consistently step in to complete a youngster's task. This often occurs when the expediency of finishing an activity results in an older family member completing what the young have set out to do. For the parent, impatience and the necessity to hurry allows no time to teach; for the child who has no time to deliberate or complete his task there is no time to learn.

When children have self-concepts that are consistent with their ability, a steady but realistic raising of aims is usual. Because he is self-confident and assured in his performance, the pupil places socially and self-approved limits on his achievement. It follows he will be unashamed of poor performance on material that is clearly too difficult for him but on the other hand he does not boast regarding successful completion of material which is easy (Sears, 1941). This is the person who feels he is someone, someone worth being, and is committed to being himself. For him positive change is possible. In contrast, the student who has adopted the unreasonable imposed goals of others becomes an overstriver and frequently announces objectives far beyond his past attainment. Uncertain about what he can really expect of himself, and unable to admit inadequacy or distinguish the unreasonable from the reasonable, he naturally lacks confidence. To reduce his anxiety, he aims beyond what he can hope to achieve as though to say, "My attainments aren't much but my goals are worthy of praise." And as failure to reach lofty goals hardly counts as failure, one's self-respect need not suffer (Cronbach, 1963, p. 482). Insecure, apprehensive, inflexible, dissatisfied—this is the human cost, the result when one lacks an appropriate concept of self that is reasonably based.

This seems clear: when one's concept of self, the goals he pursues, and the ability he possesses are discontiguous, it is likely his education will neither be satisfying nor successful. Yet success and satisfaction in classrooms must be the experience for ever-increasing numbers of children if our society is to fulfill its promise to itself. As parents and teachers are prime agents in the change process, the process by which each child's aspirations are formed, altered and reshaped, it is imperative that we work together—in the old ways, the new ways, and the ways as yet unknown to provide environmental support.

READINESS FOR INSTRUCTION

Questions of preparedness arise whenever one confronts a new endeavor. In the school setting, each successive level offers its own challenge for meeting requisites, coping with the novel, demonstrating improved performance, measuring up to ever-higher expectations. All of us hope our children will be equal to the demands that teachers and lessons impose; we hope they will be ready for instruction. Yet, even the most conscientious parents at times wonder about what should be done at home to equip the young for formal learning. There are doubts regarding the points in time or age intervals at which readiness training is most crucial. Teachers share this concern for readiness since larger numbers of children are now appearing in school who are unprepared to meet the institution's initial expectations. By the time they reach high school, some students who are unprepared for their assignments and courses come to believe that dropping out is the only feasible alternative. Educators support this tragedy when they suppose the term *readiness* can be used as a complete and final answer to the school's lack of success with an individual. Heretofore the student rather than the school has carried the load of the label. Could one say that the individual is not ready to satisfy his needs? Somehow the question does not ring true. Perhaps the term *readiness* could be used as profitably and meaningfully to assess the school's program and the preparedness of its teachers. Of this we can be fairly sure: Only as school, home, and child share in the responsibility for readiness will its occurrence eventuate.

The first notable attempt at defining readiness in terms of the young child and his beginning school experience grew out of the work of G. Stanley Hall. Concerned about the insistence of educators and psychologists that certain arbitrarily assigned aspects of preparation are needed before one enters first grade, Hall determined to find out what elements of knowledge might constitute a reasonable base for initial expectations. The practical problem chosen was, "What may Boston children be assumed to know and have seen when they enter school?" Hall indicated that almost all scholars agree the mind can learn only what is related to other things learned previously. Therefore, our point of departure for instructing children should be the knowledge they already possess as opposed to what we think they should know. Otherwise, we are showing objects requiring close scrutiny only to indirect vision or talking to the blind about color. Every teacher must know each pupil well enough to assess the content of their minds and, upon taking the measure of this knowledge, use it as a basis for presenting new concepts. Hall rejected the common persuasion that children are little men and women who possess no individuality. Instead he emphasized a need for teacher inquiry regarding the perceptive capacity and information possessed by every student as the base for selecting appropriate curricular experiences (Hall, 1907, pp. 1–52).

The questionnaire method was first used as a tool for scientific inquiry of children in Hall's Boston endeavor. At his own expense, an 18-page pamphlet was prepared covering 134 items that he thought might be revealing. Many of these questions were adapted from a similar inven-

tory administered in 1869 to investigate the individuality of children
entering city schools in Berlin, Germany, by assessing their knowledge
of the environment. Hall decided his questions should lie within the
range of what children are commonly supposed to know according to
their teachers and the writers of primary textbooks. With the cooperation
of Boston school authorities, Mrs. Quincy Shaw and four teachers from
her comprehensive system of kindergartens acted as special interrogators.
Under Hall's direction they questioned several hundred children in
groups of three on topics ranging from feelings about inanimate objects
to events in nature, religion, and identifying parts of the body. Every
answer presented by the children, no matter how readily given, was to
be carefully checked by cross examination. Unfortunately the quality of
interview technique was dubious owing to the lack of experience among
the interrogators (Hall, 1907, pp. 1–9).

Results of Hall's three-year study, published as *The Content of Children's Minds on Entering School* (1883), was translated into many languages and attracted worldwide attention. In detailing what children
think and feel, Hall offered a startling revelation of child ignorance and
preconceptions. He showed that although children see hundreds of objects daily, much of what they encounter goes unnoticed or does not
remain in the conscious. The moral was: Teachers need to show children
objects, explain relationships, and converse more with them about even
the most common things. As for preconceptions, 90 percent of the sample
group could not locate their ribs, 20 percent believed that butterflies
make butter. Other common misjudgments had it that the sun, moon,
and stars are all alive; the sun goes down at night into the ground, and
then God lights the stars with matches. In demonstrating the tremendous
chasm separating the child and adult mind, Hall's work was received with
amazement and enthusiasm. His major publication, generally referred to
as the beginning of child study in America, earned for him the title
"Father of Child Psychology."

Following Hall's innovation, the next experimental inquiry made in
quest of a natural base for school expectations was conducted in 1890 at
Annaberg, Germany, by Hartmann. Charged with the responsibility of
determining the natural course of study for the first year or two of school,
Hartmann devised a list containing 100 questions adapted from the earlier
Berlin effort. Objects and tasks on this inventory were arranged in groups
as follows: animals, plants, minerals, events in nature, time, localities,
home landscape, mathematics, religion, and social relationships. Out of
100 usable concepts, the average girl possessed 32.9 and the average
boy 30.8. One of these concepts was known to only five children, while
another concept to 1,056 of the 1,312 children tested (Hartmann, 1890).
As Hartmann's results proved valuable for determining the individuality
of children, his school entrance exam gave rise to analogous exams in
other cities of Germany. Similarly, in this country Hall's influence is

reflected in the contemporary array of readiness tests valuable in determining individuality (Ilg, Ames, 1965). The Incomplete Man Test, Knox Cube Test, Metropolitan Achievement Test, California Readiness Test, Rowe-Peterson Readiness Test, and many others all are designed to show what a child already knows or is familiar with in order that the teacher may incorporate this information for use in his teaching instruction.

Although the relationship between home influence and readiness for school is complex, it is possible to identify environmental variables and make some assessment of their collective impact. For example, a number of operational differences separate what have been termed *abundant* and *deprived* homes, the two environmental extremes in our culture. In the so-called abundant homes, most parents are conscious of their responsibility to the child in equipping him for school and so attempt to make available the guidance, materials, and types of situations that will increase his likelihood of academic success. Boys and girls reared in these settings, characterized by frequent parent-child communication, verbal exchange, and reading are encouraged to use symbols correctly, identify objects, ask questions, and think about their environment in terms of its relationships. Also, the youngsters are provided numerous manipulative toys and games to stimulate their perception and help them find pleasure in learning.

But there is another group of parents, equally supportive of the young, who either are unaware of any responsibility for readiness or else fail to recognize ways in which they might design tasks conducive to school preparedness. These deprived homes fail to provide organized opportunities for language exchange, interaction, and corrective feedback for improvement of a child's speech. Books and magazines are lacking, no one reads to children, and little encouragement or assistance is given those boys and girls who ask the many life questions of how and why. Since the parents do not participate in community affairs, the children seldom go to the park or other places in which they could see something new and establish meaningful relationships.

Because of the great increase in the numbers of deprived families and abundant families, it is understandable that the readiness concept has tended to become a referent of socioeconomic status, a term most often used, though not exclusively, to describe the basic problem of children from low-income neighborhoods. Differences in child-rearing practices between an abundant and deprived setting become more significant when their implications are understood. Take the matter of maternal competence in preparing children for school. Since middle-class children for the most part come to school adequately prepared, whereas their counterparts from poor families are ill-prepared, the problem selected by Hess and his associates at the University of Chicago was to determine what facilitating experiences are present in middle-class families that typically do not occur in lower socioeconomic homes. Through a series of questions and tasks directed to approximately 160 mothers and their four-year-old children representing the several income levels, investigators were able to glean some rather interesting data with regard to differences in maternal attitudes toward school, perception of educational purpose, and role in preparing children for learning (Hess, 1965).*

One technique used by Hess to determine perception of school purpose was to ask each mother what she would say to her child on his first day of school. Although there were differences of response within class groups, a typical mother from the lower-income home said, "I tell him to do what the teacher says, not get into trouble, not to fight, to come home right after school, and not to get lost." This view of school raises issues of dealing with authority and peers rather than presenting educational content. If learning is mentioned, it is incidental or secondary. Such a response is in contrast to the middle-class parent who was likely to say, "The teacher is like Mommy, you learn from her; if you have trouble, go to her; you are going to learn to read and write." This approach views school activity in terms of the child's learning experiences.

The mothers were also asked to explain a picture of a teacher and mother in conference. Subjects from the low-income group most often said that the mother had been called in by the school regarding some disciplinary problem. Middle-class mothers more frequently saw the conference as one in which a parent was coming to consult with her child's teacher about a learning problem. The major difference between these two types of response is in the view of the school as an institution with which the child must cope, as contrasted with a view of the school as a place of learning. The lower-class child approaches school unoriented toward learning but attuned to a need of getting along with the institution. School experience is defined to him as a problem of adapting to the teacher and to the peer situation. This presents a misconception of school purpose, with a heavy emphasis upon conformity and physical behavior rather than mental activity.

To ascertain variations in styles of maternal instruction, each parent was asked to teach her child how to assemble a jigsaw puzzle. More often than not, the middle-class mother would indicate, "This is a jigsaw puzzle that makes a picture. We remove the pieces and then put them back together so that the picture is complete again. See where all the pieces are and look at the colors so you will know where they go." Thus, the task was defined; the child had been told how to proceed. Then, spilling out the pieces, the mother gave verbal directions and encouragement as her youngster worked on his task. Mothers of the low-income group, equally supportive of their children, often dumped the puzzle without verbal directions and said, "You do it." The only guidance offered was in the

* From Robert D. Strom, *The Tragic Migration* (Washington, D.C.: National Education Association, 1964, pp. 6–8. Reprinted by permission.

frequent phrase, "Turn it around, turn it around. . . ." Thirty-five times one mother said this until finally, in defeat and frustration, her child replied, "You do it!"

Although the mother of the frustrated child was trying to help her boy, she did not know how to teach and was unable to convey the concepts needed to solve his problem. The ability to communicate concepts, to share information, and to program a simple task is seldom present in the low-income family. However, this is not the only important outcome. Imagine the child in repeated interaction with his mother coming upon problems that he tries to solve but, through lack of maternal assistance, finds impossible. The reaction of defeat, "You do it," is likely to recur and be magnified many times, resulting in feelings of apathy and despair that some problems cannot be solved. Compare his response with that of the more favored middle-class child who did not know more than he about the puzzle to begin with but who through experience realized that with some guidance there was a way to reach a solution. Upon this kind of motivational base, positive attitudes toward new learning can emerge (Hess, 1965).

The operational distinctions between deprived and abundant homes can be translated into measurable differences. During each of the first four years in a child's life these extreme environments may affect intellectual development by about 2.5 points per year or 10 IQ points during the four-year period. Later, between ages 8 and 17, extreme environments have less effect—only 0.4 points per year. During the first 17 years of life, the estimated cumulative effect of environmental influence is about 20 IQ points when contrasting deprived and abundant backgrounds as they exist in America today (Bloom, 1964, p. 72).

The greater environmental effect on intellectual development during the early years may be attributed to the fact that intelligence (as measured by IQ) is a developing function with its more rapid growth rates at life's beginning. Bloom (1964, p. 88) presents data suggesting that from birth to age 4, the individual develops 50 percent of his mature intelligence; from age 4 to age 8 he develops another 30 percent; and between the ages of 8 and 17 he develops the remaining 20 percent (see Table I-1). If as much intellectual growth occurs between birth and age 4 (50 percent) as during the next 13 years (50 percent) and if general intelligence is a developmental characteristic related to the time it takes one to learn various skills and concepts, it would seem reasonable that lack of learning in the early years might be difficult or impossible to recover fully at a later time. On the other hand, excellent learning during early childhood is unlikely to be lost. From this view of intellectual development has emerged the persuasion that we must discover ways of governing the encounters children have with their environments, especially during the preschool years, in order that as adults they will have higher intellectual capacity than would otherwise be the case.

TABLE I-1*

Hypothetical Effects of Different Environments on the
Development of Intelligence in Three Selected Age Periods

Age Period	Percent of Mature Intelligence	Variation from Normal Growth in I.Q. Units			
		Deprived	Normal	Abundant	Abundant Deprived
Birth–4	50	− 5	0	+ 5	10
4– 8	30	− 3	0	+ 3	6
8–17	20	− 2	0	+ 2	4
TOTAL	100	−10	0	+10	20

* From *Stability and Change in Human Characteristics,* by Benjamin Bloom. New York: John Wiley & Sons, 1964, p. 72 (reprinted by permission.)

A national consensus now supports the proposition that preschool experience for children of deprived homes is imperative. Recognizing the inadequate life space in which such children must function, most major cities have for some time maintained compensatory measures in the form of prekindergarten enrichment programs designed to include a dimension of experiences that are comparable to the background usually brought to school by children from middle-income families. Essentially these efforts resemble Maria Montessori's school for children of the poor, the Casa dei Bambini, begun in Rome in 1907. Just as the purpose of Montessori's Roman venture was to make learning enjoyable in a prepared environment and to overcome home conditions that might foster alienation and failure in school, so too the focus of contemporary preschool experiments is on removing academic handicaps that might otherwise confront boys and girls upon entering the elementary grades.

Project Headstart, first introduced in the summer of 1965, annually involves nearly a million deprived boys and girls between the ages of three and five. In this nationwide program of child centers, the young are being exposed for the first time to music, art, and books; they are learning size, number, and time concepts. Although they must later master symbols required in reading, writing, and arithmetic, their immediate need is to have enough direct experiences so that symbols will be meaningful. In large part this is what is meant by reading readiness in that learners must have some sort of experiences so that words have meaning. Consequently the most successful preschool experiments have emphasized a nonverbal informal approach rather than an academic formal presentation (Gray, Klaus, 1963; Deutsch, 1964; Hunt, 1964; Smilansky, 1964; Strom, Ellinger, 1966a). It is believed all boys and girls must be equipped for school when they arrive; else their initial inability to learn and resulting perception of self as inferior may set up an enduring chain of frustrations. To prevent failure, Project Headstart purports to offer deprived youngsters a more adequate chance to compete successfully in later formal academic situations.

Fig. I-5. A Montessori school in Rome. Here children attend classes held at ground level in the high rise dwelling in which they live. The long workday of many Romans means that their youngsters spend twelve or more hours with the Montessori teacher. Reprinted by permission of the Association Montessori Internationale.

Whereas major responsibility to provide readiness for elementary education can be attributed to the home, the higher a pupil advances in the grades, the more readiness becomes a function of the school. If the performance of students entering junior or senior high school falls short of our expectations, we cannot dismiss the issue by accusing home circumstance. We must assume some responsibility for the interval between age six and secondary school admission, as these years are within our province. If teacher influence is as potent as we contend, it would seem more pupils should be adequately prepared to meet the established, uniform minimum standards—or perhaps our expectations need revision insofar as many students are concerned.

Some would resolve the problems of readiness in the high school by eliminating those who present such problems. That is, by adopting a strict policy of rigid standards, the need to teach unprepared pupils vanishes since the admission criteria precludes their presence in class. But in alleviating the instructional problem by encouraging dropout, we simply

Fig. I-6. Learning to serve is a practical art that everyone should exercise. These children attend a Montessori school in Rome. Reprinted by permission of the Association Montessori Internationale.

increase the problems of society, the very problems we are charged to diminish. There is no need to underestimate the difficulties presented by the American goal of teaching all children. However, these difficulties ought not lead us to inflate the apparent successes of schools in those lands where secondary public instruction is limited only to those pupils who can exceed their fellows. In Barcelona, Spain, for example, one might well be impressed with the observed scholarship in secondary education, but it is also necessary to recognize that in Barcelona, a city nearly as large as Detroit, Michigan, there are only seven public high schools, the largest of which has an enrollment of 400 students (Strom, 1964e). We cannot go forward by going backward, by limiting the size of our secondary school population at a time when all youngsters need training for economic and vocational survival. Somehow the institution must ready itself to teach all pupils at the levels of ability they each present.

That standards in schools would rise if every student were required to demonstrate competence in his grade level before advancing into the next class is a common proposal issued by those who lack an understanding of the term *grade level*. Many children are victimized by instructors who do not understand that *grade level* is a statistical concept describing the midpoint in the achievement levels of a typical group of students. The term guarantees by definition that half of any normal group of pupils will achieve at grade level or above while the other half will achieve at grade level or below. Therefore, to expect all or even more children to reach grade level or above is to expect an arithmetic impossibility. One might as well argue that 90 percent of those who marry should be women (Frymier, 1964).

Fig. I-7. This four-year-old Italian scrubwoman is already adept at the task learned from her Montessori training. Reprinted by permission from the Association Montessori Internationale.

An opposite strategy for the readiness problem in high school is to expect less of all pupils, to water down the standards, allow all students to pass, capitulate to offering irrelevant but easy courses—eliminate a need for readiness. These and other concessions would tend to increase school holding power so that more youngsters could complete their studies, get a diploma, and enter the world of work. Proponents of this direction indicate that most employers really are not very much concerned about the high school diploma as a measure of learning anyway, since most places of work want to train employees in their own way.

Employers do look upon the diploma as an index of reliability, and suppose that if the pupil completed his work at school, he should be able to meet the business expectations of punctuality, perseverance, being able to take orders, and so forth. Whether this is true is speculative. Anyway, the suggested method provides an insufficient answer to the problem, since the curricula should be challenging to all students. This is not to say that courses of study ought to be the same for all pupils as identity of training is not the same thing as equality of opportunity.

The unique readiness problems of deprived youth in junior and senior high school often are circumvented by those who insist we have no right to impose middle-class values on members of low-income homes. This excuse fails to recognize that "some of the values the American school must teach if it is to be successful with its pupils are punctuality, orderliness, conformity to group norms, desire for work career based on skills and knowledge, desire for a stable family life, inhibition of aggressive impulses, rational approach to a problem situation, enjoyment of study, desire for freedom of self and others. *These are values of an urban industrial democratic society. They are not social class values.* It is misleading to speak of the school as a protagonist of middle-class values versus the inner-city home and neighborhood as an advocate of lower-class values with resultant conflict. This talk has just enough basis in fact to worry an inexperienced teacher but not enough to serve as a base for a positive educational program aimed at reducing the value gap" (Havighurst, 1966).

To overcome the difficulties of value readiness and retain parental favor, the school must improve the use of both its cultures. According to Havighurst (1966) educational institutions incorporate an instrumental and an expressive culture. The instrumental culture is designed to develop whatever skills, knowledge, and values are formally stated as educational objectives. In this context, learning and participation proceed largely to obtain some satisfaction beyond the process itself—to graduate, to receive commendation, to become a salesman or a physician. So there is a set of instrumental procedures that assist the student to become proficient as a reader, writer, or mathematician. On the other hand, the expressive culture consists of those activities in which pupils and teachers engage solely for the sake of the activity itself. Here the goal is the process itself, participation, and not extrinsic to activity. Popular aspects of the expressive culture include class parties, school choir, celebration of holidays, intramural athletics, playing games at recess and after school. There may be skills and knowledge that accrue from these activities, but enjoyment preempts academic gain as the major purpose. Similarly there may be expressive undertones to instrumental procedures such as when one comes to enjoy the study of history for its own sake or when one learns to love reading. In the main, however, students see a sharp division between the two cultures.

Since most students are allowed to succeed in the expressive culture in which less unfair competition prevails, it follows that this is the best element for teaching values. Not only can one come to value behaviors such as orderliness, punctuality, and the enjoyment of study from his participation in the expressive culture, but parents with little formal education themselves can generally become involved without embarrassment. Most important perhaps is that through its expressive culture the school can help many pupils achieve in the instrumental culture.

An example is The New York Guidance Demonstration Project. Sometimes called Higher Horizons, this project began its first phase (1957–1962) in a Harlem junior high school. Seven hundred pupils, representing the most able half of the school's population, were chosen for a special program. The selected students, mostly Negro and Puerto Rican, were on the average one and one-half years retarded in reading and math (median IQ of 95). A number of motivating influences from the expressive culture were introduced to enhance child affinity to the school and to encourage greater desire and respect for education. These junior high school students were taken to special cinema showings, sporting events, community activities, parks, museums, and sightseeing trips. In addition, they were given more counseling, their parents became involved in the activities, and somewhat smaller class sizes were arranged. Follow-up studies have shown that the project members entered senior high school in substantially larger numbers than their fellows in classes of previous years (Hillson, 1963). Further, of those who graduated from high school, some 168 were granted admission to a college or university as compared with only 47 students of the three classes preceding the experiment. It seems apparent that the expressive activities resulted in certain important value changes for members of the experimental group.

EPILOGUE

The problems of environmental support and facility to learn combine to effect readiness for instruction. At every level of education, from kindergarten to senior high school, teachers are concerned about the preparedness of their students. We have done a proud service in seeking to enrich child experience by operating preschool centers and by helping parents of young boys and girls better understand their responsibility. However, that greater wisdom yet needs to be demonstrated is illustrated in the speech of those who reverently refer to taking a child from where he is to where he should be and in the next breath point out that children from low-income homes are behind when they arrive in school. If one is behind when he begins, it appears illogical to cite the individual as the reference point. And the individual must be the point of reference if the term *individualized instruction* is to have any meaning. What good is a name if the name is a lie?

Equally unfortunate approaches to the readiness issue persist in secondary education, where suggestions range from eliminating the unready through rigid standards to capitulating to uniformly low expectations of all and so avoid the problem of preparedness. Others would circumvent the issue of encounter with value-readiness by declaring that we have no right to impose our views upon members of other income groups. We need to recognize that though boys and girls have been together in the same classroom over a period of years, that things are not the same for each of them. We need to recognize that even when things are similar, they are different because the people having the experiences are unique personalities. When we forget this in the classroom, the individuality of the student is denied.

Somehow we must help all pupils negotiate the transition from what they are to what their best could be—this can occur only if we in education are ready to help them. Although many local systems have made great advances in this direction, it is a fair statement to say that most schools must come to accept a greater responsibility in the matter of readiness. An institution established to equip its students for adapting to a world of change must itself remain flexible or its primary function is lost. Our future does not lie in a retreat to lesser ideals but in the enrichment and invigoration of what already is ours. The children are waiting.

CHAPTER II

Diminishing Obstacles

to Achievement

Many of us have met with periodic failure in school, encountered situations where educational advance seemed unlikely. Yet, what appeared at the time to be a myriad of unwise adult pressures, demands, and expectations, now are viewed quite differently in retrospect. In fact, we may recall certain of the reversals as being stimulating, positive, "good for us"; and some would go so far as to recommend the same adversities for all students. It is important to realize that this revised interpretation of the failure experience generally obtains only for individuals who were able to surmount the difficulties they faced, and subsequently attain their scholastic goals. In short, success can alter memory's interpretation; it can blur the recollection of feelings that accompany failure and loss; and, for some, it can engender an insensitivity to the circumstance of others who now confront problems which once were ours.

But there is another group of adults—a company of persons who, more often subject to failure in school than their peers, look back upon the academic past from a dissimilar vantage. According to these men and women, both classroom tenure and postschool life have offered a series of too difficult tasks, a number of demands calling for something beyond their ability and prowess. And, as they relate their diligence of effort and lack of good fortune, it becomes clear that memory's interpretation of school problems can be altered by subsequent failure. Indeed, most of the accounts given by this contingent—including a lengthy but dubious list of grievances—are replete with charges of teacher injustice, indifference, or incompetence. Whereas successful adults tend to ignore or play

47

down the adverse effects of early failures, the group that sustains a history of low achievement is prone to magnify and distort the same issue in a negative direction.

Given the discrepancy in recall between these adult elements, one can readily understand how difficult a task it is to identify with any degree of accuracy the major obstacles elementary and secondary pupils might anticipate in their quest for achievement. In addition, certain memories are at a discount because schools have made such pervasive changes during the interim since today's adults were in attendance. For these reasons and because youth represent a valid source of information, the primary groups selected for consideration here, in turn, are the failing and successful students of today. Though his experience be atypical with regard to frequency and magnitude of school problems, the unsuccessful pupil's history is a valuable reference in the study of failure; among its many dimensions each of us can note his own moments of fear and frustration. And perhaps we can glean insights for reducing obstacles to achievement.

THE DROPOUTS

When one has enough of failure, he can be expected to withdraw from the situation in which it occurs. As this is true for all of experience, it necessarily obtains for the schooling process as well. Each year nearly one million boys and girls abandon their studies though they have not as yet qualified to graduate from secondary school. Commonly referred to as *dropouts,* these young people leave the classroom more in hope than in confidence that they will find an out-of-school circumstance that offers them opportunity, recognition, and success—the very promises they feel education has denied them. Unfortunately, in a skilled-labor market the less educated are destined to conjure elusive dreams for desire and willingness to toil are no longer sufficient requisites for available jobs. Why then do these adolescents choose to run from learning in the first place? Why do they jeopardize their economic and social future? What are the real reasons for dropping out?

Dissatisfaction with the Curriculum

In the etiology of school failure, no factor looms larger than "dissatisfaction with the curriculum." Among *predictive dropouts* (students so categorized because it is from their IQ range, 80 to 95, more than from any other, that persons withdraw before graduating) most complaints involve the required courses of study—nature of content, degree of difficulty, and relevance to personal goals. As these youngsters are usually two years below their assigned grade level in reading and given the deficiencies they manifest with reference to mental processes like abstract reasoning, analyzing, generalizing, and inferring relationships, it is not surprising they should find many assignments beyond reason. Neither is it strange, when upon encountering matters they are unable to comprehend—expressed by the response of disinterest—that their behavior is misinterpreted by teachers as meaning a short span of attention, a restricted measure of concentration, a limitation of interest. In truth, of course, these boys and girls can be attentive, are capable of concentrating, and will sustain interests if their situation accommodates the response. The real problem lies in gaining facility to read, in learning to understand the printed page.

Reading. At the University of California's Institute for Human Development, researchers have approached the reading readiness problem from the standpoint of a substrata factor theory. In their studies, Holmes and Singer (1964) were able to identify 75 percent of the specific abilities contributing to reading power. The following subvariables account for 64 percent of the factors resulting in competent reading performance:

1. Knowledge of vocabulary in context, 16 percent
2. Ability to understand verbal analogies, 16 percent
3. Auding, defined as the ability to manipulate verbal symbols that are heard, 16 percent
4. Knowledge of vocabulary in isolation, 16 percent.

All of these factors have in common the ability to both recognize and use language as a symbolic system—the lack of which is perhaps the most basic difficulty that shows up repeatedly in the records of low-achieving children. It is little wonder that the academic experience of such pupils begins in frustration and ends in failure, since success depends on mastery of the tool of reading, and mastery of reading depends on verbal experience.

Breaking down the primary variables, researchers found that one factor, range of information, accounted for major portions of the four basic subabilities. This level 2 factor contributed:

1. 38 percent to ability to understand verbal analogies
2. 38 percent to auding ability
3. 43 percent to knowledge of vocabulary in context
4. 52 percent to knowledge of vocabulary in isolation.

All would agree that the range of information of culturally handicapped children is especially limited, in some cases to the immediate neighborhood. Therefore what is most needed is a readiness program that gives students many experiences with words, including visual and auditory discrimination with the concept of language, and with the idea of communication before they tackle the task of reading. The increasing number of kindergartens is encouraging in this regard. At present, approximately half of the states provide kindergartens for 45 percent of the nation's five-year-olds.

The necessity for readiness as an integral part of school curriculum is evident from a report given by George Spache, Head of Florida University Reading Laboratory, who contends that an urban system doing a poor job may find in its slum schools that up to 30 percent of the pupils entering junior high have not developed reading comprehension skills needed to do work on that level (Strom, 1965c). Were the validity of this assertion ever in doubt, it is again confirmed by performance of slow learners on the California Capacity Questionnaire administered in San Francisco's Reading Laboratory. Here students ordinarily score from 10 to 40 points higher on nonverbal sections of the examination. Then too, youngsters recommended for training in the special reading laboratory seem to have little difficulty with mathematic courses as long as study does not require word problem analysis. There is, for about three-fourths of the slow learners, a marked difference between their achievement by grades in verbal subjects and those in nonverbal courses such as mathematics, art, music, and some shop or sciences (Abbott, 1964, pp. 1–3). In short, the greatest problem in the reading and language arts area for the *predictive dropout* is not whether to use the Fernald method of teaching kinesthetic learners, the Spaulding unified system of phonics, or the specific language disability method of Gillingham. It is the establishment of readiness as an integral part of the curriculum.

Although readiness is less frequently discussed among high school teachers than by instructors working with elementary children, the former group is equally interested in helping less able readers. Each of the following approaches has enthusiastic advocates. One persuasion favors offering to each high school pupil only those materials he can read with a minimum of difficulty. This means that some sources need to be written on a less sophisticated level and corresponding changes are needed to simplify the content. The danger of this viewpoint is its failure to recognize that reading age and mental age are not synonymous; and that a child's interests correlate most closely with his mental age. The result: students can read the new materials that may be appropriate to their ability but find the content uninteresting. Another viewpoint is convinced that the level of difficulty need not be altered if only the nature of content is made relevant, if reading matter deals with issues of prime concern to these youngsters like dating and job-seeking. It is believed this change in the material will motivate the low achiever to come up to "grade level." This vantage ignores the difference between desire and competence. Again, children are interested but cannot read the material. A more promising strategy is the one that considers both level of reading accommodation and the interests of each pupil. In this context a common theme, written at various levels of difficulty, might be presented to an entire class so that every individual can proceed at his own rate and depth of difficulty. The shortage of texts written in multigrade levels notwithstanding, there is reason to be optimistic about the increasing number of high school teachers who are working with great success in the area of individualized reading.

Social Studies. According to dropouts, social studies is among the courses considered most difficult. Yet it is precisely in this curricular area that one is to develop understandings and attitudes vital to his success in society. Here he is expected to make such important gains as an understanding of himself, his place in the community, and an enthusiasm for the learning process. Regretably, the content area is too broad to be adequately covered by all students so that urgency of time and schedule tempts teachers to provide an excess of ready-made explanations for the less able pupil. As a consequence, such pupils lose opportunities to develop abilities in independently gaining insights into concepts. The result of teaching small parts of a large number of topics is the passive reception of disconnected ideas, not illuminated with any spark of vitality. It might be better for the slow learner if ideas were fewer in number but presented in a variety of combinations to facilitate the use of intelligent inferences and analogies (Newell, 1964, pp. 1–4).

Social studies curriculum, more than any other, can be based on the social characteristics and needs of the pupil himself. The slow learner often accepts uncritically the leadership with the greatest emotional appeal, and he may be either belligerent or obsequious in dealing with persons in status positions. Therefore, social studies should emphasize important qualities of good leadership, intelligent selection of leaders, and the choice of courses of action based on probable effects rather than on emotional appeal. To curb a tendency to be prejudiced toward people who are different or who may hold other points of view, the social studies should stress common characteristics of mankind, helping the pupil to understand why racial, cultural, and political differences exist. Feelings of inadequacy and exposure to peer rejection may be diminished in classrooms where the value and understanding of human dignity is developed by respecting the ability of all groups to contribute to society.

Not until adolescence do most children develop the sense of time that is required for historical perspective; so it is safe to assume that this sense comes even later for the slow learner. In some measure, social class background can influence this issue. The middle-class child appears more able to see the past, is working in the present to achieve goals of the future. The lower-class child tends to be interested only in the present and what is immediate in his environment. Yet the social studies should give some concept of the vast sweep of history and prehistory as well as the sense of space and variation which characterizes the planet and its people. The direct effect of time and space on the pupil as an individual often needs to be established. An example of this on the secondary level is the development of units that first identify the pupil with an issue and establish its significance to him, then place the issue in its historical and geographical setting, and conclude with a return to the here and now, where the issue is associated with current affairs of national and international significance (Strom, 1964d, 1966d).*

The predictive dropout will be a voting, reacting, working citizen. He will need to know about his own drives and physical needs, his relationship to his home, community, and nation as an elementary school child, as an adolescent, and as an adult. He needs to know basically how the government that affects him operates and the part he plays in its effectiveness. He needs to know how and why people in other times and places influence him. He needs to know in what ways his environment is different from that of others. Above all, he needs to know why his role in society is essential to others. In the last years of secondary school, social studies can be closely related to occupational preparation with opportunities to put into practice many of the social attitudes and understandings gained in prior years. This phase of the social studies should be taught by a skillful, perceptive teacher who can recognize realistic opportunities to develop concepts but who can also enable the pupil to identify principles and practices that will increase the effectiveness and satisfaction of his existence (Saterlie, 1965, pp. 286–304).

Mathematics. In mathematics particularly, where learnings are cumulative, the slow learner may soon fall hopelessly behind if pressured to keep pace with average or above-average members of his class. Studies have shown that the slow learner goes through substantially the same mental processes as his average or rapid peers, except that he seems to have a different rate of perception and moves at a slower pace (Johnson, 1966). Consequently he often needs a lengthy period to catch up or understand what is to be learned, even if it means what appears as excessive repetition.

Also, success or failure in mathematics is closely related to a pupil's ability to develop reading skills required of the subject. In a sense, mathematics is a language, calling for careful perusal with a high degree of comprehension. Therefore, study during primary years should include an extended readiness period for the introduction of quantitative concepts along with a basic vocabulary for numbers. The normal sequence of arithmetic skills can be pursued if adjusted to the individual's rate of learning, with no grade standards as criteria.

The success of modern mathematics programs with less able pupils suggests that a discovery method is appropriate. Work in New York City schools indicates that students scoring low on traditional methods of scholastic aptitude profit more from the School Mathematics Study Group (SMSG) program than pupils in high achievement brackets. This may be largely due to the fact that the program brings into play kinds of abilities not especially useful in mastering traditional materials. Edward Begle, head of the Stanford Mathematics Study Group, reports that his

* From Robert D. Strom, "Toward Realistic Curriculum for Predictive Dropouts," *The Clearing House*, Vol. 39, No. 2 (October 1964), pp. 101–106. Reprinted by permission.

organization, which has done a great service in modernizing mathematics, is now considering ways of teaching youngsters who have fallen behind in racially segregated and slum schools.

The junior high school predictive dropout is, for the most part, neither ready for nor interested in learning about such topics as taxation, banking, and interest. These learnings should be reserved for the senior high years, when there is greater likelihood of their immediate use. This does not preclude the use of practical mathematics in junior high school. However, the content should reflect adolescent experiences, such as aspects of part-time employment, wages and hours, travel distances, measurements of athletic fields, lapses of time, and recipe ingredients.

In senior high school, mathematics should also have direct relationship to industrial arts and home economics experiences. As the pupil is guided toward occupational fields, his mathematics instruction should be directed toward proficiency in specific areas including consumership and taxation. At the same time, programs should maintain basic understandings which allow for adjustment to varying situations requiring computational application. In its entire range, the program should provide not only the understanding of fundamental processes in mathematics but the recognition of their social application for the effective solution of quantitative problems in daily life.

That *predictive dropouts* severely criticize the common curricula should be of concern to educators. If we are to keep all students in school, then all required courses must be designed and taught to meet all levels of ability. Unless we can come nearer to this objective in practice, we will continue to have built-in standards of performance that will force some pupils out of school. It is precisely in the basic courses of language arts, mathematics, and social studies that antipathy or enthusiasm is nurtured, success or defeat is sealed, dropout or retention is determined.

Vocational Education

Selection of an occupational goal is frequently accompanied by a positive change in motivation. Note the student who, previously listless and unconcerned, now responds favorably to instruction, claims a new-found relevance in his studies and testifies to the benefit of having an objective. With this result in mind, schoolmen historically have urged that *predictive dropouts* be assigned a curricula of vocational courses designed to awaken a rightful commitment to the world of semiskilled or skilled labor. As low achievers obviously are out of place in the academic tract, it follows they should be given an option to elect subjects that place less emphasis upon scholarship and competition. Seemingly unable to profit from mental activity, the law of compensation dictates that such children can best work with their hands. And so, it is in shop, industrial arts, and home economics that they belong, where they will gain the previously elusive experiences of interest, enjoyment, and success.

But really? To state that pupils failing the required subjects will necessarily find vocational education interesting is contrary to research findings. Similarly, support is lacking for the assumption that success for most students is more likely in the vocational tract. For example, in a study of high schools in 128 large cities, the National Education Association's Project on School Dropouts found that while the aggregate of high schools in 1963 graduated 70.8 percent of the pupils who three years earlier (1960) were enrolled in grade ten, only 51 percent of vocational pupils in the same class remained to graduate (Schreiber, 1964, p. 53). This is not to say that vocational education cannot be found interesting nor that those who pursue its training will necessarily be unsuccessful. It is to affirm that the rate of dropouts sustained in vocational schools is appreciably higher than the rate for high schools in general.

Vocational instructors have long recognized some reasons why so many of their students find available shop courses uninteresting. These educators have responded by persistent appeal for funds in order that more relevant and up-to-date skills might become a part of the vocational curriculum. But in the past, the high school has been primarily considered an intermediate institution designed to equip students planning to attend college. Now the rising rate of unemployment among out-of-school youth has prompted the realization that identical courses for all pupils is not equality of education and that non-college-bound youngsters need and deserve instruction that will qualify them for positions in the labor market upon graduation. In realistic appraisal of the prospect that 65 percent of the nation's young will not attend college, the U.S. Office of Education recently has doubled its outlay for vocational education.

Contending that comprehensive programs of occupational preparation for high school students are long overdue, the U.S. Office of Education has termed much of present vocational training "a link to the past rather than a bridge to the future." The national agency reports that vocational education offers little status, is crippled by inflexibility, and sometimes trains youth for the wrong jobs. Currently only two in ten high school students can be expected to complete college; most of those who do not will lack job training. In one U.S. Office of Education survey involving 3,733 schools in six states it was found that only 5 percent were offering courses in retailing and 9 percent in industrial vocations. Yet 47 percent gave homemaking and 45 percent had agricultural courses—this despite the fact that the greatest increase in job opportunities over the next few years will be in clerical, sales, service, and skilled trades. Many vocational schools are neither staffed nor equipped to meet these needs (Education Training Market Report, 1965, p. 5). Under the Vocational Education Act of 1963, federal monetary assistance is available to develop new and viable curricula designed to meet manpower needs, to ensure studies are relevant. As a consequence, many high schools now are initiating courses in custodial services, shoe repair, barbering, cosmetology, laundering, valet service, nursing aides, duplicating services, painting, decorating, lawn and garden care, small appliance repair, auto mechanics, record filing, family services, and food preparation. Effecting this educational transition from a nonsensical experience to one of interest and relevance should increase the prospect of preparing many more teen-agers for a society of specialization. (See Figures II-1 and II-2).

EMPLOYMENT IN THE U. S. 1950 - 1985

BY CATEGORIES

(in millions)

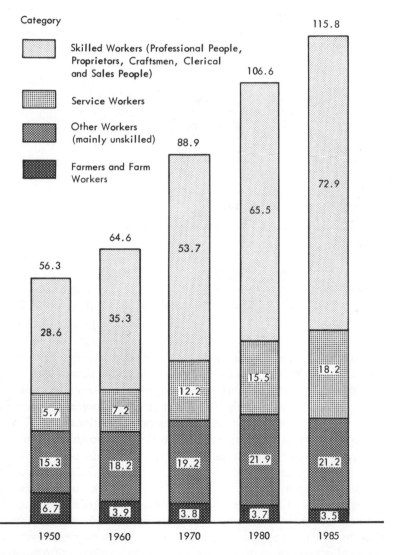

Fig. II-1. From *Letter to a College President—On the Need for Long-Range Planning* by Sidney G. Tickton (New York: The Fund for the Advancement of Education, May, 1963), p. 15. Reprinted by permission.

1—THE FALLING DEMAND FOR UNSKILLED LABOR

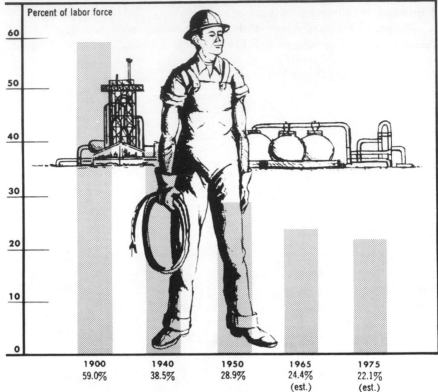

Percent of labor force

1900	1940	1950	1965	1975
59.0%	38.5%	28.9%	24.4%	22.1%
			(est.)	(est.)

Based on "Occupational Trends in the United States," 1900 to 1950, Working Paper No. 5
of the U. S. Department of Commerce, Bureau of the Census; and unpublished data
of the U. S. Department of Labor, Bureau of Labor Statistics.

Fig. II-2. From the *NEA Research Bulletin*, Vol. 38, No. 1, 1960, p. 12. Reprinted by permission.

Even the cursory view just presented is sufficient to indicate that before *predictive dropouts* can realize appropriate educational opportunity, certain archaic judgments must undergo alteration. Popular acceptance is needed for a concept that allows quality to occur within the framework of quantity. At present there are many who perceive quality only in terms of academic rigor, as a product reserved for the few whose intellectual excellence in certain subjects has been demonstrated. Adherence to this limited view of quality finds expression in schools that perpetuate a restricted formalized curricula that was appropriate in the nineteenth century when only the so-called "cultured few" attended school. When one prescribed then that "everybody" should study certain subjects, "everybody" meant anybody who was somebody, but today the term "everybody" is coming to mean everyone. Actual revision of courses both in type and content has not kept pace with changes in educational objectives as our schools ostensibly have moved from serving a select clientele to teaching the future body politic. Although most dimensions of this tragedy lie beyond assessment, one can appreciate its importance by reflection upon a statement of Kimball Wiles, past president of the Association for Supervision and Curriculum Development (1964, pp. 3, 4): "The million dropouts a year represent only a small part of the problem. The curriculum is unsatisfactory for at least 15 million more. . . . It is high time curriculum workers acknowledge this fact and begin to select from the vast reservoir of knowledge some that has relevance. . . ."

Competition

Most state and city research studies that came to the National Education Association's Project on School Dropouts during the author's tenure as Assistant Director of that unit indicated that scholastic failure is a prime factor in the decision to leave school.* For example, in the state-wide study of Iowa, 84 percent of the male dropouts and 81 percent of the female dropouts were accurately predicted by using grades and intelligence as prime indices. The testimony offered by these boys and girls yield the same results—a history of failure and frustration. As important as the evolution of their response to failure from initial anxiety, later to disappointment, and finally to indifference, is the interpretation made by their observer who very often sees the pupil response as the reason rather than the result of failure. That is, an observer may believe that the dropout apparently is unsuccessful in competitive situations more because of his negative attitude than his inability to run the race—hence the perception that greater emphasis is needed to change his attitude than to conduct a severe scrutiny of the conditions under which he maintains he cannot succeed.

Educators need to realize that competitive practices survive from the period when little was known about the individuality of growth and that in many cases they constitute a serious problem in academic evaluation. Those who argue for inclusion of competitive grading at the elementary level insist that such preparation is necessary for the type of life one can expect to encounter in our society. This misguided premise fails to consider the fact that *competition* can occur only within a range of uncertainty; that is, the range in which both success and failure are possible. *Competition* cannot occur when each participant does not have a chance, when the outcome of victory or defeat is predetermined. Note that life's competitive situations are chosen only as one perceives the possibility of success. Competition, so called in school, is hardly chosen by children

* For those interested in initiation of dropout studies, the use of a special dropout identification form, the collection of data, the bases and methods of compiling dropout statistics, and the interpretation and reporting of study findings, the author recommends *Dropout Studies: Design and Conduct,* by Daniel Schreiber, Bernard A. Kaplan and Robert D. Strom. (Washington, D.C.: National Education Association, Project: School Dropouts [in cooperation with the U.S. Office of Education], 1965), 84 pp.

but is forced upon them by compulsory school laws, anxious parents, and ill-trained teachers.

To compare the work product of one whose IQ is 85 with that of one whose IQ exceeds 130 ought to lead to a foregone conclusion. In a sense, school "competition" becomes a daily punishment for those of lesser ability. Under the circumstance in which few participants have a chance to win, it is not strange that some students protect themselves by setting a low level of aspiration, that is, by not trying. Thus, in a spelldown some children are pleased only if they are not the first to make an error; winning is far from their minds. Moreover, in competitive situations where immature minds are involved, defeating others becomes more important than doing the task well. For some pupils competition arouses conflict, others fear the threat of losing, and in some cases there are tensions induced by working against peers, which prevents wholehearted participation. Repeated frustration in the competitive arena can produce a stressful state that makes large demands on a child's emotional balance and may alter his proper relationships with companions, teachers, and parents.

Competition is not the way to bring each person to his full potentiality. By emphasizing the false standard that one should take pride where he excels, teachers too often discourage the pupil from developing his lesser talents. This is especially risky at the elementary level, where strengths are only beginning to emerge. Youngsters ought not to be forced to capitalize on just those proficiencies that develop early, lest other strengths that might develop later be excluded. Competition should never be made so important that failure to win is emotionally disruptive.

That "competition" can produce antipathy and a sense of inequity is shown by studies at the University of Michigan, where it has been determined that one of the prime difficulties in upgrading skills among older workers is their persistent belief that age cannot compete with youth under academic conditions (Donahue, 1962). Fear of competition in retraining programs render some elderly folk reluctant to participate and not infrequently results in unemployment when the old skills become obsolete. This is an example where "competition," the condition under which achievement was to flourish, has had an adverse effect on the stimulation of future learning and renders well-being and confidence uncertain. A tenable postulate is the conviction that life-long learning and activity are beneficial and will most probably take place if their occurrence is made satisfying.

In those rare instances in which predictive dropouts do experience satisfaction in learning, they quickly find that teacher judgment regarding the extent of growth is substantially less than their own estimate. This occurs in part because the desire of educators for achievement and high group standards has led some to equate the two in such a way as to eliminate any possibility of success for many children. In the realm of school evaluation the distance between practice and what we know about testing is centuries apart. We follow tradition, which dictates that pupils should be measured by comparison with others, although our knowledge of learners and the learning process has revealed that the more appropriate measure is that which assesses the growth of an individual in relation to his previous position. Under present operation, "achievement" in the classroom is more communal than personal.

Even short-term observation of a classroom can indicate the negative motivation of marks on some pupils. When identical standards are set for every student regardless of the certain difficulty and ability levels, it follows that the motivating effect on some will be limited by a feeling that high marks are out of reach. If a grade compared the pupil with others of the same ability, each pupil might then have a chance for a high mark, but this still would not be an index of personal growth. One thing we have learned from research—that all men are created unequal; individual differences exist.

Assessing achievement by group standard may be likened to the efforts of an Arkansas farmer who sought to determine a fair price on the pig he was placing for sale. In order to determine the weight of the pig, he balanced a long pole across the back fence. He tied the pig to one end of this pole and attached a large gunnysack to the other. He filled the gunnysack with rocks until the pig and rocks were of equal weight, and the pole was again in balance. Then, to determine the weight of his pig, the farmer estimated the weight of the rocks. To nullify individuality as a criterion for marking is to negate the validity of grades themselves if their purpose is, in fact, to record individual progress. To employ group curves as the standard for an individual's achievement is to guess the weight of the pig or, in our instance, the achievement of the individual. In both cases, we assign a pseudo weight after first weighing something other than that with which we are concerned. It is fair to say that the concept of individual differences has been employed least in the area where it is most needed—in the assessment of achievement. Until individual achievement is based on personal progress, our schools will continue to perpetuate a fraud upon millions of boys and girls.*

Impersonality

A notion that "no one at school really cares" is retained by a number of dropouts who state they might have remained had anyone demonstrated a personal interest in them. That they felt neglected is apparent from the frequency of negative comment regarding impersonal and punitive treatment in class. Their accounts seem to suggest (looking beyond the sour

---

* Parts of the competition discussion have been reprinted from my earlier work by permission of *The High School Journal*, "School Evaluation and Mental Health," December 1964, 48:3, 198–207, and *Journal of Secondary Education*, "Academic Achievement and Mental Health," December 1964, Vol. 39, No. 8, pp. 348–355.

grapes type of interpretation) that teacher-pupil relations can affect holding power. More specifically, as impersonality implies inattention, it
follows that classrooms so oriented are inimical to achievement. The impersonal teacher response, whether inadvertent or willful, tends to affect
staff-student associations, academic expectations, management procedures,
and instructional method.

Some dropouts recall that being ignored by the teacher was the worst
form of punishment; others recall the insult of being recognized more as
a problem than as a person. But common to both memories is an image
of favoritism, the teacher who is personal with only a select few. In this
kind of setting preference is consistently shown to certain pupils or to
their work because it typifies what is desired of all. While many such
teachers would deplore the practice of making comparisons between the
work of superior and inferior students before the class, they do not hesi-
tate to display only the work of able pupils on the bulletin board or in
room exhibits. The same circumstance obtains during recitation periods
when only pupils of the favored element are called upon. In contrast,
those who less often have teacher-accepted answers are obliged to become
listeners or, when permitted to speak, promptly reminded that the reply
is irrelevant, out of order.

Some impersonal teachers do not have favorites. Consider the instructor
who purposely avoids becoming familiar with any pupils on the premise
that it might destroy his objective base of grading. He prides himself on
being unbiased, on not becoming emotionally involved, on being impersonal. Apart from the fact that all emotion represents a bias and that one
is hired to be involved, to care about students, this instructor fails to
understand that student evaluation encompasses more than calculation.
Listen to his reply when confronted by a pupil who has questioned the
grade received: "I don't give grades, I compute them." Granting his intent,
if not his logic, that to be fair is to treat all alike, one can see the tendency
to embrace impersonal standards by requiring identical work of all class
members. Each of us share in this distortion when we allow age or grade
norms to dictate our expectations of how boys and girls should think, act,
speak, or feel; when norms serve to classify a pupil as a potential failure
or success before ever becoming involved with him; when one's IQ determines whether he is to receive respect or be held in low regard. If
impersonal expectations prevail, it is common for developmental characteristics to be ignored so that contradictory behaviors are required such
as a first-grade teacher insisting that her class remain still or do not talk.
Then too, when expectation and evaluation are impersonal, a child's self-
concept is likely to be inappropriate (Conner, 1965, pp. 174–181).

Classroom management procedures often are impersonal and sometimes
ego damaging. For instance, students may be asked to announce their
scores publicly in order to facilitate the teacher's task of recording marks.

Even though expediency is the sole intent of this practice, it does not prevent deleterious outcomes. Similarly the pupil self-view ought to be a greater concern among those who subject children to public failure at the blackboard. Again the purpose may be to illustrate error but the effect is to embarrass and threaten self-esteem. Most concepts of grouping imply impersonality. If selection for membership in instructional groups is based on the observed and measured differences teachers gain, then why is it so many instructors are able to see only three kinds of kids—usually tagging them with subtle but descriptive labels like the steamboats, rowboats, and barges? In truth, there are as many kinds of children as there are children. Moreover, reliance upon labels like "reluctant learners," and "potential retainers" tends to reinforce an image of sameness, the idea that all members of a category are alike when in fact it is only the deficit in relation to a norm that is similar instead of the nature of problems each individual separately sustains. Speed of learning is only one way and perhaps not the most useful one to differentiate instruction. Some children need more structure than others; some excell in learning by discovery; others seem to have little facility in this way and proceed best when they are "told." That grouping can sometimes effect self-concept more than it effects learning is apparent.

We breed impersonality in instructional process when individual learning rate and style are ignored. Believing the book must be finished by the semester's end, that all content must be covered in accord with the syllabus, that the workbook must be completed to justify its cost, some teachers unwittingly defeat their stated primary objectives. By providing ready-made answers to slow pupils so as not to retard group progress the instructor inhibits thinking in that he denies these persons a chance to discover, to understand, to see relationships—the basic elements of intellectual growth. At all grade levels it seems we need to de-emphasize some of the impersonal techniques like drill and memory orientation. This problem is extended within classes in which pupils are forbidden to collaborate, to work together, to associate in resolving a common problem. Because the emphasis is upon grades, talking in some cases is construed as cheating. Still it is hard to imagine how youngsters can come to learn the lessons of cooperation by always working alone, in opposition to one another. The contention that maturity will remove the propensity and incompetence is wishful thinking. Other teachers who deny group interaction justify their decision by citing negative peer influences. For a teacher to assume his proper guidance role, he must, in fact, know each individual and relate to these individuals—only then is there a prospect that negative influences might be diminished.

Each of us desires a personal response to his actions. We want to be recognized as a unique being. So important is this need that schools are charged with the responsibility of fostering individuality, to elevate self-concept, and to encourage creative behavior. There is less danger that we will be unable to fulfill this responsibility than that we shall ignore it or fail to remain cognizant of its importance. Things can be done:

1. Class sizes need to be reduced in certain schools in which overcrowding make the task of knowing each pupil more difficult. During the interim, however, we need to remember that as impersonality is more incumbent upon teacher attitude than class size, we can still diminish some impersonal responses apart from a decline in pupil membership.

2. More counseling is needed for each student, including the elementary youngster.

3. Teacher aides can be useful for performing noninstructional tasks in order to free teachers for helping students with problems.

4. Reception centers can be established for newly arrived pupils who do not come with school records. In the reception center appropriate pupil placement is determined and initial friendships are made so that transition to the new school is as pleasant as possible. For instruction to become personal, it is important that each individual receive relevant subject matter, his rate of learning be considered, and materials be appropriate to his achievement level and life circumstance.

5. Many schools need decentralization, as increase in size does tend to increase impersonality.

6. Nongraded schools should be encouraged, since they provide better pupil-teacher relationships, more appropriate curricula, and offer the chance for improved motivation.

7. Better parent-teacher relationships should be encouraged. Often the relationship between the home and the school is reflected in the child.

8. There need to be faculty meetings at times devoted to considering ways by which impersonality can be diminished.

These changes can reduce some of our error; they can provide more children with the personal help required. What we cannot ensure is a positive influence from the impersonal teacher—he or she will remain unable to convey enthusiasm, motivation, and aspiration. As important as these factors are, it becomes apparent that we must work toward helping more teachers develop personalized approaches and techniques. When that day comes, Johnny's grades may not be contingent upon the grade Jerry obtains and perhaps Linda Zuker will not be assigned to the last seat.

SCHOOL RESPONSE TO FAILURE

Homework

Historically, the most frequent response to school failure has been homework. For many years belief had it that homework is the only feasible way to maintain group pace, to motivate the reluctant, engender discipline, and overcome personal deficit (not to mention its punitive value of reducing classroom misbehavior). So popular has the practice become and its virtue so inflated that many parents and educators consider "night work" an advantageous enterprise for all pupils regardless of their academic standing. And, of course, since all homework is by nature beneficial, no justification is required for whatever kind of assignments given. Because the short school day is fully occupied with classes, the argument goes that most children should be expected to carry home whatever assigned tasks they are unable to finish during the study period allotted in school. Moreover, since learning in the required subjects is considered quantitative in that everyone must cover a certain amount of content, we might expect those persons who require longer periods of time to learn than their peers will necessarily be subject to homework in greater frequency and amount. Certainly school time cannot be wasted in order for an individual to "catch up" with the others.

Although this view implicitly recognizes differences in pupil learning rates, these differences are not allowed to modify class assignments; instead the differences are relegated to home study—only there in his home can one proceed at his own pace. The need to justify homework to countless numbers of frustrated children has often led parents and teachers to attribute a disproportionate weight to its value in the learning process—maintaining, upon evidence of pupil success, that it was the diligence, the night work, the repetitive practice and drill in arithmetic, social studies, and English that underlay the accomplishment. In a large number of instances, it is more likely the student learned in spite of his homework rather than because of it.

Even today a large number of parents believe that the teachers who most often assign homework are necessarily the better teachers, more interested in the success of children, more willing to take time and effort required for correcting papers. And, of course, the image of a teacher carrying piles of homework from the school each evening was for a long time the epitome of education (or something). So prevalent was the expectation that some teachers have felt guilty or uncomfortable leaving school at four o'clock in the afternoon with just their purse—and no pile. One could assume that whoever neglects to assign periodic homework is remiss in his duty, especially where failing pupils are concerned. After all, if a boy is failing, what better evidence might the teacher offer of interest in his welfare than to suggest additional work? So, for students unable to complete the required amount and quality of produce during school time, it has generally been accepted that they should be given a number of pages to read or problems to solve, things to finish at home by the following day. Again, as time has been considered the major difference in learning accommodation between individuals, the most common resolution has appeared to be simply a matter of assigning more drill or practice—these activities will bring success to the unsuccessful. Naturally many parents sanction any and all of these tasks, often backing up the teacher with punishment, threat, cajoling, or the frequent phrase, "It's good for you." Parents see the homework practice as the one way by which their child can keep up with or exceed the remainder of his classmates.

An educator's perception of the learning role, the teaching role, and the nature of learning can be inferred from the conditions under which he assigns homework (Strom, 1966a). Although most teachers would disapprove of lessons given as individual or group punishment, too few are disturbed by the procedure of requiring failers to complete additional work at night. If a student is unable to understand the method of attaining correct answers in school, how can it be assumed that he will learn at home? One assumption might be that for certain pupils, learning is most profitable as a nocturnal task; in which case they should attend night school. Or perhaps it is felt that parents will teach those lessons the teacher finds difficult to relate. Again, this is unlikely. In fact, teachers inadvertently undermine the respect that students have for parents when parents are faced with the precarious task of having to explain processes or techniques that they do not understand. For example, parents can feel insufficient when assistance in modern math is requested by their elementary school child. A father can explain to his youngster that he does not know the method and this requires humility; or he can "snow" the child to drive off questions and hopefully retain respect; maybe he will simply say, "What's going on at that school anyway?"

Remember too that in many cases of pupil failure there is likely to be less recourse to parental assistance than in most homes because the adults of these families may also have failed in school. In the future as levels of achievement and the nature of instruction increase in difference between each generation, parental support will need to come in ways other than the mechanics of helping with homework. Educators who persist in charging parents with the responsibility for monitoring work at home and helping youngsters with problems on the premise that it has been effective and will continue to be should reflect upon the classic statement of Will Rogers, "Things ain't what they used to be and probably never was!" Soon we must begin to ask, "What are some additional ways that parents can help children now and in the future that are different from the ones generally used in the past? What can parents do to foster the motivations and skills needed for continuing to learn the rest of one's life?"

A widespread belief in the concept of completion is the major base that underlies support for homework today. The concept of completion implies but does not ensure learning. Yet in some classrooms a major determinant of achievement is whether or not one completes assigned work. It is not that teachers are more interested in having things done than having them learned, but a persistent belief continues that practice will promote intellectual learning, that the discipline of finishing tasks will develop personal responsibility as well as promote the learning process. However, for children who lack the understanding to finish work successfully during school, drill only serves to frustrate. If practice and drill are to be effective, they must be preceded by meaning, by effective instruction. Otherwise having more homework does not necessarily mean one is learning more; it means only that he has more to do.

The concept of completion as achievement, so prominent in the days of mental discipline, is now revived, but this time as a miscarriage of gestalt closure. The gestalt principle of closure asserts that a student strives to reach a satisfying end-state of equilibrium through perceptive completion. This occurs as cognitive change allows new configurations of previously unrelated objects or ideas, enabling the learner to resolve gaps in knowledge, find missing parts, or complete partial formations. In a sense one can say that closure-completion is synonymous with a certain kind of learning.

It is important to notice certain aspects peculiar to the closure principle as it relates to the classroom. First, intrinsic motivation is operative in order to reduce the need tension created by the confrontation of a problem in which the student is ego-involved. Then, too, the attention directed to the problem sustains until cognitive change (learning) occurs, bringing new gestalt or configuration. Finally, closure results in satisfaction from resolution of the problem. It has been said that closure is to Gestalt theory what reward is to Connectionism. (These psychological modes are discussed in Chapter IV.)

Obviously, the mere completion of assigned tasks is different from gestalt closure. For one thing, the motivation is imposed, external to the learner, so that the demand is made of him but not necessarily by him. Secondly, learning will take place only if a pupil experiences closure as his project proceeds toward completion. That completion is not necessarily learning has long since been demonstrated as has the fact that enforced practice is often required at the expense of antipathy. Finally, whereas closure culminates in satisfaction, completion more often than not terminates only in a feeling of relief. In fact, a displacement of satisfaction sometimes occurs when the teacher rather than the learner is pleased with completion of assigned work. The feeling that his authority has been accepted, his responsibility dispatched, need reduction occurs for the teacher. It is, however, lamentable when student work is carried on less for personal growth and satisfaction than to please or propitiate the instructor.

Perhaps the greatest weakness of most homework assignments is a lack of constructive purpose. In the main, teacher attention is devoted solely to the student's finished product or answer rather than considering the processes used to derive solutions. Instead of diagnosing why a pupil is making errors, the expedient goal is to number his mistakes, assign a grade. In other words, achievement classification seems more central to the homework objective than does the detection of error type or the correction of inappropriate processes. It is important that a child understand the reasons for his failure if the knowledge of its occurrence is to be helpful, if his self-concept is to include an awareness of strong and weak points, if he is to improve his performance. In the field of education generally, and especially in the realm of homework, the principle of diagnostics has largely been overlooked. (See Figures II-3–II-5.) When pupils recognize that the teacher is interested only in the product and not in the process they become eager to finish and may resort to inaccurate shortcuts, thereby defeating the only tenable aim of the assignments. In fact, the failing student who recognizes that an incomplete assignment may prevent him from going to gym or outside during the recess period is prone to hand in a number of answers without even working out the problems, knowing full well that completion is the essential requirement. For students to whom completion has become a compulsion there is a tendency to equate achievement with that which they have finished. If problem-solving is the goal of most homework activity, then its substance, which is method, should receive careful evaluation. If this is not the case, the lesson is uninstructive; it cannot be diagnostic; it is without positive significance.

Periodically every teacher needs to examine his conception of homework and its relation to pupil growth. In many cases students do not finish assignments during class because of the difficulty level or an insufficient time limit given their pace of accommodation. Under these conditions homework is not the reasonable answer; more properly one would revise the assignments both in nature and in length. At a time when parents and teachers seek earlier retirement, longer vacations and shorter work weeks, it is disheartening to note that many of them condone the procedure of having students who attend school daily spend each evening in preparation for their next day's classes. In the academic realm, time is not the principal teacher; neither are parents equipped for tutorial endeavor; nor is completion an accomplishment in itself. The teacher is the key and when he believes homework is appropriate it must necessarily follow instructive purpose rather than a punitive one; he realizes that it requires little to assess error; to correct error is the main province of his profession, the challenge of a teacher. In homework, as in every other school activity, reason should prevail.

Nonpromotion

The practice of nonpromotion as a response to failure remains an obstacle to achievement even though its "beneficial" effects were repudiated long ago. Persons favoring the idea that some children should repeat grades insist the policy is defensible and, in fact, imperative, if we are to ensure mastery of content at each level, motivate pupils who

4

Tommy

1.	*somd* ✓	cellar
2.	*covle* ✓	chart
3.	*lame* ✓	lamb
4.	*oakes* ✓	oats
5.	*sonne* ✓	pigeons
6.	*lacimel* ✓	yourself
7.	*wished* ✓	washed
8.	*anpeon* ✓	anxious
9.	*wished* ✓	wished
10.	*eneal* ✓	answered
11.	*awntion* ✓	auntie
12.	*olghet* ✓	owner
13.	*tineant* ✓	ranch
14.	*uglarity*	arrived
15.	*anet* ✓	aunt's
16.	*ten* ✓	tan
17.	*scpthe* ✓	sixteen
18.	*puneo* ✓	pasture
19.	*blane* ✓	blossoms
20.	*con scrice*	cream
21.	*bonlet* ✓	bottom
22.	*sant* ✓	suppose
23.	*lanel* ✓	squirrel
24.	*warnt* ✓	quite

Fig. II-3. Selecting the appropriate homework. Everyone in Tommy's room (Grade 5) is assigned the same spelling words. Students who fail mid-week tests are obliged to complete the standing homework assignment—writing each incorrect word in three separate sentences. Will this strategy help Tommy learn to spell? Is it diagnostic? Does the frequency of error suggest a change in selection of assigned words?

appear inert, and sustain homogeneity of ability within grades. Perceiving the concepts of "social" promotion and "trial" promotion as threatening mechanisms designed to undermine or destroy school standards, advocates of nonpromotion like to fancy themselves as protectors of educational quality, defenders of scholarship. It is in this latter context, through publicizing their mission as academic guardians, that most support has been forthcoming—more so than as a response to empirical data favoring retention. Whenever one claims to protect that which all believe to be good, the popular inference is that one's opposition seek to deprecate the same cause. The retentionist then would

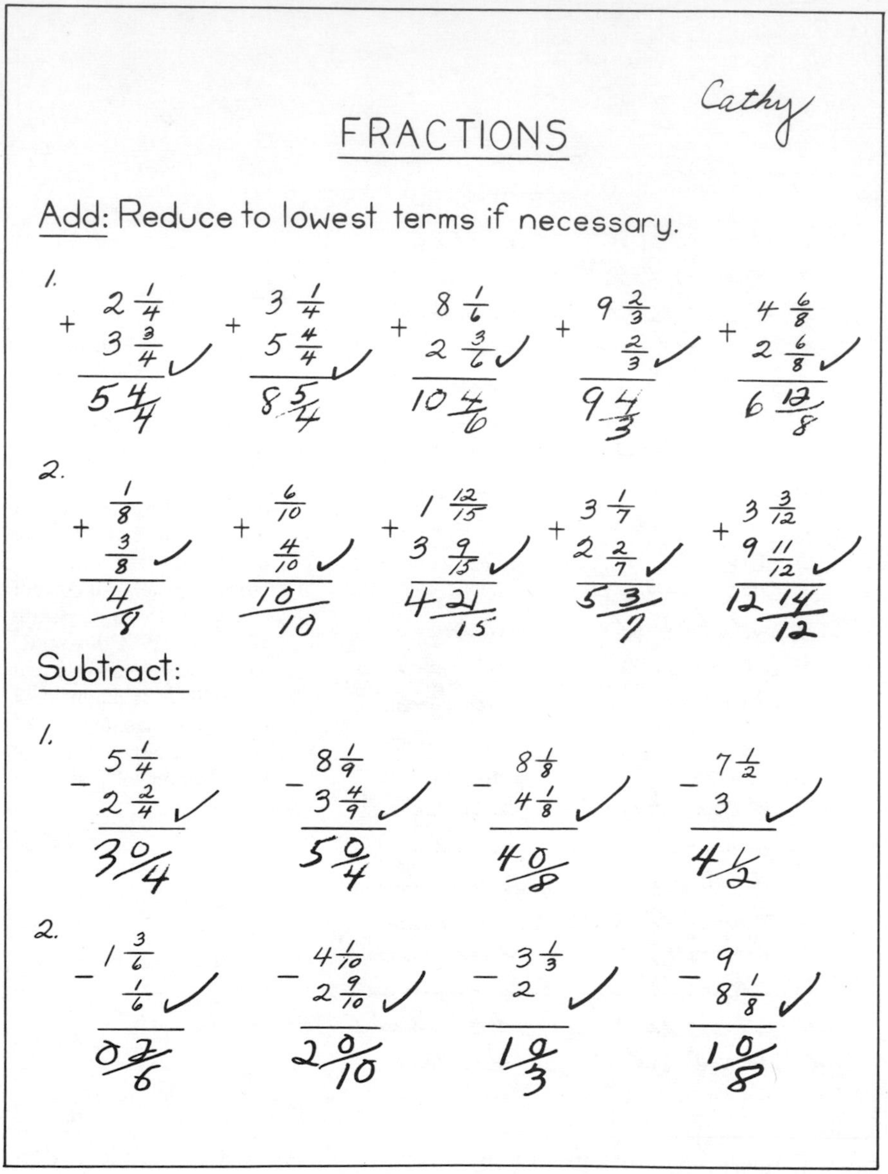

FRACTIONS

Cathy

Add: Reduce to lowest terms if necessary.

1.

$$+\ \begin{array}{r} 2\frac{1}{4} \\ 3\frac{3}{4} \\ \hline 5\frac{4}{4} \end{array} \checkmark \qquad +\ \begin{array}{r} 3\frac{1}{4} \\ 5\frac{4}{4} \\ \hline 8\frac{5}{4} \end{array} \checkmark \qquad +\ \begin{array}{r} 8\frac{1}{6} \\ 2\frac{3}{6} \\ \hline 10\frac{4}{6} \end{array} \checkmark \qquad +\ \begin{array}{r} 9\frac{2}{3} \\ \frac{2}{3} \\ \hline 9\frac{4}{3} \end{array} \checkmark \qquad +\ \begin{array}{r} 4\frac{6}{8} \\ 2\frac{6}{8} \\ \hline 6\frac{12}{8} \end{array} \checkmark$$

2.

$$+\ \begin{array}{r} \frac{1}{8} \\ \frac{3}{8} \\ \hline \frac{4}{8} \end{array} \checkmark \qquad +\ \begin{array}{r} \frac{6}{10} \\ \frac{4}{10} \\ \hline \frac{10}{10} \end{array} \checkmark \qquad +\ \begin{array}{r} 1\frac{12}{15} \\ 3\frac{9}{15} \\ \hline 4\frac{21}{15} \end{array} \checkmark \qquad +\ \begin{array}{r} 3\frac{1}{7} \\ 2\frac{2}{7} \\ \hline 5\frac{3}{7} \end{array} \checkmark \qquad +\ \begin{array}{r} 3\frac{3}{12} \\ 9\frac{11}{12} \\ \hline 12\frac{14}{12} \end{array} \checkmark$$

Subtract:

1.

$$-\ \begin{array}{r} 5\frac{1}{4} \\ 2\frac{2}{4} \\ \hline 3\frac{0}{4} \end{array} \checkmark \qquad -\ \begin{array}{r} 8\frac{1}{9} \\ 3\frac{4}{9} \\ \hline 5\frac{0}{4} \end{array} \checkmark \qquad -\ \begin{array}{r} 8\frac{1}{8} \\ 4\frac{1}{8} \\ \hline 4\frac{0}{8} \end{array} \checkmark \qquad -\ \begin{array}{r} 7\frac{1}{2} \\ 3 \\ \hline 4\frac{1}{2} \end{array} \checkmark$$

2.

$$-\ \begin{array}{r} 1\frac{3}{6} \\ \frac{1}{6} \\ \hline 0\frac{2}{6} \end{array} \checkmark \qquad -\ \begin{array}{r} 4\frac{1}{10} \\ 2\frac{9}{10} \\ \hline 2\frac{0}{10} \end{array} \checkmark \qquad -\ \begin{array}{r} 3\frac{1}{3} \\ 2 \\ \hline 1\frac{2}{3} \end{array} \checkmark \qquad -\ \begin{array}{r} 9 \\ 8\frac{1}{8} \\ \hline 1\frac{0}{8} \end{array} \checkmark$$

Fig. II-4. Teacher use of homework. In Grade 5, Cathy's homework paper has just been returned to her. Will the teacher's error checks provide clues for Cathy as to how she might improve? What has been gained by doing this lesson? Given her performance, how much more homework does Cathy seem to need regarding the reduction of fractions? What was the teacher's purpose in assigning these problems?

have his audience believe that those opposing nonpromotion sanction mediocrity.

Deferring for the moment any questions regarding incidence or effect of nonpromotion, it is fair to inquire as to who should fail. Are

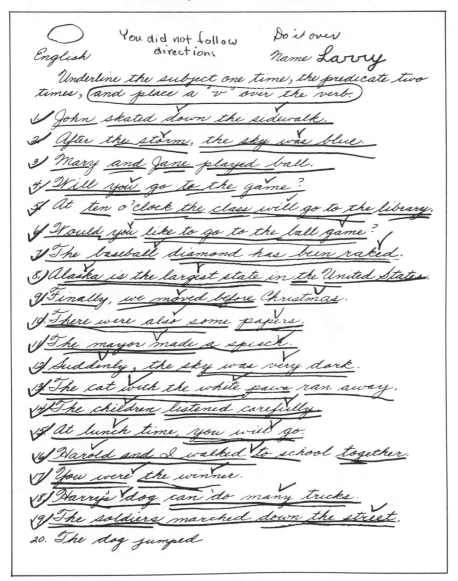

Fig. II-5. Homework, guidance, and direction. Larry reads at the third-grade level although he is in the fifth grade. Did Larry overlook the directions as the teacher infers or does Larry know what a verb is? A subject? A predicate? Can he read her response to his homework? Should drill on the parts of speech precede or follow an understanding of them? Should Larry request a conference?

the criteria for failure relevant and realistic? Surely the use of "grade level" as a class standard is unreasonable, since in a normal population only half of the members can be expected to attain the goal. Equally unfortunate is the procedure of requiring a student to repeat a year because he persistently misbehaves in class. Boys more often than girls are victim of this criterion, especially in classes in which teachers allow factors other than achievement to govern grading. Investigation reveals that even though boys and girls may have identical scores on standardized tests, their teachers often tend to give higher grades to girls (Carter, 1952). Then too, low-achieving girls may be promoted while boys with equal achievement ratings are retained (Rose, 1928). The point is that even if boys get along less well with teachers than girls, the differences in relationship should not be reflected by a greater incidence of failure among males.

The same question of realism and relevance apply to other criteria used in decisions about nonpromotion. Consider the old-fashioned virtue of regular attendance as a principal determinant of school promotion. Summarizing 27 separate investigations completed between 1925 and 1945 on the causes of nonpromotion, Lafferty (1948) states that "irregular attendance" ranked first among the stated reasons. In some systems policy requires that pupils who have been absent a certain number of days during the school year must automatically repeat the grade—this in spite of evidence that many pupils with poor records of attendance are able to maintain acceptable marks (Elsbree, 1943, p. 86). Difficulties arise also when recourse to the criterion of "maturity" is optioned as a justification for retention. Very often teachers working with low IQ children reason that promotion is unwise because the students simply are not ready for work required at the next higher grade. The fact that repeating a grade invariably results in a poorer performance than when promotion occurs is mute testimony to the weakness of such a criterion (Farley, Frey, and Garland, 1933). For students of this low-ability level, as well as for all of their age peers, the usual criteria for nonpromotion seem untenable.

Academic effects of nonpromotion have consistently proved adverse. Researchers first entered the controversy early in this century at a time when half of all elementary school graduates had failed at least one grade. Several of the many studies which offer conclusive outcomes follow:

> 1911—Using a sample of 5,000 nonpromoted students, Keyes found that while 21 percent of the repeaters improved in achievement, 40 percent achieved less than during the previous year, and 39 percent demonstrated no change (Keyes, 1911).

> 1926—In considering several thousand children who were retained, Buckingham learned that only about one-third improved after repeating the grade; the remaining two-thirds either did poorer work or showed no improvement (Buckingham, 1926).

> 1928—Restricting his concern to pupils above first grade, McKinney's inquiry revealed that only 35 percent of the repeaters did better work the second time, 53 percent did not improve, and 12 percent did poorer work (McKinney, 1953).

1936—Focusing upon retention in first grade, Arthur discovered the average repeater did not learn more in two years than the average non-repeater of the same mental age learned in one year.

It is interesting to note that nonpromotion currently involves about 20 percent of first-grade children each year (Clark, 1959).

Effects of nonpromotion have not been appreciably altered since the conduct of these early studies. That low-achieving pupils who are retained still appear to make no greater, and often less, gain in accomplishment than they do when promoted is verified by an array of more contemporary investigations (Goodlad, 1954; Worth, 1960; Wolf, 1961; Kamaii and Weikart, 1963). The conclusion is that continued reliance upon nonpromotion in itself to improve school achievement is unwarranted. If the practice is to continue it must be justified on grounds other than improved performance.

Nonpromotion often generates an adverse social response, particularly from the peer society. If as a result of being retained one's acceptance-status is significantly diminished, we can reasonably expect him to seek new avenues of affiliation. All too often this translates into an affinity toward out-of-school-age mates whose classroom experience was also unsuccessful and who may urge that he sever ties with the institution. The findings of one study suggest that a remarkably high proportion of dropouts maintain their closest peer relationship with individuals who no longer attend school (Strom, 1966e). Naturally, when in-school relationships become distant because of failure, there is less likelihood of participation in extracurricular activities. Educators with the propensity to list characteristics of persons who leave school have for many years indicated the dropout as showing relatively little involvement in social functions. Unfortunately, we have seen this less as a consequence of failure, alienation, and rejection than as an interesting phenomenon. Obviously the problem is not confined to financing attendance at extracurricular activities; to afford the ticket is not the main issue—to dress differently does not clothe failure or rid one of embarrassment. Lack of participation does not usually relate to economics but sometimes reflects an instance of default, the inevitable result of exclusion.

Relations are affected by academic loss even during the elementary grades. Left behind his promoted fellows, the failer is obliged to accept membership in a new group; his retention forces an association with children to whom he felt superior in the past. Always visible as the person who did not "pass," separated from his former classmates, and reluctant to concede that his age and greater social experience do not count for much, the nonpromoted child may encounter many instances of conflict with students and teacher. Nonetheless, a number of heroic personalities attempt to rebound from humiliation and to overcome ridicule of students in both classes, where they are known by adapting, by making an attempt to fulfill their perceived role in the new circumstance. Too often, however, this individual may find himself prevented from contributing to class activities, find his efforts ignored, or find himself relegated to carry on the obviously menial tasks of the group. Soon he realizes he has become the victim of a stereotypical view. The obvious downward mobility and loss of status within the school society add to the unpleasantness of the whole nonpromotion experience (Thomas and Knudson, 1965). It would seem that depending much on experience with his fellows, one can be made to feel more or less capable, more or less worthy, more or less acceptable. A prediction could be that only as he feels worthy will he behave in worthy ways, will he strive for those goals in school and life that are within his reach, if not his grasp.

Another deleterious outcome of nonpromotion seems to be its relationship to motivation and future progress in school. A case in point is Mercer County, Ohio, where, of 2,000 children who entered first grade at the same time, 643 dropped out before completing high school. All but 5 of these dropouts, 638, had been retained in first grade. In other words, 99 percent of the dropouts repeated grade one. In fact, as an aggregate these 643 students failed a total of more than 1,800 grades during their first six years of school. This means that each of the dropouts failed on an average of every other year for six years. These youngsters learned to fail (Dillon, 1949, pp. 35–40). Elsewhere the problem is similar. Hall's (1964) research in Dade County, Florida, shows that 74.3 percent of the dropouts there had repeated at least one grade as compared to a repeat incidence of only 17.8 percent among persons who graduated from high school. A statewide study of dropouts in Louisiana directed by Jones and Robert (1963) indicates that 72 percent of the dropouts in the state had repeated at least one year in school. Given the inextricable relationship between self-concept and performance, it should be apparent that consistent failure will only tend to restrict motivation. When one sees himself as unable to advance in school, there appears no reason to remain.

A perceptive analysis of the relationship between nonpromotion and school dropouts is presented by Thomas and Knudsen (1965, p. 91):

> In considering the content that must be mastered, it should be noted that current achievement is built upon previous success in school. Sudden high achievement following a succession of failures is unlikely to occur for at least two reasons. First, under our system of education, the marginally achieving student is faced each year with an ever-increasing gap between expectations and achievements—particularly if the educational norms of his school seem unattainable. Thus, the conditions for failure are maximized. In such circumstance, the non-school-oriented peer group may offer him the social support that he cannot obtain from the school or the family. Such a group may also offer some academic norms that deviate from those of the school and the home.

Second, nonpromotion at any stage of elementary school seems to cause problems in the later years of education. Through nonpromotion, the child has learned he is unable to accomplish the required academic work. Unless this attitude is counteracted, the child views school as an impossible or an inappropriate place for achievement and recognition. Since the school no longer holds any interest for him, he will seek accomplishment in areas outside the educational system. Consequently, students who have been "held back" at some time in their academic careers appear more likely to drop out of school.[*]

Unfortunately, many of us do not view the problem from this vantage. Instead we lament the effect as though it were the cause—we see the tardy arrival, the irregular attendance, the truancy, as principal reasons for unsatisfactory progress. Truancy is seldom the real reason for poor scholarship. In working with 110 truants, 97 of whom were judged retarded because the reading of their grade was too difficult, McElwa (1931) found that truancy was to them an escape from an embarrassing school situation—their absence was precipitated by the expectation of failure and embarrassment. Who among us enjoy the distinction of being last—and least?

During recent years a number of proposals relating to organization and instruction have been initiated to overcome certain weaknesses inherent in grade-standard achievement expectations. Each of these well-known school plans, designed for the cities of Dalton, Winnetka, Pueblo, Joplin, and St. Louis, share a common regard for individual rates of ability and learning. However, just as homogeneity fails to eventuate from nonpromotion (Saunders, 1941), so too the grouping approaches cited do not seem to result in a reduced variability of achievement within a class. Goodlad (1965, p. 59) explains the difficulty: "The variability in attainments within one child sometimes parallel the variability of an entire class. A child, like a class, is not a second, fourth, or sixth grader. Johnny can be in the fifth grade for arithmetic computation, the sixth grade for arithmetic reasoning, the seventh grade for spelling, the eighth grade for word meaning, the ninth grade for paragraph meaning and the tenth grade for language—and yet be officially registered in the sixth grade."

Perhaps we can improve learning and diminish nonpromotion through further attempts to individualize instruction and by basing our educational programs on a theory of continuous progress. According to Wilhelm (1962, pp. 62–74) whenever we tie success to the mastery of one established body of content, we have equated content with goal. This requirement demands the rejection of all who cannot master that content. Therefore, it is idle to talk about individual differences so long as there is only one way to reach a common goal, for even though goals be universal, content and method must be infinitely var-

[*] From Shailer Thomas and Dean K. Knudsen, *The Relationships Between Nonpromotion and the Dropout Problem," Theory Into Practice,* IV, No. 3 (June, 1965), 91. Reprinted by permission.

ied. This variety in content and concern for separate rates of learning represent the promise of individualized instruction—a promise that obviates the artificial hurdles of "pass" or "fail." When expectations are derived from sources extrinsic to the child, individual growth cannot truthfully be stated as the primary goal of education. As growth is personal, it follows that the advance of one student need not be contingent upon the relative gain of his peers.

The ideas of Goodlad and Anderson (1963), Brown (1963), and others regarding a nongraded or ungraded structure involve objectives that are more comprehensive than merely bringing about a decline in non-promotion practices. Yet, this has been one of the purposes served. Rigid assignment of skills to a specific grade level has no place in a nongraded school. Children are not promoted from grade to grade, they do not repeat grades—there are no grades (Goodlad, 1965). Some of the propositions basing a nongraded school are that children differ from one another; these differences must be taken into account in planning, teaching, and educational diagnosis. In the nongraded scheme, the question is not, "Is this child ready for school?" but rather, "What is the child ready for?" Criterion standards based on a sequence of learning replace normative standards as the measure of pupil progress; and sound learning is cumulative. The nongraded school structure and its basis for organizing learning experiences make the question of promotion or nonpromotion obsolete (Ellinger, 1965).

The Psychology of Consequence

Certain of the dubious responses to failure are of contemporary origin. One such strategy involves making known what might be called the "psychology of consequence." It begins with an attempt to mobilize every element of family and communal influence. Then, acting in concert, these forces are brought to bear on all young persons who might be anticipating withdrawal from school before graduating. Viewed as a benevolent effort, to let the "potential dropout"* know that people really care about him and his future, the contact objective is to reason with him, talk sense to him, help him to recognize that this decision could not be rational, and more likely will be viewed as criminal. Somehow failing students need to be warned, they need to understand that quitting carries with it a societal stigma, a sentence of being written off as a citizen, a person, a human being. And, as no one of us wishes to jeopardize his humanity, it follows that each owes it to himself and society to finish school.

A dangerous drawback of this approach is its restricted focus, in

* The term "potential dropout" is inadequate, as every student is a potential dropout. The author's term "predictive dropout" is more restrictive, used to denote pupils within the IQ range (80–95) from which the greatest incidence of school withdrawal is reported.

that the economic motivation of an individual is considered paramount. Prime emphasis is given to increasing his awareness of what a decision to leave school entails in terms of its dollars-and-cents results. Though an appeal like this is not without reason, it may be without positive effect. Erich Fromm (1962, pp. 141–151) in discussing man's relationship to self, points to an increasing tendency of our culture toward adopting a "marketing orientation." That is, man comes to experience himself less as one with fears, loves, convictions, and doubts—and more as an abstraction, alienated from his real nature, whose purpose is to fulfill a certain function in the social system. Thus, one's sense of value depends primarily on his success, on whether he can sell himself favorably in the labor market, make more of himself than that with which he began. If he fails in a profitable investment of himself, he is a failure. Clearly his sense of values depend on extrinsic factors—the world of work, the economic structure. Given the prevalence of this "marketing orientation," it would seem feasible to consider an economic appeal as having a universal base of response.

However, we err in supposing that all youngsters who leave school are unaware of the monetary hazards; they simply are no longer able to put up with the situation. In fact, their choice to migrate from student status before graduating from high school is rarely without purpose. Many of them really believe that an indeterminate destination in adult society will prove more satisfying than their present position. What makes the journey tragic is that the destination very often is unemployment. Yet to assume that fewer persons will embark on this journey simply by being warned against it is wishful thinking. Failing youngsters need something beyond the negative assurance that there are even worse failure situations in life reserved for those who leave school before graduating. In many cases the choice we offer low-achieving students is not a choice at all. There is something hollow in the option of whether to trade the chance for an unskilled life that portends low income, little status, and long hours for an opportunity to remain in a classroom, where the predicted experience is one of embarrassment, unfair competition, ridicule, and ego defeat. In spite of the "promise at the end of the rainbow" idea, the dropout—who more often sees the rain—finds the prospect a questionable advance.

One needs but to witness the rationale and action of a "return to school" campaign to conclude that adult energies are most directed toward changing adolescent attitudes. The inference is that something is obviously wrong with the decision-making of a person who chooses to evade classes. As he needs to be aware that no one should quit, an attempt is made to sketch a verbal picture of either dismal or angry public sentiment, lasting disapproval that will plague his future. What might be greater wisdom on our part is to recognize that dropping out does not necessarily reflect a weakness in character but may well represent an inadequacy of the school to provide for academic needs. There is something wrong with the methods of begging, cajoling, bribing, or selling persons on the idea of coming back to school, letting them know someone cares, giving them the a la mode encounter, and then—once the school looks as though it has done a fine job in retrieving its lost—allowing the "returned" to occupy again a position of defeat. In the author's judgment it is socially sadistic to ask boys and girls who have a history of failure to return to a setting in which they continue to serve as the pawns of success for others. In a sense these persons are not dropouts; they are squeezeouts.

B. F. Skinner (1965), professor of social relations at Harvard University, maintains that the current dropout campaign is futile; the failing adolescent should not be encouraged to return to school. Others of us who share this conviction have repeatedly been disappointed with the negative effects produced by coercive publicity. It seems that most dropouts and predictive school-leavers are not favorably impressed by a constant barrage and exposure to commercial reminders of "stay in school" and "return to school." Most of these young people have long resented the imposition tactic to which they were subject in an academic environment—especially "being told to do something on an assignment I knew I wasn't able to do." We simply compound the alienation by suggesting again, by insisting again, that as usual we know what's best for them. To them it seems the school is still a coercive institution even when one is no longer a part of it, outside of it. Far from viewing the national effort as a benevolent movement, dropouts in the main may resent it. By extending the context of pressure, enlarging the circle of experience in which a youngster must be embarrassed and ridiculed as to his withdrawal from school and reminded about the theme of "school necessity," we can induce irrevocable harm. Theirs may be the flag of defeat but we serve no gainful purpose in asking them to raise that flag in demonstration or by making sure the entire community is ready to call attention to it.

Follow-up studies in Columbus, Detroit, Los Angeles, and other cities suggest that many dropouts will return to earn a diploma by attending night classes. Often the "return mechanism" is activated after much careful thought, after repressing dissatisfying experiences, incident to the desire of improving one's position in life. The "return mechanism" is seldom activated as a result of pressure. This means that somehow we must desist in the motivation of fear and coercion, the familiar recourse to social pressure and intimidation insofar as the future education of failing pupils is concerned. To contrive devious types of motivation and then to label these "guidance" is a monument to confusion and misunderstanding.

Although the "psychology of consequence" movement has many authors, its origin can be traced to a series of events that took place during the summer of 1963. Following a White House appeal for immediate action to reduce the number of dropouts, the U.S. Commissioner of Education met with other school leaders to discuss alternatives that might be taken on such short notice. Two ideas emerged as most practical under the circumstance (USOE, 1964, pp. 1–2): (1) The mounting of a nationwide publicity campaign, and (2) the use of school counselors and other personnel to identify dropouts and potential dropouts and persuade them to return to school in the fall. Across the country, mass media gave support by preparing news releases of the value of education and also information regarding emphasis on local programs. The National Advertising Council arranged for coast-to-coast distribution of special radio and television spot appeals by the President. Approximately a quarter of a million dollars was made available from the President's Emergency Fund to help finance 63 local programs in 23 states. Fraternal and educational organizations helped in whatever way they could.

Undoubtedly certain benefits have accrued from the U.S. Office of Education dropout program. However, even a cursory inspection of the document that ostensibly describes the national outcome is disappointing. Ignoring the fact that many cherished results stated appear peripheral to the campaign's central purpose, questions can be raised about omission of data (USOE, 1964). Reportedly half of the combined group contacted—potential leavers and actual dropouts—returned to school in the fall of 1963. This is a good score if we overlook one question: What proportion of the persons contacted were potential dropouts, adolescents who were in attendance the semester preceding the campaign? An answer to this query could more clearly reveal whether the campaign had anything to do with the reported results. In sum, though few of us would quarrel with the intent of the national endeavor, it is difficult to approve either the selected program method or the assessment procedures. Certainly, to convey the idea that adults care about the young is important but it is reasonable to assume that those who do care might conceive a more effective way of relating the sentiment—in particular by making appropriate changes in the school operation and in its structure.

PROBLEMS OF THE SUCCESSFUL

Within any field of endeavor one finds that even the most accomplished individuals admit to having experienced obstacles in learning. Like their less successful counterparts, they can recall a number of school-related problems that gave them cause for alarm. But these recollections, however vivid, seldom receive due consideration in discussions that ostensibly are concerned with needed change in school structure and processes. Indeed, there are few schoolmen who solicit the negative report of graduates; an even smaller number of educators view such information as essential for deliberations relating to modification of curricula, evaluative techniques or classroom procedures. To understand some of the reasons behind this strange oversight, one must bear in mind certain contemporary changes in our economic and vocational structure that have thrust undereducated persons into a position of national cynosure. Given the economic necessity for increased school holding power, the growing visibility of unskilled dropouts, and the consequent adverse image of schools where pupils do not complete secondary grades, it is understandable that serious attention be given to keeping youngsters in class. Certainly, helping students whose academic outlook appears tenuous is a noble undertaking; we need to improve our efforts with regard to this important responsibility.

But to concurrently disregard *problems of the successful* or to relegate their difficulties to the lowest level of priority constitutes a serious omission in the quest for meaningful innovation. The difficulties experienced by students who have completed the course also demand close scrutiny if our pattern of change is to have a positive effect on greater numbers of children. It is unwise to exclude or underestimate the value of their report; to entertain their accounts regarding the classroom is requisite information for improving the classroom. We cannot be content that these pupils have "made it through"; rather we must make sure that the "through process" becomes as efficient and profitable as it can be. To favor the well-being of all students, it first becomes necessary to ascertain what difficulties they share with one another, what issues are unique to the failing group and to the group that succeeds. Up to now, whatever the reasons, we have been remiss in this important task. Beginning to look at the obstacles to achievement encountered by students who are regularly progressing, being promoted, succeeding—this represents a move toward fulfilling our commitment to the entire pupil population.

At the Ohio State University we have conducted several inquiries regarding "problems of the successful." One of these studies, involving a selected sample of 300 college sophomores, began with an attempt to identify the kinds of obstacles to achievement that they had encountered during their elementary and secondary school years (Strom, 1968). As an aggregate the students identified 50 obstacles that directly relate to mental health and satisfactory completion of academic requirements. After indicating on a check list the frequency of occurrence in which they, as individuals, were confronted by each of the obstacles, every student was interviewed relative to his written response. Before describing certain of our findings, it is necessary to remind the reader that limitations of the sampling do not permit an exercise of generalization. That is, the author makes no claim that results presented here would necessarily be corroborated in every collegiate setting. However, given this predicate of caution, it is believed that thoughtful teachers, administrators, and supervisors will wish to use the outcomes as a take-off for discussion and investigation, a resource in the determination and resolve of local-individual issues.

The Issue of Direction

Many of the students in the Ohio State University's "success sample" cited matters of direction as their major obstacles to achievement. Understandably, direction is important, for whenever objectives are obscured, response tends to be random, energy is without focus, and doubt impedes progress. On the check list the term *direction* subsumed a number of items relating to goals, counseling, and motivational support. When subpopulation distinctions were introduced for purposes of comparing members within the sample, it was found that the frequency of occurrence of *confusion about goals* directly relates to parental education. That is, the more schooled one's parents are, the less likely it is he will be confused about goals. Adolescents from homes in which parents do not complete high school show an incidence of goal confusion nearly twice as great as pupils from homes in which both parents are college graduates.

While this information would tend to merit better-educated homes, subsequent data obtained from student interviews discouraged any such inference. It seems that one reason children of well-educated parents are less often confused about goals is that goals are often imposed upon them, chosen early by mother, father, and other close relatives. Again and again pupils recounted the adult intrusion of goal selection. In some cases only a professional vocation would be considered. (You can be any kind of doctor or lawyer you like.) Apparently being less confused about goals does not ensure mental health. In certain cases it may simply mean that one's option is forfeit; that others choose for him what he is to become. On the other hand, children of less-educated parents—mothers and fathers who probably know less about the diversity of vocations—insisted only that "be what you wish to be; hopefully you'll have a more easy time of it than we [the parents] have had." To be sure, the latter parental group was less specific in providing direction but at the same time it was more tolerant in allowing the student latitude in making choices about his own future.

Lack of counseling assistance was mentioned by students of every subpopulation. Although there is evidence that better-educated parents make available more guidance, they also seem to limit the kinds of occupational information their youngsters receive, and restrict outside sources of counsel to those individuals who will reinforce or confirm earlier choices recommended by either parent. It is well to recognize that adolescent *confusion about goals* and *lack of counseling assistance* are not exclusive to the "success sample." Indeed, that these are problems that should be of concern to all is evidenced by the results of Project Talent (1965) at the University of Pittsburgh. This project involving 440,000 students in secondary schools across the nation represents the first national census of aptitudes and abilities. The Pittsburgh researchers found that students in the ninth grade were greatly confused about goals, had very unrealistic educational and career plans, but improved them somewhat during the high school years. About half of them made relatively radical changes during the first year after graduation from high school. The percentage planning various types of careers at the ninth grade, twelfth grade, and one year after high school graduation are shown in Figures II-6 and II-7 separately for boys and girls. In the case of boys, note that the ninth-and twelfth-grade choices are far out of line with regard to available jobs. Too many chose engineering and too few optioned skilled trades and technical jobs—the occupations presently growing at the most rapid rate.

The failure of boys to develop realistic career plans is well illustrated by the following Project Talent findings:

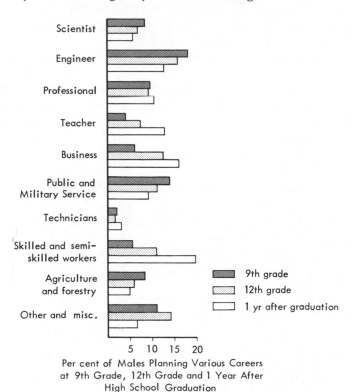

Per cent of Males Planning Various Careers
at 9th Grade, 12th Grade and 1 Year After
High School Graduation

Fig. II-6. From *A National Inventory of Aptitudes and Abilities*, Project TALENT, Bulletin No. 4, February, 1965. Reprinted by permission.

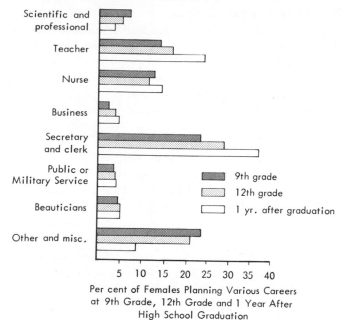

Per cent of Females Planning Various Careers
at 9th Grade, 12th Grade and 1 Year After
High School Graduation

Fig. II-7. From *A National Inventory of Aptitudes and Abilities.*

Of all young men who plan to become physicians when they are nearly through high school, half abandon the idea by the time they finish the freshman year of college.

Forty-one percent of twelfth-grade boys planning a career in law obtain general academic aptitude scores below the 50th percentile.

Thirty-three percent of the twelfth-grade boys planning careers as mathematicians obtain scores below the average of all boys in this grade in general academic aptitude.

This distortion of unrealistic objectives becomes even more poignant when considering the outcomes of local studies. In the city of Cincinnati, 1,658 junior-high students in 35 public schools were asked to state their occupational choices. Hoppock summarized the results as follows:

> What would Cincinnati be like if these students became the sole inhabitants of the city in the jobs of their choice, ten years from now? . . . Health services would be very high, with every 18 people supporting one doctor. It may be, however, that they would all be needed in a city that had no garbage disposal workers, no laundry workers, no water supply, since no one chooses to do that kind of work . . . . The two bus drivers will find that their customers get tired of waiting, and use the services of the 67 airline pilots. It may be difficult getting to Crosley Field to see the 40 baseball players (Hoppock, 1965).

Evidence that the guidance program was not functioning very effectively in American high schools during the early 1960's was obtained from the fact that between 50 and 60 percent of the Project Talent national twelfth-grade student sample indicated that they had not discussed college or career plans with a school counselor during the past year. It also seems clear that a large number of pupils do not have sufficient information regarding the world of work at the present time; the problem is even more serious for many youngsters who are not in college preparatory courses.

Adequate Motivational Support

A well-known impediment to achievement is *lack of motivational support*. Teachers generally lament the short supply of parental encouragement in certain types of homes but seldom entertain the possibility that motivational support might be at a discount in their classrooms. Our data show that approximately five times as many of the "success sample" report *lack of teacher encouragement* as a "sometimes" or "often" obstacle than the number who so indicate *lack of parental encouragement support* as a problem of similar frequency. Comparisons among subpopulations show that the likelihood of teachers failing to pro-

TABLE II-1

Percent of Students by Subpopulations Indicating "Lack of Parental Encouragement" or "Lack of Teacher Encouragement" as Obstacles to Achievement

	Percent of Subpopulation Encountering Each Obstacle								
Subpopulations	0	10	20	30	40	50	60	70	80
Parents are College Graduates	xxxxxxxxxxxxxx (20) ○○○○ (6)								
Parents Have Some College Training	xxxxxxxxxx xxxxxxxxxxxxxxxx (35) ○○○○○ (8)								
Parents are High School Graduates	xxxxxxxxxxxxxxxx xxxxxxxxxxxxxxx (41) ○○○○○○○○○ (13)								
Parents did not Finish High School	xxxxxxxxxxxxxxxxxxxxxxxxxxxxxxxxxxxxxxxxxxxxxxxxxxxx (61) ○○○○○○○○○○○○○○ (22)								

Key:

xxx = Lack of Teacher Encouragement

○○○ = Lack of Parental Encouragement

vide encouragement for pupils declines as educational background of the home increases. (See Table II-1.) This inverse relationship would seem to lend support to the assertion that teacher response is influenced by the schooling status of parents, that we may allow parental success to influence our judgment of child prospect. An indeterminate number of the teaching population perhaps reason that as children of "better" homes will more likely succeed than others, that it is they who should most receive encouragement. Undoubtedly, this conviction translates into instructional favor for a limited element of the class membership.

The research findings presented here do not confirm the popular notion that parents ordinarily are remiss in offering encouragement for their children, that the home often fails to provide school-favored motivation. On the contrary, Table II-1 suggests that although educational circumstance of the family may effect the extent to which encouragement for learning is present, the home seems to fare better in fulfilling its responsibility than does the school. Apparently much remains undone in teacher training with reference to understanding that all pupils share a need for encouragement, praise, and support from those who teach them. It is germane to cite also several of the motivational outcomes for which students of the success sample feel some responsibility: one-fourth of the sample considered *disinterest in school* as an obstacle; one-third *disliked the curriculum;* and half labeled their response to school work as *lazy.*

Coping with Pressure

Sixty percent of the total sample voiced negative perceptions about the academic expectations to which they were subject by parents and teachers. Particularly disconcerting was the incidence of *overemphasis on grades.* From the interviews, it appears that "successful" students of all subpopulations feel coerced to pursue high marks if they wish to prove self-worth, receive approval at home, aspire to higher education, or participate in extracurricular activities. That these goals should be attainable apart from a constant preoccupation with victory in the competitive arena is certain. Nonetheless, the recorded pupil remarks that follow express a rather general viewpoint that dreams will not eventuate unless high grades are forthcoming.

> I competed with twelve very able students in every course I took in high school. For some reason, the school was reluctant to concede that all of us deserved A's and tried very hard to limit the number given. I was so busy doing extra credit projects to impress the teacher, without which an A was an impossibility, that I didn't have time to think about what I was learning. All of us wanted to go to college and some needed scholarships; so we assimilated the facts, scored well on tests, and competed for the top grades. What applicable knowledge I gained was at times in spite of the school situation rather than because of it.

Overemphasis on grades came from school, friends, and family alike. All three considered grades I obtained rather than how much I learned as being more important. I never heard the statement: "What did you learn?" instead they asked: "How high were your grades?"

I feel my family did not dwell as much on the subject of grades as much as other parents I know. I was never given a dollar for every A or having privileges taken away for a low grade. But my main objective in achieving high grades was to please my parents. I found myself studying harder to raise my grades for the sole purpose of being complimented by my parents.

In the school I attended, overemphasis was put on grades in such a way that high grades were absolutely necessary to be a class officer, be in a class play, or any other extracurricular activities sponsored by the school. The teachers were more inclined to favor those students who had good grades and often gave them some extra attention, whereas the poorer students were not given as much attention as they should have received.

Within the school there were many small groups of students that usually stuck together. Looking back at my high school years, I can see that the group I was with expected high grades from its members. The groups in the school were definitely formed with grades as a major concern.

Severe competition in my high school classes was limited to a group of ten or eleven out of sixty-five pupils. In this small group, competiton was real pressure but one (in this group of ten) never worried about being able to beat the remaining fifty-five students who seemed to have gone out of the race somewhere in grade school.

Ever so many conversations among teachers focus on the unrealistic performance demands of parents, the questionable pressures the home brings to bear on children in the name of education. This projection by teachers is natural; since parents are close they represent a convenient target. However, our results—which indicate that familial pressure for good report cards is a problem of serious dimension—indicate also that teacher expectations warrant an even greater concern. For instance, 52 percent of the entire sample identify *variability of expectation standards among teachers* as a perplexing obstacle. Whereas many parents err by insisting that children be the best rather than do their best, that they bring home an enviable record, the student quest for achievement recognition becomes even more difficult when teachers seem unable to agree as to what pupil behaviors constitute outstanding prowess and so deserve the high mark. One-third of the sample population perceive an element of unfairness in teacher grading practices; the same proportion believe that grades are sometimes assigned primarily on the basis of student, family, or sibling reputation. These and other related areas of sensitivity are reflected in excerpts from the interviews:

I think my greatest problem in high school was upholding the reputation which preceded me each year. I attended a small rural high school of approximately 150 students where everyone knew everyone else. The teachers had a daily teachers' meeting around the lunch table, so it didn't take long to establish a reputation as either a good student or a poor student. Each teacher reacted differently to this reputation, but it didn't take long to decide just what the teacher expected. My math teacher knew I had an ability and an interest in math. She always made concessions for any mistakes I made. Thus I felt that I always knew how to work a problem, but I never really understood the theory. My history instructor (also the guidance counselor) was entirely different in expectations. He assigned a current events research paper to the more advanced students. We were to work on these each Monday session while he helped the slower pupils. I felt I really learned something because he expected us to be able to apply the facts to the current problems. Thus I was in the midst of two conflicting situations: in one situation my reputation made excuses for me and required a minimum of work; in the other situation, my reputation intensified the requirements and required a maximum of work.

A problem which I encountered quite frequently in high school was inconsistency in teachers' expectations. Although I generally received straight A's, there were many courses in which I had little knowledge to show for the grades which I received. I usually did only what was required. From teachers who required little, I learned little. For those who presented a challenge, I worked hard and learned much. From both kinds of teachers, however, I received the same grades, as though the work done had been equal.

Perhaps over half of the teachers graded according to their personal liking of the pupil. In my case, my older brother worked hard and received good grades. I was a year behind him and the teachers took for granted I was the same way. They were partially wrong for I did not study very much. The grades I received were not representative of my actual work. The effect of this was very evident my first quarter at Ohio State. My grades were good, but I felt very pressured and was very unaccustomed to working for my grades. I am happy that I realized the problem early enough and was able to cope with it.

I feel another problem I had was being stereotyped by the nuns. I had the same nuns in grade school as I had in high school and I did C work in grade school. When I entered high school, no one expected me to do better than average or even below average work. I entered secondary school anxious to work and get good grades but I became discouraged and began to think I had below average intelligence. When I graduated I really felt intellectually inferior and this makes college much more difficult. I feel like I am studying for something impossible for me. It is changing this attitude which has carried over from high school that I must overcome.

Grades were not even an incentive as good work was often unrewarded because of the teacher's dislike for giving A's (nobody's perfect!), liberality with B's, reserving C's and D's for those who gave him a rough time in class. The atmosphere in the class was usually one of antagonism in which I felt very uncomfortable, almost as if he was daring us to do something that he could grade us down for. I did not get my worst grades in this class but these were probably the least deserved of any I got in high school.

It was not surprising to learn that some students feel *cheating* is their only recourse for coping with excessive family and school pressures. Neither was it unexpected to find that the frequency of involvement with cheating tends to be highest among students who report unrealistic expectations by parents and teachers. What has been most difficult to accept is the report that one in four of the "success sample" were at some time or another involved in academic cheating. One would like to believe that these pupils, supposedly being groomed for positions of leadership in our society, would not resort to gain by dishonesty; but expediency is indeed a powerful motive—for some individuals it preempts integrity. If a minority of students express ambivalence about cheating with favor depending on the stakes, most of them disfavor the practice for reasons voiced by one of their colleagues:

> In high school the main obstacle I faced was cheating. Most of the teachers graded tests on the curve. This usually meant that those who had done honest studying usually fell lower than they deserved, because some had gotten the answers previous to the test or had used another device of cheating and pulled the curve up. Of course the teachers lectured and threatened about cheating but what do you expect when newly made tests are left lying out or the teacher leaves the classroom during the test? This is too much temptation for some. As my parents told me, cheating was not learning, but to me it was frustrating. It seemed unfair that many who cheated got in the upper part of their class, while some who had learned more were much lower. This is especially important now that many colleges require that their applicants are in the upper third of their class. It appears to me that some who deserve to get in may not.

Other researchers have examined the problem of dishonesty at school. In questioning over 5,000 students at 99 colleges and universities, Bowers (1965) reports that about half of the sample admitted having cheated. Few get caught, fewer are severely punished, and seldom are they expelled. According to Bowers, members of the campus community grossly underestimate the magnitude of this problem. For example, 600 college deans and 500 student body presidents were asked to estimate the incidence of cheating. The findings were that two and one half times as many students have cheated as student body presidents estimate; more than three times as many have cheated as deans estimate. Even the students themselves underestimate the proportion of their fellows who have cheated at some time; they tend to believe that only about half as many have cheated as their self-reports indicate. Additional outcomes of the Bower investigation show that large schools have higher rates of cheating than small ones; coeducational schools have higher rates than either men's or women's colleges. The lowest rate of cheating seems to occur on campuses with honor systems—where pledge codes are likely to state that "We will not lie, cheat or steal, nor tolerate among us those who do."

The Vital Relationships

   Teachers. Prospective educators are told that optimal personality development is contingent upon satisfactory relationships, that during the growing up process each of us need the kinds of affiliation that promote a healthy self-concept, a promising outlook toward life. Teachers are in a unique position to implement this counsel, since their role permits extended periods of time with children and offers the chance for great influence. It follows that we who fail to register a positive impact, a favorable influence under such opportune conditions—we have been in a sense obstacles to achievement. Many of us have a considerably less profound effect on students that we would imagine. In a study of 100 undergraduates at Harvard University, Allport (1965) learned that more than 75 percent of the students' teachers are remembered only vaguely, and credited with no appreciable influence, whether intellectual or personal. Only about 8 percent of the teachers are reported as having a very strong influence and about 15 percent are credited with a less strong but well-remembered influence. Another way of stating this finding is to say that the average teacher (assuming that all teachers are equally effective) "gets through" to less than a quarter of the class and exerts a really strong influence on not more than one student in ten.

   An obstacle of greater dimension than the failure of teachers to exercise any influence is the exercise of negative influence. Too many of us fail to use wisely our opportunities for impression. As the type of influence we convey depends on the nature of rapport, we should strive to establish confidence and respect as the basis of relationship with students. Judging from data obtained through interviews of the "success sample" it is common for teachers to violate principles of good rapport. Nearly 30 percent of the students indicate they disliked certain instructors—ordinarily because of teacher recourse to punitive behavior when confronted by difficult classroom situations. Some pupils who received teacher favor in class resented their being used as "examples" and the consequent effect this registered on peer relationships—from exclusion to the simple taunting or label of "teacher's pet." Others recall their reluctance to challenge certain teachers or question a presumably authoritarian statement because they feared the penalty of a low mark. An astonishing number believe that some teachers graded them more on the basis of conduct than on achievement, for good behavior as much as for progress. Juxtapose this statement with the finding that less than 10 percent of the sample record discipline problems in school. It would seem that more attentive study needs to focus on the real relationship between grades received in class and classroom conduct.

   A final teacher behavior found discouraging by 65 percent of the students was *unpurposeful and useless homework assignments.* A teacher reveals much about his perception of the nature of learning, the role of teacher, and learner, and their relationship by the kinds of homework he assigns. Students of less educated parents report that the necessity of doing homework was often reinforced by members of the family, who find virtue in doing extra work. On the other hand, youngsters of college-graduated parents saw many night tasks of reading or exercise drills as nonsensical—this persuasion in a number of cases was reportedly shared by their parents who perhaps more clearly recognized the distinction between "learning" and "being busy." But as one girl put it, "Because I valued my grades in school I knew I must complete my homework assignments; therefore I was forced to limit myself to two or three of these educational and enjoyable extracurricular activities. I wasted precious time copying entire sentences in grammar exercises, answering mechanical questions which merely required leafing through pages and copying answers, drilling on lists of arithmetic problems, and memorizing lists or poems. How worthless it is for teachers to assign unpurposeful homework when a child could be broadening his knowledge in other learning situations."

Peers. A majority of the "successful" believe their academic gain was curtailed in part because of peer influence. This conviction is not to be interpreted as an indictment against peer groups. Neither is it a contention that age mates deliberately contrive to undermine the advance of their classmates. Instead, most respondents explained that to them acceptance by the group was considered of sufficient importance to expend an inordinate amount of time and energy in pursuing a desired level of group esteem. In some cases this concentration of energy led to a dimunition of resource and interest for school work; the result, lower grades. Even in cases where group participation would not appreciably diminish the high rank in class, students were inclined to earn lower marks than they could since acceptance within the group was more likely for those doing merely "satisfactory work" than for those doing "extremely well."

From this interview data it seems that fear of peer exclusion is a powerful determinant of academic performance, that many of the students associate solitude with failure—to them popularity is the key to success. As popularity implies being with others, being alone is viewed with discomfort, taken as a sign of unacceptability, a circumstance to avoid whatever the cost. From this vantage it is not surprising that one in two of the sample population feel they devoted too much time to extracurricular activities, that participation in non-academic affairs became an obstacle to achievement. The lament notwithstanding, fond memories persist in relation to extracurricular affairs because organizational work for many students seemed to bring quicker results and more approval than did their studying, which led only to partial fulfillment of long-range goals—goals about which many students had misgivings.

There are, of course, successful students who find that not being part of the peer group can be an obstacle. Roughly one-sixth of the population studied feel they missed much of importance during their pre-college days by not relating well with their fellows. As a consequence, they were not invited to attend, help plan, participate, or otherwise share in those activities of significance to an age group. A number of the girls report disfavor by the peer group because they maintained close association with men who were older and already out of school. Whether precocious or just anxious to be grown up, these girls in retrospect tend to feel they missed the peer group affiliation that "might have been."

Conditions of Learning

In-school. Learning is affected by the ways in which one encounters lessons or assignments, by the ways in which one "relates" to school tasks. Achievement obstacles are minimized when the methods of task encounter include proved skills of inquiry instead of random search, habits of reading that allow rapid but thorough coverage, the expeditious retrieval of pertinent information, and a punctual response. Conversely, students whose learning style is lacking in these "relating" strategies tend to perform less well than they otherwise might. Successful youngsters, most of whom view their class assignments as a matter of personal responsibility, believe that relating to the tasks has been a problem of serious magnitude in their own instance. Indeed, over half of the sample population are persuaded that *poor study habits, difficulty in concentrating,* and *procrastination* kept them from achieving higher goals. One-third of the population indicate that *poor reading habits* and *inadequate communication skills* served to diminish their amounts of progress.

These findings may imply a necessity, a need to improve the "relating to task" behavior of students who are engaged in individual endeavors. From the interview data, it would seem that we might begin this improvement immediately by altering certain of the school conditions under which "relating" must occur. For example, the library—long considered the in-school center of solitary pursuits—often fails to provide a circumstance in which this service can be realized. Normally, students are seated six to eight at long tables, books are shelved at wall locations on each side of the room, and the librarian mans her post in front. As a result, each pupil's vision is subject to distraction, to see much beyond the book; noise is constant because people are going to and from the shelves, as well as in and out of the room. B. Frank Brown (1965), whose high school in Melbourne, Florida, has gained national attention, contends that school libraries should be carpeted; they should be at least as large as the gymnasium, fully equipped with individual carrels for visual privacy, and that each of these carrels should have a dictionary, encyclopedia, and other common reference materials. Further, Dr. Brown, who suggests that school librarians have been the least service-minded of all school personnel, maintains that the library should remain open in the evenings and on weekends as a place of study for students who lack necessary privacy at home, for others who need reference data to complete their assignments, and for those who may otherwise find this the best locale in which to "relate to their task."

A point of interest regarding in-school conditions for learning is that only 20 percent of the "success sample" named *class size* as an obstacle to achievement. No, the other 80 percent did not attend small classes! In the main, these students favor a lower teacher-pupil ratio than now exists, but many of them believe that determination of class size should depend upon several factors—especially upon the subject being taught and the person who is teaching the subject. English and mathematics are frequently cited as instances in which lower membership is preferred. In this context the Melbourne plan seems to pose another tenable alternative by enlarging class size in certain subjects in which much of the learning is programmed. In typing, for example, which seems to be 96 percent programming and 4 percent instruction, a teacher need not lecture to students, as they must learn skills by practice, repetition, and drill. Consequently it would be possible to have larger classes in typing, say 100 to 150. This situation would also obtain for classes in shorthand or drafting. The large numbers of students in typing, drafting, and shorthand would allow administrators to reduce the ratio in other classes such as English and mathematics.

Home Conditions. Although the successful students left an impression of being somewhat restrained in comments regarding learning conditions at school, their reluctance vanished when called upon to discuss deterrents encountered at home. A selected number of these obstacles are recorded in Table II-2. Considering first the matter of *work responsibilities after school,* the researcher found that employed students complain most often about the time factor. Few voice an aversion to labor but many feel that with a heavy study schedule it is difficult if not impossible to retain a work commitment also. Children of the least educated parents report they worked primarily for the purpose of contributing to meet financial needs; they felt a responsibility to "carry their share of the family load." In contrast, students of every other subpopulation indicate they engaged in work activities less in response to an economic necessity than because they wanted extra money, sought feelings of independence, or because parents insisted that working is "good for you." An exception in purpose was indicated by children of college-graduated parents. Their families tend to sanction a part-time or summer job but less often encourage it since it is believed that work responsibility will come quickly enough for youngsters. Parents of these homes less often insist that "you should work because we did." Then, too, getting a job while in school is de-emphasized by this group as less value is placed on the virtue of just working—that is, there are other ways to learn responsibility and other ways to grow in understanding one's good fortune without participating in uninviting tasks.

TABLE II-2

Percent of Students by Subpopulations Indicating
Various Learning Conditions in the Home as
Obstacles to Achievement

	Percent of Pupils Whose Parents:			
Obstacles to Achievement	*Did Not Finish High School*	*Completed High School*	*Have Some College Training*	*Completed College*
Work Responsibilities	35	21	18	16
Excessive Televiewing	25	44	44	38
Study Conditions	38	30	25	21
Family Mobility	6	9	16	20
Cultural Background	60	8	7	4

Table II-2 shows that a rather large proportion of students in each subpopulation include *excessive televiewing* as having been an unwise expenditure of time during the elementary and high school years. The period of greatest exposure to the "dark room" seems to be between ages nine and fourteen. During this age range many of the students spent as much as 25 hours per week with Dance Party, Dracula, and Dragnet. The lower rate of excess in televiewing that obtains for children of the least-educated homes was puzzling, for we expected to find the highest rate in this subpopulation. Subsequent investigation revealed that the discrepancy relates to the smaller proportion of television sets in less-educated homes of our sample than in the families of every other subpopulation. The street persuasion that less-educated persons will always buy a television set before a toothbrush would not

hold true in this sample. Pupils of college-educated and college-graduated homes were alone in having been subject to established controls
relative to types of programs allowed for view. However, few students
in either of these segments were subject to similar controls with regard
to the amount of time to be spent with television.

Home is not always the best place to study. In some cases the family fails to provide adequate facilities, proper sources of reference,
freedom from noise or other distractions. From student reports we
find that parental intrusion, offered in the name of support, is often
aggravating, since it frequently results in an argument about the
relative merits of schools and youngsters today versus their counterparts of yesteryear. It seems that in wanting to show children they
can be of assistance, some parents find themselves unable to comprehend modern math or other innovative practices and wind up arguing with the student about the best way to solve teacher-assigned problems. Even among families in which all the essentials are provided for
conditions of study, pupils recall a strange and perhaps superficial
loneliness when working alone at home. They also remember the concurrent interest in flocking to the library where one could work beside
his fellows if not speak with them. In retrospect many of these students now perceive that their primary motivation to frequent the library was less to study than to fraternize—a purpose for which many
libraries are well-structured.

A new town, a new neighborhood, a new school, new friends, new
enemies, new teachers—moving means all these things and more. Moving brings a new longing for the old town, neighborhood, teachers,
friends—and sometimes enemies. Moving means having to "walk in"
to a never-before-entered classroom in the middle of the year as a newcomer. It means being the stranger. In the new classroom one may
find different books, a higher level of arithmetic, another method of
reading, teacher expectations which are foreign and difficult. These
are but a few of the traumatic encounters moving entails. It is apparent that more-educated families tend to be more mobile. This shows
up in Table II-2; twice as many children of college-graduated parents
experience the obstacles presented by mobility as do children of parents with only a high school education. According to the students, the
beckoning of opportunity most often prompted their parents to move.
Although children of college-graduated parents most often encounter
the obstacles that invariably ensue a move, they also report more often
that parental efforts were made to minimize the negative effects, to
ease the adjustment of transition to a new environment.

There is a remarkable amount of dissonance between subpopulations as to the percentage of students who view the *cultural background* in which they were reared as being inimical to personal advance.
Sixty percent of the students whose parents have not finished high

school recall early school deficiences, which they believe arose from inadequate experience, a constricted life space. There were too few trips, books, dreams, stories, and discussions shared in the family orientation and in the neighborhood context. In some cases there were problems of home-school communication because of a bilingual background or parental reluctance to interfere with the teacher by finding out what was going on. A number of these pupils admit to having been embarrassed because of their family and even to resenting the heritage—some still feel this way since the distance is increasing as they advance in school. Children of parents with a high school education or beyond cite lack of books and parental inability to assist in homework as the two most common weaknesses in their home cultural background. For the most part, members of the successful sample are as proud of their heritage as their parents should be of their children.

EPILOGUE

A greater percentage of students now complete high school than the proportion who do not. This statement is gratifying when compared with holding-power rates during earlier years in our century. However, it does not mean that most students elude academic difficulty, are without obstacles to achievement. A substantial body of evidence reveals that difficulty in school is not exclusive to any segment of the pupil population. To be sure, there is wide variance in the severity of obstacles and the frequency with which they are encountered by different students. But if an investigation of pupil dissatisfaction in relation to school experience is to have the widest benefit, then as nearly as possible the combined judgment of both unsuccessful and successful youngsters should be included. In times past the negative report of successful students has been absent or given only perfunctory attention in affecting school change since "they made it through." As a result, without problems of successful pupils as a source of comparison, schoolmen have tended to minimize the importance of complaints offered by failing students. Little support was given the proposition that certain difficulties might be shared by students of every prospect.

In the main, dropouts severely criticize the common curriculum as being irrelevant, too difficult, and uninteresting. Aversion seems to focus on the areas of reading, social studies, mathematics, and vocational education. Almost universal resentment is expressed toward the teacher practice of ignoring learning styles, pace, level of accommodation, and sometimes one's person. Many failed youngsters feel they were unequipped to remain in the arena of competition and as a result were driven from the school context. Haunted by a statistical ghost, it seems many classrooms continue in practice to echo the fallacious belief that all students are intellectually equal (should be treated alike), and that each individual can prove his worth through hard work in competitive endeavor. The fact is, of course, that every child has personal worth apart from whatever effort he may exert in school, and the need to grade is in itself a clear indication that students are unequal. Although the weight of tradition is heavy, we must desist in viewing grades as the only incentive to learning and somehow diminish the number of teachers who are still guilty of asking children to do that which they know is impossible simply as proof for assigning a low grade.

Traditionally the most common response of educators toward failing pupil performance has been homework, nonpromotion and, more recently, a pressured counsel of "return to school." Certainly the history of consequence ensuing from each of these practices makes clear their weakness as strategies for helping children. Successful and unsuccessful students alike view homework as being of little value. Among low-achieving children who sometimes indicate they received extra lessons for punitive reasons, it was looked upon as an enterprise in frustration, since they found it difficult to complete night work at home, that they were unable to learn during the school day. A majority of the successful students judge much of their homework as unproductive, busy work—an archaic necessity to gain the grade and pacify the instructor. The fact that diagnostic concern is not a part of most assignments amounts to an admission that homework purpose is unrelated to instruction.

Similarly, research findings indicate that few reasonable bases of retention exist, that nonpromotion is on the decline and that its causes are self-perpetuating—especially in the matter of teacher misinterpretation regarding concepts such as grade level, motivation, appropriate expectation, and growth. As for the dubious practice of counseling potential dropouts and actual dropouts to return to school, one need but recognize that regard is never communicated through fear. The economic emphasis of "the return to school movement" belies whatever humane intent might be stated, whatever interests its advocates might advertise—its tenure serves but to insult and coerce the client.

From The Ohio State University Study it appears that students of every performance level seem to share the problem of confusion about goals. Among the successful, especially, there is a good deal of familial influence in goal-selection but a relative lack of guidance as to how objectives might be achieved. Apparently this circumstance has not been rectified in schools to the extent that it should, or there would be a less persistent lament among students regarding lack of counseling assistance. In addition, both low- and high-scoring students negatively perceive unrealistic teacher expectation for performance and the overemphasis on grades. Most everyone seems to view external evaluation as a threat that creates a need for defensiveness. Torrance contends that the threat makes some portion of the individual's experiencing or sensing denied awareness, and thus there is a lack of openness, which is necessary to the production of new ideas. Pressures for accomplishment also give rise to a high index of cheating and can pose difficulties for relating with the peer group. Finally, student experience indicates that conditions of learning at home and in school bear improvement if there is to be profit in solitary pursuits.

Time shows that an unjust society or institution cannot endure because those outside its benefit will revolt. In the educational setting, the revolt translates into disinterest, delinquent behavior, truancy, or dropout. In turn, such issues can escalate so as to evolve into matters of unemployment, family disruption, and crime. This ought not to be. Neither should there be unconcern about the negative judgment of successful pupils relative to school process, for these grievances, too, require consideration if student experience is to improve. Every teacher and faculty interested in student mental health needs to remain sensitive toward the obstacles to achievement faced by today's students. Since many of these obstacles are unique in history, adults cannot count on retrospect as the best source for counsel; that is, it may be there are some things we are too old to know, too old to have experienced. But we are not too old to learn—for we must learn if our generation would keep the promises it has made to the next.

CHAPTER III

Relating as a Professional

For a psychology of education to be adequate, it must be ethical. Otherwise the typical phrases voiced by educational psychologists regarding the importance of dedication and service, satisfactory teacher-pupil rapport, conjunctive efforts with the home, and faculty team approaches can have little meaning or possibility. To speak about the motivation and conduct of teachers as though these aspects of behavior occur in a vacuum is pointless, for neither professional competence nor growth is likely to occur apart from commitment to ethical principles. Nevertheless, exclusion of matters pertaining to ethical responsibility and moral choice remains as one of the long-standing curricular deficiencies in most teacher-training institutions. In select instances these concerns may receive an oblique reference, ordinarily in graduate classes of educational philosophy, but to my knowledge there is no American university that affords sufficient attention to the issue of ethical behavior at the undergraduate level. The contention of this chapter is the following: Inasmuch as the teacher's professional growth, his role in the change process, his relationship with students and their parents, and his association with colleagues are contingent upon adherence to a code of ethics, these matters should have a place in educational psychology.

MAINTAINING COMPETENCE: THE COMMITMENT TO GROWTH

Most states refuse to license the teacher who is without a degree; several states demand a fifth year as the level of training for beginning instructors of elementary and secondary grades. But even this needed extension in teacher preparation is insufficient to meet the growth needs of a career; competence enjoys a shorter life than ever before, and to sustain it requires a near constant supplement. Indeed, the problem of keeping up is no longer an issue in the sense of resolve; it is now an impossibility. Limitations of individual pace are such that no one can expect to equal the ever-changing field of knowledge he calls his specialty. No longer can a man be expected to be familiar with every book in his particular field, a fact that should diminish presumption rather than induce teacher apathy.

By way of illustration, reflect upon the enormous increase of population in scientific periodicals since their inception (see Fig. III–1).

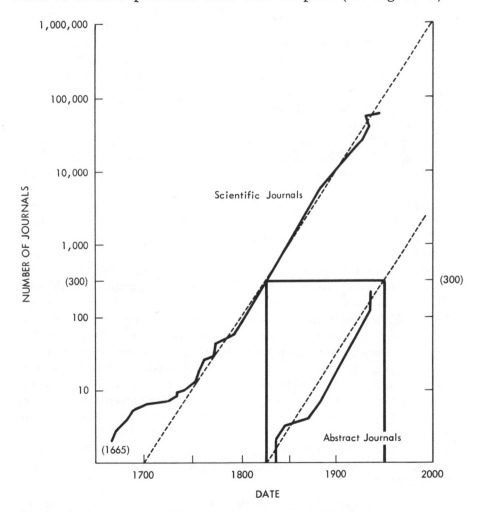

Fig. III-1. Growth rate of scientific journals and abstract journals. From *Science Since Babylon* by Derek J. de Solla Price (New Haven: Yale University Press, 1961), p. 97. Reprinted by permission.

The number of these manuscripts has increased by a factor of ten during every half century beginning from a point in 1750 when there were about ten scientific journals in the world. A remarkable conclusion derived from this data is that the number of journals has grown exponentially rather than linearly. It has doubled with some regularity. The constant involved is actually about fifteen years for a doubling, corresponding to a power of ten in fifty years and a factor of one thousand in a century and a half. In the three hundred years that separate us from the mid-seventeenth century, this represents a factor of one million (Price, 1961, p. 100).

As early as 1830 it became apparent that the proliferation of periodicals had reached a point of absurdity. No scientist could read all the contemporary materials in his field nor expect to remain conversant with the published work by scholars of ancillary disciplines that might be germane to his interest. Obviously, some new mechanism of information retrieval was needed—and so an invention as controversial as the journal itself was devised, the abstract journal. With the abstract journal as an adequate solution to the crisis, regular journals were then allowed to increase in number without restraint to the present day. And with them, a concomitant rise in the number of abstract journals seems to have followed precisely the same law, multiplying by a factor of ten in every half century. By 1950, abstract journals attained a population of about three hundred, a critical magnitude because it approximated the point at which the first abstract journal appeared (see Figure III–1). So, during the past two decades, scientists have expressed alarm about the need for abstracts of abstracts— an information problem that seems to require an electronic sorting process as a means for coping with the rising flood of literature.

It can be demonstrated that any new condensing process would bear the same relation to abstracts that the abstracts now have to original papers. This relation involves a compression by a factor of about three hundred—the number of journals that spawned the first abstracts. At present, electronic sorting provides advantages of a considerably smaller order of magnitude, perhaps a factor on the order of ten. If this factor cannot be altered, then electronic sorting offers no more than a palliative, something less than the radical solution required to meet the situation. It can only delay the fateful crisis by a few decades. Unless some way of abstracting the abstracts is found, the printed research paper may well be doomed, though it may be difficult to rid ourselves of the notion that such papers are essential (Price, 1961, pp. 98–99).*

* Responding to this point, Paul Torrance suggests that there may be some very good reasons why it will be difficult to rid ourselves of the notion that printed research papers are essential. There is a continuous need to go back to lower-order data for reanalysis, reassessment, correction of errors, and reinterpretation. The present status of research may make different vehicles than currently used necessary. For example,

But the obstacle of information retrieval is not confined to periodicals. Approximately every twenty years there is a doubling in the world population of book titles and, in turn, the volume size of great libraries. In some five hundred years of book production there must have been some twenty-five doubling periods. This yields about $2^{25}=30,000,000$ titles alive today, a figure consonant with estimates issued by the Council on Library Resources. Perhaps we can appreciate, if not comprehend, the magnitude of difficulties this data must represent to worried librarians charged with the management of ever-growing civic and university collections.* It seems that whereas the world's human population is laid to rest each generation, the world's books have a way of lingering on. Such is the stuff of cumulative growth, the distinction of scholarship in general, but of professional works in particular.

If the problem of information retrieval is monumental today, it will represent a difficulty of even greater dimension during the adult life of our children. Somehow they will need to find safeguards to ensure that worthwhile contributions not go unrecognized and that lengthy periods of delay be removed as a criterion for ideational acceptance. Years ago it was customary to anticipate the passing of a half century between the time of an innovative claim and its subsequent adoption by a large number of schools. Obviously this time lag between theory and curricular inclusion must be reduced. As is apparent from the widespread acceptance of recently conceived programs in mathematics, reading, science, and social studies, our generation has already begun to reduce the moment between idea and action. A case in point is the Stanford Mathematics Study Group program, which was adopted by 40 percent of the mathematics classrooms throughout the country (1958) only six years after its introduction in 1952. However great this reduction of the time lag may seem, it falls short of our necessity. Currently there are numerous innovations like team teaching, the Initial Teaching Alphabet, modern mathematics, and reading by color

---

as studies grow more complex and as programs of research are developed instead of one-shot studies, the usual printed article is an inadequate vehicle. Publishers will have to be willing to handle more research monographs, a trend already underway. The fragmentation is illustrated by a recent doctoral candidate of mine who published about a dozen articles, all quite different, regarding his dissertation. It might best have appeared as a monograph or book.

* As an example, Fremont Rider (1944, pp. 11, 12), librarian at Wesleyan University, has estimated: "If the Yale Library continues to grow at a rate no greater than it has been steadily growing through its more than two centuries of past existence, if it continues to grow at a rate no greater than the most conservative rate at which all our other American colleges and universities have grown ever since they started, and are now growing, then, by a series of further successive doublings, the Yale Library will, in 2040, have approximately 200,000,000 volumes, which will occupy over 6,000 miles of shelves. Its card catalog file—if it then has a card catalog—will consist of nearly three-quarters of a million catalog drawers, which will of themselves occupy not less than eight acres of floor space. New material will be coming in at the rate of 12,000,000 volumes a year; and the cataloging of this new material will require a cataloging staff of over six thousand persons."

that press for wide acceptance. Certain of these refined techniques can enable pupils to learn more effectively, whereas others may result in little or no advance. In some cities teachers will share in the determination of the merit of these innovations; in other communities teachers may serve as change agents in advocating the helpful innovative solution and dismissing the useless invention. Whatever the situation, competent teacher response presupposes that any innovation be seen in its proper context with respect to the change process.

The Change Process in Education

Egon Guba and David Clark have developed a useful schema for understanding the processes related to change in education. As illustrated in Figure III-2, the schema is organized to depict a theoretical continuum of educational change from research to action. This continuum draws attention to the diverse functions that must be accomplished before an invention can become an innovation and an innovation can become a matter-of-fact classroom procedure. The process of educational change is conceived as involving four stages: research, development, diffusion, and adoption. (These must not necessarily follow in a particular order, nor would all stages be activated in every case). It is believed that each stage has a particular objective; that whether or not these objectives are met is judged by the application of specific criteria different for each stage; and that each stage bears a particular relation to the change process. The schema categories are not necessarily processional; therefore it is possible to proceed from one stage to any other stage without returning to an identical starting point (See page 104).

Looking to the far left of Figure III-2, we see *research* as one activity in the schema for educational change. Note that the primary objective of the research process is to advance knowledge. Whether this new knowledge will bear practical application need not be especially important to the investigator. Indeed, to require practical application as a criterion for the advance of knowledge is inappropriate; the only suitable criteria for research are internal and external validity. By internal validity we mean the extent to which findings of the hypotheses are tested or the initial questions are answered with specificity. External validity is a measure of the extent to which findings are generalizable to the subjects of the questions or hypotheses under consideration. Since the relation of research to change is concerned only with providing a basis for innovation, the researcher is under no obligation to apply the new knowledge himself unless he so chooses. In sum, his tasks do not go beyond the conduct of inquiry and experimentation.

But someone must be engaged in the task of producing applications for new knowledge. This is the *development* activity shown in the next major column of Figure III-2. Development is a process that formulates a solution to an action problem (invention) through research, experience,

	RESEARCH	DEVELOPMENT		DIFFUSION			ADOPTION	
		INVENTION	DESIGN	DISSEMINATION	DEMONSTRATION	TRIAL	INSTALLATION	INSTITUTIONALIZATION
OBJECTIVE	To advance knowledge	To formulate a new solution to an operating problem or to a class of operating problems, i.e., to innovate	To order and to systematize the components of the invented solution; to construct an innovation package for institutional use, i.e., to engineer	To create widespread awareness of the invention among practitioners, i.e., to inform	To afford an opportunity to examine and assess operating qualities of the invention, i.e., to build conviction	To build familiarity with the invention and provide a basis for assessing the quality, value, fit, and utility of the invention in a particular institution, i.e., to test	To fit the characteristics of the invention to the characteristics of the adopting institution, i.e., to operationalize	To assimilate the invention as an integral and accepted component of the system, i.e., to establish
CRITERIA	Validity (internal and external)	Face Validity (appropriateness) --- Estimated Viability --- Impact (relative contribution)	Institutional Feasibility --- Generalizability --- Performance	Intelligibility --- Fidelity --- Pervasiveness --- Impact (extent to which it affects key targets)	Credibility --- Convenience --- Evidential Assessment	Adaptability --- Feasibility --- Action	Effectiveness --- Efficiency	Continuity --- Valuation --- Support
RELATION TO CHANGE	Provides basis for invention	Produces the invention	Engineers and packages the invention	Informs about the invention	Builds conviction about the invention	Tries out the invention in the context of a particular situation	Operationalizes the invention for use in a specific institution	Establishes the invention as a part of an ongoing program; converts it to a "non-innovation"

Fig. III-2. A classification schema of processes related to and necessary for change in education. Conceived and developed by David L. Clark and Egon G. Guba at The Ohio State University, 1966. Reprinted by permission.

or intuition and subsequently packages this alternative for institutional use (design). With respect to the subactivity of invention, appropriate criteria relate to judgments concerning its apparent or face validity for solving the given problem, its estimated viability in the real situation, and its probable impact, that is, the relative contribution it might make to the solution of the problem. Using team teaching as an example, these questions would be asked: Does the procedure appear to offset the weaknesses of elementary-school classroom organization? Is there face validity in the concept? (If one assumes that teachers' lack of knowledge in a variety of fields is a basic weakness in the self-contained classroom, then team teaching appears to have face validity as an invention.) What is the best rough estimate of its viability? (If it represents an exorbitant increase in school costs, it probably will not gain acceptance.) What is the best first estimate of the breadth of its impact? Is it worth pursuing in terms of potential significance to education? (Guba and Clark, 1965b, p. 3.)

The second type of developmental activity is *design*, which must render the formulated solution or intention into an acceptable, adaptable form. Here the interest is in how well the development works in the context of conditions to which it is exposed. Much greater precision can be brought to bear at this stage of development in establishing criteria for evaluating the product than was true at the invention stage. This pattern of evaluation, typically followed, is called field testing; its intent is chiefly to assess the feasibility of design of the invention in an institutional setting, the generalizability of the design to diverse institutional settings, and the performance of the design, often relative to an existing practice (Guba and Clark, 1965b, p. 3.) This allows for a "spin-out" process such as that used in the Melbourne, Florida, plan (Brown, 1963, pp. 209–210).

Engineering is required to order and systematize the components of the invented solution, and packaging is necessary to render the innovation into marketable form for classroom use. In engineering and packaging the design, teacher involvement must be given considerable attention, as must the flexibility of the program. The relationship of developmental activities to change are obvious: it is this activity instead of research that is at the heart of change; for although research may make change possible, it is development that actually produces an innovation that may be adopted. But, just as it is not except by chance the researcher's task to produce developments, so it is not the developer's task except by chance to diffuse the new developed invention.

Diffusion is seen as a process for informing persons about the existence of an invention (dissemination) and for building conviction about its utility on the basis of appropriate professional evidence (demonstration). Criteria suitable to *dissemination* include intelligibility (is the information clear?); fidelity (does the information present a valid picture?); pervasiveness (does the information reach all of the intended audiences?); and impact (does the information affect key targets appropriately?) (Guba,

1965c, pp. 11–12). The process of dissemination does not purport to effect change in schools but only to create widespread awareness of the existence of an invention.

The second activity under diffusion, *demonstration*, implies the provision of a chance for the target system to examine and assess the operating qualities of an invention. To be effective, demonstrations must be credible, convenient, and suitable for adequate evidential assessment, both positive and negative concerning the utility of the invention being demonstrated. The criterion of evidential assessment is crucial, since the aim of the demonstration is to open a further alternative for professional consideration rather than merely to huckster a particular invention.

The final stage at which the invention may actually be incorporated into a functioning school system is *adoption*, which subsumes the three activities of *trial, installation,* and *institutionalization.* If the target system becomes convinced of the efficacy of an invention, adequate opportunity for trial without substantial fear of failure should be provided in the context of the particular school setting. This trial period is not one of "trial and error" but one during which a basis can be provided for assessing quality, value, fit, and utility of the invention in a particular institution. Several general criteria can be required at this stage. Is the invention adaptable to the characteristics of the local scene? Are there problems of feasibility not detected in the early field trial? What is the action of the invention in relation to the specific circumstance?

An *installation* period is concerned with fitting the characteristics of the invention to the characteristics of the adopting institution—a complex process that may require expensive redesign and personnel training. The essential activities of this phase are introduction and accommodation to the school on the one hand and familiarization of the teaching or other staff with the innovation on the other. Appropriate criteria include the conventional administrative criteria of effectiveness and efficiency.

An *institutionalization* period is required to assimilate the invention totally, that is, to regularize the innovation and convert it into a non-innovation. The criteria for assessing whether institutionalization has been accomplished include: continuity (does the innovation persist over a period of time in the school?); valuation (do the personnel associated with the innovation, such as teachers, students, parents, and administrators, place a high value on it, and are they willing to undergo personal discomforts rather than permit the innovation to be removed?); and support (is the school willing to devote a reasonable portion of its budget and other resources to the support of the innovation?). A positive reply to these questions concludes the adoption stage. Theory has been translated into accepted practice.

Before considering the relation between teachers and innovation, it is appropriate to comment on the procession of stages. Guba and Clark, (1965a, 1965b) point out that what appears to be an inherent logic running from the left of the diagram to the right would not necessarily hold true in real life. No contention is made that every activity must necessarily begin with research and then move through development into diffusion and on to the adoption stage, eventually evolving into some kind of well-established practice. There are in fact a variety of feedback loops possible. For example, research may be entirely lacking in a given area or may be so conflicting or ambiguous as to be of little help in the practical situation. It is possible that an invention based almost entirely on experience or intuition may be developed and that only through attempts to put the invention into practice on a pilot basis will we uncover the researchable questions, which then can be pursued further in a laboratory. Obviously it is also possible for a breakdown to occur at any stage of the process, so that the attempt to install an innovation in a real school system may reveal certain fundamental flaws in its design that were not previously apparent. When this happens we may be forced into looping back to the design stage in order to rectify an error before proceeding further. Again, it is well to remember that the schema categories are not necessarily processional and that it is possible to proceed from one stage to any other stage without returning to an identical starting point.

The Teacher and Innovation

With an understanding of the change process, there may come on the part of the teacher an awareness of personal responsibility for innovation, a desire to be instrumental in school change. Experience with Title I projects of the Elementary and Secondary Education Act of 1965 suggests that this realization of self-obligation to initiate and facilitate invention is probably being experienced today by more teachers than ever before. Prospective educators can prepare for the research function as undergraduates by electing courses in tests and measurement, research design, or consumer statistics. Too often students evade these subjects because they have a reputation for being difficult. Whether this dubious distinction more often relates to the instruction than to an inherent difficulty of topic is a moot question. The important thing is that collegians should be led to realize the need for continued intellectual growth beyond graduation, to value abilities that make one capable of wise experimentation, to prize skills involved in testing novel classroom practice, and to covet techniques of diagnosing pupil error and the facility to assess instructional method. A desire to meet these needs should promote the encounter with beginning methodology of research.

There are, of course, many practitioners already on the job who lack research training. How can they become accomplished in the realm of invention, testing ideas for classroom use, interpreting journal data, and selecting the most helpful among a myriad of periodicals? Clearly the responsibility is twofold, involving the school board and each teacher.

The administration should confirm its commitment to quality instruction by providing financial support to maintain adequate in-service training. According to Schueler (1964, p. 21) we need to:

> . . . destroy the naive notion that teachers can be turned out like automobiles—that they can be given a predetermined body of knowledge, a motor of predesigned practices, and an increasing application of salary fuel and lubrication (for more is needed as the machine gets older) and sent out to fulfill a standardized function. If we pursue this analogy much further, we come to the dangerous realization that automobiles are built for quick obsolescence without presumption of tenure.

To begin with, all teachers should be given a chance to become intelligent consumers of research. This training should go beyond reading of tabled data and include the importance of accepting limitations of inquiry and findings. For example, almost everywhere a practitioner looks he may expect to find the term "no significant differences" cited as a finding. Take the case of educational television. In a review of research on technological media conducted over a six-year span Schram's (1962) conclusion about educational television was that no significant differences were shown when this type of teaching was compared with regular instruction. Again, "no significant differences" was the verdict when comparing the effect of ordinary instruction with self-teaching devices and programmed materials (Silberman, 1962). In both instances it would be a mistake to interpret the "no significant difference" finding as either a condemnation or validation of certain technologies applied to classroom instruction. Instead, the result may suggest that the media have not been used with imagination or that the wrong questions have guided research. Repetitious outcomes of the "no significant difference" kind tend to build up teacher suspicion that neither educational television nor programmed learning can be of greater worth as methods than those currently in wide use. Instead of opposing the inventions, an informed teacher would consider new ways of utilizing them (Barnes, 1965, p. 3).

Instructors need also be on guard against adopting the tendency of a novice to overestimate interpretive option. After reading a study that concludes "hooded rats do not learn from punishment," one teacher might relate the results this way: "Research shows that organisms do not learn from punishment." Or, perhaps, "It has been found that third-graders do not learn from punishment." It is tempting to use interpretive freedom, because each of us strives for applicability, but where research is done in a theoretical setting, its results cannot be expected to readily translate into a foreign circumstance. (Remember the need for the development function in the change process.) To ignore this point is to fall victim to verbal mystique, the unethical option of translating results to confirm one's bias. The chance for misinterpreting research is diminished when one is reluctant to overgeneralize findings or to assume questionable transfer. Writers can also assist in preventing the misinterpretation of

their work by departing from the conventional pattern of merely presenting results. Findings per se are only partial to the teacher-reader,
who may profit more from feedback about the concepts, ideas, and notions
on which an inquiry was based (Taba, 1965).

Another danger to which many a neophyte has succumbed is accepting
research findings as the final and ultimate authority in all matters of
debate. Barnes* points out:

> Increasingly a show of being acquainted with "what research says" is
> coming to be a popular mark of unassailable sophistication in the educa-
> tional world. Certainly, an affinity for knowledge derived from research
> bespeaks a preference for objectivity and fact. The report of researchers
> represent a kind of sanitized information uncontaminated by human pref-
> erence or whim; decisions are reached through processes quite independ-
> ent of the frailties of human thought. When sanctified in this way,
> research often exerts an influence which is not very different from the
> effect of pronouncements by authorities. The chief difference resides in
> the fact that researchers have been substituted for the authorities.

It is disappointing to witness a conversation in which thought seems
paralyzed, where ideas are replaced by an endless exchange of citations
and references to research studies and names of investigators. Sessions
of this kind offer low priority to idea, and usually degenerate to a type
of oneupmanship, a quest to find who can refer to the most recent study
or the most eminent researcher. Consider the man whose companion is
getting the better of him in a discussion. As a last resort he says, "Sigmund
Freud wrote . . . ," the implication being "Can your reputation match
his?" Naturally the discussion ends. No strategy is more popular than
the name game among the insecure, persons for whom the erosion of
thought has already begun.

As acceleration continues in the production of educational research,
one can expect enormous increases in the fund of knowledge about
schools. However, given present structures for knowledge distribution
and utilization, it is probable that this "explosion" will go largely
unassimilated by teachers. In order that educational improvement not
continue to be guided by expediency and inspired guesswork, the American Educational Research Association has formed a Committee on
Research Utilization (Miles, 1965). A major concern of this committee
is teacher readiness for research utilization. To peruse research on specific
topics, one must first be able to locate the relevant reports. A greater
teacher knowledge of information retrieval is imperative. Few instructors
are aware that progress reports of major investigations are available
several years before they appear in final published form. It is worthwhile
to request up-to-date information from university centers working with
studies such as Project English, Project Social Studies, Project Talent,
and Project Literacy. The U.S. Office of Education, National Education

* From Fred P. Barnes, *Research for the Practitioner in Education* (Washington,
D.C.: Elementary School Principals, a department of the National Education Association, 1964), p. 7. Reprinted by permission.

Association, and Science Information Exchange also are valuable sources for information about current research projects in almost any field of endeavor. For best efficiency it is recommended that each elementary and secondary school maintain a library file of contemporary projects of interest to its teachers. In addition, the school system should subscribe to a number of teacher-chosen periodicals, making them readily accessible to the staff without cost. The following resource publications are useful in locating information (see Figure III-3).

ABSTRACTS[1]

Dissertation Abstracts
Education Abstracts
Sociological Abstracts

REVIEW JOURNALS[2]

Psychological Review
Review of Educational Research

MONOGRAPHS[3]

What Research Says to the
    Teacher (NEA)
Research Resume

GENERAL JOURNALS[4]

Adult Education (American)
Adult Education (British)
British Journal of Educational Studies
Child Study
Childhood Education
Educational Leadership
The Educational Record
Elementary School Journal
Theory Into Practice
Journal of Negro Education
The Clearing House
Exceptional Children
Journal of Education
Journal of Teacher Education
National Elementary Principal
Phi Delta Kappan
School and Society
School Review

RESEARCH JOURNALS[5]

Educational

Journal of Educational Measurement
Harvard Educational Review
Teachers College Record
American Educational Research Journal
California Journal of Educational Research
Florida Journal of Educational Research
Educational and Psychological Measurement
Canadian Education and Research Digest
NEA Research Bulletin
Educational Research Bulletin
Journal of Educational Research
Journal of Experimental Research
Personnel and Guidance Journal

Psychological

Human Relations
American Psychologist
British Journal of Educational Psychology
Journal of Abnormal and Social Psychology
Journal of Experimental Psychology
Child Development
Journal of Personality and Social Psychology
Journal of Genetic Psychology
Journal of Educational Psychology
Journal of Counseling Psychology
American Journal of Orthopsychiatry
Psychological Reports
Journal of Experimental Research in Personality
Journal of Experimental Social Psychology

Sociological

Sociology of Education
Sociometry

[1]Abstracts   These sources serve as a major reference for an investigator seeking information about a particular subject.

[2]Review Journals   These journals provide more information than abstract journals by discussing reports in terms of their theoretical settings.

[3]Monographs   Presented in pamphlet form, these monographs deal with a specific restricted topic.

[4]General Journals   Although research is not the prime emphasis of these journals, studies appear occasionally.

[5]Research Journals   The comprehensive treatment of studies appear here including background data as to sampling, design, analysis, and discussion.

Fig. III-3. Selected sources of research publications for teacher reference. Adapted from a list by Fred P. Barnes in *Research for the Practitioner in Education* (Washington, D.C.: National Education Association, 1964), pp. 188–228.

Increasing Teacher Involvement

Classrooms are natural laboratories for research relative to learning and teaching. However, in the past even the best teachers lacked the knowhow to verify methods and develop innovation to assist colleagues; as a result appreciably less is known about good instruction than ought to be the case. Fortunately, more teachers than ever before understand research design, instrument construction, statistical measure, score treatment, and hypothesis testing; it can be hoped that experimentation will soon become a part of every school. For a time, though, this movement toward self-improvement will likely be resisted by a small element of the profession, those whose concept of academic freedom has led them to believe that their classroom is a haven from change. The old line that "no one can really evaluate the effectiveness of my teaching" is an example of this kind of thinking. Traditionally, individuals of this persuasion have expressed the fear of one day becoming subservient to an aristocracy of educational innovators, an elite that would dictate what to teach and how. But this fear is unjustified so long as teachers have the power to make collective decisions about innovation selection. Freedom not to utilize an innovation can be guaranteed when a teacher does not want to accept it. Democracy thrives on informed opinions and confidence in human intelligence, not on bias and sentiment. The reluctant would do well to realize that what is currently being urged is not less freedom but more—for the teacher and student to learn together.

In line with this self-improvement function each school system should maintain a research council to support inquiry by its teachers. At the outset, research investigations may be expected to lack depth and sophistication but teachers, like students, improve with opportunity and recognition. The Wisconsin Educational Research Association has for several years encouraged teachers in the state to report their investigations at the annual WERA meeting. From a meager beginning in 1960, when but a few teachers were in attendance and many of them unwilling to reveal an elemental knowledge of design and data treatment, the WERA meetings have advanced to the point where in 1965 more than sixty papers were read by teachers on topics ranging from programmed learning to the development of new tests and measures. It seems that for a long time, too long, we have curbed our greatest source of classroom invention—the teacher himself. Perhaps he more than others can provide a positive base for innovation.

School systems can profit from research carried on in conjunction with neighboring towns and districts. By pooling manpower and talent, sharing ideas, samples for study and the cost of data treatment, it is possible to increase the chance for useful innovation. Among the better examples of combination attempts are the Greater Cleveland Research Council and the Councils of Research for Pittsburgh and Milwaukee. In Milwaukee each of the participating systems annually contributes a nominal fee that permits it to share in many studies that they could ill afford to carry on independently. At the monthly meetings of Milwaukee council representatives, any system can propose an investigation; single systems need not participate in every inquiry but are obliged to take part in at least one per year. Gerald Gleason (1965), past secretary of the Greater Milwaukee Research Council, reports that each of the participating systems without exception has over the past several years increased its outlay for research and development and now enjoys a greater involvement of teachers with experimentation and innovative trial.

BECOMING A BETTER TEACHER: THE COMMITMENT TO EFFECTIVENESS*

Improvement: The Problem of Criteria

What constitutes being a "good" teacher has been an elusive search in large measure because a single set of criteria has been sought. Historically, the rating technique, with few exceptions, has permitted or encouraged persons other than the teacher to define the optimal condition for learning in his classroom.

In many cases, teachers have had little knowledge of the criteria utilized by those judging the efficiency of instructional acts. Their first response to such ratings has been to try to discover what one must be like in order to appear "good" in the supervisor's estimate. Apart from the time and emotion spent in trying to determine these unknown criteria, there is the added problem of agreement once the elusive data are made available. What is expected of a teacher by the supervisor may not coincide with what that teacher expects of himself. And when one is to be what others wish him to become as opposed to what he wants to be, the situation invites conflict between supervisor and teacher, or concession by the teacher. Either of these conditions reduces the chance of concerted effort since it is at the expense of one individual's philosophy; therefore, we can no longer sacrifice the teacher's in-class philosophy of intentions as though it were either irrelevant or at best subordinate when, in fact, it operationally represents the primary source of instruction in the classroom (Remmers, 1963).

Up to now, there has not been enough emphasis on the teacher's in-class purposes or what we have referred to as intentions. By overlooking the importance of a teacher's classroom intentions it has been possible, though unfortunate, to speak of classroom effectiveness as something quite apart from the goals of its teacher, perhaps independent of his motivation, and certainly disconnected from any self-definition of success. To ignore either self-direction or self-evaluation as an element of improvement is

* Robert D. Strom and Charles Galloway, "Becoming a Better Teacher," *The Journal of Teacher Education* XVIII, No. 3 (Fall, 1967), pp. 285–92. Reprinted by permission.

to imply that the best direction for teacher change in every instance be extrinsic. This view underestimates what might be gained when a teacher perceives his own shortcomings as obstacles to the achievement of self-defined goals. The area of one's acknowledged shortcomings is a helpful focus for those who would become better teachers.

To support the practice of extrinsic teacher direction, there has been convenient recourse to a subtle, yet restricting, terminology of what is desirable in teacher behavior. The concept of a "good" teacher as usually defined has led to the encouragement of impersonal criteria; a broader, more comprehensive notion is that of becoming a "better teacher," which has a personal referent. *"Good" connotes a singular condition and implies some degree of universality in its reference (i.e. good teachers are the same everywhere), whereas the dimension of "better" fits the uniqueness of the person to whom it is applied. Consequently, to become "better" suggests diversity; to approach "good" implies sameness. Saying that all teachers can become better is something quite different from urging all teachers to be good; "better" suggests an emerging condition emphasizing the process and growth of becoming rather than an established state, a finished stability of being.*

Improvement: The Course of Direction

Independent of what criteria obtain, there is a rather general agreement that new teachers, especially those newly assigned to inner-city positions, must alter their idealistic expectations, revamp the teaching strategies learned in college, and contrive new methods in order to be successful. It is assumed that teachers are ill-equipped to meet the demands of such a different cultural setting. Supposing that this advice is sage, and granting that beginning teachers aspire to be adequate, the relevant question urging itself is: Where does the teacher acquire appropriate information on which to base intelligent decisions for self-change? (Bloom, 1965; Frost, 1966; Passow, 1963; Reissman, 1962; and Strom, 1965.)

Obviously any counsel to change, given in the absence of specific direction, provides an additional dimension of insecurity. Not only does it serve to undermine a teacher's confidence but it fails to offer features that might enable improvement; thus, the proposition only serves to alienate its advocate. In effect the urban teacher is told that, because disadvantaged children and the neighborhood they represent are atypical, adequate teaching will require different skills than those gained during preservice preparation. The mechanisms of self-defense alone dictate a rejection of the notion that previous training is inapplicable. When the only recourse a teacher has in making the transition is an unguided process of trial and error, instructional effectiveness may or may not eventuate: it must of necessity depend on the insights gleaned from experience. Far too often the consequences of an unguided approach prove devastating to both the teacher and the students (Nicmeyer, 1966).

A second and more accepted procedure for assisting teachers derives from the belief that they can profit by obtaining a greater knowledge of the information that colleges offer. When this belief is translated into a program of in-service training, it closely resembles most preservice courses. Such an approach demands a great degree of transfer, for it relies heavily on the teacher's ability to apply what is read or heard to the context in which he must operate. Moreover, if what the teacher already knows has been judged irrelevant, it would seem absurd to compensate for the lack by simply increasing the amount.

A third proposal for increasing teacher effectiveness calls attention to the behavioral patterns of an exemplary model (Bush, 1967). The intent of this approach is to foster emulation. Obviously this can be construed as an affront by a teacher who feels that to improve one must give up his identity and be like someone else; that is, one can be more effective if he is less like himself. In short, the way to competence is not to *become* better but *to be* like one who is better. Naturally such a concession is self-defeating.

What has been recognized in most approaches to teacher improvement is that preservice training is a necessary but not sufficient condition to ensure continuous teacher competence. But the means for effecting teacher change have never been clear. The prime focus of study for a teacher on the job is not trial and error, more content, or a model image, but the teacher himself. Indeed, a profession without self-examination and introspection is untrue to itself.

To change one's behavior is difficult, unless a source of direction and guidance is available, and at the present time most teachers have no feedback regarding their behavior in the classroom. Given the assumption that the teacher desires to understand the consequences of his own behavior and wants to improve his teaching, the primary precondition for behavioral change is established. But the next condition, that of providing reliable, descriptive data relative to teaching behaviors, must also be met in order to accomplish any viable change in practice.

Data must be made available upon which to make decisions if any insight into one's own pattern of behavior is to be achieved. Information is relevant when it is connected to the self, for the self is the instrument through which lasting behavioral change takes place. In essence, growing acceptance has been given the position that continued competence based on self-insight into one's own behavior and its consequences is the major means of accomplishing professional growth; that any concept of a method of teaching must encompass the notion that method is a function of behavior; and that teacher behavior permeates every strategy the teacher employs regardless of subject matter or grade level.

Improvement: Observational Data

The net result of teacher behavior studies has been to provide descriptions of classroom activity by classifying instructional styles as dominative or integrative (Anderson, 1937), teacher versus learner-centered (Withall,

1949, 1962), direct or indirect (Amidon and Flanders, 1962), or some variation of x, y, z typologies (Ryans, 1960, 1963). Although such encompassing rubrics are useful to the researcher for his work in analyzing teaching acts, little has been accomplished in converting these rubrics into viable tactics for change and improvement of teaching. In analyzing teacher behavior, researchers have emphasized more the aspect of description than the prescription of instructional acts. Nevertheless, current systems of teacher behavior analysis also imply the acceptance of a predetermined definition of teaching that precludes the development of an evolving concept of what better teaching might be for an individual teacher. Another disturbing element in determining the relevance of research data is the teacher's difficulty in identifying his personal intentions in a researcher's impersonal report of behavior. Although the prospective value of teacher behavior research is generally accepted, a viable means has not yet been provided for enabling a teacher to change his own behavior.

The primary means of accomplishing professional growth resides in the wisdom of the teacher to use the consequences of his behavior in juxtaposition with his goals as a means for making more mature judgments and decisions. What constitutes appropriate data is inexorably related to the teacher one is and intends to be. To actualize one's own intentions and expectations is necessary, but to expect a teacher to first honor the intentions of others, to defer and subordinate his own goals, is to concede that the personal selfhood of a teacher is insignificant.

Without question, any observation procedures designed to gather data about teacher behavior must engender a regard for objectivity, reliability, and validity as necessary components (Gage, 1963). At the same time, the focus for obtaining information ought to center upon the subjective intentions of the particular teacher in question. In other words, the teacher not only is the object of observation but he also determines the scope of its focus. In this way, objective method and subjective focus coincide.

Any declaration of accomplishment implies that some pre-established goals have been met or that certain intermediate criteria have been satisfied. It follows that, in the realm of instructional improvement, gains can best be determined by a comparison between what a teacher intends to achieve and how he behaves. Consequently, in each classroom of The Better Teacher Project our work is predicated upon the statements of purpose set forth by the individual teacher.* Goals chosen by him for his situation make up the criteria for his success. In other words, success is self-defined, a necessary condition if the value of diversity is to be

* The Better Teacher Project (directed by Robert Strom) at The Ohio State University, is funded by the American Association of Colleges for Teacher Education, the Michigan-Ohio Regional Educational Laboratory, and The Ohio State University (1967); it involves teaching in the central-city Hough district of Cleveland.

realized. Apart from the important effect that goals have upon motivation, they also govern behavioral direction, both vital factors in the educative process. Of course, the goals of a teacher must be known if the function of the help-agent is to be realized.

Improvement: The Role of the Help-Agent

The role of help-agent implies that one actively seeks ways by which his talents can support intentions already held by a teacher. It would indeed be strange to purport that one is assisting a teacher without knowing something of the direction in which he hopes to achieve. In fact, where such assertions are made, two parties of different talent may work at odds with each other and, in the process, accomplish less in concert than they might separately. *Cooperation is born of mutual intent.* In order to combine the unique knowledge and experience of the teacher and help-agent, it is virtually imperative that there be some commonly known and accepted explicit set of intentions. Only under such conditions will mutual direction and motivation obtain.

When a teacher and help-agent lack a common reference system, the help-agent is more likely to direct his observation toward behaviors that are irrelevant (Berman and Usery, 1966). In the past, a recurring mistake has been for help-agents to offer prescriptions for intentions that teachers either do not embrace or do not perceive as appropriate to their circumstance. Because such conditions foster an element of intrusion, they introduce a decline in the viability of supervisory assistance.

To overcome these limitations, The Better Teacher Project will begin with the teacher by clarifying those intentions that he chooses to actualize in instructional behavior. This approach suggests that when a teacher participates in identifying intentions a greater opportunity exists for discerning a relationship between what he intends to do and what actually occurs, as well as providing an initial means for working with the teacher. Without such direction, beginning relationships can be fraught with misunderstood goals. Therefore, a major reason for using teaching intentions as a focus for instructional change is that they provide an initial point of departure for establishing a help relationship (Blanke, 1967).

Assuming that the role of a help-agent is to work in league with the teacher, the process of bringing an intention to fruition can be defined in the following way:

A *belief* is expressed in the worth of a teaching intent.

A *condition* is identified under which the intent can occur.

A *commitment* is made to test the feasibility of the condition.

The necessity of this sequence is apparent. Were one to express a belief in some intent but lack its condition, the process would be incomplete; similarly, to have the intention and understand its conditions but issue no allegiance to the intent would be to fail. In total, to fulfill the process of intention requires that one express a belief, know its best condition, and be committed to the trial.

Before the collaborative move to effect teacher change can begin, some assessment is needed to determine which among the teacher intentions are not being achieved. In this way the necessity, priority, and direction for innovation are established. Included as related sources of information are:

> 1. A historical account of teacher behavior and learner response expressed by the coding system invented for this project: Each teacher witness has been trained in use of the recording schedule and has demonstrated a satisfactory index for observer reliability.

> 2. A self-report inventory designed to reveal the teacher's subjective assessment about her success in fulfilling selected intentions. This information is later recorded on an overlay for comparison with the observer reports.

> 3. A rating form for pupils on which teacher behavior is compared with teacher intentions. We are considering use of this form with a second and more objective audience as well; that is, members of the same grade but of another school who view video tapes.

> 4. Personality and psychological test results that depict the selfhood of a teacher.* Such information represents vital matter for the help-agent whose suggestions for classroom change should be restricted to behaviors that are in consonance with the teacher's mental health.

Improvement: The Use of Feedback

Once the data-gathering process is complete, a teacher should be apprised of "how he is doing" in fulfilling his intentions in the estimate of the observer and students. Use of this extrinsic judgment about self-behavior and success constitutes what is generally referred to as "feedback" (Flanders, 1963). In a sense, the notion of feedback is as old as the profession of education itself. Teachers throughout time have used pupil-classroom reaction to determine the appropriateness of instruction, efficiency of presentation and, so to speak, "what to do next" (Yamamoto, 1967). As defined in this way, the value of feedback is necessarily minimized because (1) the teacher is unable to accommodate mentally the numerous patterns of interaction that occur over time; (2) there is a need for rapid inference; (3) and, even more important, the teacher's frame of reference stands alone as the basis for interpretation of teacher action. Other than student overt expression or lack of response, much of the information needed to improve learning and teaching is missing (Galloway, 1966).

---

* The measures selected were those found most helpful in working with Columbus, Ohio inner-city teachers for the Preface Plan Project (1966–67) directed by Robert Strom. See the Appendix, "Teacher Assessment," at the back of this book.

For feedback to be optimal in value, there ought to be data available that portray the pupil's stake in learning. In other words, the content of feedback data should be as relevant to the student's cause as to the teacher's. Certainly, a teacher needs information regarding his own instructional performance; yet, this feedback is incomplete without an interpretation of the relationship between his behavior and learner response. In short, teacher acts must be appropriate to student accommodation, not merely relevant to the teacher as performer *qua* performer. Current efforts to improve teaching typically focus upon the teacher as performer, and by so doing, omit the nature of learner behavior in juxtaposition with that of the teacher. The sharing process by which a teacher and a help-agent determine whether certain teacher intentions have been actualized in light of learner needs and responses describes feedback as something other than it is ordinarily understood to be. In this way the teacher is not encapsulated from the learner, thus making possible fulfillment of the teaching-learning process requirements. To summarize, since the role of the teacher is one of interaction with pupils, the primary sources of feedback data include a systematic observational description of teacher behavior and learner response.

By using the results of observational data graphically shown on overlay patterns and considering the psychological-personality test data depicting the kind of person a teacher is, the two parties (teacher and help-agent) set out to determine feasible alternatives that may permit the achievement of unaccomplished intentions. Having alternatives made available to him by the help-agent, the teacher can engage in subsequent behaviors that are consistent with what he wishes to do and that are also appropriate to his own style of teaching (Hinely, 1966). To admit that there are several alternate ways of actualizing an intention is to recognize that teachers do not have to engage in similar behaviors in order to maximize their effectiveness. After a teacher has tested an alternate strategy in the classroom, further observational data are collected to ascertain the success of behavioral change.

In conclusion, I submit that the traditional aim of trying to identify "good" teachers and "good" teaching has failed. Essentially it has failed because a single set of criteria has been used that defines success in an impersonal way. Until recently the complexity of accepting each teacher as a unique person with a unique set of intentions for a classroom of unique children has been deferred. Currently, there are a number of teacher behavior research projects emphasizing multiple criteria for adequate performance, along with a kind of feedback plan that promises to regard the teacher as a prime reference for self-success. Though we pursue separate directions, those of us engaged in this quest are agreed in the resolve that better teaching will most likely occur when the dignity of the individual classroom teacher is honored.

Members of the Better Teacher Project take the position that what it means to become a better teacher inevitably depends upon the person a teacher now is. Therefore, the question of self-change—a needed focus for any proposition of professional improvement—is determined by a greater awareness of self-success in achieving instructional intentions. It must be admitted that certain of a teacher's intentions are better than his behaviors, that gaps may exist between what one hopes to accomplish and what is attained. The requirements of behaviorally achieving what we know to be better is difficult. Nevertheless, when it is recognized that each teacher has his own set of intentions and unique powers, there is the prospect for a help-agent and teacher liaison to accommodate the best interests of children.

THE FACULTY TEAM: AN INSTITUTIONAL COMMITMENT

The modern school is a complex institution involving more staff than just its teacher members. Included in the cause as well are persons whom we might call "the competent others," men and women whose choice is to assist youngsters in ways apart from classroom instruction. A unique background in training enables each of these specialists to handle certain problems for which teachers are unprepared. Whether they be guidance counselors, nurses, social workers, dental hygienists, school psychologists, librarians, supervisors, or administrators, supportive staff personnel are all a vital part of the faculty team. If this group, the so-called team, were always to act in concert to focus its collective talent upon the variables that act to retard child progress, there is little doubt that a significant reduction might be achieved in the extent to which pupils experience anxiety, failure, illness, and misunderstanding. Yet in ever so many schools, combined effort is not actualized; the team is in name only.

Utilizing a Supportive Staff

Generally the responsibility for staff cohesion and mutual endeavor is perfunctorily acknowledged by teachers but then dismissed by referring to extrinsic organizational factors that operate to resist any corporate focus. According to one teacher, "Above all a continued conflict in work schedules seems to deny any possibility of frequent meetings between teacher and other specialists. We all have our own jobs to do and there really is little time left over to share ideas, consult with one another, and so forth. Not that it wouldn't be nice if we could. . . ." Another line of retreat is to lament the relative lack of supportive specialists in relation to the need that obtains. On the average there are approximately 600 students per guidance counselor in high schools, 2,000 students per nurse, and 1,000 students per social worker. A typical teacher comment is, "Because the specialists are charged with excessive work loads, it is unfair for any of us to request their help except in the most extreme cases; and while some of my students need assistance, none of them is so bad at this time as to be referred. Besides, with the present backlog in requests for referral and given so much administrative red tape and time for processing, the child of concern would likely have moved out of my classroom by the time help arrives."

This sort of evasive reasoning is in itself perhaps as much an obstacle to team enterprise as any other known factor, since ordinarily it is teacher judgment alone that serves to determine whether the student problem requires the benefit of combined strategy. For the most part, staff specialists represent a kind of latent contribution, without effect unless activated by teacher referral. Obviously this important decision about whether or not to refer a student is affected by a teacher's perception of his role in the school, his awareness of self-limitation, his understanding of the meaning and significance of referral, his cognizance regarding the function performed by each specialist, and the degree to which his supportive colleagues are respected. In turn these elements deserve mention.

At present the role of the classroom teacher is in transition; it is being redefined to student advantage. Part of this change entails the reassignment of certain tasks so that teacher responsibilities do not continue to exceed teacher competence. We are reminded that for many years school faculties were composed only of instructors to whom educated assistance was but a dream. And since no recourse to professional help was available, teachers themselves were expected to handle any and all problems involving the children of their classroom. Whatever sort of attention was needed by students, these tasks by definition were assumed to be within the teacher's orientation and ability. So inclusive, in fact, was the role as perceived by some teachers that it was long common practice for them, in pride or complaint, to describe the noninstructional job responsibilities like collecting money for milk, stamps, or tickets, administering first aid, guarding street crossings, and supervising the lunchroom, cloakroom, playground, or study hall as subsuming the function if not competence of other occupational groups such as physician, nurse, and babysitter. It is fair to say that we have not fully rid ourselves of this conception; at least a contingent still maintain that "My classroom is mine and whatever situation arises there I'll handle it." This persuasion suggests that any involvement by colleagues in one's classroom problems is tantamount to an invasion of active interference. Credence for this antique proposition is still offered by principals who give the impression to their staff that the good teacher is the one who handles his own problems, that only less competent persons involve the central office. Under these conditions, assistance is seen as an admission of personal failure and therefore only the inept would utilize services of the supportive staff.

Pretense in these matters can only penalize children. If our separate areas of academic interest are in such flux as to render competence a continued effort, it is only the most presumptuous among us who would claim facility not only in our own discipline but, by a nonreferral policy toward supportive staff, suppose our talents to include theirs. Soon we must desist in the notion that to be adequate is to be without limitation and instead realize that adequacy includes the recognition and acceptance of self-limits. It engenders as well a desire to serve the best interests of children even when occasion dictates that the best to be offered is not ours to give. The teacher who contends she never encounters problems that require supportive staff members, difficulties which are beyond her scope, either fails as a classroom witness or somehow cannot admit to being less than omniscient. To choose the inclusive role that forbids uncertainty and referral is to elect a position that can be neither effective nor professional.

Referral is not based upon an admission of defeat nor does it represent an evasion of responsibility. Rather it indicates an appropriate behavioral response of one who is committed to the institutional purpose of child growth and development; it signifies a confidence in the ability of one's fellows, a respect for their function, a concern for the student. As the best mechanism we have as yet devised for professional diagnosis, referral is an attempt to focus the most relevant talent upon a problem. In medicine, general practitioners are not embarrassed or reluctant to place the judgment of specialists above their own. So, too, we in education ought not resist the child's advantage—help from those who can help him most. An element of humility obtains in the referral act. Indeed, the most obvious way to assess humility might be by observed presumption. For being humble is far more than rejecting credit for the noble deed or simply refraining from boasting of one's accomplishment. Humility includes the awareness of personal limits.

What precisely then is the domain of these "competent others" and how does their function support pupil advance? Both questions have the same answer—growth and development. Surely in a school without guidance counselors, fewer children may be expected to manifest self-understanding, to select goals that correspond to their ability. Similarly, without social workers teachers are less likely to determine the real reasons for pupil tardiness, frequent absence, or delinquent behavior. Neither can the classroom instructor be expected to rectify misunderstandings between home and school as well as can the liaison case worker. Again, what is known of the relationship between health and personal efficiency renders the service of a school nurse invaluable. She is more able than the teacher to detect remediable physical problems and symptoms of disease, to counsel and assist parents in obtaining adequate treatment or correction. That student performance is affected on a large scale in this country by undue obstacles is shown in the statistics indicating that "presently over seven million children are in need of eye care; an additional two million sustain a hearing impairment; and an indeterminate number are daily inattentive because of dental caries." The school psychologist, librarian, and remedial specialists respectively are each important in effecting the appropriate placement of children, enabling students to better locate the stuff of learning, to diagnose and erase academic deficit. Still another group, comprised of principals, superintendent, and board of education are supportive in that they supply needed materials, provide in-service education, and arrange to make specialists available for referral. Elsewhere the author has described the responsibility of specialists (Strom, 1965c, pp. 48–70).

Student motivation with a focus, improved health and performance, conjunctive effort with the home—all these things and more the faculty team of teachers and supportive staff can accomplish. Collectively they can assist boys and girls to be adequate to their time. But whether a combined effort is activated, whether the team is allowed its existence seems to depend largely upon the teacher. To continue the phenomenon of reluctance, not to utilize the referral option and consult with specialists can undermine much of the modern school's purpose. If referral be the mechanism of optimal diagnosis in other professions, can we long continue to evade its use? Is it ethical to claim the function of other professionals? In a sense it is foolhardy to talk diagnostics apart from referral. The character of our society—its strengths, integrity, effectiveness, freedom —is definitely determined by the degree and quality of its individual members. That character is never static; it is either improving or deteriorating. Only as the entire staff of the school work together as a team, utilizing every strength and talent among its members, can the prospects of more children be optimistic.

Accepting Faculty Responsibilities

Within the informal teacher group there is periodic complaint about the assignment of faculty responsibilities. Some feel that too much extra work is required of them and that too little assistance is forthcoming. More specifically, the concerns relate to frequency and nature of faculty meetings, insufficient help with problem children, the lack of written and verbal communication regarding school procedures, encounters with an unsympathetic central administration, and the absence of teacher voice in policy decisions. Perhaps complaining about these matters can be helpful as an initial response, as a goad to action. But complaint ought not be a professional's final response to impediment since if continued it threatens to paralyze morale and to undermine personal and group efficiency. Instead, each teacher must share the obligation of making combined effort worthwhile, substituting action for lament as the medium in which the group attempts to register change. Only by working together can teachers expect to reduce their grievances and at the same time improve faculty performance.

Faculty meetings represent an example. Those who contend teachers are without personal experience in the realm of failure would do well to observe the quality variance in staff sessions at different schools.

During the weekly faculty meetings at Haley Elementary, a reasonable assumption is that one or more persons will be reading a book or correcting assignments. Several teachers have scheduled a dental appointment or other engagement to coincide with the meeting time so as to be excused. Others equally disappointed with the meetings perceive regular attendance as a sign of loyalty and dedication. The gathering has been called this week as every other solely because it is part of a series arranged before the semester began. We meet therefore because it is time—but for what? After the opening remarks have been made about the absentees, a number of reports are heard. The laborious reading of announcements which could just as well have been duplicated and left in each teacher's mailbox is meant to occupy time. During the interval that remains, since each meeting must be of a certain duration, someone is allowed to reveal his hidden agenda—ordinarily a topic he would like discussed. This is an ill-chosen procedure because in the absence of established priorities the first issue suggested, however unimportant, becomes the subject for debate. Certainly the faculty should not be expected to consider unannounced issues and teachers of all people ought to recognize that thoughtful preparation is the base for wise exchange of views. Because different issues are raised at each meeting and given but momentary consideration, action strategies are never developed and sustained effort fails to eventuate. The result is a continued staff rejection of faculty meetings as a vehicle for school improvement.

Contrast the perception of faculty meetings by Haley's teachers with that of the Walson Elementary faculty. At Walson a consensus that group endeavor might be the best instrument of progress led the staff to identify agenda concerns during the first week of school. Each teacher received the following notice from the planning committee.*

> Now that the new schoolyear is underway, it is appropriate for us to identify staff concerns that should be considered. Forms are provided for your thoughtful reactions. Return the forms to Mrs. Smith by September 15.
>
> The forms are designed to allow classification of the responses in two ways: (1) personal vs. organizational concerns and (2) immediate vs. long-range concerns. The four categories thus yielded (immediate personal, immediate organizational, long-range personal, and long-range organizational) will provide structure for future meetings and submeetings of the faculty. Each person has been given enough forms so please put only one idea on each slip.
>
> The meaning of "personal" or "individual" concern is evident. "Organizational" should be taken to mean subject matter area or grade level. "Immediate" will be interpreted that action and resolution should be effected by the end of this semester (1966–67), and "long-range" should be thought of as extending beyond the end of this semester (see Figure III-4).

* Note that the method of determining agenda does not force the choice between a personal interest and organizational need. Both are allowed to receive attention.

IMMEDIATE CONCERN   ☐ personal
                                                     ☐ organizational

_____

_____

_____

_____

_____

Long-Range Concern   ☐ personal
                                                     ☐ organizational

_____

_____

_____

_____

Fig. III-4. Walson Elementary School form for identifying meeting agenda.

As a result of the decision to determine the meeting agenda together
and to solve problems by continued effort, the Walson group over the
past several years has been able to complete exciting school research
projects and curriculum experiments. Among these teachers reluctance
to attend faculty meetings and to support the work of colleagues has been
minimized. At Walson professional responsibility has been met, the team
approach realized.

Bear in mind also that the nature of staff meetings is influenced by the
nature of informal encounter among teachers. There is usually a consonance between the sort of communication that takes place in the lounge
and the sort that occurs in the formal setting. If a group would achieve
its worthwhile purposes, each member must refrain from participating
in unprofessional verbal exchange. Perhaps no teacher behavior can more
quickly destroy the chance for noble objectives than the blatant disregard
for confidential information. Just as a doctor, lawyer, or clergyman is
charged to keep secret the privileged information revealed to them by
patient, client, or parishioner, so too the teacher should guard the private
conversation with students and their families. When the casual exchange
with fellow teachers includes personal material about students or parents,
the teacher violates a confidence. Relating private data to a co-worker
cannot be justified by simply prefacing the remark or story with, "Now

I tell you this in confidence. . . ." The act of gossip cannot be dignified
or excused; it is unprofessional regardless of its guise. The only occasion
for sharing personal information is when supportive staff members require it as background to perform their function. A fair statement is that
the most frequent disrespect of teachers toward professionalism occurs
within the lounge. Here the quality of verbal traffic must be elevated
to exceed gossip and gripe. Until this be so, a minority will delay the
larger group from meriting the term "professional."

Another ethical commitment that more teachers should honor is the
responsibility to assist colleagues. This "help process" has numerous
dimensions. For one thing the experienced faculty can support a policy by which beginning instructors are granted reduced work loads
instead of falling subject to the most difficult assignments. Moreover,
it is time to dispense with the quaint notion that since we all teach,
we have nothing to learn from one another. Sharing of ideas and techniques seldom takes place because of the "every man for himself" philosophy, a strange competition whereby teachers vie for student favor
and are careful not to reveal to one another their successful methods
as though to do so would result in personal loss. In the faculty team
approach, there is sharing because the goal of student advantage
always takes precedence over self-aggrandizement. By the same token,
staff members are encouraged to be creative, to be unique, to try new
ideas, to experiment without fear of group criticism. As the occurrence
of close association, mutual effort, and sharing increase, school faculties tend to grow in stature and efficiency.

A final issue of ethics in the colleague relationship has to do with
teacher influence upon policy decisions. Historically teachers have tended
to view the principal, supervisor, superintendent, and other administrative
personnel as outsiders, unsympathetic managers who tend to resist teacher
ideas. However often misunderstanding with these outsiders occurs, it
seems that teachers are disinclined to admit even partial responsibility.
"The fact that the administration turned us down is proof of their disinterest; after all we sent a representative." But who was sent? If the
program, the report, the request be of such significance, why is there
so little teacher deliberation in selecting representation? Instead, when
it is learned that the intended meeting will be held downtown and is
scheduled after-school hours, the evasion tactics begin. Who can go?
Who will represent us? Who lives in that direction? In some cases
this means selecting an individual more because he is convenient than
because he is informed or persuasive. Conceivably the person who is
sent may be unable to even explain the faculty position. Yet when the
administration rejects the teacher point of view, it is the board action only
that is the subject of teacher complaint. Because the only contact a board
of education or superintendent ordinarily has with teacher view and judgment occurs when there is organized representation of the staff, it

should be apparent that teachers must choose wisely and participate well if chosen. The work of Miles (1965) and Halpin (1962, pp. 1–15) regarding organizational health and faculty interaction represents signs of progress in bringing better understanding between administrative and instructional personnel.

Status and Articulation

The gain of appropriate status has long eluded classroom teachers. Until the post-sputnik era they were expected to accept low pay and little regard in return for excessive hours and responsibility. But as people become more dependent upon education for livelihood, as a society proposes to improve, the prestige of its teachers tends to rise. Reasonable salaries, pleasant working conditions, professional assistance—these and other compensations attest to the fact that teachers now enjoy a higher status than their counterparts of yesteryear. Still something more than public esteem and recognition are necessary for a group to claim itself professional. To merit the term they covet will require much more of educators. There remain the difficult tasks of erasing internal disputes about competence and establishing the much-needed relationships of articulation.

Within the teaching ranks there are long-standing distinctions of respect, a hierarchy of prestige. For years the public mind has also reserved a different level of esteem for various teachers, depending upon the student age-group one serves. That working with higher grade levels requires more of a teacher than does a younger-aged class is not a new idea. Neither is it novel to believe that those who instruct the youngest children can perform their function by knowing very little. However, since these widespread assumptions tend to relegate teachers of the young to a second-order position in the educational establishment, they should stand corrected in our time.

It is true that in most nations elementary teachers receive substantially less respect and pay than do instructors of secondary grades. But this does not mean the job of working with grade school children is less demanding or less important. The lower esteem relates to the fact that many countries have either not recognized or accepted the importance of early learning and as a consequence require little formal training of those who teach the young. Throughout Europe with the exception of England, primary teachers are not required to earn a university degree as are those who work with the adolescent group. For example, in Portugal and Spain respectively the terminal point for compulsory attendance is age eleven and fourteen. To become a primary teacher in Portugal, a nation with a reported illiteracy rate of 44 percent, the candidate need only be a graduate of the four-year elementary school, pass an examination in general education, and give a test lesson proving ability. Hence many elementary teachers, most of whom are female, begin their pedagogic career in the classroom at age eleven or twelve. Spain's elementary pupils are little better off as their teachers must be only fourteen years old, possess no incapacitating defects, have completed the first four years of secondary school, which begins at age ten, and have successfully completed an entrance examination. It is difficult to imagine that children in their formative years, needing direction from mature instructors, are taught by persons who are themselves children. One is inclined to suggest that the "baby-sitting charge" of critics has a more tenable base where conditions such as these prevail.

By way of contrast, in our country there are no differences in length of formal educational preparation between the elementary and secondary teachers. Both groups must earn a degree to be licensed; an M.A. degree for certain states. To argue whether lecturing in American history requires more skill or knowledge than teaching six-year-olds to read is an unnecessary issue. Each of the functions has an important place. The point is that as we attach increasing significance to early childhood education in our culture, we must also transfer an equal regard to those whose extensive training qualify them to offer an adequate educational background for the youngest boys and girls in school.

Status-related problems are sometimes compounded by internal disputes regarding competence. Too often public-favored teacher groups come to believe that their colleagues are less able than themselves. Invariably this judgment leads to condescending relationships and a propensity toward blaming others. Thus, the junior high school instructor can assume that Johnny's reading problem is necessarily a reflection of inadequate teaching during the elementary grades. By the same token, when senior high school personnel encounter student deficiency in required courses, they might suppose it amounts to a negative testimony against junior high school teachers. Because of cumulative deficiency, an ever-decreasing proportion of students are able to meet standard achievement expectations as their class moves up through the grades. At the end, educators of the twelfth grade could well discount the ability of all teachers preceding them were they convinced that a one to one relationship exists between student performance and instructional efficiency. On the other hand, as elementary educators are closer to the beginnings of school process, they have fewer colleagues to blame. In fact, kindergarten teachers have no previous instructors to blame except the mother, and so the home becomes a major target. Parents of course will argue that the school is at fault. This senseless cycle of evasion of responsibility and the tendency to project blame ought to cease at all levels for it offers little profit—least of all to children.

Similar disputes about competence exist among those teaching at the same grade level. Coincident with the rise in number of subject matter specialists has been an increase in vested interests so that different curricular areas now vie for prestige and school monies. In many cases this competition promotes disrespect for the function and facility of others, lack of coordination, and little support for or even opposition to the work of colleagues. The prestige battle proceeds along different lines in communities where teachers measure the value of one another by their location of assignment. Assuming that only the best staff are placed in upper-income neighborhoods, a low esteem is granted persons who labor in poverty districts. Remember, however, that just as there is no real correlation between grade level and teacher competence, so too job location is a poor criterion for assessing teacher ability. Helping children of young years or low-income families ought never be perceived as demeaning or demotive; it should not carry a dubious distinction. Rather, it is important to see service to all students as important, whoever they are, wherever they live.

The contention here is that however effective an organizational structure may appear, articulation will fail to occur unless there is mutual respect among teachers of the institutions represented. Optimum efficiency implies there be common goals and meanings as well as an absence of interpersonal barriers like distrust, suspicion, or fear. Whatever gaps in communication and action exist, they must be bridged if any of the teacher groups are to operate to satisfaction. Surely there is a need for curriculum articulation to ensure sequence of content through the grades. Further, agreement is necessary regarding grading procedures to establish a continuity between the several levels. When a pupil fails, it should be common practice for his present teachers of whatever specialization to meet and discuss strategies for success. This may require calling in the youngster's previous teachers, for they offer a better reference than the cumulative record. In ever so many instances we could benefit by consulting with colleagues of different departments or levels of instruction. To advocate interdisciplinary cooperation on the one hand and still refuse to support combined effort with fellow teachers of a different grade level is inconsistent. Through their representative, teachers should urge the formation of administrative mechanisms that will both permit and facilitate the kinds of articulation needed for the success of today's school.

HOME-SCHOOL RELATIONS: THE MUTUAL COMMITMENT

It is difficult to date the origin of cooperation between parents and teachers in this country, as they seem to have always worked together after a fashion. The nature of shared endeavors has of course changed with the years. During the early colonial period familial support was limited to reinforcing school-accepted conduct. When pupils were subject to reprimand or penalty in class, their parents were expected to augment the teacher chastisement by administering punishment of a similar or more severe nature. Years later, following initiation of the kindergarten movement, psychological studies of the learning process, and the development of testing practices, a new kind of relationship was urged between home and school. Assuming that both institutions possessed information important to the other's function, teachers and parents were encouraged to meet periodically and share ideas for helping children achieve in school. The first arranged encounters took the form of individual conferences and parent-teacher associations. These two mechanisms have been retained as the dominant modes of exchange, even though effectiveness has been a major problem ever since their inception. Most people involved may favor conferences and oppose elimination of the procedure, but they agree that meetings often prove far from adequate. On the other hand, while formal parent-teacher associations are generally advocated as requisite for school improvement, few persons would imply that the group exercises a real influence in other than its social context. What this seems to suggest is that the established and accepted vehicles for parent-teacher interaction need to evolve into more advantageous instruments of mutual endeavor. For teachers a start in this direction will necessitate increased attention to relating as professionals and fulfilling certain principles of ethics.

Conferences with Parents

In most schools released time is provided for parent-teacher consultation. Generally about three or four times a year students are dismissed early in the afternoon or excused from attendance for an entire day to provide time for the conferences. A common procedure is to arrange the schedule several weeks in advance by sending a note to each home.

> During the last week of January, Garden City Schools will conduct their quarterly parent-teacher conferences. Your assigned date and time are Wednesday, January 28, 2:30–2:45 p.m. We hope you can be present. Please confirm your appointment by returning the lower portion of this notice. If there are any questions, feel free to call.
>
> Sincerely,
> Mrs. Jane Smith
> 565-1791

....

> I will plan to meet with Mrs. Smith in Room 201 on Wednesday, January 28, 2:30–2:45 p.m.

_____

(Parent Signature)

Parental attendance is occasionally disappointing when some report themselves unable to be present and others who are scheduled find it necessary to cancel at the last minute. A quick and unprofessional teacher response to the inconvenience caused them is to engage in the lament, "What's the sense of having conferences if the parents who most need to attend don't show up? Don't they care about their kids? How can a parent be so inconsiderate as to call only a few minutes before the arranged time and announce she won't be here? Doesn't she realize the work that goes into setting up these meetings?" But there are additional cause-effect questions that may be asked. Was the assigned time inconvenient for the parent? Would it have been possible to offer an alternative schedule? If a mother has small children to care for, is it possible that the unavailability of a babysitter, sickness in the home, or lack of transportation could account for her absence? Might an unannounced problem or emergency force one to cancel an appointment? If parents do not attend the conference, can we really infer they do not care about their children?

Certainly a teacher may feel bad because parents with whom he wished to speak did not arrive, but what of the telephone? It is paradoxical that teachers spend so much time on developing the communication skills of children but fail themselves to use its most available media. For the mother with little children, the parent who is some distance from school, and the working parent it ought to be possible to arrange an exchange of views so long as there are telephones. And, isn't it true that a telephone conversation can sometimes be just as informative and helpful as the tête-à-tête? There may be numerous instances in which the conference could be more effective if carried on by telephone because some condescending conditions are eliminated; that is, the teacher does not sit behind his desk in an authoritative position with the parent stationed in the student place. Problems of eye contact that effect conversation are also overcome. But, the purpose here is not to argue the merits of face-to-face versus telephone encounters. It is to suggest that on occasions when parental attendance at the school cannot be arranged, we need not despair; the telephone represents a helpful substitute.

Successful conferences require a readiness of attitude and agenda by both parties. Mutual respect should replace defensiveness as the dominant mood. At its extreme, teacher defensiveness is illustrated by the person who sees the meeting as a time for justification, for convincing parents that his assessment of the child is correct. In these cases, most of the meeting time is used by showing the parent examples of the youngster's work. In fact, to support his case before aggressive parents of a less able pupil, the teacher may unwittingly punish the concerned child by giving him the same assignments as other students, although too difficult, in order to prove that he cannot succeed. This is an attempt to prove failure, to have a grade book in which a sequence of low marks appear. While this sort of extreme defensiveness in teacher behavior is not widespread, a significant number of teachers are somewhat defensive as evidenced by the frequent claim that "parents are unreceptive to counsel. Every layman seems to feel he knows all about the educational process simply because he once was a student. Some parents think they know as much about teaching and learning as does the teacher; the result is either dispute or a reticence to listen."

But is this judgment about parental perception warranted? In an attempt to test it on a limited scale, The Ohio State University Child Development Unit polled 555 parents representing a cross section of income and ethnic groups in six Ohio communities. Each individual was presented a list of ten occupations and asked to check those of the list that they would consider as professional given the definition that "a professional is one whose knowledge and training in a field so extends beyond that of laymen as to qualify him to give counsel and advice in his area; a person whose judgment I would solicit and regard." The fact that 493 out of 555 persons or 89 percent of those polled indicate teaching to be a profession under the defined conditions may suggest that the parental view of educators might be different from what some have supposed. From interviews with members of the sample, it was learned that many of them recognize the importance of education for success and hold their child's teacher in high regard (Strom, 1966b). If this finding is generalizable to a larger population, it means that teacher-parent conferences can become a powerful tool for the support of learning. It means also that the resisting factors may relate to teacher competence as well as to parental readiness. Whatever the case, it is clear that teachers can affect the response of parents when children are school-aged.

But readiness has more than an attitude dimension. With the limited span of time together it is essential that small talk not be allowed to dominate the parent-teacher conference. Too often the topics deal with the mutually known elements of homework, grades, and behavior. To get at the important unknowns both parties need an agenda, a list of specific questions they wish to ask or answer. Little can be accomplished by query like "How's he doing?" A profitable venture of the PTA is to devise a list of questions for which parents would like answers and a teacher list of items that they would prefer to answer and feel would be helpful to the parents. Under these conditions it would not be insulting during the conference for either party to refer to a copy of the questions as they discuss the child. Additional items beyond those listed might be examined also.

Honesty should characterize every discussion with parents. Some teachers convey misinformation because they believe a child needs encouragement from his parents. Other teachers twist the truth simply to remain in good standing with parents because they know that what parents think of them depends in part upon how they assess the child's chance for success. So the teacher may tend to give exaggerated aspirations to be popular. The unfortunate thing is that parents accept these judgments and later when another teacher actually tells them the truth, they may be unable to accommodate themselves to the second point of view. An unethical teacher early in the school career of a child can bias parents permanently so that they will not alter or change their image of the student and they simply resent later teacher information if it differs. This means the elementary teacher especially must refrain from long-term predictions because parental dreams have a way of governing aspiration and expectation. In turn this affects the way a child is treated and the kind of pressures that are brought to bear upon him.

Unless the conference is dignified by truthful exchange, there always is a risk of discrepancy in student expectations as held by parents and teachers. What is known about the relationship between motivation and stress indicates that successful performance is more likely when the objectives of school and home are in harmony. From the standpoint of guidance, working together demands similar goals and expectations. For one party to embrace or encourage unrealistic objectives is to do the child a disservice. In the future, as the age of vocational choice is reduced, pupils will need to know more about their own strengths, weaknesses, and prospects. Likewise the parents will require more information about the student's aptitudes to be of assistance in rendering the youngster's judgment adequate. No longer will "He's doing ok" be a sufficient teacher response to parental inquiry.

It is as dishonest to confuse parents as it is to lie to them. The chance to convey meaning is lost when irrelevant or ambiguous terms are used in the conference conversation. To describe a student to his parents as being "normal," "average," "exceptional," "unmotivated," "underachiever," or "overachiever" is not the best explanation. Similarly, it is of little value to speak about a child's "ability," "capacity," or "potential." All these words are empty in the absence of understood referents. Parents are not helped when told that their youngster needs more "involvement," to "apply himself," and reach "standards." Neither is it useful to expound on the teacher's role in "creating a climate" for learning, providing a "challenge," fostering a "democratic atmosphere" in which "meaningful experiences" can occur. There is much parents want to learn during the conference that they are not told. Several important reminders for the teacher are:

1. Before the conference, send home a list of relevant questions you could answer if parents wish to ask. Include a list of questions to which you seek answers. Let it be known that additional questions will of course be entertained.

2. Words chosen for conversation during the conference should have common meaning.

3. Always offer the source of reference for cited comparisons. For example, is the "standard" a class mean score, the teacher's aspiration, or grade level norm?

4. Enumerate the specific ways in which parents can help improve student progress. For example, in social studies they should regularly be provided a list of readings related to the current topics their children are studying. Since these articles and books are ones the pupils will not encounter in class the parents reading them can, like the teacher, serve as a source of knowledge to children. Similarly, parents ought to regularly receive a list of places in the community for visit in conjunction with classroom studies. These family field trips will be of greater value when the teacher's information includes questions to be asked while on the trip and aspects deserving of close observation. Aids of these kinds can help the parents fulfill a more important role in the education of their children.

5. Refrain from making student personality assessments.

6. If too much teacher observation is comparative rather than analytical, it tends to be stereotyped by the pupil's status as a leader or follower. Parents require more information about him than his social position.

7. Do not limit parental assistance to sponsoring acceptable class behavior.

8. Do not waste time showing examples of student work. Send examples home if need be and have them returned later.

The Conjunctive Association

Nearly every public school claims to support a formal association of parents and teachers. In certain neighborhoods and communities these groups have consistently proved useful while in other locales they are seemingly without effect. Just as disfavor alone does not change unsuccessful faculty meetings, so too, little is wrought by the unprofessional reaction of complaint toward an ill-functioning parent-teacher group. According to one elementary teacher:

> Our PTA get-togethers are a communal charade with the faculty conceding for the evening that parents have a voice in school affairs and conversely parents supporting the teacher need for feeling influential by showing up in response to her written request. After the teacher with the most parents in attendance wins the coveted cookie jar, and someone who never before held office is elected to head an innocuous committee, the drudgerous reports and minutes of the last meeting are read. What typically follows is presentation of a one-shot speaker, some type of student performance, discussions on how the group can raise money for needed school equipment, or a coffee hour during which everyone is encouraged to fraternize and staff are to reply to parental inquiries about student behavior and achievement.

Another teacher on the same faculty reports a different perspective:

> The fact that our PTA attendance has grown in size over the past few years would seem to indicate that the meetings are worthwhile. As a

result of a recent membership drive, we were able to persuade many seldom-seen parents to show their support for the school by joining the organization. By establishing this kind of cohesion among parents and teachers, I feel we are each demonstrating mutual confidence in the institution and its work.

These divergent points of view about the same PTA represent something more than just an interesting contrast in judgment. Further discussions with each of the individuals made clear the essential similarity of their positions—both reflect a lack of commitment with respect to assisting the home and utilizing the help parents might offer. From the complaining instructor it was learned that his source of discontent centered upon a perceived discrepancy between the useless organizational effects he observed and the noble objectives that a PTA might achieve. Nevertheless, though he envisioned a more relevant set of tasks for the association and was able to map a judicious strategy for using group energies, he made no attempt to even recommend changes on the hunch that it was not his responsibility and that were he to suggest something new, supervision would undoubtedly fall upon him as those who devise novel schemes are most always selected to direct the implementation. Lest he become involved in more work, it seemed better to register dissatisfaction simply by complaint.

The second teacher would undoubtedly be favored by the PTA members as someone who is more active, more cooperative, and more tolerant. She doesn't complain about the activities; in fact she is enthusiastic about PTA progress. Her rationale is that support and cohesion can be inferred from membership; therefore growth rate is the vital measure of an organization's effectiveness. And so, as long as we continue to assemble, especially in greater numbers, there is no reason to assume a breach. This conviction translates into the insidious procedure of leading parents to believe attendance at PTA meetings is required of them to confirm their support of the school. Everyone who cares about the children is expected to join and attend. But is it incorrect to expect parents to register support for one phase of the school (helping children) by taking part in another activity (PTA), which may bear no relation to the first phase? If a member or official of the local PTA can offer no other justification for its existence than that meeting represents a mutual show of confidence in the two represented institutions of home and school, there is something needlessly existing. If to perpetuate itself is the only goal of an organization, that organization is unnecessary.

Without question the PTA offers the best opportunity of any mechanism yet devised for making parent-teacher interaction worthwhile. The organization is already widely established and accepted but whether its appropriate functions will be achieved in each locale or serve as an impotent unit depends in great measure upon the ethics of teachers. They should recognize and assume their portion of the responsibility in determining organizational objectives, preparing for meetings, suggesting agenda and procedures, participating in activities, assessing program effect, challenging the dubious use of time and energy, and ever urging the cause of child benefit. Only as teachers fulfill these obligations can it be said they are relating as professionals.

Since purpose gives direction to behavior, optimal group functioning depends on a common set of purposes among its members. If differing primary goals are held by many persons of the same PTA, common direction and concerted effort are unlikely. Chances are that ensuing internal conflict is bound to nourish discontent, derogation, complaint, and dissension. These kinds of behavior undermine a PTA's effort to help children. Principal goals of the association ought be neither economic nor social. While participation in money-making schemes to purchase audio-visual and sports equipment for the school might be construed as benevolent, a PTA should make a more important contribution to children than merely supplementing school budget. In the same fashion only token gains are made when social objectives dominate group activity. Some would argue that socializing provides an opportunity for parents and teachers to "get to know each other" and this will enhance their working relationship. Two questions come to mind: (1) Need one get to know the school nurse or guidance counselor in order to work with them in a child's stead? (2) Is it actually believed that the nature of brief exchange between a teacher and the many parents he meets at the PTA could appreciably affect the knowledge of either party regarding the children involved? The PTA ought not be limited to a venture in communal entertainment in which the assumption is made that as parent and teacher work with the same pupil they each can profit from participating together in endeavors unrelated to the student. The association is not a status center for those unappointed elsewhere; it is not a device to provide parents with the illusion that they run the school; neither is it a place to issue oral report cards; nor a monthly gathering convened to confirm our confidence in one another; its prime function is not the presentation of art exhibits or musical concerts. This is not to suggest that presentations of student achievement have no place in school affairs but they should be scheduled on nights other than the PTA meeting.

Essentially the PTA purpose is educational—to facilitate change, increase the understanding and competence of parents and teachers, and to support pupil well-being and achievement. Much parental resistance to school change derives from the feeling that learning they have known and valued over the years is being discarded. Therefore, quite naturally they harbor doubt, misgivings, suspicion, and even animosity toward new aspects of the curriculum. To the parents' dismay, everything seems to be labeled "modern" even if it is not. The fact that mothers and fathers are unschooled in modern math, reading by color, the Initial Teaching Alphabet (ITA), and new biology can put them in an embarrassing position with the children. Confronting novel school materials, parents feel unable to help; they worry about losing the respect of sons and daughters and as a result may have some negative feelings toward the institution. Today home-school relationships can less well tolerate negative feelings than ever before. If it would, the PTA could diminish popular resistance to innovation and at the same time facilitate change by helping parents become more informed about new programs and teaching techniques before adoption. This is fair, and necessary if the school would sustain home support.

It is amazing how some local units purporting a concern for better education can so frequently manage to avoid important school issues. An abundance of problems exist that ought not be tabled in the PTA:

1. Controversial topics related to grading practices, discipline, sex education, and vocational courses bear examination by the group.
2. Other subjects for possible discussion are student televiewing habits, children and advertising, stages of personal development, and environmental influence.
3. Ways of improving parent-teacher conferences demand attention. Perhaps a list of concerns might be jointly formulated for ready reference by either party.
4. Some sessions ought be devoted to training unpaid teacher aides to assist the staff with responsibilities ranging from supervising play to conducting field trips. Grandparents should be included as teacher aid candidates.

When these purposes are honored by a PTA, the organization is worthy of its name. Long-standing grievances about meetings may be expected to diminish because new goals introduce a different type of preparation and procedure for meetings. In schools in which the PTA continues to be viewed as a showmanship affair, teachers are obliged to perform an assigned ritual of gaily decorating halls and bulletin boards with samples of student (or teacher) art work in preparation for monthly meetings. But in the increasing number of schools in which the PTA seeks to learn and share information about youngsters there is no compulsion for anyone to behave in unproductive ways. As the need for façade is obviated progress can begin.

TEACHER-PUPIL RELATIONS: THE COMMITMENT TO INDIVIDUALS

A continuing paradox involves the teacher-pupil relationship. If it is true that student motivation and success are inextricably attached to teacher behavior, one can readily appreciate why beginning instructors are admonished to conduct themselves in accord with the professional ethic. But for such advice to have meaning supposes that teacher preparation programs engender an exposure to a definitive code of ethics, some instruction in relating as a professional. Seldom is this so for, unlike persons entering medicine or law, those who teach are relatively unschooled in matters pertaining to *individual relationships.* This is not to suggest that teachers are insensitive to separate pupils nor that they are unaware of individual importance. Instead, it is to say that for the most part their training has dealt with group relationships and though they have been impressed as to the importance of professional ethics, little beyond its significance is known.

This seeming deficiency may be explained in several ways. One popular view is that appropriate conduct and ethical choice in teaching are so apparent as not to require any special course of instruction. Another faction is convinced that rapport, like other desirable but undefinable attributes, is hopefully attained in our behavior but we never can really expect to understand much about it. In other words, certain people can successfully relate to students while others cannot; you've either got it or you haven't. The important mystical and elusive features of affiliation are independent of training and have to do only with personality. Neither of these two positions is reasonable. To gain the desired rapport teachers need be cognizant regarding ways in which behaviors are mediated for good or ill and possess a repertoire of beneficial influence strategies.

By consulting the maxims of ethics in general one can derive a helpful set of rules by which to guide relations with pupils. The best-known principle of relating is embodied in the famous imperative of Immanuel Kant: "So act as to treat humanity . . . in every case as an end . . . never as a means only . . . ." By insisting that each person be treated as an entity, Kant assumed the individual to have intrinsic value. The injunction charges every person to respect the value of another and always to act with the other person's best interest in mind. In most situations the layman is capable of judging whether he is being treated as an end and if his interests are being served. Self-reliance in judging one's own interests works reasonably well as long as both parties involved have approximately the same background of information. However, this is not the case in situations in which one party is a professional. As the professional (teacher) offering a service knows a great deal more about the particular subject than does a layman (student), the latter is at a decided disadvantage when it comes to determining whether services rendered are in his best interest. Because the pupil's judgment is an inadequate check against the teacher's, it is the teacher who must assume almost sole responsibility for ensuring the fulfillment of Kant's ethic. It means that whenever the term "professional ethics" is used, the adjective "professional" modifies the noun "ethics", not by restricting its content but by adding to the professional's obligation to abide by it (Brubacker, 1962, pp. 222–231).

If the behavior of every teacher were always to correspond with professional ethics there would be no reason for posing these kinds of questions:

Is it ethical to withhold one's service from a pupil, to deny him time and attention while favoring other members of the class?

Is it ethical to establish group performance expectations that are known to be beyond the reach of certain pupils?

Is it ethical to delimit the accomplishments of some pupils so that the teacher's status is not jeopardized?

What does ethics dictate regarding the practice of grading pupils?

Are there ethical considerations in writing letters of recommendation for students?

In what ways do the principles of ethics effect teacher influence on shaping pupil aspirations?

What kinds of ethical judgments should determine disciplinary practices?

Need there be ethical decisions with respect to reporting progress to children?

Until educators can satisfactorily answer this array of inquiry, doubt will flourish, unnecessary mistakes will continue, and children will remain the greatest losers.

Obedience and Authority

Over the years a number of inhumane educational procedures have been sanctioned because they supposedly led to satisfactory outcomes. What has happened is that by justifying the means because of the end, the end itself becomes increasingly more distant and more unrealistic while the reality of the means becomes increasingly obvious and intolerable. For example, since the very survival of society seems to require obedience to authority, schools have tended to be coercive institutions. This tendency is reflected in the orientation of many teachers. In describing the kind of student they prefer, American classroom instructors by and large attach great value to attributes like obedience, industriousness, courteousness, and willingness to accept the judgment of authorities. On the other hand, they look with disfavor upon pupil talkativeness, spirited disagreement, disruption of class procedures and guessing (Torrance, 1963a, 1965a). How these conditions can nurture development of courageousness and informed and loyal citizenship is difficult to comprehend, for they appear designed to depreciate student independence of judgment, divergent thinking, challenge of authoritative position, courage of conviction, curiosity, and asking questions. Although obedience to authority seems essential to the survival of society, at its extreme an insistence upon obedience may destroy the very qualities upon which the desired society depends. No doubt the teacher need for classroom control, power, and status has prevented realization of the danger— a hazard more extended than some would suppose.

Few summers have passed since the Nazi war trials were convened to judge those men accused of crimes against humanity. During the days of court proceedings the world was horrified by testimony describing macabre processions to the death camp ovens and showers of Auschwitz and Dachau. To the international public the accused guards and attendants of concentration camps and gas chambers were guilty and deserved punishment even though the men individually entered a plea of innocence on the grounds that "I did nothing wrong; I simply obeyed orders and did what I was told." History is replete with incidents of this type, all confirming the notion that men will behave monsterously to their fellows in the name of obedience. The record shows that in obedience to the authority of enemy officers some of our own servicemen captured during the Korean conflict behaved in cruel fashion toward comrades. Contemporary studies suggest that obedience for many quite ordinary Americans may be becoming so imbued as to defeat training in ethics, moral conduct, and sympathy for other human beings.

An experiment by Milgram (1963) offers a poignant illustration of the extent to which habits of social conformity can erode humane response. It shows that submission to authority can permit people to perform acts of cruelty on command. Of the forty males Milgram selected for observation, there were represented many occupations and levels of education, with some men having less than an elementary certificate and others holding advanced and professional degrees. The youngest subject was twenty years of age, the oldest was fifty. After being told they were taking part in an experiment involving memory and learning, each individual was separately brought before the experimenter for an interview. The subjects were unaware that the stern and impassive experimenter was being assisted by a mild-mannered colleague who acted as the "victim." The experimenter interviewed each subject and with him the "victim" masquerading as another volunteer. He informed them that the intention was to investigate the effects of punishment on learning and in particular the differential effects of varying degrees of punishment and various types of teachers. In going through the motions of deciding who would play established roles, the drawing of lots was fixed so that in every case the volunteer always was the teacher and the victim always the learner.

After observing the victim being strapped into an impressive-looking electric chair, the teacher volunteer was ushered into an adjoining room where he could no longer see the victim and was faced with a complex instrument panel labeled "shock generator." The output of this generator was shown by thirty switches numbered from 15 volts to 450 volts. Above the various voltage indicators were signs of intensity effect ranging from "slight shock" to "danger," and "severe shock." A 45-volt "slight shock" was administered to each volunteer for purposes of demonstrating the generator's apparent authenticity. During the instructions each volunteer was led to believe that he was to give increasingly more intense punishment to the unseen learner victim in the adjacent room. As prearranged the learner victim gave incorrect responses to three out of four questions and received shocks as punishment for his errors. When the 300-volt level was approached the learner victim began to kick on the wall in his room. Volunteers seeking guidance at this juncture were directed to carry on. At 315 volts the noise continued. Thereafter it was silent and no further answers reappeared on the four-way signal box. Nevertheless, the experimenter encouraged each volunteer to proceed with the punishment until the maximum voltage had been reached.

Contrary to all expectations, twenty-six of the forty volunteers (65 percent) completed the voltage punishment series, actually giving the entire 450 volts to the now silent learner victim in the adjoining room. Only five men refused to go on when at 300 volts the victim's kicking protest was first heard. Most volunteers who continued the punishment were not without reservation. An observing psychologist, unseen by the volunteers, states that some of them remained calm and unmoved while others grew nervous, began to sweat, mutter, or twitch. In one case an initially poised businessman blurted out "Oh, God, let's stop it!" But he, like most of the others, kept responding in obedience to every word of the stern experimenter. Although in obvious conflict, his disposition not to harm the victim was no match for past conditioning, which dictated his obedience to those perceived as legitimate authorities. It would seem that while a majority of the volunteers entertained feelings of sympathy for the learner victim and in certain cases even voiced concern, most men overcame their humane reaction and behaved as less than men. Lest these results be dismissed because there were only forty subjects in the experiment, it should be mentioned that subsequent studies have indicated the same findings with thousands of subjects, with women as well as men (Milgram, 1965).

In reviewing Milgram's experiment, Torrance* writes:

> This entire range of responses is represented in the reactions of teachers who have written me or talked with me about unjust and punitive treatment they have had to administer to some pupils. A majority of them have justified their behavior by saying, ". . . but what could I do? I have to do what my superiors tell me to do!" A few have literally fought for pupils who were unjustly treated. In some cases they had been vindicated and have held their jobs; in other cases they have been fired or placed in an inferior position. A third group, seemingly, have not recognized anything "wrong" about their unjust and inhumane treatment of children.

The Milgram study and Torrance statement dramatize a long-standing need to alter teacher role from authority to guide. Submission of

---

* From E. Paul Torrance, *Constructive Behavior: Stress, Personality and Mental Health* (Belmont, Calif.: Wadsworth Pub. Co., Inc., 1965), pp. 388–89. Reprinted by permission.

the child mind will not permit an adult life of critical thinking, personal option, humane regard, courage, and integrity. Man may renounce much but he must be allowed to think, act, hold convictions and express his thoughts. It is tyranny to compel men not to think as they do, to demand that they express thoughts that are not their own, and to order silence when there is need for expression. Those who would educate should allow students to remain themselves, to keep their individuality and their will, to act on the basis of thought, regard, and reason rather than coercion. For when men can no longer think, they can no longer be led—only driven!

Reversing Coercive Strategies

Perhaps the amount of coercion in classrooms would decline if more teachers were familiar with the ways in which it occurs and the deleterious effect registered upon students. E. Paul Torrance, internationally recognized for research in stress and creativity, has analyzed methods of coercive influence based on records of inquisitions, witchcraft confessions, germ-warfare testimony, thought-reform programs by the Communists during the Korean conflict, and accounts of brainwashing of the native population in Red China (Torrance, 1959a, 1964a; Shein, 1956; Lifton, 1961). In conceptualizing the strategies that men have always used to force others into surrendering beliefs, identity, and even will, it seemed to Torrance (1964a) that encouragement of creative potential would require a reversal of the strategy in each case. It is worthwhile to examine several of these maneuvers with respect to teacher-pupil relationships.

Omnipotence-Omniscience

The temptation to adopt a strategy of omnipotence and omniscience is constantly before educators because of their social role. Resistance becomes more difficult when the community urges teachers to adopt this position. Many parents in attempting to ingrain child respect for learning and the school present an idyllic perception of the teacher exaggerating his authority and store of knowledge. Faced with lofty expectations by students and their families, it is not surprising that a number of instructors succumb to the temptation of adopting an almighty, all-knowing strategy. A first step is to convey to students the suggestion that the teacher knows all about each of them and has final power over them. He has aptitude, achievement, and personality test data, information from previous teachers, parents and classmates, and of course confidential reports from the guidance counselor. This information can be used in the same way that a war enemy uses bits of news gleaned from a captive's hometown paper or fellow prisoners. Students frequently believe that a teacher knows things about them which they themselves do not know. It is precisely this doubt and apprehension on the part of pupils concerning the nature and extent of knowledge a teacher has about them that permits the teacher to option a bluff.

Essentially the psychological function of bluff is to redress the balance between one's own inadequacy and the other person's superiority. The insecure teacher who believes he is expected to know all the answers or supposes that most students need to so believe is likely to employ bluff when he feels threatened by an able student. Generally the teacher justifies bluff by rationalizing that its only purpose is student benefit, in particular to keep the troublesome student in his place and protect him from "getting a big head." That being put on the spot by a youngster might jeopardize the image of omniscience is also given some consideration but supposedly not for oneself, only for the students whose learning might be adversely affected were they to lose confidence in the teacher's ability. So, having prejustified the strategy of bluff as a means for helping the threatening pupil and indirectly the entire class, the teacher begins his act.

Recognize that bluff may be deemed an unnecessary strategy in relating with some able students, especially the grade-oriented who, in becoming "seekers of the right way," have learned to follow teacher dictate without question. However, a few boys and girls will persist in challenging authority, questioning sources of information and pointing to weaknesses in teacher logic. Most members of this difficult group can be controlled through bluff. In private conference the teacher might say, "John, in many ways you are one of my better students but the tendency to interrupt the class bothers me. In considering how to handle the matter, I talked to a number of people who know you and I looked at your cumulative record—and, John, all I can say is that I am somewhat shocked by what I have learned, by what I know now." The teacher is careful not to mention specifics, knowing well that the greatest ally he has is the student's own imagination. At this point tension begins to build within the pupil as he searches his past for a possible embarrassing issue or event. In thinking back upon things he is not proud of and would not wish to have brought into the open, the pupil may reason "But how could he know that? How does anyone else know? Were we seen? What does he really know about me?" Adding to the threat of someone knowing about "the incident" in question is the teacher intimation that suggests "I would hate to reveal this information to your classmates or your parents, John, so don't push me in class or I will be forced to play my ace. Behave, do it my way and we will get along—everything will be all right!" Because the student fears teacher reprisal, he agrees to submit. The teacher retains control; the student has been bluffed.

The role of omniscience is daily enacted before the class during question periods in order to maintain a false image. Since to admit ignorance would not correspond with the intended image, various maneuvers are plied to convince pupils of teacher wisdom. One response to inquiry is snowing the group by referring to information that is either irrelevant or outside the student experience. Generally this exercise in pseudoprofundity is followed by the remark "Does everyone understand?" Because they do not wish to appear lacking, pupils refrain from indicating their lack of comprehension. For some students the fact that the teacher's remarks were incomprehensible is taken as a mark of his genius. Wisdom, of course, can communicate; it is the unwise who would confound the pupil to appear wise. Another tact is to circumvent the questions one is unable to answer by rephrasing student inquiry almost simultaneously so that the new questions correspond with the answers one hoped to offer before he entered class. Again, some students are impressed by this kind of one-way discussion. A third method involves penalizing the curious by regularly returning their inquiry with the injunction "Let's look it up." Implicit in this statement is a hunch that all answers can be found in the library and a promise that the teacher is willing to collaborate. However, it often means that the curious desist in questions after they come to learn each inquiry entails an additional assignment. Underlying each of these unnecessary strategies is the subtle threat of grading, a chance of extra work, or public embarrassment—high prices to pay for wonder. Another example of the omnipotence-omniscience strategy is when the teacher makes a mistake while writing on the board. When corrected she passes it off as something done deliberately by saying, "Very good, John, I wondered if anyone would catch that," or "I did that to see if you were awake." On the other hand, this could be used as an example that no one is perfect and even a teacher can make a mistake.

Omnipotence and omniscience strategies are anachronistic and should be replaced by those characteristic of a guide. This is not to suggest that an instructor abdicate his power as an academician. Instead the guide recognizes that pupil respect can be gained without deception. If teachers are less certain than ever before about answering each question posed it does not follow that they are less effective, for questions are more numerous today, the answers more elusive and complex. To measure the value of a reply only by the certainty with which it has been stated is erroneous. Just as the wise of every intellectual level recognize self-limitation, so the teacher needs accept his own bounds. Humility is a virtue that generally marks the great teacher. The role of guide should not be perceived as demotive. It eliminates a need for teacher presumption and gives students the active role in learning. All pupils need an anchor in reality, some kind of structure, some one or some thing to help them remove fear of the unknown—a guide serves this function. As a guide one can help a boy or girl structure their world by exploring assets and liabilities, becoming aware of sources of information, viewing the feasibility of alternative courses of action, and ascertaining his own best direction.

The Big Lie

Throughout time men have been intimidated by others who resort to "the big lie" as a means for inducing submission. Whether the untruth be a minor distortion of fact or a complete fabrication, the purpose is similar—to undermine the victim's confidence and substitute instead a dependency upon the coercing party. By arousing the student's doubt as to his adequacy, progress, or future well-being, it is possible to reduce or actually eliminate any opposition he might otherwise represent in class. Teachers sometimes use the lie to obtain behavioral conformity from those with a reputation for trouble. The lie has many forms: (1) If you don't stop talking there will be no recess for a week. (2) If you don't shape up, I can't write you a favorable letter of recommendation. (3) If you don't begin to improve, I can't pass you. (4) If you don't bring up the grade in math, we'll have to eliminate your gym period or participation on the football team. While some of these statements may represent intended action, they are in most instances lies to induce submission. Apart from the danger of being inconsistent in a threat situation, teachers should understand that unthreatening words can serve as well as others to carry influence and convey meaning. A somewhat opposite coercive strategy might be called the Big Truth. Whenever a child talks during a teacher-intended time of silence, the pupil is obliged to write "I will not talk" one hundred times.

Well-intentioned teachers perhaps never use the big lie except in special cases to wake up a pupil to the seriousness of his circumstance in hopes of motivating him to adopt a constructive course of action. However, pupils who have a reasonable contact with reality are more likely to be influenced for good purpose by a realistic facing of the probable consequences their actions could bring. Torrance explains that pupil resistance to accepting the seriousness of a danger and adapting may be caused by inadequate structure or anchor in reality.* In such cases educators can assist the student in searching for structure because in order to take adaptive action one needs to know where he stands and what he is to do. An earnest search for the truth is healthy, in fact dangers become less frightening when they are understood and methods for coping with them can be devised. The strategy of recognizing realistic dangers entails helping youngsters project the likely

* From E. Paul Torrance, "What Counselors and Teachers Can Do To Help Others Achieve Their Creative Potential." Paper presented to the South Dakota Guidance Association, South Dakota State University, at Brookings, October, 1964. 21 pp. Excerpts reprinted by permission of the author.

results of various behaviors, discovering the reasons for failure, select-ing tenable alternatives for improvement, gaining acceptance of the need for constructive criticism, and appraising themselves in realistic fashion.

Ego Inflation

The use of ego inflation is often selected as a tactic by coercive agents. In using this strategy one plays upon an individual's need for esteem and then contrives a circumstance in which the person "loses face" unless he submits. After endearing oneself to the victim, the objective is to induce a desired behavior by forcing his protection of ego, his need to remain important in someone's estimate. In the begin-ning one freely magnifies the victim's value by exaggerating his under-standing and intelligence, praising his talents and skills, lauding his poise, sensitivity, and virtue. In most cases the person has never been so charmed or felt so significant. When the victim is fully convinced he is genuinely appreciated in a way and to an extent without prece-dent, then the coercive agent threatens to withdraw the friendship, esteem, or affection unless the relationship is altered. That is, the vic-tim must now prove himself intellectually, emotionally, or through some behavior in compliance with the agent's wishes in order for their association to continue. In short, the initial "VIP" treatment is extended only under certain conditions as the agent "moves in for the kill." Whether this strategy is employed by the enemy toward a prisoner, a college man toward his date, or educators toward pupils, it comes to the same thing—taking unfair advantage of a person's need to be important to someone.

The strategy of ego inflation is understandingly tempting to an inex-perienced teacher who sees it as a useful influence for working with slow learners or excluded children. It is true that students who sus-tain a baneful image of self are easy prey to this tactic but no one wins in a game in which individuals are persuaded to accept an inflated self-image and then challenged to prove the hoped-for image. Though the big lie may be well-intentioned to motivate a youngster, elevate his aspirations, and support the occurrence of achievement, invariably it results in stress, frustration, and disappointment. The sen-sitive teacher will work toward enabling all pupils to feel important as they are without making continued esteem contingent upon aca-demic performance. When respect is related directly to achievement, less able pupils receive a diminishing level of teacher esteem. By mid-year or the end of the term the youngsters who most need support have the least.

Every student has worth aside from school accomplishment; each should be valued for reasons other than academic. Basically the stra-tegy is reversed by replacing ego inflation with respect for human dignity and worth, a concept on which are based the most satisfying of human relationships and interpersonal influences. This is not a simple matter of choice between the untruth of over-estimating a child's ability for motivation's sake or telling him the supposed truth that "he is just a stupid kid who will never amount to anything and that nothing much can be done about it." It is less a question of the truth being damaging than teacher inability to see the truth. Because they measure success in much the same way as they assess student value, some teachers are unable to accept the notion that an unskilled life could be satisfying and worth living, and that its person "might amount to something." This view prompts one to ignore the slow, assign them too difficult work, and reinforce negative self-concept.

But there is a third choice—an option higher than either ego inflation or telling the pupil one's concept of success and the good life, labeling it as "truth." This third choice takes the form of self-questioning: (1) How can I help this boy feel worthwhile as a person? (2) How can I help him assess his weaknesses and strengths? (3) How can he be led to select appropriate goals and achieve in the pursuit of those objectives? Here is the test of a genuine guide whose aspiration for each pupil is that everyone achieve whatever good in life that can be his. Under these conditions the instructor neither ignores the slow and unsuccessful nor will he assign them work that is beyond capability simply to justify a low grade. He lets it be known that he does care and that he is on the student's side. What is more, in a honest way the teacher is able to show pride in pupil gain without recourse to overestimation, exaggeration, and superfluous adjectives. It would seem that the future of many students depends on increasing this kind of teacher relationship.

Powerlessness

Control over another human being comes more quickly when the other person can be made to feel powerless, when he can be confined to concerns of physiological and safety needs. All the techniques for implementing this coercive strategy to imbue incapacity stem from the premise that to break a man down he must first be stripped of defenses and props. Metaphorically this is accomplished in ways analogous to the oldest, most clever and influential trick utilized by captors to make prisoners feel powerless, strip them of their clothes. While teachers do not divest children of garments some have a repertoire of method for stripping students of defenses to make them feel powerless. It may be achieved by constant probing, insisting that one explain the motivation for all that he does; or by an overconcern about student mode of dress, autistic thinking, lack of interest in dating, or feelings of hostility—defenses a pupil may need temporarily against more threatening things. Instead of enduring a powerless state, students should be led to experience self-pride. Whereas feelings of impotence reduce a person to animal concerns, self-esteem can elevate one to human questions. Self-awareness is an effective defense against manipulation by others and against misperception of oneself.

Those who desire self-esteem for students will respect each individual's need for various defenses, realizing that they may be necessary in protecting the pupil from anxiety until skills for coping with the pressure or forces that induce it have been developed. For example, working with four- and five-year-olds requires an understanding of the need for children of this age to depreciate the performance of others for self-power. Adults dealing with high school students should understand the necessity to rationalize as characteristic of the adolescent. In the junior high school, concern about body image, perhaps pimples, is diminished through what could appear as excessive daydreaming. To expect the adult response before adulthood is to reveal one's bias for magic. Able teachers respect the need of young people for privacy, the manner of dress and speech, or whatever prop may temporarily have been adopted to help control inner tensions and cope with environmental demands. At the same time a guide can assist each pupil in becoming aware of the reaction others have to his unusual behavior and its consequence. The self-pride strategy is implemented by being respectful of student questions and ideas, helping individuals recognize the worth of their own thinking, encouraging the use of unique strengths, establishing group standards in which its members can take pride, keeping personal information confidential, letting students "save face," and recognizing improved performance.

Friendly Enemy

Another coercive strategy is to influence a student to perceive his social environment as hostile and then communicate a notion that the teacher is his only real friend. Often this necessitates setting up a situation in which peer hostility is generated toward certain members. In one class students are urged to report their fellows who misbehave on the playground, in the lunchroom, or in the lavatory. By pupil definition those acting as informers are "ratting" and no longer deserve acceptance or esteem. After a pupil has been excluded, the teacher instills the idea that he alone remains the pupil's friend; a dependent submissive relationship generally follows. Another situation involves a teacher who, seeking to control group behavior by supposed motivational techniques, unintentionally creates conditions for pupil rejection. Some of the practices producing this consequence include giving special privileges to particular students, having selected pupils always perform the coveted tasks, and consistently referring to the work or behavior of one student as the exemplary standard. One might argue that these procedures are desirable if they achieve the intended teacher purpose of motivating the class, bestowing self-esteem and status for meritorious performance. But in many classrooms such rewards actually nourish antipathy and earn for the recipient a label of "teacher's pet." What was intended to be rewarding for him turns out, in fact, to be punishing. Peer reaction to a student perceived as teacher-favored depends of course on group norms. In low-income neighborhoods, the individual may run the risk of greater repercussion than merely being given an embarrassing label (Strom, 1965c, p. 40).

Reversing the strategy of hostile environment implies that students be helped to view their class as favorable. Considering the influence peers have on self-concept and the almost universal tendency among youngsters to rely on age-mates for support during the difficult years of growing up, it would seem prudent for educators to encourage acceptance by the class of all its members. In the future pupils may need to learn more from one another than is now the case. So rather than attempting to destroy cliques and groups out of fear for their negative influence or threat to his control, the teacher should determine to improve group functioning, especially its use of power over members. A teacher can help students understand that there can be cohesion without submission, loyalty without compromise, and that a group can succeed as a body without coercing its own members. Within the instructional groups one can show that there are more healthy company purposes than to dissuade members from their opinion toward a one-view philosophy that denies individuality. Also there is no need to vote on every issue to determine collective action and when ballot is invoked it should be understood that the majority view is not a dictate. In other words, prerogatives are allowed to the minority as long as their option is within the purpose of the larger group. In this fashion youngsters come to tolerate and respect divergent behavior among themselves without threat of ridicule or exclusion. It is soon recognized that one can belong and still retain his unique identity; he need not always conform and be the same as others. Indeed, were we all the same, some of us would be unnecessary. By helping the student group function without sacrifice to the individuality of its members, the teacher guide does not lose power, he gains respect. At the same time the group is allowed its power and reason—a combination favoring the kind of society to which we all aspire.

The forms of coercion are many and none of them belongs in the classroom. Our schools need fewer teachers who pretend omniscience and omnipotence, fewer teachers who would have students feel powerless, fewer teachers who would resort to the big lie and ego inflation, fewer teachers who would destroy, manipulate, or render cleavage in the group association of youth. Our schools need fewer teachers whose principal objective is to force compliance, obedience, and submission. These are not the goals nor qualities of an adequate teacher. To be sure, authority has a place in growth but where authority would deny the value of individual contribution, there it is tyranny. In school we dare not take away that which we are charged to nurture; no one can sanction the theft of mind. If we would have reason rule the adult life of students, it must first be allowed to develop. Critical thinking cannot be a privilege reserved for adults alone; else no adult will possess it. The mind of the young must remain their own if they would be free.

CHAPTER IV

Learning Theory,
A Resource for Method

Learning theory antedates psychology, for throughout time men have entertained notions about the ways in which information is acquired and cultural demands are assimilated. Because educators rely upon instructional strategies for modifying pupil behavior, the dominant views of learning during every era have greatly influenced teaching method and school practice. It might be said that whatever a teacher does is predicated on some theory of learning. Many of the historic guiding theorems fell to disfavor quickly; others persisted over hundreds of years, becoming traditions before they were finally dislodged; only a few theories remain in good standing today. Yet the schools continue to show signs of residual influence from archaic views that have long since been proven erroneous. The purpose of this chapter is to examine several theories of learning and consequent teaching methods that have attained widespread recognition and acceptance during the nineteenth and twentieth centuries. By restricting the focus to Faculty theory, Connectionism, and Gestalt, the intention is not to imply that other positions have been without favor or effect; it is to submit that the selected theories were predominant and most contributive.

FACULTY THEORY

Faculty theory has been called the most comprehensive error in human thought. Over the years perhaps more teachers have accepted its basic premise and instructional implications than all the other views of learning combined. And, while the theory stands in scientific disrepute today, one can infer from classroom observation that it is still very much alive in the determination of pedagogic method.

For the sake of convenience, it is said that we remember, decide, compare, or judge; these may be names for distinct functions of the mind or merely useful labels denoting complex mental processes. To reduce the intellect into discrete functions or trait units, facultists postulate that mind is the psychical correlate of body. In other words, just as the body has physical qualities, so too by analogy the mind must possess psychical attributes. Because the arm and leg have separate and unique purposes, the faculties of mind must have specific functions like feeling, knowing, and willing. During the nineteenth century craniologists expanded the number of supposed faculties to include reasoning, judgment, memory, understanding, and other mental characteristics. Tracing the faculty theory influence on the development of craniology, later known as phrenology, is more than an account of bizarre improvisation. It is the story of how medical men were startled out of their complacent neglect of the brain and nervous system; only after this had been accomplished could man develop knowledge of his mental processes and enable the methods of teachers to become appropriate.

FROM FICTION TO SCIENCE

Although Franz Gall was a man of science by intention and training, he was also the victim of a boyhood obsession. When he was nine years old, Gall first observed that those among his classmates who most showed retentive capacity had bulging eyes. While the reason for this relationship was elusive, he concluded that the secret of a good memory was possession of projecting eyes. Later (1781), as a beginning medical student at the University of Vienna, Gall sought to test his theory by making inquiries about scholars with conspicuous eyes. In his own words, "They boasted excellent verbal memories and had the advantage of me when the object was to learn by rote." Confirmation from observations by fellow students convinced Gall that there was evidence to support the hunch about a link between recollection and eye projection (Combe, 1834, pp. 22, 23). But to prove this would require knowing much more about the brain that lay behind the eyes and as yet no lectures on the subject were offered in medical schools. Instead, the interest of most physicians centered on the heart and lungs; no one bothered with the brain and skull—no one, that is, except Franz Gall, who after collecting them from postmortem rooms spent many nights in measuring, comparing, studying, and wondering.

Gall reasoned that if the eyes are swelled and the forehead is prominent, the frontal part of the brain behind the forehead must be enlarged. Thus in cases of well-developed recall the eyes are pushed forward by the memory organ located behind the eyes. At church, scanning the kneeling congregation, the young scholar noted that heads of the most devout had a marked development of the crown; at that point must be located the organ of veneration. Further observation revealed that his quarrelsome and pugnacious companions all had wide skulls in the temporal region. If memory, veneration, and combativeness are represented by skull contour, might the same be expected of the other faculties? Maybe each organ makes its own separate imprint on the skull. So intriguing was this prospect that Gall set out to investigate whether mental faculties can be determined from contours of the skull. By frequenting social events it was possible for him to observe the cranial structure of well-known persons, individuals with a reputation for accomplishment, and persons of the rising class. Whenever Gall's request was honored in school, prison, or asylum, he measured and examined heads (Winkler and Bromberg, 1939, pp. 10, 11).

Upon fingering the skulls of pickpockets at the prison, he found them all to have a certain part of the head enlarged. Gall concluded that under these bumps, titled the knobs of acquisitiveness, thriving instincts are at work. Located at the back of the skull, the bump of adhesiveness, or "seat of attachment," as it came to be called, was named after examining a woman known for her many friendships. A bulge on the temple of a five-year-old musical prodigy located tune; ideality or imagination was found in that part of the head touched by the fingers when man contemplates (see Figure IV-2). One day Gall encountered a beggar who, having squandered away a fortune, could not humble himself to work. Upon discovering a peculiar projection on the beggar's skull, Gall remembered the same bump on the bald head of an Austrian prince who consistently spoke of his noble birth. It seemed that prince and pauper suffered from an overdevelopment of pride (Jastrow, 1935, p. 296). To make sure of this diagnosis, Gall hastened to the insane asylum where, as visiting physician, he could check on an inmate whose pride was reflected in the boast of being queen of France. But the anticipated swelling was absent, and in Gall's words, "This embarrassed me at first until I reflected that among the insane pride is really vanity." Out of necessity, vanity's district was discovered beside and below the bump of pride. One by one as the number of identified qualities grew, they were incorporated into Gall's plaster busts which mapped the uncharted regions of the cranium. During this period he spent much time examining the death masks of famous artists, statesmen, soldiers, and writers that he had collected. At one point it is estimated that Gall had acquired approximately three hundred skulls of persons whose known mental characteristics were studied in relation to skull contours.

Gall recognized that even though he was without peer in knowledge of the skull, he knew little of the brain and practically nothing of the mind. Hoping that his anatomical studies, combined with an understanding of the developing "theory of cognition," would enable him to unlock the secret of how people learn, the young physician began to read assiduously about the mind. He was particularly impressed with the work of John Locke (1732), the English philosopher who suggested that thought is built of sensations to which is added mental reflection. This seemed reasonable, since the five senses represent man's only contact with the outside world. As a doctor Gall knew that impulses from the sense organs are transmitted by nerve fibers that terminate in the spinal cord and brain. Yet this explanation failed to account for the higher perceptions and sentiments of human beings. It was hypothesized that man's higher faculties are probably resident somewhere in the brain but determining the exact location promised to be a difficult task since no medical attention had been focused upon this organ. To begin with, Gall traced the fiber elements of the spinal cord up to the cerebral hemispheres and showed how they connect with the gray matter of the brain. Then, instead of slicing the brain, it was unfolded. After hours of dissection, he learned that the white matter was a continuation of the fiber tracts emanating from the spinal cord. Atop the white matter lay the gray like a folded cap, the folds termed convolutions (Winkler and Bromberg, 1939, p. 15). The revelation that the brain is more than a pulpy mass encased in a hard skull was to have many implications. For one thing, medicine could no longer ignore the brain; Gall would never be forgotten as in his work lay a sound basis for neurology. The year was 1796.

FROM SCIENCE TO FICTION

Within a short time, Gall began to offer lectures describing his science of cranial anatomy to large numbers of visiting physicians. Unresponsive to protocol and reluctant to leave his growing audience, Gall declined the Austrian emperor's invitation to become crown physician. Little did he know that the supposed friend whom he recommended in his stead would convince the king that Gall regularly jeopardized the court at Vienna in his lectures by uttering blasphemies against God and the church. As a consequence, in 1800 the lectures were interdicted by the government as being too dangerous to religion. This ban by the authorities had the unintended effect of greatly stimulating public curiosity and increasing Gall's celebrity. The restrictive censure also had the effect of forewarning its subject of the troubles yet to come, for in 1805 an imperial edict forced him to leave his native Austria.

Still confident of the developing cranial science but wary of further attack, Gall adopted a defense strategy in his lectures throughout Germany. The speeches in Berlin, Dresden, Magdeburg, and several other university towns were extremely successful because the usual recitation and dissection demonstrations were supplemented by a citation of supportive evidence; the critics were answered about the religious implications of craniology; the distinction between cranial science and that of physiognomy was explained; and new hypotheses were introduced. Each of these arguments will be considered in turn.

Ever mindful of the religious charges that led to his exile from Austria, Gall deemed it wise to quote the venerable Immanual Kant's (1724–1804) allied views with respect to faculty theory. At the time few people would dispute the great philosopher's judgment that the ultimate moral and religious reality lies not in the field of knowledge but in the process of will. Kant's adoption of the faculty theory was necessary to permit his assumption that willing and feeling are each quite separable from knowledge, a separation that made the process of will independent of causality; it made the will free to act without the control of feelings. According to Kant the *intellect* faculty remembers and analyzes; *feelings* sense pleasure and pain; and the *will* is responsible for behavior. Ever since Kant issued sanction to the notion that there are three great subdivisions of mental activity, psychologists have studied his rationale. Analysis of the process of knowing is set forth in Kant's *Critique of Pure Reason* (1781); the process of feeling and willing are treated in *Critique of Judgment* (1790) and the *Critique of Practical Reason* (1788).

Because the label "physiognomist" was bitterly resented by Gall, he utilized every opportunity to deny that cranial science was in any way related to the lay mystique of reading traits by facial features. To him traits were the operation of organs in the brain that could be known about only through prominences of the skull. In contrast, the concept of physiognomy originated with a treatise attributed to Aristotle, who reportedly read character by noting animal resemblance, accepting the proposition that human faces with animallike features imply the corresponding traits (see Figure IV-1). By that principle individuals possessed of a thick bulbous nose like a pig's will reflect that animal's lack of sensibility; a sharp-tipped nose like a dog's indicates the irritable disposition of a snarling snapping canine; a large, round, blunt nose like a lion's reveals magnanimity; and a slender-hooked nose like an eagle's is the sign of a noble though grasping nature (Jastrow, 1935, p. 248). The cult of physiognomy might have represented only a minor problem to Gall had it not gained a renaissance just previous to his own fame. Under the leadership of Johann Lavater (1741–1801), a Swiss theologian, there appeared a popular five-volume moral work *Essays in Physiognomy* (1789), with portraits of eminent men depicting in their features the known qualities of their personalities. It was when Lavater's physiognomy was at its height that the world learned of a different solution to the sources of human traits—Gall's craniology.

Each of Gall's hypotheses was advanced with a preface designed to delimit resistance. His German audience was first reminded that clinical investigations had removed the last vestige of doubt about the brain being the seat of mental life. Though names went unmentioned, most everyone

Fig. IV-1. Character signs in animal resemblances. From a sixteenth-century work by Gianbattista della Porta. From *Wish and Wisdom* by Joseph Jastrow, D. Appleton Century Co., New York, 1955, p. 246. Reprinted by permission.

in the crowd felt embarrassed that the visiting speaker was obviously referring to the disproved theory of their noted medical leader, Sommerling, who less than a decade before had claimed that the only purpose of the pulpy brain mass is to secrete fluid. Sommerling had gone so far as to infer from his experiments with hydrocephalics (someone with water on the brain) that the amount of fluids secreted is an index of intelligence. This inference along with the lay notion that the soul flows as a fluid into ventricles of the brain was no longer acceptable. The fundamental point at issue, Gall explained, was whether the big brain (cerebrum) operated as a whole or whether its areas were specifically apportioned to sight, hearing, speech, manipulation, and so forth. Increasing anatomical evidence seemed to support Gall's thesis of localization. For example, when applying direct stimulation to specific areas on the exposed brains of animals, it was learned that definite movements are registered in the digits, forelegs, hindlegs, or the head. Systematically, the nerve pathways from the several sense organs had been traced and seemed to lead uniformly to different brain areas with the eyes to the rear of the head and the ears to the temple region.

The explanation of Gall regarding localization of brain function was so convincing that few argued when later, without anatomical evidence, he took the liberty to assign theoretical properties to unknown areas of the brain. Soon there were centers isolated for reasoning in the frontal lobes because in contrast to animals, men have the power to reason, ostensibly accounting for the greater development of our frontal lobes. Using the same rationale, speech was located in the parietal lobes. There was even supposed to be a difference in the location of written and spoken language. But it was one thing to suggest that memory lies in the forebrain, and quite another to depart from science by finding appropriate seats in minute corners of the brain for all of man's supposedly fundamental traits like kindness, physical love, imitation, sadness, jealousy and modesty (Murphy, 1949, pp. 56, 57).

The zenith of Gall's fame was reached in 1807 when he took up residence in Paris to serve as physician, lecturer, and writer. Accompanying him was Johann Spurzheim, an assistant whom he had tutored in Vienna before the German sojourn. Dr. Spurzheim, formerly a divinity student, would prove to be a thorn in Gall's side when later the young man started his own campaign to achieve eminence. For the moment, however, the two engaged in a profitable lecture tour. Gall would explain to the crowd that the cavity of the skull visibly fits the mass of substances it contains and follows the faculty growth at every age of life. Thus the exterior form of the brain, which imprints itself perfectly on the internal surface of the skull, is at the same time a model of the contours of the exterior surface. Since the degree to which any trait is developed depends upon the hereditary development of the appropriate brain area, such developments tend to exert local pressure on the skull and to press it outward in the form of a bump or prominence. By feeling the skull with the fingers, one can detect those regions in which there is rich endowment, thus making possible an analysis of an individual's chief traits. Just before Spurzheim entered the arena, everyone was reminded that the brain is definitely divided into nearly forty distinct function centers separated from one another just as a map would divide the states of a country. Then, as the lecturer proceeded to elaborate on each of the discrete faculties, propensities, and sentiments, Spurzheim would carefully outline the referrent area on a demonstration cast skull. In the audience furtive hands touched their own heads as the bumps were described. The faculties and propensities each had such enchanting names and their diagnosis was so simple once an individual had located his knobs. In time the number of faculties grew to 83. See Figure IV-2.

On several occasions Gall agreed to public confrontation with the academic skeptics. In one case he was shown a skull, given no identifying information, and requested to describe the deceased. After approximating the person's age, he indicated it was the skull of a woman who during her lifetime had suffered an absence of philoprogenitiveness (mother love). Members of the audience were amazed when the skull was identified as that of Madame de Sevigne, the famed French writer whose impersonal letters to her daughter had become a literary prize. Again history agreed with Gall. Soon men of society took delight in having their skulls carved on snuff boxes; organizations devoted to craniology flourished; many stipulated in their wills that they wished their heads given to Gall. Before long he was personal physician to ten ambassadors and the man of the

Fig. IV-2. The Phrenological Head: Names, numbers and location of the organs. From *Practical Phrenology* by Orson S. Fowler, New York: Fowler & Wells, 1857, pp. 64–67.

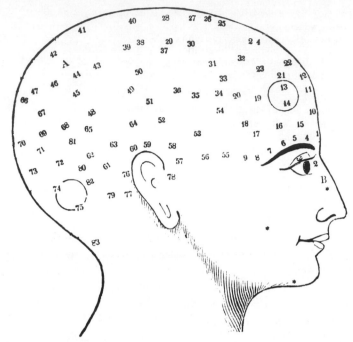

1. *Individuality.* Observation, curiosity to see things, the noticing faculty.
2. *Form.* Recollection of things by their shape, of countenances, &c.
3. *Language.* Three organs: one for expressing ideas, connected with Ideality; another for merely talking, without saying anything, called garrulity; and a third, for remembering names.
4. *Size.* Cognizance and judgment of magnitude, bulk, proportion, large and small, &c.
5. *Weight.* The balancing faculty; application of the laws of gravity.
6. *Color.* Perception, appreciation, and judgment of colors.
7. *Order.* System; arrangement; having a place for things, and things in their places.
8. *Number.* Ability and disposition to count.
9. *Calculation.* Mental arithmetic; casting accounts in the head, computing numbers.
10. *Eventuality.* Recollection of facts, events, occurrences, experiments, history, news, information, circumstances, business transactions, &c: two organs— one for remembering the scenes of childhood; the other, for recollecting recent transactions and information.
11. *Comparison of physical things*—Comparing those things of which the perceptive faculties take cognizance.
12. *Comparison of Ideas.* Discrimination, power of analyzing, illustrating, criticizing, generalizing, reasoning by indication, &c.
13. *Causality.* Power of thought; reasoning by inference; perception and application of the laws of cause and effect; conception of ideas, investigation; philosophical reasoning.
14. *Planning.* Adapting means to ends; contrivance, perceiving the shortest, surest way to effect purposes; the committee of ways and means.
15. *Locality.* Two organs; recollecting places, and love of travelling.
16. *Time.* Recollecting when things occurred; keeping time in the head; the beat in music, dancing, &c.

17. *Tune.* Disposition to sing; catching tunes by rote, or by the ear.
18. *Musical Harmony.* Perception and love of the higher qualities of music.
19. *Wit.* Repartee, perceiving and manufacturing jokes, retorts, etc., arguing by ridicule.
20. *Laughter.* Merriment; laughing easily, much, and heartily.
21. *Suavity.* Politeness; disposition to say and do things agreeably.
22. *Physiognomy.* Discernment of character; reading the characters of men from their countenances, conversation, &c; managing men.
23. *Flattery.* Disposition to praise, compliment, commend, &c.
24. *Kindness.* Disposition to do favors, oblige, serve, &c; active benevolence.
25. *Pity.* Sympathy for the distressed, commiseration.
26. *Gratitude.* Grateful for favors received; a thankful, grateful spirit.
27. *Deference.* Submission to superiors; homage, respect for age and worth; diffidence; dependence on the great and learned.
28. *Veneration.* Devotion; worship of a Supreme Being; religious awe.
29. *Faith.* Trust in Divine providence, and following its guidance.
30. *Credulity.* Belief in wonders, fish-stories, the strange, novel, &c.
31. *Imitation.* Ability and disposition to copy, take pattern, draw; imitate the ways of others; do after them; sketch; learn by being shown once, &c.
32. *Mimicry.* Ability to mock, caricature, represent, personify, &c.
33. *Sadness.* The lonely, sad, sorrowful, bad feeling, without cause.
34. *Taste.* Refinement; elegance of manners and expression; neatness of person; disgust of the coarse and vulgar; sense of propriety; gracefulness.
35. *Ideality.* Imagination; fancy; conception of the beautiful; the love of poetry, fiction, &c, and disposition to make them; reverie.
36. *Cheerfulness.* A contented, joyous, happy, cheerful feeling.
37. *Hope.* Expectation; anticipation; enterprise; looking at the bright side of the prospect; hoping against hope; counting chickens before they are hatched; never letting well enough alone.
38. *Conscientiousness.* Justice; disposition to do right; integrity, honesty; fairness; sense of moral obligation.
39. *Sense of obligation and duty towards God.*
40. *Firmness.* Decision; perseverance; stability; unity of purpose.
41. *Self-Esteem.* Self-confidence; self-assurance; ambition to do and be something great, noted, and extraordinary; aspiration after eminence; dignity.
42. *Self-Will.* Love of liberty; disposition to rule one's self; insubordination; unwillingness to serve or obey, or be under another; desire to be in business for our-self; assuming the responsibility of our own actions; love of power; a domineering spirit; determination to do as one pleases and have his own way in spite of consequences.
43. *Regard for Character.* Standing, honor, estimation, a good name, &c.
44. *Love of Display.* Fashion, style, etiquette, splendor of equipage, &c.
45. *Jealousy.* Desire to be the sole object of regard, affection, praise, &c.; spirit of rivalry, emulation, &c., desire to excel others; out do all; be noticed, &c.
46. *Fruitfulness.* This faculty makes the male sure in begetting, and the female go her full time.
47. *Continuity.* Dwelling on and pouring over one thing; the plodding, prosing, continuous disposition; patience in examining, collating, comparing, &c.
A. *Modesty.* Bashfulness; shame-facedness; blushing easily.
48. *Physical Fear.* Carefullness, caution as to dangers, losses, etc.
49. *Moral Fear.* Fear of the consequences of doing wrong, offending the Deity, &c.
50. *Guardedness.* As to papers, expression, &c.; circumspection.
51. *Combination.* Partnership; disposition to unite in business.
52. *Money-Making.* Trading; dealing largely; driving a big business.
53. *Economy.* Frugality; saving money; contracting expenses; hoarding; husbanding for the future.
54. *Ingenuity.* Dexterity in using tools, making things, turning off work, making and working machinery, etc.; building; slight of hand in all manual operations.

55. *Smell.* Love of fragrant odors, and aversion to those that are disagreeable.
56. *Thirst.* Disposition to drink; love of the water.
57. *Appetite.* Enjoyment of food; hunger; relish for food.
B. *Taste.* Love of richly-flavored and highly-seasoned delicacies.
58. *Retribution.* Revenge; disposition to punish or have satisfaction.
59. *Destructiveness.* Disposition to break, destroy; cause pain, hurt, tease, tantalize, deface, &c.
60. *Anger.* Resentment; spirit; contention.
61. *Resistance.* Self-defense; self-protection; defense of rights.
62. *Courage.* Self-possession and coolness in personal danger; intrepidity; bravery, valor.
63. *Tattling.* Telling the faults of others; when ungoverned, slander, back-biting; evil-speaking; town-talk; gossip.
64. *Secretiveness.* Management; artifice; keeping secrets; self-restraint; evasiveness; reserve.
65. *Dislike.* Aversion; dissatisfaction; fault-finding; peevishness; grumbling.
66. *Love of Home.* Attachment to the domicile of childhood and youth; love of the old homestead—of "father's house," etc.; desire to have a place of our own.
67. *Patriotism.* Love of country, and a more recent habitation.
68. *Adhesiveness.* Friendship; love of company; attachment to friends; the companionable, social, cordial, warm-hearted feeling.
69. *Love of Keepsakes.* Of presents, remembrances, etc.
70. *Parental Love.* Attachment of parents to their own children; desire to caress and pet them.
71. *Filial Love.* Love of children to their parents, or those who provide for, watch over, and advise them.
72. *Connubial Love.* Love of husbands and wives for each other.
73. *Love of Pets.* Of horses, dogs, stock, etc., and desire to improve the breed; the feeling of the shepherd.
74. *Caressing.* Pure love between the sexes; disposition to hug, kiss, caress, fondle, etc.
75. *Physical love.* Animal passion; the sexual impulse, lust.
76. *Love of life.* Enjoyment of existence; tenacity of life.
77. *Dread of Death.* Shrinking from death and annihilation.
78. *Buffoonery.* Low, comical wit; clownish sport; revelry.
79. *Organ that controls the motion of the limbs.*
80. *Organ of the Heart.*
81. *Organ of Respiration.*
82. *Organ of Digestion.*
83. *Organ of Motion.* The great center or common pole of all the muscles; desire and ability to act, or be doing something.

hour. But unlike his associate Spurzheim, who was enamored with public attention, Gall longed for only two things—to complete his writing task and to become a member of the French Academy of Science. The first aspiration he could accomplish himself but the second would never come to pass—his assistant, medical colleagues, and eventually even Napoleon would see to it that it would not.

When finally permitted a membership hearing in the Academy, Gall and his anatomical studies were carefully investigated by the best known of French scientists. Heading the five-man committee was the brilliant experimentalist Pierre Flourens, whose work with the animal brain some years later (1824, 1842) would disprove Gall's thesis. Even at the time of Gall's membership inquiry, Flourens was inclined to believe that the little brain at the back of the skull, the cerebellum, was responsible for controlling locomotion. In reply to this suggestion, Gall reiterated his position that the function of the area in question was amativeness, regulating affection, not gait. But though Flourens was able to point out a number of weaknesses in the candidate's judgment about brain functioning, he nonetheless held Gall in high esteem for his dissection experiments. In Flourens own words: "I shall never forget the impression received the first time I saw Gall dissect a brain. It seemed to me as if I had never seen this organ before." The committee favored Gall for membership and would have admitted him as a fellow were it not for an imperial dictum to the contrary. Napoleon rejected the Viennese doctor on several accounts. First of all, chauvinism was at a peak, which meant that the content and leadership in French science needed to be indigenous to France. Then too, the emperor felt slighted that the crown physician, Corvisart, spent so much time and interest in Gall's enterprise; last, and certainly not least, it was well known that in Gall's estimation Napoleon's head lacked the signs of greatness and in fact showed an overdevelopment of ambition and cruelty.

Under the circumstance, every attempt was made to discredit Gall. Many critics eager to obtain imperial approval invented bizarre stories about the physician, attributing to him the most disgusting of intentions. But this approach, sufficient to persuade the public, would not accomplish a breach between the medical world and Gall. Something more than rumor and innuendo was needed to convince the educated. Since the craniologist so often referred to his studies with inmates of prison and asylum, it was decided that he should meet Phillipe Pinel in public debate on the causes of insanity. The outcome of this encounter was determined before it took place. As expected, Gall elaborated on faculty activity, suggesting that the etiology of mania stems from an overdevelopment of combativeness while an underdevelopment of hope is perhaps the base of depressive states.

Pinel, a revered man who had won distinction in the classification of mental disorders, was a leader in the humanitarian movement and in 1792 became Director of the Bicêtre, an institution for the insane in Paris. After describing the brutalities to which mentally ill and criminally insane persons were still subject, Pinel argued that in an age of enlightenment, barbarism should cease; that capital punishment is an inappropriate penalty for petty crime; and that a wise society might correct its wrong-doers rather than punish them by inflicting pain under the guise of retribution (Murphy, 1949, pp. 39–41). He maintained that the two factors most responsible for continued injustice toward deranged persons are the conception of original sin and an emphasis on free will—both of these theses make each individual solely responsible for his delinquent behavior. But when men are poor and without food, they steal because of a stomach demand and not because of a longstanding skull bump of destructiveness.

The etiology of mental despair or jealous abnormality can more reasonably be traced to the pressure of adverse circumstance than to a mythology of bumps. Pinel was respected; his message convincing; he won the case.

In spite of mounting criticism, Gall remained confident that history would one day justify his conclusions. So, instead of seeking vindication he chose to begin the monumental writing task that would course ten years and issue six volumes. His great work *The Anatomy and Physiology of the Nervous System,* completed in 1819, was subtitled *Together with Observations on the Possibility of Determining Mental and Moral Qualities in Men and Animals by the Contours of Their Heads.* Together science and fiction are incompatible but for Gall they could not be divorced. His manuscript served to illustrate that one can accumulate an impressive array of evidence to support even a false premise. It is true, however, that whatever science there was in the doctrine was valuable and in time would earn for Gall an honorable place in the annals of medicine.

THE SPURZHEIM DOCTRINE

When Gall went into seclusion, Spurzheim grew discontented. He missed the crowds, the travel, and the excitement. So long as he was enveloped by public admiration the station of assistant was acceptable. But things had changed and the new conditions offered less appeal and reward. If Gall wished to retire or retreat, that was up to him; but for Spurzheim, still a relatively young man of 34, it appeared that new fortunes had yet to be won. He could make it by himself, establish his own doctrine, perhaps even rival the master in reputation. Given the rising tide of humanitarianism it seemed feasible to depart from Gall's teachings and instead to accommodate moral purpose by appending the list of supposed faculties with respected and desirable traits. One by one the bumps of benevolence, pity, gratitude, and faith appeared along with other culture-favored propensities and sentiments. Encouraged by public reaction to his initial presentations, Spurzheim prepared for an extended speaking tour of England (1813). And there, armed with the confidence of a winner, he gained many converts in traveling from town to town. Within weeks he was claiming from the podium that certain of the anatomical discoveries attributed to Gall were really his own. He also coined a new term to replace craniology; henceforth the truth would be known as *phrenology* (Combe, 1834, pp. 72, 73).

Years before Spurzheim had become a doctor, he was a divinity student with zealous intentions of guiding public conduct. Undoubtedly this long-standing desire was influential in the development of phrenology; the new message clearly focused upon moral principles. At a glance Spurzheim reportedly could identify the hypocrite and the sensual; he could measure the district of pride and the scope of vanity; he had the power to detect the extent of moral fear as well as discern one's amount of faith. Without hesitation this newly popular figure advertised a readiness to assist men in the selection of appropriate wives, communities in the choice of government and religious leaders, teachers in the method of instructing children, and authorities in the analysis of crime and mental disorder. Under Spurzheim's guidance supposedly anyone could expect to analyze his own character. Had phrenology been as useful as its claim, as genuine as its promise, many of our problems might be averted and others quickly resolved; psychology would be an unnecessary science and Spurzheim revered as the greatest contributor to knowledge in all time. As it is he enjoys a more dubious distinction, for the phrenological head symbolizing his work serves less as an accurate map of human faculties than it does a reminder of man's abuse of his power to think (see Figure IV-2).

Even though phrenology lacked reason, the movement was not without impact. Alarmed by the growing number of persons in support of false doctrines, Pope Pius VII in 1817 excommunicated all who would teach phrenology. For a while this censure fostered an increase of public curiosity but then Paris closed its gates to Spurzheim and his followers; before long other cities did the same. Naturally, in the minds of certain critics Gall was judged responsible for the misdeeds of his onetime assistant. Few remembered that it was the older man who years earlier had turned the medical mind away from supernatural explanations of the human soul to an organic explanation of mental and moral characteristics. Nevertheless, Gall continued to bear the brunt of insult and blame regarding Spurzheim's misconduct—in fact, criticism was still being heaped upon Gall in 1828 at the time of his death, the victim of a weak heart and a wayward discipline.

At about this time Ralph Waldo Emerson wrote from America, "We are all a little wild here with numerous projects of social reform. There is not a reading man without the draft of a new community in his pocket." Indeed the United States seemed receptive to prophets of almost every kind from hypnotists to evangelists, temperance men to abolitionists, freethinkers to Mormons. The real truth was claimed by Holy Rollers and perfectionists alike; the theosophists and revivalists both advised men how to live; Millerites and Mesmerites alike could prophesy the future. From the pulpit and the public hall came appeals and pronouncements about religion, socialism, transcendentalism, naturalism, and spiritualism—many causes each of which gained a following. Then on August 23, 1832, the *Boston Transcript* carried news about the arrival of another prophet— "Dr. Spurzheim, the celebrated phrenologist, has arrived in this city."

If he lacked honor at home, the Viennese physician made up for it abroad as huge crowds attended the 50-cent lectures offered in Boston, New York, and Philadelphia. Not only could the visiting foreigner discern the talents and dispositions of men but he could also measure them with exactitude and precision from external appearances of the skull. Soon all eyes focused on the heads of neighbors. Some women designed hair styles in such a way as to display their bumps of mirthfulness high on each side of the head while curls modestly concealed the nave of the neck where amativeness is located. Everything was going so well for the visitor when suddenly Spurzheim was stricken with typhus fever; three weeks later—November 10, 1832—he died. It is difficult to overestimate the social impact made by this man in less than three months of American residence. As one reporter covering the funeral wrote: "Dr. S. was extensively known not only in Europe but in this country and was proportionately respected and esteemed. He was the most eminent foreign scholar that has ever died among us."

Although the story of craniology and phrenology died with Spurzheim, it is interesting to note that within two years (1834) a host of charlatans revived the error after seeing its prospect as a big business. Headquarters were established in New York City and the presses began to publish guides to character, with one book reportedly selling more than 5,000 copies in three months.

Education and the Faculty View

Certainly Gall and Spurzheim were not the only facultists to achieve fame, but it was largely their influence that elevated the idea of a compartmentalized mind into academic and public favor. After that, without learned resistance, the faculty view reached into nearly every domain of nineteenth-century life, including its classrooms. Teachers in public schools received a new and comprehensive charge—to ensure development of the socially desired innate faculties, propensities, and sentiments and at the same time discourage or restrict any manifestation of less accepted attributes. A simple rationale for accomplishing this purpose involved the analogy of mind-body functions. Just as various parts of the body require muscular exercise to grow strong, so faculties of the mind may be expected to increase in power by mental exercise. According to Spurzheim, (1883, p. 89) "The influence of exercise on the functions of the five senses is generally known and admitted. It is the same with internal faculties manifested by means of different parts of the brain. Each mental power, if it be sufficiently cultivated, grows more energetic while if neglected it shows less activity."

Because the process of learning was considered to be essentially a matter of mental calisthenics, a premium was attached to whatever scholastic endeavors required great effort. Assuming that courses presenting the most difficulty would obviously be the better exercisers, they were held in high regard and recommended for every would-be scholar. In fact, for optimal intellectual development, one was advised to option only the most strenuous of curricular offerings. Consequently, Latin, mathematics, and history became the *sine qua non* of learning; to master these subjects was considered the mark of a cultured mind. Under such conditions, the primary goal of education was to produce a highly trained mind, not necessarily a useful one. If pupils found the lessons a chore, the tasks were pronounced good; if books called for rigor, so much the better. Effort and difficulty became in a way the standard for judging the educational value of a subject. Naturally this proposition tended to keep interesting and useful concerns out of the classroom because they could not be expected to produce the show of painful effort by students such as the more abstract and abstruse mental puzzles could evoke. Practical information relevant to the time and probable work life of students was omitted from lessons and assignments with the explanation that such information comes through out-of-school experience after the faculties of mind have been practically trained, disciplined, and strengthened.

In order to defend this thesis, a claim was made that each faculty has its own unique rate of growth and therefore can best be trained at a certain time (Spurzheim, 1883, pp. 117–119). Development of the faculties that appear dormant during youth were believed better deferred until a later point in time. For example, memory appears teachable at an earlier age than reason, so young children might be expected to memorize but not understand. Early memory training would furnish raw material of knowledge and provide an adjunct to reason when the latter faculty came to be exercised during adolescence. In history class the emphasis was on recollection of famous names and dates rather than on understanding cause and significance of events. Similarly, geography stressed the ability to locate obscure and unimportant places rather than to gain insight regarding effect of land and sea upon man's life style. Pupil ability was supposed to spring from the method of study, not the content. This kind of classroom orientation replete with drill, practice, and memory work was known as *formal discipline.*

By ignoring understanding as a major goal in the classroom, and delaying its encouragement to a later age in the student's life, school officials automatically diminished the importance of teacher role. With top priority granted to the exercise of mental functions, the major expectation held of teachers could hardly be to facilitate comprehension. Presumably children would fail to profit if offered lessons they might readily grasp. Indeed to assign work that could be accommodated too quickly or without much discomfort was to do the pupil an injustice; it was to render him a disservice, to take away his chance to learn. Examination of school reports of supervisors during this era suggests that a class of frustrated children might imply that here indeed is a fine, dedicated teacher—her children must work. The teacher objective, after introducing class members to a particular subject, was to ensure their continuous company (student and subject) by means of frequent homework and in-class assignments. Responsibility for a classroom was limited to enforcing the board of education demand that every course of study be completed and the syllabus be utilized as a procedural guide. Little wonder that persons desiring to teach were subject to minimal requirements of educational background. Since the important thing was to exercise the mind and because the method and expectations were the same for all pupils, instructional ability was at a discount. The teacher's role was that of supervising learners rather than teaching them; in short, he was merely a monitor, consigned to the job of "keeping school."

For the many years that formal discipline was believed the pupils' most important teacher children remained without recourse to helpful assistance. The educator's position was less one of reducing learning complexity than it was to ensure that each student encounter his fair share of difficulty. A great deal of supervision was recommended in order that teachers fulfill this proper role. In the so-called normal schools, designed for preparing teachers, the view of a compartmentalized mind continued to dominate. The following statement is from a text written for prospective instructors during the late nineteenth century.

> The mind is that which thinks, feels and wills. It is that immaterial principle which we call the soul, the spirit or the intelligence. Of its essence nothing is known; we know it only by its activities and its operations. The different forms of activity which it presents indicate mental powers which are *faculties* of the mind. A Mental Faculty is a capacity for a distinct form of mental activity. It is the mind's power of doing something, of putting forth some energy, of manifesting itself in some particular manner. The mind possesses as many faculties as there are distinct forms of mental activity (Brooks, 1879, p. 31).

Note that the explanation offers a double enumeration for all mental processes. There is not only the specific faculty of memory, for example, but the power of memory as well. As long as this convenient assumption obtained, it sanctioned the monitor role for teachers, justified the irrelevant curricula, and lent credence to inequity.

In retrospect it seems that certain of the values attributed to formal discipline were overestimated while others failed to be realized at all. Probably the greatest mistake entailed a near worship of rigorous curricula, an assumption that subject matter could be both the lesson and teacher. This viewpoint, in restricting educators to the function of curricular attendants and transmitters of fact, denied students a valuable resource for learning. Nevertheless, the design of scholarship allowed but one pattern—to exercise the selected mind compartments. If students did not understand, at least they absorbed; if pupils were viewed as reactive instead of active, it was for a lofty purpose; if they did not think, at least they listened. (That listening and learning were considered inseparable is apparent from every aspect of the scheme—even the furniture was designed with listening in mind as immobile desks held the student's body if not attention in place.)

THE TRANSFER OF TRAINING

It is a serious misjudgment to confuse eminence with infallibility, to forget that men of renown can be wrong and to suppose that in quoting their error we lend credence to our own untenable hypotheses. Yet, this was precisely the path chosen by advocates of formal discipline when, in defense of their program and procedures, they adopted the transfer of training concept first advanced by the Greek philosopher Plato. The ancient sage had insisted that reasoning gained in school mathematics would incite a pattern of rationale response for every other aspect of living. Some two thousand years thereafter, John Locke maintained a similar position (Locke, 1732; Thayer, 1921, p. 15). Likewise, to the facultists learning acquired in one kind of situation would necessarily apply to any other circumstance in which activity of the same mental function or faculty is called for. So, if one's faculty of memory became proficient in remembering Latin quotations, he will likewise be able to recollect faces, names, and street addresses. In addition to its aid in developing the power of memory, Latin was also considered an excellent subject for those choosing to improve their English. This seemingly indirect way to master one's own tongue by studying another was attributed to activation of the comparison and observation faculties when involved in the study of Latin (see Fig. IV-2). At the same time, geometry was justified for curricular inclusion because it supposedly provided exercise to the domain of reason. Likewise, history in teaching one to weigh evidence and suspend judgment was believed vital to decision-making. In this same fashion other questionable areas of content were introduced on the premise that transfer of training obtains for postschool life. Educators were quick to point out that perhaps Latin and Greek would not be used much out of school (a classic understatement in a time when nearly the entire population was engaged in agrarian pursuits) but the mental exercise and training that improved the appropriate faculties would ensure them to be no less proficient in operation outside of the school.

Late in the nineteenth century, experimental psychologists began to undermine the reign of formal discipline. After raising serious questions about the appropriateness of curricula, the effectiveness of teacher method, and the basic purpose of schooling, researchers devised experiments to test the fundamental claims of hard-riding disciplinarians, to repudiate their doctrine, and hasten the demise of the faculty view. William James (1890), who launched the controversy, initially believed that he might minimize hostility between the dominant parties (facultists and associationists) by presenting a compromise. Facultists contended that memory is an entity that literally resides in a compartment of the mind; the associationists maintained that memory is simply a name for the process by which experiences are restated through re-excitement of their physical bases in the brain. To accommodate an element of both propositions James suggested that retentiveness is a general property of the brain structure and varies from one individual to another. On the other hand, retention of a given fact or item of information is contingent not only upon the individual brain but also upon practicing a specific neural pathway of the brain.

To check his own hypothesis, James developed an experiment to find out whether memorization of certain kinds of poetry would improve retention for poetry in general; that is, whether cultivating memory for one set of materials would enhance retention for everything. When the project was completed, James announced that he and his students had been unable to establish memory transfer in learning different kinds of verse. Instead they found that someone able to remember many lines of French poetry might still remain poor in the recall of street addresses or names. James' conclusion was that practice does not appreciably improve one's ability to recall; memory cannot be developed as one would exercise a muscle; and in fact the notion that there is a general faculty of memory is unsubstantiated. Of course, these assertions stood in direct contradiction to the transfer theory embraced by the facultists. Other researchers were less kind than James as they in jest proposed that maybe there should be a bump named for memory of faces, another for names, one for locations, and still another for dates. Why not an organ for civics and an organ for algebra; one for reading and another for geography? In this fashion the skull could be tattooed with faculties until there was standing room only and still not begin to exhaust the myriad of functions for which the brain is daily employed.

Criticism notwithstanding, most school officials maintained a posture of support for the stated transfer training of formal discipline. Although much in the course of study being conducted could be justified solely on the basis that it was good for youngsters, the curriculum remained unchanged. To illustrate the degree to which the feeling in favor of the transfer theory obtained, one might consider the National Education Association Report of 1894 (p. 34) prepared by the famed committee of ten, in which was stated the belief of its majority that the choice of subjects studied in high school is relatively unimportant provided that courses offer strong and effective mental exercise and training. Whenever the question of relevance arose, its author was quickly dismissed with an explanation about transfer of training. But this answer grew ever more tenuous in the light of increasing psychological evidence to the contrary.

Only a decade subsequent to James' pioneer studies on transfer, one of his select pupils, Edward Thorndike (1901), reported almost the same findings. Working in collaboration with Robert Woodworth, Thorndike had trained individuals in tasks such as estimating the magnitude of weights, length of lines, and geometrical areas. Later, when greater weights and areas were substituted for those used during the practice sessions, it was found that the transfer effects from training were negligible. What slight carryover did occur was attributed to the presence of "identical elements" in the practice sessions and final test. This conclusion, in maximizing the importance of similar circumstance as a requisite condition for transfer, placed the charge of relevance squarely before educators. If, as Thorndike proposed, one is able to utilize in a new situation what he has learned in a previous one only to the extent that there is similarity between or that there are "identical elements" in, the two settings, then the school must concern itself more with studies bearing practical application.

By way of illustration, quoting from a classroom text, Thorndike read: "Alice has three-eighths of a dollar, Bertha eleven-sixteenths, Mary three-fourths, and Nancy two-thirds. How much have they together?" This question, said Thorndike, would appear in real life only in an insane asylum. He maintained the same is true of Greek, Hebrew, memorizing poetry, and the courses of logic. There is no evidence to substantiate the delusion that one can train a student in geometry and thereby strengthen his power of comparison; teach him mathematics and thus equip him with reason for every case; or offer history in order to cultivate latent powers of good judgment for all of life's demands. Instead, children should be taught arithmetic related to the likely adult use of numbers, assigned the kind of spelling words they would be expected to use in business and personal correspondence, and led to master the sort of reading materials that adults are likely to encounter. Many critics marshaled behind Thorndike in maintaining that unless certain things be accomplished by the curriculum, it is of spurious value, providing neither applicability nor transfer, and that transfer of training must be the major concern of school programs.

Still the formal disciplinarians would not relent in the contention that the curriculum is the principal teacher; and that certain subjects, because of inherent difficulty, lend themselves more to faculty development than do others. In desperate attempt to discount the growing body of evidence facing them, the facultists sought every available method of recourse. Some cited experiments indicating that a measure of transfer does take place between one school subject (Latin) and another (English) (Dallam, 1917); others reported voluminous compilations of the academic background for eminent persons who invariably had studied Latin, math, and history—the subjects that make for an improved mind. In answering the latter argument, Thorndike (1924) explained:

> The chief reason why good thinkers seem superficially to have been made such by having taken certain school studies, is that good thinkers have taken such studies, becoming better by the inherent tendency of the good to gain more than the poor from any study. When the good thinkers studied Greek and Latin, these studies seemed to make good thinking. Now that the good thinkers study Physics and Trigonometry, these seem

to make good thinkers. If the abler thinkers should all study Physical Education and Dramatic Art, these subjects would seem to make good thinkers. These were, indeed, a large fraction of the program of studies for the best thinkers the world has produced, the Athenian Greeks.

To demonstrate beyond a doubt that no subject matter area has a peculiar affect upon mental ability, Thorndike (1923) undertook an investigation involving more than 8,000 high school pupils. All of the sample students, engaged in taking various courses, were administered a pretest of mental ability. The following year another form of the same test was given after which score gains were analyzed for student groups having elected different subject combinations in order to ascertain whether the larger gains recorded might relate to the supposedly unique discipline values of certain subjects. Taking into account the normally expected growth for the year period, it was learned that the students who optioned so-called practical courses (bookkeeping, home economics, English) advanced approximately the same as their fellows who chose the subjects supposedly favoring greater improvement of the mind (geometry, Latin, history). All courses of the curriculum, it seemed, were similar in terms of upgrading performance on tests of mental ability. These findings have since been corroborated many times. As an example, West and Fruchter (1960) reported that students who in high school took little math and foreign language, fared just as well in the first year of college as other pupils of comparable ability whose preparation for higher education included a concentration in math and foreign languages.

For facultists, the difficulty in responding to Thorndike was compounded by the penetrating inquiry of still another articulate critic, Charles Judd. Speaking at a symposium held at the University of Michigan, Judd (1908) asked:

> Does nature study train in observation? Does washing slates lead to personal neatness? Does saying good morning to the principal lead to good manners on the playground? No—but perhaps. The mind is not composed of tight compartments in general but will become so if we train it that way. If teachers consider subjects so specialized we shall do little to generalize knowledge in our students. If we have broad views of the subjects we teach and the teaching task, we should teach as though life is not compartmentalized. *In short, the issue is one of teaching rather than how one learns because one learns as one is taught.*

This was a new view, one that would expand the transfer concept from its limited focus on the nature of subject matter to include the method of instruction; it would point up the need for greater teacher training and offer dignity to the role of educator. Thereafter men would recognize that transfer involves an important third element, the pupil—his interest in the lesson, his degree of comprehension, and the extent to which he perceives the identical elements in his learning and applicable circumstance.

For the moment, however, the important thing was that teachers had been granted a greater measure of prestige and respect; they were called upon to assume a more proper role than mere monitors of the curriculum. Without question, Judd was right in assuming that most boys and girls learn as they are taught. But he was wrong in declaring that the issue is not learning, for the best teaching methods accommodate the different styles of pupil learning rather than dictate the learning way. That is, learning should determine method of instruction rather than vice versa. But for years this point was neither accepted nor understood; method remained inflexible, uniform, and singular. Again, children do learn as they are taught but they also learn in ways other than teachers even now employ. It is through understanding more about cognitive modes that the concept of method has expanded to number a variety of techniques and one day perhaps will engender an adequate fit for children of every mind. (Cognitive styles are discussed on pp. 211–17.)

CONNECTIONISM THEORY

Who could have believed in 1897 that the young man recently arrived in New York City with only a chicken and a dream would one day be world renowned as an authority on learning? As he stood before the graduate registrar's desk at Columbia University, his prize fowl in hand, the stranger was no doubt viewed as an object of curiosity by others in the long waiting line. Seemingly unconcerned about the visual objection of his peers, the newcomer may have recalled an earlier incident when, as a Harvard undergraduate, he was threatened with eviction by the landlady of his rooming house for keeping chickens in the building. Fortunately that day had been saved by the eminent professor William James, who, intrigued by the student's ingenuity, permitted him a place for the chickens in the basement of James' own home. Based on research progress achieved while at Harvard, this young experimentalist was recommended for a doctorate fellowship at Columbia University. And, there in an attic provided him by James Cattell, head of the psychology department, he would make history at twenty-four years of age. One day he would commonly be introduced as the "dean of American educational psychology," Edward L. Thorndike.

SUBHUMAN LEARNING

Thorndike's scholarly interest in animal mentality was first generated after reading of separate research findings in Germany (Wundt, 1894, pp. 353–366) and England (Morgan, 1894, pp. 84–94), both of which took issue with the popular judgment that animals are guided either by instinct or reason. The instinct-reason dichotomy as an exclusive explanation for animal behavior had grown out of the Darwinian controversy, in particular as a result of the suggestion by evolutionists that the struc-

tural relation between men and animals might include some correspondence in their mentality. That is, if the mind of man has evolved
from its more primitive animal counterpart, one might expect to find
evidence of elemental reasoning in subhumans. Naturally such a notion
was vigorously resisted by those theologians and laymen who perceived
animals not merely as less developed than man but definitely inferior
creations. To them, reason was the domain of man alone; instinct was
the sole guide of animals. Still, many tales of observed reasoning by horses,
dogs, pigs, and cats were told as though they were matters of fact. Cases
were cited like those of Clever Hans, a horse whose talent included counting beyond 100 and the ability to recall various letters of the alphabet.
One animal, the Arabian steed Muhammed, was allegedly able to carry
out the arithmetic processes of adding, subtracting, multiplying, dividing
—and extracting square and cube root. While farfetched stories such as
these could easily be dismissed as fantasy, there were many acceptable
reports of untrained dogs and cats observed opening fence gates by
elevating the latch. These animals had apparently seen men open doors
and then reasoned how they might do the same. Unfortunately, the
animal accomplishment of opening a latch was interpreted solely as an
outcome of instinct or reasoning rather than the more extended alternative between instinct and learning. To be sure, dogs are not equipped by
instinct to open doors but how then do they learn the task? To find out
would require confronting a dog that had not previously opened a latch
with the task of doing so and following his activity from start to mastery
(Woodworth and Sheehan, 1964, pp. 68–74). It was this kind of experiment that Wundt and Morgan carried out, independent of one another,
reaching the similar conclusion that evidence does not support the assertion that dogs learn by reason; instead they appear to learn by simply
forming associations, by trial and error.

The Wundt-Morgan studies registered a great influence on Thorndike
and his developing theory of "Connectionism." Using chickens as the
first of his animal subjects, Thorndike eventually dealt with a menagerie
of cats, dogs, and monkeys, each of them forcing him to further questions
and conclusions. At the outset he constructed a maze in which three or
four possible exits led to a blind alley. The single exit of the design
led to food and other chickens. When first removed from the flock
and placed into this maze, ·individual chicks moved with aimless haste
from one blind alley into another, frequently bumping against the
wall. But in time, after exhausting the number of corridors, a chick would
reach the real exit and be granted freedom—for a moment. Then it was
carefully returned to the maze and released to find again the elusive way
out. After many trials and much wasted motion, each chick mastered the
task so that when lowered into the prisonlike maze it walked quietly to
the escape route and left.

What perplexed Thorndike at this juncture was the cause precipitating alternative courses of action by the subjects. Surely it was not thinking, as there was no evidence of reasoning capacity; and it could not be merely an outcome of exercise, for the associative laws of frequency and recency dictate that the more often and recent a behavior occurs in response to a situation, the more strongly it becomes affiliated with the stimuli. On the one hand, this meant that initial errors might be expected to repeat themselves and dominate future response; but some unknown factor was prompting the substitution of other responses for the initial ones. Further, even though repeated trial-and-error attempts eventually terminated in success, the law of frequency urges that at the start of a second problem setting, the right response will be at a disadvantage in respect to frequency since it has only happened once. On each occasion it would retain this disadvantageous position and thereby prevent improvement. However, as inexplicable as it seemed, the erroneous responses appeared gradually to diminish in favor of correct ones in spite of the supposed recency-frequency advantage held by the inappropriate responses.

Thorndike discovered the essential conditions favoring improvement by trial-and-error practice while he studied the learning curve of cats. In reporting a decreasing amount of exercise time required by cats to obtain fish dangling outside their cage, the experimenter remarked:

> When put into the box the cat would show evident signs of discomfort and of an impulse to escape from confinement. It tries to squeeze through an opening; it claws and bites at the bars or wire; it thrusts its paws out through any opening and claws at everything it reaches; it continues its efforts when it strikes anything loose and shakey . . . the cat that is clawing all over the box . . . will probably claw the string or loop or button so as to open the door. And gradually (i.e., in the course of a number of trials) all the other nonsuccessful impulses will be stamped out and a particular impulse leading to the successful act will be stamped in by *the resulting pleasure,** until, after many trials, the cat will, when put in the box, immediately claw the button or loop in a definite way (Thorndike, 1898, p. 11).

The resulting pleasure in this phrase was engendered by a new theoretical base for educational method. By recognizing the importance of satisfaction as a determinant of learning, Thorndike introduced the whole realm of affective influences. Upon the concept of *satisfying* and *annoying* reactions, later called the *law of effect,* he would build a rationale for considering pupil interest and motivation, making lessons pleasant, and offering school incentives. According to the law of effect: "The greater the satisfyingness of the state of affairs which accompanies or follows a given response to a certain situation, the more likely that response is to be made to that situation in the future. Conversely, the greater the discomfort or annoyingness of the state of affairs which comes with or after a response to a situation, the more likely that response is not to be made

---

* Author's italics, not in the original source.

to that situation in the future" (Thorndike, 1920, p. 96). This explains why animals learn their tricks, students choose to achieve, and golfers improve their score; at the same time the law accounts for how animals may be led to avoid certain situations, pupils leave the arena of competition, and golfers give up the game. Thus, the control of animal and human behavior alike might be subsumed under the law of effect. It is the great resource of all in education, government, religion, or industry who would alter the response of a man either by reinforcing old responses, adding new responses, or getting rid of those considered undesirable. In Thorndike's estimation, "The law of effect is the fundamental law of teaching and learning" (1920, p. 95).

As a severe critic of the public school and its teachers, Thorndike did not by any means absolve himself of a scholar's responsibility. Instead he chose to submit constructive suggestions for improving educational practice. Without question his early encounter with the formal disciplinarians regarding transfer of training had been a success; in ridding men of the myth that irrelevant studies prepare the young he performed a noble service; helping discredit the image of the mind as composed of discrete faculties was a significant contribution; and, of course, he was among the experimentalists who, in pointing out that instruction is more a function of the teacher than the curriculum, urged educators to assume their rightful and infinitely more important role. Thorndike had helped defeat a detrimental tradition. But could he help build a new one? What of the new pupil freedom and the new teacher chance he advocated? To what end would these contributions lead if their principal sponsor could offer no further assistance in terms of implementation? Others offered their question in a form of challenge—can Thorndike provide a working framework in which his recommendations might be accomplished? Can the evolving theory of Animal Connectionism prove an adequate guide in the education of children? Can the school ensure that its program will involve elements of transfer? Can teachers really become the helping scholar in a classroom, be prepared to understand child learning, and make lessons satisfying? Can there be a psychology for school masters, an "educational psychology"? In reply to these sorts of questions, Thorndike maintained a consistent and ready answer, "Yes."

Knowing the Learner

Man's activity is properly viewed as reactivity since in every case it is in response to a cause or incentive. Each of us behaves not because of an inexplicable directive but in reaction to some stimulation. The circumstance by which one is at any time influenced is called the *stimulus* and whatever action ensues—attention, feeling, movement, or thought—is known as the *response*. To understand the ways of children and to best govern their behavior, those who teach them need first to be made aware that every response involves being satisfied, annoyed, or indifferently affected. Whether a response results in pleasure or dissatisfaction is of great importance because the life span of a reaction depends upon its effect. That is, satisfying behavior tends to be repeated and consequently strengthened in its connection with a stimulus, whereas responses involving unpleasant effects are likely to become extinct because of disuse. Considering the significant influence that the native organization of likes and dislikes (instincts) register on habit formation, it is reasonable to expect that educators at least be familiar with the sources and types of child pleasure and avoidance.

Initially, every youngster arrives in class with a variety of organic wants and predispositions to react. School faculties would do well to consider certain of these tendencies in the determination of criteria for work habits. With respect to encountering objects, particular regard should be given the fact that children are naturally curious. When concentration appears foreign to a class or any of its several members, it is less likely that resolution lies in punishment than in presentation of more relevant lessons, bringing in matters that permit students to study up close and utilize their several senses. Recognize too that children often prefer to go beyond mere examination; they like to manipulate material and observe the results. This disposition to explore visually and to manipulate frequently includes looking an object over, holding and turning it, dropping and picking it up, poking, squeezing, shoving, pulling, and so on through the lengthy list of activities comprising the indefatigable experimentation of fancy (Thorndike, 1930, pp. 67–83). The complex of manual responses characteristic of young children, ranging from the predilection for building with blocks to the desire of digging holes, can and should be accommodated in the program of the school. True, manipulative practice may at times be destructive; nearly always it will be noisy; sometimes it will leave the room in disarray or pose some other annoying outcome to the sophisticated adult; yet all the while it remains satisfying to the youngsters.

Reasonable as the considerations cited above may now appear, they were perceived as revolutionary when first proposed. Thorndike seemed to be saying that educators should use biological tendencies to good purpose rather than deliberately resist them; that if learning is related to satisfaction then surely the school cannot expect success by constantly favoring situations that pupils find annoying rather than pleasant. In fact, educational practice might increase in effectiveness were its determination based more upon nature's dictate at each age level. To many people this line of reasoning appeared dangerous for it not only encouraged noise, movement, play, and freedom in the classroom—the very things that supposedly disrupt proper learning—but when pressed to its ultimate conclusion the proposal seemed to make man the guardian of nature's plan. Certainly a civilized society may be expected to advise more beneficial direction for its future citizen by relying upon adult experience and wisdom than by an allegiance to natural determinism. Nature should obey men—not the other way around.

Thorndike continued his appeal for an improved teacher understanding of the student's nature by suggesting that in addition to useful tendencies for encountering objects, the young are also equipped with a number of social predispositions. These social inclinations serve to urge particular responses to situations offered by the behavior of other persons. For example, whenever children are subject to the command or threat of a teacher, it is natural for them to resist the implied domination. Precisely because resistance is aroused when such measures are imposed, and taking into consideration the fact that teachers are charged to direct pupils, it ought to be apparent that there is need for more subtle types of human engineering. Too often pupil submission is gained at the price of humiliation, fear, and animosity. "To make obedience and submission a positive satisfier and productive attitude instead of a repressed and resentful state of waiting for deliverance is one of the fine arts which every teacher must acquire if he is to be effective" (Thorndike, 1930, p. 74). Further, it is known that by universal design children possess a strong desire to obtain social approval and avoid rejection. This can be accomplished only in part by academic competition. From the teacher to whom they are submissive, each youngster covets a periodic smile, a pat on the back, or an admiring glance. On the other hand, looks of scorn, a frown, the withdrawal of teacher approval, or sounds expressive of disgust bring discomfort to the young. Depending much on how the teacher manages his social sanction, children are held in esteem or low regard by their classmates. Again, how one feels effects how well he learns.

Convinced that an individual's native organization of predisposing tendencies determines in large measure his interests and aversions, Thorndike maintained that for education to improve a child's wants, it first would be necessary to take note of the original predispositions and the means of satisfying them. The desired innate and early acquired response connections should be reinforced by providing situations calling for their exercise and reward. By the same token, undesirable responses can be reduced through withholding the stimuli that elicit them or by ensuring that their occurrence results in an annoying reaction. For the most part, however, original tendencies can neither be preserved nor rendered extinct; they need be modified so as to fit the highest expectations men have of one another and themselves. For example, the random manipulation of blocks by a child can evolve into a facility with adult tools of pencil and pen. Similarly, the satisfaction derived from receiving approval from anyone during infancy is redirected by education so that special attachment is made to the sanction of respected teachers, parents, one's own higher nature, and the heroes idealized as judges. In the same fashion the infantile bent toward physical domination can be supplanted in turn by healthy rivalry with fellows, one's own past record, and finally competition against an ideal mark or objective. The early disposition to collect and hoard whatever appeals and is within reach can likewise be transformed when utilized as a stimulus to gain habits of scientific and economic thought.

Separately, each of the natural tendencies that serve to govern our likes and dislikes of people and objects, our attraction or repulsion of situations and things also can be developed into a set of interests, wants, enthusiasms, and antipathies that characterize man at his best. Unfortunately, schools have made the mistake of trying to accomplish such changes all at once and by ignoring nature. To expect boys and girls to be just, moral, wise, and considerate because we have found that these attributes favor success in the adult world is not in itself enough. Little more is gained by insisting that a student have good taste, respect justice and truth, think critically, and be accurate than by telling a tree to bear fruit or a duck to remain out of water. In short, as the eventual nature desired of man must develop from his original nature as a child, it follows that those who educate must know the student to teach the lesson. Then, in addition to knowing the child as he is apart from training, we must also know the nature of our intended product and the methods for effecting this change.

The Factors of Readiness and Practice

The medium of learning is activity, for in the process of responding to situations through trial and error one learns certain of the reactions he makes. In other words, doing is learning; we learn what is repeated. Since learning depends on activity and activity is generated by the arousal of some want, it seems reasonable that a primary consideration in teaching should involve the provision of motive—some energizing interest, desire, or craving that will promote the student's wholehearted participation.

Certainly desires cannot be expected to remain constant in type or intensity. And as they vary from time to time, their potency as tools of reward or punishment is altered. These changes of valence make it apparent that in order to control the educational process for a given age or grade group, favor must be offered to the community of wants currently in greatest intensity or readiness. Thorndike's (1930, p. 89) *law of readiness* contends: "When an individual is ready to act in a certain way, for him to act in that way is satisfying and for him not to act is annoying. Conversely, when an individual is not ready to act in a certain way, for him to act in that way is annoying." Viewed in this way readiness is directly related to maturation for the reactions that satisfy and consequently are learned include only those enabling the fulfillment of some desire, whereas reactions that fall into disuse and remain unlearned are those that block the attainment of some urge. Readiness also bears relation to the law of effect because the more ready one is to behave in a certain way or perform a specific act, the more satisfying its facility. Stated another way, the greater the readiness, the more potent the effect.

Teachers can develop readiness by diminishing conditions that interfere with pupil study (noises, distractions, and ambiguity), arousing interests through their own enthusiasm, and helping class members come to anticipate pleasant outcomes from lessons. Perhaps the motives to which education can best appeal are the desire to master or dominate, the will to overcome difficulty and secure social approval, the quest to defeat a competitor or past record of self. These motives, unlike organic cravings, are nearly always present and have proved reliable in all kinds of school settings.

Practice is a necessary condition for learning because it is through exercise that response patterns become habits. To establish any particular habit requires a certain amount of drill—less than the optimum renders a habit insecure while more than the optimum cannot appreciably improve performance. The major value of practice lies not in doing the same thing over and over. Indeed repetition is useful precisely because the exact same responses are not repeated. When called upon to encounter several similar tasks in succession, one quite naturally varies his responses; and it is these novel responses that provide the learner with the basis of selection from which to choose the behaviors that most improve his ability and reject those that weaken it. Perhaps to the eye of an observer, the student is merely doing the same thing again and again, but were this true, improvement could never take place. Improvement occurs only through behavioral variations of response followed by a pupil's adoption of his best responses (Thorndike, 1920, pp. 105–112).

Thorndike offered numerous illustrations to show that the old slogan "practice makes perfect" is false if considered as a singular guide to learning. For example, imagine that each of four cats are taught equally well to come running at the call of "Here pussy, here pussy." Later the response is exercised by feeding and caressing the first cat; petting the second; ignoring the third; and showering the fourth with a pail of water. If practice and exercise alone were sufficient to produce improvement and perfection, one might reasonably anticipate that each of these cats would learn equally well to respond more quickly to the voice of the master's appeal. However, only the first cat (fed and caressed) now comes more quickly, whereas the second (petted) appears less promptly than before; the third (ignored) appears late a few times and then does not show up at all; while the fourth desists in responding to the call even before the third. Obviously the perfection of behavior does not come about solely because of practice. As has just been shown, practice may even guarantee the extinction of a reaction if it proves annoying.

But, when the outcome of practice is satisfying, then it does in fact foster improvement.

The choice of which responses are best adopted among the variety one normally makes in a trial-error situation cannot be left entirely up to the student. Self-selection in such important matters of decision could prove disastrous in that youngsters are often less able than adults to distinguish the fine line between benefit and disadvantage. The lack of judgment that typifies children can lead them to reject certain of their more profitable responses and choose instead reactions that will in the long run prove detrimental. As a consequence, the teacher's role includes encouraging the selection of appropriate behaviors. By careful observation of activities, she can identify and reward desired responses when they appear and at the same time stamp out dubious reactions by making the pupil feel uncomfortable in some way. In helping students select for survival only the approved behaviors, the teacher acts as an adjunct to the law of effect.

THORNDIKE'S TEACHING ACT

During the period of Thorndike's prominence, the number of new teaching techniques were introduced. Toward some of these innovations he was mildly critical, toward others openly hostile, but never was he silent or without a reasoned explanation for antipathy. A sample of his judgment regarding the laboratory method follows:

> It is not scientific to spend two hours in learning by the manipulating of instruments something which could be better learned in two minutes by thought. Washing bottles, connecting electric wires and putting away test tubes, though doubtless useful tasks in connection with scientific house-wifery are not magical sources of intellectual growth. Nor is it safe to disregard what is taught so long as it is taught as an exercise in scientific method. A laboratory should teach facts important in themselves. It is disastrous to scientific habits in the young for them to find repeatedly that elaborate experimental work brings at the end some trivial or meaningless result (Thorndike, 1920, p. 178).

He was also disappointed with the discovery method and charged that the notion of pupils actually rediscovering facts is absurd.

> If they had such capacities it would be far better to set them to discovering new facts which would be more educative for them and infinitely more useful to the world. At the most, they discover facts as one might be said to discover a piece of gold who was taken to a plot in which it had been buried not too deep and told, "Dig around here. You will probably find something of value." . . . At its worst the method of discovery is a name for pretense that the child is cultivating powers of originality and self-reliant investigation, while all the time the facts are being smuggled into his possession as truly as straightforward "telling." *

* From Edward Thorndike, *Education* (New York: The Macmillan Company, 1920), pp. 178, 195, 196. Reprinted by permission.

Because Thorndike was severe in his criticism of school practice, some people came to the erroneous conclusion that he opposed all innovation in educational method. This is contrary to fact as the record shows him to have been a staunch supporter of improved preparation for teachers. On one occasion he announced "Some would say that a teacher need know only his subjects; some would add knowledge of the child to mastery of the subject but refuse to countenance method, declaring in fact that there is no method or that methods do not matter or that a teacher intuitively acquires the best method. Such ignorance and egotism fortunately have been too rare to retard the development of methods in education" (Thorndike, 1930, p. 235). Moreover, he recognized the complexity in pupil-teacher relationships and as the following global statement indicates, the need for an understanding of teacher behaviors and influence: "It is the task of the science of education to know the effect of everything that any teacher can do upon every person to whom anything can be done" (Thorndike, 1930, p. 236).

As for his own design of the teaching act, Thorndike explained that since mankind learns through a process of trial and error during which there are occasions of accidental success, the basic charge to teachers is to help pupils identify their successful behaviors and then to ensure their recurrence. Before students can experience achievement, however, the teacher must first arouse them to respond to the lesson, to engage in trial and error. Unless students are led to react, they can neither make nor repeat correct academic behaviors. It is best to initiate pupil activity, the precondition to learning, by appealing to the needs and tendencies peculiar to the learner's age group. Known as the *law of readiness* this utilization of pupil motives and interests as a determining factor in school decisions can be augmented by the teacher who, through his own set of enthusiasms, generates pupil interest in the subject. The problem of motivation is not restricted to getting a person involved in activities from which he can profit; once participation has begun the new teacher task is to help him persist in trial and error, to sustain his effort so that occasional success will occur. This means it is necessary to make learning a pleasant activity. What is more, though drill is the way by which a teacher may attempt to traffic the desired neural pathways and consequently build habits and correct pupil responses to teacher cues, it is known that the stimulus-response (S-R) bonds or connections are not strengthened by mere repetition alone but by reward *(law of exercise)*. It is as a result of achieving the incentive and experiencing the satisfaction that recurrent behavior is assured *(law of effect)*.

Throughout the entire sequence from the time a pupil is first motivated to encounter a task until at last his accomplishment is suitably recognized, the teacher is very much involved in the design for learning. A teacher's burden resides in knowing children generally (readiness stages) and each class member in particular (individual interests); being able to motivate boys and girls by presenting through drill tasks appropriate to the group; assisting pupils in the identification and adoption of their best academic behaviors; knowing when and how to discourage undesirable behaviors and reward achievement. This complex of tasks, all geared to facilitate learning, constitutes the teaching act or what is called method.

Most of the evidence Thorndike cited in support of drill as a prime method of instruction involved studies showing that improvement gains in typing and telegraphy are likely to occur when taught by practice (Bryan and Harter, 1897; Thorndike, 1920, pp. 105–112). These findings led to the mistaken assumption that drill, so helpful in skill development, can increase one's facility in any aspect of learning. As a result the Connectionism emphasis was upon drill exclusively rather than insight and understanding.

Undoubtedly Thorndike's nemesis was the population for whom his system was intended. The language and rationale of Connectionism was beyond comprehension by the typical American teacher of the time who had received but three or four years of training beyond elementary school and was salaried at less than five hundred dollars per school year (Coffman, 1911). Thorndike's confidence in the Connectionist system and his desire to have it work perhaps fostered the conviction that because its suitable application was in the school, teachers would necessarily be able to assimilate it. He overestimated teacher understanding, for they did not comprehend Connectionism. In the minds of many critics the consequent errors of teachers were a reflection of his own. But in fairness to Thorndike it is well to point out that he has often been misjudged by critics who have chosen to evaluate only his early work completed before the Connectionism school was fully developed. To consider his later writings is to be more just to the man and the system he developed. This should be the case, for Thorndike was the first experimentalist purporting to describe how pupils learn and the way in which they ought to be taught.

The Teaching Machine

Before considering the major opposition to Connectionism, it is useful to examine briefly an important departure from within. Particular attention will focus upon the ingenious way in which drill as a teaching method was extended to include its mechanized base, currently described by terms like auto-instruction and programed learning. During 1924, while Thorndike was still a major figure in American education, Sidney Pressey of The Ohio State University was engaged in developing the first mechanical device for self-instruction. Pressey's contribution grew out of an interest in objective self-scoring of achievement tests and his desire to improve education by freeing teachers from the routine of drill and paperwork. From the outset his intention was that the so-called teaching machine be looked upon as an adjunct to conventional methods of instruction, seen as an aid to facilitate drill, review, and self-testing (Pressey, 1926). Never has he deviated from this position toward one of advocating the machine as sufficient unto itself. In fact, forty years after the invention was introduced, Pressey wrote: "Adjunct auto-instruction does not substitute for a text nor eliminate the instructor" (1964, p. 4).

The adjunct approach employs procedures based on the assumption that the student has some understanding of the task as a result of conventional teaching and that he already has made an effort toward achieving mastery through participation in reading, experimentation, a field trip, or other means. Then, subsequent to grasping the structure of a unit, with much already understood, adjunct self-instruction is employed to "clarify and extend meanings, to correct misunderstandings, to confirm the student's choice, to point out his errors, and guide him to the correct answers" (1964, p. 4). As the machine does not represent an exclusive source of instruction for the student, it is unnecessary that programs cover all elements of a course or unit. Further, since the lesson plan is presented through conventional techniques, the order in which programed items appear need be neither sequential nor total. This brief background explains Pressey's relative lack of concern about the order of appearance in which questions are asked of the learner.

Multiple-choice questions have been chosen by Pressey as the mode of pupil response in self-instruction on the hunch that if wrong alternatives represent mistakes frequently made by learners, the option format will help correct wrong associations rather than form them. Thus the choices that are presented to the student have only one notably clear, correct answer and only such wrong alternatives as express common misunderstandings. Pressey's decision to utilize the multiple-choice response makes his approach more versatile than the composed or constructed answer technique later recommended by Skinner, Holland (1961), and others. This is an important concern, for the Pressey type programs are suited to the many kinds of devices incorporating automatic scoring. Moreover, the option method alone can be used equally well with persons who are very young, retarded, and handicapped. Because students are expected to correct their own mistakes in adjunct auto-instruction, the initial error rate is not considered of great consequence.

To use an early model of Pressey's machine, the pupil was first obliged to examine a typewritten question that appeared in the small window of the device. This multiple-choice item could be completed by pressing one of four keys on the machine corresponding to the correct answer. A right answer would trigger appearance of the next question. As soon as one had obtained the right response for an item a given number of times, the question was eliminated from the series (see Figure IV-3). Pressey (1932) later devised another scoring system using punched cards in which the student recorded answers by blocking out a hole in the appropriate circle. Then the card was sent through a machine, which scored the performance by summing right responses. This development served as a model for the contemporary electromechanical scoring machines. Though mindful of the limitations of his invention, including its narrow range of sensitivity, Pressey also recognized certain of its advantages. For one thing, the student is active during programing and can proceed at his own rate; mistakes are private; the teacher is relieved of drill routine; and the immediate feedback of results tends to improve performance (Pressey, 1950).

It is difficult to determine why Pressey's innovation did not immediately capture the imagination of psychologists. In his own estimate, the economic depression was a major factor. Perhaps it was because his adjunctive intention for the device did not inflate its possibility. Whatever the reason, nearly three decades passed before programed instruction came into prominence. In 1954 B. F. Skinner of Harvard University developed automated teaching machines as a means of extending to human learning the operant conditioning principles he had found useful in working with animals. At first reading, Skinner's theory of learning appears much akin to Thorndike's Connectionism, particularly with respect to its total emphasis on reinforcement. The *law of effect,* which suggests that satisfying behavior tends to be repeated, is a basic premise for Skinnerians, but they differ somewhat from Connectionists in the explanation of conditioning, believing it to be a function of one's own behavior rather than an outcome of extrinsic manipulation. According to Skinner:

> Terms for the process of stamping in may be borrowed from Pavlov's analysis of the conditioned reflex. Pavlov himself called all events which strengthened behavior "reinforcement" and all the resulting changes "conditioning." In the Pavlovian experiment, however, a reinforcer is paired with a stimulus; whereas in operant behavior it is contingent upon a response. Operant reinforcement is therefore a separate process and requires a separate analysis. In both cases, the strengthening of behavior which results from reinforcement is appropriately called "conditioning." In operant conditioning we "strengthen" an operant in the sense of making a response more probable or, in actual fact, more frequent. In Pavlovian or "respondent" conditioning we simply increase the magnitude of the response elicited by the conditioned stimulus and shorten the time which elapses between stimulus and response (Skinner, 1953, p. 65) (473).

This position is well illustrated in the work of operant theorists. Generally their experiments proceed by constructing conditions under which caged animal subjects can readily obtain food rewards by press-

Fig. IV-3a. Test-teach apparatus invented by Sidney L. Pressey and exhibited at the 1925 American Psychological Association meeting. Front shows four keys (just behind them plate housing small discs preventing more than one key at a time from being pressed). Candy reward has been delivered down chute from upright container tube in back. Test sheet on typewriter platen shows a four-choice question in window. Courtesy of the Ohio State University Photography Department. Reprinted by permission of Sidney L. Pressey.

Fig. IV-3b. Test-teach apparatus from the rear, showing wooden drum-housing top and sheet metal platen-cover raised. On drum, sliding fins project for three wrong answers to each question. Below wooden top is shift lever in up position causing drum to turn only when "right" key is pressed while all "tries" are counted on veedor back of key arms. When shift lever is down, drum turns and a new question appears whatever key is pressed, but counter adds only the right answers. Below tube is pointer to be set for number of "rights" to be rewarded. The student is automatically given a piece of candy if he attains the number of "rights" preset by the instructor on the reward dial. Courtesy of the Ohio State University Photography Department. Reprinted by permission of Sidney L. Pressey.

ing either a nearby lever or bar. It is presumed that the desirable effect of food-getting that follows lever-pressing serves to reinforce the pressing response. Since the bar-pressing response is not elicited by any known stimulus, Skinner termed it "operant" in the sense that the animal is operating on its environment. This brings up a feature unique to Skinnerian theory, namely that an animal operates on the environment instead of the environment via the experimenter operating on the animal as in the classic Pavlovian experiments. Whereas the Pavlovian situation is a passive one in that a subject remains inert while an experimenter modifies its behavior through various stimuli, operant conditioning leads to active learning as the animal is required to make some overt response that in itself leads to reward.

In his initial paper on teaching machines, Skinner (1954) maintained that any response made by an animal can be reinforced. Moreover, any desired behavior pattern can be taught by rewarding first a response that resembles what is hoped for and then strengthening successive approximations of the desired pattern. In this way an experimenter is able to shape behavior at will. According to Skinner the species involved matters little, for the same techniques that bring results in pigeons, rats, and monkeys work equally well with dogs and children. In each case the key to controlling behavior is wise manipulation of reinforcement. Skinner further suggested that typical teacher practices are inadequate for controlling learning, since reinforcements in the classroom are for the most part aversive; that is, children behave to escape consequences more than to attain any appealing rewards. Then, too, in the typical classroom setting pupils seldom receive immediate evaluation of their work; in many cases they do not find out whether their answers are correct until the following day or sometimes a week later. As a result, much of the benefit from such feedback is diminished. An even more serious problem is that failure cannot be overcome quickly because individual pupils are not reinforced after every response. Instead they receive reports about their work only after many responses have been made. To remedy this deficiency Skinner proposed the use of mechanical devices as teaching machines.

A fundamental distinction between the approach of Skinner and Pressey involves the purpose of teaching machines. In contrast to Pressey's adjunctive intention, Skinner favors machine teaching for entire courses. The two men also differ in the selective mode of pupil response. Whereas Pressey uses multiple-choice items that require that students recognize the correct answer, Skinner uses composed or constructed answers that, in favoring recall, require the pupil to form his answers of various digits by manipulating a number of sliders on the machine. Skinner chooses the composed-answer response because he considers teaching-machine learning as an operant conditioning procedure in which reinforcements are used to elicit the desired responses (see Figure IV-4). The major drawback that composed answers present is that they cannot be judged correct unless one uses the precise set of terminology previously determined by the programer, and since much of our school curricula can be conveyed in a multitude of ways, it follows that many kinds of questions are automatically excluded by devices requiring constructed-answer scoring (K. Smith, 1966, p. 253).

Skinner has given up the feature of immediate correction in order to retain composed answers in some of his recent machines. This move

Fig. IV-4. Student using a contemporary model of TEMAC teaching machine designed for use in the home setting. Photo courtesy of the Department of Photography, The Ohio State University.

has meaning if one understands Skinner's position on errors. He believes that the most important thing in self-instruction is to get a pupil to make the correct response so that it can be reinforced immediately. Therefore, programed materials ought be arranged in such a way that the learner can rarely make a mistake. In this virtually error-free situation there is no problem of correction, as the pupil is led in slow easy stages from ignorance to mastery. Anticipating the objection that programed learning is too easy if based on his principles, Skinner insists that traditional education has failed precisely because it has allowed potentially simple material to remain difficult. Advocates of this posture have followed Skinner's lead in the trend toward more simple machines.

Linear vs. Branching Style

The rapid increase in number of teaching machines during this past decade has been accompanied by a growing concern about the need to identify material types that can be offered mechanically and the necessity to determine appropriate ways for presenting programs. Two major types of programing (linear and branching) currently vie for prominence. Based on Skinner's principles of operant conditioning, the linear style involves fractionalizing the content of a subject or course into small informational units, known as frames, to be presented in sequential order. Because response strength and stability supposedly depend upon the reinforcement following correct reaction, success is built in and reinforced by the program. This is accomplished by minimizing the error factor through deliberate simplicity. In each of the frames a student is provided prompts and hints in order that his rate of mistakes does not exceed the level of 5 percent. One programer bluntly states: "Don't expect too much of the learner. Make the steps so small he cannot err" (D. E. Smith, 1959). Underlying all linear procedures, of course, is a reliance upon repetition to promote progress. In Smith's (1959) view: "If there are several ways to say the same thing, use them all. Redundancy is required." Writers of linear programs proceed on the premise that if pupils can be led item by item from very simple facts to matters of complexity, in the process they will necessarily acquire cognizance of the logical structure that inheres in a subject. In addition to the pupil's gaining a knowledge of subject structure through serial presentation, linear style offers the added benefit of prompt reinforcement through answer checks and self pacing (see Figure IV-5).

What linear advocates generally neglect to mention is that their method of presentation in fact fails to make allowances for the differences among individuals in that all pupils must answer the same questions in the same sequence. This type of program is also inflexible in the sense that a learner cannot manipulate data into novel forms

CHAPTER ONE –   **FROM EQUATIONS TO WORDS**

1.1. ONE EQUATION WITH ONE UNKNOWN

1. We have already learned how to solve the equation,
$3w = 15$. From $3w = 15$, we get $w =$ _____ .   5

2. To check the correctness of our answer, we substitute 5 for
the letter _____ in the equation, $3w = 15$. w

3. We then get $3(5) =$ _____ .   15

4. When we substitute 5 for w, we get the statement, $3(5) = 15$.
Since this is a *true* statement, we say that the number 5 is the
correct value of the letter _____ _____ in the equation, w
$3w = 15$.

5. Another way of saying the same thing is to say
that _____ is the solution of the equation, $3w = 15$.   5

6. So far we have been talking about a number which is the
solution of an equation. Every equation also has meaning
which can be expressed in *words*. The equation, $3w = 15$,
means that "three times a certain number, represented by the
letter w, _____ fifteen."   is equal to (or equals)

7. Similarly, the equation, $4n = 24$, can be expressed in words
in the following way:
"Four times a certain number is equal to _____ ."   twenty-four

8. The solution of the equation, $4n = 24$, is the value of n
which gives a true statement. Since $4(_____) = 24$, the   6
solution of $4n = 24$ is the number _____ .   6

VERBAL PROBLEMS

Fig. IV-5. Example of a linear program. From *An Introduction to Verbal Problems in Algebra* by Nathan Lazar (Willmette, Ill.: Encyclopaedia Brittanica Films, Inc., 1962). Reprinted by permission.

beyond those already indicated on the response key. And while this method can be an aid to instruction when using unambiguous materials like spelling and arithmetic, it appears ill advised for subjects of a political, ethical, or artistic nature in which "right" and "wrong" are superseded by personal opinions as the accepted mode of response. In sum, linear programs are essentially restrictive, for in disregarding pupil judgment and opinion, they tend to represent programers as the ultimate source of authority.

Whereas linear programs dictate that all pupils respond in the same fashion and sequence, the branching type approach set forth by Norman Crowder (1959) permits a student alternatives depending upon his response. For the able learner who can demonstrate mastery of a principle on its first presentation, this means that certain frames of his program can be omitted and that he may skip on to a subsequent unit. By the same token, additional information and corrective procedures are introduced whenever an error is made. Given the remedial emphasis of their design, it is understandable that branching programers are not overconcerned about the rate of pupil error. Mistakes are usually supposed to be a failure of communication originating before the error. Therefore, wrong answers are followed by revised communication using alternate approaches to an issue (see Figure IV-6). To a pupil, a program written in the branching style reads much like a conventional textbook and therefore is less subject to the Pall Effect of boredom which obtains when small-step linear presentations are used (Rigney and Fry, 1961). On the other hand, it is more difficult to engage in review when working with branching programs. The principal stated advantage of branching programs is their provision for individual pace, correction by presenting revised information rather than merely repeating it, and the applicability for subject matter areas in which alternatives are not limited to a clear choice of right-and-wrong responses.

An Outlook for Programmed Instruction

Some writers regard teaching machines as the greatest contribution to education since the invention of printing. After all, they point out, when one considers that the machine procedure affords immediate feedback, motivates pupils by success, encourages individual pace, keeps mistakes private and offers diagnostic help—these benefits and more must qualify programed instruction as the epitome of instructional design. It is a rare teacher if any who can prove so helpful to students. Perhaps in the days ahead educators armed with adequate programs might register a more profound effect upon children than is now commonly believed possible. It is conceivable that "present style texts will become outmoded as teaching aides" (Glaser et al., 1960). Within a decade or so the book as we know it may decline in favor of sequenced programs and reference handbooks (Lumsdaine, 1963). Programed books currently enjoy a great reception and in the minds of many are more practical than machines while accomplishing the same purpose. Another group of writers, equally supportive of self-instruction, counter with words of restraint indicating that grandiose claims ought not be made without

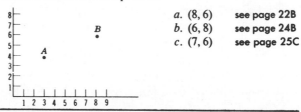

19A   From p. 23A

You are correct. (4, 1, 7) is certainly not a two-dimensional vector. Since it is a group of three ordered numbers it has three components and is a three-dimensional vector.

In the familiar Cartesian coordinate system each point on the plane is labeled with a pair of numbers. In the graph shown point A is (3, 4). We may say that every point on the plane has a vector "associated" with it. The vector (3, 4) is associated with point A. What vector is associated with point B?

a. (8, 6)   **see page 22B**
b. (6, 8)   **see page 24B**
c. (7, 6)   **see page 25C**

22B   From p. 19A

Right you are.

Let's digress for a little graph-reading practice to sharpen you for the labors ahead............

24B   From p. 19A

You answered that the vector associated with point B is (6, 8). Perhaps you have forgotten the convention used in specifying the coordinates of a point. The x coordinate value (the abcissa or horizontal axis) is placed first and the y coordinate (ordinate or vertical axis) is placed second in the parenthesis. Apparently you have not followed this convention.

Return to page 19A and try again.

25C   From p. 19A

You answered that the vector associated with point B is (7, 6). Oops! Looks like you misread the graph. Return to page 19A and give it another try.

Fig. IV-6. Example of a branching program. From Robert Carman, *An Introduction to Vectors* (New York: John Wiley & Sons, Inc., 1963). Reprinted by permission.

foundation nor speculation voiced in the absence of some research justification. These scholars argue that although programed materials can provide a useful adjunct to conventional teaching method, they are often no more effective and almost always more clumsy and expensive (Pressey, 1963; Silberman, 1962). Consequently the future of teaching machines is neither tenuous nor utopian; its ultimate importance has yet to be determined.

Although this disagreement over the contribution and future of teaching machines is but one of the many current disputes about programed learning, it is representative in the sense that each of the opposing parties have recourse to empirical support. Other instances of contradictory evidence are not hard to come by. For instance, much investigation has gone into determining the student subpopulation that stands to profit most from self-instruction. A sampling of results indicate that high achievers do better with a programed text, whereas low achievers learn more from conventional instructional (Reed and Hayman, 1962), but occasionally low-achieving students benefit more from machine teaching than high achievers (Freeman, 1959). Similarly, depending upon one's bias, research can be found to support the notion that students are enthusiastic toward programed instruction (Eigen, 1963; Engelmann, 1963) or that they find it an unsatisfactory way to learn (Roth, 1963; Fry, 1961). Essentially the same type of debate is maintained in discussions about programing variables like size of the frame step, mode of response, or the controversy over branching and linear styles.

To the casual reader the whole issue of programed instruction seems clouded by the disparity of findings; for some it may even suggest that clear answers are beyond reach or that results have been manufactured apart from genuine inquiry. A more appropriate interpretation is to recognize that the lack of agreement in outcomes among studies of ostensibly similar focus most likely relates to differences in their scope. As an illustration, whether one concludes that pupils of a given ability level do relatively better or poorer than another group of students on programs of self-instruction can depend on what factors other than ability are being considered in the study. Unless the type and difficulty of program as well as the kind of subject matter are viewed as influential factors, it is plausible to expect a lack of comparability in findings. Consider another case involving the matter of student feeling toward teaching machines. Unless the assumption is made that feeling is constant over time, an important factor in student satisfaction may depend on when the inquiry is made. That is to say, the value attached to findings in the context of satisfaction or dissatisfaction with self-instruction programs might depend on whether a pupil is asked about his reaction at the beginning of the course, during the middle, or upon termination of a course. Many students enjoy the initial novelty of autoinstruction but a continued diet can lead to boredom, the so-called Pall Effect. More important, even the youngsters who do enjoy self-instruction indicate that they do not prefer it as an exclusive method of teaching.

There are seemingly many contradictions among studies regarding programing variables. It can be demonstrated that the constructed answer is a superior mode of response to multiple choice; or it can be shown that multiple choice is more beneficial than constructed answers. The question of benefit, of course, relates to the matter of purpose, since each of these response modes have unique values and advantages. To argue about the size of frames seems an equally useless debate apart from a consideration of the type of subject matter under consideration. It may be that many frame sizes are needed. As important as the frame size is the question of whether subject matter should be segmented into bits in the first place. The variables of branching and linear style each have advantages and a number of enthusiastic advocates who claim their method is best.

All of the instances cited here can be helpful if they but serve as reminders that what at first may seem to be an inexplicable contradiction among research study findings is often in fact due to the different control factors selected by each investigator. To the extent that the variables differ in influence they effect the outcomes of studies and thereby extend the disparity between seemingly similar but sometimes very unlike investigations. In this connection the work of Gotkin and Goldstein (1964) should be examined for an overview of some ways in which programed instruction has been used in the schools, some effects the introduction of this technology has had on the curriculum and on classroom structure, and some problems of learner achievement and motivation that are beginning to emerge as the innovation spreads.

Probably the most urgent decision that leaders in the field of programed learning face today involves the selection of a theoretical model for future work. Already there are a number of reasons for doubting whether Skinner's operant conditioning principles should be the guide for developing self-instructional devices. Apart from its failure to answer the question of how pupils may be led to behave in a desired way for the first time, reinforcement theory fails to provide any answers as to what will reinforce learners (Snygg, 1962). In addition, the theory seems to ignore a number of basic principles of behavior. For one thing, the only structure that linear programs utilize is temporal sequence, even though behavior is basically space-oriented. Few if any perceptual displays are ever presented to help pupils organize the structure of a lesson or unit (K. Smith, 1966, p. 295). To repeat the boast that at least programed instruction meets individual differences of pace is a fallacy unless we assume pace to be a function apart from cognition, a term describing only speed of retention.

Pressey has been among those who have urged the new search for theories that might govern programed learning. In his judgment, the problem of transfer is the central issue. A stimulus response theory may be fairly adequate as a basis for describing how specific bits of knowledge are learned but it is totally inadequate for describing how persons learn to attack new problems or to generalize the broader applications. Therefore, Pressey suggests further research toward conceptualizing a theory to describe how the attitude of inquiry is developed on the premise that this type of student attitude might lead to wider transfer of specific knowledge. In programed learning there seems to be too much emphasis upon the learning of answers to questions and too little emphasis on how to ask questions so that understanding is a product. The key to the transfer problem may relate to this reemphasis (Pressey and Kinzer, 1964, pp. 40–41).

GESTALT THEORY

In 1910 Thorndike's theory of learning, termed "Connectionism," stood virtually without opposition. However, for the next two decades (1910–1930) its dominance was in constant dispute. Many persons, especially among the ranks of social reformers, were encouraged by John Watson's emphasis on the importance of environmental influence (see pages 18–21). Other more sophisticated leaders saw wisdom in Watson's research-based arguments against the notion of innate-preformed neural bonds. Still another contingent favored Behaviorism because of its reliance upon objective observation techniques. Collectively, these supportive groups enabled Watson and his doctrine to attain a level of visibility which for a period approached international dimension. In contrast with Watson's sudden rise to prominence, three German scholars worked relatively unnoticed in their Frankfort laboratory during 1911–1912. An impending World War, barriers of distance and communication—these factors all combined to delay the recognition of Max Wertheimer, Wolfgang Kohler, and Kurt Koffka as learning theorists, but in time they too would be internationally known, referred to as the leaders of Gestalt psychology.

REVOLT AGAINST TRADITION

In his presidential address to the American Psychological Association, Kohler (1959) recalled something of the motivation that prompted the historic Gestalt experiments in Frankfort, describing them as an attempt to escape from the "prison of psychology." In 1911, along with Wertheimer and Koffka, he was discontented with the prevailing thesis that man's experience can best be understood through its analytic reduction to basic elements that combine to introduce action when associations are formed under the influence of contiguity. It was this dubious infatuation with *elements* as the supposed clue to learning about total experiences that served as the focal point for Gestalt's unrelenting criticism of Connectionism. The three men agreed that whether the elements in question are sensations, feelings, images, or discrete neural bonds, whoever assumes them as a point of departure in the study of behavior is destined to create an artificial psychology of mosaics, compounds, complexes, bundles that are lacking in any intelligible principles of connection. The "bundle hypothesis" results in a brick-and-mortar type psychology with the bricks (elements devoid of meaning) glued together by a mortar of equally meaningless associations. Looking back, Kohler (1959) remembers: "What had disturbed us was the utter senselessness of this picture and the implication that human life apparently so colorful and so intensely dynamic is actually a frightful bore." The trio's response initiated a new psychology emphasizing not parts but wholes in the study of experience.

The school of thought popularized by Wertheimer, Kohler, and Koffka is indebted for both its name and initial direction to Christian Von Ehrenfels, an Austrian philosopher, who in 1890 published a position statement on the problem of organization in mental life. In particular, Von Ehrenfels was distressed by the inadequate explanations of his contemporaries about the nature of experience. At the time his colleague psychologists maintained that experience is but a compound of elements. To illustrate the deficiency of such a position, Von Ehrenfels chose to examine the almost universally common experience of listening to music. When one hears and recognizes a melody that he has previously listened to, we can explain that it is memory which enables his recognition. But, asked Von Ehrenfels, what is it then that makes possible our recognition of a melody played in some key other than that which was originally heard. Surely it isn't memory for one cannot remember something he has never heard. Since the elements (notes) are new, there must be something more than the sum of the tones that enables us to recognize musical transposition, an additional something that might be called *Gestaltqualität* or form quality of the whole (Ehrenfels, 1890). In transposing the melody, its whole or Gestalt quality was reproduced even though the elements or parts were not. In other words, the whole is a different entity than the sum of its parts and the parts assume their meaning only in relation to the whole. Von Ehrenfels did not pursue the nature of experiential wholes; this task would represent a major goal for the young experimentalists—Wertheimer, Kohler, and Koffka.

Wertheimer's (1912) experiments with movement demonstrated beyond a doubt the inadequacy of structural analysis by proving that the experience of watching movies involves an important property (motion), which is not to be found in the separate "still" pictures that flash upon a screen. By arranging a sequence of stills, each composed of a single vertical line in unique position, and exposing them in turn for just the right length of time, it was possible to show apparent movement in any direction. This concrete observation of apparent motion was referred to by Wertheimer as the *phi phenomenon* with *phi* representing whatever took place between *a*, the first exposure, and *b*, the second. Pure *phi* was obtained when the subjects (Kohler and Koffka) saw neither *a* nor *b* nor the movement but simply "something in motion." This same dynamic occurrence, inexplicable on *a priori* grounds, accounts for the reversal of revolution one notes when watching the spokes of a bicycle in transit.

One variation in Wertheimer's experiment included the projection of two beams of light through slightly separate slits onto a blackened screen. When projecting only one of the lights at regular intervals, a series of flashing white lines was produced on the dark background. The introduction of a second beam slightly later, which one might expect to produce two parallel lines, really produces a single line oscilating backward and forward, provided the timing is carefully adjusted. It is clear that the first line as a stimulus has been radically altered by the appearance of the second, and that a new construction has been formed that cannot be explained as a simple addition of stimuli. The new construction is a *Gestalt* or whole and cannot be analyzed into two parts. To put it another way, movement is perceived as movement, not as the mere addition of stimuli, just as water is water and not simply hydrogen and oxygen. To separate movement into elemental sensations is spurious analysis; parts of any percept must be regarded as dependent upon the whole Gestalt in which they appear. Wertheimer (1921) concluded that "perception does not arise from the sum of individual stimuli on the one side and a corresponding sum of sensations on the other . . . but of the stimulus-constellations on one side and the psychologically actual event in the Gestalt form on the other. Besides factors of the stimulus-constellations, the subjective factors which are governed by laws are also decisive."

Encouraged by their initial research findings, Wertheimer and his associates became convinced that each man perceives stimuli in organized wholes rather than as a complex of unrelated detail, and therefore the key to the study of experience lies in its total structure. It was decided "The fundamental formula of Gestalt theory might be expressed in this way: There are wholes, the behavior of which is not determined by that of their individual elements but where the part-processes are themselves determined by the intrinsic nature of the whole. It is the hope of Gestalt theory to determine the nature of such wholes" (Wertheimer, 1924). This decision to search out the dynamic principles governing perceptual organization would prove to be of extreme importance for the movement. In time these principles, most of which apply to the apprehension of visual form, totaled more than one hundred and now comprise the doctrinal position of Gestalt psychology. Though the Gestalt school no longer maintains the level of esteem it once held in psychology of perception (Floyd Allport), it continues today as the most pervasive influence in social psychology, having effected in recent years the numerous studies of group interaction and leadership, social conformity and peer power, attitude change and affiliation (Deutsch and Krauss, 1965; Asch, 1962; Heider, 1958; Festinger, 1964; Lewin, 1948; Cartwright and Zander, 1958; and Henry, 1960).

Perception: Figure-Ground and Closure

At the outset of their quest for guidelines, the young scholars received an invaluable assist from the Danish psychologist Rubin (1915), who first called attention to the *figure-ground* characteristics of sensory fields as a determinant of perception. According to Rubin, a visual perception normally divides itself into two fields; the figure, which occupies our attention, and the ground, which provides its setting. The figure is seen as a whole with definite form and looks like a thing whereas the formless ground appears not as a thing but as a substance. Because it has structure, the figure is more resistant to change than the ground. Generally the ground seems more distant, it appears less structured, less meaningful, and in a sense less lively than the figure.

This distinction can be observed in Figure IV-7 which normally is first seen as a plain vase. It is only after a brief fixation that the two profiles spring forth so that what once was ground becomes figure and vice versa. Similarly, in Figure IV-8 the two female profiles bear a reciprocal relation. The important feature is that surfaces emerge as a whole and not as piecemeal; when each appears and disappears, it does so completely. In addition, note that the switch in figure-ground relation takes place without a change in the picture itself. The revised configuration then is a product

Fig. IV-7. Rubin's vase figure. The black and white surfaces function alternately as figure and ground. From *Gestalt Psychology* by George W. Hartmann (New York: The Ronald Press Company, 1935), p. 24. Reprinted by permission.

Fig. IV-8. The two women. From "A New Ambiguous Figure," by E. G. Boring in *American Journal of Psychology*, 1930, p. 444. Reprinted by permission. (Drawn by cartoonist W. E. Hill and originally reproduced with the title, "My Wife and My Mother-in-law" in the November 6, 1915 issue of *Puck*.)

of a change within the observer and with his altered perception comes a different meaning. Then too, whichever field acts as figure for the moment functions as an integrated unit in its effect upon events; a field cannot be experienced simultaneously as figure and as ground. Naturally Rubin's findings were welcomed by the Gestalt trio as corroboration for their intention to abandon the analysis of sensory components in favor of describing experience in terms of its immediate appearances and impressions.

Gestalt psychology partially explains our motivation to learn by reference of the *law of closure* (see pp. 64–65). According to this law, a task becomes a task, or a problem is a problem in which one involves himself only when it represents to his mind an incomplete thought picture. The gap in knowledge or missing parts of visual form tend to disturb one's equilibrium and so arouse an inner need that demands reduction before a satisfying end-state can be regained through perceptive completion. Tension, or what may be called intrinsic motivation, is set up as the ever present prompter moving the learner from viewing what is initially seen as an incomplete form toward that which is more nearly complete. Through a continuous and dynamic selection of organizational patterns, cognitive change (learning) occurs, revealing the entire previously elusive Gestalt or configuration. Closure is thereby obtained, and with the satisfaction (inner reward) of solving the problem, a learner regains stasis. Closure represents to Gestalt theory what extrinsic reward is to Connectionism.

Figures IV-9 and IV-10 are presented to demonstrate the law of closure. These figures were among a number used by Street (1931) in his picture-completion test devised to determine the relation of this type of measure with that of five other verbal indices of intellective functioning. By deletion, parts of each picture have been made to form the ground so that in order to perceive the picture it is necessary to complete the structure; that is, bring about a "closure" that causes the figure to emerge from the ground. As you view Figures IV-9 and IV-10, does their incompleteness disturb you to the extent of wanting to fill them in? Notice that when cognitive change brings a Gestalt, the picture is no longer partial but now complete. Also, when each picture is seen in its entirety the need for closure is reduced, tension ends, and momentary satisfaction or what may be called the "inner reward" is experienced. Some of your colleagues do not see the picture as yet—for them the tension is sustained. In the case of Figure IV-9, 24 percent of the 754 children (grades 3–9) on whom Street's (1931, p. 7) Gestalt completion test was validated were able to recognize the locomotive engine whereas less than one percent could see the man with his camera in Figure IV-10.

Insight and Intelligence

During World War I, Kohler's research at the Tenerife Anthropoid Station in the Canary Islands led to certain findings about subhuman learning that provided great support to the Gestalt movement and also raised some serious questions about the adequacy of Thorndike's earlier work, *Animal Intelligence* (1898). Kohler had long been skeptical about the low estimates of animal mentality offered by Thorndike (who had not worked with apes), and was opposed to the Connectionist leader's judgment that blind trial and error represents the singular mode in which animals confront problems. The Gestalt leader believed that Thorndike's conclusions were unjustified because the experiments from which they had been derived did not in fact measure or even permit intelligent behavior. According to Kohler (1925, p. 3, 4): "We do not speak of behavior as being intelligent when human beings or animals attain their objective by a direct unquestionable route which clearly arises naturally out of their organization. But we tend to speak of intelligence when, circumstances having blocked the obvious course the human being or animal takes a roundabout path." Had Thorndike established experimental situations in which these conditions were met by permitting the animal a chance to survey the whole situation, he might then have been able to deter-

Fig. IV-9. From *A Gestalt Completion Test* by Roy F. Street (New York: Teachers' College, Columbia University, 1931), p. 59. Reprinted by permission.

Fig. IV-10. From *A Gestalt Completion Test*, p. 65.

mine whether animals have the power of insight to solve the problem in question; whether the subjects can grasp the notion that in order to obtain a goal it may initially be necessary to go further away from the objective; whether the animal learns by seeing relations or simply through mechanical trial and error.

Instead, Kohler maintained that all of Thorndike's arrangements simply represent blind situations. "In a complicated maze an animal cannot see the entire path to the goal and is bound to show trial and error. Thus the maze does not give the experimenter a chance to see whether insight is possible for the animal" (Wordworth and Sheehan, 1964, p. 232). The same is true of Thorndike's puzzle boxes, which were entirely too difficult for the cats. They did not know why they behaved in a certain way to bring about certain results because the relation was too obscure. The chance for transfer was thereby eliminated. Koffka (1925, p. 167) believed that without possessing some technical experience even a man placed inside such a box would be unable to comprehend his mechanisms of release, for several essential parts are placed on the outside and therefore are unseen from within.

In all of Thorndike's studies the contrived conditions were such that no opportunity was provided for insightful behavior; the fixation of successful movements and elimination of unsuccessful ones occurred without any real participation on the animal's part. The subject had not the slightest notion of why its behavior was being modified; the whole process, in which successful acts were preserved and unsuccessful acts gradually phased out, was purely and necessarily a mechanical trial and error. Under these conditions learning can be nothing but fixation and elimination; goal and direction are all but eliminated and activity becomes a medley of confused movement with learning the mere mechanical elimination of some movements.

Taking the view that animal intelligence can better be understood when subjects are studied as dynamic organisms than as machines, Köhler set out to test Thorndike's trial-and-error hypothesis, hoping to find that subhuman behavior need not be mechanical and that apes in particular, like men, arrive at solutions to problems suddenly by a process of insight in which not a series of separate clues taken in series but an integrated system of clues is responded to all at once. Each of the many ingenious experiments devised for the nine chimpanzees were known as *umweg* or detour problems. Consistent with his definition of intelligence, Kohler presented the apes with problems in which the direct path to their objective was blocked but a roundabout way left open and in full view. The problem tasks were designed after intensive preliminary observations had been made to learn the limits of difficulty and functions within which chimpanzees can possibly show insight. In Kohler's (1925, p. 265) judgment this method of task selection is essential since "negative or confused results from complicated and accidentally-chosen test material have no bearing upon the fundamental question and, in general, the experimenter should recognize that every intelligence test is a test not only of the creature examined but also of the experimenter himself." If one's theoretical position leads to the construction of problem situations that can be solved only by chance movements, then little can be gained from the research. With this in mind, the difficulties introduced were first very elemental but thereafter gradually increased in complexity so that the level of intelligence for each animal was tested. This type of procedure stands in sharp contrast to that of Thorndike, by which the cats could not possibly have had a chance to make true solutions. For our purpose, it is enough to consider only several of Kohler's problem tasks in ascending order of difficulty.

> On the second day after his arrival, Koko was, as usual, fastened to a tree with a collar and chain. A thick stick was secretly pushed within his reach; he did not notice it at first, then he gnawed at it for a minute. When an hour had elapsed, a banana was laid upon the ground, outside the circle of which his chain formed a radius, and beyond his reach. After some useless attempts to grasp it with his hand, Koko suddenly seized the stick, which lay about one meter behind him, gazed at his objective, then again let fall the stick. He then made vigorous attempts to grasp the objective with his foot, which could reach farther than his hand, owing to the chain being attached to his neck and then gave up this method of approach. Then he suddenly took the stick again, and drew the objective toward himself, though very clumsily (Kohler, 1956).*

This experiment is typical of the ones involving sticks as reaching tools. More often than not, however, the animal was in a cage and the fruit placed on the outside beyond arm's reach. Sticks were placed either inside the cage or between the bars, almost always in the visual field with the objective. Still another task required that a blanket be used to retrieve the banana located some distance outside the cage. At first Tschego made a number of useless efforts to gain the banana with her arm. After that she jumped up, went quickly into her sleeping den which opens into the cage and returned immediately with her blanket. She then "pushed the blanket between the bars, flapped at the fruit with it, and thus beat it towards her. When one of the bananas rolled on to the tip of the blanket, her procedure was instantly altered, and the blanket with the banana was drawn very gently toward the bars" (Kohler, 1925, p. 34).

Thus far we have seen that several different kinds of "tools" may be used to secure food. Another variation of the experiment involved the use of boxes and tables as implements. Instead of feeding the chimpanzee directly as usual in the morning, the meal of fruit was suspended from the cage roof. Next a box was casually thrown upon

* From Wolfgang Kohler, *The Mentality of Apes* (New York: Humanities Press, Inc., 1956). Reprinted by permission.

the floor of the cage. If the ape had never used a box before, much time was likely to be spent climbing the wall or jumping for the food while the box went unnoticed. Interruption of the ape's efforts by the experimenter, who pulled the box beneath the fruit, mounted it, and touched the banana, usually provided a sufficient hint. When the investigator stepped down and threw the box aside, the ape immediately dragged it back beneath the objective, climbed upon it, and snatched the fruit. After the animal learned this trick, and when the objective was sufficiently high, it would build a stack of several boxes to reach the goal. If this box was filled with stones, the chimpanzee removed just enough of them to permit the box to be moved, even though great effort was required—evidently a clue to its limitation of intellect. Often the keeper was pulled beneath the fruit to be used as a step.

Perhaps the most provocative of Kohler's (1925, pp. 125–128) observations concerned the jointed-stick episode with Sultan, the most intelligent chimpanzee. At the same time Sultan was put into a cage, two hollow bamboo sticks were placed on the floor beside him. Several pieces of fruit were carefully positioned on the outside of the cage at a distance too far to be reached by either stick taken separately but within reach of the two jointed sections. First, Sultan tried to reach the food with one stick after the other but failing at this he pushed one of the sticks out as far as possible and then with the second stick maneuvered the first into contact with the fruit. This showed an understanding of the problem and seemed to give the ape satisfaction, but no fruit. After some time with no progress effected toward a solution, Kohler provided Sultan a clue by sticking one finger into the hollow of the large stick in full view of the ape. This failed to help and the animal soon appeared to lose interest; the task seemed hopeless. However, Sultan continued to play with the sticks holding one in each hand and in the course of these manipulations, he accidentally got the two sticks together. At first the connections were loose and often the separate pieces fell apart until finally a firm connection was made. Once he realized that one stick could definitely be made by joining the two, things were no longer tentative; a definite triumph occurred, first in anticipation, then in action. So pleased was Sultan with his discovery that a number of bananas were drawn into the cage before he ate any of them.

Since all of the foregoing examples depict a type of behavior that must be considered "intelligent," it is important to find out how this behavior is explained by Gestalt principles. In particular, what is meant by saying that a box, table, or stick "becomes a tool"? In order for an implement to serve in retrieving fruit it first must undergo a transformation by entering a total situation as a part with causal significance in terms of the goal. Operating under the tension generated by the banana but so far without success in overcoming the critical distance, anxiety causes the chimpanzee's view of the field of action to suffer a phenomenological change. Long-shaped and movable objects are no longer beheld with strict and static impartiality but now as useful instruments for reaching the objective. This is an instance of "closure." With the situation "open" it is not just a matter of noticing an item such as a stick in that before the object can prove useful it must cease to be an isolated neutral thing to the animal and become instead part of the problem at hand. In short, the object needs to become a "tool." As a precondition for this kind of behavior, an alteration needs to take place in the object of perception. "What at the outset possessed only the character of 'indifference' or 'something to bite upon,' now engenders the function of a 'thing to fetch with'" (Koffka, 1925, pp. 209–210). Therefore, a tool is an object that has been transformed by virtue of its membership in a significant configuration; it has come to acquire meaning in terms of resolving the issue at hand.

The achievements of Sultan and his companions are all described as an instantaneous transition from helplessness to mastery through the experience known as insight. Whenever a dramatic change in the mode of attacking a problem takes place in a single trial and leads directly to its solution, the learner may be said to have shown insightful behavior. Simply stated, iinsight means that one understands the how and why of an endeavor by recognizing end-means relationships. Or in Gestalt terms, it consists of responding to patterned configurations as opposed to isolated elements. Kohler's chimpanzees were suddenly enabled to reach the previously elusive bananas because of an altered perception of the fetching implements that came to be seen as part of an organized visual whole. Kohler (1959) states: "When we are aware of a relation, any relation, this relation is not experienced as a fact by itself but rather as something that follows from the characteristic of the objects under consideration." A quick grasping of relationships, as when an animal all at once perceives the entire field of connections and their implications—this is insight. In sum, it is the perception of dynamic relations existing between parts of a whole.

For a Gestalt psychologist, "intelligence" is the reconstruction of situations to fit the conditions necessary for achieving goals, the adaptation of means to ends. We may summarize the conditions under which intelligence operates and the Gestalt theory of learning that it involves as follows: It is problematic since the organism must cope with a difficulty, purposeful in the sense of being directed toward a goal; it is characterized by insight or relational processes; it is flexible and reconstructive instead of mechanical and fixed, and it emphasizes intrinsic motivation. In this theory, learning is creative; it involves an interaction of the organism and the environment in which the situation is remade, reconstructed or transformed; it is something new and it begins when the human being or animal sees in a different way how things "hang together" when dynamic relations are perceived.

Gestalt and Problem-Solving

The Gestalt movement's emphasis upon problem-solving, insight, perceptual organization, and closure quite naturally made it a topic of discussion among prominent educators. Later, the visiting lectures of Kohler and Koffka (1924–1925) to the United States enabled many more people to understand the basic principles of what then was termed "form psychology." Many school leaders announced they found the message appealing and that it seemed to represent a better alternative for improving instructional method than did the standard drill techniques embraced by theorists of Connectionism. Momentum for the new school reached its peak in 1933 when, with the advent of Hitler, the last Gestalt leader (Wertheimer) departed Germany, bound as the others before him for America. Whatever part the distance and language barriers had previously offered as resisting gaps to the advance of configuration theory, these gaps disappeared with the establishment of Gestalt leaders into academic positions at Smith College (Koffka), Swarthmore (Kohler), and the New School for Social Research in New York (Wertheimer).

Within a short time these newly arrived scholars found themselves the subjects of great pressure to enter the controversial arena of education. On the one hand, new followers pointed to the need for classroom reform; at the opposite pole stood the Connectionists, who suggested an open competition to determine which of the two views could prevail. Deciding whether to oppose the Thorndike camp in matters educational was not an easy decision because most of the Gestalt research (except that of Kohler) had been restricted to visual perception. Nonetheless, despite their obvious disadvantage, the newcomers accepted a challenge to apply the organizational laws of perception to educational practice. Koffka's (1935) *Principles of Gestalt Psychology* was the first valiant if somewhat nebulous attempt to describe learning, memory, emotion, personality, and other factors usually judged important in the educational setting. Later, with the publication of Wertheimer's (1945) *Productive Thinking*, an additional guide was offered. Together these books, in combination with the success of Kohler's inimitable skill of debate, won for Gestalt theory a favored if not preeminent vantage.

To fully comprehend any school lesson or subject requires that the learner possess insight with respect to the part-whole relations involved. Insight therefore takes the place of repetition as the key word in a configurationist picture of learning. This insightful behavior, accounting for the solution of problems by a sudden grasp of end-mean relationships, is said to emerge whenever a previously unstructured region of one's mental life (a problem) comes to represent a new and coherent picture through cognitive change. We learn and understand when perception is so revised as to facilitate the Gestalt organization, the

picture, idea, notion, or point of issue. Tensions earlier triggered by
the missing information or visual gaps of a problem are not reduced
by just completing the task or finishing the assignment; instead closure and its satisfaction occur as one is enabled to gain the Gestalt by
organizing the configuration. In this view, trial and error is seen as
wasted motion; connecting neural pathways by repetitious activity is
considered unfortunate. We simply do not learn by repeating blind
(part) attempts that in time may produce accidental (whole) success.

Since learning is problematic, it follows that children have little
chance for gain when drill represents the dominant instructional method.
This is not to imply that practice ought be discontinued in the classroom but that it should not precede meaning; rather meaning, a product of insight, must precede drill. The necessity of this sequence can
be illustrated by examining Figure IV-11, which ostensibly depicts
the face of Christ. For argument's sake, let us say that Figure IV-11

Fig. IV-11. An unusual full-faced portrait of Christ requiring closure.

represents to a group of fifth graders not a picture but an arithmetic
process. Generally the first reaction of one who cannot comprehend
the arithmetic process (or see the face) is to defend himself by saying to himself, "This is a silly lesson; this is ridiculous." Then as others
around him begin to smile with the experience of closure, one begins
to wonder, "Am I stupid? I can't see the way to solve the problem."
("I can't see the face.") Surely the learner in this case is not assisted

either by peers or teacher who insist that "It's so simple—don't you really see it? How could you miss it? It's so easy." In fact, all that these kinds of remarks tend to do is raise further doubt as to self-ade-quacy. Neither is someone who doesn't see it or doesn't get it helped by receiving a homework charge to complete fifty similar problems or pictures by the following day. *More exposure to the task is not the key;* the real need is for greater meaning and structure to emerge in the mind of the learner through cognitive change.

Too often educators assume that children who do not understand the intended lesson or seem not to grasp the recommended process apparently were not listening when the clear explanation was given. At least the explanation was clear to the teacher. Therefore, in order for these youngsters to proceed it is supposed they need but to hear the explanation again—and louder. Such a rationale might be feasible if learning were solely a function of hearing or repetition. But the truth is that being attentive will not in itself guarantee understanding. We do not help those who can't "get it" by just telling it again; rather the material should be presented in a number of ways, one of which will likely enable each pupil to form his own Gestalt, to image the lesson's organizational pattern for himself. Most able teachers organize their presentations in a variety of ways in order to ensure a coherent structure for all students. Each new way of presentation suits a different element of the class. Sometimes this means that items of information are grouped or placed in outline form as structural clues; in other cases children find a field trip may bring meaning that a lecture cannot convey; illustrations from student life are useful as are films and discussions; the project or unit approach of integrating subjects often makes the relevance more apparent. These and a host of other types of presentation have in common the purpose of helping children perceive part-whole relations in the school curriculum.

Gestalt psychologists envision learning more in terms of perceptual organization than of memorization. As a result it is not strange to find that they interpret recall in a different way than the Connectionist. Memory is usually accounted for by the latter group in terms of the reactivation of previously used neural paths or of "traces" left behind by earlier impressions. How is it then, asks the Gestalt advocate, that having once seen a figure, we are later able to recognize it even though during the interim modifications have taken place in its position, magnitude, and color. In this case recall or reidentification must involve different neural pathways than before. If recognition be contingent upon re-excitement of the exact same fixed paths and identical traces, it is impossible to see how one recognizes anything at all since only in the rare instance would the same avenues be traversed. Because no object is ever twice reflected in the eye exactly the same way, the neural theory is killed by its own specificity. On the other hand, if the phenomena a, b, and c have been present once or oftener as members of a configuration and should one of these reappear with its "membership character" it will tend to supplement itself more or less completely with the remainder of the total pattern. This is memory according to Gestalt (Hartmann, 1935, p. 172).

The importance of teaching knowledge to students of every age group by using problem solving techniques rather than memory, practice, and drill is made apparent in the several verbal pictures that follow. First, we look in upon a group of early elementary pupils whose instructor has assigned them a series of manipulative tasks. Before the period began, this teacher helped his students select problems that would be appropriate to their individual levels of development. As they work about the room, some in groups and others by themselves, these children are learning by insight; that is, through activities of manipulative construction they come to recognize cause-effect relationships, foresee consequences of action, organize conceptual schemes by determining what leads to what, and experience the joy of discovering knowledge. In short, they are gaining understanding. Only as each pupil comprehends the solution to his problem does the teacher's role become one of communication. She then relates the name of the activity, the process, or the parts of the task to the child. By providing him a vocabulary, the teacher gives meaning to a pupil's understanding, gives him words that he can use to express what it is he knows. This sequence of providing understanding as a preface to vocabulary is vital for intellectual development. Otherwise the undesirable result is a pupil who can say more than he thinks or knows, has more words than ideas—a verbalist.

The danger of reversing understanding and vocabulary in the learning process is well illustrated in a story often told by William James of Harvard. The eminent psychologist was visiting a classroom in which children were being taught by the catechetical method. After a period of observation, James requested an opportunity to pose an inquiry. He asked, "If I were to dig a hole down into the center of the earth, would it be colder or warmer there?" None of the students responded. Interrupting the silence, their teacher suggested that they knew the answer but the question was improperly framed. Upon her query, "In what state is the interior of the earth?" a bevy of hands went up, and the respondent chosen said, "The interior of the earth is in a state of igneous fusion." What did the pupil possess—understanding or words?

When children are helped to develop understanding and then acquire vocabulary to describe what they know, a third aspect of learning necessarily ensues. The pupil is able to synthesize his learning, organize his experience, and continue to grow even after he is out of the classroom and teachers are no longer available. Unfortunately, the teaching method of some demonstrates a belief that the three steps of cognitive learning (understanding, vocabulary, synthesis) can be reversed so that instruction may proceed from synthesis to vocabulary to understanding. For example, consider the classroom in which it is assumed that children do not need to understand relationships among numbers. Here arithmetic lessons begin with knowledge that is already organized, synthesized, and embalmed in a textbook. Under this procedure, the first step in a typical encounter with a new mathematical process, say multiplying fractions, is to memorize the universal rule of multiplying fractions. Next, practice and exercise in applying this rule to derive answers are assigned to ensure that every pupil knows the operant routine. Very often adherence to this method results in a child's confronting his mentor with, "I know how to do it but do I use multiplication or division?" Does such a child really know how to solve the problem? Does he understand number relationships and mathematical structure, or does he simply know the mechanics of following an arithmetic rule? The reader who is reluctant to accept what all of us suspect applies to our own early training can try this problem. If asked what the rule is for dividing fractions, most of us could remember to invert the divisor and multiply. Let the reader ask himself, why?

In those whose elementary arithmetic is taught by rote, drill, practice, by memorizing someone else's learning rather than by understanding numerical relations and combination outcomes, there usually develops an antipathy to mathematics when, in later grades, progress is solely contingent upon comprehension. Often the little boy who could do well in memorizing his multiplication tables, although he knew nothing of the integral associations involved, finds that he cannot be an engineer, a doctor, or a physicist because higher mathematics, which requires the unalterable requisite of understanding, is closed to him (Katona, 1940; Wertheimer, 1945, p. 112). The Illinois Math, Stanford Mathematics Study Group, Minnemath, and other recent curricular programs represent a healthy transition.

It seems that there is a point in the hierarchy of knowledge above which one cannot ascend if all his learning is memory-based. A rudimentary construct of knowledge, from its lowest form, sensation, to its highest, theory, is shown in Figure IV-12. As one ascends this ladder of knowledge, he cannot proceed beyond the realm of facts and information on a rote background. Above that level, conceptual structure is vital, seeing relations is paramount, understanding is indispensable. Certainly we admire those of our number who live above the context of facts and information; in the future, social and occupational survival will demand that more of us do so.*

Criteria for Method

Instructional leaders no longer debate the relative merits of Gestalt theory versus Connectionism in the abstract, for it is generally recognized that the choice of teaching method should involve additional factors.

* From R. Strom, *Teaching in the Slum School.* Columbus, Ohio: Charles E. Merrill Books, Inc., 1965, pp. 73–76. Reprinted by permission.

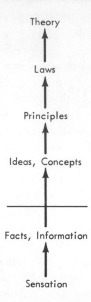

Fig. IV-12. Rudimentary construct of knowledge from a base in sensation to theory at the uppermost level.

Because learning has several dimensions (skills, knowledge, attitudes), each of which differs from the others in ways more effective for its accommodation, no single method is judged applicable for all situations. So, one can properly say that "This is the way to teach" only when the statement concludes with the type of learning intended. Drill and practice represent the best means known to develop overt physical skills requiring a high habit content for proficiency such as those dominant in typing, shorthand, golf, or football. Yet the same method of drill and repetition is ineffectual as a primary resource when it comes to developing concepts in social studies, understandings of arithmetic processes, and principles in general science. Since these latter kinds of student gain require insight of end-mean relations, they involve knowledge more than skills and so are better taught with problem-solving as the major method. (The acquisition of attitudes is considered in Chapter 7.) But the choice of teaching method is more complicated than merely matching drill or problem-solving with the dominant type of learning anticipated from a subject. To employ this procedure is to ignore the fact that learning types go together; they are not exclusive. Even though one dimension of learning is encouraged as the primary objective in a given class, pupils will still acquire something of the remaining two kinds as well. Indeed, no area of school curriculum can be judged excellent if its teachers restrict the learning under their tutelage to a single form. For persons claiming drill as the best method of teaching all lessons and who are therefore unable to account for or encourage solutions by insight, one is inclined to suggest "Think about it; you need the practice."

The desirability of multiple method can be demonstrated with any learning endeavor. For example, the football coach hoping to achieve a successful season is ill advised to rely entirely upon practice. Although the needed game skills are developed by drill, in order to win there is also a need for field strategy sessions because the action required at any point of the game is problematic; that is, it relates to the whole depending on the score, time, field location, etc. Indeed, the constant reconstruction of a shifting field is the major feature in a hotly contested game with the role of victor often depending upon player insight. In other words, learning the skills of tackling and running (drill) is important but one also must be able to find the vulnerable hole in an opponent's formation and anticipate where he will next attack (insight). At the same time, effective use of deceptive tactics hinges upon the ability of one player to lure his opponent to a given place by creating a partially closed Gestalt that he fails to complete as his opponent anticipates.

Similarly in golf, practice alone will not bring proficiency since the correction of errors requires insight on the part of the player as to the reason and way in which he should change his stance or swing. For best progress in every subject of the curriculum, whatever the priority of learning type, some attention should also be given to the remaining dimensions of learning as well. It follows that the method of teaching the dominant objective may not necessarily serve as the mode for achieving one's secondary goals in a class. An essential function of methods courses in teacher preparation is to enable prospective educators to identify the best combination of instructional techniques for use when working with specific areas of the curriculum.

Still another factor to be considered in the selection of instructional method is the teacher himself. It is a great mistake to posit a static relationship between educators and their job, to assume that the merits of any teaching method are independent of the person using it. So far is this from being accurate that one might make a case for believing a weak method, as determined by equitable criteria, in the hands of an outstanding teacher is a better instructional risk than a success-proven way employed by a less able instructor. Failure to appreciate the significance of the adaptation of professionals to their devices has resulted in much futile criticism of the lecture method in high school and college. When the lecture is optioned by a person for whom it is ill suited, such as an unorganized even though quite knowledgeable scholar with a feeble voice and distorted physique, the result will be disappointment for all concerned. But when offered by a well versed, coherent speaker whose strong voice and platform manner are a delight, the lecture becomes an effective teaching instrument. By now it should be obvious that the lecture performance of teachers at either end of the quality range ought not dictate that every other instructor should or should not employ the same method—it depends on the individual. In short, the teacher and his best methods represent an important criterion. (See the Appendix at the back of the book.)

The problem of instructional method generally arises when we think of it as something singular, an elusive master device applicable for all situations. One merely compounds this confusion by assuming that allegiance to a particular theory of learning will ensure constant success with all children. For effective teaching, other factors must be considered as well as learning theory. An abundance of evidence has made it plain that excessive concern with pure method as such is a misleading enterprise and that teacher behaviors must be dictated by elements indigenous to the circumstance. The "master method" has not yet been found precisely because the relative merit of any procedure appears to vary not only with the teacher but with the type of learning (skills, knowledge, and attitudes), subject of instruction, the age, ability level, and learning style of pupils as well as the adequacy of materials. It is not within the province of educational psychology or the methods courses to prescribe teacher behaviors for every circumstance because in the final analysis the individual teacher must make the decisions best for him. Such decisions will more likely favor the progress of every student when learning theory is understood, when theory serves as a resource for teaching method.

CHAPTER V

Educating for
Creative Behavior

To educate for creative behavior has been a stated goal in classrooms across the land since the late 1950's. At that time a rush of unexpected school criticism was issued by esteemed spokesmen representing business and industry, the military, and psychology. Although differing from one another in point of complaint, each of the critics agreed that public education lacked something crucial either in quality or type. Industrial leaders maintained that the rapid development of automation called for a new type of vocational preparation lest countless numbers of young people be useless and unemployable. The rationale was that with the increasing number of lower-order jobs being assumed by machines, a greater proportion of the work force in the future will be required to think, make decisions, have ideas, and in general function on a higher intellectual level than ever before. Unlike the past, when students were trained only for vocations commonly practiced by adults, the pace and direction of contemporary occupational life demand that many youngsters be equipped with skills to fit jobs as yet unknown.

This drive toward a new school orientation was reinforced in 1957 by high-ranking military leaders whose disappointed acknowledgment of the Soviet Union's pioneer space accomplishments led them to speculate publicly that the underlying reason for America's apparent subordination lay with the schools; indeed the lag itself offered mute testimony to our inadequate science curricula. Compounding this problem was the supposed "inability of our institutions to find a place for the creative expert and their persistence in believing that novel projects can be carried through by routine methods" (Rickover, 1959, p. 16). With the protection and prestige of the nation supposedly at stake, it was suggested that educational institutions begin to place at least as much a premium on invention and utility as upon the traditional emphasis of memory and verbal report.

A less dramatic but equally significant influence favoring the revision of the American educational scheme came from research psychologists engaged in studying the creative process and personality. Their findings suggested that creative individuals manifest many of the mental functions deemed necessary for success in the future and that these abilities are not assessed by traditional measures of intelligence (Guilford, 1950; Guilford, 1959, pp. 142–161; Taylor, 1961, p. 65). It was also announced that contrary to popular view the creative person appears more able than his fellows to adapt to novel situations, to live with the complex, to retain his individuality in a group setting—all important elements for mental health (MacKinnon, 1962a; Barron, 1963). In urging that a greater number of people develop their creative potential to improve themselves and the culture, these scholars warned that for such a goal to be realized would require the decline of certain instructional and evaluative procedures of long standing in the school that are inimical to achievement.

So, to advance the culture, to sustain it, and to improve the psychological health of its membership—all of these views appeared a reasonable base for criticism of schools, a justification of the case for creative behavior, and a powerful force in altering the course of American education.

Given the seeming mandate to pursue excellence in the classroom by encouraging creative behavior, some people expected a quick and comprehensive revolution in school operations. This expectation has failed to materialize for several reasons. In general it can be said that popular enthusiasm and naiveté combined initially to underestimate the enormity of the task. Immediately school officials indicated that in order for them to fulfill their charge, they would require the answers to certain questions. For example, if the goal is to train students to become creative adults, what are creative grown-ups like? That is, what characteristics distinguish them from their fellows? To educate youngsters to think creatively, something must be known about the creative thinking process—how does it occur? What environmental conditions act to favor or debilitate creative functioning? How might creative potential be assessed? What criteria should be used to evaluate growth in creativity? That all of these inquiries have not as yet been answered to satisfaction ought be neither surprising nor a source of great despair. Progress has been made and teachers can profit much from examining certain of the gains made thus far as well as something of the mysteries we continue to face.

THE CREATIVE PERSON

The story is told of a chimpanzee who escaped from the zoo. When after considerable searching the animal was finally located, those who found him indicated that at the time of capture he was holding in one hand a copy of the *Bible* and in the other hand a copy of *Darwin*. On the chimpanzee's face was an expression that seemed to pose the inquiry, "Am I my brother's keeper or am I my keeper's brother?" Those of us in teaching are similarly perplexed for there seems to be some doubt as to whether the creative child is one of us, one of our own kind, or whether he represents an alien species. That we are uncertain is evident by the persistence of stereotypic views regarding the nature of creative persons. Commonly they are perceived as eccentric in both thought and behavior, believed to be withdrawn, neurotic, and emotionally unstable, inept in relationships with others—in short, living a little this side of madness. To many of us, the creative individual appears less than healthy and therefore less than acceptable. But what is he really like? For the answers, we must turn to research.

A decade ago under the direction of Donald MacKinnon, psychologists at the University of California Institute of Personality Assessment and Research (IPAR) began an investigation to ascertain what personalistic and intellective factors distinguish persons judged more creative than others. Given the definition that "a creative individual is one who manifests originality and imaginative use of inventive ingenuity," experts in a number of professional fields were asked to nominate those of their co-workers who most fit the given description. From the nominations the Berkeley researchers selected for intensive study a group of individuals working as mathematicians, architects, engineers, writers, and research scientists. To ensure that the traits found to characterize the highly creative sample related to their creativity instead of their professional membership, a wider and more representative group of persons in each of the represented occupations was chosen for somewhat less intensive study. In total, about 600 participants have been involved. From the extensive IPAR inquiry it has become apparent that creative persons seldom match any of the popular stereotypes assigned to them. It is in examining some of the real likenesses and the real similarities that creative people share with one another that provide us certain clues regarding their psychobiological makeup.

Cognitive Styles

The ways by which people usually "get to know" are termed *cognitive styles* or preferred modes of experience. According to Carl Jung, neo-Freudian theorist and author of the preference concept, each of us has the availability of four functions by which to orient ourselves to the world. We can encounter experience through *sensation, intuition, thinking,* and *feeling.* The two perceptual functions considered as irrational in nature are sensation and intuition. Both sensation and intuition involve becoming aware of things—one is direct, the other indirect.

For individuals who prefer to perceive by *sensation,* there is a tendency to accept almost every event as it comes, to experience things only as they are with no recourse to imagination. Such persons find the world of actuality a sufficient source of experience without seeking ideas from the realm of what is unseen. The inclination to think about the ramifications of behavior or to question and wonder about the inherent mysteries of situations is conspicuously absent; no real valuation is made since what counts most is the strength and pleasure of sensations alone. Sensual experiences are illogical; they lack reason and reliability. Even the same stimulus may arouse a different sensation at different times. Nevertheless, those who prefer sensation as the medium of perception are often mistakenly presumed to be rational because their calm demeanor and insistence on the actual facts gives a deceptive impression of reasonableness (Fordham, 1964, p. 42; cf. Jacobi, 1964; Jung, 1923, pp. 463, 551, 568).

The second way of perceiving, *intuition,* is more indirect. In Jung's (1923, p. 568) view, "Intuition is a perception of realities which are not known to consciousness and which goes via the unconscious." Yet intuition is more than a mere perception. It is an inventive response imposing itself upon a situation with an attempt to reshape circumstance according to its vision. It has the wherewithal to inspire, and in every "hopelessly blocked situation it works automatically toward the issue which no other function could discover" (Jung, 1923, p. 463).

Whereas the attention of one whose perceptual preference is sensation focuses upon the facts as they are, to what is presented to the senses alone, the immediate givens, the individual preferring intuitive perception is future-oriented, emphasizing consistently the possibilities of an idea or situation, always alert to that which is capable of occurring, to that which is not yet realized. The intuitive person shows an aversion to staying within the familiar, the safe, obvious, and well-established order, choosing instead to play a hunch, take a chance, explore—in short, to pursue the unknown.

The two rational functions of experiential encounter deal with modes of judgment—the ways by which we reach conclusions about things. As depicted by Jung's typology, the two ways of judging are labeled *thinking* and *feeling.* Preference for the *thinking* mode is shown by a kind of decision-making that involves logical analysis, a need to reach conclusions based on objective data. Reliance upon thinking as the sole base for judgment allows one to discriminate impersonally between what is true and what is false. Because of his concern for logic, formulae, and order, it is common for a person of this bent to behave in ways that may appear to others as cold and aloof. Preoccupied with matters of thought, he may be oblivious to the needs and desires of persons round him.

By way of contrast, someone who prefers to judge by *feeling* chooses a course of action by attaching primary consideration to personal and interpersonal subjective values. His judgment discriminates between what is valued and what is not. Feeling is not a kind of emotionally muddled thinking shaped by sentiment alone, as the person who prefers judgment by thinking is apt to assume. Instead, feeling is the function by which values are weighed, accepted, or refused (Fordham, 1964, p. 39). Concerned primarily with people and human relationships, those who prefer to judge by feeling maintain an ordered scheme of things, a hierarchy of values to which they adhere. In this sense, feeling and thinking are antithetical. For example, in science, where thinking is the prime function, an equal amount of attention is afforded the trilobite as the sick child. This focus is disapproved by the feeling-preferenced person who insists on the difference in their (trilobite-child) values being recognized.

Every person, of course, has encountered some experience through each of the perceptual functions (sensation and intuition) and each of the judgmental functions (thinking and feeling); that is, we all sense and intuit, think and feel. Nevertheless, the preferred mode of an individual is often sufficiently clear to allow for his inclusion within a scheme of classification, to say, as it were, that in terms of perception one person is more sensation-oriented than intuitive while judgmentally feeling is preferred to thinking and so on.

Based on clinical observations, Jung went a step further in declaring that men and women appear to select different primal dimensions of experience. Upon this distinction he postulated the categorization of male and female sex roles, which our society seems to have accepted as a guide to maturity. (See Figure V-1). Stemming from this popular view are the many common jokes that imply that men alone do the thinking

Culture-Determined Sex Roles	Functions of Perception	Functions of Judgment
Male	Sensation	Thinking
Female	Intuition	Feeling

Fig. V-1. The perceptual and judgmental functions by which one orients self to the world. Based on Carl G. Jung's psychological theory of personality types.

and that intuition is the exclusive province of women. As a feminine characteristic, the show of feeling is permitted girls of any age, but for the same reason denied every boy. It follows that by imposing stereotyped sex roles on children, we constrict their province of experience and hence their creativity. When boys come to believe that only the sissy is open to feelings, permitted to cry, play with dolls, or be interested in form, color, movement, and ideas, certain aspects of potential are off limits. Similarly, when girls feel that it is inappropriate for them to be intellectually curious, play with guns and climb trees, or be interested in exploration and experimentation, their creative growth is hindered.

The socially practiced constriction of experience that results from sex-role expectations provides us with the first clue regarding creative personality. The most pressing question involves whether creative persons are more receptive than their fellows to dimensions of experience usually considered as appropriate to the opposite sex. In other words, how extensive is the highly creative person's field of awareness, how open is he to the several functions for gaining experience? On several indices of sexual identification by interest patterns (Minnesota Multiphasic Personality Inventory, California Psychological Inventory) the creative males studied at the Institute of Personality Assessment and Research gave more expression to the feminine side of their nature than did less creative men. It is important to note that while the creative males scored relatively higher on femininity, they did not as a group present an effeminate appearance or increased homosexual interests. In fact, they scored very well on a measure of masculinity (Strong Interest Inventory). What their elevated scores on femininity seems to mean is that these men are not so completely identified with the masculine role as to deny themselves access to other functions of experiential encounter that relate to the so-called feminine side of personality.

This inference is corroborated by performance on the Myers-Briggs Type Indicator, an instrument based on Jung's typology and designed to show a subject's preference within the perception dichotomy of sensation-intuition (whether he chooses to perceive his world in a factual realistic way or by viewing inherent imaginative possibilities) and the judgment base of thinking-feeling (whether the individual elects to arrive at decisions by logical analysis or by appreciating personal and interpersonal subjective values). MacKinnon's (1965) findings are prefaced with the estimate that in terms of perception, perhaps 75 percent of all men in the general population might classify as sensation preferents with a focus on what is immediate and attention devoted to life's givens. By way of contrast, 90 percent of the creative persons assessed by the California researchers classify as preferred intuitives—not bound to the present but manifesting a future orientation with an emphasis on what may be rather than what is. These results lend credence to the assertion that in order for men to be creative, they need to manifest intuition, a characteristic long considered reserved for the female.

Though alike in their preference for intuition as the irrational mode of perception, highly creative persons seem to differ from one another in the rational strength or judgment preference depending upon their field of endeavor. We can say that one judges or evaluates experience with thought or with feeling, thought being a logical process aimed at an impersonal analysis of the facts while feeling is a process of appreciation, bestowing on things a personal and subjective value. Whether the creative person prefers to judge by thinking or feeling is less related to his creativity as such than it is to the type of material or concepts with which he deals. In other words, artists ordinarily show a preference for feeling, whereas scientists and engineers indicate a preference for thinking; writers prefer feeling but researchers in physical science tend to be thinking preferents (MacKinnon, 1965; cf. Roe, 1956).

A third aspect of cognitive style concerns the preference between *perception* and *judgment* in dealing with the outer world or environment. In this dichotomy perception is defined as becoming aware of something; judgment entails reaching a conclusion about things. Everyone perceives and everyone judges—perception determines what is seen in situations and judgment determines what one does about it. We use both perception and judgment but we cannot use them both at the same time, so we alternate. Yet each of us has a dominant process. Rarely is there a case of a person who uses equally all four of the perceptual and judgmental processes just described. To do so would be to keep all of them relatively undeveloped and produce a primitive mentality. The reason is that the two irrational or perceptive processes (sensation-intuition) are incompatible opposites, and failing to choose one of them as the prime source is to always deny a clear signal, to be continually at odds with oneself. If either process is to develop, the other must be subjugated or shut off much of the time. The two rational or judgmental processes (thinking-feeling) interfere with each other to a degree as well. One perceptual function and one judging function can develop side by side provided one is subordinated to the other. But one process, either judgment or perception, must have control to achieve effectiveness as a person (Myers, 1963, pp. 58–60).

On the Myers-Briggs Type Indicator, highly creative persons show a strong preference for perceiving. Indeed the more perceptive a person is the more creative he tends to be. While a judging person emphasizes the control and regulation of experience and tends toward an orderly planned life, the perceiving individual is inclined to be more flexible, spontaneous, more curious, open and receptive to experiences both of the world within and outside of self. In other words, judging people run their lives and the perceptive people just live them.

A fourth mode of orientation to experience involves whether to direct perception and judgment primarily upon the outer environment or the world of ideas within. This attitude preference between what is known as *extroversion* and *introversion* affects the direction and subject of thought. Of course, no one is limited exclusively to an inner or outer world but strong preferences obtain. In fact, Jung regarded these two attitudes as sufficiently marked and widespread to be described as typical:

> There is a whole class of men who at the moment of reaction to a given situation at first draw back a little as if with an unvoiced "no," and only after that are able to react; and there is another class who, in the same situation, come forward with an immediate reaction, apparently confident that their behavior is obviously right. The former class would therefore be characterized by certain negative relation to the object and the latter by a positive one . . . the former class corresponds to the introverted and the second to the extraverted attitude (Jung, 1933, p. 85).

The direction of thinking for an extrovert is generally outward, corresponding to his prime interest in relating with people, events, and things. At his best when working with others, this type of person keeps our business and social life going. Almost always in good stead with the world, his confidence and facility to socialize do not encourage a withdrawal when disputes arise. Instead he seeks to persuade others to recognize the value of his position, and adopt it supposedly for the good of the group. Less influenced by the environment, persons of introverted attitudes seem to withdraw and focus their concentration on inner subjective factors. Lacking confidence in relationships such individuals tend to be less sociable, preferring solitary pursuits to group endeavor, and reflection to activity. At their best when working alone or in small familiar groups, introverts prefer their own thoughts to conversations, and quiet tasks to noisy ones. Self-judgment is more important to them than is a generally approved opinion—in fact they may refrain from reading a book that is popular and depreciate anything that is widely acclaimed (Fordham, 1964, p. 30).

Predictive statements about persons of either attitude (introversion-extroversion) become more precise when matched with the preferred functions of perception (sensation-intuition) and judgment (thinking-feeling). Using this principle of combination some sixteen separate types emerge. In studies at the Institute of Personality Assessment and Research two-thirds of the creative subjects revealed a tendency toward introversion as assessed by the Myers-Briggs Type Indicator (cf. Knapp, 1965, pp. 168–172). Yet it is important to mention that the extroverts in the sample, even though in the minority, scored just as high on measures of creativity as did the introverts.

As might be expected, members of the two attitude groups (introverts-extroverts) usually undervalue their opposite. To an extrovert, the introvert is likely considered as superficial and insincere while in turn the introvert views must extroverts as egotistical and dull. The influence of the introversion and extroversion attitudes on the historical development of religion, philosophy and psychology have been traced by Jung (1923) in his book *Psychological Types*. He suggests that in our culture the extroverted attitude is favored, often being described in such terms as "well adjusted and outgoing" while in the Eastern world, until recently, the introverted attitude was most desired (Fordham, 1964, p. 30).

A final aspect of cognitive style involves the *accessibility to past experience*. Whereas the modes of experiential encounter already mentioned tend to govern the type and amount of experience that one has, the issue of experience retrieval also represents a vital factor in creative functioning. Even though a wide range obtains among creative persons as to the level of their measured intelligence, they share a relative absence of repression and suppression as mechanisms for the control of impulse. By repression is meant the common tendency to force unpleasant experiences from the realm of consciousness. When some unpleasant experience occurs, the usual response is to force the experience from the level of consciousness to the level of unconscious so that one is able to live without tension. That is, stasis or equilibrium is sought. Assume a college coed has broken up with her fiancee. Her sorority sisters now urge her to forget him but what they really mean is that to remain healthy and acceptable to other persons she must put the thought of the young man out of her mind, she must repress it, since to remain steadfast on that single topic would be disruptive for her relationships with others. One can relate this mechanism of repression to the familiar adage that "The best way to learn is by experience." Since a number of our experiences have been unpleasant and, given the common tendency to force such issues from the level of consciousness to the unconscious, it should be apparent why certain among us seem not to benefit much or learn at all from traumatic encounters. What this means for education is that the creative person has an absence of repression, he lives with himself, his past experience, all that he is and has done, the good and the bad of it. Without question repression acts to diminish creativity no matter how intelligent one may be simply because it makes unavailable to the individual large aspects of his own experience, especially the life of impulse which becomes assimilated to the symbols of aggression and sexuality. In short, it seems that the creative person has more access to his experience, to himself, than do his peers.*

Achievement Orientation

If people differ systematically in what they perceive, the conclusions they reach, and how they treat their experience, we might also expect them to differ in terms of values, interests and motivation. For these

* Another cognitive style, involving the preference between learning by creativity or by authority, is discussed on pages 259–260. It is important to note that the Jungian position expressed here is but one of several promising approaches toward understanding more about the ways in which persons relate to the world, process information, and solve problems (cf. Bruner *et al.*, 1956; Gardner, 1953; Hess, 1965; Hock, 1967; Kagan *et al.*, 1960; Kagan, Rosman, *et al.*, 1964, 1965; Klein, 1958; Lee *et al.*, 1963; Wallach and Kogan, 1965; Witkin *et al.*, 1954, 1962; Yando, 1966).

reasons, another approach to creative personality has involved the study of what may be called achievement orientation. In particular it has been found useful to examine: the value hierarchy that governs types of behavior; the nature of expressed interests; the response to disorder or what might be termed "preferred level of task-complexity," and the independence of judgment. Since each of these variables acts to influence the selection and pursuit of goals, they represent important concerns for both educators and psychologists.

Values. A hierarchy of the values held by creative persons has been obtained from their dominant scores on the Allport-Vernon-Lindzey Scale (1960). This instrument purports to show for a given individual the relative standing among six basic value types: aesthetic, economic, social, political, religious, and theoretical. The Institute of Personality Assessment and Research findings suggest a rather general consistency among creative individuals that aesthetic and theoretical values are most significant; at the same time economic and social concerns rank as least important to them. The seeming incongruity between his primary choices —a cognitive and rational concern with truth (the theoretical value) and an emotional concern with beauty and form (the aesthetic value)— suggests not only that the creative person is able to withstand the inner tension produced by opposing and strong values but that he is able to reconcile them in performance. In other words, the concurrent attachment of creative persons to theoretical and aesthetic values means that to them the mere resolution of a problem is not enough; an equal demand of self is that the solution be an elegant one. In this manner, the aesthetic commitment enters all tasks—the work must depict beauty as well as truth (MacKinnon, 1965).

The relatively low position that creative persons assign to social values ought not be construed as an indication of disrespect for community nor an attempt to depreciate collective endeavor. A more reasonable interpretation is that creative individuals tend to consider popularity and group acceptance as less worthy objectives than the seeking after what they consider as being true and beautiful. It does not mean that they choose to be disliked; instead it means that their commitment is to something higher than popularity and they will not invite esteem at the cost of compulsive conformity. In short, while they prefer to be held in esteem, they refuse to achieve this status through self-compromise and find particularly adverse any pressure to behave differently in various social settings in order to please companions. They remain essentially the same in language and demeanor whether in the presence of a clergyman or with the peer group. Contrary to the assumption that this behavioral consistency represents an ignorance of social expectations, a lack of tact or ready ability to adjust, it does in fact reveal a strong allegiance to retaining one's identity, to *always* being oneself. Such individuals understand full well that being one person is sufficiently demanding without the fruitless attempt toward becoming all things to all men.

Giving the impression that he is somewhat unconcerned about public opinion and the thoughts of others may suggest that the creative person is socially irresponsible and he will no doubt be so judged if only the conventional standards serve as criteria. It is important, however, to recognize that his behavior is dictated by a set of values, a system of self-dictates that are consistent despite the fact that they may not mesh with the persons around him. Whether we approve or dislike the creative person, he is viewed as an impressive individual. Perhaps this is because to such a large extent he has realized his potentialities. Since he is not overly concerned with the opinions that others hold of him, it follows that he is freer than many of us to be himself (Maslow, 1959).

A common mistake is to assume that all persons who do not conform, who at times stand apart from the larger group, are by definition "creative." This simply is not so and much of the baneful image attached to the creative population has arisen from the popular tendency to label anything atypical under this rubric, to erroneously include persons who by no stretch of the imagination ought to be called creative. Being creative consists of something far more than manifesting odd behavior, acting unusual or different. Were these criteria sufficient then indeed the beatnik or hippie might be deserving of the term. In contrast, the creative person is neither compulsively conforming nor compulsively nonconforming; he is free to conform or nonconform on the basis of independent judgment of what is true, correct, just, aesthetic, and so on. His uniqueness does not depend upon trappings or an odd appearance but is composed of an essential personalistic and intellective difference.

Interests. We can learn something else about the achievement orientation of creative persons from performance scores on the Strong Vocational Interest Blank for Men (SVIB). The purpose of this instrument is not to measure interests as such but rather to match the similarities of a person's expressed interests with the known interests of successful men in more than fifty separate types of occupational endeavor. On the Strong Vocational Interest Blank the creative males studied at the Institute of Personality Assessment and Research show up as having interests much like those of architects, artists, musicians, physicists, and writers. They appear to have little in common with men who are bankers, carpenters, farmers, morticians, and policemen. In comparing the primary job functions of successful men whose interests are shared by creative persons, it seems that the creative mind is more interested with the meaning and consequence of ideas than in facts as such or the small details of an assignment. Obviously a banker cannot come to the end of the month and say, "This is wonderful, we are only twelve dollars off!" He must calculate down to the last detail, the last penny. Similarly the carpenter cannot look up at his work and say, "That's the finest roof I've built all year. If it were three inches longer, it wouldn't rain in here." He too must deal with the small facts, with a measure that has already been laid out for him by the architect. In this sense he is left little or no latitude for creative behavior; his concern is necessarily focused upon the given details rather than upon possibilities.

Response to disorder. In general, people prefer to avoid any confrontation with disorder, with the irregular or unusual, because this experience arouses inner tensions and raises questions about self-adequacy. For many of us the encounter with complex disarrangement brings with it a sense of confusion and perhaps a feeling of being overwhelmed (cf. Atkinson, 1957; Atkinson *et al.,* 1960; Atkinson and Litwin, 1960; Kogan and Wallach, 1964; McClelland, 1958). But does this same response to complexity hold true for creative persons? Or do they approach disorder in a different way? Some answers to these questions derive from a study by Frank Barron (1963a, pp. 180–199), the research psychologist at IPAR responsible for obtaining characteristics data on creative painters, writers, physicists, anthropologists, and economists.

Barron's investigation dealt with aesthetic preference and aesthetic expression. Materials used to determine aesthetic preference included abstract line drawings, reproductions of famous paintings, architectual designs, and cartoons. The initial group of eighty subjects asked to respond to the Barron-Welch Art Scale (BWAS), a figure preference test, consisted solely of painters representing several cities across the country. As an aggregate the artists revealed a marked preference for drawings that were of complex, asymmetrical variety often describing as dynamic and vital the same pictures that most laymen would call chaotic. But the tolerance these artists have for complex and ambiguous drawings vanishes when they are confronted by simple, symetrical figures. The dominant response toward these latter art forms is aversion. When the same art scale was presented later to doctoral candidates in science at the University of California who had been separated into two groups based on their degree of originality as rated by faculty members, the unexpected results showed a great similarity between the expressed preference of more original thinking scientists and the artists. A mutual affinity for imbalance was evident and a liking for the apparent disorder that most individuals find tension-producing and annoying. The art preference among original-thinking scientists seems to lie in cubism, impressionism, and abstract impressionism. To these men of science, works of art are choice when the unusually observed event in nature is depicted or an everyday scene is reconstructed or shown by a witness from some new position.

Essentially the same tendencies that discriminate more original thinkers from their peers on tests of aesthetic preference hold true for aesthetic expression. The stimulus materials used by Barron for tasks of aesthetic expression included the completion of drawings, interpretation of ink blots, construction of mosaics, poetic images, and arranging miniature stage properties. On the drawing and mosaic exercises, the more original thinkers seemed predisposed to bring complexity and asymmetry into their patterns. Underlying this inclination to like and to construct what is not too simply ordered there appears to be a demanding need to impose organization on the complex and disarranged. For example, even when interpreting messy ink blots on the Rorschach test, more original thinkers attempt to synthesize a myriad of details into one image. This disposition to synthesize reflects a striving to integrate diverse phenomenon into a new order, to create a more elegant and satisfying pattern than might be achieved by a less sophisticated rubric. It would appear that highly creative people are challenged by imbalance, by irregularity and the unusual; unlike most of us they see disorder as a chance, a challenge, an opportunity to introduce order, to master what seems to confound others. In coping with complexity, the creative persons derive aesthetic satisfaction from their synthesizing abilities; in sum, they have an uncanny sense of organization (Barron, 1963b; 1958; cf. Feather, 1961; Rogers, 1963).

Independence of judgment. Unless creative persons are equipped to exercise independent judgment, to stand alone at times in the face of opposing consensus, it is doubtful whether their contributions to society would ever occur. The easy path would be to conform, to embrace the dominant view, to adjust. That original thinking and independence of judgment go together has been demonstrated in a modified version of the well-known Solomon Asch (1956, 1958) experiments. By way of review, Asch involved several hundred male undergraduate students at Swarthmore College in an experiment of group interaction that places the individual under strong implicit pressure from peers to agree with an obviously incorrect group opinion. Typically the experiment included from eight to fifteen persons all of whom, with one exception, had previously agreed to conspire with the experimenter in setting up a conflict situation for the single naive member. The lone individual "on trial" was unaware that his fellows were possessed of special information and believed them to have the same tasks as himself, that being simply to match the length of a given line with one of three other lines that are themselves unequal in size. One by one each of the subjects publicly announced their judgment with the naive individual so positioned that his judgment was called for last. Confederates of the experimenter gave accurate answers regarding the lines in most cases but on the critical trials the hired majority gave a prearranged false answer. To agree with the group in their obvious error was to yield while to stand alone in defense of the correct response was termed independent. Since there are a dozen critical trials during the experiment, scores could range anywhere from zero to twelve on the variable of yielding. The individual with a yielding score of zero was judged independent. Asch found that about one quarter of the total sample were willing to allow the group consensus to preempt their own judgment; another quarter of the group persisted in the correct judgment even when opposed by a united but wrong majority.

At Barron's request, Asch made available a group of 84 subjects, half of whom had scored as independents, and the remaining half as yielders. After contrasting scores of the two groups on the Barron-Welsh Art Scale, a specially devised questionnaire, and a self-rating scale, it was concluded that independents in relation to yielders seem more open to novel ideas and innovations, more likely to prefer the complex and asymmetrical, more challenged by apparent imbalance and imperfection, and more inclined to choose the adjective "original" in describing themselves. From these results it appeared feasible to establish by actual experiment the relationship between independence in judgment and originality. This was accomplished by using a modified version of the Asch experiment along with a set of Guilford's psychological tests designed to measure originality (Guilford, 1950). Results of the experiment show that individuals who earned high scores on originality were also more independent in judgment when pressured to conform to group opinions in conflict with their own.

In summary, the Barron data suggests that independence of judgment is linked both to originality and to a preference for complexity. It further suggests that persons scoring as independents might predictably be more able to encounter contradictory phenomena. A difficult role is required when one is suddenly obliged to oppose the peer community by remaining independent in a decision—a role that perhaps can only be fulfilled by an individual who can accept discord, tolerate contradiction and complexity in his own experience, and retain a steady confidence that order is after all underneath what may appear to others as confusion (Barron, 1963b, pp. 285–305; 1963a, pp. 170–179, 200–213; cf. Mandelbaum, 1963). The ever present temptation would be to dismiss the conflict by denying those aspects of one's own experience that contradict the peer element but order achieved in this way, through exclusion of phenomena, is gained at the cost of judgment.

THE CREATIVE PROCESS

Throughout most of history myth served as the primary guide for describing creative personality. Almost always a host of negative adjectives were used when referring to the inventive mind, the original thinker, or the novel endeavor. To the ancient people, a creative individual was someone literally possessed, driven to his innovation and atypical behavior by some unseen power outside of himself. In a sense he was an instrument of a being higher than man who chose this manner of revelation. That creative behavior might be related to learning was overlooked; instead the cause of "inspiration" was attributed to the gods. And, since the forces of evil and good were known to be in constant dispute, all signs of creativity were necessarily suspect as to whether the manifestation was a deception by the forces of evil. This was particularly true in the case of creative persons who seriously questioned the beliefs, norms, and mores of their time. So, very early in history the creative process was viewed as a thing independent from the person of its residence; the so-called "inspiration" was believed disengaged from learning and thought, considered instead a function of extrinsic control by some super-human entity.

A later but still negative interpretation regarding the creative process arose from the exaggerated relationship between mental breakdown and inventive behavior. By this view the creative person was no longer considered a pawn of some unseen force but instead he was judged personally responsible for his deviant behavior. Creativity was judged an internal function, again unrelated to training, but the direct result of a sickness or diseased mind. It was so easy to dismiss the need for original thinking by pointing to its inevitable price to the person—madness! The observed propensity to be alone, preoccupied, and relatively oblivious to others was considered a symptom of this kind of sickness, a malady to be avoided at all costs. And, of course, the fact that insanity came to but few creative minds was overshadowed by citing eminent exceptions like Nietzsche and Hölderlin as though they represented the rule. It was unrecognized that the creative person's willingness to press his nature to its limits constitutes the supreme test of sanity. Instead those who failed in this attempt were singled out as proof of what happens when one is bright but tends toward being different—he goes crazy! The notion that genius and mental disorder go together became widespread and the response to this kind of person was altered. No longer considered possessed, he next was labeled as "obsessed" and therefore could be pitied, held up as an example of what others ought not become.

Because we are more knowledgeable today the stigma of being creative has nearly vanished but not the mystery of its operation—that remains preserved despite our wish to the contrary. No longer is being creative considered the same as being obsessed or insane; it is to possess a wonderful potential that should be encouraged and that can best be developed if certain internal and environmental factors obtain.

The Relation to Self

To understand something of the intrinsic factors affecting creative production, it is useful to examine Sigmund Freud's thesis regarding the relation of man to himself; in particular one's access to past experience and the nature of thought control. According to Freud, the retrievability of past experience depends primarily upon its residence, whether the once live moment is now within the conscious, preconscious, or unconscious domain. The experience that an individual remains aware of is termed *conscious*. The part of one's personal history comprising this realm is readily available and no hints are necessary to bring it forth. Experiences that seem temporarily beyond reach but that one may become aware of by the proper cues is resident in the *preconscious*. For example, upon seeing a film someone may try to remember the name of a movie star in another related movie but he is unable to do so until a companion provides a hint that triggers the already known but heretofore elusive answer. In short, the experience can be retrieved. Finally, there is the *unconscious* domain largely made up of repressed experiences that once were forced from the level of conscious. Experiences located in the unconscious are beyond our awareness regardless of whatever efforts are made to recall them or relevant hints are offered about them (cf. Jung, 1965; Neumann, 1962).

In Freud's (1923, pp. 18–29) estimate much of life is shaped by the urgings that derive from the unconscious. The key to learning about this domain centers upon the basic control mechanism (ego) that governs behavior and thought. Consider this—within the irrational unconscious there is a striving for gratification, a pleasure-bound propensity known as the *id*. The id knows no values, no right or wrong, no moral standard. Obviously life could not proceed were every person to behave solely in response to the unconscious strivings of the id. Fortunately, there is acting to restrain the id's primitive and irrational demands a censor mechanism known as the *ego*. Contradistinctive to the unconscious id, the conscious ego is capable of calculating the consequences of behavior; thus its purpose is self-preservation. Whereas the id does not care for life that does not offer pleasure, the ego does not care for pleasure that jeopardizes life. When the irrational id suggests that its person take, participate, or go ahead with any unreasonably pleasurable activity, the rational ego responds by presenting the self with reasons as to why one ought not to proceed in this way at this time. Each of us has experienced this inner dialogue while talking to himself about possible courses of action (see Figure V-2)

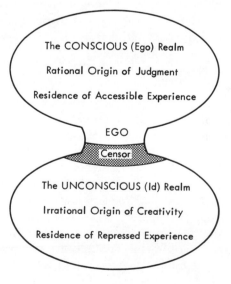

Fig. V-2. The relation of man to himself: unconscious and conscious. Based on the Id-Ego concepts of Sigmund Freud.

In order to defend one's being against the id's desires, which if continually satisfied would destroy a person, the ego must enable the person to sustain a high level of esteem. Otherwise desire would bypass the censor (ego) and lead to self-deterioration and destruction. Sometimes in order to ensure that we think well of ourselves when circumstance does not warrant it, the ego must distort reality and change the facts so that our behavior is self-viewed as commendable. Freud labeled the various ways by which the ego distorts reality as *defense mechanisms*. All of the defense mechanisms represent attempts to maintain a positive self-concept. Since the ego cannot allow a baneful image of self lest the id's desire take over and dominate behavior, each of us at times finds it necessary to distort our reality, to activate certain defense mechanisms. The defense mechanism of repression or denial of reality by burying it has already been mentioned (see p. 217). Other familiar examples of reality distortion include projection, undoing, reaction formation, and rationalization. In the case of rationalization one tries to improve his position by making excuses for existing shortcomings. Thus a boy who gets a failing mark on an assigned paper might defend himself to himself by maintaining that all the others in the class have cheated and at least he maintained his integrity. Or he might try to convince himself that inasmuch as he was the only boy in class his poor grade reflects the teacher's bias in favor of girls.

Suffice it to say that because of its censorship power the ego performs a valuable function in self-preservation. But at the same time this censorship power can act to obstruct creativity by denying the intuitive urgings that rise via the unconscious. In other words, creativity has its origin in the unconscious and whether it is allowed to emerge or not depends upon the ego. This means that each of us is faced with the dilemma that within the unconscious domain, the id, resides his greatest prospect as well as his own worst enemy.

When the ego control is relaxed, the id is free to express its fantasy through imagination. Perhaps most of us know the work of our unconscious best from the dreams we have at night. In bed there is no need to defend oneself against others in a crowded world; thus the ego (conscious) is allowed to relax while the id (unconscious) takes over and spins bizarre stories (cf. Jacobi, 1964). Sometimes we find ourselves waking up in the midst of a dream in trouble, maybe about to go over a cliff or run into another automobile because the ego has not protected us. Contrast this situation with autistic thinking or what is commonly called daydreaming, which takes place during the conscious state when the ego is in full control (Freud, 1925, pp. 44–54). When daydreaming we do not get into trouble but instead are always winning the game, gaining the merit, or becoming the hero because the ego distorts reality in our favor. Another example of ego relaxation and subsequent control by the id can be seen at the local bar. Witness the physically small man who ordinarily is quiet and restrained but now, under the influence of alcohol and the consequent relaxation of his ego, is dominated by his id as he expresses the threat to fight with anyone. Were his ego in control it might well remind him that he stands a chance of being subdued and that he is perceived by others around him as a noisy fool.

The problem of overcontrol by the ego is serious because creative ideas arise from the unconscious realm. Freud maintained that creativity originates from a conflict within the unconscious mind. In time this conflict is resolved and the id strives to express its solution. If the solution reinforces an activity intended by the ego or conscious part of personality, that is, if it is ego syntonic, it will be released as creative behavior. If the solution of the unconscious is opposed by the ego, it will be repressed or else show up as a neurosis. In other words, creativity and neurosis stem from the same source, a conflict in the unconscious, and both are driven by the energy of the id. This is not to imply that one must be mentally sick to be creative. Whereas the behavior of some mentally ill persons is directed by the id deliverances that bypass the ego, a creative individual is instead able to slacken the ego's control so that the impulses the id generates to solve its conflict can be released and cross over the threshold into consciousness (Kneller, 1965, p. 28). Not only is his ego sufficiently flexible and secure to allow the sojourn to the unconscious realm but he can return with vague feelings, impulses, and deliverances from the id, using them rather than being dominated by them as in the case of a neurotic person.

Only after the unconscious has been allowed its function to offer ideas is the rationality of the ego applied to judge by thinking and feeling these intuitive based products. Because the unconscious is recognized as the source of creative ideas, it first is allowed to deliver its produce; then logic and reason are imposed. Thus judgment is deferred rather than concurrent. Accompanying the present concern to educate for preconscious freedom, a necessity well defined by Kubie (1958) has been the development of educational methodologies like synectic group processes, T-group sessions, sociodrama, and creative dramatics, all of which offer promise for encouraging increased pupil expression of irrational wisdom (see pages 260–67).

The mystery of creative productive power eludes even those who most enjoy its presence. Throughout time some literary men have judged that their associative flow might proceed only under certain conditions. As a result some have adopted eccentric methods to ensure concentration and summon inspiration. For example, Schiller liked to have rotten apples concealed beneath the lid of his desk under his nose while composing poetry; Hart Crane played loud jazz on a phonograph. Others report a necessity to drink large amounts of coffee or tea (Auden), to smoke or pace the floor (De la Mare, Hemingway, Wolfe). We ought not think that rotten apples, cigarettes, coffee or tea have anything to do with the work quality of these men but that these are all part of a concentration that has already been achieved. De la Mare viewed his desire to smoke while writing as a need, not of a stimulus, but to canalize a distracting leak of his attention away from his work toward the ever present distractions. In Spender's (1952, pp. 114–115) judgment, "There is always a slight tendency for the body to sabotage the attention of the mind by providing some distraction. If this need for distraction can be directed into one channel—such as the odor of rotten apples or the taste of tobacco or tea—then other distractions outside oneself are put out of competition."

There have been many authors who fear becoming dry and maintain that they can relax only in certain geographical areas like Switzerland or the Riviera. This is unfortunate; the less one feels a need to rely on environment for productive power the better off he is since such a reliance narrows one's freedom of activity and tends to make him location-dependent. Hard work and discipline is more important than idiosyncrasy.

Another unnatural and deleterious method to weaken the ego control and achieve internal freedom has involved the use of psychedelic drugs (Huxley, 1954). Voltaire, De Quincey, and Edgar Allan Poe stand out as examples of men with great ability who were reduced in personal stature precisely because what they believed was a source of inspiration prevented to some degree the subsequent rational focus always necessary to perfect the id's production. In this connection it is appropriate to observe that America's reliance on drugs is unequaled in the history of mankind. We take pills to pep us up, pills to calm us down, pills to gain pounds, more pills to lose them, pills to avoid conception, and other pills to increase fertility (Berg, 1967). Especially alarming are the reports that an increasing number of adolescents are becoming involved with hallucinogens like marijuana and LSD. While there often is a conflict among reporters in the estimated size of the pupil population involved, little disagreement is offered the assertion that the mental health of those involved is in jeopardy (Cashman, 1966; Hollander, 1967; Solomon, 1964). It has been suggested that academic pressures influence some pupils to require drugs and that the student use of tranquilizers in particular must become of greater concern to teachers. In classrooms from kindergarten onward there are numerous problems that might be averted if teachers know something about the effects of drugs.

Returning to the issue of internal freedom, it is fair to say that even the least imaginative among us have at times experienced creative behavior, but usually an overprotective ego acts to deny creative functioning. Since this inner condition of excessive control is in part a response to the outside world, it is appropriate that attention now be directed toward the extrinsic factors that inhibit and facilitate creative behavior.

Societal Response to Creativity

The response of American society toward creative persons might best be described as ambivalent. We respect the contributions such persons make and the recognition they ultimately receive, perhaps even coveting the same reward in the future for our own children. But the respect and acceptance we accord his finished and proved work sometimes does not include the creative person himself. It is as though one said, "Your work is fine and should remain the same; as for yourself, changes must be made to achieve social acceptability." Reactors of this mind presume that creative production is independent of personality and thus uninfluenced by the life style of an individual. This assumption can prove tragic if the oversight is translated into an active effort to alter personality, bringing to bear pressures upon the creative individual to act with compulsive conformity in order that he might be judged normal and healthy. Compulsive conformity is probably the single greatest enemy of creativity. When likeness in certain behaviors is induced, it is at great expense to creative functioning; not infrequently the cost of change toward conformity and sameness amounts to a loss of the precondition for original thought—imagination.

If certain of the personalistic and intellective factors outlined earlier in this chapter are as crucial to creative thinking as many of us suppose, it becomes imperative that any intention of eliminating these characteristics be abandoned. At present there is a considerable body of evidence suggesting that parents and teachers in a number of cultures may unwittingly be taking away from their children important aspects of the very gift they would wish to nurture. Consider the research of Torrance (1963; 1965c, pp. 221–234), whose concern about the preservation of creativity among children led him to examine the "ideal pupil" concept as perceived by educators representing several countries. Nearly one thousand primary and secondary teachers from the United States, Germany, India, Greece, and the Philippines were presented a list of 62 student characteristics, each of which had been included because of their previous reliability in discriminating between persons of high and low creative ability. All of the teachers were instructed to place a check beside the characteristics describing the kind of person that they would like to see their students become; to double check the five characteristics considered most important and worthy of encouragement; and mark out the undesirable characteristics that ought to be discouraged or punished.

Next, to compare the teacher perceived "ideal pupil" with an "ideal creative personality," Torrance transformed the checklist into a set of cards for Q-sort rating by ten judges, all of whom had completed graduate studies regarding the nature of creative personality. The judges were directed to describe the ideal creative personality by arranging their cards in such a way that the characteristics considered most important for creative production would appear at the high end of the scale and the less important or liability characteristics at the opposite end. In pile number one the single most important characteristic was placed, the next three most important items assigned to pile number two and so on in descending order of importance through pile ten. The number of cards assigned each of the piles one through ten respectively were 1, 3, 5, 9, 13, 13, 9, 5, 3, 1, totaling 62. By combining the ratings of all judges, a composite Q-sort of creative personality was prepared for correlation with the "ideal pupil" concept of teachers that had also been score-converted to a Q-sort distribution.

The relatively low coefficients of correlation for all teacher groups suggests that every one of the five cultures engender values that act to threaten the process of creative growth. In turn, the reported coefficients of correlation between teachers and experts on creative personality were: $r = .51$ United States; .47 Germany; .35 India; .32 Greece; .30 Philippines.* It is disappointing to find from the original data of ideal characteristics ranked by teachers that they believe it more important to be courteous than courageous; to engage in independent thinking but not independent judgment; to attach greater premium on being obedient than upon asking questions; to remember well is more important than being intuitive; willingness to accept the judgment of authorities is considered of greater worth than being able to find fault with data and register spirited disagreement.

A cursory inspection of Table V-1 reveals that all five of the cultures may unwittingly be penalizing their creative membership, particularly those of the student population, by limiting adult encouragement and reward to behaviors like being courteous, obedient, handing work in on time, attaining popularity, and accepting judgment from authorities. The adverse effect that dubious criteria for reward have upon creative children is no doubt extended when certain of their self-favored behaviors are actively discouraged and at times punished. For example, Table V-1 suggests that being courageous in one's convictions, exercising independence of judgment, being unwilling to accept mere say-so and the judgment of authorities, disrupting class procedures, maintaining emotional sensitivity and occasionally regressing are behaviors construed as unacceptable, in need of correction or remediation. One thing is sure: when creative behavior does not fall within the reward structure and is in fact the object of opposition, there will be many cases among the young in which an individual forfeits his right to a productive life.

If adults are intolerant of divergent behavior and persistent in attaching derogatory labels to persons unlike themselves, it should be expected that the children with whom they relate soon will adopt a similar view. And, when such an attitude pervades the dominant segment of society, it can threaten the very progress of that society. Do you recall the adage that "Sticks and stones will break my bones but names will never hurt me"? No doubt we all have repeated this saying but few of us are psychologically equipped to endure the insult it implies. Therefore, perhaps as much in defense as in anger, we each seek retraction from the

* See pages 324–25 for an explanation of how to interpret coefficients of correlation.

Characteristic	United States	Germany	India	Greece	Philippines
Adventurous (4)	-----	-----	-----	Disc.	-----
Affectionate (6)	-----	-----	Encour.	-----	Encour.
Altruistic (7)	-----	Encour.	Encour.	Encour.	-----
Always asking questions (4)	Disc.	-----	Disc.	-----	Disc.
Attempts difficult tasks (4)	-----	-----	-----	-----	-----
A self-starter (4)	-----	-----	-----	-----	-----
A good guesser (5)	Disc.	Disc.	Disc.	Disc.	Disc.
Bashful (7)	-----	-----	-----	-----	-----
Becomes preoccupied with tasks (3)	Disc.	-----	Disc.	Disc.	Disc.
Considerate of others(6)	Encour.	Encour.	Encour.	Encour.	Encour.
Critical of others (6)	-----	-----	-----	-----	-----
Courageous in convictions (1)	Disc.	Disc.	Disc.	Disc.	Disc.
Courteous (8)	Encour.	Encour.	Encour.	Encour.	Encour.
Curious (2)	-----	-----	-----	Disc.	Disc.
Competitive (6)	-----	-----	-----	-----	-----
Desires to excel (6)	-----	Disc.	Encour.	-----	-----
Determined (4)	-----	-----	-----	-----	-----
Domineering (7)	-----	-----	-----	Disc.	-----
Disturbs class organization and procedures (6)	Disc.	Disc.	Disc.	Disc.	Disc.
Does work on time (8)	Encour.	Encour.	Encour.	Encour.	Encour.
Emotional (6)	Disc.	-----	-----	-----	-----
Emotionally sensitive (4)	Disc.	Disc.	Disc.	Disc.	Disc.
Energetic (5)	-----	-----	-----	Encour.	-----
Fault-finding (6)	Disc.	Disc.	Disc.	-----	Disc.
Haughty and self-satisfied (9)	Disc.	-----	-----	Disc.	-----

Note: Number in parentheses indicates composite Q-sort rating of experts

Table V-1. Characteristics more strongly approved or disapproved by five different cultures (by two or more standard deviations) than indicated by expert ratings of ideal creative personality (from E. Paul Torrance, *Rewarding Creative Behavior* [Englewood Cliffs, N. J., 1965], pp. 230–32).

Characteristic	United States	Germany	India	Greece	Philippines
Healthy (6)	Encour.	Encour.	Encour.	Encour.	Encour.
Independent in judgment (2)	Disc.	-----	Disc.	Disc.	Disc.
Independent in thinking (2)	-----	-----	Disc.	Disc.	Disc.
Intuitive (3)	Disc.	Disc.	Disc.	Disc.	Disc.
Industrious (5)	Encour.	Encour.	Encour.	-----	Encour.
Likes to work alone (5)	-----	-----	-----	-----	-----
Never bored (6)	-----	-----	-----	Disc.	Disc.
Nonconforming (5)	-----	-----	Disc.	Encour.	-----
Negativistic (7)	Disc.	-----	-----	Disc.	-----
Obedient (8)	Encour.	Encour.	Encour.	Encour.	Encour.
Popular, well-liked by peers (7)	Encour.	Encour.	Encour.	Encour.	Encour.
Persistent (4)	-----	Disc.	Disc.	Disc.	Disc.
Prefers complex tasks (5)	-----	-----	-----	-----	-----
Physically strong (7)	-----	-----	Encour.	-----	Encour.
Quiet (7)	-----	-----	Encour.	Encour.	Encour.
Receptive to ideas of others (6)	Encour.	-----	-----	-----	-----
Regresses occasionally (5)	Disc.	Disc.	Disc.	Disc.	Disc.
Reserved (8)	-----	-----	-----	-----	-----
Remembers well (5)	-----	-----	-----	Encour.	Encour.
Self-confident (4)	-----	-----	-----	-----	-----
Self-assertive (4)	-----	-----	-----	-----	-----
Self-sufficient (5)	-----	-----	-----	-----	-----
Sense of humor (5)	Encour.	Encour.	-----	Encour.	-----
Sense of beauty (5)	-----	-----	-----	-----	-----
Sincere (5)	Encour.	Encour.	-----	Encour.	-----
Spirited in disagreement (6)	-----	-----	Disc.	-----	-----
Strives for distant goals (4)	-----	Disc.	-----	Encour.	-----

Note: Number in parentheses indicates composite Q-sort rating of experts

Table V-1 (continued)

Characteristic	United States	Germany	India	Greece	Philippines
Stubborn (8)	Disc.	Disc.	Disc.	-----	Disc.
Sophisticated (9)	-----	-----	-----	-----	-----
Timid (9)	-----	-----	-----	-----	-----
Thorough (5)	-----	-----	-----	Encour.	-----
Talkative (7)	-----	Disc.	Disc.	-----	Disc.
Unwilling to accept say-so (3)	Disc.	Disc.	Disc.	Disc.	Disc.
Visionary (3)	Disc.	Disc.	Disc.	Disc.	Disc.
Versatile, well-rounded (6)	Encour.	Encour.	-----	-----	-----
Willing to take risks (3)	Disc.	Disc.	Disc.	Disc.	Disc.
Willing to accept judgments of authorities (10)	Encour.	Encour.	Encour.	Encour.	Encour.

Note: Number in parentheses indicates composite Q-sort rating of experts

Table V-1 (continued)

individual who offends us. But what of the case when "he" is plural, when the offenders are the peer group? Then indeed we listen and being called odd, weird, deviant, or sick does hurt and sufficiently so that most of us are inclined to alter our behavior in the direction of compulsive conformity.

To substantiate this thesis one has but to review the University of Minnesota creativity studies dealing with societal expectation and conforming behavior (Torrance, 1961; 1965d). In order to test the hypothesis that cultures differ in the amount of divergent behavior they permit, an experiment was conducted involving thousands of elementary school youngsters from Canada, Greece, the United States, and France. All of the boys and girls were asked to conjure a story about some person or animal who differed in appearance, behavior or some other way from those in his immediate environment. It was assumed that through their tales children would reveal individual perceptions about the ways in which their society deals with atypical behavior. From the fantasies submitted, it was learned that pressures for conformity differ in kind and source among cultures. Society in general served as the consistent source of pressure in narratives written by children from Greece and Canada, whereas peers were the major pressure group bringing conformity in the stories by American children. In the accounts of both Greeks and Canadians the principle form of pressure was questioning. Characters in the stories were confronted by such inquiries as: Why do you act differently? Do you comprehend our way? Why is it you choose to depart from group standards? This type of orientation emphasizes the determination of cause for differences rather than an attempt to simply eliminate difference. On the other hand, incidents reported in the American settings gave little attention to the reasons precipitating divergency but suggested instead to remove the difference through methods like ridicule, coercion, isolation, laughter, and remedial treatment.

Dangers and Advantages of Solitude

Along with the idea of creative thinking as a process requiring internal freedom and hopefully societal sanction, many persons believe working alone to be a necessity. In fact they perceive their separate state as the key to achievement. An investigator pursuing the reasons some creative persons have for this feeling will likely be told that in group settings it is extremely difficult to relax the ego either because of threat or distraction. There is also complaint about the pace of group thinking, the taking-turns procedure, the denial of intuitive process, and the greater emphasis on concurrent judgment than on deferred judgment. In general, creative persons seem to dislike the personal compromise required in groups, enforced particularly by those who do not see the implications of an idea or refuse to improve it before voicing negatives. A number view the group as a coercive body designed to dissuade one from personal opinion, to induce conformity and disrupt the creative thinking processes. Considering these types of grievances, it is not surprising that many creative persons prefer not to be involved in group work. In turn this attempt to maintain one's productive power by being separate is often erroneously construed by the group members as disloyalty, condescension, or egotism. Sometimes conflicts ensue that further separate the creative person from peers. As he continues on his own, the group may pronounce him a recluse.

Up to now this separation arrangement may have seemed to be just a slight misunderstanding, a matter of little consequence because the creative person continued to invent and contribute while the group too made its progress. But all that we know of the future suggests that major breakthroughs and discoveries are unlikely to be accomplished by single individuals. One simply cannot be aware of the many facts and changes in different fields of knowledge that impinge and bear upon important problems. An inextricable relation seems necessary, for somehow to make his contribution the creative person must be a part of the group; at the same time the group must have creative people with ideas to ensure its progress. To my mind, this needed but difficult to achieve alliance represents one of the great problems of education and the available answers are lacking in viability.

It is not uncommon that creative persons choose a relatively isolated existence, ostensibly to retain individuality, to keep alive and develop the delicate gift of imagination. Such withdrawal from human citizenship is a great mistake, most often urged by disappointing group relations as well as the knowledge of one's better performance when engaged in solitary pursuits. Surely there is nothing strange about the preference for solitude as a precondition to inventive behavior. Indeed to cherish being by oneself and so to speak "getting away from the world" for a time is an expected characteristic. But to option this separate condition, aloneness, as the way in which most all of time is to be passed cannot profit the creative individual. Instead it will serve to halt personality development. "Self-realization is not an antisocial principle; it is firmly based on the fact that men need each other in order to be themselves" (Storr, 1963, pp. 32–33). The development of an individual and maturity of his relationships cannot be seen as separate aspects of growth for they occur together or not at all. The same people who succeed in attaining the greatest degree of independence and maturity are often the ones who have achieved the most satisfactory relationships. It is unfortunate that the very term "independence" and its growth conditions have been generally misunderstood. Freud's claim that much of adult neuroticism can be attributed to a failure early in life of not becoming sufficiently independent of one's environment gave rise to a disproportionate stress on the need for independence as a desirable goal. There is no question but that independence ought to be desired but all too often independence has been misinterpreted to mean isolation, a constant state of separateness, immunity from societal involvement and pressure.

Independence is not achieved by merely living in a state of aloneness; neither can maturity come about apart from relationships with other human beings. Donne's wise and poetic warning that "No man is an island" has repeatedly been echoed by psychiatrists like Fairbairn (1952, p. 145) who, in designating "mature dependence" as the ultimate phase of emotional development, suggests that man is incomplete in the absence of personal relationships. Optimal personality development requires an acceptance of the primary need each of us has for one another. There is clinical evidence indicating that the more isolated one is the less an independent personality he becomes. At the extreme, when a person cannot establish any relationships, he is termed psychotic. Those who treat psychosis must rely on their subjective inability to contact this type of person as one index of diagnosing schizophrenia. Thus the most isolated among men are the schizophrenics. Two such people in a hospital may sleep side by side, work in the same room, and eat at the same table for years without ever acknowledging each other's presence. Each is locked in his own private world and so apparently self-sufficient or independent that he must be cared for during the remainder of his life (Storr, 1963, p. 34).

The issue for recognition is that, in the absence of relationships with others, men become more alike than more individual. In time the state of isolation leads not as some might expect to an intensification of the distinguishing features of personality but to a loss of personal identity. (For an interesting treatment of the identity loss problem, see *The Three Christs of Ypsilanti*, by Milton Rokeach (1964). In extreme isolation persons come to speak alike, they report the same disturbing experiences, and so distant is their position from health that to treat them the therapist must first learn their private language, the novel referents they have adopted for common words. For them the only way back to improved health, to regain identity and hence individuality, is by re-establishing relationships with other people, by beginning again to communicate as they once did to someone besides themselves. Paradoxically, this is to say that man is most an individual when in periodic contact with other human beings and least an individual when separated from them totally. In isolation man is collective and without a sense of identity; to be himself, the individual requires the presence of others.

Still we find a recurring wish expressed by creative persons, especially writers and artists, that somehow they might flee society and take up residence where none of this world's everyday constraints exist, a place of constant solitude that would permit the development of internal freedom, an increase in creative production, and the development of self. As for freedom, artists and writers of this intention have yet to learn the possible dangers before them so ably expressed by Erich Fromm (1950, p. 15): "To feel completely alone and isolated leads to mental disintegration just as physical starvation leads to death." As for isolation being conducive to creation, we must not forget that art and writing are forms of communication and that implicitly or explicitly the work produced in periodic solitude is aimed at somebody—the message is not for oneself alone—the greatest satisfaction is to share it (Storr, 1963, p. 37). In Virginia Woolf's (1925, p. 262) words, "The first man or the last may write for himself alone but he is an exception and an unenviable one at that and the gulls are welcome to his works if the gulls can read them" (1925, p. 262). Whereas the creative person in his periodic solitude does attempt to communicate, the totally isolated person cannot communicate. His so-called independence is his prison. This can be corroborated by visiting a mental institution and viewing the paintings of psychotic patients in therapy. However interesting the drawings may be, they are seldom aesthetically moving because they engender no attempt to communicate with other people.

When there is no attempt to communicate, so-called artistic and literary products become uniform rather than unique. Art is an attempt to depict relationships to others and to communicate rather than merely record for oneself the feelings of an autistic isolate. For example, in one study of doodles more than 9,000 of this type of drawings were collected and classified. Maintaining that doodles represent "the graphic results of playful activity done without purpose in a state of divided or diminished attention," the investigators believed that doodles might represent a useful example of graphic production that is thoroughly autistic—neither designed nor intended for communication. An interesting note from the reported findings follows:

> Doodling can be called a most asocial activity. . . . Each individual example taken from this material was made in an atmosphere of complete isolation of the individual, for which imprisonment in a telephone box can be taken as the standard symbol. . . . The isolation, freedom, and independence from standard influences had not the affect one might have expected. The products of free fantasy were conformable with a few types, and to a large extent could be called monotonous. . . . It is interesting to see that in spite of the segregation and isolation of the doodler, trends of collective psychology become active (Maclay, Guttmann, Mayer, 1938).

The fact that man in a complete state of aloneness becomes less an individual ought not demean the quest for periodic solitude since we know also that when men are by themselves for a time they do find it easier to concentrate, to become involved with the mysteries they face and to penetrate the unknown by questions of relationship, meaning, and purpose. From time immemorial religious leaders such as Moses, Christ, and Gandhi have found it necessary to retreat for a time from the life of daily affairs in order to make themselves ready for what they would reveal to men. However, in each case they returned from the place of isolation whether it be a desert, garden, countryside, or mountain to renew their contact with humanity so as to convey what they had to say and to make sure that the experience would be understood and shared. This renewed contact with the social environment is vital if retreat is to have any benefit. The state of isolation may call for questions, issues, and concerns, but personal relationships must follow if communication is to have meaning, if the individual is to develop and the self is to mature.

Creative Process as a Sequence of Phases

Although the creative process remains a mystery in many ways, there have been attempts to trace its course by describing a number of phases believed to commonly precede invention. Respectively these phases are termed *preparation, incubation, inspiration* and *verification* (Patrick, 1955; Wallas, 1926). That *preparation* is a requisite for creative production often appears as a surprise to those who have supposed "inspiration" just comes to some people and that it does not visit others. This kind of an assumption makes it easier to refrain from entering the great struggle in which all who create are engaged. After an initial self-prompting by vague insights, the creative person sets out to examine an area of difficulty. At the outset he literally floods himself with the diverse judgment of those who before him have been interested in the problem and chose to record their individual encounters. In this fashion imagina-nation receives data that it later will manipulate to form original ideas. The preparation stage is difficult, its search emphasis unromantic and characterized by many dangers that can undermine production. First, literature on the problem to be investigated may be so extensive and rigorous that the preparation task seems overwhelming. Assuming that the necessary background to proceed is going to require too much time, one may conveniently drop the issue and move instead to another concern. A related danger is that fascination with side issues encountered during the preparatory reading of material can capture attention and divert one's interest from the original purpose. Especially is this true of those whose indiscriminate curiosity leads them in every direction.

The very impatience that causes one to grapple with an issue can destroy all chance for success if the desire to begin synthesis is premature. It is difficult to overestimate this matter, particularly given the pressures upon creative persons for rapid production today. Another common error during the preparation phase is to start reacting to data too early, ordering too quickly, and thereby omitting some reading or observation that would be relevant. Again, the most important aspect of the preparation phase is to immerse oneself in the ideas of others in order to be an original thinker, to get an awareness of how others have thought and then use their pro-duce as the data on which synthesizing ability will operate. Getting out of the problem is easier at this stage than at any other since little work has been invested and the degree of involvement is not great.

So many young people judge themselves as uncreative because novel ideas have not come to them without preparation. It is good to read about the real lives of eminent people, their failures, success, and courage. This is one of the sustaining features in the preparation stage and no doubt occurs most for those who can identify with others who have in-vestigated the same problem. Preparation is a difficult time because the pressure is to create, to express—but first one must read what others have thought. To underestimate the value of preparation is to desist in prepa-ration too soon and the confidence with which one would replace preparation is insufficient. So many creative persons have given up be-cause they have been led to believe that inventive production is simple or beyond their reach. Society has told them nothing of the creative process and its difficult course.

During the second phase of creative process, termed *incubation*, the unconscious is given freedom to act upon that material that the conscious has presented. There is an irrational and intuitive encounter with the subject matter. According to the dictionary, "incubation is that phase of process which facilitates the transition of an idea from its inception to a visible manifestation." During the incubation period the creative person is ordained with unrest as he tries to get the ordering structure and re-combination that will merit his expression. At times he may seem and in fact be oblivious to situations around him. Much of the bizarre behavior attributed to creative persons is observed during this phase. Incubation is a time when much of the usually perceptive person's own daily experience goes unrecognized while his unconscious speaks to him. In short, he is preoccupied to the point where he may fail to attend to some of the most common things expected of him.

In trying to get the irrational idea into the conscious realm the creative person is dissatisfied with himself and may be difficult to be around. Sometimes conflicts ensue with family members or close friends who perceive his ignoring them as a conscious choice denoting personal affront or insult. This holds true not only in female-male relationships but teachers as well see the creative child in this way very often. Sometimes the preparation and incubation phases are concurrent, a worthwhile but dangerous situation if incubation interferes with the preparation process by constricting the focus of what is viewed or activates the unconscious operation without adequate data. A failure product often symbolizes this danger.

In the incubation stage self-doubt is an important mental health factor. Confidence is essential when unconscious activity brings up one thought combination after another; while the unconscious speaks and the conscious listens, the ego is unrestrictive. Ideas may be written down on scraps of paper but it is imperative that the conscious not disapprove ideas as they emerge, that judgment be deferred until the unconscious produce is available. The preoccupation and tension of wanting to produce the satisfying idea means that not much else in life is satisfying during this period, including the usually important things. Having to withhold one's judgment regarding what is produced lest the associative flow be terminated is an extremely difficult and demanding role requiring a high tolerance for frustration. Mental health is at a discount during this phase and although the incubation period may vary in length from minutes to months, the time span is important, for if it is protracted one may lose important relationships with people who might have tolerated a bit of atypical behavior but not a consistent diet.

Incubation is a phase in which anything disruptive to the concentration focus of the unconscious is rejected. For some individuals incubation is possible on and off over a period of time—a combination that is most favorable. But for most creative persons the attempt to produce ideas leads one to excessive lengths for sustaining touch with the unconscious in a noisy world that would deny it. At times some resort to the use of liquor or drugs—whatever is necessary to escape the distraction and sustain the activity of the unconscious until it is ready to deliver. This is without question the time when those close to the creative person must be patient with his self-impatience and seeming disregard for others. Not everyone can spend the same amount of time in incubation because it is too tension-producing. Still most creative persons prefer long blocks of time in which to work. In sum, this is a time of desire to be alone, a time when the relation to a task may preempt personal relations, when daily responsibilities seem cumbersome, and what is usually acknowledged as very important is taken for granted. To an observer it may appear as a time of self-punishment. To proceed requires excluding an awareness of phenomena other than the subject at hand; everything that is viewed or considered one may try to relate to the concern. To give up during this period is at great expense, for not achieving illumination is usually self-considered as total failure.

If the incubation phase truly represents for most creative persons what Van Gogh called a "prison" in which one is confined by conversation and debate with oneself, then the *illumination* phase might be analogous to an exoneration, release, or full pardon of an individual. It is the inspirational moment of which the artist Paul Cezanne declared, "A sort of liberation, the mysterious becoming external, everything falls into place —I see." It is the exhilarating triumph that creative persons like to describe, the sudden instant they relive, that time which is beyond words. Charles Darwin, whose search of the evolution theory came to an end on a dusty lane, recalls, "The very spot on the road whilst in my carriage, when to my joy the solution occurred to me" (Lowes, 1927, p. 443). Creative scientists, inventors, artists, and writers all look back in nostalgia at the brief but cherished illumination and often speak of it as being mystical. With illumination, the burden of tension is instantly reduced and the creative person once again gains touch with those around him. The renewed awareness of others brings changes in his behavior; to some he seems sensible again or as they say, "He is like himself."

For certain creative persons, especially those who have long awaited illumination, an effort is made to retain its joy by sharing it. Usually the account of how an idea occurred is less than exciting to other people who perceive the story teller's recent rapid transition from the preoccupation and depression they noted over a period of time to joy and conscious delight as being a further index of mental illness; they wonder at the extremes in his behavior and especially the new elation over something they consider unimportant. In the returned state to consciousness, some creative persons cannot figure out why people have become distant toward them during the interlude. Often they find that during the interim of an intensive nonconscious activity, relationships with others have been strained or disrupted. For many creative persons the creative process ends with the illumination phase, for they have achieved a tentative answer, tension is reduced, and they hasten to seek after another problem. However, persons of this bent seldom attain recognition or contribute as they might because they do not go on to make the form of their invention coherent to others.

After unconscious activity has resulted in an idea or a plan, it must become subject to conscious evaluation. For some creative persons this is difficult to accept; a few find it impossible because their emotional certainty about the worth of production precludes any criticism or adaptation. Nevertheless, the high pleasure of illumination must give way to rational judgment as a determinant of final production. If a writer is to communicate, the inspired work must first be organized and edited and the logical question of what remains undone must be answered so that a reader can share the writer's message. Similarly the scientist's elation with a successful experiment must be clearly described.

Unlike the brief illumination phase, the *verification* phase can prove to be long, arduous, and at times disappointing to someone whose patience wanes with the new eagerness to undertake another quest. The hazard of many writers and scientists, of those in technology and art, is to not follow through—an omission that has resulted in the default of much good work that could now exist. There are many writers like Coleridge and Shelley who left many fragments of unfinished work because they could not revise, feeling that inspiration cannot be improved upon and that any altering destroys illumination. Speaking of Gertrude Stein, Hemingway (1965, p. 17) said, "She disliked the drudgery of revision and the obligation to make her writing intelligible." On the other hand, certain writers have known that working out the implications of creative ideas may result in more discovery and import. Hart Crane was very exacting in his work and a look at his manuscripts indicates that there was as much doubt as decision. Notwithstanding the attachment of some writers to their work, someone must complete revisions and it is true that insight during the revision process can improve organization and structure.

What serious students find disappointing with the phase sequence approach is that its descriptive account respecting events of the mind include only those that occur after an individual has originally sensed a problem, become aware of some gap in knowledge, or experienced a vague insight into an area of difficulty. Persons fond of analogizing might compare this omission to a reader who, interested in understanding an elaborate design of intricate sequence, begins to read at midpoint in the volume that explains its quest. At the moment we have no way of knowing how much of the creative process actually precedes what now are described as established phases. Maybe what is described is not near the beginning at all; perhaps we are starting close to the end. That the undescribed aspects of invention represent an important unknown is obvious. And to those who respect the realm of unconscious it might be argued that in the creative process what takes place before one enters the first described phase is of infinitely greater importance than whatever follows. In either case, teachers can profit from learning more about the presumed sequence phases.

Creative Process in Relation to Abilities

The hypothesis that creativity is the same wherever found has been opposed by a number of psychologists who argue that the process cannot be described as singular. Its course depends primarily upon the abilities involved, which in turn are determined by the nature of the product. Writing a book, painting a picture, or conducting an experiment may all be seen as creative endeavors, but the success of each rests upon different abilities. The author, artist, and scientist may not confront their task in the same manner. Indeed, to separate process from the abilities utilized is to oversimplify the issue, for we cannot hope to describe process apart from the mental functions that direct its course and the goals to be reached. Thus a prior question seems to be what abilities are involved in the creative process? J. P. Guilford (1950; 1963), who conceptualized the structure of intellect (see pages 13–15) believes that most of the known creative abilities—*flexibility, fluency, originality,* and *elaboration*—can be subsumed under the rubric of divergent thinking. Unlike the thinking emphasized in most classrooms requiring convergence upon a single correct and accepted answer, divergent thinking entertains a number of alternatives for problems to which single solutions seem inappropriate. *Redefinition* and *sensitivity* are also factors judged important for creative production.

Being *sensitive* to a problem appears necessary to engage the creative process. Two persons can witness the same event quite differently in the degree to which they are sensitive to it. For example, the advanced training of chemists and teachers tends to make each of these groups sensitive to entirely different aspects of experience. Perhaps the chemist alone in his lab can be relatively insensitive to interpersonal relationships and yet remain successful on the job, but not so the teacher. Similarly, the educator may be doing a good job with children and have little sensitivity toward temperature; not so in the chemist's case. Solving problems in any field begins with appropriate sensitivities.

Because sensitivity has been considered a feminine trait in our culture, the schools have been reluctant to train children for extending the range of environmental stimuli to which they respond. Along with providing an awareness or feeling toward a problem, sensitivity seems to engender a compunction to favorably change the situation. This tendency has been observed among creative individuals at all ages. After his work involving the motivation of patent inventors, Rossman (1931; 1964) distinguished them from their less inventive peers by noting that whereas noninventors tend to complain about environmental defects, inventors are intrigued by finding better ways of doing things to improve conditions. Similarly, at the kindergarten level, Torrance (1965c, p. 307) found that less creative children have little difficulty in being able to catalogue the defects in toys and pictures presented to them but appear devoid of constructive response. When confronted with a plastic toy dog and requested to think of ways in which it might be changed to be more fun, most noninventive youngsters suggest that it should move but offer no way of having this accomplished. They appear locked in the role of critic and insensitive to ways of improving things. On the other hand, inventive children who also feel that the plastic dog should be mobile to be more fun, indicate alternatives like attaching a string to pull it, wheels, a motor or battery, some mechanism for winding or a magnet placed in the nose.

Perhaps the fluency factors best illustrate the point that there is a relationship between creative process and field of endeavor. Defined as the "proliferation and ease with which ideas are generated and expressed," fluency is usually divided into four types—ideational, word, associational, and expressional. *Ideational fluency* refers to an ability to produce a large number of ideas in a situation requiring few restrictions other than time. Although an emphasis on the number of ideas produced may seem relatively unimportant as a criterion, there is evidence that quantity does lead to quality. That is, the person with more ideas more frequently seems to have better ideas. Besides the agreement of notables like Edison and Whitehead who support the view of a relationship between quantity and quality of ideas, studies have shown that even in group activity the greater the variation of ideas presented, the more likely the final aggregate decision will be reasonable (Ziller, 1955). In assessing ideational fluency, the subject is asked to enumerate as many ideas as possible about an assigned topic in five minutes. Another task requires listing within a specified time all the things one can think of that are round. The total number of responses constitute the ideational fluency score.

To perform well on *word fluency,* a factor that correlates positively with creative success in college arts and science courses (Drevdahl, 1956), one needs to demonstrate a rapid show of words that fulfill indicated requirements. For instance, the person is faced with an assignment in four minutes to issue as many words as he can that end with a specified suffix or listing a number of words that rhyme with a designated word. *Associational fluency* refers to one's awareness of relationships and the ease with which he can provide meaning in congruent manner. Usually this ability is measured by requiring the person to offer synonyms for given words or to complete simile phrases. The fourth type of fluency is termed *expressional fluency*, indicating the rapidity by which words are combined within an established time. Generally expressional fluency is ascertained by word-arrangement tasks calling for an organized written discourse using prescribed words. In review, whereas the fluency factors might be of little importance for creative production in a physics laboratory, they seem crucial for an area like creative writing. Guilford's (1959, pp. 385–386) contention is that, "Ideational fluency should give the writer something to write about; expressional fluency should help him put his words into organized discourse; [and] associational fluency should give him the word finding ability that he needs."

The word "flexibility" is often mentioned as a requisite for everyone in this era of rapid change. Generally described as the ability to shift from one train of thought to another, flexibility is shown by individuals who are able to change with ease. The thinking of such persons is not bound by history or tradition; familiar social restraints do not obstruct their consideration of new viewpoints. *Spontaneous flexibility* is unlike fluency in that its emphasis lies not with the number of ideas produced but rather on the number of categories into which ideas are produced. There is little doubt that some people get into a rut and become unable to change tracks, devise new approaches, or see alternatives. In the Minnesota studies the extent of rigidity was assessed by asking subjects to think of as many unusual, clever, or interesting uses for tin cans as possible (Torrance, 1965c, p. 302). What follows are the percentages of persons in each of the sample groups who were unable to break away from the idea that cans are containers: schizophrenics, 87 percent; graduate students, 40 percent; college sophomores, 33 percent; upper elementary children, 15 percent. From these figures graduate students appear more rigid than sophomores in college, yet less so than schizophrenics; on the other hand, elementary children are the most flexible of the lot. What is known as *adaptive flexibility* refers to the ability to sense out of the ordinary solutions and try them out. Frequently this may involve such principles as reversing procedures or changing positions, and departing from the traditional methods of doing things in favor of more novel approaches.

Although almost everyone mentions *originality* as an important aspect of creative thinking, agreement is lacking about what the term means. One suggestion is that to be original is to do something without precedent, the first of a kind in existence. This definition becomes impossible when we try to measure originality since verification of a new idea would require finding out whether anyone throughout time has ever thought of it. The same difficulty obtains if two inventors simultaneously arrive independently at the same conclusion. Under this circumstance it would be unwise to regard as creative only the one credited with the patent simply because his idea was officially registered first. Neither is there merit in attaching value to behavior simply because it is novel. Surely the content of man's dreams and hallucinations are unique but they often lack relevance and worth to a conscious world. For purposes of measure, Wilson, Guilford and Christenson (1953) hypothesized that originality is a phenomenon possessed by all men to a degree and therefore characterized as a continuum. Instead of defining as original only that which is new or without precedent, three alternative criteria were used—uncommonness of response, remoteness of association, and cleverness.

Assuming a continuum for uncommonness of response, originality was operationally defined as the ability to produce ideas that are statistically infrequent for the population of which the subject is a member. On an unusual-uses test, persons were confronted with several objects each having a common use and asked to enumerate six additional functions for the separate items. The remoteness of association definition for originality was tested by presenting 25 paired words with the relationship between them not immediately apparent. Here the individual was asked to suggest a third word linking each of the pairs. Finally, originality was assessed by a panel of judges responding to the plot titles that individuals submitted for several stories they had been assigned to read. There three approaches to the assessment of original response seem sensible. If the nature of novel ideas makes them impossible to judge by conventional standards, then deleterious labels like "silly" or "odd" should not be the criteria but rather we ought to be restrained in the immediate tendency to deem new ideas as unworthy without examination. To break out of the mold or get off the beaten track should not be judged as wayward but will be considered so if its occurrence is always punished in the classroom.

There are, of course, other abilities affecting creative process. In brief, to work out the implications of an idea and fill in the details of a structure is known as *elaboration.* Sometimes original thinkers achieve less than they might because they lack elaborative ability; and others who follow them may receive much credit for explicating the same issues as a translator. Elaboration involves following through on ideas. In his essay "On Genius," John Stuart Mill said, "As much genius is often displayed in explaining the design and bringing out the hidden significance of a work of art as in creating it." Finally, the ability to *redefine* is of significance in creative production because it entails the transformation of an existing object into one of a different function, design or use; it implies a freedom from fixedness and the skill to reinterpret what is known.

Age and the Inventive Process

Age is believed to be an important variable in the inventive process. One assumption is that inventive thinking does not proceed in the same fashion at all chronological points. It may be as one grows older that his thought processes are revised as a result of changes in physical energy, perception, the need for achievement, societal expectations, and information. Perhaps the creativity of a young mind is manifest in ways different from that of an adult. If this be so, we may inadvertently be punishing creative children. To speak of the inventive process as something singular as though the child and adult pattern are the same may be misleading. Indeed there is reason to believe that appreciable differences do exist in the creative process between members of different generation groups. During the preschool and primary grades, children are encouraged to fantasize, engage in role play, and conjure. To facilitate the pretending function, they are told stories of imaginary characters whose adventurous exploits depict "good" behavior. It is typical for adults to spin tales and experience delight with the enthusiastic response of youngsters. But then as boys and girls begin to advance through the elementary grades, there is a reversal in the adult reaction to creative behavior and sponsorship of fantasy. All of a sudden pretending has no place and the display of imagination is discouraged.

Since the fantasy product of children has no utility value in the adult world, some parents decide boys and girls must give up this satisfying but useless enterprise early and instead occupy their thoughts with concerns that can better prepare the mind for life in these times. With the rejection of content on which child imagination operates, there is an attempt to introduce a focus on new content—the realistic and factual. These elements, it is believed, will more likely motivate achievement than will a dreamy orientation of fantasy. Children need to learn that the world is not all roses, that animals don't really talk, competition is keen, and that the rewards go to persons who are alert and less visionary, people in the right arena—that of realism.

Reinforcing the discount of child imagination is an adult fear of its product. Imagination supposedly will render a person unacceptable if it dominates his mature life. Moreover, this unreal part of the mind, this irrational and uncontrolled aspect of being, is considered the source of man's inhumanity to man. It follows that since violence is bad and peace is our goal, we ought not allow children to pretend encounters of a hostile nature. Rather they must be exposed to the realistic, become cautious and peace-loving. Lest more irrational men destroy themselves and introduce destruction into life, we must introduce reason early to all children—the earlier the better. In sum, a rational base for behavior is necessary; all that is irrational must be curtailed—one cannot afford imagination above a certain age.

Another adult contingent tends to disfavor child fantasy, believing that it represents the origin of misconduct. By this reasoning there already is so much lying and cheating in the world, and somehow we must work toward more integrity and truthfulness. Pretending is interpreted as lying, making up stories is a breach of morality and develops the tools of dishonesty, a tendency to be eliminated before it becomes inseparable from personality. Grown-ups of this persuasion fail to realize two very important things: First, the child mind is insufficiently developed to use imagination in the adult-accepted utility way; that is, it does not produce anything saleable or profitable. Unable as yet to attach imagination to abstraction, the child pretends just for the fun of it, an outcome of little value in the estimate of certain parents and teachers. A second and frequently overlooked point is that fantasy serves a useful motivation and mental health purpose during childhood in that achievement usually has to be imagined before it is actualized. Children have fewer achievements than they prefer. Much of what they perceive as recognized accomplishment lies beyond what their mind or strength would allow. Therefore, it is only natural that they should frequent an imaginary world in which the desired goals can be reached.

It should also be expected that the product of imagination will be related as though it represents a fact. This deserves elaboration. Assume a first-grade boy has described how on the way home from school he heard a cry for help and upon investigation witnessed an infant drowning.

He dived in, saved the would-be victim and received the undying gratitude of its parents as well as the onlookers who had gathered to watch
his rescue operation. The fact that no body of water lies between his
school and home, that he cannot swim, and that his clothes are perfectly
dry, does not detract from the story—the rescue should have happened
if it didn't. It illustrates how he would act if such a situation arose. So he
might as well believe it is true. But every so often this kind of child report
is treated as a moral issue with a scolding or spanking because an
untruth cannot go without punishment—this response from parents who
at the same time are telling his younger brother and sister about the
Easter bunny and Santa Claus (it leads one to think that only popular
lies are acceptable). Of course, the parents might do well to encourage
real achievement like teaching the youngster to swim, but the point is
that for the child a narrowed and often ignored line separates fact from
wish, what is from what one would like it to be. Imagination is able to
bridge this gap and a boy who first imagines himself a hero is more likely
to become one.

Another relevant illustration of fantasy's benefit to motivation is reported by Hadfield (1962, pp. 156–157), who tells of taking a four-year-
old girl to a party. So shy and bashful was the escort's charge that whenever guests approached or spoke with her, she would bury her face in
his coat. All during the festivities, she did not speak at all until it came
time to leave. Then she remarked how very much she would like to come
back again. Upon arrival at home the girl related to her mother how she
had played and spoken with all of the other children. Again this so-called
lying represented what the girl would have liked to have been doing
and therefore what she imagined herself to have done had being bashful
not interfered. On a subsequent visit perhaps she will do what the shy-
ness had first prevented. But to her way of thinking no clear boundaries
separate fantasy from fact. Indeed the first leads to the second and this
holds true for most children in that achievements have to be imagined
before they are put into effect. This principle obtains for adults as well—
a man without fiction is a man without; he lacks not only the primary
source by which to sustain creative production but a great mechanism of
defense that can dilute the power of stress and so enable mental health.

Whether the adult rejection of child imagination stems from a concern
for realism, or truth, a fear of moral misdirection, or weak achievement
motivation, it comes to the same thing—many of us simply fear fantasy.
By way of contrast is the view of Albert Einstein, scientist and humanitarian. In his estimate, "Imagination is more important than knowledge,
for knowledge is limited, whereas imagination embraces the entire world
—stimulating progress, giving birth to evolution." This introduces a
strange dilemma; on the one hand our society advocates acceleration on
a scale never before known, if possible finishing the formal school course
in less time than normally expected so as to allow early entry to a voca-

tional position. At the same time, imagination, the very base of the intended productivity, is considered less than valuable until utility-directed on the job. It may be that the very institution charged with preparing a child for creative achievement undermines this objective. If children would be creative as adults in science, art, or technology, then imagination must be preserved and developed, fantasy must be allowed to persist in the form of pretending, and other nonutility fashions until such time as abstraction can absorb the force of imagination and demonstrate the power of originality in adult-accepted form, until imagination is ready to impose its power on what grown-ups accept as useful (cf. McClelland, 1955b). That adults need to be more tolerant of child imagination is not a new complaint. As far back as the eighteenth century it was alleged that J. Rousseau, the famous child development leader, forbade his children to attend public lessons before age twelve, believing that if schoolmasters were to discourage imagination before this age it could prove devastating.

Given the adult feelings just described, it ought not be surprising that a great deal of research shows that children unnecessarily sacrifice creativity at about the fourth grade. At that point the previously rising creative growth curves begin to decline. This tendency was first noted in 1900 by Kirkpatrick, whose ink-blot study showed primary children to be more imaginative than boys and girls of the intermediate grades. During an investigation of written compositions, Colvin and Meyer (1906) reported a general decline in imagination from grades three through twelve. In her song-creation experiment, Weideman (1961) found that fourth-graders submitted a smaller proportion of songs than any other grade but at the same time they expressed a perfectionist trend in being the most interested group in judging work done by others. The same discouraging trend toward decreased production at the fourth grade is illustrated in Torrance's (1964b) study of children's writing.

It seems that about the fourth grade male and female roles assume significance, peer standards become very important, and one is expected by teachers and parents to start acting more like a grown-up. The curriculum content shifts its emphasis from the so-called unreal to the real; animals in the stories no longer talk nor serve as principal characters but instead represent background. Lessons now are formalized and organized; students are inadvertently urged to be critical of one another; guessing or atypical response is discouraged; credit is given only for what is written down and grade symbols become more important than ever before. Under these conditions, imagination is subject to discount. In response to the question, "What are all of the possible things Mother Hubbard could do when she found no dog bones in the cupboard for her dog?" younger children were quick to reply, but fourth graders found the problem extremely difficult since they were so preoccupied with a notion that she should have prevented this predicament, that they could not entertain alternatives of how she might extricate herself (Torrance, 1964, pp. 5–6). Our society may inadvertently be diminishing its talent through exclusion of imaginative growth during middle childhood. If this were not so, many more youngsters might grow up to be productive adults.

But age bears another relation to creativity, namely that the development of process is closely linked with the issue of pace. If the rate expectations in school work be uniform and all are supposed to proceed in unison, then the development of creativity among the precocious stands in jeopardy. In warning of this danger, Sidney Pressey (1955) points out that stereotypes about precocity have led us to believe that the learning pace of such youngsters must be restricted for their own benefit. Generally this assertion is justified by undocumented claims that precocious children are less than healthy, that their intellectual advantage serves to penalize them in terms of social adjustment, and that they need help in making friends and getting along with others. Therefore, to facilitate the able child's acceptance by his peers and society, his intellectual pace should be slowed down rather than accelerated. Intellectual development is thereby sacrificed, ostensibly for the sake of social adjustment. By this course, the youngster's creative processes may not be activated and at a time we know to be crucial for intellectual development. It is a sad commentary that some educators find it necessary to think of growth as more related to adjustment than development.

Insights as to how the creative process might be facilitated in the early years can be derived from a consideration of history's precocious young. In the Europe of two centuries past, one finds a rash of notable precocious musicians who before reaching their teens were well on the way toward becoming accomplished performers. To mention a few— Mozart, Chopin, Haydn, Mendelssohn, Shubert, and Dvorak. In our own time it is just as easy to enumerate athletic champions who attained eminence as adolescents—Jack Nicklaus, Cassius Clay, Marlene Bauer, Maureen Connolly, Babe Didrickson, Don Schollander, and Bob Mathias. To account for the difference in talent abundance between the two eras, we are reminded that during the time of Chopin music served as a major interest and avenue of acclaim for people of all economic stratas just as today athletics is universally esteemed. But being born at a certain time and possessing certain constitutional factors, important as they may be, cannot account for the development of the prodigies mentioned. Some of the favorable factors of environment that most of these eminent persons enjoyed were an excellent early opportunity to develop, encouragement, guidance, and instruction from family, friends, and teachers, close association with others in the same field, and many chances for acclaim and success.

The serious question that comes to mind is why, by comparison with music and athletics, precocity is so rare in science, technology, art, and literature. In addition to the greater weight our society has placed upon social adjustment than intellectual advance, Pressey (1955) suggests that whereas music teachers and athletic coaches have always been interested in identifying and developing able performers, classroom teachers usually lament their lack of time or method to do so. In addition, the continuing opportunity for intensive practice and rapid progress to be found in music and athletics are often unavailable in other areas of the curriculum. In other words, the precocious child in elementary school who is interested in trigonometry finds he must wait to learn it until he gets into that year of high school when such a course is offered, when his peers are ready. Meanwhile he is expected to be content with overlearning and dubious status. Unlike the athlete or musician who gains acclaim early, the student of science may have little chance to receive peer favor and adult recognition beside that which accrues from marks. In fact, members of his club or special interest group may be the only persons who really encourage him at all. In this context, Pressey (1955) raises an important issue:

> Suppose that Mozart or Bobby Jones had not been allowed to begin his music or his golf until the other children did, or to practice more or progress faster or had had only the instruction of the school class in music or physical education. Suppose that they had been kept from playing with older children or adults in the fear that they might become maladjusted, kept from associating much with other musicians or golfers because that would be narrowing and undemocratic, kept from public performances or tournaments because that would be exploiting the poor child! It surely may be questioned whether they would have then reached the preeminence they did. Abuses in the aforementioned directions are, of course, possible. But it is also an abuse to withhold opportunities from precocious youngsters who are eager to advance and excel. The opinion is ventured that the last type of abuse is now, in this country, the more common one.

Although society has recently come to favor early admission to school, there is continuing opposition to the established fact that able children can best proceed at their own rate without danger to social development. The concept of acceleration has been least effective because some have assumed it can be accomplished only by skipping grades. Instead by admitting precocious children on the basis of readiness rather than chronological age into a nongraded structure, it is likely that some will, moving at their pace, complete public school more rapidly and that the same group will finish college more quickly if credit be granted upon successful examination (Pressey, 1963, pp. 1–4; 1967, pp. 73–80). They might then approach their career at an earlier age. One study at The Ohio State University of sixteen-year-old early entrants indicated that 50 percent went on to graduate school as compared with only 30 percent of the eighteen-year-old entrants paired with them according to test ability and program type. Among the early entrants, 63 percent graduated in

less than the typical four-year period (Pressey, 1932; 1949, p. 11). These
results have been corroborated by a number of similar studies (Terman
and Merrill, 1937; Pressey, 1967).

A third point of view about the age-creativity relationship implies that
there is a biological "time of plenty," an age period during which inventive behavior will most likely flourish. Advocates of this position insist
that we can infer distinctions in the development of creative process by
plotting the most common ages at which creative productions occur. By
this method of compilation, much supportive evidence has emerged for
the contention that intellectual creativity reaches its peak early in adult
life and therefore that conditions during the young years ought to be made
conducive for imaginative production. Lehman (1966) has matched
nearly 700 recognized contributions to psychology with the inventor's
chronological age at the time of contribution. As indicated in Figure
V-3, the peak period among contributors now deceased is close to forty
years of age. By way of contrast, the apex for living inventors approximates thirty years of age.

The "time of plenty" view is not a pessimistic commentary. It simply
points up certain facts about age and production. The reasons for these

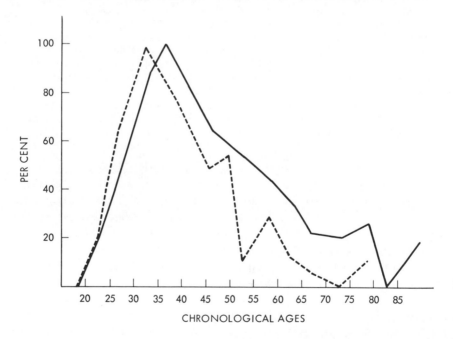

Fig. V-3. Age versus contributions to psychology as listed by E. G. Boring (1950).
(Solid line: 563 superior contributions by 187 contributors now deceased and born
subsequent to 1774—an average of 3.01 contributions each. Broken line: 120 superior
contributions by 68 still living contributors—an average of 1.76 contributions each.)
From "The Psychologist's Most Creative Years," by Harvey Lehman, in *American
Psychologist*, XXI, No. 4 (1966), 366. Reprinted by permission.

facts have retained their mystery though new hunches are continually being advanced and tested. On the one hand, the data would seem to urge young people to put forth their best effort before reaching middle age. If there is a sparkle of originality within, it ought to be released while the spirit, energy, perspective and commitment of youth remain. At the same time, Lehman (1966) reminds us:

> Since group means tell nothing at all about individual performance, since each of the large number of some one individual's contributions may possess far more merit than the master works of certain other individuals, since there are numerous heart-warming exceptions to the general trend, and since, moreover, life should consist of far more than the production of scientific contributions, the present study provides no good reason why anyone should feel at any age level that his usefulness is at an end.

Although less is known of the creative process than desired, its necessity in the future is without dispute, since persons of every generation, group, and society have need of their own dreams, ideas, and innovations. For these needs to be fulfilled, we must preserve the imagination of the young, encourage its development in school, and respect persons whose thoughts are not our own.

Measurement and Creativity

The single most controversial issue in the debate over whether to educate for creativity is focused upon its relationship to intelligence. Leaders in the field have been severely criticized for basing their work on a convenient but questionable assumption, namely, that there is a domain of creativity, an established cohesive psychological dimension of individual differences that exists independent from what has been traditionally called general intelligence. Another postulate that has drawn much criticism is that the current variety of indices labeled as "creativity tests" actually share in common the measure of this distinct psychological dimension. A number of scholars who believe creativity might at best be subsumed as a minor aspect of general intelligence reject the idea of referring to both concepts as though they were comparable in level of generality. After all, to do so implies that each of the rubrics, creativity and intelligence, do in fact subsume a unified dimension of cognitive activity. And, while there is evidence that the familiar G concept, referring to the satisfactory intercorrelation among tests of intelligence, allows us to label a certain aggregate of abilities as comprising "intelligence," it is doubtful whether any such relationship of internal consistency obtains among tests measuring this so-called realm of creativity. A few examples supporting the negative view will clarify the nature and importance of this dispute.

Working with a sample of 531 youngsters, ranging in placement from sixth grade to senior high school, Getzels and Jackson (1962) compared IQ performance with the results attained on five tests described as indices of creativity. Respectively these creativity tests called for an ability to:

make up arithmetic problems from assigned information, compose endings for fables, detect geometric figures hidden in a complex pattern, devise alternate meanings for certain stimuli, and suggest uses for given objects. All five of these creativity measures for boys and four in the girls' case were significantly correlated ($p < .05$) with IQ.* It was also found that no greater correlation obtained among the creativity tests than between them as an aggregate and the IQ measures. This suggests that whatever similarities the tests of creativity share among themselves they also share with intelligence tests. In other words, the indices of creativity seem about as independent of one another as they, in the aggregate, are from intelligence. Consequently there is no warrant for supposing that a unified psychological dimension of individual differences labeled creativity exists apart from general intelligence. Given this conclusion, it also appears questionable whether scores of separate component measures ought to be summed to yield an overall index score as though they have the same psychological meaning. The low correlation among them indicates that the creativity measures are in fact independent indices of different things; to add them up as though they possess something in common that was distinct from what they share with tests of general intelligence is unjustified.

In 1962 Cline and others compared the results of 95 male and 66 female high school pupils on an IQ measure with seven measures of creativity resembling the task types cited in the Getzels and Jackson study. The results showed a sizable correlation between creativity and intelligence. The average correlation between the indices of creativity and intelligence was higher than that among the tests of creativity. In 1963 Cline and others completed a similar study using 79 male and 40 female high school pupils. It was learned that for boys 6 of 7 creativity tests and 4 of 7 for girls were significantly correlated with IQ at the .05 level. Again, the creativity tests correlated more strongly with intelligence than they did with one another in the case of both sexes. That is, the tests of creativity seem to have nothing in common beyond that which they share with tests of intelligence. Since a battery of creativity measures relate more strongly to a standard index of intelligence than they do with one another, internal consistency appears to represent a major problem in creativity testing (Wallach and Kogan, 1965; cf. Torrance, 1966c).

From each of the three studies just discussed a similar conclusion was drawn: There is no warrant for referring to creativity as a comparable but separate domain from intelligence. To accept this conclusion, however, implies that we accept the measurement approach on which the procedures have been based; it denies the possibility that the methods used in the studies described have perhaps been too varied to define an existent domain independent of general intelligence. To entertain such a

---

* The certainty or confidence level with which any assertion is made often is expressed in probability form. For an explanation see page 301.

possibility forces us to the serious question of what psychological processes are the ones to deserve focus. One useful clue as to what ought to be measured derives from a perusal of the introspections of manifestly creative individuals who, to a remarkable degree report a similarity in the processes of their own creative work with respect to combining information, blending elements from dissonant thoughts, drawing together distant concepts, and playfully juxtaposing remote ideas.

Using the accounts of eminent persons as a reference, Mednick (1962) has defined creative thinking as the process of "forming associate elements into new combinations which either meet specific requirements or are in some way useful." When so defined creative thinking is distinguished from original thought by the imposition of requirements on uniqueness. Although 418 might be a very original response to the question of how much is $9 + 5$, it can only be designated as creative if it meets the criterion of being useful. Original ideas are frequently expressed in mental institutions but few of these would classify as creative. And, even though it might be difficult to reach agreement in certain fields of creative endeavor as to what constitutes being "useful" we can use arbitrarily imposed criteria in experimentally contrived situations with success if they are explicated to the subjects.

From Mednick's definition of creative thinking, one can deduce some of the factors that will differentiate among individuals in terms of their probability of reaching creative solutions. In general it can be said that any ability or tendency that facilitates bringing together otherwise mutually remote ideas will favor the inventive orientation; conversely, whatever personalistic elements act to deter the contiguity of remote associations will inhibit creativity. The first and obvious requisite for combining remote elements involves a repertoire since one can combine only what exists for him. In other words, to effect a creative solution the necessary cognitive units must exist in some kind of stored form in the first place or else they could not be generated under any conditions. Hence the ceiling performance of an individual's capacity to generate cognitive units is governed by the extensiveness of his response repertoire. This fact by itself will tend to increase the significance of any demonstration that creative thinking, as defined by Mednick, is relatively separate from general intelligence.

How an individual's associates are organized is a concern second only to the existence of remote elements, for on this issue rests the probability and speed of attaining a creative solution. As an illustration, two patterns of associate response strength are depicted in Figure V-4. The horizontal base line (abcissa) indicates that responses may range in hierarchy from the stereotypic or conventional at the high end to those that are unique and original at the low end. The relative speed of response is shown by the vertical line (ordinate).

Although stereotypic responses possess greater strength for almost

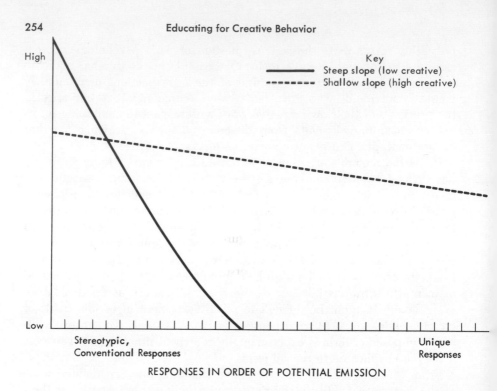

Fig. V-4. Two hypothetical patterns of associative response. Adapted from a figure of associative hierarchies by Wallach and Kogan (1965).

everyone, we differ from one another a great deal with respect to the availability of our unique associates. For example, when presented with the stimulus word "table," a low creative individual restricted to stereotypic responses like "chair" would be characterized as having an associate hierarchy with a steep gradient (see Figure V-4). Once beyond the initial conventional responses to the stimulus, his associate strengths for other ideas or words lower in the hierarchy rapidly drop. That is to say, he stops when the stereotypic associates have been exhausted. In contrast is the high creative person whose associative hierarchy is characterized by a shallow gradient. While the high creative person's strongest response to the stimulus word "table" is also "chair," this response is not overly dominant. So, given enough time, it is more likely that he will be able to get to the less probable and remote kinds of associations to the word "table." And, it is among these more remote responses that the combinations for a creative solution is to be found. This means that the shallow gradient defines a high creative person whose associative organization is marked by a repertoire of cognitive elements exceeding in size that of the steep gradient individual who is low in creativity.

We can predict that the high-creative, shallow-gradient person will respond relatively slowly and steadily emit many responses and some that are unique, while the low-creative, steep-gradient person will initially respond at a higher rate because of his associate strength concentration on the conventional but emit fewer responses in the long run and less probably attain the creative solution. While unique responses possess greater associative strength for the creative person, his level of associative strength still remains lower for unique than stereotypic responses. Thus, while unique responses will not be given at all by low creative, steep gradient persons the rate of producing unique responses will be relatively slow for even the high creative person. Supporting this prediction is the research of Bousfield *et al.* (1954), who in measuring the rate of depletion of the associative reservoir found a high negative correlation between rate of association and total number of associations.

The major reason the curves in Figure V-4 do not intersect the ordinate at the same point is that the response strength for stereotypic associates is far greater for the low creative person. Mednick suggests that creative persons actually manifest an aversion to issuing conventional responses. There is an interesting exception to the patterns of associate response strengths in Figure V-4. When a group of thirty research scientists were divided into dichotomous groups (high-low) for rated creativity, the low-creative group issued more stereotypic responses to 80 percent of the words presented them from a list chosen for its tendency to elicit stereotypic response. The obvious interpretation of this finding is that the associate response organization of highly creative persons is characterized by less stereotypy. According to Mednick (1958, 1962), a less obvious but possible interpretation might be that some highly creative individuals could have a steep but deviant associative hierarchy. By this is meant a strong dominant associative response but one that deviates from the popular pattern. One prediction that could be made of this type of person is that he will more likely be a one-shot producer—an occasional phenomenon among novelists (Reynolds, 1966). If such a person does create further products, they will tend to closely resemble his first product. This by way of contrast to the shallow-gradient creative person, who may be expected to be a multiple producer engaged in several kinds of creative expression.

Several implications for an approach to creativity testing derive from Figure V-4. Particularly significant is the fact that stereotypic responses tend to precede unique ones in order of production whether an individual is classified as high or low creative (Christenson *et al.*, 1957). Given the belated position of unique associates it would seem improbable that persons able to generate them could be identified unless there be provided an adequate period of time in the testing period. By the same token, the temporal constraint acting to penalize highly creative persons favors the low creative, whose initially more rapid fluency of stereotypic responses may make him look outstanding so long as time is called before he exhausts his reservoir of convention. When no time limits obtain, of course, the low creative "runs out of gas" with the depletion of stereotypes. This information along with the knowledge that high-creative persons generate unique associates in less frequency than low creatives produce stereotypic responses should indicate that time limits ought not be imposed if a fair assessment is to be made of how able one is in generating the unconventional. For the high-creative person unique associates will proceed at a slow and steady rate over a period extending far into the time when the low creative is no longer generating anything. In order that creative persons be able to demonstrate superiority over their less inventive peers in the production of unique associates, temporal freedom is imperative. Perhaps individuals taking creativity tests should be permitted as much time as they desire.

Another condition of merit for creativity testing comes from the many creative artists and scientists who express agreement that the relaxed precondition of creative process is violated whenever a threat of evaluation exists, whenever one is led to believe that his immediate performance will reflect on self-worth. That such constraints disrupt the creative process is apparent from Dentler and Mackler's (1964) study in which subjects earned significantly higher scores on an unusual-uses test when the conditions of administration were relaxed than under several evaluational conditions. This leads to new considerations about the type of context within which creativity might best be expected to reveal itself. Translated into operational innovation it suggests that a gamelike setting should replace the familiar evaluative procedures and that time limits should be abandoned. Together these two variables, lack of temporal freedom and a gamelike context, represent a possible explanation as to why the studies cited earlier have failed to differentiate statistically between the creativity and intelligence domain. Then, too, perhaps the definition of creative thinking has been too diffuse in certain of these studies.*

Wallach and Kogan (1965) are responsible for a major study of the creativity-intelligence distinction that has enabled us to resolve a long-standing controversy. These investigators set out to determine whether creativity, defined as the ability to produce many associates and many that are unique, is independent of individual differences in the traditional domain of general intelligence. A second purpose was to ascertain whether creativity, like the G concept of intelligence, engenders a sub-

---

* Torrance, whose sustained studies during the past decade have enabled the development of a verbal and figural test battery of creative thinking for children, adolescents, and adults, suggests that since a person can behave creatively in an almost infinite number of ways and given the diversity among definitions of creativity, "the concept of an overall validity coefficient for tests of creative thinking ability is grossly inappropriate. It is much more useful to think in terms of a variety of kinds of criteria of creative behavior and of a variety of kinds of creative thinking ability involved in these criterion behaviors" (1966c). This approach has guided the development of his own test tasks, which sample a wide range of abilities in the universe of creative abilities (Guilford, 1966; Yamamoto, 1966).

stantial degree of generality across different types of tasks (verbal-visual). Serving as the sample group were all of the fifth-graders of a middle-class suburban public school system. In total, 151 youngsters (70 girls and 81 boys) participated, all of whom completed a series of creativity instruments calling for the production of associates. The tests employed resemble closely an earlier battery of procedures devised by Guilford but with certain notable exceptions in their administration. In the Guilford test setting, a premium has been placed on performance and no attempt was made to dissuade the test taker from viewing the whole affair as unlike the usual test encounters in class. But speed and evaluative emphasis are conspicuously absent in the Wallach and Kogan study; instead a gamelike atmosphere and temporal freedom obtain. For each instrument (all are oral) the number of unique associates and total number of associates serve as correlated variables.

On the *instances* procedure, one is asked to generate possible instances of a class concept that is specified in verbal terms. For example, name all the round things you can think of. The number of unique responses to an item is defined as the number of associates given by only one child to the item in question. So, while "lifesavers" is a unique response for round things, "buttons" is not. The *alternate uses* procedure requires generation of possible uses for a verbally specified object. Example: Tell me all of the things you could do with a shoe. A unique response for this question might be "to trap a mouse," while to "throw at a noisy cat" is not. Another procedure urges one to come up with possible *similarities* between two verbally specified objects. When asked to "tell me all the ways in which milk and meat are alike," a conventional response is "they come from animals"—more unique is "they are government inspected." In addition to the foregoing verbal techniques, there are two procedures involving abstract patterns and line-visual stimulus materials for which the subject is to generate possible meanings or interpretations. The sample group was also given ten indices of general intelligence, including verbal and performance subtests of the Wechsler Intelligence Scale for Children (WISC); verbal and quantitative aptitude scores from the School and College Ability Tests (SCAT); and the Sequential Tests of Educational Progress (STEP), an index of academic achievement in various subject content areas.

After the measures of creativity and intelligence had shown themselves reliable, the dimensionality of these indices was examined. As an aggregate the creativity instruments proved highly intercorrelated (average .40);* the same internal consistency held true among the tests of general intelligence (average .50). However, the correlation between creativity and intelligence was extremely low (.10). These relationships encourage the conclusion that the dimension of individual differences in ability to

* See pages 324–25 for an explanation of how to interpret coefficients of correlation.

generate many cognitive units and many that are unique is definitely independent from what has traditionally been called general intelligence, while at the same time being a cohesive and pervasive domain in its own right. That is, in an assessment context free from evaluative threat and temporal constraint the ability to generate unique associates derives from a source different from intelligence as historically perceived. We can with some confidence assert that the ability of a child to exhibit creativity, as defined in the Wallach and Kogan (1965) research has little to do with whether or not he reveals the behaviors that bring high scores on tests of general intelligence. This finding becomes even more significant when we recall that all of the creativity measures were oral, calling for verbal facility, and that verbal facility also plays a major role in the assessment of general intelligence.

Moreover, the results suggest that we may be able to educate to a higher degree many people with whom we have up to now been unsuccessful. Operationally, intelligence has been the complex of abilities needed to master reading and arithmetic—subjects not conspicuously demanding of creative behavior. It should be mentioned that while the creativity and intelligence domains are unique, a given person might be high in both of them. One estimate is that if we identify a group of children who are either highly creative or highly intelligent, 30 percent will be both. Finally, the relative orthogonality of the two domains (creativity-intelligence) has been illustrated at a point in the life cycle (ages ten and eleven) well below the age when maximal differentiation of types of cognitive performance might be expected (Wallach and Kogan, 1965). Nevertheless, the distinction between creativity and intelligence as modes of thinking is already clear in an elementary school population. These data combine to pose an inquiry of educators—what can be done in schools to educate for creativity?

THE SCHOOL AND CREATIVE BEHAVIOR

School personnel have made two prominent errors of omission with respect to educating for creativity. The size of the student population who possess creative potential and the subject matter areas in which creativity might be developed have both been underestimated. Creativity is not limited to art and music, as some suppose (cf. Andrews, 1965; Roe, 1956). In fact, much of the work in art and music is reproductive rather than creative-productive in the sense that originality has little chance to appear when an individual's purpose is to master or duplicate the performance of something already completed by another person. Invention is not restricted to certain aspects of the curriculum but rather has a place in every subject from science to shop, home economics to human relations (cf. Smith, J. A., 1966).

Recognize too that everyone owns creativity to some degree. Yet for most adults and many children it is seldom in evidence, less often recognized, and almost never rewarded. Somehow the creative potential is held back by an excessive consciousness of self, hidden as it were behind an overprotective ego that prevents the kind of relation to task that is required to activate the creative process. Even highly creative persons are unproductive at times when they deny expression of their inventive functioning. Whether we choose to lecture the individual for succumbing to compulsive conformity or lecture the group for bringing undue pressure to bear on its membership, the fact is that almost all the reasons for an early decline in creativity seems culture-caused rather than biological. During the same period of life when what is termed "intelligence" shows substantial growth, the level of creative behavior shows a reduction.

Most of what boys and girls learn prior to attending school comes through guessing, questioning, searching, manipulating, even playing around, but always trying to find the truth. During early childhood, creativity develops more rapidly than intelligence because lacking a vocabulary children must learn by guessing, discovering, and testing. According to Torrance (1961a), "Creative learning takes place in the process of sensing difficulties, problems, missing elements, gaps in knowledge, making guesses, formulating hypotheses about these deficiencies, testing hypotheses, possibly revising, retesting and communicating results." The tension aroused when one senses that a thing is missing or untrue is accompanied by a desire for relief. This is what prompts one to guess and to inquire by asking questions. Being uncertain as to whether the guesses are correct, discomfort continues and it becomes necessary to test hypotheses, correct errors, and modify conclusions. Once a discovery is made, the tendency is to want everyone to know about it. All of this is why it is so natural for children to prefer learning in creative ways.

But generally the school favors another way to approach learning— by authority. One learns by authority whenever something is accepted as true because an authority says so. This authority may be the teacher, a parent, the newspaper, a textbook, or an encyclopedia. In time the authority can become "they," the peer group consensus. The point is that most youngsters enter school with a cognitive style or preference for learning creatively; whether this affinity persists depends upon the degree to which authoritative learning is imposed and the relative weight afforded creative behavior as being an achievement.

Preserving Creativity

Given the great number of children with creative prospect and the fact that it represents a natural evolving process, the first concern among educators ought to be one of preservation. Creativity will develop if allowed to grow, if teachers permit and encourage a course already begun (cf. Gowan *et al.*, 1967). A primary clue comes from the process itself—

allowing inquiry, manipulation, questioning, guessing, and the combination of remote thought elements. Generally, however, the preferred cognitive style of learning creatively is discouraged. Studies indicate that discontinuities in creative development occur at several grade levels and that these losses are accompanied by a decline in pupil curiosity and interest in learning. At the same grade levels at which creative loss occurs, increases are noted in the incidence of emotional disturbance and egregious behavior. Among Anglo-American cultures, the greatest slump in creative development seems to coincide with the fourth grade; smaller drops take place at kindergarten and seventh grade. Children at each of these grades perform less well than they did one year earlier and less well than children in the grade below them on measures of divergent thinking, imagination, and originality. This problem was long ignored, since it was judged to be a developmental phenomena instead of man-made or culture-related (Torrance, 1962). Not long ago it was first recognized that in certain cultures the development of creative thinking abilities are continuous. And, even in our own country, under selective teachers who encourage creative boys and girls and reward creative behavior, no slump occurs at grade four.

Believing that the fourth-grade slump might be eliminated by planned intervention, Torrance (1965f) and his associates have developed a series of dramatized records, most of which present an aspect of the difficulties eminent persons have faced in their struggle for creative achievement as well as certain of the ways by which they attained their contribution. Included among the episodes are Benjamin Franklin's perseverance in the midst of rejection; Thomas Edison's steadfast commitment to invention though considered by teachers as mentally deficient; the Wright brothers' virtual failure in the bicycle business and the communal criticism they received for the impractical idea of an airplane; and the ridicule of visionary men like Henry Ford and explorers Lewis and Clark. Throughout these records listeners are impressed with the need for courage and independence of judgment. None of the heroes presented is depicted as an all-American boy but in the reality of what is known about him from history including his novel ideas and personal idiosyncrasies. At strategic points the records may be stopped in order for students to pose alternatives and guess what happens next. In devising the materials, an attempt was made to find exercises viewed by children as provocative and yet within the competence range of fourth-graders so that they might engage in tasks analogous to those achieved by the eminent persons.

Other records in the same series deal with the need to keep fantasy alive until imagination can show its force in an adult-accepted manner. This effort, designed to offset the excessive quest for safety, realism, certainty, and objectivity that characterizes the fourth grade is accomplished by dramatized legends. For example, in one sequence the young Italian Giovanni develops from a coward into a hero by using his imagination, cleverness, and ingenuity to outwit a wicked giant. The stop device is used in this drama whenever Giovanni finds himself in new difficulty. Some of the expected outcomes are: an awareness of the development of courage in the hero, the development of ability to see new relationships and draw tentative conclusions from information given, practice in making multiple hypotheses, and elaborating the implications of an idea.

Familiarizing children with the nature of creative thinking by viewing episodes in the lives of prominent people is important. It would be desirable, of course, if the creative process were always exemplified in teacher behavior, but unfortunately some instructors are afraid of imagination. They admit being fearful "to let go" in front of children, to pretend, conjure, laugh, regress, or in any way exhibit attributes of behavior that might raise questions about their dignity as a teacher. This reluctance among educators and candidates for teaching to behave in ways that are creative is poignantly demonstrated by the 3,000 who participated in trial testing "Sounds and Images," a recorded group of exercises in which sound effects are used to encourage imagination and courage among children (Torrance, 1963b, pp. 23–27). This record consists of four sound effects each of which is repeated three times. The first sound is easily recognized, simple, and well organized, but the succeeding ones increase in strangeness, are less coherent, and less obviously related. The fourth effect consists of six strange and unrelated sound elements placing a burden on the listener's ability to synthesize unrelated elements into a coherent whole. Each time the sounds are repeated, listeners are urged to let their imagination go a bit further and create more original images and word pictures. The activity is structured so that there is a built-in warm-up, freedom from evaluation that makes divergent thinking legitimate, and an invitation to regress and enjoy it.

Upon conclusion of the record, listeners are asked to select their most interesting response for each of the sound effects. Among the teacher sample, many preferred their first or second response, expressing the feeling that they could not defend their third response because it did not reflect realism. Some refused to let colleagues see the third response because of embarrassment. By far the largest number of teachers simply closed up after the first response refusing to go beyond except in elaboration (Torrance, 1963b). Under these conditions, it is easy to realize why many teachers find it hard to preserve, encourage, or develop student imagination. The need to alter teacher view regarding the acceptance of divergent ideas is apparent.

Increasing Pupil Understanding of Creativity

Beyond the responsibility for preserving creative behavior, there lies a responsibility for its development. This might best be accomplished by increasing the emphasis upon synectics, a method of group creative problem-solving based on the idea that inventive function can be increased when people understand something of the psychological processes operating in creativity (Gordon, 1961). In particular the importance of the preparation phase in the creative process needs to be recognized. The lore about creative production seldom includes any aspect other than inspiration. Anton Chekhov insisted, "To deny artistic creation involves problems and purposes would be to admit that an artist creates without premeditation, without design, under a spell. Therefore, if an artist boasted to me of having written a story without a previously settled design, but by inspiration, I should call him a lunatic" (Ghiselin, 1952, p. 6). The same necessity for hard work is evident in the view of Paul Valéry, who speaks of "Une ligne donnée" of a poem. One line is given to the poet by God or nature and the rest he must discover for himself.

Just as preparation should be extolled so too students need recognize the importance of nonintellectual factors in thought production—especially sensitivity and emotion (Bugental and Tannenbaum, 1965). Writing about the artist, Picasso said, "He is a receptacle of emotions come from no matter where: from the sky, the earth, a piece of paper, a passing figure, a cobweb. This is why one must not discriminate between things. There is no rank among them. . . . The painter passes through states of fullness and of emptying. That is the whole secret of art. I take a walk in the forest of Fontainebleau. There I get an ingestion of greenness. I must empty this sensation into a picture" (Zervos, 1952, p. 51; cf. Gilot and Lake, 1964; Lowenfeld and Brittain, 1965).

It should be known that as creativity has its source in the unconscious, this unconscious must be allowed to work on a solution if one is to emerge. This is to say we often mistake the time for struggle, the time for will and reason to intervene. To struggle before the unconscious has had an opportunity to work on a solution is to lose for the rational will has no power in the realm of irrationality. It is only when the picture has come into being (from the unconscious) that one can struggle and make it grow to completion. According to Ernest Hemingway (1965, p. 13): "I learned not to think about anything that I was writing from the time I stopped writing until I started again the next day. That way my subconscious would be working on it. . . ." Many writers have failed because they constantly focus the conscious on their work even when they are not working; in this way the premature intervention of will and reason prevents the subconscious from dealing with the issue at all and posing creative solutions.

Speaking of the will, Ghiselin (1952, pp. 16–17) writes, "One can save oneself much trouble by recognizing the limitations of the will in creation. . . . Will belongs to the conscious life only. It is effective in attaining objects in view but it cannot enable us to move in directions that have not yet been discovered. Will rather tends to arrest the undetermined development, by laying the emphasis of a heightened tension upon whatever is already in mind. When what is required is work to be done on something already defined, such an emphasis is useful." It is important to recognize that the will does function in two important stages of creative process, namely in the preparation stage, without which there can be no significant activity, and in the work of verification or revision that ordinarily ensues the inventive activity and completes or refines the product.

Youngsters also need to know that being uncertain about having the ability to produce is not unusual. Even the best-known scientists wonder at times if they will devise another major experiment; artists and writers feel the same about their pictures and books. Answering the writer's query about "drying up," Gertrude Stein said:

> You will write . . . if you will write without thinking of the result in terms of a result, but think of the writing in terms of discovery, which is to say that creation must take place between the pen and paper not before in a thought or afterward in a recasting. Yes, before in a thought but not in careful thinking. It will come and if you have anything you will get a sudden *creative recognition*. [Then speaking for her fondness for Sherwood Anderson, Miss Stein indicated] You see, he had that creative recognition, that wonderful ability to have it all on paper before he saw it and then to be strengthened by what he saw so that he could always go deep for more and not know that he was going (Preston, 1952).

Pupils are frequently discouraged by their pace of production. Teachers and parents add to the frustration when they construe lack of speed as lack of ability, being slow as an indication of failure. It should be known that the time needed for production depends on the individual. Mozart and Beethoven represent notable contrasts in musical production. Mozart thought out quartets and symphonies entirely in his head while traveling or exercising. Then upon returning home he would write them in their entirety. Yet Beethoven often wrote his work note by note, fragments at a time that he recorded in a little booklet for years. Often his initial ideas were so clumsy as to make one wonder how, at the end, such beauty could emerge. At the outset of his career as a writer, Ernest Hemingway (1965, p. 154) felt that, "I didn't know how I would ever write anything as long as a novel. It often took me a full morning of work to write a paragraph." This same man later was able to write a classic novel in six weeks.

The emotional factors of perseverance and courage are needed throughout the creative process. Courage is required to move alone toward uncertainties, counter to one's peers, to do battle with one's own prejudice only less than those of others. It takes perseverance to begin a task again and again, to reach the desired product. Van Gogh and Kuniyoshi allegedly made many paintings of the same subject in order to refine the insights expressed in representing them. D. H. Lawrence reportedly wrote *Lady Chatterley's Lover* three times. To rework and revise after a long and arduous undertaking is difficult. The same can be said of most of the creative process. Persistence brings both success and failure. More than most of us, the creative person knows failure because he does not run away from tasks. Many of us do not fail because we never become involved; at the same time we can never fully succeed. Persistence enables one to sustain a question, a problem or task and work it through to completion. The history of those who have contributed the most to society is an account filled with persistence and courage (cf. Feather, 1961; Maddi, 1965). Some of us lose our courage to venture when we hear the words, "Who ever heard of that?" It takes courage to answer, "Nobody, I hope, it's my idea." It takes courage to answer the statement, "We've never done that in this school," with "Oh, good, then I can be the first to try it." And it takes real stamina to hear the words, "How stupid," and answer with conviction, "No, creative!" (Halek, 1965).

Requisite Classroom Conditions

Creative behavior would increase almost at once if there existed a public tolerance for novel ideas. Educators should be concerned about the greater number of critics than innovators our schools graduate. Students are trained almost from the beginning to concentrate on analysis, to take things apart, to spend most of their energies in finding fault, detecting weakness, criticizing and rejecting that which is different from the usual and accepted. In itself, this is not bad but by itself it cannot be otherwise. Analysis must not be singularly prized to the exclusion of synthesis. Instead pupils should be helped to synthesize, to put things together and give them structure, to bring order out of chaos, to be original, to learn how to improve ideas and situations, to be as critical of one's own ideas as that of others, and to use tests in judging the worth of ideas.

The easiest, most common and dubious way to determine the worth of ideas is to accept only the message of eminent men, and discount the views of all without reputation. In other words, the value of an idea is related primarily to the status of its spokesman. It has been found that students who assume a constructive attitude toward available information rather than a critical attitude were able to produce a larger number of solutions and more that were original (Torrance, 1964). Similarly when groups reach a point in their development that they accept as right all the solutions of high status members because they have been right so frequently in the past, there is danger of ineffectiveness and breakdown. No matter how wise an authority may be, it is always necessary to evaluate and consider the idea itself.

Even where authority worship does not obtain, the mistrust of irrational production may represent an obstacle to the fair evaluation of novel ideas. Nearly every child is admonished to continually strive for a realistic perspective, a factual outlook. He may also be instructed in techniques for testing ideas. Nevertheless, among persons of every grade and age, inventive and imaginative ideas are consistently rejected without any testing whatsoever. The fact that some notions are arrived at irrationally often results in dismissing them without the same consideration afforded ideas generated in rational fashion. Judgment is not deferred; instead, all solutions based on guesses are judged to be of little significance. To demean the place of imagination is a great mistake, a mistake that has seldom been made by persons who have attained eminence. For example, Einstein said that, "Imagination is more important than knowledge." Goethe indicated that, "To act is easy—to think and imagine is hard." In the words of Anatole France, "To know is nothing at all; to imagine is everything." Lord Chesterton put it this way: "There are no rules for a castle in the clouds."

A third opposition to new ideas stems from the greater emphasis that teachers place on norms of behavior than on the production of original work. In certain schools, more attention is given to adjustment than to achievement; unfortunately some instructors perceive the two terms as synonymous. Thus, to pose the unique idea or question is frequently to be seen as wayward, rebelling against tradition, or depreciating socially approved patterns of response. This means that the same originality and zeal with which youngsters approach tasks on the school newspaper, in drama, athletics, social affairs, and dating must be denied in working on school assignments and tests precisely because there it will be undervalued. An important teacher role is to ensure that a tolerance for ideas be established, by his own conduct in class, and testing ideas as a basis for group decision-making. Where habits of subjecting ideas to testing exists, there a basis for tolerance has been established.

The tolerance allowed new ideas should be accompanied by a respect for their spokesmen. To view people who think unlike ourselves as being less worthy is to miss the advantage that differences can offer. To be sure, all who deviate ought not be labeled "creative," for some unique ideas are useless—but to sort them out is the purpose of testing. History shows that teachers and students alike have been impatient with the highly creative minority. Einstein, Roosevelt, Kennedy, and Churchill were judged no better than average pupils. Our top space expert Wernher von Braun actually failed high school mathematics and physics. From their study of over 400 acknowledged geniuses Goertzel and Goertzel (1962) estimate that at least 60 percent of these persons had serious difficulties in school! Many did not have good grades and left school for a time. A number of them were made to feel guilty about their divergent thinking ability. The response of too many creative persons over the years has been that of self-abnegation. This renunciation of one's own talent is illustrated by a bright fourth-grade Minneapolis boy who, when asked to conjure some fantasy about a flying monkey, wrote the following:

Once there was a little monkey who was always doing what his mother told him not to do. One day he told his sister, "I can do something that you will never be able to do. I can fly." His sister said he couldn't, so he climbed the tree, gave a leap and began to fly. His sister ran as fast as she could to the mother monkey. The mother was surprised and angry. She told the little monkey to go back to the house but he refused. So that night when father monkey came home, the mother told him all about it. And he went out and got the little monkey and said for him not to fly anymore or all the other animals would think he was crazy and out of his head.

It ought to be impressed upon students that whatever the nature of creative talent may be, those persons considered as outstanding merely have more of what all of us own. Therefore, each of us should have expectations of self that exceed just the simple, the easy to accomplish, and the sure thing. The lesson is that we can all become more creative than we are. While it may be useful to adopt the maxim, "Know thyself," this is of little relevance unless one first achieves the maxim, "Be yourself." Without question, compulsive conformity is the greatest enemy of creative thinking. Being different may simply mean being oneself, since in not compulsively conforming and acting just as others do, we differ from them. And from a mental health view, to get along with myself I must first be me.

Valuing one's own ideas goes along with being oneself. Evidence that children do not place much value on their own ideas comes from child observations, sociometric studies, and research on creative writing—all suggesting that peer pressures for conformity effect a decline in creative development at about fourth grade. The need for consensual validation is intensified at that time and one becomes afraid to think until he knows the peer judgment. The same pressures increase as one advances through the grades. This is especially so for youngsters in low-income areas. Among 45 seventh-graders of the inner city who had been chosen as predictive dropouts, 95 percent felt that their ideas would be laughed at or not be taken seriously by the rest of the class; 70 percent indicated a belief that the best answer is the one that the class decides is right. These children believed they have no chance of obtaining approval for ideas and as a result have stopped responding creatively (Torrance, 1966a). Those who have been led to lack faith in their own ideas more quickly defer to group judgment. By the way, even some highly creative persons lack confidence; they too have doubts which can destroy their progress if doubt is reinforced by the group.

Everyone should allow himself and others the chance to encounter experience without imposing the unnatural restraint of historical sex roles. Members of both sexes tend to shut out certain important aspects of awareness. By its nature, creativity involves sensitivity and independence of thinking and judgment. But in our society sensitivity and being receptive are considered female; independence of thinking and judgment are seen as masculine. This means that only the divergent personality maintains both sensitivity and independence of thinking and judgment. Likewise, intuitive display is judged off limits for males. Boys are taught that they should guard their masculinity by denying themselves access to certain kinds of experience, by not talking a lot, construed as girlish and intolerable among boys. That sex differences appear early among seventh- and eighth-grade predictive dropouts is apparent by the fact that 90 percent of the girls and only 15 percent of the boys indicate the best answer should be that which the teacher thinks is right. It appears that among predictive dropouts, girls tend to be overly receptive and boys overly rejecting of authority (Torrance, 1966a). It is a mistake to repress sensitivity, for to become thick-skinned is to become unbaffled, to assume everything is understood, to have no questions and ostensibly no problems. The creative person is sensitive to problems, intuits solutions and puts them to the test. Children need to realize that solutions to problems do not always come after prolonged study but might come like a flash after a rest or while involved in something different. They should respect their intuition and test it out; sex roles ought to be anathema in thinking for they serve only to restrict productivity.

Freeing the Creative Mind for Production

Curiosity is often cited as the single most important element of creative behavior but insufficient unto itself without the proper tools of inquiry. If 'wanting to know' is to prove satisfying, then 'how to learn' or find out is imperative. Learning does not occur by just doing something. We learn best when we are interested in the matter and possess the necessary investigative skills. In other words, we must first learn to do if doing is to be fruitful. Many imaginative young people seem destined to spend much of their school life in nonproductive ways simply because they have not been taught to use powerful skills of research that are introduced much later in the educational scheme. Historiography, descriptive and inferential statistics, and library knowhow—these are some of the research skills that are reserved for the older mind. But for even the young child who has ideas there must be a way to try them out and test them apart from popular reaction. For his commitment to a hypothesis to persist and develop, he must be able to evaluate his own ideas.

An even prior skill is the formulation of hypotheses based on insightful questions. So many of us as pupils and teachers fail to perform well because we have not learned how to inquire, how to ask questions; and on this issue rests much of creative development (Torrance and Hanson, 1965). To foster creativity we must maintain the age of inquiry as long as possible. Reasoning comes from learning to question. The best educators throughout the ages have recognized the importance of questions. Here one of them, Abelard, whose famous book *Sic et Non* altered medieval education, writes of the place of inquiry and doubt in learning:

> In truth, constant or frequent questioning is the first key to wisdom; and it is, indeed, to the acquiring of this [habit of] questioning with ab-

sorbing eagerness that the famous philosopher, Aristotle, the most clear-sighted of all, urges the studious when he says: ". . . . Indeed, to doubt in special cases will not be without advantage." For through doubting we come to inquiry, and through inquiry we perceive the truth. As the Truth Himself says: "Seek and ye shall find, knock and it shall be opened unto you." And He also, instructing us by His own example, about the twelfth year of His life wished to be found sitting in the midst of the doctors, asking them questions, exhibiting to us by His asking of questions the appearance of a pupil, rather than, by preaching, that of a teacher, although there is in him nevertheless, the full and perfect wisdom of God" (Mayer, 1960).

The second necessity in freeing the creative mind to produce involves conditions of study. Although a great deal is known about the study conditions creative persons have preferred, no real attempt has been made to determine the conditions favored by individual school children. Just as it has been convenient to assume that all learn in the same fashion, so it is convenient to believe each of us can best study under the same circumstances. Yet the history of invention shows that periods of quiet and aloneness yield the birth of most new ideas. Many creative persons point out that they needed to walk while they think—a practice some religious groups still use for meditation. Other creative persons prefer sitting and gazing, often interpreted as daydreaming by the observer. But can we allow children to study alone in school without considering them reclusive, to pace up and down or attend a study hall in which there is soft music? We seldom ask or seem to care if children study best with music, alone or with others, with television, chewing gum or not, pacing or, for that matter, lying down. Students are not asked whether they study best at home, in the library, or at school. They are seldom asked what things disturb them when they study.

A third requisite for freeing the mind to produce involves evaluation. People of varying levels of creative ability react differently to the same kinds of schoolwork. Highly creative children favor complex tasks, prefer open-end to structured assignments, enjoy learning more by inquiry than by being told, and are more productive on frustrating tasks. When permitted to learn in their preferred way, all is well. However, even when they are permitted this option, there is the problem of whether what has been learned serves as the primary material for evaluation or not. If what one has learned is not the subject of evaluation and his chosen abilities are not called for on the examinations, then failure is likely and will perhaps bring a reorientation of learning style.

Many teachers have underestimated the possibility that elementary and high school students might succeed in productive thinking, that they can conceivably generate ideas that have not been memorized. This has led to an overestimate of pupil receptivity, which in turn has resulted in an evaluation emphasis on recall and reproduction to the exclusion of creativity and decision-making. Most classroom tests are of the single-answer type involving only convergent thinking. Some teachers use multiple-choice tests or reproductive tests because they are easier to score, requiring only that pupils recognize a correct answer. A study conducted in the state of Minnesota indicated that 90 percent of the tests given at junior high school level were directed solely toward convergent thinking. Under these conditions, children cannot be led to believe that problem-solving is most important or that originality and imagination have a value in the school. The work of Gordon (1961) and Osborn (1963) suggests that evaluation be suspended during efforts to produce original and useful ideas or fundamental improvements. There is also some reason to believe that creative feedback is better than evaluative report (Torrance, 1966b).

Another aspect of evaluation besides thought production is that concerning intermediate achievement and the teacher decision to refrain from evaluating student work. Creativity is not tied to volition; it cannot always be summoned by choice or the assignment of a teacher. To insist on completion of a task as a requisite is to ignore or downgrade incomplete work. It often takes a long time to obtain the relaxation necessary for proper concentration and this process is disrupted by placing rigid time limits on production or testing. In short, teacher expectations must emphasize thinking rather than always a well-written, neat, and completed paper. Just as unfortunate is the compulsion to assign an evaluative weight to every pupil paper submitted. Perhaps credit needs to be given for original ideas and self-initiated learning and the pupil ought be involved in this evaluation. Much of school learning in the future depends on what types of evaluation teachers will encourage or discourage.

By educating for creative behavior, perhaps we can provide for individual differences in learning; maybe we can enable the designs by which more of the world will live with peace and less poverty. Certainly we can promise the future a better man.

CHAPTER VI

Evaluation in the Classroom

The present reliance of educators upon measurement and research as necessary ways to obtain information about student potential, individual achievement, and instructional efficiency is unique to this century. To be sure, teachers throughout time have devised tests of accomplishment in order to determine the truth about pupil progress. And, while certain among the historic evaluative models have been noteworthy, for the most part they represent methodological schemes lacking in the characteristics now judged as requisite for the acceptability of a measuring instrument.

ORIGINS OF MEASUREMENT

Standardized Achievement Tests

Prior to 1845, oral examinations served in most classrooms as the dominant if not singular procedure for the evaluation of learning. In those days the citizens committees, from which modern school boards have derived, responsible for education were charged to visit annually each school in the district. On such occasions every pupil was formally examined by the committee. This practice of pupil oral interrogation was generally acknowledged as suitable; apparently little thought was given to what might happen one day if the school population ever reached a point where continuation of the method would prove unmanageable. That day finally arrived for Boston in 1845 when pupil enrollment became so large that the visiting committee of laymen examiners were unable adequately to perform their task of spending a designated amount of time with each pupil. Nevertheless, the commitment to a tradition and the expediency of the situation combined to dictate a compromise, namely that only a perfunctory exchange take place with each student. It was by way of remedy for this difficulty that Horace Mann, then secretary of the Massachusetts Board of Education, recommended that uniform written examinations be considered as an alternative to the traditional oral approach. Because Mann's proposal represents an important event in the history of school evaluation, its circumstance deserves explanation.

It seems that, angered by certain of Mann's statements about the quality of education in their districts, the committee leaders and teachers representing several Massachusetts towns were formally charged by the secretary to repudiate his judgment by agreeing to a written achievement comparison of the children in their charge with other similar-aged youngsters attending classes in different school districts. Accordingly, tests in arithmetic, astronomy, grammar, history, and geography were used to rank the schools in order of merit. The discrepancies in achievement results revealed in the testing of more than five hundred students (average age 13) substantially justified Mann's criticism. Fortunately, he was wise enough to recognize the inappropriate method of testing and not its advocates as the more dangerous enemy to the cause of children. So instead of belittling an already embarrassed opposition, Mann chose rather to prepare an enthusiastic defense for the written test as an examination procedure exceeding in merit the traditional limited oral model. As editor of *The Common School Journal*, he presented the aforementioned survey results in a fair manner, predicting rightly that no school committee would go back to the old and uncertain practice of public oral examinations once the greater value of written tests had been understood (Mann, 1845; Caldwell, 1923). The transition from oral to written tests meant that henceforth all pupils would confront the same questions, teacher appraisal would supersede the judgment of outsiders; indeed, the instructor would become the exclusive examiner.

Before long Mann was joined in his position as advocate for the new assessment technique by other educational leaders who recognized the inherent possibilities of written tests. Some of the limitations of oral procedure were enumerated: questions differ in merit and difficulty; pupils interrogated later in the session might be advantaged by the mistakes of preceding students; able youngsters may miss extremely difficult questions while less able pupils are credited for answering simple inquiries; instructors ask leading questions that imply solutions and thereby defeat the objective of the test; and insufficient time is available to permit an adequate examination of all pupils (Tiegs, 1939, p. 4). Since the essay form offered the same task to all pupils it was considered more thorough, impartial, and free of favoritism than was oral inspection; results of the new procedure were considered more tangible and its design more likely to disclose accurately the comparative progress of different pupils; the ease or difficulty of various items could readily be determined and defects of teaching or studying more clearly revealed. In whatever manner the arguments supporting written examinations were expressed, they seemed to receive favor as the new method became widely adopted. Subse quently all members of the same classrooms could respond to uniform questions in their own way—an important first requisite for standardiza tion of tests.

Still there remained the problem of teacher response in marking essay papers with subjectivity varying in direction and extent according to the prejudice and mood of the individual scorer. In other words, the uni formity of testing items brought about through written examinations was not accompanied by a uniformity in marking practices; in fact, the ap plication of objectivity to scoring method using preestablished keyed re sponses still lay several decades ahead. The notion of age-grade norms or general performance standards as a base for comparability among stu dents did not appear until the early years of 1900.

An event sometimes referred to as the beginning of educational research constitutes the second major influence favoring the development of stand ardized achievement tests. The setting, dated late in the nineteenth cen tury, took place at a moment in time when public school leaders were bombarded by requests and demands of various formal pressure groups whose intention was to force the inclusion of home economics, manual training, and other so-called practical arts into the curriculum. Incidentally, the tactics of these pressure groups serve to remind us of the greater merit then attributed to argument than evidence as a basis for persuasion and change. Most superintendents opposed the recommendation for ad ditional courses on the premise that "there is barely enough time in the school day to teach subjects already an established part of the curriculum." This reply typified the assumption held by most educators, namely that the results obtained in any course of study are directly proportionate to the amount of time expended.

But one man, J. M. Rice, doubting the wisdom of his colleagues in this matter, finally concluded: "I came to recognize that this was all talk, that no one really knew the facts because there were no standards to serve as guides." Therefore, Rice determined to settle the practical issue of proper time allotment to be devoted to a course by subjecting the problem to empirical inquiry—a new way to settle questions in educa tional practice. A spelling test of fifty words, uniform although not stand ardized, was administered to approximately 30,000 students representing more than twenty city school systems (Stanley, 1964). The results of this first serious attempt to obtain uniform measurement of instructional efficiency were tabulated in relation to the amount of programmed time devoted to spelling. In presenting his findings at the 1897 meeting of the Department of Superintendents of the National Education Association, Rice declared that students who had studied spelling a half hour each day for eight years were no better spellers than their peers whose spelling instruction had been limited to fifteen minutes per day for eight years (Rice, 1897).

The investigator was immediately denounced as a heretic by many schoolmen; others discounted the sensibility of using a measure of how well people could spell for evaluating the effect of instruction in spelling. After all, the argument went, the function of spelling lessons is primarily to develop the student's faculty of memory rather than merely learning to spell. One observer at the convention described the audience reaction as follows: "The educators who discussed his [Rice] findings and those who reviewed them in the educational press united in denouncing as foolish, reprehensible and from every point of view indefensible the effort to discover anything about the value of the teaching of spelling by finding out whether or not the children could spell" (Ayres, 1918, p. 11). Notwithstanding the stern criticism heaped upon Rice, his evidence was convincing to large numbers of influential people and served to further detract from the already waning status of faculty psychology. It is interesting to note that today there are perhaps no elementary schools in America that allot more than fifteen minutes per day to spelling. And what is more, Rice, reviled years ago as a heretic, is today revered as the inventor of the comparative test, the ideational author of objective measurement in American education.

Even though the Rice spelling research findings were not enthusiastically received in most quarters, they did offer a source of inspiration to men like Thorndike, Courtis, and Stone, who shortly thereafter began construction of the first standardized educational tests. The prospect of standard scales and instruments initially became feasible in 1904 when the first text devoted to measurement appeared, a volume providing educators some procedural knowledge of statistical concepts and their application to classroom problems. So influential was this book, *An Introduction to the Theory of Mental and Social Measurements*, that no other work on the subject appeared for more than a decade. Its author, Edward L. Thorndike, perhaps more than anyone else, gave stature to the measurement movement not only through his many publications on statistics but by the standardized test scales he and his students composed. In 1908 Stone, a pupil of Thorndike, published his Arithmetic Reasoning test, which is generally considered the first standardized test—the measures used by Rice hardly fulfilled all the necessary conditions. A year later, Courtis (1909), who found Stone's tests unsatisfactory for the purpose of establishing norms of achievement for different grades, constructed his own arithmetic test. During the interim, Thorndike himself constructed the first standardized achievement scale for Handwriting of Children and this was followed by similar efforts in elementary school subjects like English composition (Hillegas, 1912) and spelling (Buckingham, 1913).

The distinction between tests like that of Stone and scales such as those of Thorndike and Hillegas is that the former are composed of exercises to be done by students, whereas the latter consist respectively of a series of samples of handwriting and English composition with which pupil performance can be compared. When Buckingham's spelling scale appeared in 1913, the difficulty of the words included had been determined according to the percentage of correct spellings by high school pupils. These words were then arranged in order of increasing difficulty so that a spelling scale was produced such that practically all children except beginners could spell the first words and very few could spell the last ones. Standardized tests were not made available at the high school level until after 1916 with most of them appearing after 1920.

Departments of Educational Research

The development of standardized tests provided an opportunity to actualize one of J. M. Rice's innovative dreams. Recognizing the potential benefit of his own modest investigation in spelling, Rice had in 1902 suggested that departments of educational research be established to determine the effectiveness of school practices in every city (Rice, 1912, p. 15–16). He specifically mentioned the U.S. Bureau of Education and the National Education Association as likely organizations to assume leadership in this type of endeavor. The plea of Rice was that "If just one enterprising city would undertake the task, others would surely follow." During the ten years between the time of this recommendation and its eventuality, many scholars acknowledged a need for research departments but felt disposed to lay the notion aside because there were not as yet enough standardized instruments available for the purpose of gathering data on achievement. Nevertheless, prominent educators continually sponsored the idea during the intervening years between 1902 and 1912. Probably the single most important outlet for the advocate expression was *The Journal of Educational Psychology*, first printed in 1910 with the editorial comment: "The time is ripe for the study of schoolroom problems in the schoolroom itself . . . educational practice is still very largely based upon opinions and hypothesis, and thus will it continue until competent workers in large numbers are enlisted in the application of the experimental method."

Coincident with the awareness of educators that objectives, methodology and curricula ought to be subject to critical analysis was the taxpayers' concern regarding wise allocation of funds and to the degree possible a limitation of school expenditures without sacrifice to quality. It was believed that the purposes of both scholars and laymen could partially be accomplished by learning just how well monies were spent and reporting this news to the community. Thus began the "School Efficiency Movement" in Pittsburgh in 1907 and it spread so rapidly to other cities that within a decade more than one hundred studies of public school systems had been made (Whipple, 1918, p. 183–90; Chapman, 1927). Although the declared intention of most school surveys was merely to inform the public, the rapid development and acceptance of standardized tests by 1915 and measures of intelligence by 1918 fostered a transition to self study by school systems for purposes of improvement. For example, the New York City study of 1913 was the first in which educational tests were used to judge instructional efficiency. Courtis, a member of the New York City commission, administered his Series A Arithmetic tests to 30,000 pupils. The "School Efficiency Movement" exerted a strong positive influence on the further development and use of standardized tests. In a short time departments of research were established in a number of major cities including Baltimore in 1912, New Orleans and Rochester in 1913, Boston, Kansas City, and Detroit in 1914.

It was at this time that Courtis, who had led the vanguard for Rice's comparative testing proposition, introduced a valuable innovation of his own. Whereas previously Courtis had only solicited the cooperation of teachers and superintendents in standardizing the measures he constructed, he now foresaw the desirability of having within each state some sort of center for distributing tests, receiving and compiling scores obtained, and conducting inquiries with respect to unusual conditions. The first among these centers, which at the outset focused exclusive attention to the construction and use of tests, were established in 1914–1915 at the Universities of Minnesota, Indiana, Iowa, Oklahoma, and Kansas State at Emporia.

By 1918 the pioneer era of the measurement movement had drawn to a close; the idea of research in education had become firmly entrenched. The extremely hostile and skeptical view toward research that Rice faced in 1897 when he reported the spelling investigation findings had changed. While some educators still remained adamant, more were neutral and the number of advocates ever increasing. The measurement movement had passed its critical phase from the standpoint of survival and acquired considerable momentum. Already achievement tests were being widely used in elementary schools, school surveys were providing new direction for curriculum, bureaus of research in city systems and universities were improving test construction and data treatment. True, there were yet few achievement tests at the high school level, the only indices of intelligence were individual tests and too few books on measurement were in print. These limitations were extended by the lack of general knowledge about statistical techniques but the dream now stood a chance and would more likely come true because it was shared.

Problems in Scoring

Another factor urging the development of standardized tests grew out of the increasing awareness by educators regarding just how poor the existing measures of achievement were. Numerous studies concerning the accuracy of school marks revealed high subjectivity and inconsistency; invariably they concluded that instruments ought be composed that would enable a more accurate measure of achievement. Many investigators made clear the unreliability of examinations and grades. Myer in 1908 reported on the marks given by forty instructors at the University of Missouri over a five-year period. That wide variation obtained is shown by the proportion of A's assigned in philosophy (55 percent) in contrast to the proportion of A's given in chemistry (1 percent). At the same time, teachers of English II had failed 28 percent of the students while not a single person failed Latin I. Several years later, Johnson (1911) published a similar research account involving teachers at the University of Chicago high school where, over a two-year period, 17.1 percent of the marks in German were A's as contrasted with 8.4 percent of F's. Quite the opposite held true in English, in which 6.5 percent of the marks were A's and 15.5 percent F's. The reasonable interpretation to be drawn is not that English is harder than foreign languages but that, in these two schools, English instructors are harder. Given the subjectivity of marking, the grade received could be more a function of teacher personality than student performance—a state of affairs then labeled by Thorndike as "scandalous" (Stanley, 1964; Thorndike, 1922).

A series of another type inquiry raised even more questions about teacher examinations and marking procedures. While it might be plausible to explain the variation of success or failure rate in certain subject matter areas on the basis of pupil background and intellect, the presentation of further data casts doubt upon this convenient assumption. Pupil experience and mental age cannot be cited as the cause for great differences in performance when several people mark the same pupil's paper and certainly not when one person marks the same student product on two different occasions. Yet both of these conditions were found to exist. When Starch and Elliot (1913) asked 115 high school mathematics teachers to mark the same geometry paper, the resultant marks ranged from 28 to 92—and this from teachers of one of the supposedly most objective subjects in school (see Table VI-1). Note that when the same high school English examination was marked by 142 different English teachers, a range of about 40 points separated the high and low marks. An even greater variance holds true for college literature (50 points), junior high school science (60 points), and physiology (70 points). Moreover, it appears to make little difference whether or not the markers are especially prepared in the field of the examination. In geometry, for example, graded only by mathematics teachers, the range is greater than for marks assigned to junior high school science papers some of which were marked by instructors not even teaching science (Tiegs, 1939, p. 10).

Even more distressing were the findings that teachers issued different marks when they rescore the same papers without knowledge of their former judgment. Ashbaugh (1924), working with 48 Ohio State University seniors and graduate students who were teachers, had them rate a seventh-grade paper in arithmetic three times with an interval of four

TABLE VI-1

Variability in Marking Five Essay Examinations*

Marks Assigned	7A † Physiology	H.S. ‡ English	Essay Examinations H.S. ‡ Geometry	College † Literature	Jr. H.S. † Science
	1	2	3	4	5
90–100	4	61	2	2	5
80– 89	8	67	18	9	7
70– 79	3	11	40	13	12
60– 69	2	2	35	0	13
50– 59	9	1	16	8	4
40– 49	4		2	2	0
30– 39	0		1		1
20– 29	1		1		
10– 19					
0– 9					
No. of Markers	31	142	115	34	42

* From Ernest W. Tiegs, *Tests and Measurements in the Improvement of Learning* (Boston: Houghton Mifflin Co., 1939), p. 9. Reprinted by permission.

† Studies by Ernest W. Tiegs

‡ Studies by Daniel Starch and E. C. Elliott

weeks between ratings. Only one of the 48 persons assigned the same score every time and only seven gave the same score twice. The mean difference between pairs of scores on successive trials were: 8.1 points between the first and second trials; 7.3 points between second and third trials. In another study of marking reliability among 28 Wisconsin high school teachers of English, Hulten (1925) found that the marking judgment varied each two-month interval when they graded the same composition. Fifteen of the teachers who gave passing marks on the first trial would have failed the pupils the second time they graded them; 11 who failed the pupils the first time would have passed them the second time. Investigations in English composition are significant because every essay examination is a series of compositions and when teachers of English cannot agree with each other or with themselves as individuals on a second scoring, the state of affairs is indeed unfortunate (Ross, 1954).

Although standardized tests eliminated the influence of scorer bias, examinations of this type were relatively unavailable at the high school level until later in the 1920's. The few that were in print were opposed by some school boards as being too expensive. In response to this dilemma McCall (1920) wrote an article which seems to have been the first public discussion of the so-called new type or objective examination. McCall's contention was that teachers need not depend solely on standardized tests but might construct similar measures of their own for classroom use by adapting the professional test-maker's design and procedures. In this fashion teacher-made objective tests can be constructed essentially the same way as are standardized tests so that whoever marks them will obtain the same result and this result once obtained represents a much more stable and accurate measure of ability and achievement. At first the true-false item received the most emphasis but soon a popularity grew for multiple choice, simple recall, completion, and matching forms. By 1924 the first of many books dealing with the adaptations of standardized tests by teachers was published with an emphasis on the improvement of objective examinations (Ruch, 1924). Four years later Odell's (1928) *Traditional Examinations and New Type Tests* appeared. It is fair to say that interest in the teacher-made objective measures exerted a revolutionary influence on the character of evaluative models in the classroom. In fact the results of a national survey of high school testing only a short time later revealed that 74 percent of the teachers were using informal objective tests (Lee and Segel, 1936).

Test Misuse and the Issue of Competence

During the 1920's a widespread acceptance of achievement batteries and intelligence tests led to a somewhat indiscriminate enthusiasm. This of course is not unlike the early stages for any later accepted movement in that it is characterized by a lack of awareness regarding shortcomings. Only time and test usage would alter this sentiment. For the moment test results were accepted without question, providing an erroneous base for many decisions of pupil promotion, grouping, and instruction. If educators were too busy to learn how test results ought be analyzed, this did not detain them from the fashionable use of test results with personal interpretation. Too few schoolmen were concerned about competence in handling score data; the mere use of objective instruments was considered a virtue in itself. Many persons of the time were impressed by the advantages of objective tests but oblivious to the limitations; in fact every voice of criticism was dwarfed by enthusiasm to the contrary.

Many authors during the early 1920's believed that if their data were objective, the conclusions must be indisputable and, conversely, that if the data lacked objectivity the conclusions were undependable. Typifying the faith then extant in objective methods is a report of the "Winnetka Social Science Investigation," in which its authors assert: "This work has proceeded to the point where we know definitely what persons, places, dates and events must be known to the child if he is to become an intelligent member of society. We know further the relative importance of these items . . ." (Mohr, 1922). The entire article clearly indicates that in the minds of its authors the basis for asserting that they "know definitely" what children ought to learn is the objectivity of the methods they employed. Later in the same discussion they described their investigation as being "strictly scientific," which seems to mean that its conclusions were reached independent of the bias and opinion of the researchers. Monroe (1928, p. 48) dates the peak period of this worship of objective methods as being 1922–1923.

By the mid-1920's research had obtained public favor and quantity production was realized, facilities for conducting studies were increasing, and there existed a widespread faith in objective measurement as a way to settle educational issues. Then into this pervasive arena of optimism the question of researcher competence was raised. Lamenting the prevailing uncritical attitude toward instruments and the ignorance about data analysis and interpretation, test experts made the point that instruments cannot provide judgment but only scores; and that for scores to be meaningful, appropriate interpretation is required—a function beyond the ability of untrained self-styled researchers. Little credence was extended the futile argument of the novice that research of the time was at least better than before 1918—such statements were dismissed as pointless since techniques and measures were much less developed in 1918.

A review of Monroe's (1928, p. 79–80) revealing summary regarding the poor quality of research articles appearing in *The Journal of Educational Research* for the period January, 1920, to June, 1927, is representative of the criticisms that began to emerge. The total number of articles printed in *The Journal of Educational Research* over the period of time specified was 467, 72 of which (or 15 percent) seemed to qualify as experimental investigations by which an attempt was made to evaluate some method or procedure related to instruction. After critically examining the research techniques used by the various investigators, it became apparent that most of their conclusions would have to be discounted. Of the 72 experimental studies only 5 of them (or 7 percent) were classified as having involved satisfactory techniques or procedures open to but minor criticism; 20 studies (or 28 percent) were labeled as involving reasonably satisfactory research procedures but offering unjustified generalizations; and 47 studies (or 65 percent) of the total were listed as being open to such serious criticism that the conclusions could not be accepted as dependable. Commenting upon these findings the editor of the journal in question agreed that "We have observed in many of the practices of educational research a tendency to shallowness." Trabue (1925) claimed: "We must use greater care to make certain that the conclusions we state in our reports follow logically from the data presented. Too many reports state conclusions that are not fully supported by the research data included in them." Whipple (1927) stated the case even more strongly: "I cannot evade the conviction that 'relatively speaking' the published research in education is on the whole inferior in ultimate quality and more especially inferior in significance to the published research in other branches of scientific endeavor. Too many contributions seem essentially futile. After you read them, you feel like saying: 'Well, suppose it is true; what of it?' "

As soon as the authorities in measurement began to point out certain shortcomings of popular research production, a recession occurred for the enthusiastic view that "anyone can do it." Of course, some teachers were insulted by the inference that they had acted in ignorance but in the main educators were pleased to be rid of the pressure to keep steady company with tests—a job for which they obviously were ill prepared. At the same time the teachers gave up the presumption of being test experts, an error was made in assuming that they could not become adept in this field, that knowledge of testing was "out of their line." As a consequence, experimentation, research design, testing, and statistics were considered "off limits" to teachers and the exclusive province of the measurement specialist—a continuing great mistake, in my judgment. A number of contemporary surveys both in the United States and in other countries show rather clearly that today's teachers are grossly lacking in evaluation skills and measurement competencies and that they are reluctant to invest in the development of more skills or better ones. One of the hopes for the future is to develop more adequate skills during initial teacher education programs (Torrance, 1967; cf. Ebel, 1961). As for the 1920's, one can say that it was a period of intense enthusiasm for testing, hopes for research ran high; the merits of each were somewhat less.

Evaluation as a Goal

The latter half of the 1920's was characterized by a growing recognition of the limitations in objective measurement and the necessity for increased competence among researchers. Then too, it was a period when there was demonstrated a need for philosophical methodology as well. That is, with the measurement movement on safe ground it became necessary to humanize it, to make it sensitive, to include ways of pupil growth not considered theretofore. Responding to the criticism that tests were too narrow and did not always show what had been learned, a new orientation was considered that broadened the scope of concern to engender more than just skills and memory. Attention was directed toward new outcomes of instruction like attitudes, interests, and the ability to utilize information. Gestalt psychology helped solidify this viewpoint in urging that the "whole child" become the focus rather than just the memory component of his being. An awareness grew that to help youngsters requires the availability of knowledge about their interests as well as abilities, attitudes, and aptitudes. In addition to humanizing the movement and thereby adding new advocates, enlarging the scope of assessment meant that to know more about students entailed the use of greater and not lesser numbers of instruments. The notion of achievement determination was consequently extended to include previously unused types of evidence about pupil accomplishment—testing being only one of them. This move toward a more comprehensive scope was symbolized by the substitution of the term *evaluation* for that of *measurement* as an ultimate goal.

Ralph Tyler (1931) was the first to outline procedures for test construction and validation that reflected the essential dependence of an achievement testing program on the objectives of instruction, and included the recognition of new forms of pupil behavior indicating attainment of the desired instructional outcomes. Tyler (1934) probably was more responsible than anyone else for the extension of achievement testing to subsume the intangible purposes of learning. He also was instrumental in upgrading evaluation practices of the standardized testing movement by his guidance in the famed Eight-Year Study involving the member schools of the Progressive Education Association. Under Tyler's direction the assessment group completed in 1942 a series of indices for measuring such instructional outcomes as the ability to interpret principles in the sciences, the ability to interpret literary data, and analogical reasoning. Such instruments tapped certain intangible yet functional behaviors instead of the more tangible, formal instructional effects in academic areas (Greene, 1954, p. 26–27).

With the attainment of a more comprehensive and humane province for evaluation, there arose a new interest in certain evaluative tools that had been invented earlier but long ignored—namely questionnaires, checklists, anecdotal records, sociograms, and the analysis of group dynamics. Concurrently, tests and scales were exposed to close scrutiny for improvement. Perhaps the most influential publication in measurement during this period was the *Buros Mental Measurements Yearbook*, first published in 1938, which listed and described the educational, psychological, and personality tests of the day. This annual volume continues as a great resource. With healthy criticisms centered on weak tests and the development of new measures under way, the evaluation movement advanced to the extent that in 1944 an estimated 60 million tests were administered to approximately 20 million persons in the United States (Reavis, 1947). This figure is, of course, considerably larger today owing in part to the availability of federal funds, which especially since 1958 have made possible both the purchase of more standardized tests and the employment of personnel to administer them. Then too, the public school and higher education population have increased such that as an aggregate the total number of students presently approximates 60,000,000 (Chauncy, 1961).

Measures of Intelligence

During the same era when educators were developing better measures of learning in the form of achievement tests, there was a growing concern about assessing the capacity of children to learn, which took the form of intelligence tests. In order for the measures of education, achievement tests, to be most meaningful, it was deemed expedient to have acceptable indices of educability. The roots of this concern can be traced back to 1879, when the first experimental laboratory in psychology was established at Leipzig, Germany. Because its founder Wilhelm Wundt was particularly interested in the analytic reduction of consciousness into quantitative elements, most of the lab's problems focused upon physiological measures of sight, hearing, feeling, and reaction time. Wundt recognized that in order to successfully perform the work of his intention it would be necessary to obtain careful research design and precision of measurement. The consequent emphasis he gave to development of accurate measures greatly influenced his students and through them the entire intelligence testing movement.

By way of illustration, it was James Cattell who, in 1885, introduced to America the measuring of individual differences in reaction time and later (1890) suggested the term "mental tests," which came to be the identifying label of the whole measurement movement. In assuming that sensory responses reflect differences in intelligence, Cattell made the same mistake as his teacher, namely restricting the province of mental testing to matters of sensory discrimination, in which the differences among persons are least. The same limitation of scope in mental testing characterized the English point of view although they too added invention and refinement to statistical instruments. Sir Francis Galton initially suggested a graphical method of representing correlation; in turn his student Karl Pearson, Charles Spearman, and Cyril Burt (the first appointed school psychologist) have contributed to the knowledge of statistical analysis.

Before the improvements in measurement technique that had accrued from Germany, England, and the United States could register their combined influence, it was necessary to redirect the point of concern in mental testing from the physiological realm of sensation, in which differences among individuals are least, to that of the higher mental processes, in which the individual differences are greatest. The man most responsible for accomplishing this redirection in mental testing was Alfred Binet. That great men can also be uncertain and naive is illustrated by Binet, whose career orientation shifted from law to medicine and finally to psychology. Previous to his fame as test-maker par excellence, he experimented with measuring heads and other of the bizarre methods dictated by phrenology, graphology, and palmistry. Then, dissatisfied with the approach of reducing consciousness into faculty or sensory components, he composed in 1905 a scale of items to discriminate levels of intelligence while conforming to predictive criteria. This first successful effort measured intelligence and expressed individual differences in accurate quantitative terms. (See pages 11–12.)

American psychologists engaged in testing were particularly enthusiastic about Binet's scale, partly because of its predictability. Until that time the invalidity and unreliability of most measures served to jeopardize the future of the movement. For instance, the initial usage of the Pearson product moment technique of correlation involved the relationship between the academic performance of American college students and scores on Cattell's tests of sensory and motor performance. Wissler (1901) found little more than chance relationship betweten the tests and college work. To a certain extent this explains why Binet's work was so welcome in this country. Even before Binet's death in 1911 American psychologists began to adopt his (1905–1908) intelligence scales. Goddard (1911) first used them at Vineland as early as 1905; Kuhlmann (1912) extended the range from Binet's lower limit of three years downward to age three months. Perhaps the most notable revision occurred in 1916, when Louis Terman of Stanford University standardized the test, calling it the Stanford-Binet. The well-known 1937 and 1960 revisions of this test are still with us. It was Terman who popularized the use of intelligence quotient, often identified as the IQ, which is the ratio of mental age to chronological age multiplied by 100. Terman adopted this idea from Stern, who in 1912 suggested that the ratio of mental age to chronological age be called a mental quotient. In recent years it has become common practice to report IQ scores in terms of a deviation approach so that results obtained from tests produced by different publishers might correspond. This method calls for conversion to a standard score scale after which outcomes of separate intelligence tests can be compared (Strom, 1966a; see pp. 325–30).

However ingenius and useful the early intelligence measures appear to have been, the Binet scale and its descendants engendered two major disadvantages. First they were highly linguistic; successful administration called for the testee to understand English. And secondly, they were individual so that only one person could be examined at a time. Solutions to both of these limitations arose concurrently. In 1917 the United States entered World War I and with only a short supply of officer leaders faced the extraordinary task of training and positioning great numbers of recruits. The American Psychological Association responded to the emergency situation by offering staff resources to the Department of War. It soon became apparent that apart from being unsatisfactory for illiterates and foreign-speaking soldiers the individual tests of intelligence were too time-consuming to administer. The Binet and its revisions required a

trained examiner one hour or more to test a single adult. Expediency
dictated a group test of some kind. Therefore, a committee of psychologists working primarily with the as yet unpublished work of Arthur Otis
developed the Army Alpha as the first in a long list of group intelligence
tests. Alpha could be administered to more than 100 doughboys all at
once in the same time it took for a single Binet. Of course this did not
overcome the language problem, since Alpha was highly verbal, pre-
suming a sixth-grade reading ability. Necessarily a separate nonverbal
performance test was developed for foreign-speaking soldiers. This non-
language measure intended for recruits who could neither read nor speak
English was termed Army Beta and represented the first such index
using both the group and performance ideas. In total, approximately two
million men took one or the other of these (Alpha or Beta) test forms
in 1917–1918.

From the end of World War I until the middle 1920's public interest
toward intelligence testing grew and many new group tests were published. Alpha and Beta were released for general use and Otis (1918)
completed the first group intelligence measures designed for use in
schools. In some ways perhaps the increased activity in measurement was
greater than was best for the movement's cause. It seems probable that
much of the noncritical use of tests and unwarranted interpretation of
results so common during the decade ensuing the war may in large
measure be traced back more or less to the wholesale methods used in
the Army. Although techniques improved, the principal indices of general intelligence employed during World War II (Army General Classification Test and The Army Individual Test of Maturity) were essentially
the same in purpose and measure as the Army Alpha and Beta of a quarter
century before.

Measures of Prediction

One final aspect of testing deserves mention—the assessment of aptitudes. Whereas achievement indices show a pupil's accomplishment at a
given point in time, aptitude tests purport to predict what a person might
achieve if provided suitable training. That is, aptitude tests tap an
individual's potential for accomplishment in a given performance area
prior to direct acquaintance with that area. Actually, the attempt of
Spearman (1904) and others to subdivide general and specific mental
ability into a g factor and many specific factors represented the first
aptitude testing (see pp. 11–12). But even though these efforts to measure specific traits preceded Binet's work, they were dropped when the
French psychologist demonstrated that measures of more complex behavior were superior. Subsequently, after it was learned that tests of
general intelligence lacked the power to predict success for specific
types of performance, the aptitude test movement was revived. Munster-
berg's 1913 aptitude test for streetcar motormen and telephone girls was

quickly followed by Seashore's tests of musical aptitude in 1915; Thurstone devised a clerical aptitude test in 1919 and a mechanical aptitude instrument by Steinquist appeared in 1922. To these authors as well as to Clark Hull for his book *Aptitude Testing* (1928) the measurement movement owes a great debt.

Between 1930 and 1955 factor analytic techniques were being devised that have since led to the identification of certain group factors of intelligence believed disparate both from the specific aptitudes and factors of general intelligence. At the time test group factors were first considered for inclusion within tests of mental ability, they also introduced the notion of separate linguistic and quantitative or verbal-nonverbal scores. Thereafter a number of batteries for the measurement of general and differential aptitudes as well as primary abilities were developed, each designed to distinguish several group factors of intelligence (Greene, 1954, p. 31).

Some authorities maintain that the years since Sputnik, 1957, have been without major innovation in measurement and testing. In the words of one expert, speaking about the era 1945–1966: "It would be difficult to mention a significant breakthrough in method or technique that could be clearly ascribed to this period" (Noll, 1965). Others of the profession, myself included, feel that we have had a major breakthrough in broadening the concept of intelligence. Attitudes concerning its fixedness and the fixedness of its development process have radically changed. There is now a wider view of the human mind, an expanded concept of mental functioning, which urges children to learn in creative ways, to use abilities previously unconsidered by instruments of intellective assessment. No doubt the expansion of uses for factor analysis will enable the refinement of existing measures and the composition of new ones. Finally, the increasing concern about cognitive styles as different ways of knowing promises to have a great impact upon education in the future.

THE GOOD TEST

Validity

The first inquiry a teacher ought to make about a test concerns validity, for regardless of whatever other characteristics an instrument might possess, its final acceptability and chance of being pronounced "good" rests upon this necessary attribute. By *validity* is meant the degree to which a measuring tool fulfills the purpose for which it is intended. Therefore, since validity has to do with the truthfulness of a test, it must be determined in relation to some pre-established purpose. In other words, there is no such thing as general validity; no test is just valid—its truthfulness must be in relation to something and is properly described in connection with this intended context. It follows that an evaluation index judged highly valid in achieving one purpose may be seen as invalid for another objective, appropriate in a certain setting and out of place elsewhere, right for use with a particular group of students but useless in the next classroom. Were a junior high school history instructor to administer a test of memory concerning the battlesites of World War II, he would on the basis of the test scores alone be unwarranted in drawing any conclusion about whether his students have a sense of patriotism. Likewise, the same memory test would lack validity if given to the third-graders in the school system because students of this age level possess no background of information about the war in question. Validity is always a specific attribute depending not only on content but also on factors involving proper usage such as the population group being tested.

Since the degree of validity of an instrument indicates the extent to which its objectives are being achieved and because tests vary from one another in terms of objectives, so there are several ways to approach the determination of validity. The nonempirical approach, used to obtain content and construct validity, is logical and rational calling for an analysis of test content in relation to course material. On the other hand, empirical or statistical procedures are employed in the determination of concurrent and predictive validity. Each of these several approaches to validation will now be considered.

Nonempirical approaches

To what extent does test content represent the actual substance of a course and do the items offer a proper difficulty level for students in the class? These questions, which call for a judgment about the relevance and cross-sampling of subject matter, make up the principal issues regarding *content* validity or, as it is sometimes called, *curricular* validity. This nonstatistical validity derives from a reasoned analysis and professional judgment rather than any empirical evidence. However, the fact that reason instead of measurement constitutes its underlying base does by no means simplify the determination of content validity. To gain insight regarding the view of qualified experts on course objectives demands careful analysis of textbooks, reports by national committees, curriculum guides, and the writings of subject matter specialists. The composite of these data serves as the basic source for decision-making about test content. Most curriculum leaders support the increasingly popular practice of involving teachers in the formulation of instructional goals for their particular grade or subject. After teacher committees have defined objectives and identified behavioral outcomes that will confirm the realization of goals, the next step is test construction. Much of the work in composing tests depends on the specificity with which the committee on objectives fulfills its expectations. If the course intentions are vague and the anticipated results are not precisely expressed, the validity of its test is adversely affected. Likewise, if the stated goals are too distant, the test-maker has difficulty. Even though ultimate goals cannot be

achieved in a short time some effort ought to be made to define intermediate accomplishments in order that the test-maker can proceed in
devising measures (Greene, 1954, pp. 68, 69).

A second nonempirical type of validity deals with constructs. In order
to account for certain aspects of human behavior we resort to constructs
like "cautiousness," "conformity," and "the ability to apply principles."
While these labels offer a way of identifying responses, they are not self-
validating (Ahmann, 1960, p. 60). Consequently, any instrument believed
to reflect a particular construct must be validated in order to determine
whether verifiable inferences can be made from its scores. When a reasoned analysis is made of the mental processes that comprise some concept goal like "scientific thinking" or "openmindedness" the type of validation is known as *construct* or *concept* validity. As the public school
emphasis upon problem solving and divergent thinking increases, it is
probable that less attention will center upon the traditional facts and
information orientation than upon method and process—the focus will be
on construct validity.

If goals are set forth in terms of constructs rather than small facts, the
task of obtaining validity is understandably enlarged. Somehow the concept goals must be reduced to test operational behaviors. Content is not
the concern so much as are the mental functions and processes applied
to content, the ways of manipulating data in achieving solutions (Thorndike and Hagen, 1959, p. 113). From this view validity is not thought of
principally in terms of subject matter that is at best the stimulus but in
terms of mental operations. In other words, the focus shifts from the
curriculum to the learner. As in content validity, the sources of information for analysis may be committees, texts, national groups, or a combination of these. In the end professional judgment is offered as to how
adequately the test items correspond with the sample of behaviors representing the construct goal.

The danger of restricting test validation procedures to subjective judgment was recognized as early as 1922: "In the elementary schools we now
have many inadequate and even fantastic procedures parading behind
the banner of educational science. Alleged measurements are reported
and used that measure the fact in question about as well as the noise of
the thunder measures the voltage of the lightning. To nobody are such
more detestable than to the scientific worker with educational measurements" (Thorndike, 1922, p. 8; cf. Campbell and Stanley, 1963). One
study of the validation methods used for 184 important achievement tests
constructed before 1928 showed that the most dominant method was
"personal opinion of the author" (Peter and Crosley, 1929). The gravity
of this situation was reduced somewhat as scholars grew more adept in
the use of empirical methods to obtain evidence of validity. Although
some persons still presume that the only kind of validity most teachers
need be familiar with is content and construct, the facts are otherwise.

In reality, teachers must frequently appraise the empirical validity co-efficients reported in conjunction with standardized instruments.

Empirical approaches

The second major source of evidence for test validation involves statistical procedure. This empirical type of evidence stemming from the amount of agreement between test scores and some criterion external to the test itself may either be concurrent or predictive. Often these two terms, concurrent and predictive, are treated as separate kinds of validity when they might better be described as instances of empirical validity, differing from one another in time sequence alone. When test scores and an outside criterion like report card marks are obtained at approximately the same time, the resulting relationship is known as an index of *concurrent* or status validity. And, should this relation between test and criterion be expressed as a coefficient of correlation, it is called a concurrent validity coefficient. In the case of *predictive* validity, there is a lapse in time between when test scores and some future criterion like job success can be determined. That is, concurrent validity is important when, by indirect means, an instrument is used to determine a pupil's present status or behavior, whereas in the case of predictive validity the required criterion behavior lies in the future.

A frequent mistake is to suppose that empirical validation is necessarily superior to all other approaches because it eliminates the need for assumptions, opinions, judgment, and other subjective forms of response. Indeed, the major problem presented by instances of both concurrent and predictive validity is the selection of a criterion, the subjective choice of a standard. Consider the newly composed intelligence test, which, in order to be declared acceptable, must first be shown to correlate to a high degree with an existing accepted measure of the same mental function. When the new test and the established test (or so-called criterion measure) are juxtaposed the resulting correlation is a congruent validity coefficient, distinguished from a concurrent coefficient only in that the criteria are test scores. The point is that in order for evidence of congruent validity to carry any weight there first must be much evidence to support the criterion measure's validity. Only then does a high correlation of the new test with the criterion perpetuate whatever validity the criterion may have.

Similarly, when school marks become the criterion for validation, it is with the assumption that in the end a test is valid if the pupil scores relate closely to acknowledged achievement. That is, a biology test must have high validity if those who score well on it are the same persons who attain superior marks in the class; and conversely so, if the low scorers earn low marks. Although teacher marking is known to be unreliable, it is still likely that a test that shows which pupils, in the teacher's view, are outstanding and less able probably is highly valid. Underlying the empirical approach is a conviction that the test is valid if high correlations are shown between its scores and the criterion measure; also implicit is a confidence that the criterion may be accepted as a measurement standard.

The selection of a criterion for estimating predictive validity is equally difficult. Aptitude tests administered in the junior high school frequently are validated on the basis of some recognized accomplishment in high school vocational education courses or by postdiploma success on the job. This has worked rather well in the first instance (aptitude score–course success) but in the second (aptitude score–job success) predictability is more difficult for there is always a chance that the job success criterion may be the product of factors extrinsic to the ability of the person for whom prediction is being made. Conceivably success in business may be independent of one's ability, as in the case of a salesman whose dollar volume is as much or more influenced by the job territory than by his selling ability. Moreover, successful performance may not even show up on the recommendation for promotion form if the rater allows personal differences with the ratee to influence his judgment.

Given the importance of choosing a suitable criterion measure for validation, Thorndike and Hagen (1959, pp. 118–119)* have recommended four qualities that teachers ought to bear in mind as desired features: (1) relevance, (2) freedom from bias, (3) reliability, and (4) availability. A criterion is judged relevant to the extent that the criterion measure score is governed by the same influences that account for job success. Since no empirical evidence can indicate the relevance of a particular criterion measure, the necessary recourse is professional judgment. Just as the course relevance of an achievement test is best decided by teacher judgment, so employers represent the proper decision source as to factors related to job success. By freedom from bias is meant the provision of each individual with the same chance to make a good showing. In sales, for instance, one man may appear much better on paper than another because of the assigned territory, variation in work conditions or equipment, temperament and competence of the person doing the rating. Obviously it will be hard to extract meaning from the correlation between test scores and the criterion measure if the latter is contingent more upon elements in the environment than the employee. A criterion score must be reliable (consistent) if it is to be predictive; otherwise there is no point in searching for a suitable predictor. Finally, the criterion measure must offer availability in terms of being fairly proximate, convenient, and not cost-prohibitive to obtain. An example of proximity might be success in an automotive training class rather than the distant and ultimate goal of becoming a good mechanic.

It should be clear that the need for human judgment at some point is

* From Robert L. Thorndike and Elizabeth Hagen, *Measurement and Evaluation in Psychology and Education* (New York: John Wiley & Sons, Inc., 1959), pp. 118–119. Reprinted by permission.

inescapable in every approach to the assessment of validity. In the case of concurrent and predictive validity, a decision must be made that the criterion itself is valid. Additional judgments are necessary in deciding how to obtain usable measures of the criterion itself. With regard to content and construct validity the judgment is more directly applied to the question of relationship between the test situation and the universe of behaviors comprising course goals.

To ask how high a validity coefficient must be in order to be acceptable is like asking "How high is up?" Usually the value of a given predictor depends on the effectiveness of other available predictive instruments. If a new aptitude test shows a correlation of .75 with the criterion measure and the only previously available predictor offered only .45, favor is naturally given to the new measure. A predictor's usefulness is not, however, exclusively dependent upon how well it correlates with the criterion measure but also on how much new information it offers. If for instance a test is already available with a validity coefficient of .60, it would be more desirable that a new measure show a correlation of .55 than .63 if in the first instance it is judged independent from rather than highly interrelated with the .60.

Generally speaking, the higher the correlation between a test and its criterion measure the better. But to properly interpret coefficients of validity additional factors must be considered. The availability of natural criterion make some tests easier to validate than others. Lacking good criterion one cannot expect high validity; in fact, there are instances in which the test is a better measure of the attribute than the selected criterion. Also one of several possible criteria may be more relevant than the others for the intention. Sometimes tests that work well with certain groups are inappropriate for others in the sense that the standards differ. Then there is always the question of variability, since coefficients of validity tend to be higher in cases of heterogeneity. Thus even a crude test can discriminate well if differences be large while a very good test may inadequately discriminate if the group be homogeneous. All of these contingencies caution one to never flatly assert that "The higher the validity coefficient, the better. Other things being equal, this is true—but other things must be equal" (Lyman, 1963, pp. 28–30).

Reliability

By *reliability* is meant the extent to which a test agrees with itself. If on successive administrations of an examination the individual scores remain nearly the same or if two forms of an instrument can be relied upon to yield similar results, then the essential conditions for reliability have been met. As a measure of self-consistency, reliability differs from validity, which is a measure of how the test agrees with the intention for which it was constructed. That is, validity coefficients are determined by a relationship to some external criterion measure, whereas in reliability the desired consonance of agreement is with some kind of internal criterion. Unlike validity, which is specific in nature and concerned with the truthfulness of an instrument, reliability is general in nature dealing only with test consistency. By itself, consistency is of questionable merit, since tests like people could be consistently wrong. However, even though a high index of reliability cannot ensure that the test be "good," its absence is sufficient reason for doubt; in fact low reliability does guarantee the test will be known as "poor." Although reliability is not dependent upon validity, the opposite case does obtain. That is, a test may be reliable (consistent) without being valid (truthful), but test validity depends in part upon reliability to determine its ceiling. In sum, a measure is only as valid as it is reliable because the ideal instrument tells the truth (validity) consistently (reliability) (Ross, 1949, pp. 83–84).

Something about the validity of a test can be determined by merely inspecting it; this is not the case with reliability. To be sure, a glance will reveal something about the scoring procedures used as well as the test length. And it is true that tests objectively scored are, in the main, more reliable than those marked subjectively; it is also known that, generally speaking, instruments of greater length prove more reliable than shorter ones. But since exceptions to these commonalities do exist, neither length nor objective scoring are themselves sufficient guarantees of reliability. To obtain the data on which an estimate of reliability should be predicated calls for: administration of an equivalent test; or readministration of the same test; or subdivision of a test into equal parts.

Equivalent forms method

When two supposedly equivalent forms of a test are available, an index of reliability can be determined by administering both forms to the same persons and subsequently calculating a coefficient of correlation from the two sets of scores. If there is close agreement between the test and its intended criterion, the alternate form, youngsters who score high in one case will earn superior marks on the other as well; the converse holds with respect to consistent position in low performance. A maximum degree of relationship, indicating the unlikely perfect consistency is shown in a coefficient of ± 1.00 while .00 indicates an inconsistent, unreliable relationship. A common procedure in standardizing instruments involves the construction of alternate forms, which are primarily used to correct possible sources of test error, particularly the variation due to content sampling. The need for correction arises in view of the necessity for test-makers to choose a limited sample of tasks to represent some universe of behaviors. In covering the same area of knowledge functions by using different questions, equivalent forms are alike in range and degree of item difficulty. An additional advantage of alternate forms is that they minimize the effect of practice that exists when the same test is given twice.

Both forms may be taken at one examination setting or two, depending on the time required, the age and maturity of persons being tested and the nature of the test materials. If the examiner is not interested in stability over time, the tests might as well follow each other immediately. Should a time interval be allowed between the test administrations, there will have been a chance for three sources of variation to enter their effect —those arising from the test itself, the individual over time, and variation due to sampling of tasks. To demonstrate consistency under these conditions is the most rigorous expectation that can be held for a measure. In the judgment of Thorndike and Hagen (1959, p. 128): "Evidence based on equivalent test forms should usually be given the most weight in evaluating the reliability of a test."

Several problems combine to delimit usage of the alternate form procedure as a method for determining test precision. For one thing, it dictates that two equivalent forms be available and that sufficient time be allowed to administer both measures. The fact is that most achievement tests, especially the teacher-made variety, are produced in single form only. In addition to the lack of an alternate form, it may be impossible to arrange a second testing either because there is not enough time or it represents a burden upon available resources. Whatever the practical dictate, be it expediency or convenience, such factors have prompted test-makers to become more receptive to procedures that extract an estimate of reliability from administration of only one form of a test. These procedures for establishing reliability are at best compromises and cannot be granted the same approval reserved for the preferred method of parallel forms where a time lapse of days or weeks occur between administrations.

Test-retest method

When only a single test form is available its reliability can still be established by repeating the test. Using the scores obtained on the first and second administration as correlates, the examiner computes a coefficient of reliability. Obviously, much of the potential benefit offered by the test-retest method rests on the time lapse between settings. If the measure is readministered at approximately the same time of its first use, one can presume that the individual taking the examination has not changed much and therefore whatever sources of error exist lie in the measuring. Otherwise, if for some reason such as excessive test length it becomes necessary to separate the two trials, especially in the case of achievement tests, this delay will likely introduce other variables. Should a pupil discuss the issues on the test or look them up during the time between the first and second administration a change occurs in the status of his knowledge—that is, a variation takes place within the individual. Then too because the task remains the same in both settings the retest score does not indicate what changes might be expected were another sampling of items used. Furthermore, in cases of testing in which the material is the same, the error for an individual is constant for both exams, since it affects both scores alike, thereby making the test look as though it is reliable instead of unreliable. Finally, there is reason to suppose that answers offered on the second administration of a test are related to the first in that the task does not represent the same problem as it once did with responses probably influenced by memory of the initial responses or knowledge acquired about the items subsequent to the first setting. A retest is hard to justify both from the standpoint of the student motivation required in encountering the same items twice and practically speaking in terms of finding time in an already crowded pupil schedule.

Split-half method

The difficulties associated with establishing reliability by the test-retest and equivalent forms methods led to a search for more feasible techniques. Among the favored alternatives the split-half procedure has gained the widest recognition and use in recent years. By this technique, requiring a test of only one form, the items are divided presumably into two equivalent halves, the scores of which are correlated to yield an index of the accuracy with which the test is measuring its taker. Ordinarily the test is divided into chance halves by computing one score for the odd-numbered items and another for the even. When the scores on one half are correlated with scores on the other, the reliability of the half test is obtained. From this coefficient the reliability of the entire test can be estimated by using the Spearman-Brown Prophecy formula. This general formula is employed to predict the increase in reliability expected when the test is lengthened by the addition of items like those in the original.

$$r_n = \frac{nr_s}{(n-1)r_s + 1}$$

In this formula "The Reliability, r_n, of a test n times as long as a shorter test of known reliability, r_s, is equal to n times the reliability of the shorter test, divided by $(n-1)$ times the reliability of the shorter test, plus 1" (Ebel, 1965, pp. 314–315). Assume a given test of 25 items has a reliability of .60 and that its author by the addition of equivalent items increases the test length 4 times. The test now includes 100 items. According to the formula above, the lengthened test's reliability is found by dividing 2.40 by 2.80, yielding a quotient of .85.

$$r_n = \frac{4 \times (.60)}{3\,(.60) + 1} = \frac{2.40}{2.80} = .85$$

When the task is simply to predict the reliability of the test twice the length of another as in the split-half method of reliability estimation, the formula reads:

$$r_1 = \frac{2r_s}{r_s + 1}$$

Suppose that on a given test the correlation of odd-numbered items with even-numbered items is .70. The whole test estimate of reliability will be .82.

$$r_1 = \frac{2 \times (.70)}{.70 + 1} = \frac{1.40}{1.70} = .82$$

By using a variant of the Spearman-Brown Prophecy formula, it is possible to determine how many times a test must be lengthened to attain some intended reliability (Tiegs, 1939, p. 384). To raise the obtained reliability of a test from .70 to the desired level of .90, the formula is:

$$r_d = \frac{Nr_o}{1 + (N-1)r_o}$$

where r_d is the desired coefficient of reliability,
N is the number of times the test must be lengthened,
r_o is the obtained coefficient of reliability.
Substituting in the formula:

$$.90 = \frac{.70N}{1 + (N-1)\,.70} = \frac{.70N}{1 + .70N - .70}$$

$$.90 = \frac{.70N}{.30 + .70N}$$

$$.90\,(.30 + .70N) = .70N$$

$$.270 + .630N = .70N$$

$$.270 = .70N - .63N$$

$$.270 = .07N$$

$$N = \frac{.270}{.07}$$

$$N = 3.88$$

To obtain a .90 coefficient of reliability the test must be made 4 times its present length.

The popularity of the split-half method ought not to lead one to over-look its major limitations (see Table VI-2). Since both of the scores for the correlation derive from a single measure, they each represent a person as he is at the same point in time. Consequently there is no possibility for the day-to-day variation within a person to enter its effect. Instead a split-half estimate of reliability supplies information only regarding the precision with which a student can be tested at a particular time moment. Also there are some difficult assumptions to be met if the procedure is to have optimal value. By definition each half of the test should be equal with respect to its statistical properties in average difficulty and variability; the items added must be of the same quality as those already existing; and this inclusion of items should not alter the average correlation among items. Another assumption that involves the variables of fatigue, motivation, and boredom is that increasing the test length will not change the way in which examinees respond to it. Apart from pupil variation and equivalence factors, conditions of administration can represent an obstacle, for the split-half estimate of reliability tends to be inflated when used with speeded tests. Despite the favor extended alternate forms and the numerous shortcut methods advanced for estimating reliability based on split-half data (Rulon, 1939; Stanley, 1951), the Spearman-Brown formula continues to be the most used and reported in test manuals.

TABLE VI-2

Relation of Test Length to Test Reliability*

Items	Reliability
5	.20
10	.33
20	.50
40	.67
80	.80
160	.89
320	.94
640	.97
∞	1.00

As the table shows, "the higher the reliability of the test, the smaller the increase in reliability with added test length. Adding sixty items to a twenty-item test could increase its reliability from .50 to .80. But adding eighty more items to the eighty-item test would raise its reliability only from .80 to .89. To achieve perfect reliability, an infinite number of items would have to be used, which of course means that perfect reliability is unattainable by lengthening any unreliable test."

* From Robert L. Ebel, *Measuring Educational Achievement* (Englewood Cliffs, N.J.: Prentice-Hall, Inc., © 1965), p. 337. Reprinted by permission.

Kuder-Richardson formulas

Dissatisfied with the split-half method, Kuder and Richardson (1937, 1939) devised new procedures based on item statistics for obtaining an estimate of reliability from a single testing. The rationale maintains that just as larger parts, say halves, of a test need be parallel in order to obtain good reliability estimates of the whole, so items must be parallel in the Kuder-Richardson approach. Presumably the items within one test form have as much in common with one another as they do separately with the corresponding items in alternate test forms. That is, one assumes the items in a form are homogeneous, all measuring one common factor; they are factorially univocal. After fractioning the test into n parts of one item each, the basic Kuder-Richardson formula 20 reads:

$$r_{11} = \left(\frac{n}{n-1} \right) \left(\frac{\sigma^2 - \Sigma pq}{\sigma^2} \right)$$

where r_{11} is the estimate of reliability,
$\qquad$ n is the number of items on the test,
$\qquad$ σ is the standard deviation of the test,
$\qquad$ Σ means "take the sum of" and covers the n items,
$\qquad$ p is the proportion of correct responses to each item in turn,
$\qquad$ $q = 1 - p$ (or the proportion failing the same item).

Because formula 20 requires knowledge of statistics on item difficulty, several modified versions have been proposed. The less complicated Kuder-Richardson formula 21, which yields a close approximation to formula 20 reads:

$$r_{11} = \frac{n}{n-1} \left[1 - \frac{M_t \left(1 - \frac{M_t}{n} \right)}{\sigma^2} \right]$$

Where M_t is the group's mean score:
$\qquad$ other symbols retain the same meaning as
$\qquad$ indicated in formula 20.

There is little question that the Kuder-Richardson formulas have merit. To determine how much precision is lost in applying these procedures generally, Brogden (1946) made a thorough and systematic analysis by setting up artificial tests with widely varying compositions and he found the results to show little bias; these conclusions apply to formula 20 and not the less exact 21. The major limitations embodied by Kuder-Richardson approaches stem from the basic assumption of a unifactor test and parallel items; this circumstance is rarely encountered in actual practice. In addition, the formulas take no account of variation within individuals over time, and since they are inappropriate for speeded measures must be consigned to instances of power testing. The more widely the items in a test vary in difficulty, the more seriously the Kuder-Richardson method, especially formula 20, may underestimate reliability. In the case of formula 21, which demands no information on item difficulty, an underestimate is always given because items invariably do differ in the level of performance required. Indeed before accepting the Kuder-Richardson 21 index of reliability as a good estimate one would first need be satisfied that few of the test items are extremely easy or difficult. It is well to remember also that the Kuder-Richardson approach is applicable only to tests in which items are scored by giving one point for correct and none if incorrect. Should there be a correction for guessing or if other forms of weighted marking are employed, then more complex formula variations are necessary.

Interpreting coefficients of reliability

Thus far several methods for determining test reliability have been presented that involve sources of data from a single measure (retest, split-half, Kuder-Richardson, 20–21) or more than one test (equivalent forms). There are also a host of analysis of variance approaches (Hoyt, 1941; Jackson and Ferguson, 1941; Ebel, 1951; and Linquist, 1953), and certain generalized formulas for reliability (Guttmann, 1945; Horst, 1949; Cronbach, 1951) that lie beyond the scope of this book but can be found in texts essentially concerned with measurement. For our purpose, Table VI-3 offers a comparison among the familiar procedures of estimating reliability. Notice that four sources of variation are listed that separately or in combination can influence the accuracy of an individual's test score. The table reveals which sources of variation occur with each technique of estimate. A simple inspection shows that the methods are not equivalent in that they are subject to different sources of variation. Only one procedure, parallel forms with a time interval, allows all four sources of variation to enter their effect. For each of the remaining methods some source of variation is hidden that may bear importance in the test situation. When the same test is readministered the item-sampling variation is neglected; to complete all the testing in one setting fails to take into account the day to day variation of an individual; and when in a single time limit all the testing takes place as a unit, the neglected source of variation is speed of response (Thorndike and Hagen, 1965, p. 131). From the standpoint of practicality it is unwise to insist that a certain method for estimating reliability be used in every situation; things go best when the purpose determines choice of technique. Table VI-3 can be especially useful whenever one finds it necessary to appraise test reliability as reported in some periodical or test manual.

A natural and significant inquiry concerns the desirable magnitude of reliability coefficients. Of course, it is advantageous for tests to be as reliable as possible. However, as is true in the case of coefficients in general, it is misleading to establish any arbitrary standard for what may

TABLE VI-3

Sources of Variation Represented in Different Procedures for Estimating Reliability*

	Experimental Procedure for Estimating Reliability					
Sources of Variation	Immediate Retest, Same Test	Retest after Interval, Same Test	Parallel Test Form without Time Interval	Parallel Test Form with Time Interval	Odd-Even Halves of Single Test	Kuder-Richardson Analysis, Single Test
How much the score can be expected to fluctuate owing to: Variations arising within the measurement procedure itself	X	X	X	X	X	X
Changes in the individual from day to day		X		X		
Changes in the specific sample of tasks			X	X	X	X
Changes in the individual's speed of work	X	X	X	X		

* From Robert L. Thorndike and Elizabeth Hagen, *Measurement and Evaluation in Psychology and Education* (New York: John Wiley & Sons, Inc., 1959), p. 131. Reprinted by permission.

be considered a "high" or "satisfactory" index of reliability. What might be viewed as high or satisfactory in one situation may be judged "low" or "unsatisfactory" in another depending upon the thing being measured, procedure employed, test length, range of talent, and objectives for which the scores are used. Whereas a reliability coefficient of .60 may be adequate in comparing average scores for large groups of individuals, a coefficient of .95 may be inadequate in cases where extremely accurate descriptions of persons are desired. The disadvantage of interpreting coefficients of correlation on the basis of size alone is also shown by the fact that while standardized tests usually exceed .90 in reliability and tests of intelligence are generally above .85, this is in marked contrast with typical validity coefficients. A validity coefficient of .50 may be quite acceptable; a reliability measure of the same magnitude would be unsatisfactory for almost any test. Lindquist (1942, p. 200) urges that no attempt be made to establish a single classification for reliability coefficients as "high," "low," or "medium" but instead evaluate each test on a relative basis in comparison with coefficients of reliability obtained with other available tests of the same traits.

Considering the fact that measures of reliability, regardless of how they may be reached, are influenced by variables other than formal content of the test itself, it would seem that the value of such measures have been overemphasized. No doubt test-makers have given too much attention to reliability and too little to establishing validity, which might yield a better return. One reason of course is that it is easier to determine measures of reliability. Too much harm has occurred when uncritical test-users have naively assumed that reliability ensures validity. Add to this the fact that most instructors will find it unnecessary to compute reliability coefficients for ordinary classroom tests, other than final examinations. It would seem that teacher study of methods for determining reliability is somewhat lacking in application. But bear in mind also that anyone answerable for assigning academic marks has a responsibility for understanding possible sources of unreliability in his marks; such knowledge is also invaluable in the selection of tests to be purchased; and to read research reports with understanding, it is a necessity.

The standard error of measurement

The reliability of an educational measuring procedure can be statistically expressed in two ways—one is the reliability coefficient, a useful index and the only one possible when comparing tests whose measures are expressed in different units. The standard error of measurement (SEM) is preferred to the reliability coefficient when describing the accuracy of an individual's score, for it shows the expected variation if repeated measurements are made of the same person. Owing to the somewhat random nature of effects of the error factors involved, the repeated measurements of an individual tend to form a normal probability curve (see Figure VI-1). The amount of variation for these repeated measures is given by the standard deviation of the probability curve and is known as the standard error of measurement. This means that the standard error of measurement is the standard deviation of the normal distribution that is repeated an unlimited number of times. Thus it is an index of scatter or chance variation in the measure. The lower the standard error of measurement the more reliable the measure. In educational testing we seldom obtain more than two scores on a given measuring procedure for each individual but from these two it is statistically possible to estimate the variation of a larger number of repeated observations. Any test score or comparison of that score must be made with an awareness of the standard error of measurement for even with high estimates of reliability, appreciable errors are possible in some cases. In fact, shifts of 5 to 10 points in IQ scores are not uncommon as results of errors of measurement.

Sometimes referred to as the standard error of obtained scores, the standard error of measurement is a rather direct indicator of the probable extent of error for any score in the set to which it applies. This matter becomes more clear when reliability, defined as the proportion of true variance in scores, is made into a prediction problem by stating that reliability is the proportion of variation in obtained scores determined by or accounted for in true scores. Now the concern becomes one of predicting true scores from obtained scores. Assuming a normal distribution of errors at every true-score level, it is possible to draw inferences regarding the probability of errors of different scores. Given any obtained score, conclusions may be drawn about the probable limits of corresponding true scores. However, whether errors of measurement remain uniform at every true-score level is a moot question (Guilford, 1954, p. 351).

The standard error of measurement formula is:

$$S_m = \Sigma \sqrt{1 - r_{11}}$$

where S_m is the standard error of measurement,

$\quad \sigma$ is the standard deviation of test scores,

$\quad r_{11}$ is the reliability coefficient.

For a test with a reliability of .64 and a standard deviation of 10 points the standard error of measurement is:

$$S_m = 10 \sqrt{1 - .64}$$

$$= 10 \sqrt{.36}$$

$$= 10 \times .6 = 6$$

In this case a set of measures for a particular person would have a standard error of measurement of 6. We know that a fairly constant proportion of cases lie within any specified number of standard deviation units from the mean. According to Figure VI-1, for a normal curve 31.74 percent of the cases or about 1 in 3 differ from the mean by as much as one standard deviation; 4.56 percent by as much as 2 standard deviations. Applying this information to the instance above in which 6 is the SEM, it would seem there is about 1 chance in 3 that an obtained score for an individual differs by as much as 6 points or 1 standard error from his "true-score" (see Figure VI-1.) There is about 1 chance in 20 that the obtained score differs from the true score by as much as 12 points or 2 standard errors. So we can think of a 45 score as meaning rather surely a score between 33 and 57.

A definite advantage of the standard error of measurement is its independence from the talent range in the group for which it was established. On a reading achievement test, it would have nearly the same value if determined for a group of second to sixth-grade children as for a class of fourth-graders only. The principal disadvantage of the standard error of measurement is that it is expressed in terms of the unique unit in which the scores are reported. Whereas the coefficient of reliability is an abstract index independent of the size-measuring unit involved in its determination, the standard error cannot be compared for different measures and is hard to interpret for even one test, owing to the uncertainty of meaning or absolute size of the unit at issue. One reasonable suggestion is that if persons concerned about test score interpretation would adopt the practice of writing after each score the value of its probable error, the periodic mistake of attributing significance to accidental variations in test performance would decline (Lindquist, 1942, pp. 222–223).

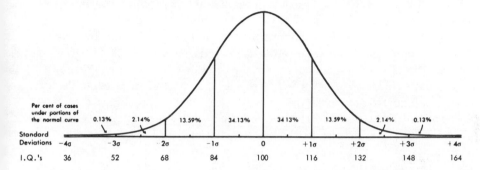

Fig. VI-1. Use of the normal curve in determining the probability of a person having a given IQ. Terman and Merrill (1937) have reported studies indicating that the IQ distribution according to the Stanford-Binet scale approximates the normal probability curve with a mean of 100 and standard deviation of 16. Therefore, by referring to Fig. VI-1 certain probability statements can be made. For example, the chances are roughly 2 out of 3 (actually 68.26 percent) that a person's IQ lies between 84 and 116; or chances are 19 out of 20 (actually 95.44 percent) that an individual's IQ lies between 68 and 132.

Before concluding this discussion, it is well to interject a new term, *level of confidence.* The certainty or confidence level with which any assertion is made can be expressed in probability form. Lindquist (1942, pp. 107–108) uses the illustration of marked cards to explain the matter. Imagine that among 100 cards, 95 are marked. After shuffling the deck, a single card is drawn at random. We can with a high degree of confidence, even before viewing the selected card, assert that it is marked since only 5 of the entire lot are otherwise. The degree of certainty basing this particular assertion about the unread card being marked is known as the 5 percent level of confidence. The smaller the percent indicated, the greater the degree of confidence for any assertion. For the normal distribution we know that 95.44 percent of the cases will fall within 2 standard deviations of the mean, or that approximately 5 percent may deviate further from the mean. So we may confidently assert at the 5-percent level that any pupil score randomly chosen from a normal distribution will depart from the mean by less than 2 standard deviations (actually 1.96σ). This assertion of probability would be reported as $p < .05$.

Practicality

Validity and reliability, both of which deal with the theoretical accuracy of measurement, are without question the two most important characteristics of a good test. Nevertheless, anyone who assumes responsibility for testing students is soon made aware that practical considerations of usability also affect decision-making. The most significant aspects of usability are objectivity; ease of administration, scoring, and interpretation; and economy.

Objectivity is ensured when scoring is uninfluenced by the bias judgment of whoever marks an examination. It is shown by the degree to which equally competent scorers obtain the same results. Usually objective examinations are so worded that one answer only is acceptable for an item. The advantage of this procedure is that it precludes disagreement about the range of correct responses and, disregarding chance errors, no variation should exist in the marks assigned to a particular test by different scorers or by the same scorer on different occasions. Objective tests are frequently criticized as being inherently weak because most of them arc limited to assessing the recall and recognition of information instead of the application of knowledge and other higher-level mental operations. Still there is no empirical evidence indicating that understanding and the application of knowledge cannot be measured objectively (Noll, 1965, p. 93). If teacher-made examinations perpetuate more restricted goals than the pupil might desire, it is probably because the teacher lacks test construction skill. On the other hand, published tests have to be objective; otherwise, if each examiner scored tests according to his own bias, interpretations based on comparison of test results with class, school, or age norms would have no meaning. One of the major values standardized tests possess is that personal judgment is largely eliminated in the scoring and interpretation of results—this in sharp contrast to the often unreliable teacher-made test.

Ease of test administration is a practical consideration. The Stanford-Binet has a high index of validity and reliability but might be considered low in usability because as an individual test it is time-consuming and requires a specially trained examiner. Proper administration also implies that planning be given the tasks of distributing and collecting materials, issuing oral and written instructions, the use of sample items and timing of subtests. Another aspect of practicality is the ease with which scoring proceeds. Scoring is facilitated by an answer sheet on which item responses are positioned in a straight line rather than randomly placed all over the page. If the test is meant to be diagnostic there will most likely be subscores, a necessary inconvenience to the teacher. Obviously, when marking is mechanically done, only objective test items can be considered. With the exception of rating scales that require that score values be of unequal weight, test items should all bear equal importance. Some of the newer techniques for weighting items purport to increase validity and reliability but since they require use of the computer, they are impractical at present.

For a test to possess utility, it must satisfactorily serve a definite need in the use situation; unless constructed to enable some predetermined objective, any test is questionable. To assist the examiner in fixing appropriate meaning to obtained scores, test manual authors are obligated to suggest ways by which results can be used. Manuals should also include a statement of the test's intended function, procedures for examiners to follow, evidence of reliability and validity and intercorrelations of subtests. Since the lack of alternate forms imposes severe restrictions on many types of educational research, information about the availability of equivalent tests should be indicated. Then too, there is a need for providing adequate norms; wherever possible, derived scores should be capable of being read directly from tables of norms without the necessity of computation.

School budgets usually dictate that considerations of economy be made in testing programs. This does not imply that economy will be achieved by selecting from just the least expensive instruments on the market. By the same token it is erroneous to assume that the most costly measures are necessarily better than the others. Greene (1954, p. 81) suggests that the economy of the testing program should be computed in terms of the validity of the tests per unit of cost. There are many ways to save money without damaging the testing program. For example, by purchasing tests having separate answer sheets, the booklets can be reused and the space required for storing student profiles reduced. Optimally, only if two tests are equally good for the stated purpose should expense be the deciding factor (Noll, 1965, p. 101). For educators who cannot find adequate time to score tests, there are many publishers that offer completion of this task at low rates.

In summary, the essential features of a "good" measuring instrument are validity, reliability, and practicality. In other words, a "good" test measures its intention consistently and at a minimum price in terms of energy, time, and dollars.

ANALYZING TEST RESULTS

The Frequency Distribution

Teachers cannot hope to tell much about group performance from a lengthy, unordered list of individual scores that reflect only the random fashion by which they were collected. About all we can glean from Table VI-4 is that none of the students earned a perfect mark, they each re-

TABLE VI-4

Unranked Scores of 36 Junior High Pupils
on a 100-Item Mathematics Test

86	67	69	92
68	95	79	75
58	79	85	64
97	54	63	71
83	77	80	85
91	73	76	73
89	60	70	79
62	89	83	82
79	72	87	89

sponded correctly to more than half the items, and their scores range from 54 to 97. Data presented in this form do not enable an adequate description of the group. Moreover, their disarray poses an unreasonable expectation of the reader to grasp and hold many unlike facts in isolation. Somehow, before these scores can assume their proper meaning and interpretation, they must be rearranged and analyzed.

One scheme for classifying the scores is to place them in order of size from highest to lowest (see Table VI-5). By this series arrangement, commonly employed when class membership is small, each score retains its identity while contributing to a new and more ordered form. Notice that the same group of scores in Table VI-4 reappear in Table VI-5 but are there shown in order of size and with corresponding ranks. Now it is possible to recognize that Charles Johnson's 86 ranks him ninth in the class of 36 or about one-fourth of the way from the top. This same type of observation can readily be made for any member of the class. However, when there are more than about 20 pupils in a course, the ranking method often proves unsatisfactory. According to the teacher's grade-book, Shirley and Ted both earned an 85. Because it is incorrect to view either of these two same scores as higher than the other, they are assigned a fractional rank. Since nine pupils scored higher than Shirley and Ted, the next two positions (10, 11) are averaged to yield their joint rank of 10.5. Similarly, in the case of the four children earning 79's, a score exceeded by fifteen others, rank is determined by averaging 16, 17, 18, 19 for a position designated as 17.5. The time and effort required to rank scores in this manner produce a list that is long, hard to handle, and totally inadequate for making comparisons with classrooms of a different size membership.

A better way to present test results and facilitate interpretation requires the construction of a frequency distribution that includes, by order of

TABLE VI-5

Ranked Scores of 36 Junior High Pupils
on a 100-Item Mathematics Test

Order of Size	Rank Order	Order of Size	Rank Order
97	1	79	17.5
95	2	77	20
92	3	76	21
91	4	75	22
89	6	73	23.5
89	6	73	23.5
89	6	72	25
87	8	71	26
86	9	70	27
85	10.5	69	28
85	10.5	68	29
83	12.5	67	30
83	12.5	64	31
82	14	63	32
80	15	62	33
79	17.5	60	34
79	17.5	58	35
79	17.5	54	36

size, all the possible score values within the obtained range (see Table VI-6). Since 97 and 54 represent the earned extremes, every integral between them is placed in the test score column, symbolized by the letter X. The number of times each score value occurs is tallied in the tabulation column and thereafter entered to the frequency (f) column. The symbol N at the base of the (f) frequency column signifies the total number of pupil test scores. By this procedure the more frequently obtained measures stand out, revealing in a graphic manner just how the scores are distributed along a linear scale of values. Like the unordered or ranking approach, this method allows each score to retain its identity but it results in an even more lengthy and cumbersome arrangement. In fact, to include all the scores between 54 and 97 requires 44 lines.

Whenever the score range appears too large to handle, say in excess of 25 points, it becomes necessary to condense the frequency distribution by grouping nearby scores together and subsequently treating them as equal for computational purposes. Then, instead of showing the fre-

TABLE VI-6

Ungrouped Frequency Distribution of Scores for
36 Junior High Pupils on a 100-Item Mathematics Test

Score(X)	Tabulation	f	Score(X)	Tabulation	f
97	/	1	75	/	1
96			74		
95	/	1	73	//	2
94			72	/	1
93			71	/	1
92	/	1	70	/	1
91	/	1	69	/	1
90			68	/	1
89	///	3	67	/	1
88			66		
87	/	1	65		
86	/	1	64	/	1
85	//	2	63	/	1
84			62	/	1
83	//	2	61		
82	/	1	60	/	1
81			59		
80	/	1	58	/	1
79	////	4	57		
78			56		
77	/	1	55		
76	/	1	54	/	1
				$N=\Sigma f=36$	

quency of occurrence for each integral value separately, the distribution
indicates the number of scores falling within equal intervals along the
linear scale. In this grouped frequency distribution (Table VI-7) the
number of adjacent scores being combined together is known as a *class
interval*. Although no general rule need be followed to establish interval
size, it is unwise to consider fewer than 12 classes or more than 20—a
sufficiently small enough number to think about effectively and yet not
so few that important differences are masked. Essentially the choice of
interval size involves a compromise between losing data detail and achieving a workable arrangement of scores. A broad interval is used at sacrifice to accuracy but results in a more condensed form.

The range is used in determining which among the commonly preferred intervals (1, 2, 3, 5, 10, or 15) to select for the particular distribution. Again, the class interval is the size of the group into which scores are to be classified. A practical rule of thumb is to choose an interval that will divide the score range into approximately 15 groups. In Table VI-7, where the highest score is 97 and the lowest is 54, the range that is one more than the difference between the highest score and the lowest is $(97 - 54) + 1 = 44$. Dividing 44 by 15 yields 2.93. And since it is impractical to use any class interval except a whole number, the fractional

TABLE VI-7

Grouped Frequency Distribution of Scores for 36 Junior High Pupils on a 100-Item Mathematics Test

Score Interval	Tabulation	f	d	fd	fd²
96–98	/	1	+6	+ 6	36
93–95	/	1	+5	+ 5	25
90–92	//	2	+4	+ 8	32
87–89	////	4	+3	+12	36
84–86	///	3	+2	+ 6	12
81–83	///	3	+1	+ 3	3
				+40	
78–80		5	0		
75–77	///	3	−1	− 3	3
72–74	///	3	−2	− 6	12
69–71	///	3	−3	− 9	27
66–68	//	2	−4	− 8	32
63–65	//	2	−5	−10	50
60–62	//	2	−6	−12	72
57–59	/	1	−7	− 7	49
54–56	/	1	−8	− 8	64
				−63	
		N36		+40	453

$$-63$$
$$36 \quad -23$$
$$c = -.64$$
$$i = \quad 3$$
$$ci = -1.92$$

unit is disregarded in favor of the next higher unit—in this case 3. Construction of the table should include the highest and lowest earned scores. To expedite tabulation begin each class with a multiple of the class interval. Since the highest class begins with 96, a multiple of 3, it will accommodate the greatest score, 97; each succeeding class drops back 3 points below the one just above it. The next class starts at 93, 90, etc., until the lowest, 54, is reached. It is important to realize that all of the intervals are of equal value and the lower limit of each is divisible by the interval value (3) itself—this is convenient, it eases computation, and reduces the possibility of error. Yet, it would be just as satisfactory to use limits that are not multiples of the interval. In fact, some authorities recommend selecting the interval limits in a way such that its midpoints are multiples of the interval (so that in Table VI-7 the top interval would read 95–97) but this appears a less natural way of viewing class intervals (Noll, 1965, p. 461).

After deciding upon the size and limits for class intervals, take the first score of the original list (Table VI-4), locate its appropriate interval, and place a tally mark opposite in the tabulation column. Proceed in this fashion until all of the test scores have separately been recorded. Accuracy in plotting the frequency distribution is imperative because any error will invalidate the accuracy of whatever statistical computations follow. Care is necessary to avoid this most common error—placing the tabulation of a score in the wrong class interval. To properly complete the task, tallies are totalled for each row showing that number in the frequency (f) column and then obtaining the sum of the frequencies (Σ means to "take the sum of"). This sum, N, should equal the total number of original scores, thereby providing a rough check in the accuracy of the tabulation.

The grouped frequency distribution of Table VI-7 differs from the ungrouped distribution of Table VI-6 in that the original scores are no longer recognizable, their individual identities having been lost as a result of grouping. Distinctions cannot be made among scores falling within the same class. For example, the four 79's and single 80 are consolidated into a frequency of 5 for the 78–80 interval. The reader of Table VI-7 has no way of knowing how the 5 scores of interval 78–80 are distributed. Consequently, even though it be easier to see how the scores are spread over the entire range, it is impossible to ascertain the frequency of occurrence for any particular score value. Again, for the interval 87–89 one cannot tell how many of the 4 scores are 87's, 88's, or 89's because such information is hidden in the grouping. Given this loss in identity of individual scores, it will be necessary in later computations to use the midpoint of each interval to represent the value of all measures contained in the interval. We assume that all instances for any class fall at the midpoint of that interval, except when the median or percentiles are computed—then it is assumed that cases are spread evenly across the interval. The midpoint is that value lying halfway between the *real limits* of the interval, which extend .5 below and .5 above the stated interval. If the interval contains an even number, the midpoint will be a decimal value and thus inconvenient. In any interval containing an odd number of units, however, the midpoint will be an integral number. Usually when selecting class intervals an odd number is optioned in order that the midpoints will be whole numbers.

In review, the purpose of a frequency distribution is to impose structure upon an array of unorganized information, to condense test data into a form more readily grasped by showing the number of times each score value (or class interval) of measures occurs. With an appreciation for and an understanding of the frequency distribution, we are introduced to the realm of statistics, an area of study focused upon the collection, tabulation, analysis, and presentation of data. Statistical methods of analysis and synthesis enable its user to scientifically collect and describe quantitative numerical factors too numerous and complex for simple observation and interpretation. In other words, statistics provide the educator with a research tool for extracting the significant truths concealed in masses of numerical data. Although an increasingly higher level of order has been attained in Tables VI-4 through VI-7 respectively, inspection of these presentations reveal very little about central tendency or averages of the scores, their dispersion, relationships, or other significant facts. For this reason, teachers need to know the computation procedures necessary to analyze and summarize the data presented in score distributions.

Measures of Central Tendency

The process of condensing test scores into a grouped frequency distribution is requisite for analysis and interpretation. But beyond this, to properly describe the data it is necessary to locate some single index representative of the entire table that can reveal the trend of scores as to whether on the whole they be high or low. Because the indices assumed to represent a distribution generally are found near the center of the scores, they are referred to as averages or measures of central tendency. Any measure of central tendency is designed to provide a single value that is most typical of a set of scores. For example, on a standardized test the norm is that score made by the typical student of a certain age or grade; that is, the norm is the average score earned by a representative group of pupils. Whenever standardized instruments are administered the teacher is naturally interested in how his class or institution compares with test norms. All comparisons with norms are in terms of averages (Ross, 1949, p. 227). If at a certain school the average score in each of three tenth-grade rooms were respectively the same as the norm, above the norm score, and below it, these classes might in turn be identified as typical, better than average, and poorer than average. Given the wide uses of averages in school work, it is useful to consider the *mode, median,* and *mean*—three common measures of central tendency.

Mode. An easy way to identify the typical score of a set is to find the measure within it that occurs most frequently—this is the mode, an average obtained by inspection. As the most commonly obtained score or the midpoint of the class interval that has the greatest frequency, the mode is easy to find and understand but there its advantages end. The mode is considered an unstable and therefore untrustworthy average, particularly with small groups, since it is sensitive to minor changes in data. For instance, the changing of an individual score in Table VI-6 could decidedly alter the mode of 79. Were one of the persons making 79 to have scored 89 instead, the mode would rise to the latter figure because more pupils would have that mark than any other. Likewise, the modal interval on Table VI-7 would change from 78–80 to 87–89. Sometimes there are two outstanding frequencies (bimodal) or more (multimodal) in a given distribution. Whatever the case, the mode is seldom reported in testing literature in deference to the mean and median, both averages of greater stability and usefulness.

Median. A more acceptable reference for the average or typical measure than the mode involves determining that value which divides the upper half of a group from its lower half—this is called the median. By definition the median is that point along the score continuum above and below which 50 percent of the instances lie; a measure the same as the 50th percentile. Described as the counting average, the median is often recommended for general use by teachers when the number of cases is small and a high degree of accuracy is unnecessary. Unlike the mode, which may be greatly influenced by a single measure, a score far beyond the median contributes no more to its determination than does a score just above it. In the same fashion an extremely low mark alters the median position to the same degree as does a score just barely below the median. Contrary to the mean, which is affected by each of the scores in proportion to their size, a median is preferred whenever one desires to avoid the influence of extreme scores.

The following steps enable determination of a median from Table VI-7.

1. Compute ½N. That is, the total of the frequencies is divided by 2. In this case $\frac{1}{2}N$ $\overset{\text{or } N}{\underset{2}{\rule{1cm}{0.4pt}}} = 18$

2. Find the approximate median. Starting at the low end of the distribution of scores, count upward in the (f) frequency column as far as possible without going by 18, the $\frac{N}{2}$ previously obtained. In this problem the frequencies $1 + 1 + 2 + 2 + 2 + 3 + 3 + 3$ yield a total of 17. We can go no higher, since to include the next frequency, 5, would bring us beyond 18. Therefore, the approximate median is 77.5, the lower limit of the class interval (78–80) containing the median.

3. Decide upon the necessary correction. Subtract the frequency total arrived at in step 2 from $\frac{N}{2}$. That is, $18 - 17 = 1$. This indicates that one

more score is required to constitute one half, and the additional measure must come from the next class (78–80) where there is a frequency of 5. To put it another way, we need to go ⅕ of the distance into this next higher interval. Since this class interval is 3, this means the correction is ⅕ of 3 or .60. The step just described is based on an assumption that an interval's scores are uniformly distributed.

4. Locate the actual median. Add the correction in terms of scale distance to the lower real limits of the interval in which the median lies to find the actual median. A correction of .60 is added to 77.5, the lower real limits of the interval containing the answer, for a median of 78.1.

By using the steps just outlined to compute a median, we have employed this formula:

$$Md = l + \frac{\frac{1}{2}N - s_b}{f} i$$

where $l =$ lower limit of the class containing the median,

$N =$ total number of cases in the frequency series,

$s_b =$ number of cases below the class containing the point desired,

$f =$ number of scores in class containing median,

$i =$ represents the interval.

Mean. Although teachers regard each of the central tendency measures as a form of average, most laymen think of the term average as pertaining only to the arithmetic mean. When reference is made to the average price, salary, or temperature, it is the arithmetic mean which is used. This most familiar form of average can be defined as the sum of all scores in a frequency distribution (ΣX) divided by the total number (N) of such measures. Formula $M = \frac{\Sigma X}{N}$ The arithmetic mean indicates the size that the numerical values would be if all were exactly alike in value while the total number of measures remained the same. By this method, the mean of 78, 80, 81, 82, and 83 can easily be found: $M = \frac{404}{5} = 80.8$. Computing the mean in this manner is appropriate if scores are few in number or part of an ungrouped series.

Should there be enough measures to justify the construction of a frequency distribution, it becomes possible to employ a shortcut method. Here the arithmetic mean is defined "as a point on the scale such that the sum of the deviations of the values larger exactly equals the sum of the deviations of the values smaller than it is" (Greene, 1954, p. 318). By analogy, the mean may be likened in physical terms to a point on a scale at which the fulcrum must be placed in order to balance its moments of force. If the physical lever be out of balance, its fulcrum must be moved toward the heavier end as a correction until equilibrium is obtained. Similarly, a sort of trial balance is taken when calculating the arithmetic mean and, if the moments of force appear too one-sided, the place of rotation is moved toward the heavy end until the difference between the two forces reaches zero (Greene, 1954, p. 319).

To illustrate the rationale of using deviation units, let us consider the problem cited above, namely finding a mean for 78, 80, 81, 82, and 83. Observation would suggest that 81 is a good guess as the mean. In such case the 82 is a point too large while 83 is two points above the guessed mean. By the same token 80 is a point too small and 78 is three points too small. The total of differences above the guessed mean is three and the total of differences below it is four. This indicates that the guessed mean of 81 is too large by the amount of this difference divided by the number of cases. That is to say, $1 \div 5 = .2$, the amount too large. Subtracting .2 from 81 yields a mean of 80.8. Notice that this corresponds exactly with the mean found when dividing the sum of the total scores by the number of test scores ($M = \dfrac{\Sigma X}{N}$).

By going through the steps required to compute an arithmetic mean for Table VI-7, a better appreciation of the process can be gained.

1. Decide upon a guessed mean. Since we assume that all scores in each interval have the value of the midpoint, the midpoint of some interval will be chosen as the guessed mean. Although any class can be selected, it is best to choose one near the distribution's center. For Table VI-7 the guessed mean is 79, midpoint of the (78–80) class interval whose lower and upper limit respectively are 77.5 and 80.5.

2. Lay off deviations from the guessed mean by intervals. The values in the deviation (d) column are found by assigning a zero to the class in which the guessed mean is located and then counting, in terms of the number of intervals, how far each deviates from the interval containing the guessed mean (78–80). Deviations above the guessed mean are positive and those below it are negative. So the deviation value of the 81–83 interval is +1 because it is one interval above while the 75–77 interval is —1 and so on.

3. Multiply the frequency (f) of scores in each class by its corresponding deviation (d) from the interval containing the guessed mean. These products are recorded in the column headed fd. From the top the first product in this column reads $1 \times 6 = 6$ and the second $1 \times 5 = 5$. Products below the guessed mean will have negative signs.

4. Sum the values in the fd column, taking account of the plus and minus signs. To avoid computation errors, the plus and minus entries ought to be summed separately, and then combined to obtain the final total. Note that the sum of plus values is 40 and the sum of minus values is 63. This results in an algebraic total of —23. Had the plus values been greater than the minus ones, the consequent sum for the frequency distribution column would have been positive.

5. Determine the correction for the guessed mean by first finding the deviation of scores. To do this divide the sum of the frequency distribution column (Σfd) by N to get $\Sigma fd/N$, retaining the proper sign. Since there are 36 scores in the distribution and each contributes equally to the —23 units, the average correction in terms of classes in the quotient of —23 $\div$ 36 = —.64. Next, convert the mean of the deviations of the scores to the scale value. Since there are 3 units in each interval, it is necessary to multiply —.64 by 3 in order to make the correction into scale units. The consequent value of —1.92 represents the amount by which the guessed mean must be corrected.

6. Find the true mean by algebraic addition of the correction (—1.92) to the guessed mean (79.00). The negative sign of the correction shows that the guessed mean is too high and must be changed downward. 79 + (—1.92) = 77.08, the true mean.

To check the accuracy of computing the mean, it is only necessary to select a different class interval as the guessed mean and repeat the same calculations. If the arithmetic is correct the mean will result as the same value. Whatever the initial class selection, the formula for this shortcut method remains the same:

$$M = M^1 + \frac{\Sigma fd}{N} i$$

where $M =$ true mean,

$M^1 =$ guessed mean,

$\Sigma fd =$ sum of frequencies, multiplied by their respective deviations,

$N =$ total number of frequencies,

$i =$ class interval.

Choosing the measure of central tendency

Any merit comparison between the several measures of central tendency should include an awareness of their differences in assumption and process. In computing the median for a grouped frequency distribution, it is assumed that each measure expands or contracts in such a way so that it shares the scale distance through an interval equally with the other scores in that same class. By way of contrast, when computing the arithmetic mean, each of the scores is assumed to have the value of the midpoint of the interval in which it is recorded. So, all five scores in the 78–80 interval are considered as having a 79 value when finding the arithmetic mean but judged to occupy ⅕ of the scale distance through that interval (⅕ x 3 = .6) when calculating the median. The median and mean differ also in the process by which they are determined; the median is found in counting ranked scores until the middle measure is reached, whereas the mean is located by identifying the point at which the scores balance.

If the distribution of scores is symmetrical or nearly so, there will be little difference between the balance point and the middle point; consequently mean and median will correspond, having about the same numerical value. However, were a score distribution skewed, that is, piled up at one end, the mean and median would be expected to substantially differ. Since the mean is greatly influenced by extreme scores, being pulled toward the heavy end of the distribution, the median is generally recommended when the scores are skewed because it fits logically into the percentile scale and continues to divide the group in half. Often both the mean and median are reported to indicate whether the distribution is skewed. If a test is too difficult or easy, there may be some zero scores and some perfect scores. In neither case have the students of these extremes been properly measured—so the median is preferred. On the other hand, in settings where it is statistically important that each score be permitted its full weight according to its magnitude, the average to use is the mean.

Several other considerations deserve mention. Use of the mean is limited to distributions of unit-scale scores; it would be devoid of meaning with measures of rank order expression. This limitation is not shared by the median which may be used with either type measurement symbol and therefore qualifies as the most widely applicable descriptive measure of central tendency (Bradfield, 1957, pp. 148–150). From the standpoint of theoretical statistics, the mean, which is algebraic in nature, has the advantage of the median, arithmetic in nature, since it figures in the computation of other measures such as the standard deviation, coefficient of correlation, and analysis of variance. Obviously the mode is the poorest average among the measures of central tendency; whether the median or mean is judged best depends on the purpose and circumstances. In any case it is well to realize that a single "score has no meaning except in comparison to other scores in the same series, or to the central tendency or average of all scores in the series" (Noll, 1965, p. 43).

Measures of Variability

The averages for a given class, age, or grade, provide useful reference points with which an individual score may be compared; yet no distribution is fully described by its indices of central tendency. Indeed none of the averages reveal anything about the form in which scores are distributed. It is conceivable that two classes in the same building might share similar averages and still differ greatly in terms of their range or spread of performance levels. In one room student achievement scores could extend from grade 3 to grade 9 while another room of the same average might enroll youngsters almost all of whom achieve at the 6th-grade level. One room has a performance range of 6 grades while the other by comparison has a negligible amount of variability and is therefore more homogenous. Even though these classes show the same central tendencies no informed teacher would regard them as comparable for the variability suggests that they will present different instructional problems. Obviously, it is important for an instructor to be able to determine the variability of a group, that is, some measure of the extent to which scores and distribution tend to spread above and below the average. Each of the popular variability measures—range, semi-interquartile range, and standard deviation stand for distances with the greater distances corresponding to larger variability or score scatter.

Range and semi-interquartile range

The distance between the highest and lowest scores in a distribution augmented by one is known as the *range*. More precisely, the range is the difference between the upper limit of the top score interval and the lower limit of the bottom score. Sometimes, when comparing school classes, it is more important to be aware of their respective spread in scores than to know the averages for each group. However, since the range depends entirely upon just the two extreme measures of a set, it is capable of great change with the shift of a single score. In Table VI-6 the top mark is 97 and the lowest mark is 54, resulting in a range of 44 ($97 - 54 + 1 = 44$, or $97.5 - 53.5 = 44$). Were the person who attained 54 to have performed less well and instead achieved a mark of 34, the range would thereby have extended 20 points ($97 - 34 + 1$) to become 64. Because the range is a crude indicator that can readily increase or diminish the apparent scatter of a score set, it is seldom viewed as a dependable or trustworthy measure of variability.

Whereas the range can be greatly influenced by a single measure located at either the bottom or the top of a set, this does not hold true for the semi-interquartile range, generally designated as Q. As a refinement of the crude range, the semi-interquartile range omits the high and low 25 percent of the measures where scatter and unreliability are most likely to occur and presents instead a measure of dispersion for the more consistent and concentrated middle 50 percent of the distribution (Noll, 1965, p. 46). In a sense, "This statistic defines itself: *Semi* (half) *inter* (between) *quartile* (one of three points dividing the distribution into four groups of equal size) *range* (difference or distance); in other words, the statistic equals one-half the distance between the extreme quartiles, Q_3 (seventy-fifth percentile) and Q_1 (twenty-fifth percentile) (Lyman, 1963, p. 51).

Expressed by formula, the semi-interquartile range is determined as follows:

$$Q = \frac{Q_3 - Q_1}{2}$$

Finding quartiles is just like locating the median with one exception made in the first step. While the fractional element of N in computing the median is always $\frac{1}{2}$, it now is changed to indicate whatever proportion is desired below an intended point. In other words, it would be $\frac{1}{4}N$ for Q_1 and $\frac{3}{4}N$ for Q_3. Computing Q_1 and Q_3 from Table VI-7 will enable a solution for Q.

$Q_1 = \frac{1}{4}N = \frac{1}{4}$ of $36 = 9$ cases counting up from the low end of the
$\qquad\qquad\qquad$ distribution
$\quad = 68.5$ (lower limits of the interval in which Q_1 falls)
$\quad = 68.5 + \frac{1}{3}$ (the necessary distance into the interval) $\times 3$ (size
$\qquad\qquad\qquad$ of interval)
$\quad = 68.5 + \frac{1}{3} \times 3$
$Q_1 = 69.5$

$Q_3 = \frac{3}{4}N = \frac{3}{4}$ of $36 = 27$ cases counting up from the low end of the
$\qquad\qquad\qquad$ distribution
$\quad = 83.5$ (lower limits of the interval in which Q_3 falls)
$\quad = 83.5 + \frac{2}{3}$ (the necessary distance into the interval) $\times 3$ (size
$\qquad\qquad\qquad$ of interval)
$\quad = 83.5 + \frac{2}{3} \times 3$
$Q_3 = 85.5$

$$Q = \frac{Q_3 - Q_1}{2}$$

$$= \frac{85.5 - 69.5}{2}$$

$$= \frac{16}{2}$$

$$Q = 8$$

Whether a semi-interquartile range of 8 is judged great or small is relative, the contingency being how large comparable measures are for other pupil groups administered the same test. When the semi-interquartile range of one class exceeds another in size, the difference reveals the degree to which the former membership is more heterogeneous than the latter. Q is a preferred measure for working with skewed distributions and, since it belongs to the same family of statistics as the median (both calculations are based on percentiles), the semi-interquartile range is used as the index of spread whenever the median is employed as the measure of central tendency.

Standard deviation

The standard deviation, represented by the Greek letter σ or sigma, is usually considered as best among the several measures of variability. Test-users need to understand standard deviation well, for its many purposes include providing a basis for standard scores, a way of indicating test score reliability, a manner of showing the accuracy of values predicted from a correlation coefficient, and a common statistical test of significance (Lyman, 1963, p. 51). Since the sigma is based on the deviation of each score from the arithmetic mean, this statistic offers a true index of dispersion that is less variable than other measures from one sample to the next.

Suppose that the arithmetic mean for an ungrouped series of 6 scores (8, 4, 6, 12, 14, 16) is calculated to be 10. To ascertain the degree that these scores are scattered from the mean of 10 the mean amount is subtracted from each score. This subtraction from the set (8, 4, 6, 12, 14, 16) respectively yields differences of −2, −6, −4, +2, +4, and +6. In each case these plus and minus sums depict the separate deviation of scores from the mean, the greater sums representing larger distances. Assuming that the average of the six deviations will provide a general index of spread, we add them. However, the sum obtained is necessarily zero because the mean depicts a point of balance between positive and negative deviations. So, to find the desired average and still deal with the plus and minus signs, all deviations are squared ($- x - = +$). Then the squared deviations are summed and divided by the number of cases to determine their average. The square root of this average value is calculated to compensate for squaring the individual deviations with the result known as sigma. In other words, *standard deviation* is the "square root of the average of the squared deviations from the mean" (Thorndike and Hagen, 1965, p. 95). Considering the problem above:

$$\sigma = \sqrt{\frac{(-2)^2 + (-6)^2 + (-4)^2 + (+2)^2 + (+4)^2 + (+6)^2}{6}}$$

$$= \sqrt{\frac{4 + 36 + 16 + 4 + 16 + 36}{6}}$$

$$= \sqrt{\frac{112}{6}}$$

$$= \sqrt{18.66}$$

$$\sigma = 4.3$$

When calculated from a guessed mean in a frequency distribution, the standard deviation formula is expressed as follows:

$$\sigma = i \sqrt{\frac{\Sigma f d^2}{N} - c^2}$$

Most of the steps required to determine sigma are the same as employed in obtaining the mean. The single new term presented is Σfd^2, which stands for the sum of frequencies times the squares of their respective deviations. For Table VI-7:

1. Guess the mean (79).
2. Lay off deviations above and below the guessed mean.
3. Each f is multiplied by its d. For scores presented in classes, deviations are considered as having the midpoint of the interval in which they are located. This allows a deviation expression in terms of classes rather than scale units.
4. Find Σfd, the algebraic sum for the fd column; in this case, -23.
5. Obtain the correction. $-23 \div 36 = -.64$. Note that the correction is not multiplied by the class interval; unlike the mean it is left in terms of intervals rather than converted into scale units.
6. Multiply each d by its respective fd and place the product in the fd^2 column.
7. Determine Σfd^2. Since the negative deviations are squared all values in the fd^2 column are positive.
8. Substitute in the formula for sigma. c^2 is subtracted from Σfd^2 whether c is negative or not; the end result is shown in terms of score units as opposed to classes.

$$\sigma = i \sqrt{\frac{\Sigma fd^2}{N} - c^2}$$

$$= 3\sqrt{453/36 - (.64)^2}$$

$$= 3\sqrt{12.5833 - .4096}$$

$$= 3\sqrt{12.1737}$$

$$= 3 \times 3.49$$

$$\sigma = 10.47$$

To better understand the importance of the standard deviation statistic (σ), it is necessary to refer to the so-called normal curve, a symmetrical bell-shaped distribution with many cases in the middle and few at the extremes (see Figure VI-1). In this kind of distribution sigma represents the distance from the mean at which the normal curve changes from convex to concave. Given the direct mathematical relationship sigma bears to the proportion of cases in a normal curve, it can be shown that the same proportion of instances will always be found within the same deviation limits. In a normal distribution 34.13 percent of the scores fall between the mean and 1 sigma away; so 68.26 percent of the cases lie between -1 sigma and $+1$ sigma. Although these exact figures will not hold true for nonnormal or skewed distributions, approximately ⅔ of the scores will always be found between −1 and +1 sigma. Between the points 2 sigmas above and below the mean approximately 95.44 percent of the measures will occur and 99.74 percent of the measures between −3 sigmas and +3 sigmas. As an example, the individual earning the score 1 sigma above the mean will be in better stead than roughly 84 percent of the group—the 50 percent below the mean and the 34.13 percent between the mean and +1 sigma. If the pupil had a score corresponding to +3 sigmas, we would expect this to be exceeded by only a negligible proportion of students (0.15 percent).

Or take the problem just completed regarding Table VI-7, in which the standard deviation is 10.47. This means that approximately 68 percent of the scores will be found between 1 σ on either side of the mean. Obviously, this is not completely true, for no distribution having as few as 36 scores is likely to closely approximate the normal curve. Yet, about two-thirds of the scores can be expected between −1 and +1 sigma. For this problem the points are 77.08 + 10.47 and 77.08 − 10.47 or 87.55 and 66.61. Actually 23 scores or about 63.88 percent of the total lie between these two points.

Choosing the measure of variability

When measures of variability are considered as a group, the standard deviation is generally pronounced "best" and the range judged "poorest," the latter being subject to the same shortcomings that hinder the mode as a measure of central tendency. However, like the mean, the standard deviation is readily affected by extreme scores. This suggests that to avoid the influence of deviant scores, the median should be used as the average measure and with it the semi-interquartile range as an index of variability. In the same way, whenever the mean is used as the measure of central tendency, the corresponding measure of variability is standard deviation. A final reminder is that the standard deviation of small numerical value represents a fairly homogeneous frequency distribution in which scores cluster closely about the mean, whereas the larger standard deviation indicates that the frequency distribution is heterogeneous with test scores widely scattered above and below the mean.

Measures of Relationship

Whenever more than a single set of measures is available for a given student population, it is possible to assess the relationship of these sets. For instance, teachers can determine the extent to which intelligence test scores and achievement scores covary or the association of reading and arithmetic performance and so on. Essentially, correlation is the study of paired numerical facts resulting in a coefficient expression of the amount and direction of relationship between the series examined. The direction of relationship can be learned from the coefficient sign. If pupils who are high in one distribution tend to be high in the second and students

low in the second are low in the first, there is a direct relationship indicated by a positive sign $(+)$. That is, a tendency obtains for the two
values to vary in the same direction. Usually the positive sign, $+$, is
omitted; if no sign appears the coefficient is understood as positive. On
the other hand, negative $(-)$ coefficients represent an inverse relationship where the tendency is for scores to vary in opposite directions so
that pupils high in one distribution are low in the other and conversely
so. While the coefficient sign indicates the direction of an association, the
coefficient size must be considered to learn about the degree of closeness
in a relationship. Magnitude may take any value from .00 indicating no
relationship to $+1.00$ or -1.00, equally perfect relationships. Whether
positive or negative, all values of the same size represent equally close
relationships (Ross, 1949, pp. 241–242; Wood, 1961, pp. 77–80).

Spearman rank order method

Perhaps the easiest method to determine correlation is the one authored
by the British psychologist, Charles Spearman. The Spearman rank order
technique, symbolized by the Greek letter *rho* and written as ρ is generally
used when the number of cases is small, data is in ordinal form, and great
precision is not a major issue. Table VI-8 provides the set of scores for
correlation using this formula:

$$\rho = 1 - \frac{6\Sigma D^2}{N(N^2 - 1)}$$

1. Establish rank order among the scores in each set. For the sake of
convenience, it is recommended that one score series be recorded in order
of size. The chemistry scores, designated in Table VI-8 as the X variable,
have been so arranged while the physics scores, hereafter referred to as
variable Y, do not appear in order of size. Whenever 2 or more scores of
the same size occur in a set, they are assigned their average rank. Under
the X variable, for example, 59 is recorded 5 times. Since there are 8
scores above 59, all the 59's are assigned the average of the ensuing 5
ranks, (9, 10, 11, 12, 13), which is 11. Notice that the person earning the
highest chemistry score (variable X), designated by a rank of 1 was
second highest in physics (variable Y). At the opposite extreme the individual scoring last (20th) on variable X ranks 17th on variable Y.

2. Determine the differences in rank between the two sets of measures
and record them in the D column. The first student earned a rank of 1
on the X variable and 2 on the Y. Using X as a base this means the student's rank on X was 1 better than on Y, shown as $+1$. The second pupil
had a rank of 2 on X and 1 on Y, indicating that the rank score on X fell
1 below the Y score, and indicated as -1. Keeping the signs before the
differences permits an accuracy check since the respective sums of the
$+D$'s and $-D$'s should be equal; in the illustration each sum is 36.

TABLE VI-8

Calculation of rho by the Rank Order Method of Charles Spearman

Scores		Ranks		Differences in Ranks	
Chemistry X	Physics Y	Chemistry X	Physics Y	D	D^2
63	69	1	2	+ 1	1
62	72	2	1	− 1	1
61	67	4	3	− 1	1
61	62	4	7.5	+ 3.5	12.25
61	55	4	17	+13	169
60	64	7	5.5	− 1.5	2.25
60	61	7	9.5	+ 2.5	6.25
60	64	7	5.5	− 1.5	2.25
59	61	11	9.5	− 1.5	2.25
59	55	11	17	+ 6	36
59	62	11	7.5	− 3.5	12.25
59	59	11	13.5	+ 2.5	6.25
59	60	11	11.5	+ .5	.25
58	55	15	17	+ 2	4
58	66	15	4	−11	121
58	51	15	20	+ 5	25
57	60	17	11.5	− 5.5	30.25
56	55	18.5	17	− 1.5	2.25
56	59	18.5	13.5	− 5	25
55	55	20	17	− 3	9
N=20					
				+36	ΣD^2=468.50
				−36	

3. In the D^2 column, record the squares of the differences between ranks. The sum of this column, ΣD^2, is 468.50.

4. Substitute in the formula:

$$\rho = 1 - \frac{6\Sigma D^2}{N(N^2 - 1)}$$

$$= 1 - \frac{6 \times 468.50}{20(20^2 - 1)}$$

$$= 1 - \frac{2811}{7980}$$

$$= 1 - .35$$

$$\rho = .65$$

TABLE VI-9

Calculating rho by the Product-Moment Method of Pearson

Scores		Deviations		Deviations Squared		Products of Deviations
Chemistry X	Physics Y	Chemistry x	Physics y	x^2	y^2	xy
63	69	$+ 4$	$+ 8$	16	64	32
62	72	$+ 3$	$+11$	9	121	33
61	67	$+ 2$	$+ 6$	4	36	12
61	62	$+ 2$	$+ 1$	4	1	2
61	55	$+ 2$	$- 6$	4	36	-12
60	64	$+ 1$	$+ 3$	1	9	3
60	61	$+ 1$	0	1	0	0
60	64	$+ 1$	$+ 3$	1	9	3
59	61	0	0	0	0	0
59	55	0	$- 6$	0	36	0
59	62	0	$+ 1$	0	1	0
59	59	0	$- 2$	0	4	0
59	60	0	$- 1$	0	1	0
58	55	$- 1$	$- 6$	1	36	6
58	66	$- 1$	$+ 5$	1	25	$- 5$
58	51	$- 1$	-10	1	100	10
57	60	$- 2$	$- 1$	4	1	2
56	55	$- 3$	$- 6$	9	36	18
56	59	$- 3$	$- 2$	9	4	6
55	55	$- 4$	$- 6$	16	36	24

$M'_x=59$ $M'_y=61$ $+16$ $+38$ 20)81   20)556 $+151$

$(N=20)$ $\underline{-15}$ $\underline{-46}$ 4.05   27.8 $- 17$

$20)\underline{+ 1}$ $20)\underline{- 8}$ $-$ $\underline{.0025}$ $\underline{-.16}$ $20)\underline{+134}$

$$c_x=+.05 \quad c_y=-.4 \quad \sigma_x^{\,2}=4.0475 \quad \sigma_y^{\,2}=27.64 \quad \frac{\Sigma xy}{N}=6.7$$

$$c_x^{\,2}=+.0025 \quad c_y^{\,2}=-.16 \quad \sigma_x=2.0 \quad \sigma_y=5.3$$

$$r=\frac{\dfrac{\Sigma\, xy}{N}}{\sigma_x\,\sigma_y} - c_x\,c_y = \frac{6.7-(.05\times-.4)}{2\times5.3} = \frac{6.7+.020}{10.6} = .63$$

Pearson product-moment method

The most recommended and widely used method of correlation, based upon the deviations from the means of each set, is attributed to Karl Pearson. This is the product-moment method which yields the Pearson r.

$$r = \frac{\frac{\Sigma xy}{N} - c_x c_y}{\sigma x \; \sigma y}$$

Like most statistical measures, the seeming difficulty of this one disappears when its formula is broken down into steps for solution of a problem. The same data (Table VI-8) used to find the Spearman ρ (rho) appears in Table VI-9 for determining the Pearson r.

1. Determine the deviation for each score from the mean of its set. Because the true mean is seldom a whole number, it is easier to use the guessed mean as a basis for obtaining deviations. In this problem the guessed mean of X is 59, for Y it is 61. Deviations from X and Y are represented by the same letters, only in smaller size, x and y. Signs of the deviations must be shown.

2. Find the squares for each deviation placing them in the appropriate column labeled as x^2 and y^2.

3. Obtain the product for each pair of deviations; that is, multiply each x by its matching y placing the products in the xy column. The first three products from the top are as follows: $4 \times 8 = 32$; $3 \times 11 = 33$; $2 \times 6 = 12$.

4. Substituting $\Sigma xy/N$ is 134, the algebraic sum of the xy column, dividing by N which is 20. This gives 6.7. c_x is the algebraic sum of the x column divided by N, and c_y is the algebraic sum of the y column divided by N. In this problem c_x is $+ .05$ and c_y is $- .4$. Their product $c_x c_y$ is $.05 \times - .4 = - .020$. But as the formula is $\Sigma xy/N - c_x c_y$, the substitution is $6.7 - (- .020)$, or $6.7 + .020$. σ_x and σ_y are found by the usual formula:

$$\sigma x = \sqrt{\frac{\Sigma x^2}{N} - c^2 x} = \sqrt{\frac{81}{20} - (.05)^2} = \sqrt{4.05 - .0025} = 2$$

$$\sigma y = \sqrt{\frac{\Sigma y^2}{N} - c^2 y} = \sqrt{\frac{556}{20} - (-.4)^2} = \sqrt{27.8 - .16} = 5.3$$

5. Complete the process.

$$r = \frac{\frac{\Sigma xy}{N} - c_x c_y}{\sigma_x \sigma_y} = \frac{6.7 - (.05 \times - .4)}{2 \times 5.3} = \frac{6.7 + .020}{10.6} = .63$$

Notice that the product-moment method in this case yields almost exactly the same value, .63, as the Spearman rank order method, .65. Both methods indicate the tendency for students in chemistry to do well in physics and conversely. The closeness between .63 and .65 is not a coincidence, for the difference between the r and ρ is usually likely to be less than .02 although rarely ever exactly the same (Ross, 1949, p. 240).

Interpreting relationships

It would be nice to be always able to say with certainty how close a relationship is indicated by a coefficient of some size, say .80, but this is unlikely. Indeed, to describe this association, .80, as being "high" or "substantial" between any two sets of measures is dubious and misleading. Perhaps .80 might be regarded as a close degree of relationship between intelligence test scores and achievement scores but would certainly not be viewed as close in correlating two forms of the same achievement test. "High" and "low" are relative terms that cannot be uniformly applied by a simple correspondence with coefficient size apart from consideration of the variables. Still there does appear in the literature of testing a tentative classification of values for coefficients with which the reader ought to be familiar. Usually correlations between .00 and $\pm$ .20 are referred to as negligible relationships; .20 to .40 is considered low; .40 to .60 definite but relatively low; between .60 and .80 marked to substantial and .80 to 1.00 high to perfect positive or negative correspondence. Again, while it may be useful to know these limits, the best interpretation of any coefficient of correlation is made by comparing it to the values commonly obtained with respect to the same variables.

A word of caution is necessary concerning the role of coefficients as predictors. A correlation of $+$ 1.00 for two variables would mean that an estimate of achievement based on one would be 100 percent accurate in predicting the other. Aptitude tests predicting job success fare considerably less well. The important point is that while perfect correlation, 1.00, means absolute accuracy in the estimate of a relationship, it does not follow that .50 will be 50 percent correct in predictive situations. By using Kelly's coefficient of alienation, written as k, it is possible to find the percentage of forecasting accuracy for certain values of r. As a measure of the departure from perfect agreement, k can temper optimism in cases in which prediction of one variable is to be made from the assessment of another. Using the correlation of .80 referred to above, the formula would read:

$$k = \sqrt{1 - r^2} = \sqrt{1 - .80^2} = \sqrt{1 - .64} = \sqrt{.36} = .60.$$

Where r is .80, k is .60, meaning that the departure from perfect agreement is 60 percent. Put another way, in this case it is possible to predict the values in one set from those in the other only 40 percent better than chance. A point of interest in studying Table VI-10, which lists the percentages of forecasting accuracy for certain values of r, is that a correlation of .80 appears more than 4 times better as a predictor than a correlation of .40.

TABLE VI-10

Percentages of Forecasting
Accuracy for Certain Values of r*

Coefficient of Correlation	Percent of Forecasting Efficiency
1.00	100
.99	86
.98	80
.95	69
.90	56
.866	50
.80	40
.75	34
.70	29
.65	24
.60	20
.50	13
.40	8
.30	5
.20	2
.10	½

* From Harry A. Greene, Albert N. Jorgensen and J. Raymond Gerberich, *Measurement and Evaluation in the Secondary School* (New York: Longmans, Green & Co., 1954), p. 383. Used by permission of David McKay Company, Inc.

Measures of Relative Position

At this juncture we change our focus from measures that describe group performance to measures that tell something about the relative position of individuals within groups. As indicated in the earlier discussion regarding the construction of frequency distributions, the simplest way to depict relative position is to rank order. This scheme of classification, whereby all raw scores are arranged in order of size, calls for rank assignments to each measure with a position of 1 given the top score. Whenever there is a large number of measures or several persons obtain the same score, this procedure becomes cumbersome, lengthy, and of questionable value. Then too, merely knowing the rank of a score is not enough, since that same rank might have an altogether different meaning for a group of incomparable size. A rank of 5th in a graduating class of 30 can mean something quite different from being 5th in a group of 3,000.

Percentile Rank. To compensate for the inherent shortcomings of simple rank order, the percentile rank has been adopted to describe an individual's relative position. The percentile rank for any score in a small ungrouped set is easily found by determining what percentage of the total scores lie beneath the specified measures. If, out of a group of 36 scores, 25 of them (or 69 percent of the total) fall below the raw score

TABLE VI-11

Grouped Frequency Distribution Data from Table VI-7 to be Used for Construction of a Cumulative Percentage Curve

X	f	Cumulative Frequency	Cumulative Percentage	
96–98	1	36	100	
93–95	1	35	97	
90–92	2	34	94	
87–89	4	32	89	
84–86	3	28	78	
81–83	3	25	69	
78–80	5	22	61	
75–77	3	17	47	← This is the P rank of 77.5
72–74	3	14	39	
69–71	3	11	31	
66–68	2	8	22	
63–65	2	6	17	
60–62	2	4	11	
57–59	1	2	6	
54–56	1	1	3	
	N=36			

of 84, then the percentile rank of 84 is 69 for this specific distribution and is designated as P_{69}.

The process is a bit more complicated when calculating for distributions of group intervals. In such cases it is expedient to construct an ogive graph, or what might be called a "cumulative percentage curve." When fully completed the ogive proves a handy shortcut to the percentile rank of any raw score in the series and facilitates locating the median, quartiles, and deciles as well. In order to build an ogive for Table VI-11, start at the base of the f column and add each of the frequencies separately, placing every new sum in the cumulative frequency column. Next, divide each figure in the cumulative frequency column by the number of cases in the distribution, $N = 36$, indicating the result in the cumulative percentage column. By this method each figure in the cumulative percentage column stands for the percentile rank of a boundary point. Having this information makes it possible to construct Table VI-12 of percentile ranks and boundary points from which the cumulative percentage curve or ogive is plotted (Bradfield, 1957, pp. 155–157; (see Table VI-12 and Figure VI-2).

TABLE VI-12

Boundary Points and Percentile Ranks for Table VI-11

Boundary Point	Percentile Rank
53.5	0
56.5	3
59.5	6
62.5	11
65.5	17
68.5	22
71.5	31
74.5	39
77.5	47
80.5	61
83.5	69
86.5	78
89.5	89
92.5	94
95.5	97
98.5	100

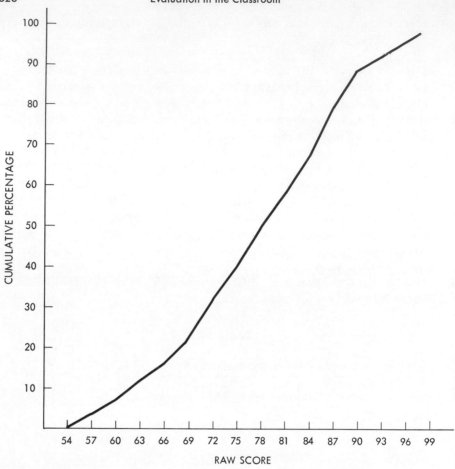

Fig. VI-2. Cumulative percentage curve or ogive on frequency distribution data from Table VI-7 (See also Tables VI-11 and VI-12.)

Standard Scores. A major limitation of percentile rank is that its units are unequal, the distances between them being much less at the center than at the extremes of a distribution (see Figure VI-2). To overcome this difficulty, *standard scores* are preferred as a measure of relative position because their units retain the same meaning all through a distribution. The scores are called standard because they are based on the standard deviation, an index that is essentially the same from test to test. The standard score for a particular raw score indicates the difference or distance in sigma units that the particular score is from a stated group's mean. In other words, the standard score for a specified raw score is equal to the raw score's deviation from the mean divided by the standard deviation. The letter z is used when referring to the basic standard score from which all other linear standard scores derive. Any raw score smaller than the arithmetic mean yields a negative z; raw scores larger than the mean yield positive z scores.

$$\text{standard score } (z) = \frac{X - \overline{X}}{\sigma}$$

where X = a specified raw score,

$\overline{X}$ = mean raw score for the same group,

or

$X - \overline{X}$ = deviation of raw score from the mean,

σ = standard deviation.

Substitute, using the facts of this case. Steven earned a score of 87 on a mathematics test for which the group mean is 77 with a standard deviation of 10. Steven's score was 55 on a geography test for which the group mean is 60 with a standard deviation of 5.

$$z = \frac{X - \overline{X}}{\sigma}$$

$$= \frac{87 - 77}{10}$$

$$= \frac{+10}{10}$$

$z = +1$ for the raw score of 87 in mathematics

$$z = \frac{X - \overline{X}}{\sigma}$$

$$= \frac{55 - 60}{5}$$

$$= \frac{-5}{5}$$

$z = -1$ for the raw score of 55 in geography

Steven's z score in mathematics is 1 standard deviation above the mean while he falls 1 standard deviation below the mean in geography. Assuming a normal distribution, Steven did as well or better than 84 percent of his peers in mathematics, whereas he surpassed only about 16 percent of them in geography (refer to Figure VI-1). Unless there is a bad skew, standard scores beyond plus or minus 3 are unlikely, and the probability of encountering a score beyond 5 sigmas in a normal distribution is almost unheard of—less than one three-millionth.

A couple of factors combine to detract from the convenience of z scores. For one thing, plus and minus signs are easily overlooked or copied incorrectly; then too, since decimal points are involved they might be erroneously placed. Both of these drawbacks are eliminated by adding some constant like 50 to each score and multiplying every standard deviation score by 10. Other values than 50 or 10 may be used but the same scale and like norming groups must be used in order for results from different tests to be comparable. Except for these features of an arbitrary mean of 50 and standard deviation of 10, T scores are similar to z scores in rationale.

$$T = 10(z) + 50,$$

$$\text{where } z = \frac{X - \overline{X}}{\sigma}$$

Considering Steven's z score in mathematics, $+ 1$, and geography, $- 1$, the corresponding T scores are found through substitution.

Mathematics T score $= 10(+ 1) + 50 = \quad 10 + 50 = 60$
Geography T score $\;= 10(- 1) + 50 = - \; 10 + 50 = 40$

As measures of relative position, the percentile rank and standard scores enjoy wide usage. Of the two, percentile rank is generally better understood, although percentiles suffer from being unevenly spaced throughout a distribution. On the other hand, while standard scores are expressed in presumably equal units, they have the demerit of being more difficult to comprehend, especially hard to interpret for skewed distributions, and are confined to unit-scale raw data. A choice between these measures of relative position should always be governed by the nature of the data and the user's intention (Bradfield, 1957, p. 158).

TEST CONSTRUCTION

The issue of asking good questions has been raised several times. Nowhere is this weakness more apparent than in the tests teachers regularly administer to students. Apparently forgetting that evaluation of pupil progress is a major aspect of a teacher's role, the tendency is to look upon the task of preparing examinations and assigning marks as an undesirable duty, some unreasonable demand or necessary evil imposed by and for the sole benefit of the school board and administration. My hunch is that the dissatisfaction of many teachers with poor tests during their own school career as students has not necessarily motivated them to construct better instruments for the children they now serve. In any case, since test results constitute a primary source of judgment for determining marks, teachers need to strive for well-devised measures. Commenting on the shortcomings of teacher-made tests, Wood (1961, p. 1) states the probable causes to be "inadequate consideration by the teacher of the objectives of instruction, *technical defects in construction*, the teacher's failure to appreciate those factors that make scores undependable, or his inability to apply even rudimentary statistical treatment to test scores . . . the teacher often completes his educational program with little understanding of testing principles and practices" (cf. Ebel, 1961, 1962). By the way, this does not exempt teachers in colleges and universities, where Wood contends the appraisal of educational achievement has a "horse-and-buggy look." Hopefully this undesirable image will not continue indefinitely; it need not if more prospective teachers become adept at test-making.

Objective Tests

There are many kinds of objective tests, most of which have eliminated the problem of scorer unreliability. The feature of objective marking accounts for high scorer reliability and the consequent term "objective" test. Although easier to score and more often used in the United States[*] than essay examinations, objective measures are harder to prepare and can encourage guessing. On the other hand, by presenting many items, the objective test offers opportunity for wide sampling of course content and enables more rapid feedback of results to students. Objective kinds of measures are especially recommended when classes are large, reuse of the test is considered, freedom from scorer bias is desired, or the instructor feels more confident of his ability to write unambiguous objective items than his prowess as a critical reader of essays. The several forms of objective tests to be described in relation to their usual limitations and manner of improvement are *true-false, simple recall, completion, matching,* and *multiple choice.*

True-False. The alternate response form, or what is generally referred to as true-false testing, was at one time the most popular type among objective examinations. In classrooms today this form still rivals multiple choice as the dominant device even though there is little to recommend it. That experts in measurement hold the true-false form in low regard is evidenced by the omission of such items from most standardized tests. This judgment is dictated by the weakness of true-false as a diagnostic instrument, the necessity for greater length than other objective type measures to obtain comparable reliability, and the factor of guessing.

[*] Objective type examinations are also used extensively in countries like Japan, Sweden, and, for the first time, in India, which has recently embarked upon a national program of objective testing encompassing the training of educators to construct and interpret measures of this type. There is also a trend toward using more objective type tests in the emerging and developing countries of Africa, the Netherlands, Germany, Argentina, and Chile. By way of contrast, essay examinations have traditionally been and remain the predominant type test in England and throughout most of Europe. A combination of objective and essay testing seems to be in the plans of measurement experts from most countries (Torrance, 1967).

In conceding the limitations of true-false items, its advocates prefer to cite such ostensible advantages as ease of construction, complete objectivity of scoring, applicability to a wide range of issues, and the opportunity to present in the same length of time more items than any other objective measure.

Whenever the alternate response test is used, and that should be in situations for which no other type is applicable, items should be carefully worded so that the content of the statement rather than its form governs the response. In particular, it is wise to refrain from using what are known as specific determiners; that is, tell-tale words or clue expressions that identify a statement containing them as true or false. Strongly stated words like "never," "entirely," "none," "every," or "always" have been found to occur mostly in false statements, whereas expressions of moderation like "may," "perhaps," "sometimes," "could," and "occasionally" are more likely to occur in true items (Ahmann, 1960, p. 115; Stanley, 1958; Ross, 1954). Either these expressions should be eliminated altogether or else the items in which they are found be balanced so that approximately the same number are true as are false. Test-wise pupils can be counted upon to spot specific determiners and when such individuals are enabled to obtain correct answers without knowing what the item calls for, the test is discriminating among pupils on a basis other than the intended ability.

Just as damaging to a test as providing unwarranted clues is the presentation of words that are unclear or ambiguous. To convey meaning, quantitative language is preferred to vague and possibly misleading references like "recently," "long ago," "modern," or "old." To phrase an item "President Kennedy was assassinated recently" is unclear. A better way to put it might be "President Kennedy was assassinated in 1963." Similarly, "The Second World War took place a long time ago." This item could be more clear if stated as "The Second World War took place during 1941–1945." Sometimes the ambiguity a pupil faces stems from having to make judgments without being told which among the several standards presented in class to use in decision-making. The frequency with which pupils complain of not knowing the basis for choice would seem to urge test writers to make an effort to incorporate within an item whatever standard of truth is to be used in judgment.

Omitting information that students need for deciding responses is also unfair. Quite the opposite error is to so entangle statements as to confound all but the writer. Examples of this mistake are part of the experience of each of us. The range of confusion is fantastic. In its most mild form, item writers merely extract textbook material verbatim and include some negative term to make the item false. Other writers resort to the frequent use of double negatives and while the pupil well-versed in grammar understands that two negatives equal an affirmative, his peers interpret such statements as emphatic negatives. At its extreme, the lengthy obscure true-false statement can result in an incorrect response by even the knowledgeable pupil who would respond accurately if the question made sense. A classic story in this context involves the time Grandpa Snazzy was called to witness in court:

> The attorney said: "Now, Mr. Snazzy, did you or did you not, on the date in question or at anytime perviously or subsequently, say or even intimate to the defendant or anyone else, whether friend or mere acquaintance or in fact a total stranger, that the statement imputed to you, whether just or unjust and denied by the plaintiff, was a matter of no moment or otherwise? Answer—did you or did you not?"
> Grandpa thought a while and then said, "Did I or did I not what?" (Ross, 1954).

Certain of the suggestions for improving true-false items call for a basic reorientation. One approach suggests that pupils cross out that part of the statement that is incorrect; another contingent would have the student correct the wrong statement. Some would favor the allowance of weights for responses according to pupil judgment (see Ebel, 1965, pp. 130–133). Since all of these procedures increase the labor of scoring, it is understandable that they have not been widely accepted. Usually about the best way to improve true-false tests is to extend the length. In most instances, it is desirable that a true-false test be about 75 items in length with 50 items the bare minimum unless the measure is designed for only a narrow range or is intended for instructional purposes alone. To facilitate scoring it is recommended that simple indicators like + for true and 0 for false be used since these can hardly be mistaken for each other. To facilitate the teacher task of summing the number of correct answers, items should be arranged in sets of 5 on the answer sheet with a double space between sets. Finally, if the true-false test is speeded, it is worthwhile to consider a "correction for guessing" formula.

Completion and Simple Recall. Since they are closely related, simple recall and completion tests are considered together. Recall items typically appear as direct questions or phrases to which a pupil responds with one or several words. Completion items differ in that certain key words have been omitted for the pupil to fill in. Both types require the student to produce the answer rather than recognize the correct response from a teacher-made list. They are similar in eliminating the guessing factor but also share the problem of laborious scoring because the responses are not completely objective. On completion tests the missing words often are written on blanks scattered all over the page. Unless the teacher is to argue that there is only one way to state the answer, a dubious procedure, he cannot foresee all of the variant acceptable responses and so cannot turn the scoring over to another person; thus these objective forms take longer than others to score.

Especially adapted to factual data of the who, what, when, and where variety, completion and simple recall tests are more difficult to construct than it would seem. For one thing, pupils need to know the type of response they are expected to make; therefore the test-maker must refrain from including phrases of indefinite conclusion. For example, "Walt Disney was born in _____." For this item the pupil does not know whether he is expected to give the date, place, or circumstance of Disney's birth. In the item's present form, feasible answers might be "December" or "1901" for the date; "Chicago" or "the Midwest" for the place; and "middle income" or "the north-side tenement district" as the circumstance. By a minor revision in wording, the intention is made clear. "Walt Disney was born in the state of _____." The same kind of revision would improve an item like, "Columbus came to America in _____." Another guideline concerning unwarranted clues involves leaving out key words and phrases rather than unimportant details; otherwise questions are too easy or too difficult. The answer may be as obvious as "The well-known amusement center in California created by Walt Disney is known as _____"; or as unnecessarily difficult as "Walt Disney's well-known amusement center in California is located near _____." Notice that the blanks above are of uniform length because if they vary the pupil has an additional clue. An even more serious but less frequently occurring error is to include a dot for each letter in the answer. One further suggestion for improving recall-completion items is to avoid overmutilated statements, since by leaving out too many key words the intended meaning is lost and the statement becomes absurd. For example, "The _____ is obtained by dividing the _____ by the _____." It is impossible to know whether this item refers to arithmetic or statistics and if statistics then whether it intends IQ or some other quotient. Commenting on the absurd form that completion items can take, Wood, 1961, p. 29) recalls seeing one that read "_____, working with _____, discovered _____."

As in the case of all objective test forms, it is foolish to compose unnecessarily complicated situations to assess what a student has learned. Consider the following example:

> If a man out hunting saw a bear 300 yards to the east of him and he walked 300 yards north, shot straight south and killed the bear, what would be the most probable color of the bear? ———

According to its author the item's correct response of "white" is derived in this way: "The only place on the globe where the conditions named could result in the death of the bear would be at the north pole. The man, therefore, was 300 yards from the pole when he sighted the bear. When he reached the pole, the only direction in which he could shoot and still hit something on the earth was south. Having located the place geographically, it may be deduced that the only bear which could survive in this latitude is the polar bear, and polar bears are white" (Tiegs, 1939). In one sense I agree with the writer of this item—not regarding the manner or substance of his presentation but that polar bears are white!

Matching Forms. The task on a matching test is to select from a column of alternatives the correct response that goes with each of the premises in the other column. In this way men and movements, concepts and definitions, inventors and discoveries, cause and effect and other types of learning which involve the association of two things, may be assessed. Use of this form enables the inclusion of large quantities of factual information without requiring a lengthy period of time for testing. Generally the matching test contains at least 5 and not more than 15 items, since a large list wastes the reader's time and shorter ones increase the possibility of guessing correctly. The principal limitation of most matching tests is the tendency of item writers to provide heterogeneous alternatives, thereby providing irrelevant clues to the correct answers. In this sense, the form of the statements dictate the student answer rather than the content of the item. Consider the following illustration regarding a high school physics test.

( ) 66. Determined the speed of light recently.   (1) Index of refraction

( ) 67. The property of light that varies inversely.   (2) The foot candle

( ) 68. The intensity of illumination of a candlepower light at a distance of one foot.   (3) Michelson

( ) 69. The ratio of the velocity of light in the air and its velocity in any medium.   (4) Total reflection

( ) 70. What happens when light tends to pass from a denser to a rarer medium at an angle greater than the critical angle.   (5) Intensity

(6) Faraday

In this series the premise of item 66 suggests a man's name. Since only two names appear in the response column, the student who recognizes Michelson as a contemporary scientist ("recently") and knows that Faraday is not, can easily select the correct answer. Item 67 calls for a "property"; the response list contains only one property, "intensity." The words "candle" and "foot" in the premise of item 68 strongly suggest "the foot candle" response. "Ratio" suggests "index" for item 69. And, for item 70, "total reflection" is the single answer that corresponds to the question form, "what happens when . . ." (Lindquist, 1936, p. 78).*

To avoid irrelevant clues, it is recommended that only homogeneous material appear in each set of premises and responses. If a list of responses contains proper names, dates, places, and so on, the pupil's task is simplified since he can proceed by common-sense elimination. Some teachers admit that they know it is a weakness to mix in a matching set

* From E. F. Lindquist, "The Theory of Test Construction," in Herbert E. Hawkes, E. F. Lindquist, and C. R. Mann (eds.), *The Construction and Use of Achievement Examinations* (Boston: Houghton Mifflin Co., 1936), p. 78. Reprinted by permission.

such dissimilar associations but claim there are not enough justifiable names and dates, cause and effect situations, or men and movement issues to constitute a set of more than three or four items. In such cases the matching test is an inappropriate mode of examination. Another common fault in constructing matching tests is to include the same number of elements in the premises column as in the responses column. Inasmuch as the usual practice is to apply each response but once, a student knowing all the answers except one will automatically earn a perfect score. The same opportunity with somewhat reduced chance for success exists if the pupil knows all but two answers. By including more responses than premises and by designing some responses as correct more than once, like Hemingway and Fitzgerald in Figure VI-3, the problem of the test being too easy is overcome (see Figure VI-3). By the same token, there is no point in presenting a needlessly time-consuming task for students by including too many elements (15 is a workable limit) or a list of responses without some logical order. There is a need to present responses in a systematic arrangement to facilitate the necessary scanning. This means that if the response list is comprised of dates, they ought to be given in chronological order; for other alternatives, alphabetical order will assist pupils in locating the intended answer. The responses in the column should then be numbered consecutively.

Directions: Write in the blank preceding each of the various books in Column A that number appearing beside the correct author's name in Column B.

Column A	Column B
_____ A FAREWELL TO ARMS	(1) Steven Crane
_____ BRAVE NEW WORLD	(2) Charles Dickens
_____ MOBY DICK	(3) Theodore Dreiser
_____ TENDER IS THE NIGHT	(4) Henry Fielding
_____ THE GREAT GATSBY	(5) F. Scott Fitzgerald
_____ THE SEA WOLF	(6) Ernest Hemingway
_____ THE SUN ALSO RISES	(7) Victor Hugo
_____ ULYSSES	(8) Aldous Huxley
_____ WAR AND PEACE	(9) James Joyce
_____ YOU CAN'T GO HOME AGAIN	(10) Sinclair Lewis
	(11) Jack London
	(12) Herman Melville
	(13) John Steinbeck
	(14) Leo Tolstoi
	(15) Thomas Wolfe

Figure VI-3. Example of a Matching Set. Notice that there are more alternatives than premises, certain alternatives are used twice, and both column presentations appear in alphabetical order.

Multiple Choice. The type of objective test that has the most to recommend it is multiple choice. In practice this form is popular among teachers and often used in standardized instruments. Typically an item presents several responses only one of which is correct or better than the others. The standard by which the best response is to be selected is included in the item itself. Since the best alternative need not be the only correct one, it follows that for multiple choice item-writing the teacher enjoys more freedom in selecting concepts to be assessed than is the case with true-false items. In fact, the content can call for a measure of discrimination between levels of goodness. This versatility is perhaps the outstanding feature owing to multiple choice for it can in fact measure both recall and judgment without introducing the problems of subjective scoring or ambiguity. What is more, successful guessing becomes less a difficulty with multiple choice provided there are a sufficient number of distractors (4 are recommended). The undesired responses for an item, which include all but one of the responses, are known as distractors.

Constructing plausible distractors represents a great obstacle in successful multiple choice item-building. To begin with, distractors must correspond in grammatical form with the stems so that each response makes a complete sentence when read alone with the main portion of the item. Positive items are best. While the negative item is easier to produce, calling as it does for what is *not* an important view among these, or what is *least* likely to transpire, such an approach serves to penalize the student who prefers to indicate feasible solutions rather than unaccepted ones. Whether the distractors are brief or lengthy, they must not present irrelevant clues to the desired response—this most troublesome problem in test construction offers no exception to multiple choice items. By way of illustration:

The Frenchman who first explored Lake Michigan was:
(1) Kosciusko
(2) Nicolet
(3) Raleigh
(4) Gilbert
(5) San Martin

The item above was administered to 444 pupils who previously had responded to the following item.

He first explored Lake Michigan:
(1) Rochambeau
(2) Cartier
(3) Duquesne
(4) Genet
(5) Nicolet
(6) Champlain

Only 66 of the 259 students who got the right answer to the first item, responded correctly to the second. Obviously, the first item was simple to anyone able to recognize that four of the responses are not French names but who otherwise would have been unable to recall or even recognize the correct response (Lindquist, 1936, pp. 75–76).*

Sometimes teachers who lack one or more distractors for an item and either cannot think of another or feel pressed for time resort to "none of the above" as an alternative response. This response is properly restricted to situations in which every choice can definitely be identified as right or wrong; however, it has no place in items designed to measure judgment about varying degrees of adequacy. Thus, "none of the above" applies more to statements of fact than judgment—and perhaps could better be assessed through the completion type examination. Wood (1961, p. 55) maintains that "all of the above" has even less to recommend it as a tenable alternative. Consider a five-choice item in which the last choice, "all of the above," is correct. Should a pupil know that any of two of the first four responses be correct, he can reasonably infer that "all of the above" is correct. Here again, the test-writer's intention is better met with a different type of examination (true-false).

Scoring the multiple choice test is more efficient if a key is made in such a way that holes indicate the position of correct answers. When applied to an answer sheet, the pencil marks appearing in the holes can be counted. Check to be sure there are no multiple marks for any item. When properly prepared, the correct answers should be randomly distributed with approximately the same proportion of correct responses appearing in each position (a, b, c, d, e). To facilitate summing the number of correct answers, items should be arranged in sets of 5 on the answer sheet with a double space between sets. If the test has items differing in number of alternatives from other items, those of a similar number of response choices should be grouped together so as to facilitate use of a "correction for guessing." The correction formula is recommended generally if the number of alternatives to an item be fewer than 4. Theoretically, and this has been verified in practice, a multiple choice test with a given number of items can be expected to indicate comparable reliability in its scores to a typical true-false test of nearly twice the number of multiple choice items (Ebel, 1965, pp. 60–61).

Correction for Guessing

For most classroom objective tests every pupil has an opportunity to consider each item since the measuring purpose involves power rather than speed. Items on a power test are arranged in ascending order of difficulty, whereas speed tests measure the accuracy and rapidity with which one can respond to standardized items of a uniform degree of difficulty. In the case of timed tests, frequently used in elementary edu-

---

* From E. F. Lindquist, "The Theory of Test Construction," in Herbert E. Hawkes, E. F. Lindquist, and C. R. Mann (eds.), *The Construction and Use of Achievement Examinations* (Boston: Houghton Mifflin Co., 1936), pp. 75–76. Reprinted by permission.

cation for skills assessment, the temporal constraint is such that even the fastest pupil is unable to go over all the items in the period allotted. The necessity of this circumstance for timed tests is apparent; were ample time allowed everyone to consider each item, a pile up of scores would occur at the high end of the scale, thereby restricting the information provided about differences among individuals within the group. On such tests, if the score is the number of correct answers, any success one has with guessing will raise the score. Therefore, it is not strange that some pupils see an advantage in guessing blindly on the unfinished items. After all, they rightly reason that chances are one in two that an unread true-false item can be correctly guessed.

Assume that two students have taken the same test—one pupil completes 60 of the 100 questions, all of them correct, and omits the remainder for a total score of 60; the other pupil also gets 60 finished, all of them correct, and finds that only a moment remains before time is called. Hastily he proceeds to randomly mark responses for each of the unread remaining items and ends up with a final score of 80. Students should be encouraged to omit items they do not reach or cannot handle rather than blindly guess. Unless corrected, the second student's (mark of 80) appears as being higher than the first pupil's (60) although their performance was essentially the same.

To eliminate the blind guesser's seeming unfair advantage over someone omitting the same unread items requires that an amount equal to the guesser's expected gain from blind guessing be subtracted from his score. So, for true-false tests expecting that he would guess as many correct answers as wrong ones, the formula would be:

$$S = R - W,$$

where $S =$ score corrected for guessing,
$R =$ number of right answers,
$W =$ number of wrong answers,
(omitted answers are excluded).

Using this formula for the boy whose score of 80 was based on a knowledge of 60 items and guessing for the remaining 40 items, $S = 80 - 20 = 60$.

On items of multiple choice with 3 or 4 alternatives in which the chances of guessing an item answer correctly are respectively 1 in 3 and 1 in 4, the formula reads:

$$S = R - \frac{W}{N - 1}$$

where $S =$ score corrected for guessing,
$R =$ number of right answers,
$W =$ number of wrong answers,
$N =$ number of responses presented for each item.

For a multiple choice of 3 alternatives

$$S = R - \frac{W}{2}$$

Example: 40 item test with 34 right and 6 wrong

$$S = 34 - \frac{6}{2} = 31$$

For a multiple choice of 4 alternatives

$$S = R - \frac{W}{3}$$

Example: 40 item test with 30 right, 6 wrong and 4 omitted

$$S = 30 - \frac{6}{3} = 28$$

Correction for guessing is unnecessary when the number of alternatives for an item exceed 4 since the chance of guessing correctly is not large.

It should be understood that the correction for guessing is recommended primarily for speeded tests, in which the greatest likelihood of omitted items and blind guessing exists. When applied to objective tests in general, the value of the formula is more psychological than mathematical, simply encouraging the omission of too difficult and unread items. The truth is that with power tests a correction makes little difference. Yet an instructor can use it in good conscience if he so desires. But "his conscience can usually be just as clear, and his life simpler if he avoids it" (Ebel, 1965, p. 233).

Essay Examinations

Essay type tests differ from most objective examinations in permitting students to compose their own response rather than select from a list of teacher-given alternatives. It is this feature of composed answers that essay advocates and opponents usually speak about. On the plus side, it is desirable that pupils be able to organize information and express ideas fluently in their own words but to do so requires that fewer items be used with essay testing than with objective forms—hence a more limited and narrow sampling of content. An equally great problem is the subjectivity of scoring and consequent unreliability. The reader may recall evidence produced earlier in this chapter to the effect that teachers cannot always agree with one another in marking essays; in fact, some cannot agree with themselves when asked to repeat a marking (see pages 275–78).* Suffice it to say that the essay is chosen less often by teachers in the United States as an instrument of measure than objective tests. Ordinarily recommended for use with small classes, the essay form can be a dependable measure provided certain precautions are taken.

A more valid sampling of pupil knowledge is possible by increasing the number of essay questions and reducing the discussion time allotted

---

* As the nature of essay exams become more diverse, it is perhaps unfair to continue the practice of lumping them all together. Although it be a difficult task, there already exist sets of criteria for evaluating essay items requiring decision-making, synthesizing, creative applications, restructuring, organizing, and so forth. The various volumes of taxonomies of educational objectives that have been developed can be helpful in selecting measurable purposes (cf. Bloom *et al.*, 1956; Stanley, 1964).

to each question. Although a well-organized paragraph might constitute a reasonable answer to most of the items pupils face on these tests, the tradition of including only one or two questions for an hour's testing persists. Another way to elevate validity is to ensure clarity for every question; that is, to enable everyone to know what is being asked. If some pupils respond to what the teacher intends and others interpret the question differently, these two student groups can hardly be evaluated by the same scale. Typically the student is instructed to "summarize," "describe," "explain," "evaluate," or "discuss." Perhaps the least direction is provided by insisting the student "discuss" a specified issue. If the problem read to "discuss learning theory," the student would not know whether to begin with a historical treatment or a comparison of the well-known theories or an evaluation of their influence on teacher behaviors. As a rule the student finds it necessary to start writing and continue until time is called hoping all the while that the teacher intended the approach he has taken. To obviate this mixup, the instructor should indicate clearly the type of pupil response intended. For example, "Discuss the implications of connectionism and Gestalt theory for elementary teachers." Or, "Compare the role of the teacher according to faculty learning theory with the role advocated by Gestalt theory."

Concern about scorer unreliability and sampling declines somewhat when a key is prepared before the testing and grading process takes place. Often the key, designed to establish a hierarchy of value weights for various responses, will highlight weaknesses of a question and result in its further refinement. Moreover, armed with a key, the teacher can avoid restricting the range of scores. Lacking this type of a guide it is common for teachers, who are ostensibly using a 10-point scale to assign a minimum score of 3 or 4 to pupils who write anything, assuming they must have learned something. At the other extreme, there is a reluctance to score any paper as 10 since "no one is perfect." Consequently, the 10-point range may exist in name only, functioning from 4 to 9 and even then poorly, since the weights are devised as one proceeds in scoring.

At times examiners feel uncomfortable about the dubious content-sampling their essays present and decide to compensate by using optional items. This procedure of virtually allowing students to plan their own test by choosing say two among four items is indefensible in that the option means pupils are not really taking the same test. And, in such cases, any effort to assess them by using the same instrument is at once defeated. The same measure need be given to all "whose relative degree of achievement in a particular area are to be compared. The scale points denoting different qualities of performance are more likely comparable if all pupils face the same situation" (Wood, 1961, p. 105). In sum, there are no logical reasons to support the notion of different tests for different students when they are enrolled in the same course with identical curricula.

Anyone who reads essay examinations should be aware that the values assigned one paper often are influenced by the merit of the paper happening to precede it in order of scoring. Examiners are also somewhat susceptible to the practice of being more lenient with the second half of a paper if impressed by the first half; conversely, if the first half of a test is judged poor, this impression tends to influence marking of the second half. Another questionable practice is to mark a paper differently if the identity of its author is known. To eliminate such instances of the "halo" effect, it is best to assign each essay a number so that the reader is not influenced by the author's identity and is led to read the responses for all of the pupils for a single question before going on to the next question.

In review, the essay examination requires a pupil to produce answers using his own words and organization rather than responding to teacher-made alternatives. Essay questions are fewer and more general in nature than are objective items, meaning that more test time is spent thinking and writing rather than in reading and thinking, as is the case with objective tests. Unlike objective tests, which are hard to prepare and easy to score, the essay type is relatively easy to prepare but difficult to score; it is time-consuming to both the pupil (test-taking) and the teacher (scoring). Essays are usually lacking in diagnostic use and permit bluffing, whereas objective tests lend themselves to diagnosis, permit guessing but not bluffing or question-distortion to fit whatever knowledge a student may have retained. Generally speaking, the essay is recommended when the classes are small, the test is not to be reused, and the teacher has more confidence in his ability as a critical reader than as a writer of objective items. If classes are large, the test is likely to be reused, and the instructor is more confident of his ability as a writer of objective items than a critical reader of essays, then an objective exam is most appropriate (cf. Lindquist, 1955; Sanders, 1966).

Item Analysis

Teacher responsibility for a test does not conclude with its administration; the worth of any measure must be established rather than assumed. To accomplish this means gathering some minimal information about the test items with respect to level of difficulty and relationship to the entire instrument. Before presenting the steps in this data-gathering process, termed item analysis, it will be helpful to gain a certain understanding about the function of test difficulty. By difficulty is meant that attribute which, when present in large degree, causes numerous incorrect responses and, present in slight degree allows a large number of correct responses. For a good test, items are arranged in order of difficulty so that the initial questions can be completed by all pupils, whereas items appearing last in the series are expected to tax even the most able. Were the situation reversed and difficult items placed first in a series, the morale of average and weak pupils would be adversely affected. And, since the only purpose for having very difficult items involves their ability to discriminate among high-ranking pupils, they are better positioned near the end of the test where only the more able will get to them; if the less able should encounter such items, the items appear sufficiently late in the test to seriously jeopardize total performance.

In general it can be said that most classroom tests do not contain an adequate level of difficulty to function well in discriminating among levels of achievement; in short they are too easy. Obviously information about the relative differences among pupils is lost when the average score runs from 70 to 80, as is often the case. In many classes this high-average situation is a natural one based on the popular but fallacious teacher assumption that passing marks should fall between 70 and 100 percent of the total items. The fact is that for any given individual the most reliable test of his ability is one comprised of equally difficult items on which he is able to score 50 percent. Whoever gets a perfect score or zero on a test has not been adequately measured. According to Richardson (1936), "A test composed of items of 50 percent difficulty has a validity which is higher than tests of any other degree of difficulty" (see also Gulliken, 1945).

An index of item difficulty (p), showing the percentage of students who get the correct response, is found by dividing the number of right answers by the total number of pupils $\left(p = \dfrac{R}{N} \right)$. Since most classroom tests are constructed to assess students of unequal ability, items need to range from those that nearly everyone can answer to others that almost no one can master. When this degree of variance obtains in the level of difficulty, some items are so easy that even the least able students can get 50 percent of them right, while other items are so difficult that the top performers can manage only 50 percent correct. The entire test should reflect a difficulty level such that the average pupil in the group scores roughly 50 percent of the possible total. It follows that a test that is of appropriate difficulty for one class may be either too simple or high-powered for another.

There are three notable exceptions: for diagnostic and mastery tests, the content is determined by importance of the subject matter rather than its difficulty level; so a diagnostic test on the facts of multiplication could show an average of near perfect scores in one class and below 20 percent correct in a weak group. In the cases of speeded tests, where rate is at issue rather than power, all items should be of uniform difficulty instead of arranged in ascending order of difficulty.

Acting on the assumption that a total test is measuring some intended unitary factor and perceiving its improvement to involve elimination of items not positively correlated with the whole, it becomes desirable to obtain a measure of item–total test relationship. In courses in which en-

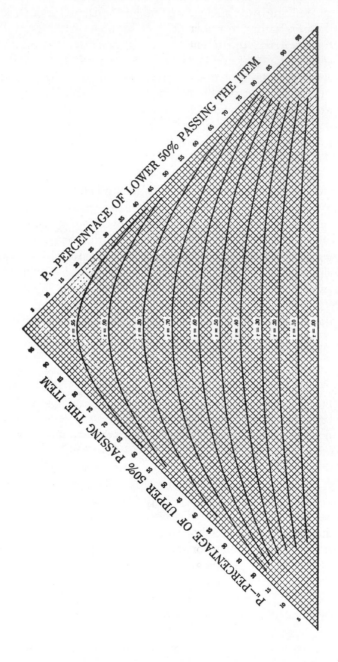

Fig. VI-4. Chart for computing Tetrachoric r with the criterion dichotomized at the median. From Dorothy Adkins Wood, *Test Construction* (Columbus, Ohio: Charles E. Merrill, Inc., 1961), p. 85. Reprinted by permission.

rollment is large, above 100, or when several classes have been administered the same test, a measure of the discriminating power for each item can readily be found using a tetrachoric coefficient of correlation. After placing all scores within an upper (p_u) or lower (p_l) group based on the median, the percentage of students passing each item is obtained for both p_u and p_l. Referring to the computing chart (see Figure VI-4), "locate the point on the vertical axis which corresponds with the percentage in the upper group (p_u) and extend an imaginary line to the right, parallel to the horizontal axis. Then locate the point along the horizontal axis corresponding to the percentage in the lower group (p_l) and extend an imaginary line downward parallel to the vertical axis" (Wood, 1961, pp. 85–86). The tetrachoric r is read where the two lines intersect. So for a p_u value of 65 and a p_l value of 40, r would be estimated as .39. Should there be a need for interpolation, work along the shortest distance (diagonal) between curves. The coefficient is positive when p_u exceeds p_l; a negative r obtains when p_l is larger than p_u (found by reversing the p_l and p_u scales). Although the sign and approximate size of a coefficient can be known when in both p_l and p_u the percentage of students passing an item approaches either 100 or 0, the influence of chance is so great that an accurate estimate of r cannot be made.

For some high school teachers and many elementary instructors, the small number of pupils whom they test will not warrant use of a tetrachoric coefficient of correlation. Instead they may wish to obtain item validity through a simple inspection of performance by the upper and lower criterion groups. Some writers recommend that the upper quarter and lower quarter of the class be compared. Any item on which percentage of correct responses by p_u exceeds that of p_l is correlated positively with the criterion and the item should be kept as part of the test. Should the percentage of p_l and p_u who pass an item be similar, that item is of no value since it correlates near zero with the criterion. Perhaps it should be revised if it is to function in the test. Those items in which the percentage of correct responses by members of the low group (p_l) exceed those of the high group (p_u) are actually detracting from test validity and should therefore be omitted.

In conclusion, the teacher who would improve his classroom influence must learn to ask better questions, construct better tests, and become a better judge of student performance.

CHAPTER VII

Mental Health

and Personality Development

People are more often seen in terms of being congenial or unfriendly, patient or anxious, considerate or domineering than they are as being informed or unread. We tend to assess one another primarily in reference to our own individual concepts of mental health and appreciated features of personality.* This is not surprising, since life includes many important aspects other than intellectual growth, vocational competence, and economic security. In the home, on the job, about the community—wherever persons meet, there is always the potential problem of encounter, of getting along. The degree to which one is able to relate in a satisfying and constructive way with himself and others is of obvious importance and has long been acknowledged for the adult population. Only recently, however, has the teaching profession become convinced that the experience of childhood and adolescence also engenders a sufficient condition of anxiety, doubt, pressure, and despair to warrant careful study and response. Contemporary research indicates that in order for the school influence to enter its proper effect, it is absolutely vital that teachers understand not only how children learn but how they develop and mature as persons.

* According to Torrance, "A society's concept of the meaning of mental health and personality adjustment determines in a large measure its child-rearing procedures, its educational practices and most of its institutions. A classroom teacher's concept of the meaning of mental health strongly influences his relationships with students, his disciplinary procedures, his evaluation procedures and the content of the curriculum (1965d).

A good case can be made for the thesis that people are largely a product of their relationships with the quality of self being determined by the kinds of associations experienced. This is not to imply that inborn factors of temperament are without impact but rather to suggest there is long-term value in providing the best of possible relationships for emergent personalities. However simple this recommendation may seem, it is difficult to eventuate because the nature of adult-child rapport is usually such that the grown-up's expectations govern whether either party finds the affiliation satisfying or annoying, rich or frustrating. This problem is compounded by the generation factor in that for many grown-ups the concept of normality has but one chronological reference. Consequently, they perceive all juvenile behavior as deviant since it differs from the accepted adult conduct. Actually, what is normal depends upon how old one is. Indeed, the much-quoted adage "act your age" is one that parents and teachers should more often allow. To separate action from age is to deny the order of human development—to ignore the process of becoming.

By perceiving child behavior mostly in terms of what is acceptable in the realm of adult affairs, grown-ups necessarily reject nature-determined aspects of development like aggression, negativism, bragging, and daydreaming, all of which must be permitted some tenure if the healthy attributes like courage, independence, curiosity, and commitment are to be achieved. Quite naturally cultural demands represent the prime source of direction in rearing youngsters, but nature's orientation also requires understanding and support. And strange as it may seem, the purposes of society and biology are consonant on this score—both favor the development of maturity. While boys and girls increase their knowledge, they also undergo an important sequence of biologically predetermined psychosexual stages, each of which introduces new problems of interpersonal relationships. Unless the elders who comprise a youngster's primary group are aware of the behaviors characteristic for his maturational stage and the attendant biological values, chances are they will maintain inappropriate expectations and convey a sense of undue disappointment in him. Probably they will misinterpret his intentions and motivation, failing to recognize that what their best response toward him ought to be depends on the developmental stage in question and should not remain constant over time. Many young people live with unnecessary pressure, doubt and self-abnegation; they lack confidence, hope, and satisfaction because those to whom they are responsible do not comprehend the nature of personality development.

As adults we cannot expect youngsters without our experience to act as we do, in accord with norms beyond their years. Yet some parents and teachers find it annoying or unacceptable that youngsters establish their own norms; often these norms are evaluated by the glib unreflective observation that "kids aren't what they used to be." I hope not—if they are, something's wrong, for where cultures change the life of the junior members is altered as well. And although we cannot fully know what it is to be a child today, to fulfill our role as parents or teachers, we must know what childhood is and how its purposes can best be met to ensure a mentally healthy person. In a society of rapid transition it is imperative that those responsible for initiating the young not permit an enthusiasm for early acculturation to exclude the consideration of maturation in determining expectations. A single orientation for guiding growth to maturity is inadequate—both society's plan (*acculturation*) and nature's design (*maturation*) are essential; how these purposes can be made consonant is the theme of this chapter.

BECOMING SEPARATE

The Realization of Separateness

One criterion for a mature relationship is that other people be seen and regarded as separate persons. The nature of infancy prevents this condition, for to the newborn the world is completely private, the realm of not-self goes unrecognized, there is no concept of others or even things. The only acknowledged reality is sensation. And somehow even without words an infant is able by using a system of negative (crying, refusal, fretting) and positive (cuddling, smiling, cooing) signs to convey his need status. The needs are reported to adults who in his estimate have no being of their own, no separate life apart from his, but exist only to serve him when tired, hungry, or wet. Noting the baby's cues—everwatchful caretakers respond to satisfy his expressed and observed needs. He in turn falls off to sleep whenever the inner demands of hunger and thirst have been met; until need requires them again, the elder servants can cease to be—baby knows they are easily called back to life.

Under such conditions—that to express desire is to obtain satisfaction— it is understandable that most infants are led to experience a sense of great confidence and trust, a state sometimes called *infantile omnipotence*. Paradoxically, it is the absolute helplessness of an infant and not his power that brings maximal assistance from adults. For the time being, total dependency is his greatest strength; he need only express discomfort and help is on the way, coo or gurgle and excited compliments abound, burp and a friendly shoulder is occupied. It is the adult picture of infancy as being helpless that permits the opposite omnipotent view for infants. During the first months few boys and girls are denied this perception of life and when they are it is at great expense to development. Unable to alleviate neglect, infants deprived of love and care have no recourse but to suffer. The continuing effect of this experience is usually an outlook of suspicion and pessimism toward the world instead of a more healthy sense of confidence and trust. Before age one, the response to deprivation is a passive mistrust without anticipated release as opposed to the active aggression or resentment of environment that occurs later

(Baldwin, 1967, pp. 354–357; Bowlby, 1965, pp. 21–58; Hurlock, 1964, pp. 261–265).

The treatment of those we claim to love is a key to our maturity. It is impossible to speak properly of the love relationship of an infant; he cannot love others since he does not recognize their separate existence. However, during infancy there are valued objects, the use of which reflects a solipsistic orientation, the feeling that self is the center of the world and that persons and things share the single purpose of providing gratification. Since others lack a separate existence, an attempt is made to consume orally or incorporate them. Because the oral region is the sensation center during the first year, we speak of the *oral stage* (Watson, 1965, pp. 263–269). Even more significant than the infant's fantasy of being able to consume what is valued by him, to take into himself what is liked, is the brevity of attention. When milk or food are finished, the container is rejected; the same holds true for toys and the pacifier, for when each has fulfilled its function it is pushed away. As soon as an object offers its gratification, its strength of attraction declines for the infant. In sum, the pattern of relationship during life's initial year toward valued objects is that they are first possessed, then consumed to gratify, and thereafter ignored until a new valence is established.

Although society is rightfully unopposed to infants perceiving the world and its residents as private property, we disapprove certain residual influences of oral stage behavior when encountered among adults. Freudian theorists have postulated that, if because of early deprivation, overindulgence, or problems of adjustment, a large amount of sexual energy be fixated upon valued objects, a depletion will occur in the supply of libido available for more mature types of object relationships. Consider those adults whose partners have been left without attention after fulfilling their function in sexual gratification. Some grown-ups daily enact the oral attitude toward cathected objects beginning with a demand for the other person when desire is intense and ignoring her at all other times. The suggestion that this type of behavior is more widespread than generally supposed derives from Strom's (1967) study of male sexual behavior as reported by college females. Another form of orality during the grown-up years centers upon food; especially is this the case in compulsive overfeeding of a child, an oral act whereby the adult equates food with love. Also there are instances of oral passivity among men and women who hold an unfounded optimism that somehow someone will show up, extricate them from trouble and save the day (cf. Baldwin, 1967, pp. 356–357; Frank, 1966, pp. 163–171; Church, 1966).

The point for recognition is that however aversive orality may be in adult form, it is necessary during infancy. Little ones must be allowed to make demands of others before they are ready to make demands of themselves; the separateness of self must be experienced before there can be regard for others; no love for others is possible before others are known to exist. A major biological value of infancy is that the dependence of its members facilitates assimilation of certain attitudes basic to mental health. To find the immediate world friendly rather than antagonistic, trustworthy rather than neglectful, calm and caring rather than anxious and unkind, is a natural and universal need of infancy. To the extent that these attributes characterize a social environment, the chances are increased that a basic attitude of trust, optimism, confidence, and friendliness will be adopted toward life. On the other hand, failure to provide a supportive context is to render more likely the attitudes of suspicion, pessimism and antagonism (Bowlby, 1965, pp. 201–235; Erickson, 1959; Finney, 1961; Spock, 1966).

If ever the infant is to relate properly he must become concerned about others; but even before that others must be recognized as owning an existence apart from his own. The private world must enlarge in population if others are to be esteemed and his ego status is to proceed. To advance as a person it is necessary to leave the realm of *primary narcissism*, a term that is applied to one whose psychological world lacks external objects and personal relationships, a being for whom the only pleasure lies in sensation. Piaget (1952, p. 158) has shown that a sense of self is still undeveloped quite late into the first year. When a new response is learned because it was rewarded, an infant is unable to make the connection between correctness of behavior and receiving the prize; he cannot differentiate between times when the act will bring reward or not and instead presumes something in his generalized behavior brings its own reward. Usually the awareness of others as distinct from self arises as a result of discovering spatial relations. By grasping and kicking objects one comes to experience the boundaries of his own body; he learns there is a not-self existence or world beyond the me (cf. Chess, 1965).

Coincident with the growing awareness of separateness is a concern for its meaning in terms of safety and well-being. The wholeness of total dependency and consequent illusion of omnipotence is replaced by perceiving self as part of the larger world and perhaps not its major determinant. Moreover, realizing that mother and surrogates are becoming less anxious to fulfill every request, that his desire and intentions are less often gratified on demand than they were but a few months earlier, the frustration of being dependent upon others is revealed. One finds that physical limitations are restrictive and there are many events over which one has little power or control.

Imitation, the Beginning of Relationships

The realization of separateness leads not only to fear and anxiety, the realization of dependence and helplessness, but necessarily the beginnings of a concern for personal relationships. Many problems are attendant upon this recognition, starting with the fear of mother's departure, the anxiety of being a separate and obviously weak individual. Although the infant does not like being moved from place to place, he welcomes movement per se and likes to be rocked for movement means someone is near; conversely, absolute silence suggests aloneness and desertion. Often when the infant is crying the mere rocking, signifying mother's presence or still better the sound of her voice is enough to reassure and terminate the upset. According to Storr (1963, pp. 83, 139) the "fear of being abandoned" may be one of the basic fears of mankind. When people are absolutely alone over a protracted time mental disorder results because personality cannot be maintained under conditions of emotional isolation (see pp. 233–36). So it is not strange that a child worries about the absence of those upon whom he depends in part because they provide for his physical well-being but also because the preservation of the developing structure of his personality is contingent upon a sustained relationship with the persons who accept him. Whereas during the omnipotent period he neither recognized nor cared about parental wishes, he has now become aware of his separate existence and consequent dependency. It becomes important to please the parents lest they abandon or punish; there is a necessity to behave like those on whose benevolence one's continued security depends. Thus the foundation is established for the relationship with parents that begins with imitative behavior.

Were it not for imitation, many children would perish; all of them would find adjustment to life far more difficult. Although the innate propensity to recreate the actions of others who are more experienced obtains throughout life, it is most powerful during the second year. The biological value of imitation is that it enables one to take over appropriate responses to life situations for which one has no proper hereditary reaction. Rather than learning danger by the direct experience of pain or injury, a child observes his mother's careful avoidance of fire and subconsciously behaves in the same way. This conforming response cannot be explained as reasoning on the child's part, for the cerebral cortex is not at this age sufficiently developed to permit reason.

That the toddler finds it easier to do something when shown than when told is apparent from his imitation of action even when he cannot understand the verbal explanation. Thus imitation is the most effective teaching medium at this stage. Observe a child mimic your action of wiping off a desk and yet when told to stop, he listens in seeming concern and then proceeds to wipe some more. This is because if you are doing it the act must be right as far as he is concerned; words to the contrary are less influential than your example. So much is imitation a subconscious process that if the child is behaving in accord with his natural propensity to conform he even dislikes the intrusion of being told; to insist that he copy your behavior will likely bring a refusal not because he is stubborn but because imitation is basically a subconscious rather than a deliberate process—to make it deliberate confuses him. An important reminder is that while the tendency to imitate is innate, that which a given child mocks depends upon his social environment. Therefore, adults need to be mindful to do in his presence only those things they would have him do, to be as they would have him become.

First Demands of the Self

At the same time that the child is vicariously acquiring certain adult responses to experiences he has not known, he also is having to learn responses for direct experiences that adults cannot share with him. It is in the life dimensions in which children and adults share the least that the greatest conflict is generated. For the toddler the first step in becoming separate is to make demands of self, to gain self-control, and to engage in autonomy. This fact is in sharp contrast to the popular impression that between ages one and two children are so demanding; it is more perceptive to observe them as assertive since they are in fact beginning to make more demands of themselves and less demands of their parents (Gesell and Ilg, 1943, pp. 132–133; Watson, 1965, pp. 277–280).

Despite the unconscious fear of parental abandonment, the toddler is trying to assert the natural beginnings of an independence from them; he is starting the long and difficult preparation to leave childhood and its role of dependence behind. This intention is defined by acting in ways that many impatient and unknowing grown-ups find distracting. For example, he wants to feed himself, an independent act. After carefully lifting the cup with both hands, he succeeds in bringing it to his face only then to tilt the bowl in excess. Enthusiastically he shoves the spoon into the cereal and manages to reach the mouth with at least some of its content. Perhaps it is the frustration of adults, who would prefer to do it for him, to feed him and so eliminate the constant mess, that leads us to conclude that he is demanding and stubborn rather than that he is trying to become independent and we are impatient. In truth he is striving for independence, as demonstrated by the exerted demands being made of self. Credit is due his age rather than a comparison to our more adept manner of feeding ourselves; whether we deserve any merit depends on our response to his forceful attempts.

The strength of gross motor behavior among toddlers is another source of dismay to parents when it ought to bring quite the opposite response. If confined in a playpen, the toddler will throw out the toys. A common parental strategy is to lecture the child that he should take care of his things, be responsible, bear in mind the many chores mother already has, and consider ways to make life easier for his parents. Use of this strategy to get him to stop often proves more a motivator for him to continue throwing. The casting behavior of throwing whatever is held is a characteristic trait during the second year and it represents an emphatic release. The power to release hold of an object voluntarily is a complicated pattern of action involving an intricate development of the controlling nerve cells in the brain. To develop this control takes time as the child must learn to modulate his release and to time it accurately, to make it obedient to his projection. He is learning how to control and to release. Like any other growing function, this requires practice through exercise.

By the way, it is important to omit the intrusion of adult-supported motives; that is, throwing toys does not mean that it is time for Dad to buy a football, an object far too cumbersome to assist growth, however pleasant the paternal illusion of a son's athletic interest may be. We sometimes impute inappropriate motives by assuming that a child is ungrateful for what we have given him as he flings the costly toys about. The fact is he couldn't care less about the toy cost and if the parents are worried about objects being broken, they ought to select more durable playthings. Many kids today are considered more destructive than they in fact are because of parent inability to select durable toys. To return to the issue, it will take years of neural motor organization before a youngster can throw in a mature manner, but casting is a rudimentary step in the development of this rather complicated ability and must be significant or it would not be so universal in the behavior of fifteen-month-old children (Gesell and Ilg, 1943, pp. 131–140).

However gratifying the ego effect may be of independent feeding and learning voluntary control over the release of objects, the young child still has very strong needs for recognition by others. But his position now in relation to the mother brings him less frequent attention. Whereas during the time of breast-feeding the lactogenic hormone and her own physical comfort favored close attachment, and still later the infant's lack of mobility required her near-constant observation, she now catches up on her household chores, leaving him alone in the playpen or some distant room. The biological function of self-display as a recourse to neglect is to gain attention. While this form of behavior is quite natural, it tends to shift toward sexual deviation if its purposes are not met. In the attempt to have others notice and commend, the infant studies what pleases people as well as what they dislike, approve, or avoid. This careful observation of grown-up values is one of the earliest sources of a child's social behavior for he is determined not to be ignored.

In most cases the child's consequent antics bring adult laughter and renewed parental pride. But in some cases it is necessary for children to resort to sexual exhibition. Here the little fellow who believes himself uncared about seeks to determine how he might become attractive, and assumes that the display of sex organs that gives him pleasure will provide the same for others. So, in a pathetic appeal for notice he displays his private parts. Such behavior ought not be repressed by punishment nor allowed to be the only means of evoking adult concern. Boys and girls of every age require affection because they are persons—a single yet sufficient reason!

Living with Order, Control, and Choice

The change in primary source of sexual satisfaction from the mouth to the anal region at about age one is generally accompanied by parental concern for toilet training. This is another instance of expecting control and consistency too soon. Usually the sphincter muscles are not developed until fourteen months of age. About one-third of all children develop bladder control by eighteen months, three-fourths by two years, and almost all by age three. If toilet training be introduced too early, it can jeopardize the teaching role of the mother. In fact, maternal frustration can destroy the teacher-learner relationship leading her to conclude that as a teacher she is ineffective. Mothers who feel this way are generally sold on the value of preschools without knowing anything about them.

To hurry integration of the child's retention-elimination impulses, some mothers attach the display of affection to toilet success. And the child in turn finding that bowel movements at the right time and place can be traded for kindness and regard develops a perception of love as being an exchange of possessions similar to the way in which love and food are synonymous during the oral stage. Unfortunately, with this notion of trading as the basis of affection, the concept of love and ownership become inextricably related. For those of us who lament this fact, it should be recognized that it is at least an advance beyond the oral phase in which the relation to valued objects ended in object consumption. The trading idea is more mature in at least admitting that relationships involve two complimentary trading parties. Accordingly, persons as well as valued objects are treated as possessions to be carefully guarded, selfishly cherished, and controlled. No loss in attraction occurs because of consumption, for consumption itself is refused, since possessions are too valuable. That this vantage affects interpersonal relations is apparent from observation; when in contact with contemporaries the child perceives them not as persons like himself but as objects for manipulation and exchange. He pulls, pinches, pushes, and strokes them as if they were inanimate. Although quite content to be engaged in solitary play, back to back with peers, he obviously is unready for group activity, especially social cooperation (cf. LeShan, 1967).

Cleanliness, order, and punctuality represent the major toilet-training effects upon personality (Watson, 1965, pp. 277–280). A compunction for each of these attributes may be observed of the anal-staged eighteen-month-old whose most interesting psychological characteristic is the desire to complete situations. He likes to sweep the floor, hand mother his empty dinner plate, put toys away, close the door, and hand Daddy the paper; even when he sits down it is done in a decisive manner as if to report "There, that's finished!" He is making elementary judgments about accomplishment even if they are not put into words, being expressed more with the body than verbally. In play he likes to carry objects from one location to another and in this way learns what a place is; he even likes to put things back in order, a tidiness soon outgrown. But these behaviors serve to remind us that a great deal of organization is taking place in spite of the apparent aimlessness in activity. Otherwise, how can one discover without exploring or explore without traveling; and how can one find out where he began from without returning (Gesell and Ilg, 1943, pp. 141–158). It seems that, after all, there is a logic in this back and forth behavior—the logic of development that cannot be hastened by words, things must first be acted out by the large vocabulary of expressive gestures and sounds he owns. His favorite words are "all gone," "thank you," "bye bye," all of which register completion.

The Problem of Self-will and Decision-making

At two years of age the child is dominated by self-will; temper tantrums occur whenever an obstacle prevents fulfilling desire (Ausubel, 1950; Macfarlane, Allen, and Honzik, 1954; Landreth, 1958; Piaget, 1965). As a person he now appears totally different from the passive quiescent youngster of a year earlier whose major interest was to shut out the world; different as well from the curious one-and-a-half-year-old bent upon touching, handling, and exploring all within his reach. By now he is able to discriminate between the objects he sees; he has become acquainted with the world in which he must live; the biological value of the exploratory phase is complete. No longer is he content to learn what more there is of the household environment; the task now is to exercise power upon the world and make it conform to his dictate. But although nature has provided this stage to permit the biological value of learning management of one's environment, many parents find themselves in disagreement. If the child's temper tantrums are seen in reference to the acceptability of temper behavior in an adult setting, parents may be inclined to conclude, "He has a will of his own and must not be permitted to grow up that way. A man at the office is just like that and no one likes him. We cannot permit it of our son." The fact that the man at work is thirty years old and the child is two shows parental ignorance in comparing the two persons. If the man at the office is unacceptable, ostensibly the boy will be—that is, if he doesn't do any growing between age two and his placement in the world of adult affairs.

All this syllogistic reasoning leads parents to the affirmation that "We must break his will; then he will be acceptable, conformed, civilized, and cooperative." But will he? The fact is that to destroy the normal aggression of a two-year-old by an appeal to fear is not to evoke his cooperativeness; it is to render him docile, to make him a person lacking in initiative and strength of character. For without recourse to the assertiveness provided by nature, people are unable to fend for themselves, to meet responsibility, and to protect others. The important place of aggression in personality development will be discussed shortly (see pp.

360–362, 373–379); but suffice it here to say that aggression usually evolves into a healthy confidence that one can alter his circumstance and that life is not the product of fate but of choice and effort. The two-year-old's self will represents his source of resolution, perseverence and determination—all noble features of character that make up the will itself when it later develops at about age four. The distinction between self-will and will is one of control source; in self-will momentary impulses dominate behavior, whereas will is the function and activity of the personality as a whole in the pursuit of its ends. So, to handle the self-willed child appropriately is not to eliminate or repress aggression but to provide through toys and physical exertion a vent for its course.

Another frequent response of parents to the self-willed child involves reasoning with him (cf. Rousseau, 1965, pp. 38–41). This mistake is enacted in almost every supermarket. Observe the mother whose two-year-old has just insisted upon procuring an item from the shelf that neither she nor the child needs. Part of her attempt to return the item entails a lengthy explanation to the child that the article represents an unnecessary expense, an impractical selection, and if he quietly relinquishes it without an embarrassing fuss she may later reciprocate with some different and more valued object or favor. Apparently she does not realize that a two-year-old cannot be reasoned with because the power of reason is undeveloped. One of the main functions of the brain cortex is inhibition and control. If the primitive impulses of self-will are allowed complete freedom, they clash with each other and the total personality. This is precisely the status of mind at age two; the child is a slave to his impulses because the cortex of the brain is not as yet fully developed. There will be times in the supermarket when the child must have the assistance of his parents to establish control, a task that cannot be accomplished by their losing their temper or reasoning to the wall but by quiet firmness, the parent's will substituting at the moment for the child's self-will.

Parenthetically, imitation is a useful corrective for tantrums. Remember that tantrums arise when children are frustrated in what they wish to do; and further, that at this age they want to do mostly what their mother is doing, be it washing dishes, sweeping the floor, or cleaning the bathtub. So it is reason and not luck that some parents have children who show few tantrum signs at age two; they have provided plenty of examples and outlets for assertiveness, remembering that two is an age of assertiveness and not necessarily tantrums.

Between the self-willed phase of age two, in which primitive impulses act to determine momentary direction, and the conforming age of three, when behavior is more consistent and choices between familiar alternatives are welcomed, stands the two-and-a-half-year-old youngster whose behavior extremes qualify him among parents as being at the most exasperating age. Generally the spanking curve reaches its peak during this time.

What adults find difficult to accept are the child's transitions from noisy activity to being quiescent, from intense desire to gain some object to indifference toward a possession, from laughter to whining, calling for food and then rejecting it, from screaming to speech of a whisper level. This oscillation from one behavior to its opposite is not motivated by an attempt to "test" or "try" the parent, as some wives tales would have it. Neither do the behavior extremes represent fluctuations in mood. Instead the back-and-forth demands reflect a child's difficulty in attaching his narrow experience base to the nature-urged task of decision-making now being made possible by the developing cortex. As he comes to recognize more distinctions between paired opposites and alternatives, the experience base broadens and enables the organizing of options so that by age three he will with ease make one choice when facing several alternatives. At present, however, he is learning to make one choice by exercising two, trying as it were to go both ways at once, less because of stubbornness than because the capacity for voluntary choice is still weak; it is hard to think of one alternative to the exclusion of the other. In following both courses of action he no doubt appears obstinate to an observer but a closer look reveals the method of nature by which censors and extensors are brought into contiguity, the alternatives of yes and no, grasp and release, start and stop, pull and push, enter into balanced equilibrium (Frank, 1966; cf. Landreth, 1958).

Suggestibility and Acquired Experience

Nearing their third birthday most youngsters enter the phase of *suggestibility*, a favorite though underestimated time by parents. Unknown perhaps by those who care for him, the child over the next few months will take over their attitudes, feelings, and moods—a complicated advance beyond the early imitation stage, when he adopted only adult actions. The suggestible orientation of conformance and being anxious to please is judged remarkable by parents who several months ago wondered if he would grow up wild. It is common practice to attribute the drastic positive change in his demeanor to whatever strategies parents employed during the self-willed stage. Upon hearing the glowing accounts of such parents one is tempted to remark, "Listen, the boy is anxious to satisfy you now chiefly because he is three, not because of your persuasive ability, just as at two he was passionate and assertive because he was two and not because of the hereditary influence of some belligerent uncle."

Psychic dependence describes the suggestible phase during which an emotional and mental reliance upon grown-ups is established such that their attitudes, emotions, and feelings become the child's curriculum. Should the mother be kind and considerate, these expressions will be adopted even though impulse is to the contrary; the same holds true for the paternal example. By way of illustration, imagine a boy who atop his mud-ridden tricycle enters the just-waxed utility room that adjoins the garage. Eying her son, the mother can in a defensive tone shout, "That bike doesn't belong in here—get it out!" More than likely the equally loud response will be, "I won't take it out." Then, altering her tone the mother states, "The wheels of the bike have mud on them. And, you don't want to mess up mother's clean room, do you?" Chances are the boy may say, "No" and without further comment redirect his vehicle toward the exit. Here is suggestibility, for when the woman was domineering so was the child; her change to being conciliatory prepared him to so behave. To assume that this incident can be explained as an instance of child reason is incorrect. What brought the altered response was not reasoning at all but the woman's change in tone. That the floor had just been waxed was irrelevant to the child—he couldn't care less. The mother's shift in mood was responsible for the boy's shift in attitude.

This explanation becomes even more clear upon recognition that suggestibility is a subconscious process. In other words, the suggestible person automatically takes over the feeling, moods, and attitudes of those about him without consciously being aware of doing so. This is because suggestibility is a function of the brain's subcortical centers, whereas reasoning and criticism relate to the higher cortex, which is relatively undeveloped at this age (cf. the cerebral cortex discussions of Woodburne, 1967, pp. 289–316; Lawson, 1967, pp. 3–26, 92–100; Travers, 1967, pp. 201–233).

Because suggestibility is subconscious it follows that to teach an idea deliberately may be less effective than merely to insinuate it. Two fathers and their sons were observed at a resort making their way to the beach via some sharp rocks. On the first day both boys complained about the painful encounter, "Oh, it hurts." In reply, one father acknowledged the pain, "Yes, it does hurt," and proceeded on while the other father told his boy, "Nonsense, it doesn't hurt at all." When next it was time to visit the water the youngster whose dad previously admitted pain did not complain precisely because suggestibility is a subconscious and not a conscious process. Having indicated his own displeasure about the terrain the father was in fact suggesting to his boy that like it or not to reach the sea the obstacle would have to be crossed. On the other hand, the parent who said, "Nonsense, it doesn't hurt," probably felt this was a good suggestion for the boy but all it really implied to the young partner was that Dad is a fool because it obviously hurts. Indeed the father was wincing as he cautiously proceeded over the debris (Hadfield, 1962, pp. 119–121).

Or take the common case of parents who accompany a child to the hospital for a tonsillectomy. Hoping to allay his fear they enthusiastically report the general health difference to be expected once the operation is over. Usually the pitch is, "You'll be okay, and everyone will be kind, and your throat will feel better and everything will come out all right, you'll see." Certainly the parental intent in this case is above reproach, for they believe the suggestion to the child ought to be comforting. However, the actual response is something quite different, as the child senses that an undesirable experience is going to transpire if Mother and Dad are so anxious to reassure him. The subconscious inference drawn by the child from the reassurance has far more impact than the reasoning of reassurance itself. No doubt a relaxed show of confidence by the parents would serve their intention better.

These examples reveal the greater influences of subconscious than conscious suggestion in working with three-year-olds. One more instance familiar to all of us should suffice. During the days preceding a dinner-party mother pleasantly notes her daughter's shadow behavior; that is, when the mother sweeps, the daughter does, and so on. At the dinner affair, like most parents, she reports her daughter's conforming behavior as though the child were responsive to whatever direction she is offered. Later, in the hallway as the guests are preparing to leave, she calls the daughter out, hands her the broom and says, "Cindy, sweep up. Sweep for mama." After three unsuccessful commands, which evoke only a blank stare from the girl, the guests become anxious to leave. Following the mother's explanation that her daughter is obviously too tired to respond, the hostess bids goodbye to her guests. No sooner have they left and she begins to tidy up by sweeping than the girl is observed doing the same thing. In vain the mother would like to call the friends back to observe that her report about the daughter was true and thus diminish embarrassment; but alas they are already out of the driveway and probably now discussing her delusion about the gifted child that is too stupid to even sweep the floor. The point is that if the child is told to imitate by saying, "Do as I do," she probably will refuse; and not because she is contrary for the sake of resistance alone. The refusal occurs because suggestibility is naturally a subconscious process and to try and make it conscious is to interfere with the natural way.

The suggestible process obtains for more than actions—it includes moods, feelings, and dimensions of morality. Thus a youngster will take over a concern for the oppressed, a dislike of minority groups, certain hopes and fears—all these are assumed involuntarily without being told and often the more likely if not told. Apart from using example, of course, one can use words. At this age mothers who would direct behavior are best advised to appeal to suggestibility by saying things like, "I wouldn't do that if I were you," instead of "Don't do that!" Since he is less influenced by reasoning than by reasonableness of tone, it is easy to see why a great compliment is due mothers of three-year-olds who do not often raise their voice.

Like imitation the biological value of suggestibility is that it saves the youngster the necessity of going through a great deal of experience by the potentially dangerous route of trial and error. Unlike imitation, which is of action, suggestibility includes words and attitudes of mind, feelings, and emotions. The child cannot prove everything for himself nor experience all that he needs to know. He must learn before he learns, so to speak, by taking advantage of the experience of others and this is the one chance, the one time that adult experience is most relevant. Nature provides him with the suggestibility to take over parental experience; he is thus enabled to adopt the acquired experiences of others and to profit from such experience. This is of incalculable advantage in the struggle for existence, a necessary means of adapting to life. Yet we ought to recognize that he can pick up fears and prejudices as easy as tolerance and integrity; it all depends on the proximate models—his family.

The Importance of Assertion and Sexuality

The phase of personality organization that immediately follows *suggestibility* is known as *identification*. According to Jung (1938, p. 551), this term implies an estrangement of a subject from himself in favor of another person in whom the subject is to a degree disguised. For child life this means that the successive takeover of grown-up behaviors, which began with actions and then feelings, moods, and attitudes, is now extended to incorporate the entire adult personality. A boy of four may be expected to impersonate his father as though he and the parent were one and the same person. The purpose of this duplicate being is not to provide an exercise in self-delusion but to retain love and a sense of power, both features of life desired and needed by persons at every age. Because his security still depends on parental approval and protection, the child feels that he must conform and be like them or what they expect of him in order to sustain their affection. Not daring to be entirely himself, owing to the risk of a loss in security, he attempts to model himself after those he must please. As a consequence the direction of personality now shifts from its prior self-course toward that of the parent model.

At the same time that the child seeks to be like his parents through an introjection of their personality, he necessarily attempts to be rid of whatever qualities they disapprove. Soon he begins to view various elements of himself as undesirable and so denies or represses them, perhaps condemning the same attributes when they are met in other personalities. The mechanism by which unaccepted elements of the self are attributed to others is known as *projection*. While any unconscious or conscious dimension of self that is felt alien to the personality can be dissociated or projected, the mental content usually relates to those components of self that people in modern society find hard to face—namely the aggressive drive for power and sexual impulse (Bromberg, 1963, pp. 193–195). Because neither of these aspects of personality is permitted expression in childhood, each often generates domestic conflict. For as long as the parents serve as principal love objects, the full expression of sexuality is improbable; similarly, while parents maintain control, a child's self-assertion is incomplete. Since the urge to power and sexual drive comprise the basis for emergence as a separate individual, their position requires further explanation.

The assumed linkage between dependence and aggression indicates that since each child is dependent he therefore will be aggressive. And further, that to become a separate personality the young must somehow oppose the loving parents by self-assertion or else remain forever locked in identification with them, mere replicas of the former generation. Recognizing that the acceptance of other people as separate persons is a criterion for mature relationships makes it clear that identification with another individual is a bar to having an adult relationship with him. Normal development is characterized by a progressive decrease in identification and is indicated by a child's assertiveness to become separate. Unfortunately some parents seldom oppose their children at all, preferring instead to give in to all demands and subordinate their personal lives to the youngster's wishes. By behaving in this concessive fashion they inadvertently deprive the child of anyone whom he can legitimately oppose. To wage a conflict with someone who immediately concedes makes a fight impossible and urges one to either become a tyrant or suffer the guilt of self-recrimination about quite natural feelings of aggression. An unassertive mother whose sole motive appears to be retreat and whose manner conveys the impression that she has surrendered any claim to a personal existence for herself will likely inculcate the belief that to oppose anyone else is wrong. This in turn can have the effect of a child denying his aggressive impulses, which are so important to development. The epitome of loving a youngster does not involve granting his every wish but does include a recognition that his opposition and challenge to parental authority are a necessary part of becoming. For parents to refuse to fight back when children raise the disputes they need is to treat the youngster as less than a person and to fail to maintain a relationship with him. Thus one situation that promotes the disassociation of aggressive feelings among children is to encounter the type of parent who rarely exerts authority and always gives in (McCandless, 1967, pp. 142–153; Sears, Maccoby, and Lewin, 1964; Storr, 1963).

Other parents pose the problem of issuing authority in such a manner as to so frighten children that they dare not oppose grown-ups. This circumstance is as unfortunate as the concession orientation because development is impeded when aggressive feelings are not allowed expression. If to challenge one's parents inevitably brings harsh punishment, a child quite naturally seeks to deny feeling urges that threaten the peace by promoting parental anger. Because aggression may be dissociated if parents are either too concession- or too authority-oriented, the proper but difficult balance lies between these extremes. Owing to the large numbers of homes in which this balance is elusive, it is understandable that for many people aggressive feelings have been dissociated. On the other hand, nature makes no compromise, and when natural outlets for feeling are blocked, the vent is turned inward so that in the case of aggression it results in neurotic symptoms during the growing and older years. The magnitude of this problem is reflected in the fact that for a number of years psychiatrists have devoted more attention to under-standing the place of aggressive impulse in personality development than to the phenomena of sexuality (Oberndorf, 1964, pp. 208–250; Bromberg, 1963, pp. 200–238).

The reasons accounting for child dissociation of aggressive impulse are readily apparent but explaining the case for sexuality is somewhat more complex. Indeed, for a society like our own it may be initially unrecognized or at least seem puzzling that sex impulses are felt to be alien. After all, the condemnation of infantile sexuality has progressively declined as more parents have been exposed to the doctrines of Freud (1905; 1907; 1908; 1923; 1938). Yet sexuality does persist as a contributing factor in the etiology of neurotic conflict. Youngsters reared in situations of sexual freedom seem to suffer the same difficulties during adolescence as do their more conventionally brought up peers. It seems likely that, whatever the upbringing circumstance, there will be a certain amount of guilt and anxiety about sex feelings precisely because there is no way in which the erotic impulse can fully be satisfied in the family setting. So long as parents control child behavior, sexuality will need to be a rejected part of personality. It cannot be allowed its natural course in behavior, at least between parent and child, without that relationship being impaired.

Realizing this, most parents early discourage any child display portending intimacy, a problem that first appears at about age four, when the pleasure center shifts from the anal region to the genitals. Freud (1923; 1924) termed life's fourth and fifth years the *phallic* period and its chief manifestation the *oedipus complex,* based on Sophocles' Greek tragedy, by which sons experienced a rival desire of the father's place in mother's estimate.* At this age a boy may request to sleep with his mother, make

---

* The play, *Oedipus Rex:* Oedipus was, in ancient Greek legend, the son of Laius (king of Thebes) and Jocasta. Laius had been warned by Apollo's oracle that if he had a son by Jocasta, that son would kill him as punishment for his past misdeeds. Therefore, when Oedipus was born, Laius caused his feet to be pierced with a spike and bound together (this accounts for his name, Oedipus, which means "swollen-footed"), and ordered him to be exposed on Mount Cithaeron. However, the shepherd who took the infant was too tender-hearted to leave him to die on the mountain side. Instead, he gave him to a shepherd from another district. The second shepherd gave him to Polybus, king of Corinth. Polybus and his wife Merope, being childless, brought Oedipus up as their own son. When he was grown to manhood, Oedipus was taunted about his origin. Hints were thrown out that he was not the true son of his father. Uneasy in his mind, Oedipus secretly set out to consult the oracle at Delphi. To his horror the oracle told him that he would slay his father and sire children by his mother. Determined to prevent the fulfillment of this awful prophecy, Oedipus did not return to Corinth but made his way to a new land. On his way from Delphi where three roads crossed, Oedipus met an older man in a chariot, who ordered him out of the road. Oedipus refused to move and a quarrel arose. Oedipus was struck and defended himself. The stranger, angry in his turn, lashed out at Oedipus with his goad. Enraged, Oedipus set on him and killed him and all his company, save one who escaped. He then proceeded on his way. On the outskirts of the city of Thebes, he was stopped by a Sphinx. This monster had been terrorizing Thebes by stopping passers-by and compelling them to answer a riddle: What goes on four legs in the

an effort to see her undressed, and designate her as the mate when asked whom he will one day marry. Aware of the child's new kind of attachment toward her, the mother may react in any one of a number of ways contingent upon her view of self, relationship with the father, and concept of childhood. By far the most common maternal response is to tolerate child advances and questions but kindly disapprove them. The fact that oedipal attachments or, in the case of girls, electra strivings, are not inborn, that the availability and training role of mothers in this culture favors their closer relation than fathers with children, and the known relationship Freud had with his own parents makes the oedipal design less an explanation of universal child tendency than an autobiographical observation (Fromm, 1963, pp. 59–65; Hadfield, 1950, pp. 385–388; Mussen, 1963, 273–276; White, 1960).

There is of course another side to incest, when the grown-up initiates the relationship, and this type is universally condemned, for in it a child cannot be treated as a person because he cannot participate on equal terms. The child is thus used rather than loved by the very person to whom he ought to be able to turn for protection and security, treated by that person not as an individual but as a thing. The full expression of sexual love in adulthood is possible only when each partner feels on equal terms, when giving and taking is equal and each is accepted as a whole and separate person.

---

morning, two legs at noon, and three legs in the evening? Whoever failed to give the correct answer (and all had failed) was slain by the Sphinx. Oedipus, when the riddle was put to him, answered that it was man: In infancy he crawls on all fours, in youth he walks upright on his two legs, and in the evening of his life he needs the aid of a staff. On hearing the correct answer the Sphinx killed herself and Thebes was freed of her ravages. When Oedipus arrived in the city, he learned that the king had recently been murdered, and that the regent, Laius' brother-in-law Creon, had proclaimed that whoever vanquished the Sphinx should become king of Thebes and marry the former king's widow, Jocasta. By her Oedipus became the father of two sons, Eteocles and Polynices, and of two daughters, Antigone and Ismene. Oedipus and Jocasta dwelt in perfect harmony and Thebes prospered. Then a plague struck the city. Cattle and men died, no young were born, the sound of weeping filled the streets. Oedipus sent Creon to the oracle at Delphi to learn the cause of the plague. On his return Creon reported that the plague would be lifted when the murderer of Laius was found and punished. Oedipus now issued a proclamation decreeing that whoever had knowledge of the murderer and sheltered him would be shunned by all Thebans and subject to banishment. He called down terrible punishments on the murderer and on those who knew of him and concealed their knowledge. The seer Teiresias was brought to the city on the advice of Creon. Teiresias at first refused to do more than hint at the identity of the murderer but, goaded by the anger of Oedipus, at last revealed that it was Oedipus himself who had murdered Laius. The tragic story gradually unfolded. The shepherd who supposedly had exposed Oedipus as an infant was found and confessed that he had given the child to a shepherd of Corinth. News came from Corinth of the death of Polybus, and at the same time, the fact that he was not the real father of Oedipus was revealed. All of the pieces of the story fell into place and it became horrifyingly clear that the prophecy the oracle at Delphi had made to Oedipus had come true. He had slain his father and became the father of his own sisters and brothers by his mother. Jocasta hanged herself when she learned the truth. Oedipus despairingly blinded himself and as a consequence of his own order, was shunned by all the people of Thebes.

Apart from the sexual intimidation incest imposes, there is an issue of greater import. During adolescence sexuality is the major drive that promotes independence; it compels one to seek intimate relationships outside the family, since sexual expression is not accepted within. Were the drive of sexuality allowed free expression within the family (incest), there would be little prompting to become independent and to establish extrafamily relations—persistent dependence and immaturity would be the consequence. Obviously an incestual relation between parent and child is opposed to individuality, self-realization, and maturity. By making sex either too easily accessible or too frightening, incest may encourage the continuation of immaturity and hence preclude the development of adult attitudes. So, on rational as well as emotional grounds, incest is inimical to growth if we accept maturity as a goal for personality.

If sexuality cannot be brought into the adult-child relationship without damage, it is apparent that sex impulses like those of aggression may become dissociated from the total personality and felt to be alien to it, even though the parents may never have been derogatory about the display of infantile urges. Some parents exercise self-blame upon witnessing anxiety in their young. We need to recognize that to emerge as a separate person the child will necessarily be subject to some anxiety and that it will be displayed mainly in those aspects of personality that are artifically dichotomized as sexuality and aggression and that this obtains even when the best of child-rearing practices are followed. Therefore, it is understandable that in adulthood those aspects of self that are denied and hence projected by a person and that give rise to symptoms are intimately attached to the twin motives of power and sex that comprise the individual roots of one's emergence as a separate individual (Fromm, 1964, pp. 95–114; Storr, 1963, pp. 88–101).

Morality and the Ego Ideal

Formation of the *ego ideal* constitutes yet another stage in the organization of child personality (Freud, 1962, pp. 18–29). Remember that in imitation the actions of adults are assumed and later during suggestibility there is a takeover of moods and feelings; subsequently the entire personality of the adult is impersonated by identification. During the ego-ideal stage the child scraps the person but keeps the character, which now becomes a part of his own personality. No longer does he declare, "I am powerful like my dad," but rather, "I am powerful." A self-guiding principle has been established by which primitive impulses are harmonized and controlled; the center of control has switched from other persons to within, from extrinsic to internal discipline, from being told how to behave to self-dictation. In this fashion children develop behavior standards and moral sense by a natural process. In fact, if a child were never offered one moral dictum he would still find a code of right and wrong through the process of identification. More than anything else, the mental health of a child depends on the nature of the ego ideal adopted—if too severe it will repress impulses and thereby weaken character; conversely, if lenient he is without power to guide and control impulses. A healthy ego ideal is capable of directing all the forces of personality toward a common end (White, 1963, pp. 173–179).

One consequence of incorporating an ego ideal is the formation of a duality in personality. On the one hand, there is the natural self with its innate impulses and desires versus the moral self or ego ideal, which owes its existence to identification. Unique to the psychology of man, this duality represents the cause of our ageless conflict between impulse and will, between the self we naturally are and the self we wish to become. Another outcome of ego-ideal incorporation is self-consciousness. In other words, one part of the dual personality is conscious of the other. At this stage children begin to use "I" in conversation instead of their given name; now "I had a dream," not "Peter had a dream." The biological value of self-consciousness is that it enables children to see themselves as others see them, to observe their own behavior and match it against what they wish to become and what others desire them to be. Self-consciousness is one of the most important aspects in the development of social and communal life; it bases morality through founding within the child conscious standards by which to live and ideals for which to strive, thereby enabling men to rise above other forms of life (Hadfield, 1950,; Laing, 1958).

Self-consciousness leads to self-criticism, for the one follows the other. Self-criticism can be annoying; it is seldom pleasant to be scolded, especially by oneself, since we carry our critic everywhere. Just as parents criticized him, the child now censures himself. He may still grow angry on occasion but thereafter feels shame when comparing his behavior with his standards. This function of self-criticism defines conscience. *Conscience* is the judgment that the ego ideal or moral self passes upon the infantile, undeveloped ego and natural self. The biological function of conscience is to check the impulses of the natural self so that actions of the personality are harmonized (Hall and Lindzey, 1966, pp. 32–36; Mussen, 1963, pp. 276–280; White, 1964, pp. 174–175). Formation of the ego ideal also brings self-control. A boy says, "I am brave," and doesn't cry; this requires restraint, not repression, for the lad is aware of his fears but controls them, whereas in repression he would deny being afraid. True self-control is engendered between the ages of three and five, when the child adopts his own ego ideal. That explains why there are fewer tantrums at this age than earlier. Instead of having a tantrum, he is more likely to try to master the thing he wants to do.

Some theologies maintain that conscience and moral direction are given to each of us by God. It would be better to say that moral sense is not inborn but that its ingredients reside with every child (cf. Rousseau, 1965, pp. 41–46). A moral sense of some sort is inevitable because of the natural processes of suggestibility, identification, and, as a consequence, adoption of an ego ideal. But the nature of the moral sense depends on the environment in which the child is brought up and the people with whom he identifies. Unfortunately, a child can adopt a mother's irritability as well as her kindness and humor (M. Hoffman, 1963). That is why conscience, like all the functions of human personality, requires both exercise and education.

To the question of what constitutes a good ego ideal, the psychologist must reply that certain ideals are more capable than others to achieve personality coordination. For example, because self-indulgence is divorced from the demands of reality and life, it is incompatible with mental health. Similarly ruthlessness is inappropriate because it suppresses the impulses of tenderness and affection, which are a part of man's nature. Such ideals are considered wrong not because they are incompatible with social and religious demands but because they fail to bring about the coordination of the personality that is the criterion of mental health.

When the ego ideal is well established in the personality and in control of impulses, it constitutes the will. Will is the function and activity of personality as a whole in the pursuits of its aims. A free will is one free to do this unhindered by uncontrollable impulses or neurotic complexes (cf. the self-willed phase of age two). If these impulses and complexes dominate the individual, he cannot carry out what is intended and the will is not free. The will derives strength from the native impulses that comprise its driving force, and receives direction from the ego ideal. A strong will and personality is one in which the maximum of native forces have been mobilized toward healthy aims in life for the use of the personality as a whole.

The main reason a child should be moral is that man achieves his highest fulfillment as a member of a community. In the community he finds protection and security in the form of police, the hospital, and the army, whereas isolated he would fall victim to enemies, disease, and deterioration. Only in community can he attend schools, cafes, museums, clubs— as solitary individuals we would enjoy none of these. The community is the medium through which man's life develops and his happiness made complete. In other words and contrary to general opinion, only as a member of a community can a man attain true freedom and fulfillment of personality. But if we enjoy the privileges that society provides, we have obligations toward others who also want to enjoy the same. If we do not want others to steal from us we in turn must not take from them. Laws are generally regarded as restrictive but they are made so that all should enjoy freedom. In a higher sense only by the pursuit of some aim can a person coordinate and harmonize the conflicting forces within his personality so that it is balanced and in peace; otherwise his life is a chaos of conflicting forces. So, in social and moral life ideals and aims of some sort are necessary for mental health (Hadfield, 1962, pp. 133–146; Piaget, 1965, pp. 327–408; Medinnus, 1962).

The widespread parental appeal to child fear is undesirable as a motive for morality, and usually proves ineffective. Morality based on fear may make a child well behaved but placing him in constant anxiety lest he incur displeasure means that he may do nothing rather than do something wrong. While a certain degree of fear is stimulating, an excess can be paralyzing. The boy or girl made "good" through fear and threat may be filled with latent hostility and resentment and when they attain independence in adolescence may thrust off all forms of restraint. A proper parental aim should be not merely to produce good behavior but to instill a right disposition; that is, raise children who wish to behave well, not just to share but to be generous, not just to be polite but to be considerate, not just to discuss problems but to care about them.

To conclude the explanation of becoming separate, it is necessary to reiterate that the importance of life's initial years is no longer in dispute. For a time Freudians stood alone in contending that the basis of character is determined by the age of three and that the traits formed prior to this time cannot be basically changed (Jones, 1953, p. 13). Subsequently, Adler (1930, p. 48) and his disciples have indicated that a lasting life style is adopted by the age of four or five. Add to this the increasing evidence regarding intellectual development during the first years and the result comes out to be an unprecedented concern for child growth and development (Bloom, 1964, pp. 72–89). This is a good sign if societal intention is to diminish its incidence of mental disorder, delinquency, prejudice, anomie, and apathy. With a generous amount of security at the beginning, boys and girls have a better chance to reach the goal of maturity; without security they develop a pathological craving for it, and they show it by the display of insistent demanding, egotism, and jealousy. When needs are gratified and expectations are appropriate, then and only then can a child complete successfully each stage of development, abandoning his habits and advancing on to the next higher phase of becoming. "Having known acceptance and affection in the environment, the child learns more readily to accept himself, to tolerate the ways of the world and to handle the conflicts of later life in a mature manner" (Allport, 1962, p. 32; cf. Maslow, 1954). With the formation of an ego ideal, the basic organization of a child's personality is complete; he is now a separate person whose next task is to become himself.

BECOMING ONESELF

Until a child becomes a separate person from the parents, possessed of reason, will, and an ego ideal, he cannot pursue the difficult but necessary goal of becoming himself. Recall that in order to maintain security during the early years certain aspects of parent personality are introjected that may not be in accord with one's inherited temperament; these not-self elements must now somehow be expelled. Other parts of self were disapproved by the parents and so denied or projected. To become oneself it is necessary that the unadmitted elements be acknowledged and accepted. By identifying with and projecting upon other persons outside of the family, the child gradually is able to disclose heretofore dormant potential, to discover his own personality and rechart whatever deviation from his own roots as has been imposed as a result of immaturity. Since the extent to which any of us become ourselves affects the degree to which we can be satisfied with and contribute to life, this quest is of major significance (cf. Missildine, 1963, pp. 42–50; Storr, 1963, pp. 88–101; Hall and Lindzey, 1957, pp. 195–196; Byrne, 1966, pp. 269–271).

Earlier it was suggested that in the absence of companionship, personality cannot develop. Moreover, for individuality to emerge the presence of others is required in whom one finds aspects of himself. It follows that to live with parents alone as the only companions is a regrettable circumstance not just because their role precludes equality and sexuality but they also may lack the attributes required to bring forth certain aspects of a child's potential. Nature has anticipated this contingency by implanting a tendency to impersonate so that if a child be exposed to a variety of people he may incorporate into himself all those characteristics most salient to his personality. In my judgment the impact of this process in personality development has been grossly underestimated, especially in our culture, in which relationships with influential persons outside the family begin so early. Without question much personality development takes place beyond the age of five (cf. Babladelis and Adams, 1967; Hamachek, 1965; Medinnus, 1967).

Discarding the Not-Self

One of the first persons outside the home to become important to a child is his teacher. If she is liked and serves as a temporary focus of identification she may evoke latent features of his personality. Generally, the traits a teacher is able to draw forth are those not represented in either parent and have consequently remained dormant until brought out by someone else. Feeling that an esteemed grown-up approves of him it is common for a young boy to adopt his teacher's mannerisms in toto; however, time will reveal how much of what has been taken over does in fact belong to the child's own personality. Many of us perhaps remember with nostalgia our greater affinity to elementary than secondary teachers; obviously this phenomenon relates less to the issue of competence than to time of influence.

Regardless of whoever the child identification model may be—parents, teachers, peers, or mass-media heroes—it is likely that some aspects of personality introjected may not coincide with the inherited temperament (Spock, 1966; cf. Laing, 1965). For some persons this means attempting to act like their parents throughout much of life; others find it necessary to reject teacher-parent views in favor of ideas more compatible with self-convictions. For most of us there must be a break with the past in terms of its behavioral dictate; self-realization includes becoming aware of and therefore ridding oneself of inappropriate introjected attitudes (Missildine, 1963, pp. 51–55). But discarding elements of the not-self can occur only when emotional security is established, a circumstance most probable in classrooms and families in which adults are sufficiently secure to allow divergence from themselves and mature enough to regard the young more as separate individuals than as replicas of themselves (cf. Mead, 1966c).

It is parents and teachers themselves in need of reassurance who insist that children conform compulsively to their opinions and attitudes. To tolerate people who differ from oneself is an index of maturity and a necessary criterion for deep love and lasting relationships. Men and women who treat children as extensions of themselves rather than as separate persons are disappointed when it is learned that the young have their own goals, identities, and interests. Research shows that children who most identify with parents are likely products of an anxious upbringing and will probably turn out to be the same type of parents who cannot accept departure from their standards (Storr, 1963, pp. 84–87; Fleming, 1966, pp. 61–70; Raubinger, pp. 84–88). To cast off early identifications adopted solely for sustaining security and parental approval is an advance in personality; unfortunately this healthy process is less often seen as such in many homes.

Coercive child identification is based on a type of fear that reasons "I must be as my parents and teachers are or they will punish me." The "good" is what adults cherish and the "bad" is what they will not allow. Boys and girls often think of themselves as able or unworthy in terms of achieving goals set for them by other people. Even among grown-ups there are those who act more on the basis of expectations introjected during childhood and never discarded, although no longer appropriate, than they do upon reasoned conscious choice. In such cases the superego demands are usually harsh, unyielding, and irrelevant to the present. For people dominated by a restrictive superego that developed in childhood and has not changed, arguments of reason seem to make little impression. In seeking one's own identity, one needs to discard identifications with those on whom he was earlier dependent and persons with whom he feared to disagree as a young child. At the same time he needs and tends to identify with others who attract him and can favorably influence him by bringing out those aspects of himself that otherwise would remain unrecognized.

Some children find themselves without an adult model. A common reason for too early peer identification is parents who have refused to allow identification with themselves. By so doing adults deny the young a needed sense of vicarious power. Before a child earns his own esteem, he is sustained by the status derived from identification with parents (Ausubel, 1958). Children lacking a chance to identify with parents are more likely to identify early with peers (Lesser and Abelson, 1959). This is often the case in neighborhoods of low income where a peer subculture of great strength develops long before its middle-class counterpart (cf. Strom, 1965c; Bloom, Davis, and Hess, 1965; Keach, Fuller, and Gardner, 1967; Kontos and Murphy, 1967). To identify exclusively with peers early in life is unfortunate, since it prevents what might be gained by identifying with adults. Children identifying primarily with peers may be expected to differ from others whose main identification is with parents in that they lack inner conscience controls that to a considerable degree depend for development upon the love relationship with parents (Hoffman, 1962). Such controls are unlikely to evolve if parents reject the child's effort to identify. As a consequence, early peer identification leads one to be other-directed rather than inner-directed. In Freud's terminology this type person has an externalized superego, his standards vary with the group to which he belongs at any particular time. We can predict that children denied early parent identification will associate more with peers and will adhere more rigidly to peer codes. Quite probably rejected children identify more closely with agemates than their unrejected contemporaries and since they lack inner controls become prospects for delinquency. Daily we read of delinquent gangs composed of youngsters from broken homes in which no parental ties exist. If Ausubel's (1958) theory is correct, the early peer-identifying child pays a price of lack of autonomy and of inner controls; still he finds the identification satisfying for without it the environment would be too threatening to face with equanimity (Johnson and Medinnus, 1966, pp. 330–331).

According to Boehm (1957) autonomy from adult control takes place earlier in the United States than in Europe presumably because American parents are less secure, less certain that their way is the right one, and therefore more readily yield than European parents to pressures from children. Then too, groups in America appear more cohesive because Europeans allow far less unsupervised interaction among youngsters (McKenney, 1953). Because of its greater temporal contact, the American peer subculture has developed more clearly articulated norms and techniques of coercing membership. Under heavy peer pressure the American child encounters weaker parental resistance as he adapts to the demands of his friends. Since peers provide enough security for children, they can risk moderate parental rejection; thus one's fellows represent a prime force aiding in the emancipation from parents. "It is indeed possible that changes in the orientation of American culture over a period of time as well as differences between American and European cultures may result in part from the growing socializing role of peers in this country from generation to generation and from the greater functions served by the peer society in the United States than in Europe" (Johnson and Medinnus, 1966, p. 332).

Accepting the Unadmitted Self

For optimal development of the personality, it is necessary to rid oneself of alien introjected attitudes and convictions that were adopted from teachers and parents. But there is also the need for an opposite process —recognizing and facing those self-characteristics that have been denied and rejected in the development process. Whereas by introjection the characteristics belonging to others are attributed to oneself, projection is the mechanism by which characteristics belonging to oneself are attributed to others. In questing for identity it is as vital to recognize the parts of oneself that are projected upon others as to discard those personality features of others that have been taken over by the self.

At its extreme, projection takes the form of disillusion. Among psychotic patients, for example, there is the conviction that it is others who plot to destroy me and not myself who is distrustful of comrades; that others who whisper about me behind my back and not my own fantasy that peoples a supposed conspiracy. In other words, that which is unacceptable is totally disowned but found to be projected upon other people. It is only extremely dependent persons who cannot come to admit any of the characteristics that they as children knew to be judged "bad" by their parents and that therefore if admitted would have threatened one's security. The finding that schizophrenics are generally "compliant" or "good" children supports this notion. However, projection is not indigenous to the sick; it is used by each of us as we condemn in others the unadmitted and unacceptable parts of ourselves. The woman unable to accept her own dependence is the person who cannot entertain the thought of bearing children; similarly the gossip is opposed to anyone who talks about neighbors and friends. To study those people we dislike is a painful but potentially rewarding experience, for it reveals the projected and hence unadmitted parts of one's own being.

The principle that we tend to condemn in others the unadmitted parts of ourselves is easy to accept, but coming to grips with infantile aggression and sexuality that have been repressed is a difficult experience accompanied by fear and anxiety. Psychologists have found that to assimilate what is projected is as hard as to expel what has been introjected. Generally, the unadmitted aspects of personality show three features: (1) they tend to be projected upon others; (2) they remain infantile; and (3) they bring disturbance in the form of symptoms. The attitudes and beliefs of personality disowned in childhood remain infantile and preserved so that it is as though a child coexisted with the adult in terms of thinking and feeling. Under treatment, many patients find it difficult to admit sexual compulsions and infantile fantasies but when denied aspects of self are fully faced to the extent that they can be revealed to another person, the compulsive quality generally declines, and the energy gain becomes available to the entire personality. That which cannot be fully admitted to another person is that which cannot be completely accepted by the individual himself; that which is unacceptable to the individual as being part of himself is inadmissible to another person. Most of us would like to believe that what we are able to admit to ourselves about ourselves in private has been accepted and that it is only the content of experience residing in the unconscious that we find hard to tolerate. But the trouble people have in telling about their bothersome fantasies that may be entirely conscious suggests there exists a great difference between self-admission and actually revealing it to someone else. Here again, the maturing process seems to require the presence of others—the acceptance of rejected infantile elements of personality cannot take place in isolation. Indeed, this is a major reason for psychotherapy (Bettelheim, 1960, pp. 177–236; Fromm, 1962, pp. 166–168; Jung, 1958, pp. 77–78; Menninger, 1964, pp. 99–123; Storr, 1963, pp. 91–93).

It is generally acknowledged that the unadmitted rejected parts of personality are those that cause symptoms of mental illness but in the absence of a self-realization concept it is hard to see why this ought to be so. It seems that what has been rejected tends not only to persist and repeat itself in infantile form but to also demand recognition. Rejected parts of the personality are like children clamoring to be allowed into a room—they will continue to disturb until admitted. It is as if even the most infantile elements of personality, the parts we should like to be rid of, were possessed of a dynamic energy demanding that they too seek expression. Ultimately personality seeks realization as a whole and regardless of how much the ego may try to reject that which it finds intolerable, the rejected parts will make their appearance as symptoms or as projections upon others.

Like identification, projection has positive as well as negative effects. Young children tend to glamorize and idealize older peers and adults and at times we find surprising the intensity of feelings demonstrated toward some apparently dull or undistinguished person. It can be shown that such people usually epitomize the undeveloped parts of a child's own personality and they strongly attract because they stir a subjective response. Therefore the personality elements that can be said to be unconscious are in fact recognized by the individual concerned but at the beginning are thought to belong to others rather than to himself. Irrational attraction and adoration for a teacher, a parent, or an older child, for example, can inspire and is explained in terms of projection. To the very young every adult is invested with a certain charm simply because they can do things children cannot; the very attribute of being "old enough" is in itself an attraction.

There are two courses of action when a child projects upon his teacher an element of his own capacity that until evoked was latent and unrecognized. The normal and hopeful route is that the child proceeds from projecting to that of identification and so begins to model himself after the educator. As the child himself becomes capable of what he previously thought possible only by the teacher, not himself, the emotional fervor of the attachment declines. We only become emotionally involved with those who have got something for us and when we ourselves have it they no longer attract us to the same degree. A child grows out of someone to whom he was attracted because he has been able to develop in himself that which was originally projected upon the other. Even in adult life we all tend to overvalue skills we do not ourselves possess but we also no longer admire in others that which we could easily do ourselves. The second and less desirable course for the child is to rest in the attitude of adoration, by which he feels that the teacher continues to be wonderful but that he himself is incapable of achieving such stature. It is not that describing his teacher in terms like "fantastic," "tremendous," and "amazing" are themselves inappropriate but, if identification does not take place and projection is not withdrawn, growth is unlikely, and in certain situations projection without identification is an important feature of homosexuality (Group for the Advancement of Psychiatry, 1965, pp. 69–78; Hadfield, 1950, pp. 377–385; Kinsey, 1965, pp. 446–501; Storr, 1963, pp. 106–115).

The Need for Power and Aggression

All the while children are finding and identifying elements of their own personality in others, expelling aspects of the introjected not-self and accepting unadmitted parts of the "me," they are attempting to assert the emerging individuality, to try its power, to prove that impressions can be made and that change can be registered—that I can be a somebody. This concern with the prospect of control over situations is both satisfying and natural for one who so recently and still to an extent serves as an object of control by others. Part of the process of becoming an individual consists of building confidence in the emerging self by proving one's worth; it requires inner assurance, and how better to gain this goal than for the subject to convince himself and supposedly others that in him resides power? Even a casual observation of boys and girls in the four-to-seven-age range is enough to reveal their egocentricity and preoccupation with individual achievement, recognition, and consequent discount of sociability. It is a time for showing off, for announcing, "Look how fast I can run," or "See what I built," or "Watch me!"

The purpose for soliciting attention at age four is to exhibit independence, whereas at age two the quest for adult attention was due to insecurity, a feeling of dependence, and a fear that one might be unattended. Sometimes parents, relatives, and teachers fail to realize or accept the fact that boasting and showing off is natural for the four-year-old. Grown-ups prefer instead to depreciate this type of behavior without reservation, since self-praise is considered obnoxious when met in another adult. Again, recourse to the single reference standard of grown-up behavior prevents accepting any form of child behavior like boasting as potentially valuable. The persistence of some adults in refraining from praising children and in criticizing all boastfulness lest vanity ensue is a continuing error, a failure to realize that we cannot expect maturity without permitting its development. To become oneself it is necessary to make a transition from that security defined as total reliance upon others to a form of reliance within. As people lacking a sense of power can find security only via dependence, gaining power is important to growth and independence. Power is one aspect of maturity and if it is to grow, the small beginnings need be acknowledged rather than discouraged. It is the least powerful and insecure at every point in life who will most often elect to brag. It follows that to boast about one's achievements at age four is quite a different matter from doing so at age thirty.

Power usually appears in a destructive fashion before its constructive orientation. For example, it is common to witness a four-year-old in one day crush the neighbor's flowers, persecute the cat, tear down small limbs from a tree, pull off the wings of a butterfly, stamp the ants, and harass a child younger than himself. Seen in the context of grown-up life, this kind of wanton destruction cannot be condoned and generally prompts a comprehensive lecture about private property (the neighbor's flowers), the dependence of animals upon men (humane society), the social reaction to bullies (disfavor and delinquency), and the nature of respect. All this is likely followed by a threat or punishment. Yet it is not that the boy has anything against flowers or trees, that he hates cats or butterflies, or, for that matter, has anything against smaller folks. Instead he uses these relationships to inflate the ego; they permit his expression of power—he destroys in order to build his self-confidence and prove his strength. Obviously he ought not be encouraged to enlarge the scope of destruction and would less often choose these measures were games and exercises provided in which energy could be spent for constructive accomplishment.

Disappointed with their child who boasts and seems to own a destructive disposition, many parents feel impelled to turn the issue upon themselves, "What have we done wrong in raising him? Where have we failed?" This rhetorical question is often followed by the resolve, "He must not turn out to be aggressive and bad." Implied here is the notion that aggression and hostility are synonymous, that all forms of aggression are undesirable and that the causes of aggression should be determined and eliminated. Among the theories set forth to explain child aggression three views particularly emphasize aspects of parent-child relationships. In the first case, grown-ups are believed to generate aggression by any situation, condition, experience, or relationship that brings the child frustration; to impose frustration and deny aggression is to court disaster.

The second explanation stresses identification by which the child models his behavior after the parent; thus the way in which a parent handles his or her own aggression influences the child's response. Third, to be permissive about aggression is to increase the child's tendency to behave in that fashion. Note that all three of these explanations center upon the environment and ignore the biological basis for aggression, namely separation and independence (Dollard, 1939, pp. 27, 40; Hartrup, 1959; Horney, 1939; Johnson and Medinnus, 1966, pp. 467–472; Levin and Sears, 1956; Otis, 1955).

No brief is made here for labeling destructive aggression as "good." The point is that for personality to develop some show of aggression is necessary and to root its explanation in the environment alone fails to fully account for both its occurrence and its potential value. A more reasonable postulate suggests that aggression is innate and will progressively decline in importance as development proceeds. In other words, there seems to be an inextricable relationship between dependence and aggression. To be dependent upon someone implies a certain restricting power by that person, which in turn produces frustration and hence aggression. It follows that when dependence or inequality is at its maximum there will likely occur the maximum aggression (Sears, 1965). But as children become independent, more separate and differentiated from their parents, the overt aggression naturally lessens, as in time will sibling rivalry and immature competitive questing. At the point of maximal development only so much aggression exists as is necessary to maintain the personality as a separate entity. So, there will always at every age level be a wide variance among people in terms of their amount of aggressive behavior.

It is unfortunate that aggression is not generally considered as positively related to dignity and maturity when in fact any affirmation of the personality is aggressive. Most of us find it difficult to think of aggression as having any meaning apart from hostility. Nevertheless maturity is characterized by assertion and affirmation of the personality without hostility and without competitiveness, both characteristics indicative of child personality. The more one has succeeded in self-realization, the less he will be compelled toward hostility and competition. Common experience yields much evidence that it is the person who has least succeeded in reaching his potentialities who is the most hostile and that the best way to deal with the rebel is to place him in a position of responsibility. Obviously the lack of maturity of teachers and parents can hinder a child's development because the less mature an adult is the less he can tolerate rebellion in children and the more he requires them to be obedient. It is largely immature persons who cannot tolerate differentiation from themselves. Differentiation is a necessary condition for individuality because if two people should have the same views, hold the same opinions, and indicate the same interests they are not separate but identical. The wish to see in one's students or sons an image of oneself is narcissistic. The idea that it is wrong or dangerous to oppose anyone else is easily induced but the behavior this suggestion brings is debilitating to the personality as a whole because individuality implies opposition and differentiation (cf. Mussen, 1963, pp. 283–289; Storr, 1963, pp. 165–177; McCandless, 1967, pp. 142–153; Mead, 1966b).

Fortunately for parents and teachers, they represent only a peripheral target for the power display partly because of their greater strength and status and partly by nature's design, namely the onset at about age six of what Freud termed the psychosexual phase of latency (cf. White, 1964, p. 119). Feeling that the romantic attachment to his mother is involving him in an unsuccessful rivalry with the father and sensing a consequent growing resentment of the male elder's possession of her, the boy in childlike logic assumes that dad must be similarly jealous of him. He also believes that if their mutual antagonism were ever aired the father could defeat him on every count. The outcome of fearing father's jealousy is a transition of the romance with mother from one of attachment to aversion, and not only toward her but all of her sex whatever their age (cf. Baldwin, 1967, pp. 362–368). By the time he is seven the boy is apt to squirm if mother shows affection toward him in the presence of others and he will find love affairs on television or in the movies a silly sight at which he can but groan as if in pain. This natural sexual taboo is often given as an explanation of why during latency children turn with glee and relief to impersonal interests like science, nature, and various hobbies.

The latency phase from approximately age six through eleven is a time during which the power motive is realized in a peer setting. The primary source of libidinal concern is no longer the opposite sex parent but one's agemates. Boys chose to play with boys most often and girls are judged much less appealing than they will be in just a few short summers; and the same is conversely so in the estimate of girls. Friction between the sexes is common as boys take every opportunity to assert themselves, trying to resemble one of the television or sports heroes they so admire. In the early grades pranks often occur with boys driven to distraction when teased by the girls who, although the same age, are likely to be larger physically and superior in academic performance.

Conflict is not limited to boy-girl encounters, of course. That boys are more aggressive than their female peers shows up early and is recognized by even the youngsters themselves (Levin and Sears, 1956; Walters, 1957). The boy's identification with the father indicates an association with the relatively aggressive model for his eventual role and in this country it is expected that boys be more aggressive than girls. Not only is aggression tolerated among boys but reinforced by statements like "Hit him back!" (Sears, 1957). The fact that greater expectations are held of sons than daughters is probably also a factor. On the other hand, girls are not encouraged to be aggressive (Torrance, 1966, p. 63). Although fully aware of these cultural expectations, many educators choose to ignore them. Even in the preschool most aggression is treated as undesirable and its outlet denied (Baldwin, 1967, pp. 460–462). Teachers fail to realize that adult aggression is verbal but children cannot spend it all in this way. And so a child is told, "We don't wrestle here in school"; instead he is given clay or a paintbrush to release his emotions. Maybe both boys wish to wrestle, yet many teachers, librarians, and Sunday School instructors reply in concert, "This is not the place to fight!" Perhaps there should be more mats to dive on, bags to punch, places in school for noise to be allowed, times to run, and room to roll.

On the playground the situation is not much better. Bragging initiates a myriad of comparisons and arguments about who can do what and who cannot. Among little boys in early elementary school the desire for power so often leads to fighting and arguments they can hardly be left alone at recess without a reported misunderstanding. The little girls, of course, are quite willing to turn the boys in. Cooperation is at a discount, with the favorite trick being to quit once a person has had his turn at bat. There is no team spirit since each is concerned with himself and properly so. How do some teachers react to the periodic fights? Stopping the encounter and insisting that both parties show no anger shows a lack of knowledge about emotions; to insist the boys "go inside for fighting" is not much help either for they need to spend their aggression rather than repress or eliminate it; to have the opponents promise "never to do it again" is also to exact an unreasonable demand. Too many children are given only verbal outlets as though it is wrong to have and to show feelings in any way other than by words. We ought not tell children to respond other than how they feel, to insist they say, while still angry, "I'm sorry I hit you." It is of dubious value to place the social graces above feeling and to assume it is more important to be correct than sincere, to say what is right than to feel sorry. To do so is to encourage inauthentic relationships. Perhaps it might be better to listen to the reasons for anger and not insist that children always feel guilty for opposing anyone. Expecting boys not to emotionally reply to a challenge is to look for tall angels in a class of would-be men.

The child need for power is also an identification motive as shown by the model types introjected (Mussen and Distler, 1959). Most every four-year-old boy prefers to see himself as a race-car driver or operator of heavy construction equipment. In announcing either assumed identity he uses the volume required to speak above the competing occupational sounds of a speed motor or tractor. Similarly, the Florence Nightingale dream of little girls stems less from a humanistic bent than from the fact that when someone is sick the nurse is the most important person in the house even to the point of directing the mother. The little girl's fantasy behavior confirms this notion of a nurse's power, bossing the entire household including of course the patient. These child desires for power are not without immediate benefit. Appeal to this sense of power now, not the outgrown suggestibility. A little boy of five or six cannot be expected to be especially kind to his little sister; however, if she is in jeopardy the role of a powerful big brother prompts his quick support. Sometimes little girls watch their baby siblings not out of any maternal affection but because the responsibility evokes pride and power (cf. Neider, 1966).

By the time children approach the middle elementary grades they begin to direct power against authority figures. Dad is reminded that "My teacher says . . . ," "The book states . . . ," "The law says . . . ," and "You're driving over the speed limit." Adding to the broadening base of authority, a boy wants to be like other boys in dress and speech rather than striving to be only like his father or teacher. The process of independence is underway and earlier than the traditional view that its rise begins during adolescence. In school, teachers may expect the beginnings of challenge to their authority through wisecracks or making him the subject of a peer-group joke. This behavior indicates that children are trying out the role of opposition, enacting the antisocial position to confront sources of control. As a rule, we are less pleased about this kind of activity than should be the case. Often the adult response is to depreciate its benefit to the point of excluding opposition—perhaps calling all of it bad and labeling those who disagree with their elders as outspoken, stubborn, disrespectful, spoiled, and uncooperative. If we will not permit a trial zone of challenge behavior for them, who will? Or should they really believe that opposing anything and anybody is wrong? The word "no" is sometimes appropriate, even for children.

One reason some teachers perceive aggression as "bad" is that much of what they see is not the natural propensity for assertion but instead a reaction to frustration. In Columbus, Ohio, there was an instance of a candy store robbery in which most all the stock was taken. What angered the community and stimulated discussion was the fact that the thieves had chosen to urinate all over the store. Surely this could not bring them more candy; it was clearly senseless. When there was no material gain to be derived from such a misdeed, why did it occur? The thieves did it precisely because for some young people purposeless retaliation or aggression displacement seems the only way to respond to a target one dare not or cannot face. Some of the aggression that takes place in the school setting is explained in the same way. Consider the in-class conditions that sponsor child anger and upset. It is important to differentiate this kind of aggression from the natural dictate. Forcing children who cannot read to attempt it aloud is to invite aggression; to insist that one fail at the board or publicly announce his low grades is to foster aggression; to place one in an embarrassing public position in any way is to invite aggression. If teachers value obedience more than spirited disagreement there is no outlet for aggression; it must lead either to overt hostility or to apathy and anomie. Educators who will not accept pupil speculation prompt aggression. All this unnecessary aggression is increased by the school's historical responses to failure (see pp. 62–77).

In many schools it seems there is a greater concern about the control of aggression than its proper expression, a proposition which, if carried to its ultimate, would make control unnecessary, since there would be no feelings to restrict. Somehow the need to show power in consolidating one's personality must be recognized and accepted. This society has a strange ambivalence about how aggressive behavior ought to be assessed. Among children aggression is discouraged and restricted; yet in adult life assertion carries a premium with the hard-driving ambitious male considered the exemplar of success. A fair conclusion is that we approve aggression in its covert, sophisticated forms but, except in formalized events like athletics, we reject primitive stages of aggression characteristic of child behavior.

Peers and the Socialization Process

Part of becoming oneself involves the sociability of achieving acceptance by peers, gaining a sense of community, and beginning to direct personal power toward fulfilling group purpose. That the processes of citizenship begin to evolve within the seven-to-twelve-age range is quite clear. First of all, the preoccupation of comparing oneself with agemates who are complimented or taken to task begins to wane as does the tendency to depreciate peer accomplishment. At the same time an appreciative attitude regarding the work of others is being assumed, there is a coincident move to regularly make critical remarks about one's own achievements and not to write off as unimportant the tasks wherein one fails. As in the phase of suggestibility, the moods and actions of others continue to be taken over, except that the process is now fully conscious and the peers join with parents as being major influence agents upon personality direction.

These changes bring children a new social position. Recall that as a result of marginal status in the culture and the manifest inability to fend for himself, a four- or five-year-old's feelings of self-esteem derived from what his parents did or were, an esteem independent of his performance ability. During middle childhood a different process obtains. He is experiencing the press of many forces that tend to desatellitize him, to make him independent in experience from his parents. Both in class and with the peer group he is urged to compete for a primary status based on social skills, and academic and athletic prowess. It is learned that peers initiate and legislate their own values, offering a new type of status in their community based on loyalty and self-subordination, a status that is earned, not derived, and direct, not vicarious. This tends to devaluate the view of parents and undermine their omnipotence in his eyes (Ausubel, 1963, pp. 109–141). From this point forward, reports by parents of their past experience is not enough for him; he cannot settle for the vicarious and must have his own experience—and that can best be shared with those whose life is like his own, the only associates with whom he can communicate fully and with whom he must now learn to cooperate if he is to become a citizen—his peers.

The increasing interest in one's peer group necessarily alters the nature of parent-child relationships and can lead grown-ups to misread the causes of certain behavior, especially attributing to the peers a disproportionate negative influence. It may be something as simple as "Johnnie's friends endanger his health by their negative example. When playing ball on a cold day, they throw off their coats and he naturally feels pressured to do the same." But is this the whole of the matter? Or could taking off the coat be accounted for in another way? Physicians agree that the period from eight to twelve years of age is the most healthy season in life, the years of greatest vitality and least illness, the time when children most rapidly recover from fatigue, sleep most soundly, and least feel the cold. The good appetite they manifest means that a large amount of food is consumed and burned up in the body raising energy and heat. This in fact is why the middle childhood group of either sex dislike being encumbered by a jacket, hat, and gloves and why mother is judged "fussy" if she insists upon it. So, in this case, neither the peer group influence nor child disrespect is as much an explanation as is physiology.

Another parent may contend that "My polite little boy turns into a boisterous savage when in the association of his friends; they seem to sponsor only primitive and roughneck activity like playing war, climbing trees, backyard hunting and camping—all activities that bring havoc and noise to the house and neighborhood not to mention damaging the shrubs. And although he has never stolen anything before, there have recently been occasions when his group has been seen taking apples from the neighbor's tree. What else can I surmise but that the peers are having an undesirable effect upon my boy?" One alternate and verifiable conclusion is that this interest in primitive behavior is less related to social coercion than physiological development. Moreover, for a community of children to begin cooperative endeavors, the first arena must be their own interest. This can mean that they need to work together capturing the enemy hill or rocket supply (apple tree) before concerning themselves with the quiet community and how to legislate peace—tasks that appear even beyond our own talent. As offensive as theft may be it is rather common among members of this age family since they perceive all groups other than their own as hostile and therefore fair game. Since truth is granted a lesser allegiance than the peer group, responsible adults must see their job as less one of crime and punishment than one of enabling young assemblies to fit truth beside loyalty and power in the hierarchy of goals.

Although a child's contemporaries foster self-discipline and encourage conscientiousness, this influence often escapes the notice of parents. Instead we are inclined to see the slovenly, argumentative demeanor that children adopt to differentiate themselves from us. For some grown-ups this observation translates into an impression that the seeming disrespect can be attributed to an excessive social influence by peers whose impact might better be directed toward academic achievement. Numerous parents fail to realize that excessive academic pressures can be unhealthy and that all work and no play does make Jack a dull boy because study gives expression to only part of his personality; it leaves undeveloped some of the important qualities nature endows. Indeed it could be argued that character and mental health are probably more affected by out-of-school extracurricular activities than in the instructional setting. In any case social influence in a world where men encounter one another daily is more important than we have yet recognized; how to get along may be more difficult and quite as necessary as how to gain knowledge. It may be that the school should capitalize at this age level upon the common interest in primitive sports like camping, climbing, and swimming, in which competition is more with nature than with each other and where cooperation rather than exclusion is the key to success.

But isn't it true that peers undermine juvenile interests by making them transient and superficial? Not really. Between ages eight and twelve, moods correspond with physical energy in being strong but short-lived. Hobbies are earnestly taken up and then dropped as quickly, much to the chagrin of parents who finance the interest. Understandably adults would prefer that a youngster's interests relate to their own or at least persist for the life of purchased objects. And while this might hold true for less durable toys in childhood, it is not so in the middle grades, with the expensive stamp collection that in a matter of months may be shelved in favor of some new venture. These interest fluctuations imply change rather than stability and it holds true for friends as well as objects with the emotions of love and hate being strong but momentary. Seeing the child's interests depart from their own grieves those parents who attempt to retain the things a family holds in common by possessiveness (mother) or authority (father). Adult understanding is needed to build the kind of desired confidante relationship. This means accepting the fact that the child is through with psychological dependence, he must be allowed his own experience, interests, and choice of friends; it means that the activities dominant at this age should be encouraged rather than subordinated to our wishes; it means he will be disappointed if parents are affectionate toward him in the presence of peers; it means he probably will not express gratitude for the many ways in which he is assisted; it means that for the moment parents are bygone heroes replaced by new ones from literature, films, and television. But also it means that while the parent model does not continue as a singular one, that role remains important and, although he may not acknowledge the love and assistance given, he does in fact appreciate it. Unless he is understood in these things the only conclusion junior can draw is, "They don't understand me,"—and for too many boys and girls this conclusion is accurate.

Prejudice as a Bar to Development

How children as a group view internal differences ought to be more a concern of this society than how the young can be led to become more like us and less like their peers. Certainly communal living is a necessary condition for citizenship, but this goal can be permanently impaired in elementary school if certain students are not regarded as part of the first self-governed assembly. In the loosely formed, adult-directed community of the initial grades, discrimination is not a problem. In fact, first- and second-graders often elect to play with or sit beside someone of another ethnic group or race. Then, about the fifth grade, this friendliness seems to vanish and children begin to associate almost exclusively with peers whose background resembles their own. According to ten-year-olds, few if any positive features can be attributed to members of minority groups (Blake and Dennis, 1943). What seems to happen as children of the middle grades form themselves into subsocieties is that they primarily cohere with those who have been brought up with similar standards in order to reassure themselves that one is the right kind of person, a reasonable conviction that is reinforced by the group's practice of excluding all those who differ. This clanishness often leads to intolerance and prejudice (Hurlock, 1964, p. 397; Davitz, 1955; Broderick and Fowler, 1961). While it can be shown that by twelfth grade most children have become less rejecting of minority groups, even attributing some positive features to them, this cannot offset the deleterious and possibly lifelong effects upon personality entered during the middle years of public schooling (Allport, 1958, pp. 282–296; Spock, 1964, 1964a, 1966, 1966a).

For those who serve as objects of prejudice, some of the psychic energy that should be spent to advance ego status is necessarily diverted to protecting the self. There is no way to speak about prejudice without involving self-concept; they are inseparable. The manner in which one is treated by others tells him what he is as well as who he is. And to suggest that a child disregard the low estimate others hold of him is to presume he is unaffected by peers; how they feel about him is important, for it influences how he feels about himself as well as how they treat him. For millions of children the supposedly harmless discrimination of peers is ego-damaging. Some minority group youngsters are unable to think of themselves as individuals, since they are always viewed as representatives of an ethnic or racial group. Under such conditions a child might say were he able to word the feeling, "My self-concept is divorced from me —I am a member of a minority group, of the not-group, unseen as an individual; my personal merit precedes my existence since it is the same for all of my kind." To appraise oneself in a negative way is to more likely experience negative than positive emotions and so to behave in an unpleasant way toward others. Self-concept is the key to human behavior and when it is altered, personality changes. If a child accepts the negative image of himself as held by the dominant group, he is less likely to become himself; being not-self is perceived as better. We encourage the not-self being or the denial of self-features through prejudice and thereby stunt personality development.

But it is not only the objects of prejudice who are hurt. Defined as "thinking ill of others without sufficient warrant," prejudice retards those who embrace it as well. Because he will not accept others as equal, the prejudiced person is also unable to mature. His recourse to exclusion without encounter, judgment before contact, means there is no chance for him to identify with or learn from those who are prejudiced against. For the prejudiced person some men are considered as less than men, a view that destines him to remain a child, whatever delusions he may entertain to the contrary.

It is apparent that to regard the initial six years of life as totally responsible for one's basic social attitudes is incorrect. By the same token it is an error to assume that the prejudice first manifested at about age eight is inborn. After determining the extent to which 240 children of grades four through six expressed prejudiced attitudes toward minority groups, Harris (1950), questioned the mothers of these children. Far more often than the parents of unprejudiced children, mothers of the prejudiced stressed obedience as a youngster's most important lesson, insisted that children never oppose them nor keep a secret from them, preferred they be quiet rather than noisy, and suggested anger as the best adult treatment for temper tantrums. Under training conditions like these a child no doubt learns to be on guard, to police his impulses lest they conflict with parental mood or rules and thereby trigger punishment or the withdrawal of love. According to Allport (1958, pp. 283–285) such children learn that it is power and authority rather than trust and tolerance that dominate human relations. And so the stage is set for a hierarchical view of society, a persuasion that equality ought not really prevail. The effect goes even deeper as the child comes to mistrust his impulses, believing he must not have temper tantrums or disobey; he must fight these evils in himself and by projection comes to fear evil impulses in others—it is they who are not to be trusted. If this type of training forms the ground for prejudice, the opposite style seems to predispose toward tolerance. A child who feels secure and loved whatever he does, one who is not subject to exhibitions of parental power, is likely to develop equality and trust as basic attitudes. Not having to repress his own impulses he probably will not project them upon others and so is less likely to develop suspicion, fear, and a hierarchical view of human relationships.

Becoming Responsible Through Feeling

Apart from the cliques and subsocieties designed to confirm self-direction, middle-graders as an aggregate are attempting to prove to themselves and the world that they can organize and practice a form of social life without continued reliance on imposing grown-ups. Since they are particularly trying to free themselves from parental dependence, these children eagerly look toward teachers they respect for new ideas about the world, a fact that affords the educator who is liked a singular opportunity to convey an appreciation for people from all kinds of backgrounds (cf. Cronbach, 1963). In this way the personality is beneficially influenced. That the years from six to ten are more crucial for personality development than we have generally supposed is indicated by recent studies of the Fels Research Institute, which also suggest the possible impact of teachers helping children improve the status and confidence of peers (Kagan, 1964).

Part of becoming oneself and assuming the role of citizen is to feel responsible and to express that which is felt. In the absence of feeling there is no responsibility and where men do not care about the status of others the concept of community is hollow. For the school to resemble a trial community requires that its teachers encourage the aspects of personality made evident in authentic relationships—those elements referred to when speaking about being deeply concerned, really caring, experiencing involvement—the very features that sometimes appear disconnected from the overt and intellectual behavior of pupils. In many subtle ways children are early advised to divorce themselves from feeling. Although it might be as helpful to find out what someone feels as to learn what he thinks, it frequently is made clear in class that no instances of heated dispute will be accepted. After all, the image of a learned person is one whose confidence in objectivity surpasses any regard for irrational emotional wisdom. Consequently, outbursts of anger are inappropriate in class, arguments on the playground must never run their course, no tears of joy or despair should be shown—indeed there is little place in school to display genuine emotion. Instead, laughter is regulated at the same time that pupils are advised to read poems with feeling. Along with being taught to distrust feelings is the lesson of denying the expression of feelings. To the question, "How are you?" there are only a limited number of acceptable answers like, "Fine," "Good," "Okay," or "Well." Given the reply "I didn't sleep last night worrying," the interrogator becomes embarrassed, and doesn't know what to say next—his question didn't intend involvement (cf. Fromm, 1962, pp. 141–152).

Repression of feeling includes even facial expression and the paralanguage of body movement. Then when students hit the halls, they come alive in a very literal sense. Some of them become quite boisterous in releasing pent-up emotional resources that should have been linked into the learning process instead of being disconnected from intellectual behavior and repressed. As a consequence, many of the classroom experiences are superficially internalized; that is, they do not become part of the personality system and register change in behavior. Instead, learning amounts to little more than storing information in easily accessible and readily erased components of the brain's retrieval system. This is why students who get an "A" in social studies can so quickly forget almost all they learn and why they seldom show the slightest alteration in actual social conduct because of this knowledge about human society that passes so superficially into and out of the personality by way of a lecture, text, or notebook (Bloomberg, 1966; 1967).

Students retain these habits taught them by the school system into adult life so that as "citizens" they can read detailed accounts of slums, war, air polution, and overpopulation; discuss them sensibly; and then put them out of mind completely without ever once really experiencing anything in the way they feel those things in which the whole personality is involved. These persons can watch a race riot on television and upon turning it off remark, "This network sure has good coverage." Hopefully, the citizen we wish to develop through experiences in the educational system should also learn to have concern for issues involving the well-being of the community and to express that concern through action. Here too the professional educator has by and large provided a negative model. It is probably still true that most primary and secondary school teachers cringe at the thought of behaving in a way that some school board member might label as "controversial" or "political." The situation is a little better in colleges and universities. What students at every level learn about concern and action from their teachers is carried over into community life: maintain the status quo, resist changes that affect your own narrow round of life, talk knowingly as an expert spectator about the vital issues confronting the larger community, but don't actually try to influence them. This type of behavior might best be described in the jargon of a children's textbook: "Look at the issue. See the issue. See the important issue. Talk about the issue. Talk some more about the issue. Look at the next issue . . . ," and so on. By watching his teachers the student learns that to be concerned about an issue means to observe it, and to be active means only to talk (Bloomberg, 1966; 1967; cf. Fromm, 1964b, pp. 108–142; 1962b, pp. 83–106).

As the schooling process continues to lengthen, we must somehow ensure that it does not compete with the equally essential need of pupils for experience and responsibility, that it does not make unattainable the very development at which it aims. If we do not educate for responsibility, "we can have no adults but only aging children who are armed with words and paint and clay and atomic weapons, none of which they understand" (Kubie, 1958, pp. 104–136). Unless students are concurrently exposed to emotionally maturing experiences along with the academic

advance, they can only become erudite adolescents. The mere passage
of time makes maturity possible but never guarantees it. However extended an education may be, it fails the student if a chance for individual
responsibility be omitted. Men cannot be wise and yet remain immature;
truly the need of today and its people is for greater not lesser men (cf.
Raths, Harmin, and Simon, 1966; Maslow, 1959a).

For a person to become an involved citizen requires that he not think
feelings without having feelings. More than ever before and largely because of mass media, people are told how they ought to feel and what
they are supposed to feel about all kinds of situations. In colleges many
prospective teachers are told what they are to feel about children and
then later they sometimes experience guilt when such feelings are not
experienced. Erich Fromm (1965, pp. 132–133, 213–219) suggests that
feelings may be more genuine in a peasant community, where people are
less exposed to mass media and are not indoctrinated as to what they are
supposed to feel. We are already at the point where many people do not
know what they feel and this means they do not know who they are. It
is tragic when men know the right words, know what to say, when to
say it and how to reply but do not experience the feelings, the reality of
what their words should mean. A life of vocabulary is not the same as a
life of meaning. The verb "to educate" is not just transitive, it is also a
reflexive verb. True maturity can eventuate only when the verb is reflexive; then it is not a case of learning someone else's experiences,
thinking someone else's feelings—it is having our own! This is crucial,
because personal responsibility is unlikely to come about when one is
always told what to do and how to feel rather than when he feels himself
what should be done. Hopefully the aim of education still is to develop
mature persons, citizens who in addition to knowing about issues also
feel, care, and are responsible—persons whose achievement does not
cease with becoming separate but includes the greater accomplishment
of becoming themselves.

BECOMING MATURE

Having become separate and finding themselves through others the
young next enter an important time known as adolescence. The term
adolescence derives from the Latin meaning "to grow into maturity."
During the adolescent years, generally considered as the twelve-to-
eighteen age span, one is expected to bridge the gap between childhood
and adulthood (cf. Eisenberg, 1965). Since teen-agers sooner approximate
grown-ups in physical size than in social and emotional stature, it is
likely that family and school may at times demand behavior beyond one's
years—usually prefaced by the superficial observation, "You are not a
child anymore." The problem of unrealistic expectations is of course not
unique to modernity; boys and girls of many generations have probably

known it. However, what is new is the adolescents' longer period of economic dependency and greater learning than those of adolescents of the past, a sometimes volatile combination where it discourages early marriage, allows longer parental dominance, and so defers independence. Many young people are told that their generation has not learned life's lessons of responsibility—"Your mother and I had to work; it wasn't easy then as it is now." Yet when the adolescent announces an intention to seek part-time employment a frequent parental reply is "No! We are working and sacrificing so that you won't have to, so that you can have all the things we never had—just enjoy yourself!" In many cases the implicit meaning is to be grateful and remain dependent.

If adults are ambivalent about the economic dependency and imposed irresponsibility of youth, they express an even greater concern about the supposed level of adolescent morality. It seems that teen-agers are urged to date earlier than ever before but encouraged to get serious later, exposed to considerable sexual stimulation via mass media, provocative music, and dance but remain detached and unemotional; to have access to a car and contraceptives yet still be unaffected and innocent (cf. Christensen, 1952; Douvan and Adelson, 1966, pp. 174–228). Moreover, the number of sources from which adolescents derive their values has increased, thereby adding to the uncertainty about which goals are right, what to believe in and look forward to. Another circumstance serving to reduce the change of adult guidance involves discrepancies in personal and communal values witnessed by adolescents. They are told all men have the same rights, yet they daily observe discrimination against themselves and others because of age, race, financial station, or creed. Such inequities form their focus for change to make the world a better place— but they cannot exercise the franchise before reaching the legal age of twenty-one.

Compounding the adult reluctance to accept him as grown-up is the teen-ager's observation that he is a member of a society whose premium is upon youth rather than age; that in fashion and use of leisure time adults work to appear younger than they in fact are. Even a casual observation reveals the image of youth in mass media being used to sell everything from soap to automobiles, and that to stay young is the common American dream. Obtaining a responsible place in society, gaining acceptable sexuality, determining values by which to live, and manifesting the desire to become mature rather than remain a child—bearing these issues in mind the popular question of whether adolescent life is more difficult now than in the past is necessarily unanswered, for whoever tries to compare succeeding generations starts with the hopeless disadvantage that he belongs to one and cannot fully know the other. Nevertheless, however different the era, certain purposes of adolescence remain constant: It always has been and yet is a time for growing up, for acquiring additional important aspects of personality, for realizing that one does not become a man merely by having a developed body, living in a house, feeding one's face, and agreeing with the neighbors. Manhood is achieved by becoming mature in relationships with members of the same sex, the opposite sex, with the culture, and with oneself.

The Psychosexual Significance of Puberty

It has long been a tradition in many cultures to regard the twelve-to-fourteen-year-old members as positioned upon the threshold of sexual maturity and therefore ready for citizenship. Even today there are places in the world where groups carry on elaborate forms of ritual to celebrate the onset of puberty. As a total society, Americans do not feel constrained to recognize early adolescents as full-fledged adults just because they begin to show overt physical changes. But regardless of the low significance Americans attach to physiological development in terms of a criterion for granting acceptance to adult status, something of the body's transition must be known if the basis for teen-age mental health is to be understood. The sudden spurts in height and weight, the lanky appearance and temporary loss in coordination all stem from the rapid growth of limbs and are not due to sexual development as some would suggest. On the contrary, when the sex glands become active they actually impede the growth process, a fact well illustrated by the shorter, more heavy and stocky appearance of early-maturing teens than their lanky later-maturing peers. There is also a difference between the sexes as to the times of growth spurt. Shorter until age ten, the girls become taller between eleven and fourteen because their growth design initiates earlier than for males. Accompanying this anatomical growth is a corresponding physiological advance that explains the greater precocity of girls in the late elementary and junior high years (cf. Gebhard, 1965). Most teachers are aware that the girls pester boys quite sometime before the boys become interested (Horrocks, 1965, p. 723; Kinsey, 1965, pp. 125-131; Muess, 1966, pp. 4-12).

Until the influence of Freud, it was assumed that sexuality actually begins with puberty. As a result of psychoanalytic study indicating that sexuality is manifest even during infancy, the way was paved to understanding nature's extremely important *principle of anticipation.* According to this principle, the physiological capacity for any function anticipates the biological necessity for its use. Consider the organs of reproduction as an example: Girls first experience their menstrual period in preparation for maternity but it is not until a minimum of two years or so after the first flow that females are capable of bearing children. Boys and girls of eight and nine years are quite able to engage in sexual intercourse long before the natural age of procreation. And in some uncivilized clans, early sexual relations are encouraged. However, the fact that nature anticipates the sexual need does not mean that its precocious exercise is desirable. The fact that such affairs are labeled precocious implies that we recognize a time more proper for exercising the sexual function than at its first appearance.

Although it is an error to associate puberty with the emergence of sexuality, the reasons for doing so warrant consideration. In preparation for parenthood there are changes in the sex organs, including menstruation in the girl and capacity for ejaculation by boys. Then too, emotions and sexual feelings become much stronger at this time. Before puberty it takes external stimulation like masturbation to arouse sex feelings; from puberty onward these feelings can be stimulated internally as the result of the development of sexual gland secretions, particularly of the pituitary gland at the base of the brain. This gland provides the gonadotrophic hormone that originates both sex feelings and the sex cycle and stimulates to action the gonads or testicles in the male and ovaries in the female. So proximate is the pituitary gland to the brain that sexual response can be evoked as much by imagination from within as by external stimulation. This circumstance obtains for adolescence and beyond, whenever sex fantasies are operative.

To fully appreciate the significance of puberty one needs to realize that the time of its arrival is steadily becoming sooner. Statistics for females of the United States indicate that the average year and month in which the first menstrual period occurs, known as the *menarche,* has continuously declined approximately one third of a year per decade during the last century. At present the menarche for American girls is fourteen years and two months (13.1 in the Kinsey studies), figures considerably lower than most other cultures for which data is available: India, 14.1; Brazil, 14.5; Russia, 15.8; Finland, 15.10; Eskimos of Greenland, 16.0 (Hadfield, 1962, p. 192; Horrocks, 1965, pp. 712–715; Kinsey, 1965, pp. 80–83).

Whatever the age when girls and boys come to show signs of puberty, it does not indicate a capability of reproduction since the age of nubility does not coincide with menstruation and emission; instead there is a gap of adolescent sterility, an infertile time that follows puberty. Evidence for this thesis derives from studies of the Hindu girl who marries before puberty but does not cohabit with her husband until after the menarche. Roberton (1843) found that even when such unions are consummated immediately the space between menarche and conception approximates three years. The same interval between first menstruation and pregnancy is reported by Mondaire's (1880) research dealing with Chinese women. Similarly Malinowsky (1927) observed that although young girls from the Trobriand Islands are promiscuous, they rarely become pregnant until several years beyond the menarche. It is apparent that nature discourages early bearing of children by providing a delay between the initial preparation for reproduction and the time of actual capability to reproduce (cf. Montagu, 1957; Mills and Ogle, 1936, pp. 607–615).

The same sterility so to speak appears on the psychological side, for although amorous feelings greatly increase at puberty they are not immediately directed toward erotic intimacy. This is because by itself sex is insufficient to enable lasting relationships between men and women; nature therefore has designed additional phases leading to maturity before sexual intercourse is appropriate. Defined as "that group of functions and activities whose natural end is reproduction," sex is generally associated with the internal or external stimulation of the genital organs. As such, it is an important but single component among the many comprising love during adolescence (Fromm, 1962b, pp. 52–57, 106–133). Whereas sex, anger, and fear are instincts, love is a sentiment; love is a group of positive emotional tendencies centered around some person, idea, or object. The object of love may be a wife, girl friend, children, religion, country, sport. Some of the emotions ranging around a love object are tenderness, respect, devotion, pride, sex, friendliness, loyalty, and protectiveness. Since each of these elements, which appear during adolescence, has a unique biological function to fulfill in the development of a complete and mature personality, it is erroneous to perceive teen relations as characterized only by sex (cf. Ames, 1964, pp. 124–148; Fromm, 1962b, pp. 102–133; Hadfield, 152, pp. 131–144; Hurlock, 1955, pp. 394–395).

The components of love found in adolescence do not of course appear all at once but rather in phases of ordered sequence, each making its contribution to the final fulfillment of love, marriage, and parenthood. Too many adults assume that when the reproductive organs develop at puberty, they immediately generate a desire for sexual intercourse. Instead, the typical adolescent in his or her lovelife passes through four consecutive phases: (1) a loyalty attachment to some group of the same sex; (2) personal affection for a bosom friend of the same sex; (3) an affinity toward a group of the opposite sex; (4) and finally, after an interlude of romance, a complete falling in love takes place with an intimate partner of the opposite sex. Respectively these separate phases deserve elaboration.

The Benefit of Homosexual Attachment

As boys and girls enter adolescence, a marked change can be observed in group relationships. The tendency toward sex cleavages becomes more pronounced than before. Whereas both sexes played together on equal terms between ages eight and twelve, they no longer do so. Instead, members of the puberty set form closely knit homosexual gangs to which loyalty and obedience are sacrosanct. Part of being loyal implies the rejection of all other groups, especially those made up of the opposite sex. At this age boys consider girls silly; they groan at lovemaking on television and in the movies and place dancing far down the list of preferred activities. Conversely, girls regard boys as rough and impolite. This mutual revulsion serves a useful biological function since even in early adolescence boys are becoming capable of reproduction but it is not as yet desirable that they should father offspring.

One can of course find some incidence of dating during the puberty period but this early and unnatural entrance to heterosexual social life often means "what is learned is only manner-deep, the acquisition of the exterior graces; the deep bewilderments go untouched. It represents a skewed maturation—social maturity preceding psychosexual maturity and in preceding, influencing it" (Douvan and Adelson, 1966; cf. Mead, 1965; Coleman, 1965). For example, the author has observed dances held for boys and girls as young as age twelve. While such affairs resemble the adult fashion in terms of couples arriving together, what frequently follows is that girls gather on one side of the room and boys on the other. Out on the dance floor one is most likely to observe two girls dancing with each other. Nature would have it so.

Male gangs occur in greater frequency than female gangs. They cohere in part because of some shared interest, need, or distress but in most cases because of a commonly admired leader. Under his direction the same boy perceived by adults as rebellious and disobedient can appear submissive and accommodating. In developing a sense of comradeship, loyalty is felt toward fellow members less because of personal reasons than because they are part of the assembly. Under these conditions it is an unwise parent who risks a son's humiliation and disaffection by insisting the boy not dress as the gang would have it; too many of us assume conformity of mind when we witness likeness of apparel. The point is that one does not lose his individuality by joining a group; neither does he forfeit freedom because it is in a community that we experience our greatest liberty. What one does lose and should lose by belonging to a gang is egotism and self-centeredness. These are replaced by submission, loyalty, and respect, important attributes for citizenship, marriage and parenthood (Hadfield, 1962, pp. 210–215; Horrocks and Buker, 1951; cf. Kawin, 1963, pp. 70–72).

Despite its many benefits the gang and its leader are too impersonal to satisfy all of one's needs during the homosexual phase. Therefore, in time boys and girls develop the need for an intimate friend of the same sex, someone with whom secrets and problems can be shared (Blos, 1962; Farelli, 1957; Kawin, 1963, pp. 306–308). This relationship does not originate merely by seeing a peer who evokes some kind of yearning and affection; but on the contrary, the desire and yearning are felt first. Two reasons account for this need of a nonsexual relationship with a bosom friend. First, it is essential to have another person in whom to confide because at this juncture a teen-ager is beginning to feel many strange impulses, mysterious sensations and feelings within the body as well as strange ideas in the mind that he cannot comprehend. Feeling unsure of himself he needs another person to speak with, to discover whether that trusted peer is experiencing the same impulses. A second reason for the friendship is the strength of physical urges that are of sufficient tension to demand some kind of relief. Somehow expression must be given these urges by telling another person about it, preferably one of the same chronology and similar feelings. This longing also accounts for another phenomenon of adolescence, namely the keeping of diaries. If a boy or girl has no bosom pal or even if they have, there is still a need to pour out the most secret thoughts into these diaries, which become treasured possessions.

Even though the adolescent has an urge to express his feelings in these ways he is not as a rule prepared to tell parents for they live in another world and cannot share the emotion. As a result, bosom friends share everything, they whisper in quiet places and allow no one to hear their thoughts. This confidentiality does not mean they are up to trouble but is in fact quite normal. In this regard, the like-sex friendship of girls seems to be more intense and important when compared with the like-sex friendship of boys (Douvan and Adelson, 1966). However, a bosom pal cannot fulfill the parental function during this period of handling certain fears. In some ways the wise mother is of much greater benefit than a premature confederate, especially as it relates to understanding body image. During puberty girls experience a widening of the pelvis in preparation for childbearing and the growth of "puppy" fat on the hips. In consequence they become knockkneed and seem to waddle when running instead of proceeding straight-legged as before. All this proves to be a source of annoyance and shame until the slim mother reveals that she was just as plump and awkward at the daughter's age. There is also the appearance of hair on the pubis and armpits which some girls regard as ugly. As the boys laugh, a girl's self-consciousness increases, especially about her breast development, which she may attempt to hide by stooping the shoulders forward. The physical reasons for awkwardness should be explained to adolescents. Otherwise they can develop feelings of inferiority and excessive self-consciousness. Here obviously is a situation in which adult recall, mother's adolescent experience, is most relevant and can be of great help.

In this culture girls make the transition from homosexuality to heterosexuality earlier than boys (Kinsey, 1965, pp. 122–126). Usually the shift occurs at about thirteen or fourteen for females but seldom before fifteen in males. For a study of feminine adolescent development see Douvan and Adelson (1966), Williams and Kane (1959) and Neider (1966). In the case of both sexes the transition from homosexuality to heterosexuality is characterized as a moody retreat from almost every form of interpersonal relationship, a time when neither the gang nor even the bosom friend can understand the need to walk, ride and think alone, to be by "myself." Parents who observe the brooding introspection but are unaware of its meaning often pose inquiries like: "Why aren't you with the fellows any more? John used to be your best friend and came over to the house daily—now we never see him at all. What's the matter with you anyway, don't you want any friends?" To these well-intended but foolish questions, most teen-agers curtly reply, "I just would rather be alone."

Don't worry! He will soon elect to be part of a group again but with one difference—the chosen company will be peers of the opposite sex.

Before considering patterns of relationship with the new-found opposite sex, another matter deserves explanation. It has already been stated that during puberty boys and girls usually feel an antipathy toward each other and that this keeps the sexes apart during the initial phases of reproductive development, thereby preventing them from becoming parents long before they are ready. To this seemingly built-in yet temporary revulsion there is one notable exception—the opposite parent who is able to foster a tryout zone for the imminent adult role. To prove to his mother and himself that he is approaching manhood, a teen-ager may politely open the car door, see her across the street, and fancy that he is protecting her. Because behavior that conflicts with the intended role is embarrassing, it is distasteful to have mother order him about or kiss him in public. The most helpful outcome of this relationship is that it keeps alive heterosexual feelings in a nonsexual way; it encourages a form of chivalry that later is properly directed toward the wife. Like most play that is anticipatory, the teen-ager is playing at being a husband from a safe distance, all the while increasing in confidence and understanding about how a woman should be treated. The same type of association occurs between daughter and father with her holding his arm and taking pains to provide comfort upon his arrival home from work. This tryout zone in the role of wife is valuable to a girl for it encourages character aspects like tenderness and devotion before the maturity of reproductive functions.

Adolescent Polygamy and Its Merit

It seems that no sooner have adolescents reached the stage of identity with their own sex than they begin to be fascinated by that which they lack—the attributes of the opposite sex. Being attracted by peers of the opposite sex is an experience that usually arrives between fifteen and eighteen years of age but contrary to popular surmise this new affinity is not based upon an immediate desire for physical intimacy. Before the press for sexual union occurs, a number of changes take place in the nature or components of love. At the outset, sexual curiosity and the mere desire to attract are uppermost in the teen-ager's estimate; only later do the elements of romance and erotica prevail. In time all of these aspects unite to bring a feeling known as "falling in love." There is also a gradual development in the love object selection. Polygamy or the attraction to many precedes monogamy, the choice of one. During the polygamous phase a sixteen-year-old feels no inconsistency or self-recrimination in his attention to a number of girls simultaneously, all of whom of course are pledged his undying devotion. Likewise, any one of the girls he admires may at the same time express love for a recording artist, the school football captain, a cousin, and the young married man next door. It isn't that one beloved is not enough; instead the dimensions of love remain insufficient because the adolescent is immature.

Although finding many members of the opposite sex attractive seems not to pose serious difficulty, making an admission of the fact is quite another matter. It is difficult for boys to concede the suddenly recognized beauty in girls who up to now have been seen as silly and unnecessary. By the same token girls consider it an embarrassing reversal of their previous attitude to now acknowledge the once crude and rough males as being attractive. Since they cannot admit to themselves what is happening, young people frequently tease peers who are seen with someone of the opposite sex to indicate that they at least have not been caught and made to surrender. It is likely that when a boy starts to tease his companions about girls, it is because he is on the verge of capitulation himself and his offensive behavior is meant to hide his own feelings—a complex of emotions about which he is still half-ashamed but nevertheless driven by.

The way in which teasing is accepted often depends upon the source. As a rule it is unwise for parents to make fun of the adolescent's transient affections. Regard as normal the report that one week Phyllis is the only girl in the world and the following week she is forgotten because Diana takes her place. At the time of each infatuation the teen-ager is totally committed—temporarily (Ellis, 1949). The short length of fidelity will need to extend if marriage is to be a feasible proposition but at the moment being a flirt provides valuable experience in how to select a mate. First, a girl may be enchanted by a good-looking boy but soon finds that he thinks more of himself than her; next a flattering young man is chosen until it is learned that his endearing remarks are offered to every girl; later perhaps a considerate boy is dated until he proves to be more submissive than protective. On and on the trial of suitable partners continues (Ames, 1964, pp. 107–123). All the while boys too are learning from their temporary choices—pretty girls are not always intelligent and capable of desired conversation; shapely girls may also be vain and selfish; and academic girls may be bossy. Parents should recognize the necessity of allowing nature's motivation for numerous boy and girl friends because this experience does increase the likelihood of selecting an appropriate life partner. For grown-ups who fear the prospect of pregnancy, it is well to remember that since other qualities need to develop in both sexes before they fall in love, the desire for intercourse is seldom prominent at this time.

Sex curiosity is a common feature of the polygamous phase. Underlying this curiosity about the physiology of sex are the strange and satisfying feelings which such contemplation arouses. The object of excitement at the beach is the sight of the other sex which stimulates erotic feelings. If a youth be sufficiently aroused to the point of masturbation or nocturnal emission, it generally stems from his conjuration of witnessing girls undress rather than gaining a sexual union (Hurlock, 1955, p. 360; Ramsey, 1943). Masturbation at this age is common and is natural considering the extra strong feelings emerging now. Yet, some teen-agers have been led to regard the act as terrible, shameful, and promoting insanity. Boys especially experience much guilt for fear they are hurting themselves and also because they can't tell anyone about it. The actual harm of adolescent masturbation is psychological and not physical. Its excessive practice most often involves those who feel deprived of affection, persons for whom the whole of love concentrates on physical satisfaction the urge to which becomes compulsive. In marriage such people seek only to satisfy themselves and not the partner. But when masturbation occurs in adolescence simply as a relief of tension, little psychological harm is done, despite the notions of those who would oppose it on religious grounds.

When investigating a case of excessive masturbation, it is necessary to discover what is the mental fantasy or image by which one excites his or her own sex feelings. In early puberty the image is usually of nothing more than the feelings themselves; it is purely autoerotic. But generally there is a stimulating fantasy, which it is important to discover because it is obviously less psychologically perverted if the image is one of ordinary attraction to one of the opposite sex than of a persistently homosexual nature (Pomeroy and Christenson, 1967). One unfortunate effect of masturbation that applies to the girl rather than the boy should be mentioned for it is sometimes judged as the cause of frigidity.

In female sexuality the focus of sexual excitation before puberty is externally confined to the clitoris and after puberty passes internally into the vagina in anticipation of sexual intercourse. Therefore, if a girl masturbates by external stimulation before puberty and continues to do so thereafter, the center of excitement tends to remain external which means that although as a wife she enjoys external stimulation and may get an orgasm that way she experiences no particular pleasure in sexual intercourse within the vagina and has no orgasm. Marriage therefore may be a disappointment to both husband and wife.*

A second feature of the polygamous phase is to become attractive to the opposite sex, to make conquest and in so doing ensure oneself that the intended adult role is possible. In males sexuality is aggressive, a fact that can mean forcing compliance of the female but if properly directed takes the form of protecting her. Unlike men, females lack sufficient strength to force their gratification and instead are equipped with the will to seduce. Female sexuality is receptive-seductive in contrast to male aggression. Almost everyone has seen an example of sex play illustrating this difference. Notice the adolescent boy bullying a girl and twisting her arm while she pleads with him to stop. But then as soon as he stops she

---

* From J. A. Hadfield, *Childhood and Adolescence* (Baltimore: Penguin Books, 1962) p. 167. Reprinted by permission.

begins to provoke him again. He enjoys showing his strength by bullying and she likes to be mastered; both conform to their own sexual nature.

Those who study development realize the biological significance of the adolescent desire to attract; it is to ensure marriage and procreation. However, to the polygamous teen-ager being attractive is in itself a goal and irrespective of any desire for sexual union. To a boy or girl at this age the desire to attract is conscious and deliberate but motiveless. So at a party the girl's first concern and unspoken question of all whom she encounters is "How do I look?" She delights in compliments yet would be offended at any suggestion of sexual intercourse and may discontinue dating an older boy who is so inclined. For the time being she wants only to attract with no thought of intimacy. Some girls fail to realize the implication of provocation and need to be cautioned that while being called attractive is enough for her, it may not bring the same level of satisfaction to an older date of eighteen or nineteen who is sexually aroused and may insist that she give what she is still unprepared to offer (cf. Gebhard, 1965).

The polygamous stage in adolescence resembles an earlier phase of civilized man's evolution. Even today most primitive tribes and animals remain polygamous by design. Since only a few children survived in the days of old, polygamy served to bring numerous offspring. But in the higher stages of evolution the development of a strong maternal instinct for care of the young makes polygamy less necessary while monogamy offers the advantage of a more cohesive family life, the most beneficial setting for rearing children. Nevertheless, though polygamy is unacceptable for adult life in our culture, it still serves a useful purpose during adolescence in improving one's ability ultimately to select a single companion with whom to cohabit.

Romance and Falling in Love

From being attracted to several members of the opposite sex, each boy and girl suddenly finds that there is only one person for him. And with this recognition the polygamy of dating per se is replaced by the monogamous practice of "going steady." Mutual admiration is the major characteristic of romantic monogamism. The girl who was laughed at yesterday is now viewed on a pedestal as the boy wonders how he could have so long been blind to her charms and what is more how the other boys continue to resist her. Similarly, to the girl this pimple-ridden boy is the most handsome and perfect of companions. First romances often bring a decline in appetite and weight less because the parties feed on love as poets would have it; a more unromantic but accurate explanation is that any strong emotion like fear, love, or anger stops the gastric juices and thereby hinders digestion so that the food appetite is reduced.

The romantic couple accept each other as confidante in much the same

way as the same-sex bosom-pal arrangement of several years before. This
attachment is expressed by communicating secrets. By exposing the feelings of hope and fear, one runs the risk of being ignored or laughed at.
So the usual romantic experience entails trying out new words and ways,
advancing and withdrawal—opening up and exposing the self. During
this tryout zone the boy learns what will be expected of him in an adult
relationship, he learns to commit himself to another person, to love in a
giving as well as a pleasure-seeking way and to find that many nonsexual
activities are a part of the love experience. On occasion, when emotions
surpass expressive ability, lovers just sit and hold hands. Generally the
romantic relationship does not include sexual intercourse; in more cases
than not the couple perceive their union as incompatible with physical
intimacy. Indeed, a boy may feel that his mate is too pure for conquest,
her personality too ideal, and subject to spoiling if sex were part of the
situation (Biegel, 1951). As a natural phase of maturation this romantic
interlude is neither so serious or lasting as an observer would suspect;
it is playing at lovemaking, an anticipation of the real thing. Parents' and
teachers' unawareness of what this phase means can erroneously suppose
that boys and girls should not go steady because they will "get into
trouble." No doubt there are enough instances where this might be so
but in the normal boy-girl context the danger is fictional since they desire
and value romance more than sexual experience.

Grown-ups would do well to minimize negative comment about the
romantic attachment of youth and instead gratefully acknowledge the
reduction of egocentricity between childhood and the teen years that
makes adolescent love possible. Beginning with total incorporation and
thereafter possession, the love experience during its early stages of development is essentially selfish in nature; pleasure-seeking dominates with
little regard for others. By age fifteen the nature of love has in most lives
expanded to include attributes like appreciation, tenderness, understanding, and concern—all for the beloved person. This evolution from love as
self-seeking to love as desiring happiness for the love object is a sign
of maturity and requisite to the lasting success of intimate relationships.
It is no longer just an issue of "What do I want?" but "I wish to consider
also her interests and needs." A major behavioral advance in personality
at this time is the healthy adaptive response of regard and care for the
beloved; that is, obtaining pleasure from giving it and achieving the
mutual union so different from the mechanical union of two for the pleasure of one.

A number of values accrue from experiencing the romantic phase of
heterosexuality. For one thing, adolescents get to know one another more
intimately than in the polygamous context, a fact that educates in the
ultimate choice of a mate. The sustained companionship with one individual instead of many gives rise to minor interpersonal problems that
form a trial arena in which to learn accommodation, compromise, and

conciliation. Since to love begets a desire for pleasing the beloved, adolescents strive to demonstrate courtesy and consideration. Boys begin to dress up without parental demand, clean their fingernails and act less crudely while girls spend many moments preparing for dates (Sollenberger, 1940; Stone and Barker, 1939).

It should be mentioned that the more rapid physiological and emotional development in girls means that girls are more responsible than boys during late adolescence. Accordingly nature has determined that sexual relations have greater significance for the girl than the boy, so if to him intercourse is just for fun, she is likely not to share that view but rather consider the responsibility of bearing children (Sugarman and Hochstein, 1965). This probably accounts for the curious way in which a girl who "goes wrong" is more condemned than a boy, for to do so she must overcome more natural resistance within. Consequently, many a seventeen-year-old girl will reject a boy her own age for another suitor of twenty-two who is able to provide the kind of care and protection she needs (cf. Pomeroy and Christenson, 1967). At school or camp she may even prefer her young teacher to the better-looking yet less mature peers; unless taken advantage of these relationships generally are both harmless and temporary.

The step beyond romance known as *falling in love* implies that devotion, protection, tenderness, companionship, sexual attraction, respect, and admiration—all the elements of rapport—are combined in an attachment to some particular girl or boy. When it happens, the lover is hardly able to concentrate on anything else than the object of attraction. It is a time for self-forgetting, vowing to desire and protect forever. In the case of the girl it means admiring a boy's strength, wishing to please him, and wanting to bear his children. That heterosexual falling in love or experiencing compulsive attraction is based upon projection is universally accepted. When we refer to someone as fantastic or super or beautiful, this magical quality is due to the projection of a subjective element—an undeveloped part of our own personality. Each of us recognizes that the lover sees the beloved as not identical with the person seen by everyone else. Falling in love involves an overvaluation and distorted picture of the loved object. To us a girl appears quite ordinary but to him she is gorgeous; to us a man seems commonplace but to her he is a fabulous hero. It is inevitable that beauty resides in the eye of the beholder and that the image of the beloved represents the expression of a subjective need rather than a portrait of an actual being (cf. Jourard, 1958, pp. 233–255).

But what is this subjective need and how does the countrasexual image emerge? It is apparent that the sexual instinct itself seeks fulfillment and that its frustration or lack of object will give rise to an imaginary substitute so that men without women or the other way around will people their dreams with a missing party. But to "fall" for someone is an experience inadequately described in terms of a craving for genital satisfaction, since this can be experienced by two people who do not in fact care for one another. To remain consistent in assuming that the irrational magical quality associated with falling in love is always due to the projection of a subjective element, one cannot escape the hypothesis that all those who become capable of falling in love with someone of the opposite sex are bisexual. For it is clear that no experience is more magical than falling in love and also true that no experience is more manifestly subjective. In his state of infatuation the lover seems to conceive of union with the beloved as the be-all and end-all of existence. Lovers feel as if they were made for each other, as if no one else could possibly fulfill their need, as if no one could be as fortunate as themselves, as if they separately were incomplete without the other person. Here the projection of a subjective element is obvious.

The mutual projection that occurs between lovers seems to indicate a search for completeness, a reaching out after wholeness, a union between conscious and unconscious, so that to the man the woman appears to contain all that is missing in himself and all that would complete his life. And while the fundamental part of what is missing is a partner with whom he can have intercourse, this is not the only need she promises to fulfill. For him she personifies whatever in his particular culture is called feminine and for her he is the embodiment of masculinity. The image that each projects upon the other exhibits the psychological as well as the anatomical attributes that distinguish the sexes; and the fact that the psychological attributes vary from time to time and place to place does not invalidate the concept (Storr, 1963, pp. 121–123; cf. Fromm, 1962b, pp. 54–57; Bonner, 1965, pp. 147–164).

Of course it is natural and biologically desirable that sexual passion play the major role in the love of early adults because of nature's concerns for the procreation of species. A second concern of nature is the survival of offspring, a condition not fully met by the maternal instinct. Since children are best reared in a home of two parents, the maternal and home-building instinct of many girls controls their sexual component so that a man's sexual desire for intercourse before marriage may be denied much as she too may desire it because she wants the assurance that he really loves her. This is what the late adolescent girl means when she says that she wants to be loved for herself; that is she wishes to be assured that he wants to protect and care for her in a permanent fashion. Most girls know that practice doesn't make perfect in sexual relations and that to be mechanically experienced is not to be wiser. They are also aware that premarital sexual relations make it easier for either partner to fall back on outside affairs after marriage and that extramarital relations are a prime cause of family dissolution, which in turn harms the children. Essentially this is why society holds high the principle of the monogamous condition however much it may have fallen short in practice.

Mature Dependence

The developmental scheme for maturity was long viewed as terminating in marriage and the attainment of genital primacy on the assumption that achieving satisfactory heterosexual intercourse was the final aim of human relationships. Naturally the appeal that each sex has for the other leads to intimate heterosexual association and the establishment of the genitals as the main channel for the giving and receiving of love. But the achievement of genital primacy and becoming an adult member of one's own sex is not the whole of development. A further stage exists in which heterosexual projection is withdrawn, a stage of development in which being "in love" is superseded by loving, in which projection is replaced by relationship. This final stage of emotional development is termed *mature dependence*:

> What distinguishes mature dependence from infantile dependence is that it is characterized neither by a one-sided attitude of incorporation nor by an attitude of primary emotional identification. On the contrary, it is characterized by a capacity on the part of a differentiated individual for cooperative relationships with differentiated objects. So far as the appropriate biological object is concerned the relationship is of course genital; but it is a relationship involving evenly matched giving and taking between two differentiated individuals who are mutually dependent, and between whom there is no disparity of dependence. Further the relationship is characterized by an absence of primary identification and an absence of incorporation (Fairbairn, 1952, p. 145).

The attitudes described above as incorporation and identification are connected with and may underlie the more familiar concepts of dominance and submission. To incorporate another person is to overwhelm and destroy him—to regard him as less than an entire person. This is sadism. To identify with another person is to submerge one's own identity in that of the other, to be overwhelmed and treat oneself as less than an entire person. This is masochism. In interpersonal relationships maturity demands that neither oneself nor the other shall disappear but that each personality shall contribute to the affirmation and realization of the other (Storr, 1963, p. 43; cf. Fromm, 1962b, pp. 107–133).

This is not to deny the continuing need of each sex for the other; anatomy alone demands that it be recognized. But the absence of compulsion, the withdrawal of projection, must be recognized as a developmental state beyond that in which an individual is at the mercy of such feelings. However delightful being in love may seem, it is an advance to be able to love without the distortion of the other person that the projection of the contrasexual image necessarily involves. Were a man marooned on an island with one female companion, it is quite probable that his objective need would invest her with the glamour that she would not appear to possess under more normal circumstances. It is only when we no longer compulsively need someone that we can have a real relationship with him. None of us is ever completely whole nor can our need for each other and therefore our distortion of each other be entirely dispelled but if we are sufficiently fortunate in our partner and if our relationship be progressive and not merely a static achievement, we may approximate to a stage in which because each fulfills the other's need, each is also treated as a whole person by the other. Whereas formerly two people in love served only to complete what each felt to be lacking, now two whole people confront each other as individuals.

Becoming as a Function of Choice

Part of becoming mature involves the selection of ideals and goals by which to direct self-conduct and personal evaluation. These ideals, first manifest at about age sixteen, should be viewed as a basis for understanding motivation and behavior during late adolescence. They also account for the important distinction between child and adult conscience. Psychologists have long described the conscience as an instance of opportunistic learning much like any other cultural practice except that punishment rather than reward serves as the decisive agent. During early childhood the external voice of parental authority is being internalized so that the same demands made by others will in time automatically be made of oneself. However applicable this theory may be to the initial stages of conscience, it is unsatisfactory for describing the adolescent and adult experience. Were conscience stable over time and limited to providing self-recrimination for violation of taboos outlined in child training, there would be no way to explain how as grown-ups we disown our first codes of conduct in favor of those we devise ourselves. As it is, each of us develops a separate code by which self-judgment proceeds so that when we experience guilt it may be for reasons totally unrelated to the once important family prohibitions (Allport, 1962, pp. 68–71; cf. Bonner, 1965, p. 79; Baldwin, 1966, pp. 321–322, 366–368).

What seems to transpire between early childhood and late adolescence is a shift from habits of obedience to a commitment toward ideals, from behavior rooted in fear to action prompted by intention. Whereas the child conscience is motivated by a threat of punishment that one must not do certain things and one must do other things, the "feel" of adult conscience seldom relates to extrinsic authority or self-inflicted punishment; instead one struggles within about a value-related obligation. When goals and ideals come to be embraced as self-appropriate, they are accompanied by a sense of obligation which is a definite advance upon the juvenile compulsion to follow rules. Allport indicates that "ought" is not the same as "must." I must stay within the speed limit and pay my taxes or undesirable restrictions will follow. On the other hand, I "ought" to help a disabled neighbor, "ought" to vote in the local election, and "ought" to send a birthday card to grandmother. When a self-referred value judgment is made as if to say, "This action is consistent with my self-image and the other is not," then a sense of self-obligation is felt that is free of fear. This explains why some persons are driven more by ideals than coercion. Of course the conscience can be arrested in development like any other aspect of personality and many adults who have not made the must-ought transition continue to suffer from infantile guilt (Allport, 1962, pp. 72–74; 1950, pp. 86–98; cf, Fromm, 1961, pp. 104–108; Jourard, 1958, pp. 372–383).

Several factors combine to effect the shift from the must-conscience of childhood to the ought-dictate of adult life. As a result of introjection and identification, internal demands grow more important than external sanctions. Concurrent with the adoption of a value system the negative feelings of fear and prohibition are replaced by a concern for preference in self-image. Self-guidance comes to mean more than mere habits of obedience in terms of regulating conduct. The conscience would surely decline were prohibition and parental identification its only source but what actually takes place is that the conscience is kept alive and relevant to new experience by generic self-guidance. This new monitor of growth initiates a change in emphasis from tribalism to individuality, from opportunistic to oriented becoming; it fosters the conviction that a state of wholeness is possible though there is a constant dispute between our intention and how we behave.

Even if certain ideals are unattainable they still exert a powerful influence on contemporary behavior and in so doing effect the course of becoming. It is unfortunate that the growth process has most often been referred to in terms of a reaction to past and current stimuli while ignoring the equally important factor of futurity. "As a matter of fact a great many states of mind are adequately described only in terms of their futurity. Along with striving we may mention interest, tendency, disposition, expectation, planning, problem solving and intention" (Allport, 1962, p. 51; cf. Bonner, 1965, pp. 131–146). It seems that people are busy leading their lives into the future, whereas psychology has for the most part been occupied in tracing them into the past. (For a summary regarding Allport's psychology of the individual, see Hall and Lindzey, 1957, pp. 257–295).

Since in some ways becoming mature is a product of choice and because ideals do direct behavior from adolescence onward, the selection of what kind of goals to embrace and what kind of a person to be are extremely important issues (Combs, 1961). It is easy to dismiss the matter by citing the increase of agencies and institutions concerned about the affairs of youth. Yet this fact ought not blind our recognition that few if any of the conflicting sources advising youth are experienced in the problems of today's teen-agers. For parents to remark, "When I was a kid we weren't allowed to do that," is an insufficient guide to conduct (cf. Mead, 1966a). Chances are the referent experience did not even exist when the parents were adolescents. A generation ago, how many high school girls had to decide about whether to use the contraceptive pill? How many boys had to decide in sixth grade whether to attend a dance or whether to go steady while in junior high school?

Adding to the problem of choosing what kind of adult to become is the prior question about whether to strive for maturity at all. From every side teen-agers hear persons urging that they "grow up," but for themselves prefer to resemble youth. A mature person does not desire to always be known as young; if one's direction lies behind rather than before him, less attention can be given to growth than ought to be. It has been said, "You are only young once," but once is enough if you work it right. And to give youth the impression that becoming mature is in fact a concession rather than an accomplishment is the greatest injustice we can do.

The Image and the Fact

Most adults are concerned about the noticeable decline in communication with youth that occurs during late adolescence. Hoping to remain informed about the teen-age set, even though in less frequent contact with them, some parents grow receptive to outside sources that claim first-hand witness of youth's energy, sources that ostensibly make it their business to observe and report the ways in which adolescents behave. When this purpose is honored, news media do a service by helping adults better understand both the wide array of activities available for teen-agers as well as the diversity that obtains among young people themselves. However, what seems to happen more than it should is that adolescents are shown as singular in type and negative in behavior. Emphasis is given the anxious and wayward dimensions of a minority rather than the healthy and proud attributes of most. Consider the following:

> One third of high school brides are pregnant before marriage; each week twenty pregnant girls drop out of the Chicago Public Schools; girls seventeen and under account for 22 percent of all illegitimate births. In 1964 girls of high school age alone aborted 180,000 pregnancies (Gross, 1966, p. 22).

> At least half of all high school students in the Los Angeles area have tried marijuana at least once; one in four of them use it regularly (*Time*, 1967, p. 22).

> 200,000 Americans in the fifteen-to-nineteen age bracket will be infected with syphilis this year (Lippincott, 1966, p. 23). Reported cases of syphilis among teenagers have more than tripled since 1956 (Gross, 1966, p. 22).

> By 1975 one boy of every five under eighteen years old will be known to the police courts (Dinitz, 1965).

> Twenty percent of American college students use drugs, ranging from pep pills to marijuana, the amphetamines to the psychedelics (LSD, mescaline and Psilocybin) (Hollander, 1967, p. 22; cf. Cashman, 1966, pp. 78–91).

The third leading cause of death among fifteen-year-old boys in Scarsdale, New York, is suicide (Patterson, 1965, p. 36a).

Unmarried female students at Pembroke College of Brown University have been given contraceptive pills by the campus health director (Lawrence, 1965, p. 23).

Sexual promiscuity and the pill, crime and delinquent behavior, drugs and maladjustment, anxiety and insecurity—these are some of the features proposed as accurate in the portrait of today's youth. But there are more. We are told that although this generation can expect a lifespan longer by thirty years than their counterparts of a century ago, modern adolescents cannot defer gratification but instead embrace a philosophy of immediacy, of instant hedonism. "This generation has no utopia. Its idea is the happening—let it be concrete, let it be vivid, let it be personal, let it be now" (Gallagher, 1967, p. 20; cf. Rand, 1964). The same theme of impatience causing them to disregard all tradition in the realm of sexual relations applies to social change. Unable to wait for academic rules to be reversed by the democratic process, they engage in a kind of revolt that would destroy the very process in which they wish to assume power. "They don't seem to be willing to wait very long for answers" (Kerr, 1966, p. 5). And when it comes to answers about how life should be lived they can be counted on to reject them cynically in part because they have cast off everything their parents believe in and now occupy a spiritual vacuum. At the same time these adolescents have the audacity to declare "God is dead," they speak of searching for their own identity (cf. Wingo, 1965; Kneller, 1964). So distant are many members of the "now" generation that, unlike their predecessors, who at least went home for spring vacation, they prefer instead to roam in migratory groups to Fort Lauderdale or the Bahamas. Seemingly unable to communicate with their families, they huddle with their own kind; such is the nature of today's youth.

Confronted by this kind of adolescent image and discouraged by the present relationship with their own teen-ager, it is understandable that many adults become victims of worry, imagining all sorts of harmful possibilities that might harm the son's or daughter's intended future. At the same time grown-ups are experiencing fear, they attempt to dismiss the reported teen-age image as distorted and unrepresentative, an exercise in overgeneralization. But doubt-ridden by what they do not know about their own offspring and bothered by what others suggest he or she is likely to be, parents have but one recourse—to become their own witness. Although much of adolescent life is spent with peers alone and therefore lies beyond parent observation, parents find that what can be seen presents a less frightening image than one might suppose. Adolescents spend much energy in the conduct of dubious marathons to see who can play chess the longest, stuff the most persons into a telephone booth, fly a kite the highest, stay awake the longest, or remain in a shower the greatest length of time. Whereas competition in these endeavors is serious, the wisdom of expending energy for such purposes is questionable—in fact an obvious sign that the group is still juvenile. Watching an adolescent delight in having the car to ride around with his friends for no apparent purpose or seeing him mount a skateboard with confidence also leads many an adult observer to conclude that kids are hardly dangerous, just irresponsible—indeed seventeen going on twelve.

But is it wise to assume that all the foolish expenditures of adolescent energy stem exclusively from a lack of commitment to responsibility? Or could it be that teen-agers favor responsible outlets for their energy yet face a lack of opportunity? When the latter case obtains, we wrong the "now" generation by inferring their entire intent from action alone; to do so presupposes that whatever they intend is possible. In my judgment the major problem today is less one of irresponsible young people than youth denied their desired responsibility (cf. Coleman, 1965; Mead, 1965). And this is not without dire consequence for society. Whoever feels a sense of responsibility about what can and should be done in a particular instance yet is rendered powerless to affect the change suffers from impaired mental health. Make no mistake about the weight of responsibility felt by our present adolescent society. More than any generation before them, they are exposed through mass media to the ills and needs of man with all its dimensions of poverty, war, injustice, and disease. To question how able their future response to these issues will be is to overlook how they now behave. Apart from the many who participate in VISTA and the Peace Corps, there are some 250,000 youth tutoring children of the poor; countless others contribute volunteer services to hospitals and community while still another group is gainfully employed in part-time work. In addition, bear in mind that these youngsters enjoy a greater freedom than teen-agers of any prior time. Wherever there is freedom, there is the responsibility of having to make appropriate choices about behavior. And teen-agers do a far better job in this realm than adults credit them with.

Adolescents know that their proper relationship to the culture is responsibility, not receptivity; they realize that unless their life has purpose and effect, it will be empty and void. This perception is well expressed in a novel entitled *Where the Boys Are* by Glendon Swarthout (1960). The story involves American college students who during the annual spring vacation swarm by thousands down to the broad beaches of Fort Lauderdale, Florida. What follows is adapted from a speech, in effect a soliliquy spoken by Basil who is "one of the boys" during a long evening with his girl in a deserted section of the beach.

"This," he says, "is the bad news for kids today: we are undramatic. We have been rooked out of every generation's birthright, which is conflict. The Twenties had a reputation to build, the Thirties an economic struggle, The Forties a world war. We have no damn contrast. We have pimples but no suffering, money but no wealth, delinquency but no evil . . . television but no insight.

"We have roll without rock . . . tolerance without love . . . sex without delight . . . death without sting.

"We have sweatsocks instead of sweat . . . we have IQ's instead of intellects—in short, we have everything to live for but the one thing without which human beings cannot live—something for which to DIE slightly, not mortally but sufficiently—and we need it so pathetically and crucially that I am sorry for us to the coolest shadows of my soul!" (Swarthout, 1960, pp. 125–126).

What Basil seems to suggest is that his generation does not wish to be known for initiating a philosophy of indifference, for living uncommitted lives, or for expressing fear of becoming involved. Instead the young people of today prefer to be committed to great causes and responsive to the needs of their fellow men. But this requires a chance during adolescence to try out responsible aspects of the adult role before assuming that station. Conversely, if parents declare adolescents irresponsible and then disallow responsibility, the fiction will come true. It is this unfortunate but common condition in our society that underlies the urgency of Basil's remarks. It may be that "Where there is no vision the people perish"; but have we closely considered that unless the vision of youth can be acted upon it may also vanish?

APPENDIX

Teacher Assessment

Most people who work in a help-agent role with teachers have been subject to questions which seem to treat the inquirer as insignificant. It is always difficult to answer the question: "If Johnny did this or that in my classroom, how should I as a teacher respond?" The implication appears to be that "I as a teacher" is separate from "I as a person"; that is, the proper classroom response must resemble a chess move, some action or remark independent of the personalities involved. Whenever the method for improving teacher-pupil relationships is assumed to be singular, whenever it is believed to be the same for everyone, then the teacher and pupil involved are by definition perceived as insignificant variables. To offer another person alternatives by which he can attain his goals requires knowing something more about him than that he is having difficulty. Help-agents simply cannot offer prescriptive devices apart from a knowledge of its user. In other words, what teacher method is best necessarily relates to who a teacher is as an individual. In my judgment, we err in perceiving the method questions solely in relation to subject matter or pupil age. Since method is also a function of behavior, its best course must relate to teacher identity.

To the extent that a help-agent is unaware of a teacher's individual psycho-social attributes, he may inadvertently suggest behavioral alternatives that are inconsonant with the teacher's personality. For example, to suggest to a teacher who has a high need for structure and has a low tolerance for frustration that he employ strategies involving ambiguity and the attendant anxiety is foolish. Similarly, it may be unwise to counsel a teacher low in measured creative potential to invite much pupil speculation. This is not to say that some teachers cannot, with help, over a period of time accommodate divergent pupil response; it is to imply that suggested alternatives take into account the current personal structure of the teacher for whom intended. With this in mind—each teacher's dignity and mental health—I endeavored through the administration of certain psychological-personality instruments to better know the Preface plan participants who during the 1966–1967 school year would be seeking my assistance. A brief description of the indices chosen to better acquaint myself with the teachers and enable those working with them to offer better counsel follows. A word of caution: The amount of training required on the part of whoever is to properly administer and use the results of these measures is in most cases comparable to membership in the American Psychological Association. In fact, certain of the tests are unavailable without evidence of proper credentials. (In addition to the twelve instruments described, there were also included several measures of local design for which normative data is incomplete. Respectively, these devices relate to teacher motivation, self concept, and reaction to classroom incidents.)

California Psychological Inventory (Gough, 1964). Unlike many of the standard assessments designed for use by persons concerned with problems of deviant behavior, the CPI deals with personality features having a wide pervasive applicability to human behavior and which in addition are related to the healthy aspects of personal functioning rather than to the morbid and pathological. Intended primarily for use with "normal" (non-psychiatrically disturbed) subjects, the CPI has since 1951 been administered to more than 750,000 persons between the ages of twelve and seventy. Each of its eighteen scales is intended to cover one important facet of interpersonal psychology, with the total set providing a comprehensive survey of a person from this social interaction reference.

To emphasize some of the psychological and psychometric clusterings that exist among the various scale purposes, author Harrison Gough has grouped them into four broad class categories:

I. Class I. Measures of Poise, Ascendancy, and Self-Assurance
   1. Dominance: To assess factors of leadership ability, dominance, persistence, and social initiative.
   2. Capacity for Status: To serve as an index of an individual's capacity for status (not his actual or achieved status). The scale attempts to measure the personal qualities and attributes which underlie and lead to status.
   3. Sociability: To identify persons of outgoing, social, participative temperament.
   4. Social Presence: To assess factors such as poise, spontaneity, and self-confidence in personal and social interaction.
   5. Self-Acceptance: To assess factors such as sense of personal worth, self-acceptance, and capacity for independent thinking and action.

6. Sense of Well-being: To identify persons who minimize their worries and complaints and who are relatively free from self-doubt and disillusionment.

II. Class II. Measures of Socialization, Maturity, and Responsibility

7. Responsibility: To identify persons of conscientious, responsible, and dependable disposition and temperament.
8. Socialization: To indicate the degree of social maturity, integrity, and recititude that the individual has attained.
9. Self Control: To assess the degree and adequacy for self-regulation and self-control and fredom from impulsivity and self-centeredness.
10. Tolerance: To identify persons with permissive, accepting, and non-judgmental social beliefs and attitude.
11. Good Impression: To identify persons capable of creating a favorable impression and who are concerned about how others react to them.
12. Communality: To indicate the degree to which an individual's reactions and responses correspond to the modal ("common") pattern established for the inventory.

III. Class III. Measures of Achievement Potential and Intellectual Efficiency

13. Achievement via Conformance: To identify those factors of interest and motivation that facilitate achievement in any setting where conformance is a positive behavior.
14. Achievement via Independence: To identify those factors of interest and motivation that facilitate achievement in any setting where autonomy and independence are positive behaviors.
15. Intellectual Efficiency: To indicate the degree of personal and intellectual efficiency that the individual has attained.

IV. Class IV. Measures of Intellectual and Interest Modes

16. Psychological-mindedness: To measure the degree to which the individual is interested in, and responsive to, the inner needs, motives, and experiences of others.
17. Flexibility: To indicate the degree of flexibility and adaptability of a person's thinking and social behavior.
18. Femininity: To assess the masculinity or femininity of interests.

Edwards Personal Preference Schedule (Edwards, 1959). Personality inventories are generally made up of statements relating to traits in such a way that a "yes" response indicates that the subject believes the statement is characteristic of himself and a "no" response that it is not. On the EPPS, the influence of social desirability in responses has been minimized. Assume that two statements represent different personality traits and that each is equal with respect to social desirability scale values. Under these conditions, selecting from a pair of statements, the statement more characteristic of oneself renders the factor of social desirability less an influent than in a yes-no item choice.

In another respect, Alan Edwards' EPPS departs from most personality inventories which purport to indicate an individual's degree of adjustment, anxiety, emotional stability or, in some instruments, the clinical syndromes of maladaptive response—hysteria, paranoia, or schizophrenia. For purposes of counseling where it often is desirable to report scores back to the testee, such inventories present definite problems. These connotations are less likely to be attached to the fifteen normal, yet relatively independent, manifest need variables measured by the EPPS.

1. Achievement: To do one's best, to be successful, to accomplish something of great significance, to be a recognized authority.
2. Deference: To get suggestions from others, to find out what others think, to follow instructions and do what is expected.
3. Order: To have written work neat and organized, to make plans before starting on a difficult task, to have things organized.
4. Exhibtion: To say witty and clever things, to tell amusing jokes and stories, to talk about personal adventures and experiences, to have others notice and comment upon one's appearance.
5. Autonomy: To say what one thinks about things, to be independent of others in making decisions, to feel free to do what one wants, to do things that are unconventional.
6. Affiliation: To be loyal to friends, to participate in friendly groups, to do things for friends, to form new friendships.
7. Intraception: To analyze one's motives and feelings, to observe others, to understand how others feel about problems, to put oneself in another's place.
8. Succorance: To have others provide help when in trouble, to seek encouragement from others, to have others be kindly, to have others be sympathetic and understanding about personal problems.
9. Dominance: To argue for one's point of view, to be a leader in groups to which one belongs, to be regarded by others as a leader.
10. Abasement: To feel guilty when one does something wrong, to accept blame when things do not go right.
11. Nurturance: To help friends when they are in trouble, to assist others less fortunate, to treat others with kindness and sympathy, to forgive others.
12. Change: To do new and different things, to travel, to meet new people, to experience novelty and change in daily routine, to experiment and try new things.
13. Endurance: To keep at a job until it is finished, to complete any job undertaken, to work hard at a task, to keep at a puzzle or problem until it is solved.
14. Heterosexuality: To go out with members of the opposite sex, to engage in social activities with the opposite sex, to be in love with someone of the opposite sex, to be regarded as physically attractive by those of the opposite sex.
15. Aggression: To attack contrary points of view, to criticize others publicly, to tell others off when disagreeing with them, to get revenge for insults, to become angry, to blame others when things go wrong.

Study of Values: A Scale for Measuring the Dominant Interests in Personality (Allport, Vernon, and Lindzey, 1960). In his book, *Types Of Men,* Edward Spranger defends the view that the personalities of men are best known through the study of their values or evaluative attitudes. Using Spranger's classification, Allport, Vernon and Lindzey have devised a study of values primarily intended for use with college students or with adults of equivalent education. The *Study of Values,* originally published in 1931 and revised in 1960, aims to measure the relative prominence of six basic interests or motives in personality; the theoretical, economic, aesthetic, social, political, and religious. Respectively:

1. The Theoretical: The dominant interest of the theoretical man is the discovery of truth.
2. The Economic: The economic man is characteristically interested in what is useful.
3. The Aesthetic: The aesthetic man sees his highest value in form and harmony.
4. The Social: The highest value for this type is love of people. In the *Study of Values,* it is the altruistic or philanthropic aspect of love that is measured.
5. The Political: The political man is interested primarily in power.
6. The Religious: The highest value of the religious man may be called unity.

The Rosenzweig Picture-Association Study for Assessing Reactions to Frustration (Rosenzweig, Fleming, and Clarke, 1947). The picture-frustration study, or as briefly referred to, the PF instrument, represents a limited projected procedure for disclosing patterns of response to everyday stress that are of widely recognized importance in both normal and abnormal adjustment. Each of the twenty-four cartoon-like pictures comprising the test depicts two people involved in a mildly frustrating situation common to most of us. At the left of each picture a figure is shown saying words that help to describe the other person's frustration or to prove themselves frustrating to him. A blank caption appears above the frustrated person on the right. All expressions of personality and facial features are purposely omitted from the pictures. The situations included are comprised of two types: ego blocking and superego blocking. Ego blocking issues are those in which an obstacle, personal or impersonal, interrupts, disappoints, deprives, or otherwise frustrates the subject. Superego blocking represents some accusation, charge, or incrimination of the subject by someone else.

The person taking the test is instructed to successively inspect each situation and fill in the blank captions with the first appropriate reply entering his mind. It is assumed that the person taking the PF test will either unconsciously or consciously identify himself with the frustrated individual in each pictured situation and in the replies given project his own bias. To assess this, bias scores are assigned to each response regarding the direction of aggression and type of reaction. Subsumed under direction of aggression are: (1) extra-punitiveness—when aggression is turned upon the environment; (2) intropunitiveness—when aggression is turned upon the subject; and (3) impunitiveness—when an evasion of aggression glosses over the frustration. Subsumed under reaction types are: obstacle dominance in which the barriers occasioning the frustrations stand out in the responses; ego defense in which the subject's ego predominates; and need persistence in which resolution of the frustrating situation is emphasized.

Gordon Personal Inventory (Gordon, 1963). Developed from a factor analysis approach, the GPI may be used with students of high school and beyond. The four personality traits which it measures are important ones in determining the adjustment of normal individuals in numerous educational and social situations: cautiousness, original thinking, personal relations, and vigor. High and low scores on each of the scales are interpreted as follows.

Cautiousness: Individuals who are highly cautious, who consider matters very carefully before making decisions and do not like to take chances or run risks, score high on this scale. Those who are impulsive, act on the spur of the moment, make hurried or snap decisions, enjoy taking chances, and seek excitement, score low.

Original Thinking: High scoring individuals like to work on difficult problems, are intellectually curious, enjoy thought-provoking questions and discussions, and like to think about new ideas. Low scoring individuals dislike working on difficult or complicated problems, do not care about acquiring knowledge, and are not interested in thought-provoking questions or discussions.

Personal Relations: High scores are made by those individuals who have great faith and trust in people and are tolerant, patient, and understanding. Low scores reflect a lack of trust or confidence in people and reflect a tendency to be critical of others and to become annoyed or irritated by what others do.

Vigor: High scores on this scale characterize individuals who are vigorous and energetic, who like to work and move rapidly, and who are able to accomplish more than the average person. Low scores are associated with low vitality or energy level, a preference for setting a slow pace, and a tendency to tire easily and be below average in terms of sheer output or productivity.

The Guilford-Zimmerman Temperament Survey (Guilford and Zimmerman, 1949). One of the most often employed instruments to obtain a comprehensive picture of individual personality is the *Guilford-Zimmerman Temperament Survey*. Comprised of 300 items, the survey yields a score index for each of 10 traits that have been identified by factor-analysis procedures. The utility of the traits concept has been amply demonstrated in their clinical applications and in vocational counseling and placement. The ten traits are:

General Activity   Objectivity
Restraint   Friendliness
Ascendance   Thoughtfulness
Sociability   Personal Relations
Emotional Stability   Masculinity

Watson-Glaser Critical Thinking Appraisal (Watson and Glaser, 1952). Some of the important abilities involved in critical thinking are measured by the Watson-Glaser instrument which purports to serve both as a test of such factors and as a tool for their development. Most of the content resembles arguments, problems, and statements that each of us daily encounter in our reading, televiewing, or discussion with other people. Each of the 99 items making up five subtests call for critical thinking about one of two subject matter types. Some items deal with problems of a neutral nature like the weather about which people generally do not have strong feelings. Though parallel in structure, other items relate to economic, social, or racial issues about which people generally have strong feelings and indicate their bias or prejudice. Certainly the emotional impact of each item will vary from person to person but the inclusion of areas of common prejudice or controversy is necessary to provide a partial sample of an individual's thinking about concerns in which he has personal involvement. Naturally any subject's total critical thinking score will probably be reduced by any lack of objectivity. The five subtests are:

Test 1: Inference. Designed to sample ability to discriminate among degrees of truth or falsity or probability of certain inferences drawn from given facts or data.

Test 2: Recognition of Assumptions. Designed to sample ability to recognize unstated assumptions in given assertions or propositions.

Test 3: Deduction. Designed to sample ability to reason deductively from given premises; to recognize the relation of implication between propositions; to determine whether what seems an implication or necessary inference between one proposition and another is indeed such.

Test 4: Interpretation. Designed to sample ability to weigh evidence and to distinguish between unwarranted generalizations and probable inferences which, though not conclusive or necessary, are warranted beyond a reasonable doubt.

Test 5: Evaluation of Arguments. Designed to sample the ability to distinguish between arguments which are strong and important to the question at issue and those which are weak and unimportant or irrelevant.

Torrance Tests of Creative Thinking (Torrance, 1966). In both his verbal and figural tests, Torrance has devised activities that make use of what is known about the nature of the creative thinking process, the qualities of creative products and creative personalities. An attempt is made, however, to assess the products that result from the administration of these two tests in terms of Guilford's divergent thinking factors: fluency, flexibility, originality, and elaboration.

For example, one straightforward model of important elements for creative thinking is the ask and guess subtest, included in the verbal battery to allow a subject a chance to express his curiosity, show an ability to develop hypotheses and think in terms of possibles. The number of relevant responses one produces gives a measure of ideational fluency, while the number of shifts in thinking or categories of questions, causes or consequences, yields an index of flexibility. The statistical infrequency of these questions, causes or consequences or the extent to which the response represents a mental leap or departure from the obvious and commonplace gives the measure of originality. The detail of specificity incorporated into the questions and hypotheses are measures of an ability to elaborate. Additional verbal tasks entail product improvement, unusual uses, unusual questions, and responses to improbable situations.

The figural tasks may require one to think of a picture in which the provided shape is an integral part. An effort is made to elicit an original response by asking subjects to think of something that no one else in the group will produce. The instructions encourage the adding of ideas that will make the picture tell as complete a story as possible. Thus, the product is evaluated for originality and elaboration. Other figural subtests involve incomplete figures and parallel lines which should elicit the creative tendency to bring structure and completeness to whatever is incomplete, while the circles and closed figures require the ability to disrupt or destroy an already closed form.

FIRO B (Shutz, 1966). FIRO stands for "Fundamental Interpersonal Relations Orientation." It signifies the basic idea that each person orients himself in characteristic ways toward other people, and the basic belief that knowledge of these orientations allows for considerable understanding of individual behavior and the interaction of people. The postulate is that every individual has three interpersonal (or group) needs: inclusion, control, and affection.

The interpersonal need for inclusion is defined behaviorally as the need to establish and maintain a satisfactory relation with people with respect to interaction and association. On the level of feelings the need for inclusion is defined as the need to establish and maintain a feeling of mutual interest with other people. This feeling includes being able to take an interest in other people to a satisfactory degree and having other people interested in the self to a satisfactory degree. With regard to the self concept, the need for inclusion is the need to feel that the self is significant and worthwhile.

The interpersonal need for control is defined behaviorally as the need to establish and maintain a satisfactory relation with people with respect to control and power. With regard to feelings, the need for control is defined as the need to establish and maintain a feeling of mutual respect for the competencies and responsibilities of others. This feeling includes being able to respect others to a satisfactory degree; and having others respect self to a satisfactory degree. The need for control, defined at the level of perceiving the self, is the need to feel that one is a competent, responsible person.

The interpersonal need for affection is defined behaviorally as the need to establish and maintain a satisfactory relation with others with respect to love and affection. At the feeling level the need for affection is defined as the need to establish and maintain a feeling of mutual affection with others. This feeling includes being able to love other people to a satisfactory degree; and having others love the self to a satisfactory degree. The need for affection, defined at the level of self concept, is the need to feel the self is lovable.

According to Shutz, this type of formulation stresses the interpersonal nature of these needs. They require that the organism establish a kind of equilibrium, in three different areas, between the self and other people. In order to be anxiety-free, a person must find a comfortable behavioral relation with others with regard to the exchange of interaction, power, and love. The need is neither wholly satisfied by having others respond toward the self in a particular way nor is it wholly satisfied by acting toward others in a particular way. A satisfactory balance must be established and maintained. The six indices of the FIRO-B are:

Wanted Inclusion   Wanted Affection   Wanted Control
Expressed Inclusion   Expressed Affection   Expressed Control

The Myers-Briggs Type Indicator (Myers, 1963). The purpose of this indicator is to implement the theory of type expressed by Carl G. Jung, the neo-Freudian. It was Jung's assumption that much apparently random variation in human behavior is actually quite orderly and consistent because of certain basic differences in the way people prefer to use perception and judgment. By perception is meant those processes of becoming aware with respect to things or people or occurrences or ideas. By judgment is meant the processes of reaching conclusions about what has been perceived. If people differ systematically in what they perceive and the conclusions they come to, they may as a result show corresponding differences in their reactions, in their interests, values, needs, and motivations, in what they do best and in what they like to do best. With this as a working hypothesis, the *Myers-Briggs Type Indicator* purposes to ascertain from self report the basic preferences of people with respect to perception and judgment in order that the effects of these preferences and their combinations may be better understood.

The indicator contains separate indices for determining each of four basic preferences which under this theory structure the individual personality.

Preference as Between	Affects Individual's Choice as to
Extroversion or Introversion	Whether to direct perception and judgment upon environment or world of ideas
Sensing or Intuition	Which of these two kinds of perception to rely on
Thinking or Feeling	Which of these two kinds of judgment to rely on
Judgment or Perception	Whether to use judging or perceptive attitude for dealing with environment

Runner Studies of Attitude Patterns (Runner, 1965). The Runner instrument is designed for people whose daily work requires that they be able at least to recognize and, hopefully, develop resources in other people. It pertains to desires for excitement and personal growth on the one hand versus desires for comfort and personal security on the other. Almost all of the 118 items are derivations or elaborations of this basic conceptual dichotomy of desire for new experience and growth as opposed to desire for comfort and security. It is convenient to think of the twelve scales as related to four discrete types of personal orientation:

1. *Control Oriented,* including
   Emphasis on rules and tradition
   Practical Planfulness
   Hostility
   Passive Compliance
2. *Freedom Oriented,* including
   Experimental Orientation
   Inituitive Orientation
   Resistance to Social Pressure
   Pleasure in Tool Implemented Handskills
3. *Recognition Oriented*
   Extraversiveness
   Desire for Power and Authority
4. *Anxiety Oriented*
   Performance Anxiety
   Social Anxiety

Bibliography

Abbott, Mary K. *The Culturally Handicapped and the Reading Process* (San Francisco: Public Schools Community Improvement Project, 1964), pp. 1–3.

Abernathy, John. "Reflections on Gall and Spurzheim's System of Physiognomy and Phrenology," *The Surgical and Physiological Works* (Vol. II). Hartford: Longman, Hurst, Rees, Orme and Brown, 1825, pp. 45–80.

Adler, Alfred. *Problems of Neurosis.* New York: Cosmopolitan Book Co., 1930, p. 48.

Ahmann, J. Stanley, Glock, Marvin D., and Wardeberg, Helen. *Evaluating Elementary School Pupils.* Boston: Allyn & Bacon, 1960, pp. 60, 115.

Allport, Floyd H. *Theories of Perception and Concept of Structure.* New York: John Wiley & Sons, 1955. 709 pp.

Allport, Gordon W. *The Individual and His Religion.* New York: The Macmillan Company, 1950, pp. 86–98.

———. *The Nature of Prejudice.* Reading, Mass.: Addison-Wesley Publishing Company, Inc., 1958, pp. 282–296.

———. *Becoming.* New Haven: Yale University Press, 1962, pp. 32, 51, 68–71, 72–74.

———. "Crises in Normal Personality Development," *The Teachers College Record,* Vol. 66, No. 3 (December 1964), pp. 235–241.

———, Vernon, Philip E., and Lindzey, Gardner. *Study of Values: A Scale for Measuring the Dominant Interests in Personality (Manual).* Boston: Houghton Mifflin Company, 1960. 19 pp.

Ames, Louise Bates. "Is Your Child in the Wrong Grade?" *Ladies Home Journal,* Vol. 84, No. 6 (June 1967), pp. 119–120, 131.

Amidon, Edmund J. and Flanders, Ned. *The Role of the Teacher in the Classroom.* Minneapolis: Paul S. Amidon & Associates, 1962. 63 pp.

Anastasi, Anne. *Differential Psychology* (3rd ed.). New York: The Macmillan Company, 1958, pp. 295–300.

Anderson, Harold H. "An Experimental Study of Dominative and Integrative Behavior in Children of Preschool Age," *Journal of Social Psychology,* Vol. 8, No. 1 (1937), pp. 335–345.

Andrews, Frank M. "Factors Affecting the Manifestation of Creativity Ability in Scientists," *Journal of Personality,* Vol. 33, No. 1 (March 1965), pp. 140–152.

Arthur, Grace. "A Study of the Achievement of Sixty Grade 1 Repeaters as Compared with that of Nonrepeaters of the Same Mental Age," *Journal of Experimental Education,* Vol. 5, No. 2 (December 1936), pp. 203–205.

Asch, Solomon E. "Studies in Independence and Conformity: A Minority of One Against a Unanimous Majority," *Psychological Monographs,* Vol. 70, No. 9 (1956), pp. 1–70.

———. "Effects of Group Pressures Upon the Modification and Distortion of Judgments," in E. E. Maccoby, T. M. Newcomb, and E. L. Hartley (eds.), *Readings in Social Psychology.* New York: Holt, Rinehart and Winston, 1958, pp. 174–182.

———. *Social Psychology.* Englewood Cliffs, N.J.: Prentice-Hall, 1962. 646 pp.

Ashbaugh, E. J. "Reducing the Variability in Teacher Marks," *Journal of Educational Research,* Vol. 9, No. 3 (March 1924), pp. 185–198.

Atkinson, John W. "Motivational Determinants of Risk-Taking Behavior," *Psychological Review,* Vol. 64, No. 6 (November 1957), pp. 359–372.

———, Bastian, Jarvis R., Earl, Robert W., and Litwin, George H. "The Achievement Motive, Goal Setting and Probability Preferences," *Journal of Abnormal and Social Psychology,* Vol. 60, No. 1 (January 1960), pp. 27–36.

———, and Litwin, George H. "Achievement Motive and Test Anxiety Conceived as Motive to Approach Success and Motive to Avoid Failure," *Journal of Abnormal and Social Psychology,* Vol. 60, No. 1 (January 1960), pp. 52–63.

Ausubel, David P. "Negativism as a Phase of Ego Development," *American Journal of Orthopsychiatry,* Vol. 20 (October 1950), pp. 796–805.

———. *Theory and Problems of Child Development.* New York: Grune and Stratton, 1958.

———, and Ausubel, Pearl. "Ego Development Among Segregated Negro Children," in A. Harry Passow (ed.), *Education in Depressed Areas.* New York: Teachers College, Columbia University, 1963, pp. 109–141.

Ayres, Leonard P., "History and Present Status of Educational Measurements," *The Measurement of Educational Products,* Seventeenth Yearbook of the National Society for the Study of Education, Part II. Bloomington, Ill.: Public School Publishing Company, 1918, pp. 9–15.

Babladelis, Georgia, and Adams, Suzanne. *The Shaping of Personality.* Englewood Cliffs, N.J.: Prentice-Hall, 1967. 517 pp.

Baldwin, Alfred L. *Theories of Child Development.* New York: John Wiley & Sons, 1967, pp. 321–322, 354–357, 360–368, 460–462.

Barnes, Fred P. *Research for the Practitioner in Education.* Washington, D.C.: Department of Elementary School Principals, National Education Association, 1964, pp. 3–11.

Barron, Frank. "The Psychology of Imagination," *Scientific American*, Vol. 199, No. 3 (September 1958), pp. 151–156.

———. *Creativity and Psychological Health*. New York: D. Van Nostrand Co., 1963a, pp. 180–199, 200–213.

———. "Creative Vision and Expression," in Alexander Frazier (ed.), *New Insights and the Curriculum*. Washington, D.C.: Association for Supervision and Curriculum Development, National Education Association, 1963b, pp. 285–305.

Bartholomoi, F., and Schwabe, J. "Der Vorstellungskreis der Berliner Kinder beim Eintritt in die Schule," *Berlin Statistches Jahrbuch*, 1870, pp. 59–77.

Beadle, George, and Beadle, Muriel. *The Language of Life, An Introduction to the Science of Genetics*. Garden City, N.Y.: Doubleday & Company, 1966. 238 pp.

Berg, Ronald H. "Drugs, the Mounting Menace of Abuse: Why Americans Hide Behind a Chemical Curtain," *Look*, Vol. 31, No. 16 (August 8, 1967), pp. 11–17.

Berman, Louise, and Usery, Mary Lou. *Personalized Supervision*. Washington, D.C.: National Education Association, 1966. 55 pp.

Bernard, L. L. *Instinct, A Study in Social Psychology*. New York: Holt, Rinehart & Winston, 1924. 550 pp.

Bettelheim, Bruno. *The Informed Heart*. New York: The Macmillan Company, 1960, pp. 177–236.

Biegel, H. G. "Romantic Love," *American Sociological Review*, Vol. 16, No. 3 (1951), pp. 326–334.

Bindra, Dalbir. *Motivation: A Systematic Reinterpretation*. New York: The Ronald Press Company, 1959, pp. 5–10.

Binet, Alfred. "Nouvelles Recherches sur la Mesure du Niveau Intellectuel chez les Enfants d'Ecole," *L'Année Psychologique*, Vol. 17 (1911), pp. 145–201.

———. *Les Idées Modernes Sur Les Enfants*. Paris: E. Flamarion, 1909. 344 pp.

———, and Simon, Theophile. "Méthodes Nouvelles pour le Diagnostic du Niveau Intellectuel des Anormaux," *L'Année Psychologique*, Vol. 11 (1905), pp. 191–244.

———. "Le Développement de l' Intelligence chez les Enfants," *L'Année Psychologique*, Vol. 14 (1908), pp. 1–90.

Blake, R., and Dennis, W. "The Development of Stereotypes Concerning the Negro," *Journal of Abnormal and Social Psychology*, Vol. 38, No. 4 (October 1943), pp. 525–531.

Blanke, Virgil E. "Planned Change, Public Education and the State," a paper presented in Scottsdale, Arizona, to conferees at an eight-state project, Designing Education for the Future. April 5, 1967. 21 pp.

Bloom, Benjamin S. *Stability and Change in Human Characteristics*. New York: John Wiley & Sons, 1964, pp. 72–89.

———, Davis, Allison, and Hess, Robert. *Compensatory Education for Cultural Deprivation*. New York: Holt, Rinehart and Winston, 1965. 179 pp.

———, Englehart, M. D., Furst, E. J., Hill, W. H., and Krathwohl, D. R. (eds.). *Taxonomy of Educational Objective: The Classification of Educational Objectives, Handbook I: Cognitive Domain*. New York: Longmans Green, 1956. 192 pp.

Bloomberg, Warner. "Professional Education in the Urbanized Society: Teachers for Citizens or Trainers of Denizens?" a paper presented at the Danforth Foundation Conference, Stony Lake, Michigan, September 3, 1966. 19 pp.

————. "The School as a Factory," a paper presented to the Interdistrict Institute, Homewood-Flossmoor, Illinois, February 13, 1967. 17 pp.

Blos, P. *On Adolescence: A Psychoanalytic Interpretation.* New York: The Macmillan Company, 1962. 269 pp.

Boehm, Leonore. "The Development of Independence: A Comparative Study," *Child Development,* Vol. 28 (1957), pp. 85–92.

Bonner, Hubert. *On Being Mindful of Man.* Boston: Houghton Mifflin Company, 1965, pp. 79, 131-164.

Bousfield, W. A., Sedgewick, C. W., and Cohen, B. H., "Certain Temporal Characteristics of the Recall of Verbal Associates," *American Journal of Psycholgoy,* Vol. 57, No. 1 (March 1954), pp. 111–118.

Bowers, William J. "Student Study Shows College Cheating High," *Columbus Dispatch,* Columbus, Ohio, January 24, 1965, p. 3.

Bowlby, John. *Child Care and the Growth of Love.* Baltimore: Penguin Books, 1965, pp. 21–58, 201–235.

Bowman, Paul H. "Family Role in the Mental Health of School Children," *Mental Health and Achievement,* eds. E. Paul Torrance and Robert D. Strom. New York: John Wiley & Sons, 1965, pp. 7–14. Washington, D.C.: U.S. Office of Education, 1958. 151 pp.

————, and Matthews, Charles V. *The Motivation of Youth for Leaving School.* Report on Cooperative Research Project #200.

Bradfield, James M., and Moredock, H. Stewart. *Measurement and Evaluation in Education.* New York: The Macmillan Company, 1957, pp. 148–158.

Broderick, C. B., and Fowler, S. E. "New Patterns of Relationship Between the Sexes Among Pre-adolescents," *Marriage and Family Living,* Vol. 23 (1961), pp. 27–30.

Brogden, H. E. "The Effect of Bias Due to Difficulty Factors in Product-Moment Item Intercorrelations on the Accuracy of Estimation of Reliability," *Educational Psychological Measurement,* Vol. 4, No. 4 (Winter 1946), pp. 517–520.

Bromberg, Walter, *The Mind of Man.* New York: Harper & Row, 1963, pp. 193–195, 200–238.

Brookover, W., Thomas, S., and Patterson, A. "Self-Concept of Ability and School Achievement," *Sociology of Education,* Vol. 37 (Spring 1964), pp. 271–278.

Brooks, Edward. *Normal Methods of Teaching.* Lancaster, Penn.: Normal Publishing Co., 1879, p. 31.

Brown, B. Frank. *The Nongraded High School.* Englewood Cliffs, N.J.: Prentice-Hall, 1963. 223 pp.

————. "Using Research in Program Development," a speech delivered at the Ohio Association for Supervision and Curriculum Development, Curriculum Research Institute, November 15, 1965, Columbus, Ohio.

Brubacher, John S. *Modern Philosophies of Education.* New York: McGraw-Hill Book Company, 1962, pp. 222-231.

Bruner, Jerome S., Jacqueline, J., and Austin, G. *A Study of Thinking.* New York: John Wiley & Sons, 1956. 330 pp.

Bryan, William L., and Harter, Noble. "Studies in the Physiology and Psychology of the Telegraphic Language," *Psychological Review*, Vol. 4, No. 1 (1897), pp. 27–53.

Buckingham, Burdette Ross. "Spelling Ability: Its Measurement and Distribution," in *Teachers College, Columbia University Contributions to Education*, No. 59. New York: Bureau of Publications, Columbia University, 1913. 118 pp.

————. *Research for Teachers*. New York: Silver Burdett & Co., 1926.

Bugental, J. F., and Tannenbaum, Robert. "Sensitivity Training and Being Motivated," in E. Schein and W. Dennis, (eds.), *Personal and Organizational Change Through Group Methods: The Laboratory Approach*. New York: John Wiley & Sons, 1965, pp. 107–113.

Burks, B. S. "The Relative Influence of Nature and Nurture Upon Mental Development," *National Society for the Study of Education, 27th Yearbook*, Part I. Bloomington, Ill.: Public School Publishing Company, 1928, pp. 21–316.

Buros, Oscar. *The Mental Measurement Yearbook 1965*. New Brunswick, N.J.: Rutgers University Press, 1965. 1713 pp.

Burt, Cyril L. "The Inheritance of Mental Ability," *American Psychologist* Vol. 13, No. 1 (January 1958), pp. 1–15.

————, and Howard, M. "A Multiple Factorial Theory of Inheritance and its Application to Intelligence," *British Journal of Statistical Psychology*, Vol. 9 (1956), pp. 93–131.

Bush, Robert N. "The Science and Art of Educating Teachers," in *Improving Teacher Education in the United States*. Bloomington, Ind.: Phi Delta Kappa, 1967, pp. 35–62.

Byrne, Donn, *An Introduction to Personality: A Research Approach*. Englewood Cliffs, N.J.: Prentice-Hall, 1966, pp. 269–271.

Caldwell, Otis, and Courtis, Stuart. *Then and Now in Education, 1845–1923*. New York: World Book Co., 1923, p. 37.

Campbell, Donald T. and Stanley, Julian. *Experimental and Quasi-Experimental Designs for Research*. Chicago: Rand McNally & Company, 1963. 84 pp.

Carter, Robert, "How Invalid Are Marks Assigned by Teachers?" *Journal of Educational Psychology*, Vol. 43, No. 4 (April 1952), pp. 218–228.

Cartwright, Dorwin, and Zander, Alvin. (eds.). *Group Dynamics: Research and Theory*. Evanston, Ill.: Row, Peterson & Co., 1958. 642 pp.

Cashman, John. *The LSD Story*. New York: Fawcett Publications, 1966, pp. 78–91.

Cattell, J. McKeen. "Mental Tests and Measurements," *Mind*, Vol. 15 (July 1890), pp. 375–381.

Cattell, Raymond B. *The Scientific Analysis of Personality*. Baltimore: Penguin Books, 1965, pp. 32–38.

Chapman, H. B. "Organized Research in Education," *The Ohio State University Studies*, Bureau of Educational Research Monographs, No. 7. Columbus: The Ohio State University Press, 1927. 221 pp.

Chauncy, Henry. "Report of the President 1960–1961," in *Annual Report 1960–1961*. Princeton, N.J.: Educational Testing Service, 1961.

Chess, Stella, Thomas, Alexander, and Birch, Herbert G., "How Babies Differ," *McCall's*, Vol. 92, No. 10 (July 1965), p. 73.

Christensen, H. T., "Dating Behavior as Evaluated by High School Students," *American Journal of Sociology*, Vol. 57, No. 6 (May 1952), pp. 500–586.

Christensen, P. R., Guilford, J. P., and Wilson, R. C. "Relations of Creative Response to Working Time and Instructions," *Journal of Experimental Psychology*, Vol. 53, No. 1 (January 1957), pp. 82–88.

Church, Joseph (ed.). *Three Babies: Biographies of Cognitive Development.* New York: Random House, 1966. 323 pp.

Clark, Bill. "Emotional Problems: A Major Factor in Retention," *Southeastern Louisiana College Bulletin* (January 1959), p. 39.

Cline, V. B., Richards, J. M., and Abe, C. "The Validity of a Battery of Creativity Tests in a High School Sample," *Educational and Psychological Measurement*, Vol. 22, No. 4 (Winter 1962), pp. 781–784.

Cline, V. B., Richards, J. M., and Needham, W. E. "Creativity Tests and Achievement in High School Science," *Journal of Applied Psychology*, Vol. 47, No. 3 (June 1963), pp. 184–189.

Coffman, Lotus D. *The Social Composition of the Teaching Population.* New York: Teachers College, Columbia University, 1911, pp. 79–81.

Coleman, James S. "Social Change: Impact on the Adolescent," *National Association of Secondary School Principals Bulletin*, Vol. 49 (1965), pp. 11–14.

Colvin, S. S., and Meyer, I. F., "Imaginative Elements in the Written Work of School Children," *Pedagogical Seminary*, Vol. 13 (1906), pp. 84–93.

Combe, George. *Lectures on Phrenology.* New York: Samuel Colman, 1834, pp. 22–23, 72–73.

Combs, Arthur W. "What Can Man Become?" *The California Journal of Instructional Improvement*, Vol. 4 (1961), pp. 15–23.

Conlin, Marcia R., and Haberman, Martin. "Supervising Teachers of the Disadvantaged," *Educational Leadership* (February 1967), pp. 393–397.

Conner, James. "The Teacher in a World of Increasing Impersonal Relations," in E. Paul Torrance and Robert D. Strom (eds.), *Mental Health and Achievement.* New York: John Wiley & Sons, 1965, pp. 174–181.

Courtis, Stuart A. *Manual of Instruction for Giving and Scoring the Courtis Standard Tests in the 3 R's* (Series A). Detroit: Department of Cooperative Research, Detroit Public Schools, 1910.

Cronbach, Lee J. "Coefficients Alpha and the Internal Structures of Tests," *Psychometrika*, Vol. 16 (1951), pp. 297–334.

————. *Essentials of Psychological Testing.* New York: Harper & Row, 1960. 475 pp.

————. "How Can Instruction be Adapted to Individual Differences?" in Robert M. Gagne (ed.), *Learning and Individual Differences.* Columbus, Ohio: Charles E. Merrill Books, 1967, pp. 23–39.

————. *Educational Psychology* (2nd ed.). New York: Harcourt, Brace & World, 1963, pp. 472–490.

Crowder, Norman. "Automatic Tutoring by means of Intrinsic Programming," in E. Galanter (ed.), *Automatic Teaching: The State of the Art*, New York: John Wiley & Sons, 1959, pp. 109–116.

Crutchfield, Richard S. "Independent Thought in a Conformist World," in S. M. Farber and R. Wilson (eds.), *Conflict and Creativity.* New York: McGraw-Hill Book Company, 1963, pp. 208–228.

Dallam, M. Theresa. "Is the Study of Latin Advantageous to the Study of English?" *Educational Review*, Vol. 54 (1917), pp. 500–503.

Darwin, Charles. *The Origin of Species by Means of Natural Selection.* New York: D. Appleton & Co., 1860. 432 pp.

———. *The Expression of the Emotions in Man and Animals* (2nd ed.). London: Murrary Co., 1904. 397 pp.

Davitz, J. R. "Social Perception and Sociometric Choice of Children," *Journal of Abnormal and Social Psychology,* Vol. 50, No. 1 (1955), pp. 50, 173–176.

Dentler, R. A., and Mackler, B. "Originality: Some Social and Personal Determinants," *Behavioral Science,* Vol. 9, No. 1 (1964), pp. 1–7.

Deutsch, Martin. "Facilitating Development in the Preschool Child: Social and Psychological Perspectives," *Merrill-Palmer Quarterly,* Vol. 10, No. 3 (1964), pp. 249–263.

Deutsch, Morton, and Krauss, Robert M. *Theories in Social Psychology.* New York: Basic Books, 1965, pp. 14–36.

Dewey, John. "The Need for Social Psychology," *Psychology Review,* Vol. 24 (1917), pp. 266–277.

Dillon, Harold. *A Major Educational Problem.* New York: National Child Labor Committee, 1949, pp. 35–40.

Dinitz, Simon. "Adolescents: A Neglected Minority," quoted by Mary McGarey in the *Columbus Dispatch,* Columbus, Ohio, April 11, 1965.

Dollard, J., Doob, L. W., Miller, N. E., Mowrer, O. H., and Sears, R. R. *Frustration and Aggression.* New Haven: Yale University Press, 1939, pp. 27, 40.

Donahue, Wilma. "Adult Learning and Potentialities," in L. H. Evans and G. E. Arnstein (eds.), *Automation and the Challenge to Education.* Washington, D.C.: National Education Association, 1962. 190 pp.

Douvan, Elizabeth, and Adelson, John. *The Adolescent Experience.* New York: John Wiley & Sons, 1966, pp. 174–261.

Drevdahl, J. E. "Factors of Importance for Creativity," *Journal of Clinical Psychology,* Vol. 12, No. 1 (1956), pp. 21–26.

Dugdale, Richard L. *The Jukes: A Study of Crime, Pauperism, Disease and Heredity.* New York: G. P. Putnam's Sons, 1877. 120 pp.

Dunlap, K. "Are There Any Instincts?" *Journal of Abnormal Psychology,* Vol. 14 (1919), pp. 307–311.

Ebel, Robert L. "Estimation of the Reliability of Ratings," *Psychometrika,* Vol. 16 (December 1951), pp. 407–424.

———. "Improving the Competence of Teachers in Educational Measurement," *The Clearing House,* Vol. 36, No. 2 (October 1961).

———. "Measurement and the Teacher," *Educational Leadership,* Vol. 20 (October 1962), pp. 20–24.

———. *Measuring Educational Achievement.* Englewood Cliffs, N.J.: Prentice-Hall, 1965, pp. 60–61, 130–133, 233, 314–315.

Education Training Market Report, Vol. 1, No. 2. Washington, D.C.: Edu-Tech, Inc., April 27, 1965, p. 5.

Edwards, Allen. *Edwards Personal Preference Schedule (Manual).* New York: The Psychological Corporation, 1959. 27 pp.

Ehrenfels, Christian Von. "Über Gestaltqualitäten," *Vierteljahrschrift für Wissenschaftliche Philosophie,* Vol. 14 (1890), pp. 249–292.

Eigen, L. D. "High School Student Reactions to Programmed Instruction," *Phi Delta Kappan,* Vol. 44, No. 6 (1963), pp. 282–285.

Eisenberg, Leon. "A Developmental Approach to Adolescence," *Children,* Vol. 12, No. 4 (1965) pp. 131–135.

Ellinger, Bernice D. "Nonpromotion: A Review Essay," *Theory Into Practice*, Vol. 14, No. 3 (June 1965), pp. 122–127.

Ellis, Λ. "A Study of Human Love Relationships," *Journal of Genetic Psychology*, Vol. 75, 1st half (1949), pp. 67–71.

Elsbree, Willard S. "Pupil Progress in the Elementary School," *Practical Suggestions for Teaching*, No. 5. New York: Teachers College, Columbia University, 1943, p. 86.

Englemann, M. D. "Construction and Evaluation of Programmed Materials in Biology Classroom Use," *American Biology Teacher*, Vol. 25 (1963), pp. 212–214.

Erickson, E. "Identity and the Life Cycle," *Psychological Issues*, Vol. 1, No. 1, Mono. 1. New York: International Universities Press, 1959.

Fairbairn, W. Ronald. *Psychoanalytic Studies of the Personality*. London: Travistock Publications, 1952, p. 145.

Farley, Eugene S., Frey, Alvin J., and Garland, Gertrude. "Factors Related to the Grade Progress of Pupils," *Elementary School Journal*, Vol. 34, No. 3 (November 1933), pp. 186–193.

Feather, N. T. "The Relationship of Persistence at a Task to Expectation of Success and Achievement Related Motives," *Journal of Abnormal and Social Psychology*, Vol. 63, No. 3 (1961), pp. 552–561.

Festinger, Leon. *Conflict, Decision and Dissonance*. Palo Alto: Stanford University Press, 1964. 163 pp.

Finney, J. C. "Some Maternal Influences on Children's Personality and Character," *Genetic Psychological Monograph*, Vol. 63 (1961), pp. 199–278.

Flanders, Ned. "Intent, Action and Feedback: A Preparation for Teaching," *Journal of Teacher Education*, Vol. 16 (September 1963), pp. 251–260.

Fleming, Robert S. "Spilling Over: A Further Look at Pressures," in *Children Under Pressure*. Columbus, Ohio: Charles E. Merrill Books, 1966, pp. 61–70.

Flourens, Pierre J. M. *Recherches Expérimentales sur les Propriétés et les Fonctions du Systeme Nerveux dans les Animaux Vertébrés*. Paris, 1824, pp. 236–241.

―――. *Recherches sur le Développement des Os et des Dents*. Paris: J. B. Bailliere, 1842. 460 pp.

Fordham, Frieda. *An Introduction to Jung's Psychology*. Baltimore: Penguin Books, 1964, pp. 30, 39, 42.

Fowler, Orson S. *Practical Phrenology*. New York: Fowler & Wells Co., 1857, pp. 64–67.

Frank, Lawrence. *On the Importance of Infancy*. New York: Random House, 1966. 207 pp.

Freeman, J. T. "The Effects of Reinforced Practice on Conventional Multiple Choice Tests," *Automated Teaching Bulletin*, Vol. 1 (1959), pp. 19–20.

Freud, Sigmund. "My Views on the Part Played by Sexuality in the Aetiology of the Neurosis (1905), in Phillip Rieff (ed.), *Sexuality and the Psychology of Love*. New York: Collier Books, 1966, pp. 11–19.

―――. "The Sexual Enlightenment of Children (1907)," in Phillip Rieff (ed.), *The Sexual Enlightenment of Children*. New York: Collier Books, 1966, pp. 17–24.

―――. "On the Sexual Theories of Children (1908)," in Phillip Rieff (ed.), *The Sexual Enlightenment of Children*. New York: Collier Books, 1966, pp. 25–40.

————. "The Infantile Genital Organization of the Libido (1923a)," in Phillip Rieff (ed.), *Sexuality and the Psychology of Love.* New York: Collier Books, 1966, pp. 171–175.

————. *The Ego and the Id,* (1923b), ed. James Strachey. New York: W. W. Norton & Co., 1962, pp. 18–29.

————. "The Passing of the Oedipus Complex (1924)," in Phillip Rieff (ed.), *Sexuality and the Psychology of Love.* New York: Collier Books, 1966, pp. 176–182.

————. *On Creativity and the Unconscious* (1925), trans. Joan Rivere. New York: Harper and Row, 1965, pp. 44–54.

————. *The Basic Writings of Sigmund Freud,* trans. and ed. by A. A. Brill. New York: The Modern Library, 1938a. 1001 pp.

————. "Splitting of the Ego in the Defense Process (1938b)," in Phillip Rieff (ed.), *Sexuality and the Psychology of Love.* New York: Collier Books, 1966, pp. 220–223.

Fromm, Erich. *The Fear of Freedom.* London: Routledge and Kegan Paul, 1950, p. 15.

————. *The Sane Society.* New York: Holt, Rinehart and Winston, 1962, pp. 141–151, 166–168.

————. *The Art of Loving.* New York: Harper & Row Publishers, 1962, pp. 52–57, 83–133.

————. *Sigmund Freud's Mission.* New York: Grove Press, 1963, pp. 59–65.

————. *The Heart of Man.* New York: Harper & Row, 1964a, pp. 95–114.

————. *Escape from Authority.* New York: Harper & Row, 1964b, pp. 108–142.

————. "An Interview with Erich Fromm," *McCall's,* Vol. 93, No. 1 (October 1965), pp. 132–133, 213–219.

Frost, Joe L., and Hawkes, Glenn R. (eds.), *The Disadvantaged Child.* Boston: Houghton Mifflin Company, 1966. 445 pp.

Fry, E. B. "Programming Trends," *Audio Visual Instruction,* Vol. 6 (1961), pp. 142–143.

Frymier, Jack M. "Ninety Percent Should Be Women," *Education,* Vol. 84, No. 8 (April 1964), pp. 498–500.

————. *The Nature of the Educational Method.* Columbus, Ohio: Charles E. Merrill Books, 1965, pp. 107–155.

Gage, N. L. "Paradigms for Research on Teaching," in N. L. Gage (ed.), *A Handbook of Research on Teaching,* Chicago: Rand McNally & Co., 1963. pp. 94–141.

Gallagher, Buell. "Man of the Year," *Time,* Vol. 89, No. 1 (January 6, 1967), p. 20.

Galloway, Charles. "Teacher Non-Verbal Communication," *Educational Leadership* (October 1966), pp. 55–63.

Galton, Francis. *English Men and Science: Their Nature and Nurture.* London: The Macmillan Company, 1874. 270 pp.

————. *Inquiries Into Human Faculty and Its Development.* London: The Macmillan Company, 1874. 270 pp.

Gardner, R. W. "Cognitive Styles in Categorizing Behavior," *Journal of Personality,* Vol. 22, No. 1 (1953), pp. 214–233.

Gebhard, Paul. "The 1965 Kinsey Report," *Ladies Home Journal,* Vol. 82, No. 6 (June 1965), p. 42.

Gesell, Arnold, and Ilg, Frances. *Infant and Child in the Culture of Today.* New York: Harper & Row, 1943, pp. 131–158.

Getzels, J. W., and Jackson, P. W. *Creativity and Intelligence.* New York: John Wiley & Sons, 1962. 293 pp.

Ghiselin, Brewster (ed.), *The Creative Process.* Berkeley: University of California Press, 1952, pp. 6, 16–17.

Gilot, Françoise, and Lake, Carlton. *Life with Picasso.* New York: McGraw-Hill Book Company, 1964. 350 pp.

Glaser, R., Homme, L. E., and Evans, J. L. "An Evaluation of Textbooks in Terms of Learning Principles," in A. A. Lumsdaine and R. Glaser (eds.), *Teaching Machines and Programmed Learning: A Source Book.* Washington, D.C.: National Education Association, 1960, pp. 437–445.

Gleason, Gerald. "School-University Cooperative Research," a paper presented to the Ohio Association of Supervision and Curriculum Development, Research Institute, Columbus, Ohio, November 15, 1965.

Goddard, H. H. "A Revision of the Binet Scale," *Training School Bulletin,* Vol. 8 (June 1911a), pp. 56–62.

———. "Two Thousand Children Measured by the Binet Measuring Scale of Intelligence," *Pedagogical Seminary,* Vol. 18 (June 1911b), pp. 232–259.

Goertzel, V., and Goertzel, M. G. *Cradles of Eminence.* Boston: Little Brown and Company, 1962. 362 pp.

Goodlad, John I. "Some Effects of Promotion and Nonpromotion Upon the Social and Personal Adjustment of Children," *Journal of Experimental Education,* Vol. 22 (June 1954), pp. 301–328.

———. "Meeting Children Where They Are," *Saturday Review,* Vol. 48 (March 20, 1965), pp. 57–59, 72–74.

———, and Anderson, Robert H. *The Non-Graded Elementary School* (rev. ed.). New York: Harcourt, Brace and World, 1963, pp. 30–43.

Gordon, Leonard. *Gordon Personal Inventory (Manual).* New York: Harcourt, Brace & World, 1963. 20 pp.

Gordon, William J. *Synectics.* New York: Harper & Row, 1961. 180 pp.

Gotkin, Lassar G., and Goldstein, Leo S. "Programmed Instruction in the Schools: Innovation and Innovator," in Matthew B. Miles (ed.), *Innovation in Education.* New York: Bureau of Publications, Teachers College, Columbia University, 1964, pp. 231–48.

Gough, Harrison. *California Psychological Inventory (Manual).* Palo Alto: Consulting Psychologists Press, Inc., 1964. 40 pp.

Gowan, John Curtis, Demos, George D., and Torrance, E. Paul. *Creativity: Its Educational Implications.* New York: John Wiley & Sons, 1967. 336 pp.

Grafton, Samuel. "Teachers Who Make Children Hate School," *McCall's,* Vol. 92, No. 4 (January 1966), p. 68.

———. "Pressures That Push Children into the Wrong Careers," *McCall's,* Vol. 93, No. 9 (June 1966), p. 67.

Gray, J. Stanley. *Psychological Foundations of Education.* New York: American Book Company, 1935, pp. 48–52.

Gray, Susan, and Klaus, R. A. *Interim Report: Early Training Project.* Nashville, Tenn.: George Peabody College and Murfreeboro, Tennessee City Schools, 1963.

Greene, Harry A., Jorgensen, Albert N., and Gerberich, J. Raymond. *Measurement and Evaluation in the Secondary School.* New York: Longmans Green and Company, 1954, pp. 26, 27, 31, 68, 69, 81, 318, 319.

Gross, Leonard. "Sex Education Comes of Age," *Look,* Vol. 30, No. 5 (March 8, 1966), p. 22.

Group for the Advancement of Psychiatry. *Sex and the College Student.* New York: Atheneum, 1965, pp. 69–78.

Guba, Egon. "Methodological Strategies for Educational Change," a paper presented to the Conference on Strategies for Educational Change, Washington, D.C., November 8–10, 1965. 38 pp.

———, and Clark, David. "An Examination of Potential Change Roles in Education," a paper presented at the symposium on Innovation in Planning School Curricula. National Education Association Center for the Study of Instruction, Arlie House, Virginia, October, 1965a.

———. "One Perspective on Change," an interview by Virgil Blanke in *Strategies for Educational Change Newsletter,* Vol. I, No. 2 (October 1965b), Columbus, The Ohio State University, pp. 2–4.

Guilford, Joy P. "Creativity," *American Psychologist,* Vol. 5, No. 9 (September 1950), pp. 444–454.

———. "Measurement and Creativity," *Theory Into Practice,* Vol. 5, No. 4 (October 1966), pp. 186–189.

———. *Psychometric Methods.* New York: McGraw-Hill Book Company, 1954, pp. 351, 380.

———. *Personality.* New York: McGraw-Hill Book Company, 1959, pp. 142–161, 385–386.

———. "Potentiality for Creativity and Its Measurement," *Proceedings of the 1962 Invitational Conference on Testing Problems.* Princeton: Educational Testing Service, 1963, pp. 31–39.

———, and Zimmerman, Wayne. *The Guilford-Zimmerman Survey (Manual).* Beverly Hills: Sheridan Supply Company, 1949. 12 pp.

Gulliksen, Harold. "The Relation of Item Difficulty and Inter-Item Correlation to Test Variance and Reliability," *Psychometrika,* Vol. 10 (June 1945), pp. 79–91.

Guttmacher, Alan R., Tyler, Edward R., and Moss, Richard. "Infertile Husbands and Wives," *Ladies Home Journal,* Vol. 84, No. 5 (May 1967), p. 24.

Guttmann, L. "A Basis for Analyzing Test-Retest Reliability," *Psychometrika,* Vol. 10 (1945), pp. 255–282.

Hadfield, J. A. *Psychology and Mental Health.* London: George Allen & Unwin Ltd., 1950, pp. 377–388.

———. *Mental Health and the Psychoneuroses.* London: George Allen & Unwin Ltd., 1952, pp. 131–144.

———. *Childhood and Adolescence.* Baltimore: Penguin Books, 1962. pp. 119–121, 133–146, 156–157, 167, 194, 210–215.

Halek, Loretta. "Atmosphere for Creativity," *Delta Kappa Gamma Bulletin,* Vol. 31 (Summer 1965), p. 11.

Hall, Calvin, and Lindzey, Gardner. *Theories of Personality.* New York: John Wiley & Sons, 1966, pp. 32–36, 195–196, 257–295.

Hall, G. Stanley. *The Contents of Children's Minds on Entering School* (2nd ed.). New York: E. L. Kellog & Co., 1883. 56 pp.

————. *Aspects of Child Life and Education.* Boston: Ginn & Co., 1907, pp. 1–52.

Hall, Joseph. *A Study of Dropouts.* Miami, Florida: Dade County Public Schools, Department of Research and Information, 1964, p. 21.

Halpin, Andrew W., and Croft, Don B. *The Organizational Climate of Schools.* Washington, D. C.: U.S. Office of Education, 1962. 187 pp.

Hamachek, Don E. (ed.), *The Self in Growth, Teaching and Learning.* Englewood Cliffs, N.J.: Prentice-Hall, 1965. 576 pp.

Harris, D. B., Gough, H. G., and Martin, W. E. "Children's Ethnic Attitudes: Relationships to Parental Beliefs Concerning Child Training," *Child Development*, Vol. 21 (1950), pp. 169–181.

Hartmann, B. *Die Analyse des Kindlichen Gedankenkreises als die Naturgemässe des ersten Schulunterrichts.* Annaberg, Germany: H. Graser, 1890.

Hartmann, George W., *Gestalt Psychology.* New York: The Ronald Press Company, 1935, p. 172.

Hartrup, W. W., and Keller, E. D. "Nurturance in Preschool Children and its Relation to Dependency," *Child Development*, Vol. 31, No. 4 (1960), pp. 681–689.

Havighurst, Robert. "Overcoming Value Differences," in Robert D. Strom (ed.), *The Inner-City Classroom: Teacher Behaviors*, Columbus, Ohio: Charles E. Merrill Books, 1966, pp. 41–56.

Heider, Fritz. *The Psychology of Interpersonal Relations.* New York: John Wiley & Sons, 1958. 322 pp.

Hemingway, Ernest. *A Moveable Feast.* New York: Charles Scribner's Sons, 1965, pp. 13, 17, 154.

Henry, Nelson B. (ed.). *The Dynamics of Instructional Groups: Sociopsychological Aspects of Teaching and Learning, 59th Yearbook*, Nat'l. Soc. for the Study of Ed. Part II. Chicago: University of Chicago Press, 1960. 286 pp.

Hess, Robert D., "Maternal Teaching Styles and Emotional Retardation," in E. Paul Torrance and Robert D. Strom (eds.), *Mental Health and Achievement.* New York: John Wiley & Sons, 1965, pp. 15–23.

————, and Shipman, Virginia C., "Early Experience and the Socialization of Cognitive Modes in Children," *Child Development*, Vol. 36, No. 4 (1965), pp. 869–885.

Hilgard, Ernest R. "Human Motives and the Concept of Self," in C. L. Stacey and M. DeMartine (eds.), *Understanding Human Motivation*, Cleveland: Howard Allen, 1958, pp. 196–210.

————. "A Perspective on the Relationship Between Learning Theory and Educational Practices," in Ernest R. Hilgard (ed.), *Theories of Learning and Instruction, 63rd Yearbook*, National Society for the Study of Education, Part I. Chicago: The Society, 1964, pp. 402–418.

————. "The Place of Gestalt Psychology and Field Theories in Contemporary Learning Theory," in Ernest R. Hilgard (ed.), *Theories of Learning and Instruction, 63rd Yearbook*, National Society for the Study of Education, Part I. Chicago: The Society, 1964, pp. 54–77.

Hillegas, M. B. "A Scale for the Measurement of Quality in English Composition by Young People," *Teachers College Record*, Vol. 13 (September 1912), pp. 331–384.

Hillson, Henry T. *The Demonstration Guidance Project* (George Washington High School, 1957–1962). New York: Board of Education, 1963. 31 pp.

Hinely, Reginald T., Coody, Ben E., Galloway, Charles, and Sandefur, Walter S. "An Exploratory Study of Teaching Styles Among Student Teachers," *Journal of Experimental Education* (Winter 1966), pp. 30–35.

Hock, Ellen R. "The Relation of Culture to the Reflection-Impulsivity Dimension," unpublished M.A. thesis, The Ohio State University, Columbus, 1967. 54 pp.

Hogan, Barbara. "The Silent Teens," *Potomac, The Washington Post*, February 16, 1964, pp. 4–9.

Hoffman, Martin, "Childbearing Practices and Moral Development: Generalizations from Empirical Research," *Child Development*, Vol. 34, No. 2 (1963), pp. 295–318.

Holland, J. G., and Skinner, B. F. *The Analysis of Behavior*. New York: McGraw-Hill Book Company, 1961. 337 pp.

Hollander, Charles. "Man of the Year," *Time*, Vol. 89, No. 1 (January 6, 1967), p. 22.

Holmes, Jack A. *Speech, Comprehension and Power in Reading*. Berkeley: University of California Press, 1964.

Hoppock, Robert. "The Use and Misuse of Occupational Information," an address to Ohio Guidance Personnel delivered in Columbus, Ohio, June 17, 1965.

Horney, Karen. *New Ways in Psychoanalysis*. New York: W. W. Norton Co., 1939.

Horrocks, John E. "The Adolescent," in Leonard Carmichael (ed.), *Manual of Child Psychology*, New York: John Wiley & Sons, 1965, pp. 712–715, 723.

———, and Buker, Mae. "A Study of the Friendship Fluctuations of Pre-adolescents," *Journal of Genetic Psychology*, Vol. 78 (1951), pp. 131–144.

Horst, P. "A Generalized Expression for the Reliability of Measures," *Psychometrika*, Vol. 14 (1949), pp. 21–31.

Hoyt, Cyril. "Test Reliability Obtained by Analysis of Variance," *Psychometrika*, Vol. 6 (1941), pp. 153–160.

Hull, Clark. *Aptitude Testing*. New York: World Book Co., 1928. 535 pp.

Hulten, C. E. "The Personal Element in Teacher's Marks," *Journal of Educational Research*, Vol. 12, No. 1 (June 1925), pp. 49–55.

Hunt, J. McV. "The Psychological Basis for Using Preschool Enrichment as an Antidote for Cultural Deprivation," *Merrill-Palmer Quarterly*, Vol. 10 (1964), pp. 209–245.

Hurlock, Elizabeth B. "Evaluation of Certain Incentives Used in Schoolwork," *Journal of Educational Psychology*, Vol. 16 (1925), pp. 145–159.

———. *Adolescent Development*. New York: McGraw-Hill Book Company, 1955, pp. 360, 394–395.

———. *Child Development*. New York: McGraw-Hill Book Company, 1964, pp. 192, 261–265, 397.

Huxley, Thomas H. "On the Natural Inequality of Men, (1890)," in *Method and Results* (Vol. I). New York: D. Appleton and Co., 1894, pp. 290–335.

Huxley, Aldous. *The Doors of Perception/Heaven and Hell*. New York: Harper & Row, 1954. 185 pp.

Ilg, Francis, and Ames, Louise. *School Readiness: Behavior Tests Used at the Gesell Institute*. New York: Harper & Row, 1965. 396 pp.

Jackson, Donald. "Crack-Ups on the Campus," *Life,* Vol. 58, No. 1 (January 8, 1965), pp. 60–73.

Jackson, R. W., and Ferguson, George. *Studies on the Reliability of Tests,* Department of Educational Research Bulletin #12. Toronto: University of Toronto, 1941.

Jacobi, Jolande. *The Psychology of C. G. Jung.* New Haven: Yale University Press, 1964. 193 pp.

James, William. *The Principles of Psychology,* Vols. I and II. New York: Holt, Rinehart & Winston, 1890, pp. 383–441, 663–665.

Jastrow, Joseph. *Wish and Wisdom.* New York: D. Appleton Century Co., 1935, pp. 246, 248, 296.

Johnson, Franklin, W. "A Study of High School Grades," *School Review,* Vol. 19 (January 1911), pp. 13–24.

Johnson, G. Orville. "Motivating the Slow Learner," in Robert D. Strom (ed.), *The Inner-City Classroom: Teacher Behaviors,* Columbus, Ohio: Charles E. Merrill Books, 1966, pp. 111–130.

Johnson, Ronald, and Medinnus, Gene. *Child Psychology: Behavior and Development.* New York: John Wiley & Sons, 1965, pp. 330–332, 467–472.

Jones, Mary Cover. "Elimination of Children's Fears," *Journal of Experimental Psychology,* Vol. 7, No. 5 (1924), p. 382.

Jones, Ernest. *The Life and Work of Sigmund Freud.* New York: Basic Books, 1953, p. 13.

Jourard, Sidney M. *Personal Adjustment: An Approach Through the Study of Healthy Personality.* New York: The Macmillan Company, 1958, pp. 233–255, 373–383.

Judd, Charles. "Relation of Special Training to General Intelligence," *Educational Review,* Vol. 36 (June 1908), p. 42.

Jung, Carl G. *Psychological Types.* London: Routledge & Kegan Paul, 1923, pp. 463, 551, 568.

————. *Modern Man in Search of a Soul.* New York: Harcourt, Brace & World, 1933, p. 85.

————. *The Undiscovered Self.* London: Routledge & Kegan Paul, 1958, pp. 77–78.

————. *Psychological Reflections,* ed. Jolande Jacobi. New York: Harper & Row, 1961. 340 pp.

————. *Psychology of the Unconscious.* New York: Dodd, Mead and Company, 1965. 566 pp.

Kagan, Jerome. "American Longitudinal Research on Psychological Development," *Child Development,* Vol. 35, No. 1 (1964), pp. 1–32.

————. "Impulsive and Reflective Children: Significance of Conceptual Tempo," in J. Krumboltz (ed.), *Learning and the Educational Process,* Chicago: Rand McNally, 1965, pp. 133–161.

————, Moss, H. A., and Sigel, I. E. "Conceptual Style and the Use of Affect Labels," *Merrill-Palmer Quarterly,* Vol. 6, No. 4 (1960), pp. 261–278.

————, Rosman, B. L., Day, D., Albert, J. and Phillips, W., "Information Processing in the Child: Significance of Analytic and Reflective Attitudes," *Psychological Monographs General and Applied,* Vol. 78, No. 1 (1964), pp. 1–37.

Kamii, Constance K., and Weikart, David P., "Marks, Achievement and Intelligence of Seventh Graders Who Were Retained (Nonpromoted) Once in Elementary School," *Journal of Educational Research*, Vol. 56, No. 9 (May–June, 1963), pp. 452–459.

Kant, Immanuel. *Critique of Pure Reason*, trans. S. M. Meiklejohn. London: Bell and Daldy, 1872. 517 pp.

————. *Critique of Practical Reason*, trans. Thomas Abbott. London: Longmans Green and Company, 1883, 368 pp.

————. *Critique of Judgment*, trans. James E. Meredith. Oxford: Clarendon Press, 1961. 180 pp.

Katona, G. *Organizing and Memorizing: Studies in the Psychology of Learning and Teaching*. New York: Columbia University Press, 1940. 318 pp.

Kawin, Ethel. *Later Childhood and Adolescence*. New York: The Macmillan Company, 1963, pp. 70–72, 306–308.

Keach, Everett T., Fuller, Robert, and Gardner, William E. *Education and Social Crisis*. New York: John Wiley & Sons, 1967. 413 pp.

Kerr, Clark. *Meet the Press* (National Broadcasting Company). Washington, D.C.: Merkle Press, September 25, 1966, p. 5.

Keyes, Charles Henry. *Progress Through the Grades of City Schools*. New York: Bureau of Publications, Teachers College, Columbia University, 1911.

Kinsey, Alfred, Pomeroy, Wardell, Martin, Clyde, and Gebhard, Paul. *Sexual Behavior in the Human Female*. New York: Pocket Books, 1965, pp. 80–83, 122–131, 166–173, 446–501.

Kirkpatrick, E. A. "Individual Tests of School Children," *Psychological Review*, Vol. 5, No. 7 (1900), p. 274.

Klein, G. S. "Cognitive Control and Motivation," in G. Lindzey (ed.), *Assessment of Human Motives*. New York: Holt, Rinehart & Winston, 1958, pp. 87–118.

Knapp, Robert R. "Relationship of a Measure of Self-Actualization to Neuroticism and Extroversion," *Journal of Consulting Psychology*, Vol. 29, No. 2 (April 1965), pp. 168–172.

Kneller, George F. *Existentialism and Education*. New York: John Wiley & Sons, 1964. 170 pp.

————. *The Art and Science of Creativity*. New York: Holt, Rinehart & Winston, 1965, p. 28.

Koffka, Kurt. *The Growth of the Mind*. New York: Harcourt, Brace & World, 1925, pp. 167, 209–210.

————. *Principles of Gestalt Psychology*. New York: Harcourt, Brace & World, 1935. 720 pp.

Kogan, Nathan, and Wallach, Michael. *Risk Taking: A Study in Cognition and Personality*. New York: Holt, Rinehart and Winston, 1964, pp. 95–124.

Kohler, Wolfgang. *The Mentality of Apes*. New York: Humanities Press, 1956. pp. 33, 34, 125–128, 265.

————. "Gestalt Psychology Today," *The American Psychologist*, Vol. 14, No. 12 (December 1959), pp. 727–734.

————. *Dynamics in Psychology*. New York: Grove Press, 1960. 156 pp.

Kontos, Peter G., and Murphy, James J. (eds.). *Teaching Urban Youth*. New York: John Wiley & Sons, 1967. 346 pp.

Kubie, Lawrence S. *Neurotic Distortion of the Creative Process*. Lawrence: University of Kansas Press, 1958, pp. 104–136.

Kuder, G. F., and Richardson, M. W. "The Theory of the Estimation of Test Reliability," *Psychometrika*, Vol. 2 (September 1037), pp. 151–160.

Kuhlmann, F. *A Handbook of Mental Tests*. Baltimore: Warwick & York, 1922.

Lafferty, H. M. "Reasons for Pupil Failure—A Progress Report," *American School Board*, 118 (July 1948), pp. 18–20.

Lamarck, Jean P. *Philosophie Zoologique*. Paris: G. Bailliere, 1830. 475 pp.

————. *Histoire Naturelle Des Animaux Sans Vertèbres*. Brussels: Meline, Cans et Compagnie, 1837, pp. 11–115.

Landreth, Catherine. *Early Childhood Behavior and Learning* (2nd ed.). New York: Alfred A. Knopf, 1958. 388 pp.

Lavater, Johann C. *Essays in Physiognomy*, trans. Henry Hunter. London: J. Murray Co., 1789. Vol. I, 281 pp.; Vol. II, 444 pp.; Vol. III, 437 pp.

Lawrence, Muriel. "Sex and the Student: Should Colleges Cooperate?" *Columbus Citizens Journal*, Columbus, Ohio, November 23, 1965, p. 18.

Lawson, Chester. *Brain Mechanisms and Human Learning*. Boston: Houghton Mifflin Company, 1967, pp. 3–26, 92–100.

Leahy, Alice M. "Nature-Nurture and Intelligence," *Genetic Psychology Monographs*, Vol. 17, No. 4 (1935), pp. 235–308.

Lee, C. L., Kagan, J., and Rabson, A. "Influence of a Preference for Analytic Categorization Upon Concept Acquisition," *Child Development*, Vol. 34, No. 2 (1963), pp. 433–442.

Lee, J. Murray, and Segel, David. *Testing Practices of High School Teachers*, U.S. Office of Education Bulletin, No. 9. Washington, D.C.: U.S. Government Printing Office, 1936, p. 6.

Lehman, Harvey C. *Age and Achievement*. Princeton: Princeton University Press, 1953. 358 pp.

————. "The Psychologist's Most Creative Years," *American Psychologist*, Vol. 21, No. 4 (April 1966), pp. 363–369.

LeShan, Eda. "What Children Learn When They Play," *Redbook*, Vol. 129, No. 3 (July 1967), p. 67.

Levin, H., and Sears, Robert R. "Identification with Parents as a Determinant of Doll Play Aggression," *Child Development*, Vol. 27, No. 2 (1956), pp. 135–153.

Lewin, Kurt, *Resolving Social Conflicts*. New York: Harper & Row, 1948. 230 pp.

Lifton, Robert J. *Thought Reform and the Psychology of Totalism*. New York: W. W. Norton Co., 1961. 510 pp.

Lindquist, E. F. "The Theory of Test Construction," in Herbert E. Hawkes, E. F. Lindquist, and C. R. Mann (eds.), *The Construction and Use of Achievement Examinations*. Boston: Houghton Mifflin Company, 1936, pp. 17–106.

————. *First Course in Statistics*. Boston: Houghton Mifflin Company, 1942, pp. 107–108, 222–223.

————. *Design and Analysis of Experiments in Psychology and Education*. Boston: Houghton Mifflin Company, 1953, pp. 357–382.

————. *Educational Measurement*. Washington, D.C.: American Council on Education, 1955. 819 pp.

Lippincott, Rick. "Syphilis, A Growing Problem—Columbus Cases Rise," *Columbus Dispatch*, Columbus, Ohio, March 24, 1966, p. 23.

Locke, John. *Some Thoughts Concerning Education.* London: A. Bettesworth and C. Hitch, 1732. 331 pp.

———. *Conduct of the Understanding,* ed. Thomas Fowler. Oxford: Clarendon Press, 1901, pp. 6–12, 45–46.

Lowenfeld, Viktor, and Brittain, W. Lambert. *Creative and Mental Growth* (4th ed.). New York: The Macmillan Company, 1965. 412 pp.

Lowes, John Livingstone. *The Road to Tanadu: A Study on the Ways of the Imagination.* Boston: Houghton Mifflin Company, 1927, p. 443.

Lumsdaine, A. A. "Instruments and Media of Instruction," in N. L. Gage (ed.), *Handbook of Research on Teaching.* Chicago: Rand McNally & Co., 1963, pp. 583–682.

Lyman, Howard B. *Test Scores and What They Mean.* Englewood Cliffs, N.J.: Prentice-Hall, 1963, pp. 28–30, 51.

Macfarlane, Jean W., Allen, Lucile, and Honzik, Marjorie P. *A Developmental Study of the Behavior Problems of Normal Children Between Twenty-One Months and Fourteen Years.* Berkeley: University of California Press, 1954. 221 pp.

MacKinnon, Donald W. "Architectus Creator Varietas Americanus," *Journal of the American Institute of Architects,* Vol. 24 (1960), pp. 31–35.

———. "The Highly Effective Individual," *Teachers College Record,* Vol. 61, No. 7 (April 1960), pp. 367–378.

———. "Fostering Creativity in Students of Engineering," *Journal of Engineering Education,* Vol. 52, No. 3 (December 1961), pp. 129–142.

———. "The Nature and Nurture of Creative Talent," *American Psychologist,* Vol. 17, No. 7 (July 1962), pp. 484–495.

———. "Testing to Identify Creative People," a speech delivered at The Ohio State University, Columbus, February 19, 1965.

Maclay, W. S., Guttmann, E., and Gross, Mayer. "Spontaneous Drawing as an Approach to Some Problems of Psychopathology," in *Proceedings of the Royal Society of Medicine,* 1938.

McCall, William A. "A New Kind of School Examination," *Journal of Educational Research,* Vol. 1, No. 1 (January 1920), pp. 33–46.

McClelland, David C. "Measuring Motivation in Fantasy: The Achievement Motive," in David C. McClelland (ed.), *Studies in Motivation,* New York: Appleton-Century Crofts, 1955. pp. 401–413.

——— (ed.), *Studies in Motivation.* New York: Appleton-Century Crofts, 1955. 552 pp.

———. "Risk Taking in Children with High and Low Need for Achievement," in John Atkinson (ed.), *Motives in Fantasy, Action and Society,* Princeton: D. Van Nostrand Co., 1958, pp. 306–321.

McDonald, Frederick J. "The Influence of Learning Theories on Education (1900–1950)," in Ernest R. Hilgard (ed.), *Theories of Learning and Instruction, 63rd Yearbook,* National Society for the Study of Education, Part I. Chicago: The Society, 1964, pp. 1–26.

McDougall, William. *An Introduction to Social Psychology* (5th ed.). London: Methuen, 1916. 431 pp.

———. *The Energies of Men.* New York: Scribner's Sons, 1933, pp. 97–106.

McElwa, Edna Willis. "A Study of Truants and Retardation," *Journal of Juvenile Research,* Vol. 15 (July 1931), pp. 209–214.

McKenney, Ruth. "Paris! City of Children," *Hoilday,* Vol. 13, No. 4 (April 1953), pp. 63–68.

McKinney, B. T. "Promotion of Pupils a Problem of Educational Administration," unpublished doctoral dissertation, University of Illinois, Urbana, 1928.

Maddi, Salvatore, R. "Motivational Aspects of Creativity," *Journal of Personality,* Vol. 33, No. 3 (September 1965), pp. 330–347.

Malinowsky, B. *Sex Repression in Savage Society.* New York: Harcourt, Brace & World, 1927. 285 pp.

Mandelbaum, David C. "The Interplay of Conformity and Diversity," in S. M. Farber and R. Wilson (eds.), *Conflict and Creativity,* New York: McGraw-Hill Book Company, 1963, pp. 241–52.

Mann, Horace. "Boston Grammar and Writing Schools," *Common School Journal,* Vol. 7, No. 19 (October 1, 1845), pp. 289–304.

Maslow, Abzraham. *Motivation and Personality.* New York: Harper & Row, 1954. 411 pp.

———. "Creativity in Self-Actualizing People," in H. H. Anderson (ed.), *Creativity and Its Cultivation.* New York: Harper & Row, 1959a, pp. 83–95.

———. (ed.). *New Knowledge in Human Values.* New York: Harper & Row, 1959b. 268 pp.

Masters, William, and Johnson, Virginia. *Human Sexual Response.* Boston: Little, Brown & Co., 1966, pp. 64–67.

Mayer, Frederick. *A History of Educational Thought.* Columbus, Ohio: Charles E. Merrill Books, 1960, p. 143.

Mead, Margaret. "Early Adolescence in the United States," *Bulletin of the National Association of Secondary-School Principals,* Vol. 49 (April 1965), pp. 5–10.

———. "The Changing Cultural Patterns of Work and Leisure," presented to the Seminar on Manpower Policy and Program, Washington, D.C., February 16, 1966a. 38 pp.

———. "On Aggression," *Redbook,* Vol. 128, No. 1 (November 1966b), p. 34.

———. "The Gift of Personal Independence," *Redbook,* Vol. 128, No. 2 (December 1966c), p. 26.

Medinnus, Gene. "Objective Responsibility in Children: A Comparison with Piaget's Data," *Journal of Genetic Psychology,* Vol. 101, 1st half (September 1962), pp. 127–133.

———. *Readings in the Psychology of Parent-Child Relations.* New York: John Wiley & Sons, 1967. 371 pp.

Medley, Donald M., and Lantz, Donald L. "Application of Teacher Behavior Research," a speech delivered at the American Educational Research Association, New York City, February, 1967. 22 pp.

Mednick, Sarnoff. "An Orientation to Research in Creativity" (Research Memo No. 2). Berkeley: University of California, Institute of Personality Assessment and Research, 1958.

———. "The Associative Basis of the Creative Process," *Psychological Review,* Vol. 69, No. 3 (1962), pp. 220–232.

Melton, James. *Education and the Gestalt Theory of Generalization.* Columbus: The Ohio State University, Ph.D. dissertation, 1932, pp. 99–167.

Mendel, Gregor. *Versuche Über Pflanzen-hybriden.* New York: Hafner Publishing Co., 1865. 47 pp.

Menninger, Karl. *Theory of Psychoanalytic Technique.* New York: Harper & Row, 1964, pp. 99–123.

Miles, Matthew B. *Learning to Work in Groups: A Program Guide for Educational Leaders.* New York: Bureau of Publications, Teachers College, Columbia University, 1959. 285 pp.

———— (ed.), *Innovation in Education.* New York: Bureau of Publications, Teachers College, Columbia University, 1964. 689 pp.

————, "Induction of Organizational Change in School Systems," a paper presented to the Ohio Association for Supervision and Curriculum Development, Research Institute, Columbus, Ohio, November 16, 1965.

————, *et al.* "Development-Diffusion-Adoption," a paper by the American Educational Research Association Committee on Research Utilization, Washington, D.C., 1965. 6 pp.

Milgram, S. "Behavioral Study of Obedience," *Journal of Abnormal and Social Psychology,* Vol. 67, No. 4 (October 1963), pp. 371–378.

————. "Group Pressure and Action Against a Person," *Journal of Abnormal and Social Psychology,* Vol. 69, No. 2 (August 1964), pp. 137–143.

————. "Some Conditions of Obedience and Disobedience to Authority," *Human Relations,* Vol. 18 (1965), pp. 5–20.

Mills, C. A., and Ogle, C. "Physiological Sterility of Adolescence," *Human Biology,* Vol. 8, No. 4 (December 1936), pp. 607–615.

Missildine, Hugh. *Your Inner Child of the Past.* New York: Simon and Schuster, 1963, pp. 42–55.

Mohr, Louise, and Washburne, C. W. "The Winnetka Social-Science Investigation," *The Elementary School Journal,* Vol. 23, No. 4 (December 1922), pp. 267–275.

Monroe, Walter S., Odell, Charles W., Herriott, M. E., Engelhart, Max O., and Hull, Mabel R. *Ten Years of Educational Research 1918–1927.* Urbana: University of Illinois Press, 1928, pp. 48, 79–80.

Montagu, M. F. A. *The Reproductive Development of the Female with Special Reference to the Period of Adolescent Sterility.* New York: Julian Press, 1957. 234 pp.

Morgan, C. Lloyd. *An Introduction to Comparative Psychology.* London: Walter Scott, 1894, pp. 84–94.

Muess, Rolf E. *Theories of Adolescence.* New York: Random House, 1966, pp. 4–12.

Munn, Norman. *The Evolution and Growth of Human Behavior* (2nd ed.). Boston: Houghton Mifflin Company, 1965, pp. 40–42.

Murphy, Gardner. *Historical Introduction to Modern Psychology.* New York: Harcourt, Brace & World, 1949, pp. 39–41, 56–57.

Mussen, Paul, Conger, John, and Kagen, Jerome. *Child Development and Personality.* New York: Harper & Row, 1963, pp. 273–280, 283–289, 532–533.

Mussen, Paul, and Distler, Luther. "Masculinity, Identification and Father-Son Relationships," *Journal of Abnormal and Social Psychology,* Vol. 59, No. 3 (November 1959), pp. 350–356.

Myer, Max. "The Grading of Students," *Science,* Vol. 28, No. 712 (August 21, 1908), pp. 243–252.

Myers, Isabel Briggs. *The Myers-Briggs Type Indicator Manual.* Princeton: Educational Testing Service, 1963, pp. 58–60.

National Education Association. *Proceedings of the National Council of Education, 1894.* St. Paul. Pioneer Press Co., 1895, pp. 33–43.

National School Public Relations Association. *Education U.S.A.* Washington, D.C.: The Association, a Department of the National Education Association, April 16, 1965, pp. 3–4.

Neider, Charles. *Susy: A Childhood.* New York: Horizon Press, 1966, 223 pp.

Neumann, Erich. *The Origins and History of Consciousness,* Vol. I and II. New York: Harper & Row, 1962. 493 pp.

Newell, Lillian. "Developing Concepts in Social Studies," San Francisco: Public Schools Community Improvement Project, 1964, pp. 1–4.

Newman, Horatio H., Freeman, Frank N., and Holzinger, Karl J. *Twins: A Study of Heredity and Environment.* Chicago: University of Chicago Press, 1937. 369 pp.

Newsweek. "Mowgli: 1960 Model," Vol. 56, No. 23 (November 28, 1960), p. 82.

Niemeyer, John H. "The Importance of the Inner-City Teacher," in Robert D. Strom (ed.), *The Inner-City Classroom: Teacher Behaviors,* Columbus, Ohio: Charles E. Merrill Books, 1966, pp. 1–20.

Noll, Victor. *Introduction to Educational Measurement* (2nd ed.). Boston: Houghton Mifflin Company, 1965, pp. 33, 43, 46, 93, 101, 461.

Oberndorf, Clarence P. *A History of Psychoanalysis in America.* New York: Harper & Row, 1964, pp. 208–250.

Odell, C. W. *Traditional Examinations and New-Type Tests.* New York: Century Company, 1928. 469 pp.

Openshaw, Karl. "Instrumentation for the Categorizing of Teacher Behavior in Classrooms," in M. Usdan and F. Bertolaet (eds.), *Teachers for the Disadvantaged,* Chicago: Follett Publishers, 1966, pp. 128–186.

Osborn, A. F. *Applied Imagination.* New York: Charles Scribner's Sons, 1953. 317 pp.

Otis, Arthur S. "An Absolute Point Scale for the Group Measurement of Intelligence," *Journal of Educational Psychology,* Vol. 9, No. 6 (June 1918), pp. 239–261, 333–348.

Otis, N. B., and McCandless, Boyd. "Responses to Repeated Frustration of Young Children Differentiated According to Need Area," *Journal of Abnormal and Social Psychology,* Vol. 50, No. 3 (May 1955), pp. 349–353.

Page, Ellis B. "Teacher Comments and Student Performance: A Seventy-four Classroom Experiment in School Motivation," *Journal of Educational Psychology,* Vol. 49, No. 4 (August 1958), pp. 173–181.

Panel on Educational Research and Development for the President's Science Advisory Committee. *Innovation and Experiment in Education.* Washington, D.C.: Government Printing Office, 1964, pp. 11–13.

Passow, Harry A. (ed.). *Education in Depressed Areas.* New York: Bureau of Publications, Teachers College, Columbia University, 1963. 359 pp.

Patrick, Catherine. *What Is Creative Thinking?* New York: Philosophical Library, 1955. 210 pp.

———. "The Adolescent," a speech delivered in Columbus, Ohio at the Children's Hospital to the Sixth Annual Pediatric Postgraduate Conference on Medical Care, April 1, 1965a.

Patterson, Paul. "Adolescents: A Neglected Minority," *Columbus Dispatch.* Columbus, Ohio, April 11, 1965b, p. 36A.

Petermann, Bruno. *The Gestalt Theory and the Problem of Configuration.* New York: Harcourt Brace, 1932. 319 pp.

Peters, Charles C., and Crossley, Elizabeth. "The Relation of Standardized Tests to Educational Objectives," in *Second Yearbook of the National Society for the Study of Educational Sociology.* New York: Bureau of Publications, Teachers College, Columbia University, 1929, pp. 148–159.

Piaget, Jean. *The Origins of Intelligence in Children.* New York: International Press, 1952, p. 158.

―――. *The Moral Judgment of the Child.* New York: The Macmillan Company, 1965, pp. 327–408.

Pierce, James V., and Bowman, P. H. "Educational Motivation Patterns of Superior Students Who do not Achieve in High School," Report on Cooperative Research Project #208. Washington, D.C.: U.S. Office of Education, 1960, p. 62.

Pomeroy, Wardell B., and Christenson, Cornelia V. "Characteristics of Male and Female Sexual Responses" (SIECUS Discussion Guide No. 4). New York: Sex Information and Education Council of the United States, April, 1967. 11 pp.

Pressey, Sidney L. "A Simple Apparatus Which Gives Tests and Scores—and Teaches," *School and Society,* Vol. 23, No. 586 (March 20, 1926), pp. 373–376.

―――. "The New Program for the Degree with Distinction at The Ohio State University," *School and Society,* Vol. 36, No. 922 (August 27, 1932), pp. 280–282.

―――. "A Third and Fourth Contribution Toward the Coming Industrial Revolution in Education," *School and Society,* Vol. 36, No. 934 (November 19, 1932), 668–672.

―――. *Educational Acceleration: Appraisals and Basic Problems.* Columbus: The Ohio State University Press, 1949, p. 11.

―――. "Development and Appraisal of Devices Providing Immediate Automatic Scoring of Objective Tests and Concomitant Self-Instruction," *Journal of Psychology,* Vol. 29 (1950), pp. 417–447.

―――. "Concerning the Nature and Nurture of Genius," *Scientific Monthly,* Vol. 81, No. 3 (September 1955), pp. 123–129.

―――. "Teaching Machine and Learning Theory Crisis," *Journal of Applied Psychology,* Vol. 47, No. 1 (February 1963), pp. 1–6.

―――. "A New Look at Acceleration," in *Acceleration and the Gifted.* Columbus: Ohio State Department of Education, 1963, pp. 1–4.

―――. " 'Fordling' Accelerates Ten Years After," *Journal of Counseling Psychology,* Vol. 14, No. 1 (1967), pp. 73–80.

―――, and Kinzer, John R. *The Effectiveness of Adjunct Auto-Instruction.* Tucson: University of Arizona, 1964, pp. 4, 40–41.

Preston, John Hyde. "A Conversation with Gertrude Stein," in Brewster Ghiselin (ed.), *The Creative Process.* Berkeley: University of California Press, 1952, pp. 164–167.

Price, Derek J. de Solla. *Science Since Babylon.* New Haven: Yale University Press, 1961, pp. 92–124.

Project Talent 1965, University of Pittsburgh. *Project Talent Bulletin,* No. 4 (February 1965), 10 pp.

Ramsey, G. V. "The Sexual Development of Boys," *American Journal of Psychology*, Vol. 56 (1943), pp. 217–233.

Rand, Ayn. *The Virtue of Selfishness*. New York: Signet Books, 1964. 144 pp.

Raths, Louis E., Harmin, Merrill, and Simon, Sidney B. *Values and Teaching*. Columbus, Ohio: Charles E. Merrill Books, 1966. 275 pp.

Raubinger, Frederick. "Some Possible Causes of Pressures," in Ronald C. Doll and Robert S. Fleming (eds.), *Children Under Pressure*. Columbus, Ohio: Charles E. Merrill Books, 1966, pp. 84–88.

Reavis, William C. "Testing is Big Business," *School Review*, Vol. 55 (May 1947), pp. 259–260.

Reed, J. E., and Hayman, J. L. "An Experiment Involving use of English 2600, an Automated Instruction Text," *Journal of Educational Research*, Vol. 55 (1962), pp. 476–484.

Reissman, Frank, *The Culturally Deprived Child*. New York: Harper & Row, Publishers, 1962. 140 pp.

Remmers, H. H. "Rating Methods in Research on Teaching," in N. L. Gage (ed.), *Handbook of Research on Teaching*. Chicago: Rand McNally & Co., 1963, pp. 329–378.

Reynolds, Paul R. "The Hollywood Screen Writers," *Saturday Review*, Vol. 49, No. 28 (July 9, 1966), pp. 52–53, 60.

Rice, J. M. "The Futility of the Spelling Grind," *Forum*, Vol. 23 (April–June, 1897), pp. 409–419.

———. *Scientific Management in Education*. New York: Hinds, Noble and Eldridge, 1912, pp. 15–16.

Richardson, Marion W. "The Relation Between the Difficulty and the Differential Level of a Test," *Psychometrika*, Vol. 1, No. 2 (June, 1936), pp. 33–49.

———, and Kuder, G. F. "The Calculation of Test-Reliability Coefficients Based Upon the Method of Rational Equivalence," *Journal of Educational Psychology*, Vol. 30, No. 9 (1939), pp. 681–687.

Rickover, H. G. *Education and Freedom*. New York: E. P. Dutton & Co., 1959, p. 16.

Rider, Fremont. *The Scholar and the Future of the Research Library*. New York: Hadham Press, 1944, pp. 3–19.

Rigney, J. W., and Fry, E. B. "Current Teaching-Machine Programs and Programming Techniques," *Audio-Visual Communications Review*, Vol. 9 (1961), p. 3.

Robert, Louis D., and Jones, Wallace L., Jr. *The School Dropout in Louisiana 1962–1963*. Baton Rouge: State of Louisiana, Department of Education, 1963, p. 14.

Roberton, J. "Early Marriage So Common in Oriental Countries No Proof of Early Puberty," *Edinburgh Journal of Medical Surgery*, Vol. 6 (1843), pp. 1–18.

Roberts, J. A. F. *Introduction to Medical Genetics*. London: Oxford University Press, 1959.

Roe, Anne. *The Psychology of Occupations*. New York: John Wiley & Sons, 1956. 340 pp.

Rogers, Everett M. "What are Innovators Like?" *Theory Into Practice*, Vol. 2, No. 5 (December 1963), pp. 252–256.

Rokeach, Milton. *The Three Christs of Ypsilanti*. New York: Alfred A. Knopf, 1964. 336 pp.

Rose, Marion. "Promotion and Failure as Affected by Sex," unpublished Master's thesis, University of Kansas, 1928.

Rosenzweig, Saul, Fleming, Edith, and Clarke, Helen. *Revised Scoring Manual for the Rosenzweig Picture-Frustration Study (Form for Adults)*. Provincetown, Mass.: The Journal Press, 1947. 46 pp.

Ross, C. C. *Measurement in Today's Schools*. Englewood Cliffs, N.J.: Prentice-Hall, 1949, pp. 83–84, 227, 233, 240–242.

———, and revised by Julian Stanley, *Measurement in Today's Schools* (3rd ed.). Englewood Cliffs, N.J.: Prentice-Hall, 1954, pp. 43, 149–150.

Rossman, J. *The Psychology of the Inventory: A Study of the Patentee*. Washington, D.C.: Inventors Publishing Co., 1931. 252 pp.

———. *Industrial Creativity: The Psychology of the Inventor*. New York: University Books, 1964. 252 pp.

Roth, R. H. "Student Reactions to Programmed Learning," *Phi Delta Kappan*, Vol. 44, No. 6 (1963), pp. 278–281.

Rousseau, Jean Jacques. *Emile*, trans. William Boyd. New York: Teachers College, Columbia University, 1965, pp. 38–46.

Rubin, Edgar John. *Visuel Wahrgenommene Figuren*. Copenhagen: University of Copenhagen, 1915.

Ruch, G. M. *The Improvement of the Written Examination*. Chicago: Scott Foresman & Co., 1924. 193 pp.

Rulon, P. J. "A Simplified Procedure for Determining the Reliability of a Test by Splitting Halves," *Harvard Educational Review*, Vol. 9, No. 1 (January 1939), pp. 99–103.

Runner, Kenyon, and Runner, Helen. *Runner Studies & Attitude Patterns (Handbook)*. Golden, Colorado: Runner Associates, 1965. 35 pp.

Ryans, D. G. "Characteristics of Teachers," in *American Council on Education*. Washington, D.C.: The Council, 1960. 416 pp.

———. "Assessment of Teacher Behavior and Instruction," *Review of Educational Research*, Vol. 33 (1963), pp. 415–441.

Sanders, Norris M. *Classroom Questions: What Kinds*. New York: Harper & Row, 1966. 176 pp.

Saterlie, Mary. "Realistic Studies for Potential Dropouts," in E. Paul Torrance and Robert D. Strom (eds.), *Mental Health and Achievement*. New York: John Wiley & Sons, 1965, pp. 286–304.

Saunders, Carleton M. *Promotion or Failure for the Elementary School Pupil?* New York: Teachers College, Columbia University, 1941.

Schaar, John H. *Escape from Authority*. New York: Harper & Row, 1964. 335 pp.

Scheinfeld, Amram. *The New You and Heredity*. Philadelphia: J. B. Lippincott Co., 1950, pp. 394–410.

Schram, Wilbur. "Learning From Instructional Television," *Review of Educational Research*, Vol. 32, No. 2 (April 1962), pp. 156–167.

Schreiber, D. *Holding Power/Large City School Systems*. Washington, D.C.: Project School Dropouts, National Education Association, 1964, p. 53.

———, Kaplan, B. A., and Strom, R. D. *Dropout Studies: Design and Conduct*. Washington, D.C.: Project School Dropouts, National Education Association, 1965. 84 pp.

Schueler, Herbert. "Boston," in *The Development of the Career Teacher: Pro-*

fessional Responsibility for Continuing Education. Washington, D.C.: National Commission on Teacher Education and Professional Standards, 1964, pp. 21–29.

Shutz, William. *The Interpersonal Underworld (FIRO, A Three-Dimensional Theory of Interpersonal Behavior).* Palo Alto: Science and Behavior Books, Inc., 1966. 242 pp.

Sears, Pauline S. "Levels of Aspiration in Relation to Some Variables of Personality: Clinical Studies," *Journal of Social Psychology,* Vol. 14 (1941), pp. 311–336.

Sears, Robert R., Maccoby, Eleanor E., and Lewin, H. *Patterns of Child Rearing. Evanston:* Row, Peterson, 1957, pp. 246–247.

———. "The Socialization of Aggression," in Judy Rosenblith and Wesley Allinsmith (ed.), *The Causes of Behavior.* Boston: Allyn and Bacon, 1964, pp. 96–103.

Shearer, Lloyd. "Life in the Deep Freeze," *The Washington Post,* Washington, D.C., July 19, 1964, pp. 2–5.

Shein, Edgar H. "The Chinese Indoctrination Program for Prisoners of War," *Psychiatry,* Vol. II (1956), pp. 149–172.

Shepherd, Jack. "When College Students Crack Up," *Look,* Vol. 31, No. 12 (June 13, 1967), p. 23.

Shields, James. *Monozygotic Twins.* New York: Oxford University Press, 1962. 264 pp.

Silberman, Harry F. "Self-Teaching Devices and Programmed Materials," *Review of Educational Research,* Vol. 32, No. 2 (April 1962), pp. 179–193.

———. "Characteristics of Some Recent Studies of Instructional Methods," in J. E. Coulson (ed.), *Programmed Learning and Computer-Based Instruction.* New York: John Wiley & Sons, 1962, pp. 13–24.

Skinner, B. F. "The Science of Learning and the Art of Teaching," *Harvard Educational Review,* Vol. 24 (1954), pp. 86–97.

———. *Science and Human Behavior.* New York: The Macmillan Company, 1953, p. 65.

———. "Problems in the Schools" (an interview), *Columbus Dispatch,* Columbus, Ohio, October 14, 1965, p. 31A.

Smilansky, Sarah. *Progress Report on Kindergartens.* Jerusalem, Israel: Henrietta Szold Institute, 1964.

Smith, D. E. P. "Speculations: Characteristics of Successful Programs and Programmers," in E. Galanter (ed.), *Automatic Teaching: The State of the Art.* New York: John Wiley & Sons, 1959, pp. 91–102.

Smith, James A., *Setting Conditions for Creative Teaching in the Elementary School.* Boston: Allyn and Bacon, 1966. 207 pp.

Smith, Karl U., and Smith, Margaret F. *Cybernetic Principles of Learning and Education Design.* New York: Holt, Rinehart and Winston, 1966, pp. 253, 275–289, 295.

Snygg, Donald. "The Torturous Path of Learning," *Audio-Visual Instruction,* Vol. 7, No. 1 (1962), pp. 8–12.

Sollenberger, R. T. "Some Relationships Between the Urinary Excretion of Male Hormone by Maturing Boys and Their Expressed Interests and Attitudes," *Journal of Psychology,* Vol. 9 (1940), pp. 179–189.

Solomon, David (ed.). *LSD: The Consciousness-Expanding Drug.* New York: G. P. Putnam's Sons, 1964. 268 pp.

Spearman, Charles. "General Intelligence: Objectively Determined and Measured," *American Journal of Psychology*, Vol. 15 (April 1904), pp. 201–293.

————. "The Proof and Measurement of Association Between Two Things," *American Journal of Psychology*, Vol. 15 (1904), pp. 72–101.

Spender, Stephen. "The Making of a Poem," in Brewster Ghiselin (ed.), *The Creative Process*. Berkeley: University of California Press, 1952, pp. 114, 115.

Spock, Benjamin. "Children and Discrimination," *Redbook*, Vol. 123, No. 5 (September 1964), pp. 30–32.

————. "Protecting Children From the Harm of Discrimination," *Redbook*, Vol. 123, No. 6 (October 1964a), pp. 26–27.

————. "The Beginning of Character," *Redbook*, Vol. 127, No. 6 (October 1966).

————. "Treating Children with Respect," *Redbook*, Vol. 128, No. 2 (December 1966a), p. 33.

Spranger, Edward. *Types of Men*. Translated from fifth German edition of *Lebensformen* by Paul J. W. Pigors. Halle: Max Aiemeifer Verlag. American Agent: Stechert Hafner, N.Y.

Spurzheim, J. G. *Education: Its Elementary Principles, Founded on the Nature of Man*. New York: Fowler & Wells, 1883, pp. 89, 117–119, 130–131.

Stanley, Julian C. "A Simplified Method for Estimating for Split-Half Reliability Coefficient of a Test," *Harvard Educational Review*, Vol. 21, No. 4 (Fall 1951), pp. 221–224.

————. "The ABC's of Test Construction," *National Education Association Journal*, Vol. 47, No. 4 (April 1958).

————. *Measurement in Today's Schools* (4th ed.). Englewood Cliffs, N.J.: Prentice-Hall, 1964, pp. 14–17, 173–175.

Starch, Daniel, and Elliott, Edward C. "Reliability of Grading Work in Mathematics," *School Review*, Vol. 21 (April 1913), pp. 254–259.

Stone, C. P., and Barker, R. G. "The Attitudes and Interests of Premenarchael and Postmenarchael Girls," *Journal of Genetic Psychology*, Vol. 54 (1939), pp. 27–71.

Stone, Clifford W. *Arithmetical Abilities and Some Factors Determining Them*, Contributions to Education, No. 19. New York: Teachers College, Columbia University, 1908. 101 pp.

Storr, Anthony. *The Integrity of Personality*. Baltimore: Penguin Books, 1963, pp. 32–34, 37, 43, 83–101, 105–115, 121–123, 159, 165–177.

Stott, Leland H. *Child Development: An Individual Longitudinal Approach*. New York: Holt, Rinehart and Winston, 1967. 513 pp.

Street, Roy F. *A Gestalt Completion Test*. New York: Teachers College, Columbia University, 1931. 47 pp.

Strom, Robert D. "Comparison of Adolescent and Adult Behavioral Norm Properties," *Journal of Educational Psychology*, Vol. 54, No. 6 (December 1963), pp. 322–330.

————. "Raising Aspirations of Youth," *Catholic Education Review*, Vol. 62 (May 1964a), pp. 289–297.

————. *The Tragic Migration*. Washington, D.C.: National Education Association, 1964b, pp. 6–8, 9, 27–29.

————. "How Europeans Face Up To Their Dropout Problem," *The Clearing House*, Vol. 38, No. 7 (March 1964c), pp. 431–433.

————. "A Realistic Curriculum for Predictive Dropouts," *The Clearing House*, Vol. 39, No. 2 (October 1964d), pp. 101–106.

————. "The European Attitude," *Education*, Vol. 85, No. 1 (September, 1964e), pp. 14–16.

————. "School Evaluation and Mental Health," *The High School Journal*, Vol. 48, No. 3 (December 1964f), pp. 198–207.

————. "The Dropout in a Society of Specialization," *California Teacher Association Journal*, Vol. 60, No. 4 (October 1964g), pp. 4–6.

————. "What is the School Speedup Doing to Children?" *The Elementary School Journal*, Vol. 65, No. 4 (January 1965a), pp. 206–207.

————. "Education—Key to Economic Equality for the Negro," *Journal of Negro Education*, Vol. 34, No. 4 (Fall 1965b), pp. 463–466.

————. *Teaching in the Slum School*. Columbus, Ohio: Charles E. Merrill Books, 1965c, pp. 20–26, 40, 48–70, 73–76, 91.

————. "The Dropout Problem in Relation to Family Affect and Effect," in E. Paul Torrance and Robert D. Strom (eds.), *Mental Health and Achievement*. New York: John Wiley & Sons, 1965d, pp. 24–31.

————. "Teacher Aspiration and Attitude," in Robert D. Strom (ed.), *The Inner-City Classroom: Teacher Behaviors*. Columbus, Ohio: Charles E. Merrill Books, 1966a, pp. 21–39.

————. "Family Influence on School Failure," in Glenn R. Hawkes and Joseph L. Frost (eds.), *The Disadvantaged Child: A Book of Readings*. Boston: Houghton Mifflin Company, 1966b.

————. *The Preface Plan: A New Concept of Inservice Training for Teachers Newly Assigned to Urban Neighborhoods of Low Income* (Final Report, U.S. Office of Education, Project No. 6-1365). Columbus, Ohio: The Ohio State University, August 1967a. 110 pp.

————, and Galloway, Charles. "Becoming a Better Teacher," *Journal of Teacher Education*, Vol. 18, No. 33 (Fall 1967b), pp. 285–292.

————. "Sex and the Educated Adolescent: A Study of Ohio State University Undergraduates," Columbus, 1967c. (Privately distributed.)

————. "Problems of the Successful," *The High School Journal*, Vol. 51, No. 4 (April 1968).

Sugarman, Daniel, and Hochstein, Rollie. "Sex and the Teenage Girl," *Seventeen* (July, 1965).

Swarthout, Glendon, *Where the Boys Are*. New York: Random House, 1960, pp. 125–126.

Taba, Hilda. "The Effect of Feedback of Research Results to Classroom Teachers," an address presented to the Ohio Association for Supervision and Curriculum Development, Research Institute, Columbus, Ohio, November 14, 1965.

————, and Elkins, Deborah. *Teaching Strategies for the Culturally Disadvantaged*. Chicago: Rand McNally & Co., 1966. 295 pp.

Taylor, Calvin. "A Tentative Description of the Creative Individual," in Walter B. Waetjen (ed.), *Human Variability and Learning*. Washington, D.C.: Association for Supervision and Curriculum Development, a department of the National Education Association, 1961, p. 65.

Terman, Lewis M. *The Measurement of Intelligence*. Boston: Houghton Mifflin Company, 1916. 362 pp.

————. "The Discovery and Encouragement of Exceptional Talent," *American Psychologist*, Vol. 9 (1954), p. 221.

————, et al. *The Stanform Revision and Extension of the Binet Scale for Measuring Intelligence*. Baltimore: Warwick and York, 1917. 170 pp.

————, and Merrill, Maud A. *Measuring Intelligence*. Boston: Houghton Mifflin Company, 1937, pp. 33–51.

Thayer, Vivian T. *The Misinterpretation of Locke as a Formalist in Educational Philosophy*. Madison: University of Wisconsin Studies in Social Sciences and History, No. 3 (1921), p. 15.

Thomas, Shailer, and Knudsen, Dean D. "The Relationship Between Nonpromotion and the Dropout Problem," *Theory Into Practice*, Vol. 4, No. 3 (June 1965), pp. 90–94.

Thompson, G. G., and Hunnicutt, C. W. "The Effect of Repeated Praise and Blame on the World Achievement of Introverts and Extroverts," *Journal of Educational Psychology*, Vol. 35, No. 5 (1944), pp. 257–266.

Thorndike, E. L. *Animal Intelligence*. New York: The Macmillan Company, 1898. 109 pp.

————. *Notes on Child Study*. New York: The Macmillan Company, 1903, pp. 40–124.

————. *An Interpretation to the Theory of Mental and Social Measurements*. New York: Teachers College, Columbia University, 1904.

————. "Handwriting," *Teachers College Record*, Vol. 11 (March 1910), 83–175.

————. *Educational Psychology: The Original Nature of Man*, Vol. I. New York: Teachers College, Columbia University, 1913. 327 pp.

————. *Education*. New York: The Macmillan Company, 1920, pp. 95–96, 105–112, 178, 195–196.

————. "Measuerment in Education," in *National Society for the Study of Education 21st Yearbook*, Part I. Bloomington, Ill.: Public School Publishing Co., 1922, pp. 2, 8.

————. "Mental Discipline in High School Studies," *Journal of Educational Psychology*, Vol. 15, No. 2 (1924), pp. 83–98.

————. *The Measurement of Intelligence*. New York: Bureau of Publications, Teachers College, Columbia University, 1927. 613 pp.

————, and Gates, Arthur I. *Elementary Principles of Education*. New York: The Macmillan Company, 1930, pp. 67–83, 89, 236.

————, and Woodworth, R. S. "The Influence of Improvement in One Mental Function Upon the Efficiency of Other Functions," *Psychological Review*, Vol. 8 (1901), pp. 247–256.

Thorndike, Robert L., and Hagen, Elizabeth. *Measurement and Evaluation in Psychology and Education*. New York: John Wiley & Sons, 1959, pp. 95, 113, 118–120, 128, 131.

Thurstone, Louis L. "Primary Mental Abilities," *Psychometric Monograph*, No. 1. Chicago: University of Chicago Press, 1938, pp. 2–10.

Tiegs, Ernest W. *Tests and Measurement in the Improvement of Learning*. Boston: Houghton Mifflin Company, 1939, pp. 4, 10, 58, 384.

Time, "Man of the Year," Vol. 89, No. 1 (January 6, 1967), pp. 18–23.

Torrance, E. Paul. *The Struggle for Men's Minds*. Wright Patterson Air Force Base, Ohio: Orientation Group U.S.A.F., 1959.

————. "Are the Gifted Being Challenged to Think and Learn Creatively?" An address presented to the Sacramento State College Association for Gifted Children, Sacramento, California, October 14, 1961.

————. *Guiding Creative Talent.* Englewood Cliffs, N.J.: Prentice-Hall, 1962. 278 pp.

————. "The Creative Personality and the Ideal Pupil," *Teachers College Record,* Vol. 65, No. 3 (December 1963a), pp. 220–226.

————. *Creativity.* Washington D.C.: The Department of Classroom Teacher, American Education Research Association of the National Education Association, 1963b, pp. 23–27.

————. "What Counselors and Teachers Can Do to Help Others Achieve Their Creative Potential," an address presented to the South Dakota Guidance Association, South Dakota State University, Brookings, October 3, 1964a.

————. *Role of Evaluation in Creative Thinking* (Cooperative Research Project #725). Minneapolis: Bureau of Educational Research, University of Minnesota, 1964b.

————. "Teaching Creative Behavior in the Classroom," an address delivered at The Ohio State University, Columbus, March 5, 1965a.

————. "Continuity in the Creative Development of Young Children," in E. Paul Torrance and Robert D. Strom (eds.), *Mental Health and Achievement.* New York: John Wiley & Sons, 1965b, pp. 274–285.

————. *Constructive Behavior: Stress, Personality and Mental Health.* Belmont: Wadsworth Publishing Company, 1965c, pp. 3, 388–389.

————. *Rewarding Creative Behavior.* Englewood Cliffs, N.J.: Prentice-Hall, 1965d, pp. 221–234, 302, 307.

————. *A New Movement in Education: Creative Development.* Boston: Ginn & Co., 1965e, p. 22.

————. "Fostering Creative Behavior," in Robert D. Strom (ed.), *The Inner-City Classroom: Teacher Behavior.* Columbus, Ohio: Charles E. Merrill Books, 1966a, pp. 57–74.

————. "Does Evaluative Feedback Facilitate Creative Thinking?" Unpublished paper, Minneapolis, 1966b. 4 pp.

————. *Torrance Tests of Creative Thinking: Norms Technical Manual* (Research Edition). Princeton: Personnel Press, Inc., 1966c, pp. 17–22, 23–56.

————. "A Summary: The International Workshop on the Possibilities and Limitations of Educational Testing," Berlin, West Germany, May 17–23, 1967. 5 pp.

————, and Gupta, Ram. *Programmed Experience in Creative Learning.* Minneapolis: Bureau of Educational Research, University of Minnesota, 1964, pp. 5–6.

————, and Hanson, Ethel. "The Question-Asking Behavior of Highly Creative and Less Creative Basic Business Teachers Identified by a Paper-and-Pencil Test," *Psychological Reports,* Vol. 17 (1965), pp. 815–818.

————, and Strom, Robert D. (eds.). *Mental Health and Achievement.* New York: John Wiley & Sons, 1965. 417 pp.

Trabue, M. R. "Special Applications of the Scientific Method to Educational Measurement," *School and Society,* Vol. 21 (April 1925), p. 486.

Travers, Robert M. *Essentials of Learning.* New York: The Macmillan Company, 1967, pp. 201–233.

Tyler, Ralph W. "A Generalized Technique for Constructing Achievement Tests," *Educational Research Bulletin,* Vol. 8 (April 1931), pp. 199–208.

————. *Constructing Achievement Tests.* Columbus, Ohio: The Ohio State University, 1934.

————, and Smith, Eugene R., and the Evaluation Staff. *Appraising and Recording Student Progress.* New York: Harper & Row, 1942. 550 pp.

U.S. Office of Education. *The 1963 Dropout Campaign,* Bulletin 1964, No. 26, OE-20060, pp. 1–2.

Wallach, Michael A., and Kogan, Nathan. *Modes of Thinking in Young Children.* New York: Holt, Rinehart & Winston, 1965. 357 pp.

Wallas, Graham. *The Art of Thought.* New York: Harcourt, Brace & World, 1926.

Walters, J., Pearce, Doris, and Dahms, Lucille, "Affectional and Aggressive Behavior of the Preschool Children," *Child Development,* Vol. 28, No. 1 (1957), pp. 15–27.

Watson, John B. *Behavior: An Introduction to Comparative Psychology.* New York: Holt, Rinehart & Winston, 1914, pp. 106–107.

————. *Behaviorism* (rev. ed.). New York: W. W. Norton Co., 1930, pp. 104, 158–195.

Watson, Robert I. *Psychology of the Child.* New York: John Wiley & Sons, 1965, pp. 263–269, 277–280.

————, and Glaser, Edward. *Watson-Glaser Critical Thinking Appraisal (Manual).* New York: Harcourt, Brace & World, 1952. 12 pp.

Weideman, Ruth A. "An Experiment with Grade School Children in Making Creative Song with Varied Stimuli," Masters research paper, University of Minnesota, Minneapolis, 1961.

Weismann, August. *Essays Upon Heredity and Kindred Biological Problems,* Vol. I. London: Oxford University Clarendon Press, 1891, pp. 71–106.

Wertheimer, Max. "Experimentelle Studien: Über das Sehen von Bewegung," *Z. Psychol.,* Vol. 61 (1912), pp. 161–265.

————. "Untersuchungen zur Lehre von der Gestalt," *Psychologische Forschung,* Vol. 1 (1921), p. 54.

————. "Über Gestalttheorie," an address before the Kant Society, Berlin, Germany, December 17, 1924, p. 2.

————. *Productive Thinking.* New York: Harper & Row, 1945, p. 112.

West, J. V., and Fruchter, B. "A Longitudinal Study of the Relationship of High School Foreign Language and Mathematics Study to Freshman Grades," *Journal of Educational Research,* Vol. 54, No. 3 (1960), pp. 105–110.

Whipple, G. M. (ed.). "Bibliography, Divisions H and I: City Surveys and State, County and Other Surveys," in *National Society for the Study of Education, 17th Yearbook,* Part II. Bloomington, Ill.: Public School Publishing Co., 1918, pp. 183–190.

————. "The Improvement of Educational Research," *School and Society,* Vol. 26, No. 661 (August 27, 1927), p. 251.

White, Robert W. "Competence and the Psychosexual Stages of Development," in *Nebraska Symposium on Motivation 1960.* Lincoln: University of Nebraska Press, 1960, pp. 97–108, 133–138.

————. *The Abnormal Personality.* New York: The Ronald Press Company, 1964, pp. 173–179.

Wilhelms, Fred H. "The Curriculum and Individual Differences," in Nelson B. Henry (ed.), *Individualizing Instruction.* Chicago: University of Chicago Press, 1962, pp. 62–74.

Williams, Mary McGee, and Kane, Irene. *On Becoming a Woman*. New York: Dell Publishing Co., 1959, pp. 107–148.

Wilson, R. C., Guilford, J. P., and Christensen, P. R. "The Measurement of Individual Differences in Originality," *Psychological Bulletin*, Vol. 50, No. 5 (September 1953), pp. 362–370.

Wingo, G. Max. *The Philosophy of American Education*. Chicago: D.C. Heath and Company, 1965. 438 pp.

Winkler, John K., and Bromberg, Walter. *Mind Explorers*. New York: Reynal and Hitchcock, 1939, pp. 10, 11, 15.

Wissler, Clark. "The Correlation of Mental Tests and Physical Traits," *Psychological Review*, Monograph Supplement, Vol. 8, No. 16 (1901).

Withall, John. "The Development of a Technique for the Measurement of Social-Emotional Climate in Classroom," *Journal of Experimental Education*, Vol. 17 (March 1949), pp. 347–361.

———. "Conceptual Frameworks for Analysis of Classroom Social Interaction," *Journal of Experimental Education*, Vol. 30 (1962), pp. 307–370.

Witkin, H. A., *et al. Personality Through Perception: An Experimental and Clinical Study*. New York: Harper & Row, 1954. 571 pp.

———, *et al. Psychological Differentiation*. New York: John Wiley & Sons, 1962. 418 pp.

Wolf, James M. "Retention Doesn't Pay Dividends," *Special Education Bulletin*, Canal Zone Special Education Program, V (June 1961), pp. 3–4.

Wood, Dorothy Adkins. *Test Construction*. Columbus, Ohio: Charles E. Merrill Books, 1961, pp. 1, 29, 55, 77–86, 105.

Woodburne, Lloyd. *The Neural Basis of Behavior*. Columbus, Ohio: Charles E. Merrill Books, 1967, pp. 289–316.

Woodworth, Robert S. *Dynamic Psychology*. New York: Columbia University Press, 1918, pp. 44–76.

———. *Heredity and Environment: A Critical Survey of Recently Published Materials on Twins and Foster Children*. New York: Social Science Research Council Bulletin, No. 47 (1941), 95 pp.

———, and Sheehan, Mary R. *Contemporary Schools of Psychology*. New York: The Ronald Press Company, 1964, pp. 68–74, 232.

Woolf, Virginia. *The Common Reader*. London: Hogarth Press, 1925, p. 262.

Worth, Walter H. "Promotion or Nonpromotion?" *Educational Administration and Supervision*, Vol. 46 (January 1960), pp. 16–26.

Wundt, W. *Lectures on Human and Animal Psychology*, trans. J. E. Creighton and E. B. Titchener. London: Sonnerschien Co., 1894, pp. 353–66.

Yamamoto, Karou. "Do Creativity Tests Really Measure Creativity?" *Theory Into Practice*, Vol. 5, No. 4 (October 1966,) pp. 194–197.

———. "Evaluation in Teaching," an address presented to the Preface Plan Project Workshop, The Ohio State University, Columbus, February, 1967. 19 pp.

Yando, R. M. "The Effect of Teachers' Cognitive Tempo on Children," unpublished Ph.D. dissertation, Columbus, Ohio State University, 1966. 64 pp.

Zervos, Christian. "Conversations with Picasso," in Brewster Ghiselin (ed.), *The Creative Process*. Berkeley: University of California Press, 1952, p. 5.

Ziller, R. C. "Scales of Group Judgment: A Determinant of the Accuracy of Group Decisions," *Human Relations*, Vol. 8, No. 2 (1955), pp. 153–164.

Name Index

Subject Index